THE GRE

F. Mannino/Lara Pessina/MICHELIN

Sicily

Director	David Brabis
Editorial	Maura Marca
English Edition	Mike Brammer, Alison Westwood, Helen Isaacs
Practical Points	Alison Westwood, Helen Isaacs
Mapping	Alain Baldet, Geneviève Corbic, Aurélie Huot
Picture Editor	Cathérine Guégan, Stéphane Sauvignier
Technical Assistance	Audrey Horne, Titus McCready
Lay-out	Michel Moulin, Jean-Paul Josset
Graphics	Christiane Beylier
Cover	Agence Carré Noir
Production	Pierre Ballochard, Renaud Leblanc
Marketing	Ellie Griffith
Sales	John Lewis (UK), Gayle Sparks (USA)
Public Relations	Gonzague de Jarnac, Paul Cordle
Contact	The Green Guide Michelin Travel Publications Hannay House 39 Clarendon Road Watford Herts WD17 1JA United Kingdom b (01923) 205 240 Fax (01923) 205 241 www.ViaMichelin.com TheGreenGuide-uk@uk.michelin.co

Published in 2003

The Green Guide: Spirit of Discovery

Leisure time spent with The Green Guide is also a time for refreshing your spirit, enjoying yourself, and taking advantage of our selection of fine restaurants, hotels and other places for relaxing: immerse yourself in the local culture, discover new horizons, experience the local lifestyle. The Green Guide opens the door for you.

Each year our writers go touring: visiting the sights, devising the driving tours, identifying the highlights, selecting the most attractive hotels and restaurants, checking the routes for the maps and plans.

Each title is compiled with great care, giving you the benefit of regular revisions and Michelin's first-hand knowledge. The Green Guide responds to changing circumstances and takes account of its readers' suggestions; all comments are welcome.

Share with us our enthusiasm for travel, which has led us to discover over 60 destinations in France and other countries. Like us, let yourself be guided by the desire to explore, which is the best motive for travel: the spirit of discovery.

Contents

Practical Points

Insights and Images

M. Magni/MICHELIN

Sicilian puppet

G. Bludzin/MICHELIN

Drystone walls in the Iblei Moutains

Selected Sights

D. Boggini/MICHELIN

Traditional Sicilian cart (detail)

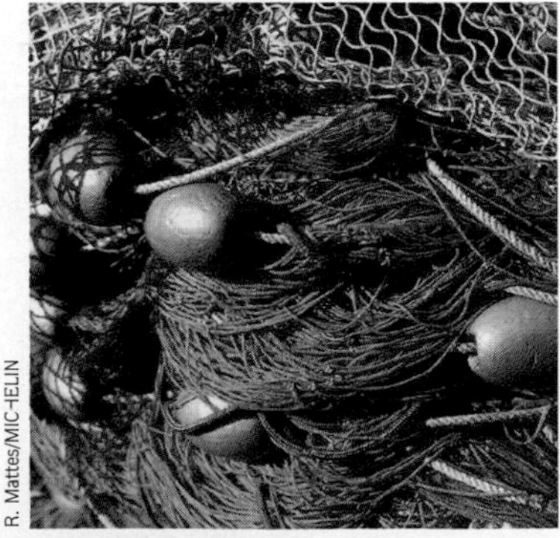
R. Mattes/MICHELIN

Fishing nets, Porticello

Maps and plans

Companion publications

All Michelin publications are cross-referenced. For each sight covered in the Selected Sights section of the guide, a map reference is given under the heading "Location". From our range of products we recommend the following:

- **Michelin map 565 Sicilia,** which covers the island of Sicily and includes an alphabetical index of towns, as well as maps of Agrigento, Catania, Messina, Palermo and Siracusa. Scale 1:400 000.

TRAVELLING TO SICILY:

- **Michelin map 735 Italia,** a practical map which provides the visitor with a complete picture of Italy's road network. Scale 1:1 000 000.
- **Michelin Road Atlas Italia,** a useful, spiral-bound atlas with an alphabetical index of 70 towns and cities. Scale 1:300 000.

Internet users can access personalised route plans, Michelin maps and town plans, and addresses of hotels and restaurants featured in *The Red Guide Italia* through the website at www.ViaMichelin.com

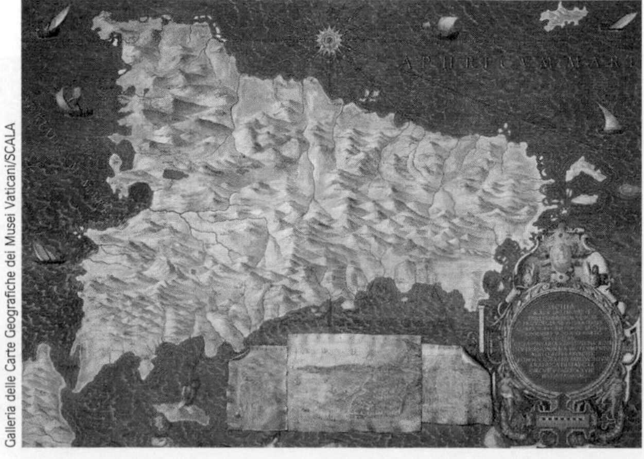

Galleria delle Carte Geografiche dei Musei Vaticani/SCALA

List of maps

Town plans

Touring maps

Plans of archaeological sites

Plans of churches

Key

Selected monuments and sights

Tour - Departure point

Catholic church

Protestant church, other temple

Synagogue - Mosque

Building

Statue, small building

Calvary, wayside cross

Fountain

Rampart - Tower - Gate

Château, castle, historic house

Ruins

Dam

Factory, power plant

Fort

Cave

Troglodyte dwelling

Prehistoric site

Viewing table

Viewpoint

Other place of interest

Sports and recreation

Racecourse

Skating rink

Outdoor, indoor swimming pool

Multiplex Cinema

Marina, sailing centre

Trail refuge hut

Cable cars, gondolas

Funicular, rack railway

Tourist train

Recreation area, park

Theme, amusement park

Wildlife park, zoo

Gardens, park, arboretum

Bird sanctuary, aviary

Walking tour, footpath

Of special interest to children

Special symbols

Gendarmerie (Carabinieri)

Temple, Greek and Roman ruins

Beach

Abbreviations

H	Town hall (Municipio)
J	Law courts (Palazzo di Giustizia)
M	Museum (Museo)
P	Local authority offices (Prefettura)
POL.	Police station (Polizia) (in large towns: Questura)
T	Theatre (Teatro)
U	University (Università)

	Sight	Seaside resort	Winter sports resort	Spa
Highly recommended	★★★	☼☼☼	✻✻✻	⚲⚲⚲
Recommended	★★	☼☼	✻✻	⚲⚲
Interesting	★	☼	✻	⚲

Additional symbols

ℹ	Tourist information
═ ═	Motorway or other primary route
❶ ❶	Junction: complete, limited
	Pedestrian street
	Unsuitable for traffic, street subject to restrictions
	Steps – Footpath
	Train station – Auto-train station
S.N.C.F.	Coach (bus) station
	Tram
	Metro, underground
P R	Park-and-Ride
♿	Access for the disabled
	Post office
	Telephone
	Covered market
	Barracks
	Drawbridge
	Quarry
⚒	Mine
B F	Car ferry (river or lake)
	Ferry service: cars and passengers
	Foot passengers only
③	Access route number common to Michelin maps and town plans
Bert (R.)...	Main shopping street
AZ B	Map co-ordinates
▶▶	Visit if time permits
⏲	Admission times and charges listed at the end of the guide

Hotels and restaurants

20 rooms €118 €180	Numbers of rooms: price for one person/two people, including breakfast
double rooms	Double occupancy only
€5	Price of breakfast when it is not included in the price of the room
half-board or full board €78	Price per person, based on double occupancy (half or full board obligatory)
100 apart/room week. €200/300	Number of apartments or rooms, minimum/maximum price per week ("agriturismo" or units rented on a weekly basis only, in summer)
100 beds €15	Number of beds (youth hostels, refuges, etc) and price per person
150 sites €19	Number of camp sites and cost for two people with a car
€10/26	Restaurant: minimum/maximum price for a full meal (not including drinks)
	No credit cards accepted
P	Reserved parking for hotel patrons
	Swimming Pool
	Air conditioning
	Hotel: non-smoking rooms Restaurant: non-smoking section
♿	Rooms accesible to persons of reduced mobility

The prices correspond to the higher rates of the tourist season

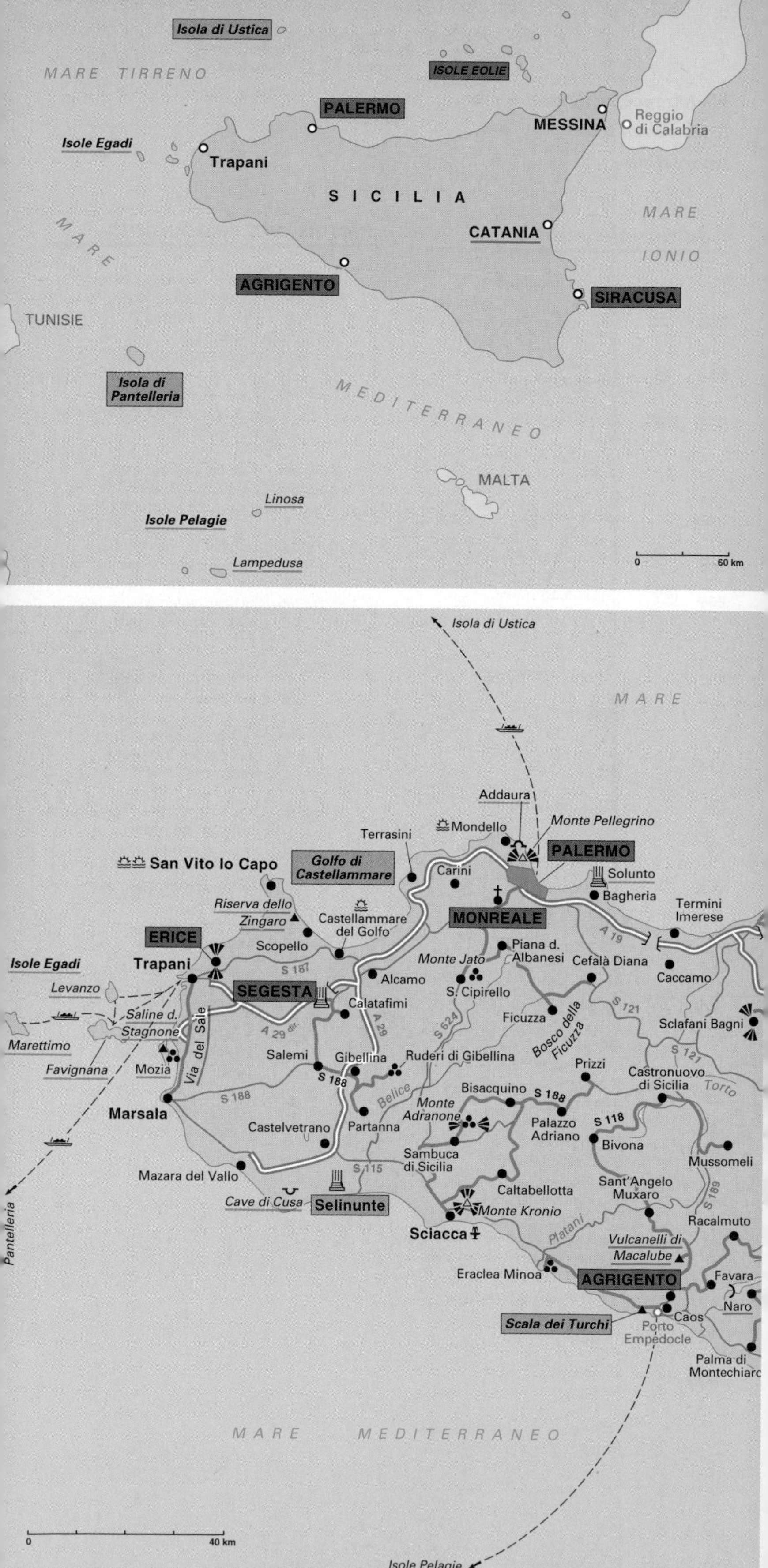

Isola di Ustica
MARE TIRRENO
ISOLE EOLIE
PALERMO
MESSINA
Reggio di Calabria
Isole Egadi
Trapani
SICILIA
MARE
MARE
IONIO
CATANIA
AGRIGENTO
SIRACUSA
TUNISIE
Isola di Pantelleria
MEDITERRANEO
MALTA
Linosa
Isole Pelagie
Lampedusa
0
60 km
Isola di Ustica
MARE
Addaura
Mondello
Monte Pellegrino
Terrasini
PALERMO
San Vito lo Capo
Golfo di Castellammare
Carini
Solunto
Bagheria
Riserva dello Zingaro
Castellammare del Golfo
MONREALE
Termini Imerese
ERICE
Scopello
Piana d. Albanesi
A 19
Isole Egadi
Trapani
Monte Jato
Cefalà Diana
Caccamo
S 187
Alcamo
Levanzo
SEGESTA
S. Cipirello
Calatafimi
S 121
Saline d. Stagnone
A 29 dir.
A 29
S 624
Ficuzza
Bosco della Ficuzza
Sclafani Bagni
Marettimo
Via del Sale
S 121
Favignana
Mozia
Salemi
Gibellina
Ruderi di Gibellina
Prizzi
Castronuovo di Sicilia
Torto
S 188
Belice
Bisacquino
S 188
Marsala
S 188
Monte Adranone
Palazzo Adriano
S 118
Castelvetrano
Partanna
Bivona
Mussomeli
Sambuca di Sicilia
S 115
Mazara del Vallo
Caltabellotta
Sant'Angelo Muxaro
S 189
Cave di Cusa
Selinunte
Monte Kronio
Racalmuto
Sciacca
Platani
Vulcanelli di Macalube
Pantelleria
Eraclea Minoa
AGRIGENTO
Favara
Naro
Scala dei Turchi
Porto Empedocle
Caos
Palma di Montechiaro
MARE MEDITERRANEO
0
40 km
Isole Pelagie

Principal sights

PALERMO	★★★	Highly recommended
Selinunte	★★	Recommended
Modica	★	Interesting
Gangi		Other sight described in this guide.

Seaside resorts, spas and winter resorts are classified according to the quality and range of facilities offered.

Itinerary described in this guide: look up one of the sites in the index at the back of the guide to find the page where the tour is described.

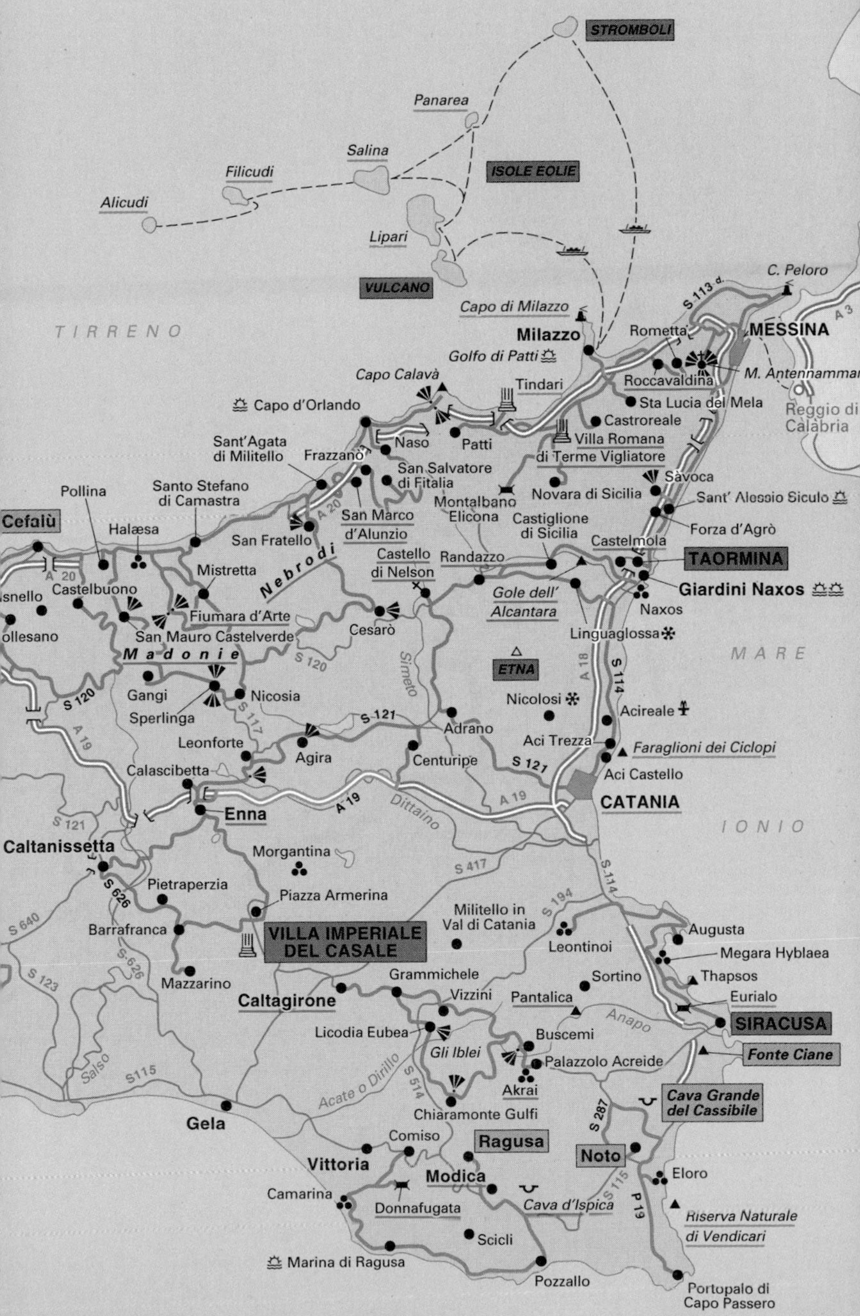

Driving tours

For descriptions of these tours, turn to the Practical Points section following.

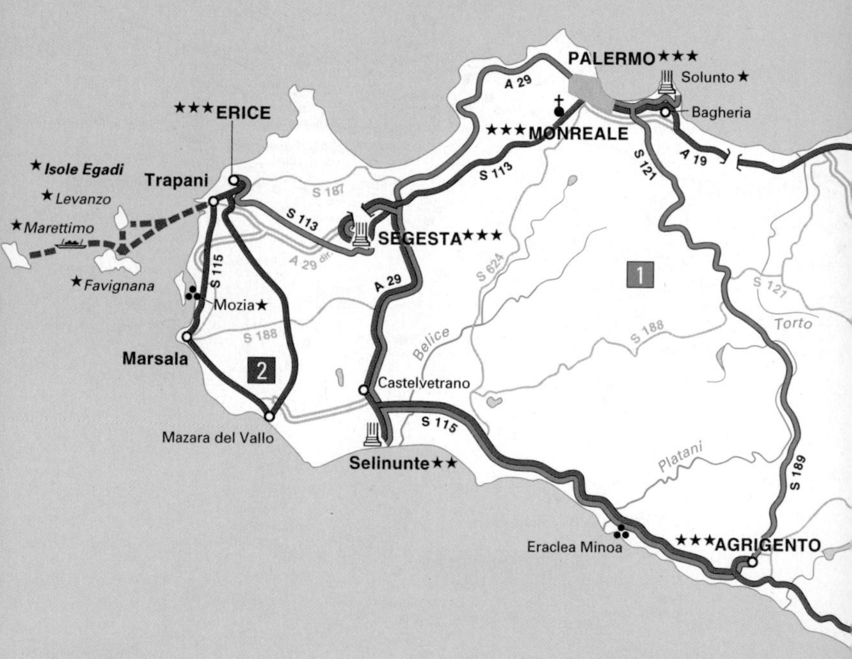

1 Archaeological sites and antiquities: 500 km/310 mi (9 days including 3 in Palermo and 2 in Agrigento)

2 Saltworks and tuna fisheries: 150 km/90mi (8 days including 4 in the Egadi Islands)

3 Reach for the heights: 250 km/155mi (5 days)

4 Baroque Sicily - demise and revival in 1693: 350 km/220mi (9 days including 3 in Siracusa)

5 The Demone Valley: 400 km/250mi (10 days including 4 in the Aeolian Islands)

6 Grand Tour of Sicily: 850 km/530mi (15 days)

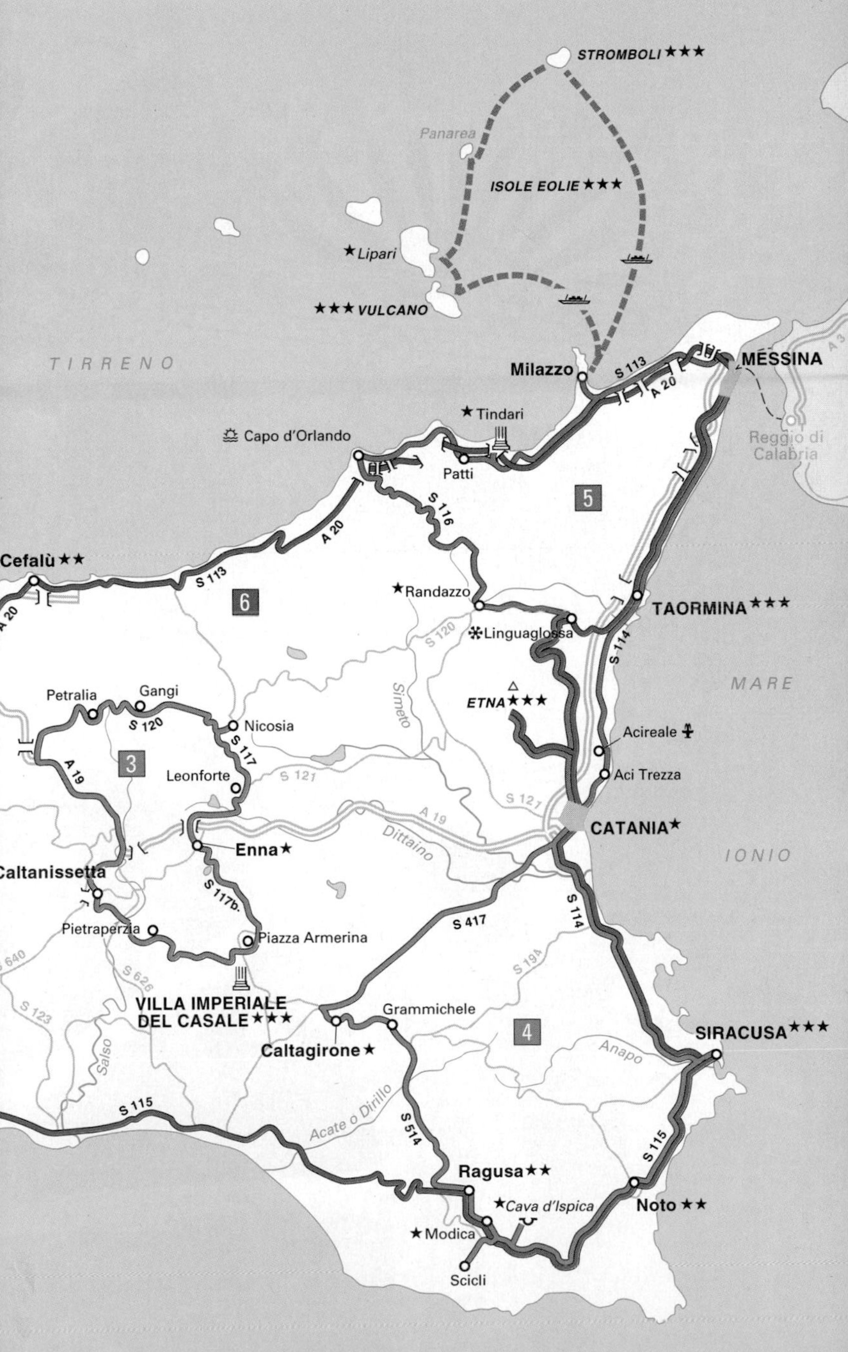

Lara Pessina/MICHELIN

Practical Points

Planning your Trip

Useful addresses

Information on Sicily is available from the Assessorato Regionale del Turismo, delle Comunicazioni e dei Trasporti, Via Notarbartolo 9, 90141 Palermo; ☎ 091 69 68 201; Fax 091 69 68 135.
Local tourist offices are listed under the "Location" heading in the Selected Sights section of this guide.

Internet

The Internet is a useful source of information, enabling visitors to contact tourist offices, consult programmes and brochures and make bookings on line. The following websites provide information on Italian history and art, as well as giving practical suggestions for making the most of your time in Sicily.

Italy

www.enit.it/default.asp (Italian Tourist Office)
www.museionline.it/ (information on museums in Italy)
www.beniculturali.it/ (Ministero dei Beni Culturali)
www.fs-on-line.com/ (Italian State Railways)

Sicily

www.regione.sicilia.it (official website of the Sicily region)
www.coloridisicilia.it/isola/index.htm
www.bestofsicily.com/magazine.htm (English magazine on Sicily)
www.parks.it/regione.sicilia/index.html (natural parks and nature reserves)
www.wwfsicilia.it/default.asp (World Wildlife Fund, section on Sicily)
www.festedisicilia.it/ and www.insicilia.it/sicilia_eventi_spettacoli.htm (festivals and events)
www.insicilia.it (tourism in Sicily)
www.siciliano.it (Sicilian search engine, with an excellent book section)
www.viaggioinsicilia.com/default.htm (theme-based tours)

Sicilian provinces

Agrigento: www.aaa-agrigento.it/turismo/turismo.html and www.lampedusa.to/ (Lampedusa)
Caltanissetta: www.aapit.cl.it/
Catania: www.turismo.catania.it/, www.comune.ct.it/conoscerect/filodarianna/filodarianna.htm (city tours), www.parcoetna.ct.it/ (official website for the Etna National Park)
Enna: www.ennaonline.com/aast/home.asp
Messina: www.azienturismomessina.it/, www.netnet.it/aasteolie/ and www.portaledelleolie.it/index.php (Aeolian Islands), www.taormina-network.it/ (Taormina)
Palermo: www.aapit.pa.it/, www.arcidiocesi.palermo.it/?omelie=1&benic=1 (part of the archidiocese website, with information on churches in Palermo), www.cefalu-tour.pa.it/ (Cefalù)
Ragusa: www.ibla.net/
Siracusa: www.flashcom.it/aatsr/
Trapani: www.apt.trapani.it/, www.egaditourism.it (Egadi Islands), digilander.libero.it/isoladipantelleria/ (Pantelleria)

Tourist organisations

(see also Embassies and Consulates, below)

Italian State Tourist Office – ENIT (Ente Nazionale Italiano per il Turismo) – For information, brochures, maps and assistance in planning a trip to Italy, contact the ENIT in your own country or log onto the ENIT website, www.enit.it
1 Princes Street, London W1B 2AY; ☎ (020) 7408 1254; 24-hour brochure request line: ☎ 090 65 508 925 (calls charged at premium rate)
630 Fifth Avenue, Suite 1565, New York, NY 10111; ☎ (212) 245 4822
12400 Wilshire Boulevard, Suite 550, Los Angeles, CA 90025; ☎ (310) 820 0098
175 Bloor Street, Suite 907 – South Tower, Toronto M4W 3R8; ☎ (416) 925 4882

Italian embassies and consulates

Details on visa requirements and other information can be obtained from your nearest Italian embassy or consulate:

Embassies

14 Three Kings' Yard, London W1K 2EH; ☎ (020) 7312 2200; Fax (020) 7499 2283; emblondon@embitaly.org.uk; www.embitaly.org.uk
3000 Whitehaven St, NW Washington, DC 20008; ☎ (202) 612 4400; Fax (202) 518 2154; www.italyemb.org
275 Slater Street, 21st Floor, Ottawa, Ontario K1P 5H9; ☎ (613) 232 2401; Fax (613) 233 1484; ambital@italyincanada.com; www.italyincanada.com

Consulates

38 Eaton Place, London SW1X 8AN; ☎ (020) 7235 9371; Fax (020) 7823 1609; itconlond@btconnect.com
Rodwell Tower, 111 Piccadilly, Manchester M1 2HY; ☎ (0161) 236 9024; Fax (0161) 236 5574; italconsulman@btinternet.com

32 Melville Street, Edinburgh EH3 7HW; ☎ (0131) 226 3631; Fax (0131) 226 6260; consedimb@consedimb.demon.co.uk
690 Park Avenue, New York NY 10021; ☎ (212) 737 9100; Fax (212) 249 4945; info@italconsulnyc.org; www.italconsulnyc.org
3489 Drummond Street, Montreal, Quebec H3G 1X6; ☎ (514) 849 8351; Fax (514) 499 9471; cgi@italconsul.montreal.qc.ca; www.italconsul.montreal.qc.ca
136 Beverley Street, Toronto, Ontario M5T 1Y5; ☎ (416) 977 1566; (416) 977 1119; CGToronto@toronto.italconsulate.org; www.toronto.italconsulate.org

Formalities

Documents

Passports – British visitors travelling to Italy must be in possession of a valid national passport. Citizens of other European Union countries only need a national identity card. In case of loss or theft report to the embassy or consulate and the local police.

Visas – Entry visas are required by Australian, New Zealand, Canadian and US citizens (if their intended stay exceeds three months). Apply to the Italian Consulate (visa issued same day; delay if submitted by mail). US citizens may find the booklet **Your Trip Abroad** useful for information on visa requirements, customs regulations, medical care etc when travelling in Europe – available from the Superintendent of Documents, PO Box 371954; Pittsburgh, PA 15250-7954, ☎ (202) 512 1800; Fax (202) 512 2250; www.access.gpo.gov

Driving Licence – Nationals of the European Union require a valid **national driving licence**. Nationals of non-EU countries should obtain an **international driving licence**, obtainable in the US from the American Automobile Association, US$18 for members and US$20 for non-members. The AAA can be contacted at AAA National Headquarters, 1000 AAA Drive, Heathrow FL 32746-5080; ☎ (407) 444 7000; www.aaa.com Other documents required include the vehicle's current **log book** and a **green card** for insurance.

Health

As the UK is a member of the European Union, British subjects should obtain **medical form E111** from the Ministry of Social Security, Newcastle-upon-Tyne, or from main post offices, before leaving home. Separate travel and medical insurance is highly recommended – check with your local travel agent before departure.

Customs regulations

As of 30 June 1999, those travelling between countries within the European Union can no longer purchase "duty-free" goods. For further information, there is a free leaflet, **Duty Paid**, available from HM Customs and Excise, Finchley Excise Advice Centre, Berkeley House, 304 Regents Park Road, London N3 2JY; ☎ 0845 010 9000; www.hmce.gov.uk The US Customs Service offers a free publication **Know Before You Go** for US citizens, www.customs.gov

Pets (cats and dogs)

A general health certificate and proof of rabies vaccination should be obtained from your local vet before departure.

Seasons

Climate

In Giuseppe Lampedusa's *The Leopard*, the Prince of Salina describes the Sicilian climate as "six months of 40°C [104°F] temperatures". Although Lampedusa exaggerated to make his point, the southern coast and its immediate hinterland (where the sirocco winds are at their strongest) do indeed suffer from excessively high temperatures in summer. The northern and eastern coasts and the islands off Sicily enjoy a milder climate, protected by the mountains running along the coast which shield them from the hot winds heading up from Africa. The inland mountains have cooler summers, with temperatures dipping in the evenings, and harsh winters. Catania is an exceptionally hot city, with conditions made unpleasant by traffic pollution and smog. As a general rule, July and August are the most uncomfortable

The beach at Cefalù

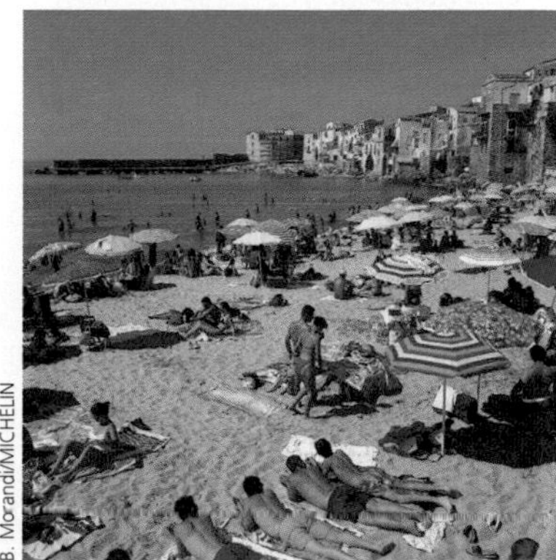

B. Morandi/MICHELIN

months on the island, while April, May, June, September and October offer pleasantly warm temperatures. Rainfall is scarce, although the lack of water that has afflicted the island for centuries does not usually affect visitors, as most hotels have their own water cisterns.

Best time to go

Climate is an important consideration when planning a trip to Sicily. In many ways, **spring** is the ideal time to visit: the weather is mild, blossoming trees add a touch of colour to the countryside, and the busy tourist season has not yet started (although you may well come across school groups visiting some of the major monuments). However, Etna is usually covered with snow and therefore inaccessible until early May, the sea at this time of year is still a little cool for bathing, and the tourist season on the offshore islands only runs from April/May to October. Visitors interested in local traditions and festivals are advised to visit the island during the **Easter holidays**, when most of Sicily's major festivals take place. **Summer** is the most popular time to visit: by now all the island's tourist facilities are up and running and museums and monuments offer extended opening hours. However, the disadvantages of visiting at this time of year are the weather, which in some areas (eg the central inland region, the southern coast, Catania and Palermo) is almost unbearable, and the hordes of tourists which crowd the most popular sites. **Autumn** is a more pleasant time to visit the island, offering similar conditions to spring. **Winter** is perfect for anyone planning a purely cultural trip, although care should be taken to check opening times of museums and monuments. If travelling inland in the winter months, be sure to take the weather into consideration, as the mountains can be wet and snowy at this time of year.

Public holidays

A working day is *un giorno feriale; giorni festivi* include Saturdays, Sundays and the following public holidays:
January 1 (New Year)
and 6 (Epiphany)
Easter Sunday and Monday
(lunedì dell'Angelo)
April 25 (St Mark's Day and liberation in 1945)
May 1 *(Festa dei Lavoratori)*
Sunday nearest June 2 (Anniversary of the Republic)
August 15 (The Assumption – *Ferragosto*)
November 1 *(All Saints – Tutti i Santi)*
December 8 (Immaculate Conception), 25 and 26 (Christmas and St Stephen's Day).

Time difference

The time in Italy is usually the same as in the rest of mainland Europe (one hour ahead of the United Kingdom) and changes during the last weekend of March and of October between summer time *(ora legale)* and winter time *(ora solare)*.

Budget

Compared with other parts of Italy and with the exception of the most popular tourist sections of the island, the cost of living is not particularly high in Sicily. The most visited areas, such as Taormina, Agrigento, Cefalù, Etna and the Aeolian Islands, are world famous and prices reflect this, especially in high season.
Accommodation options for visitors on a budget include campsites, hostels and the increasingly popular *agriturismi*.
For suggestions on how to make your money go further, especially when buying airline or train tickets, see *Concessions* below.
If you are on a **tight budget** it is possible to manage in Sicily on a daily allowance of €50. This sum includes accommodation in a double room in a **Budget** category hotel (options in this category also include youth hostels, *pensioni*, bed and breakfast accommodation and campsites; if staying in the latter, your daily budget could come down even further), a snack at lunchtime (a slice of pizza, pastry or roll) and an evening meal in a trattoria or pizzeria (€15). The **Moderate** category is for those on an **average budget**. Allow around €80 per day including a room in a comfortable hotel, a snack lunch and dinner in a medium-priced restaurant (for around €30).
If you choose to spend more you can select a hotel from the **Expensive** category and enjoy dining in gourmet restaurants.
This daily budget excludes any additional costs such as entrances to museums and monuments. Guided tours (especially those on Etna) and boat trips can also be quite expensive. Agrigento, Palermo and Siracusa all offer reductions on combined tickets to museums.

Special needs

Many historic monuments do not have modern lifts or wheelchair facilities. For detailed information prior to departure contact **RADAR** (Royal Association for Disability and Rehabilitation), 12 City

Forum, 250 City Road, London EC1V 8AF; ☎ (020) 7250 3222; Fax (020) 7250 0212; radar@radar.org.uk; www.radar.org.uk
For information in Italy on which monuments are accessible to disabled travellers, contact the **Associazione Italiana Assistenza Spastici**, Via Vitadini 3, Milano; ☎ 02 58 32 00 88, or **CO.IN** (Consorzio Cooperative Integrate), Via di Torricola 87, 00178 Roma; ☎ 06 71 29 011; Fax 06 71 29 01 25. Information in English on hotels, restaurants, museums and monuments with facilities for the disabled is available at www.italiapertutti.it
Sights in the guide marked with the symbols ♿ or (♿) have full or partial access for wheelchairs.

Transport

Airlines and rail companies offer special rates outlined in *Concessions*.

Getting there

Flights

Several international airlines fly into Palermo, Catania and Reggio Calabria, especially during the summer season when additional charter flights are laid on. At present, the only low-cost airline to fly directly to Sicily (Palermo) from the UK is Ryanair from London Stansted. For further information on this service log onto www.ryanair.com
The main Italian airlines operating to Sicily are Alitalia and Meridiana.

Alitalia:
4 Portman Square, Marble Arch, London W1H 9PS; ☎ (020) 7486 8432; Fax (020) 7486 8431. Reservations can also be made on ☎ 08705 448 259; www.alitalia.co.uk
4-5 Dawson Street, Dublin 2; ☎ (01) 677 5171; Fax (01) 677 3373.
666 Fifth Avenue, New York, NY 10103; ☎ (212) 903 3300; 1 800 223 5730 (toll-free); Fax (212) 903 3350; www.alitaliausa.com
Viale Marchetti 111, 00148 Rome; ☎ 06 65 621; www.alitalia.it

Meridiana:
Meridiana operate flights from London to Palermo via Naples, and to Catania via Florence.
For the London sales office, call ☎ (020) 7839 2222; info.london@meridiana.uk.com; www.meridiana.it To contact the main office in Italy, call ☎ 0789 69 300.

The following American airlines operate flights to Italy:
American Airlines – www.aa.com
Continental Airlines – www.continental.com
Delta Airlines – www.delta.com
Northwest Airlines – www.nwa.com
United Airlines – www.ual.com
USAirways – www.usairways.com

Tour operators offering flight-only or package holidays to Sicily include:
Citalia – ☎ (020) 8686 0677; www.citalia.com
Italy Sky Shuttle – ☎ (020) 8748 1333; www.traveleshop.com
The Magic of Italy – ☎ 08700 270 480; www.magictravelgroup.co.uk
Page and Moy Ltd – ☎ 08700 106 400; www.page-moy.co.uk

By air

Sicily's two main airports are **Falcone e Borsellino** in Palermo and **Fontanarossa** close to Catania on the east coast; the latter is well located for visitors intending to stay around Taormina and Siracusa. There is also an airport in **Reggio Calabria**, which although on the Italian peninsula, lies close to the Straits of Messina.
Other Sicilian airports are located at **Trapani Birgi**, which links Trapani with Pantelleria, Rome and Milan, and on the islands of **Pantelleria** and **Lampedusa**, from where direct flights operate to and from major larger Italian cities in summer. *For detailed information, see PANTELLERIA and LAMPEDUSA.*

By rail

The train operates via the Straits of Messina, with coaches being loaded directly onto the ferry at Villa San Giovanni. Ticket prices are all inclusive. For information, apply to the **Ferrovie dello Stato** (Italian State Railways), ☎ 848-88088 (information in Italy); www.fs-on-line.com
Information on trains to Italy is also available from Ultima Travel, 424 Chester Road, Little Sutton, South Wirral CH66 3RB; ☎ (0151) 339 6171; Fax (0151) 339 9199.

By coach

Coach services to Italy from Victoria Coach Station in London are operated by Eurolines, 4 Cardiff Road, Luton, Bedfordshire LU1 1PP; ☎ 08705 143 219 (calls charged at standard rate); Fax 01582 400 694; welcome@eurolinesuk.com;

G. Bluczin/MICHELIN

www.eurolines.co.uk Alternatively, contact National Express, 52 Grosvenor Gardens, London SW1; ☎ 0870 901 3190; 08705 80 80 80; www.nationalexpress.com

The Segesta Internazionale bus company operates daily coach services between Rome, Palermo and Trapani. Journey time between Rome and Palermo is 12hr. *For further information see p 280.*

By boat

Ferries operate to Palermo from Genoa (20hr), Livorno (17hr), Naples (11hr or 4hr 30min by hydrofoil) and Cagliari (13hr 30min). *For further information see p 280.*

By car

The Michelin companion maps and plans for this guide are listed after the main contents page at the beginning of the guide.

Until the bridge over the Straits becomes a reality, the link between Sicily and the rest of Italy is provided by ferries and hydrofoils between Reggio Calabria or Villa San Giovanni and Messina. Ferrovie dello Stato (Italian State Railways) provide a car-ferry service, but only from Villa San Giovanni (☎ 0965 75 60 99). The time of the crossing depends on the type of ferry (whether it is transporting only cars or train carriages as well), and varies between 25-45min. A ferry service is also operated by Società Caronte Shipping, ☎ 0965 75 14 13. Because of the frequent service (every 30min), booking is not necessary. Just turn up at the dock.

From Reggio Calabria, there are also services for foot-passengers only, both by ferry (Stazione Ferrovie dello Stato, ☎ 0965 86 35 25) and hydrofoil (Aliscafi SNAV, ☎ 0965 29 568).

Getting about

Also see the Map of Driving Tours on p 12.

By car

Travelling by car is certainly one of the best ways of covering the island for people who intend to visit not only the main towns and cities, but also the smaller, more remote centres. However, this clearly does not apply once your destination has been reached: Palermo traffic is so heavy and chaotic that you would be well advised to leave your car somewhere safe and rely on public transport to get around, or walk. Walking is also the best option in smaller towns and villages, where the narrow, medieval streets make driving difficult.

The **motorways** *(autostrade)* in Sicily do not cover the whole island. Motorway stretches include Palermo-Messina-Catania (A 18 and A 20), with a dual-carriageway section between Castelbuono (10km/6mi east of Cefalù) and Acquedolci (Furiano exit); Palermo-Trapani-Mazara del Vallo (A 29); and Palermo-Enna-Catania (A 19). Tolls are payable on the sections between Messina and Furiano (A 20), Catania and Messina (A 18), and Cefalù and Buonfornello (A 20). All other motorways are free of charge.

Away from the fast highways, most towns are generally served by good roads. The only difficulties drivers are likely to encounter are on roads to small mountain towns and villages, where the views are often stunning but the roads tend to be winding and therefore slower.

Highway code

Traffic drives on the right and the **minimum driving age** in Italy is 18 years.

Seat belts must be worn in the front and back of the vehicle. Drivers must wear **shoes** and carry spare lights and a **red triangle** to be displayed in case of a breakdown or accident.

A valid driving licence must be carried at all times.

Motorways (*autostrade* – subject to tolls) and dual carriageways *(superstrade)* are indicated by green signs; ordinary roads by blue signs; tourist sights by yellow signs.

Italian **motorway tolls** can be paid with money or with the **Viacard**, a magnetic card which is sold in Italy at the entrances and exits of the motorways, in Autogrill restaurants and in the offices of ACI (Automobile Club Italiano), Via Marsala 8, 00185 Rome; ☎ 06 99 81.

The following **speed restrictions** operate:

50kph in built-up areas;
90-110kph on open country roads;
90 (600cc) – 130kph (excess of 1 000cc) on motorways depending on engine capacity.

Parking

The main car parks are marked by the symbol 🅿 on the city maps. Visitors are advised not to leave valuable items in their cars and to ensure that all luggage is out of sight in the boot.

MAPS AND PLANS

A list of Michelin maps that would be useful for getting to Sicily and finding your way around the island is given at the beginning of the guide *(see Maps and Plans)*.

ROAD RESCUE SERVICES

A road-rescue service is provided by the ACI (Automobile Club Italia). For information, call ☎ 06 49 98 23 00. For the emergency service ☎ 803 116 (24-hour service).

PETROL/GAS

Fuel is sold as *super* (4-star), *senza piombo* (unleaded 95 octane), *super plus* or *Euro plus* (unleaded 98 octane) or *gazolio* (diesel).

Manned petrol stations are usually closed noon-4pm and at night. Petrol can be bought 24hr a day and on Sundays from automatic petrol pumps.

CAR HIRE

All the main car hire agencies have offices in the major cities and at the airports. Some tour operators offer "fly-drive" packages. Call the following numbers for further information (numbers accessible from within Italy only):

Avis: ☎ 199 100 133; www.avis.co.uk

Hertz: ☎ 199 112 211 – if calling from a mobile, dial ☎ 0248 233 662; www.hertz.co.uk

Europcar: ☎ 800 014 410; www.europcar.co.uk

Maggiore: ☎ 848 867 067; www.maggiore.it

By rail

The rail network is fairly limited in Sicily and does not cover the whole island. The main services operate along the coast, linking Messina-Siracusa (3hr), Messina-Palermo (3hr), Palermo-Agrigento (2hr) and Palermo-Trapani (2hr 30min). Services to the mountainous interior are relatively infrequent.

By coach

The coach network offers the best way of exploring the island for visitors without their own transport, offering regular services to many towns and cities. For further information, contact the local tourist office *(see Location at the beginning of each chapter in the Selected Sights section)*.

Where to Stay and Where to Eat

Addresses listed in the guide

For all budgets

The **Directory** sections in the main text of the guide list a selection of hotels and restaurants chosen for their value for money, typical Sicilian cuisine, location or character, including historic hotels, old converted buildings, such as *bagli* (fortified buildings) and convents.

Types of accommodation

The hotels listed in the guide are divided into three price brackets. Hotels included in the **Budget** section are usually small and basic, but are fairly comfortable and situated in a particularly good location; expect to pay less than €70 for a double room. This category includes campsites, youth hostels and modest *pensioni*. Those with a larger budget will find hotels offering greater comfort and charm in our **Moderate** category, where prices range from €70 to €130 for a double room. A selection of luxury and atmospheric hotels offering a wide range of facilities and guaranteeing a memorable stay is given in the **Expensive** section, with double rooms starting at €130. In the more popular and expensive towns and cities, visitors should bear in mind that some hotels in this category would elsewhere be included in the Moderate category.

For regions and cities popular with tourists, it is advisable to book accommodation well in advance, especially if you plan to go from April to October. In general from November to March, prices are considerably lower and many hotels offer discounts or special weekend deals.

For each establishment, the first figure refers to the price of a single room, the second figure to the price of a double room. Exceptions to this are highlighted (rural guesthouses, for example, which generally only have double rooms). Breakfast is usually included in the price although this may not be the case in smaller hotels. When not included in the price of the room, the cost of breakfast immediately follows the price of the room. Whatever type of accommodation you choose, it is advisable to check prices before booking, as rates can vary depending on the time of year and availability of rooms.

HOTELS AND PENSIONI

It is not always easy to distinguish between a hotel and a *pensione*. Generally, the word *pensione* is used to describe a small family-run hotel, which is sometimes situated within a residential building and which offers simple, basic rooms, often without a private bathroom. Some *pensioni* do not accept credit cards.

RURAL ACCOMMODATION

Rural guesthouses were originally conceived as an opportunity to combine accommodation with the chance to taste the products made on the farm (among them olive oil, wine, honey, vegetables and meat). In the last few years Sicily has witnessed a huge growth in popularity of such guesthouses, some of which are as elegant as the best hotels, with prices to match. As a result, in some you will find a menu that makes use of the farm's own produce while in others you may be provided with a kitchenette in an apartment that will offer you complete independence; others still may only offer breakfast. The guesthouses included in the guide usually accept bookings for one night only, but in high season the majority prefer weekly stays or offer half or full board as well as requiring a minimum stay. Prices for the latter are only given when this formula is compulsory. Bear in mind that the majority of these rural guesthouses only have double rooms and prices shown here are based on two people sharing a double room. People travelling alone should try asking for a discount. In any case because of the ever-increasing popularity of this type of accommodation it is advisable to book well in advance.

To get an idea of what is on offer in this category consult the following guides: *Turismo Verde in Sicilia*, published by the Consorzio Villaggio Globale (an offshoot of the Italian Farming Confederation in Palermo; ☎ 091 30 81 51); *Vacanze e Natura* (published by Associazione Terranostra; ☎ 06 46 821; www.terranostra.it; *Agriturismo e Vacanze Verdi* (published by Associazione Agriturist, Corso Vittorio Emanuele 101, Rome; ☎ 06 68 52 342; Fax 06 68 52 424; www.agriturist.it); and *Guida all'Agriturismo*, published by Demetra and *Vacanze Verdi* published by Edagricole. Other interesting accommodation options are published in the *Guida del Turismo alternativo* (*Sicilia occidentale* and *Sicilia orientale;* in Italian only), available from bookshops and newsagents, or directly from the Sicilian Tourist Service, which provides an information and booking service (Piazza Don Bosco 6, Palermo; ☎ 091 36 15 67; Fax 091 63 72 482; www.stsitalia.it). Information is also available from **Turismo Verde**, Via Caio Mario 27, Rome; ☎ 06 36 11 051; www.turismoverde.it

BED AND BREAKFAST

A varied category, where often the difference between a hotel and a bed and breakfast is indistinguishable. The house or apartment is also often the home of the hosts, who let out a few of their rooms. Guests are usually required to stay for a minimum period and credit cards are rarely accepted. Generally speaking, a bed and breakfast offers a cosier atmosphere than a hotel at competitive prices.

To get an idea of what is on offer contact **Bed & Breakfast Italia**, Palazzo Sforza Cesarini, Corso Vittorio Emanuele II 282, 00186 Rome; ☎ 06 68 78 618; Fax/☎ 06 68 78 619; www.bbitalia.it, or **Bed & Breakfast Bon Voyage**, Via Procaccini 7, 20154 Milan; ☎ 02 33 11 814; Fax 02 33 13 009. Information is also available on the following websites: www.bedandbreakfast.it; www.primitaly.it/bb/; www.bedebreakfast.it; www.dolcecasa.it; and www.caffelletto.it

CAMPSITES

A good option for visitors on a tight budget, campsites generally have a restaurant, bar and food shop and some have swimming pools. Some sites also have bungalows and caravans; for prices contact each site individually. Prices shown in the guide are daily rates for two people, one tent and one car.

An International Camping Carnet for caravans is useful, but not compulsory; it can be obtained from the motoring organisations or the **Camping and Caravanning Club,** Greenfields House, Westwood Way, Coventry CV4 8JH; ☎ (024) 7669 4995; www.campingandcaravanningclub.co.uk

For more information contact the **Federazione Italiana del Campeggio e del Caravanning**, Via Vittorio Emanuele 11, 50041 Calenzano (FI); ☎ 055 88 23 91; Fax 055 88 25 918; www.federcampeggio.it The organisation publishes a map of campsites and a list of those which offer special rates to holders of the international camping card. It also publishes an annual guide, *Campeggi e Villagi Turistici in Italia*, in collaboration with the TCI. Local tourist boards also supply information on campsites.

YOUTH HOSTELS AND RELIGIOUS BOARDING HOUSES

Hostel accommodation is only available to members of the Youth Hostel Association. It is possible to join the organisation at any of the YHA hostels; membership then provides access to the many YHA hostels located around the world. There is no age limit for membership, which must be renewed annually. In Italy youth hostels are run by the **Associazione Italiana Alberghi per la Gioventù** (AIG), situated at Via Cavour 44, 00184 Rome; ☎ 06 48 71 152; www.ostellionline.org

Case per ferie (holiday homes), generally to be found in the big cities, offer simple but clean and reasonably-priced accommodation, the only disadvantage being the curfew: visitors are expected to be back by 10.30pm. For more information contact the tourist offices and CITS, Centro Italiano Turismo Sociale, Associazione dell'Ospitalità Religiosa, ☎ 06 48 73 145.

Where to Eat

For each restaurant listed we have given the minimum and maximum price for a full meal, excluding drinks. The sections entitled **For all budgets** list restaurants in ascending order of price, based on the minimum price given. For the major tourist centres, we have divided restaurants into two categories: **Budget** (meals available for less than €25) and **Moderate** (over €25).

In Sicily, lunch is usually served from 1 to 2.30pm and dinner from 8.30pm. Booking is recommended especially in high season. Although the distinction between different types of restaurants is not as obvious as it once was, in general, a *ristorante* offers elegant cuisine and service, whereas a *trattoria* or *osteria* is more likely to be a family-run establishment serving home-made dishes in a more relaxed, informal atmosphere; prices are usually lower in the latter. In typical trattorias, the waiter will often tell you what dishes of the day are on offer. If ordering these, make sure that you know how much you are paying ahead of time to avoid any unpleasant shocks when the bill arrives! (a list is usually available; if in doubt ask to see it). Be wary of choosing the tourist menu, which usually has very limited choice. Trattorias used to have almost exclusively house wine on offer (served by the carafe), but you can now expect to find a proper wine list which often has a good selection of local wines. For further information on Sicilian cuisine, see *Sicilian Food and Wine.*

SNACKS

For those who prefer not to sit down for a large meal at lunchtime or who are on a limited budget, bars, *pasticcerie* (pastry shops) and cafeterias offer a range of snacks and local specialities such as *arancini (rice balls)*, *panelle* (fried chickpea pancakes) and slices of pizza. Alternatively you may prefer to lunch on an ice cream or crushed ice *granita* with a brioche and cream.

R. Mattes/MICHELIN

TAKING A BREAK

Cafés and *pasticcerie* are ideal for a quick break in between sightseeing. The best on the island are listed under the heading **Taking a Break** either in the Directory section or within the running text of individual chapters.

And don't forget The Red Guide

THE RED GUIDE ITALIA

For a more exhaustive list of hotels consult *The Red Guide Italia* which provides a whole host of details on Italy's hotels and restaurants. Establishments that offer particularly good value for money are marked with the **Bib Gourmand** symbols.

Choosing Where to Stay

The map of Places to Stay on p shows places of interest marked to denote suitability for different kinds of trips.

Those interested in **cultural centres** should look for place names framed in green. For visitors on brief trips who want to stay in one of the many cities of artistic interest, destinations suitable for an **overnight stop** are underlined in green.

Among the many other **places to stay** look for areas shaded in green (nature parks) and for the symbols ⚕ **(spas)**, ⛱ **(seaside resort)** and ❄ **(winter sports resort)**.

Places to stay

- Seaside resort
- Spa
- Winter resort

Seaside resorts ⛱, spas ♆ and winter resorts ✻ are classified according to the quality and range of facilities offered.

- Cultural centre
- Overnight stop in town
- Protected parkland and nature reserves

0 — 40 km

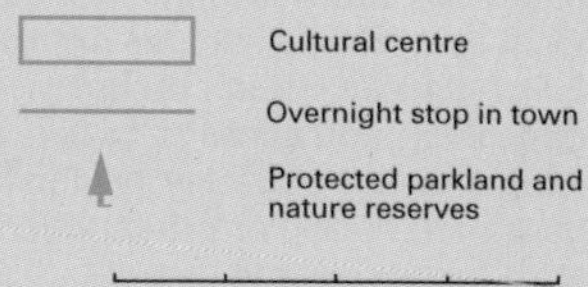

Ustica
MARE
Mondello
PALERMO
San Vito lo Capo
Terrasini
S. Nicolò l'Arena
Campofelice di Roccella
Castellammare del Golfo
Zingaro
A 19
TRAPANI
S 187
S 121
Isole Egadi
Saline di Trapani e Paceco
A 29 dir.
S 624
Stagnone
A 29
S 121
Torto
S 188
Marsala
Belice
S 188
S 115
Marinella di Selinunte
Foce del fiume Belice
Sciacca
Platani
S 189
Siculiana
Torre Salsa
AGRIGENTO
Porto Empedocle
MARE MEDITERRANEO
Lampedusa

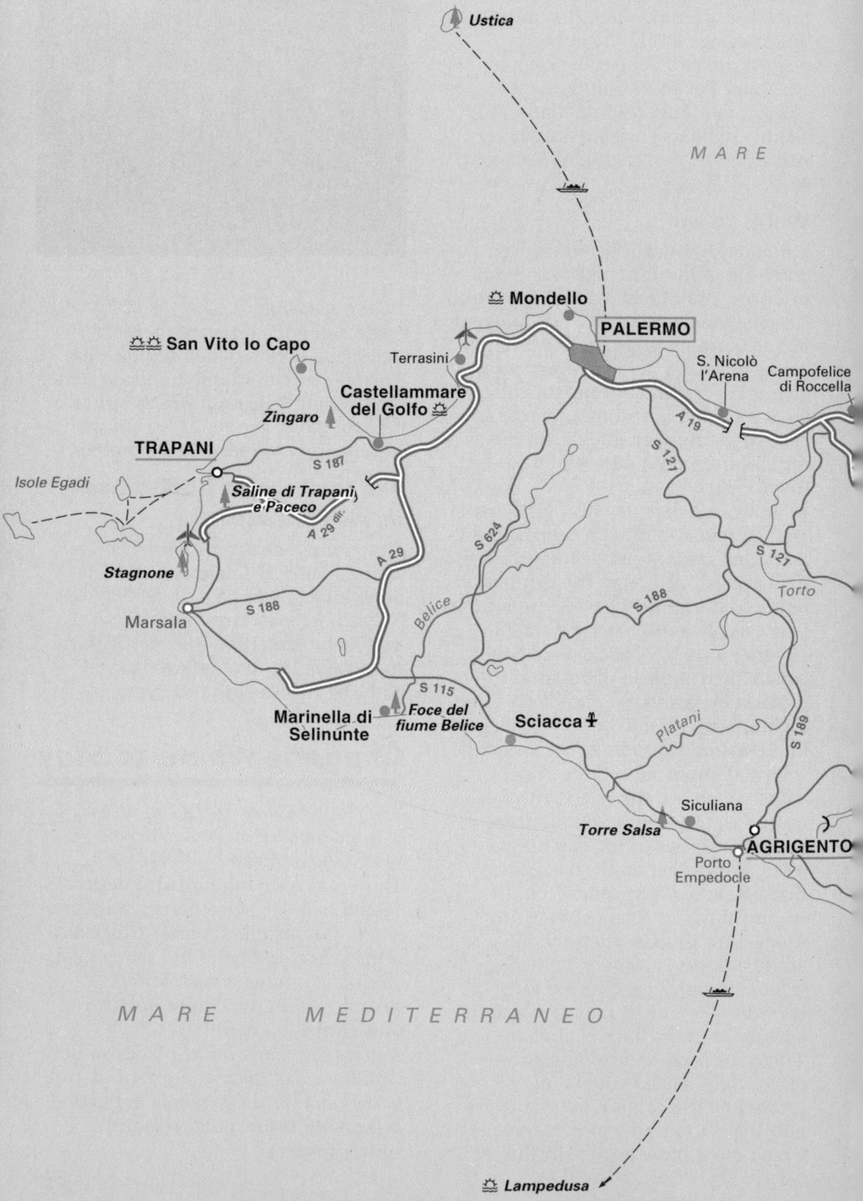

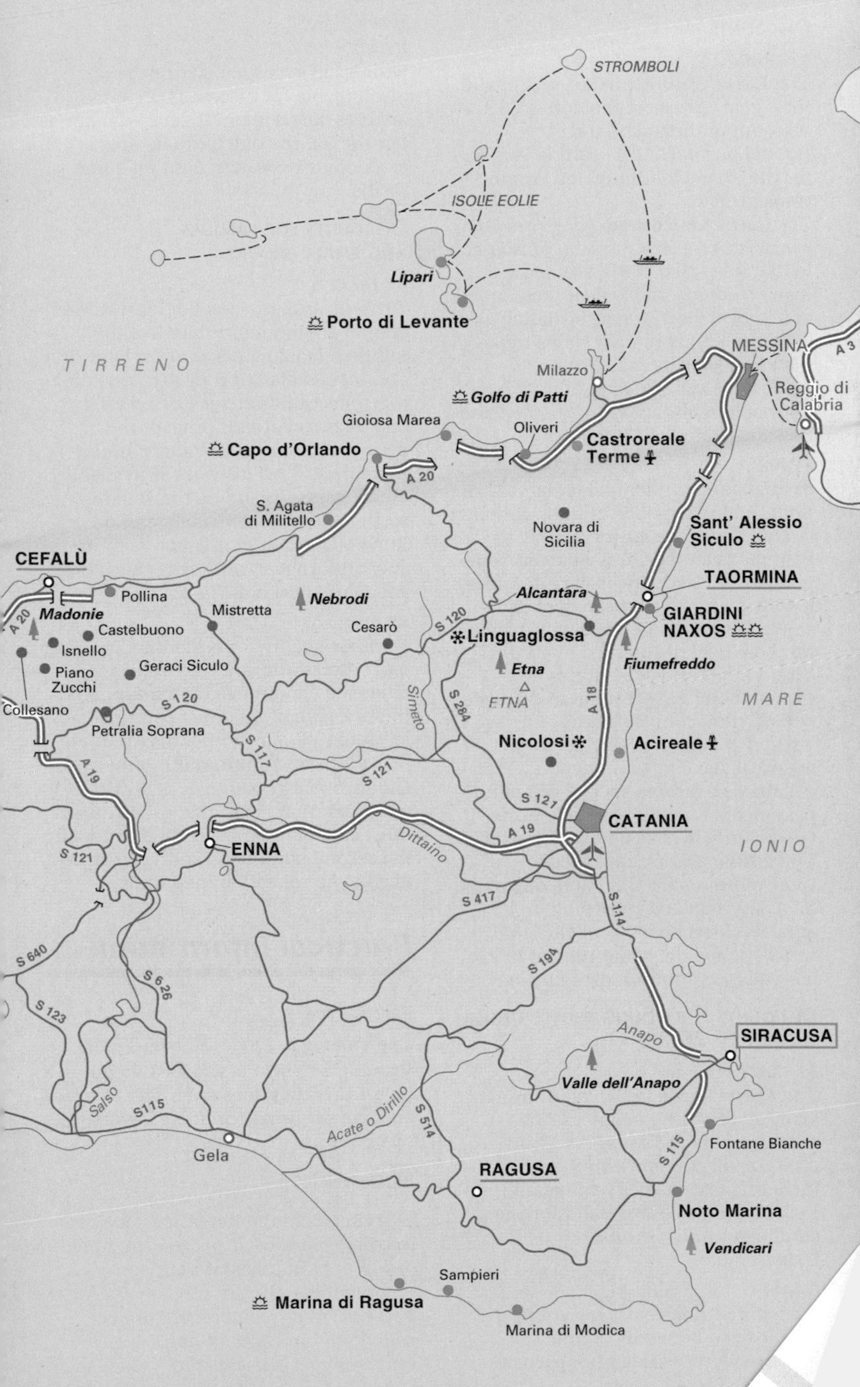
STROMBOLI
ISOLE EOLIE
Lipari
Porto di Levante
TIRRENO
MESSINA
A 3
Milazzo
Reggio di Calabria
Golfo di Patti
Gioiosa Marea
Oliveri
Castroreale Terme
Capo d'Orlando
A 20
S. Agata di Militello
Novara di Sicilia
Sant' Alessio Siculo
CEFALÙ
TAORMINA
Pollina
Madonie
Mistretta
Nebrodi
Alcantara
GIARDINI NAXOS
A 20
Castelbuono
Cesarò
S 120
Linguaglossa
Isnello
Geraci Siculo
Etna
Fiumefreddo
Piano Zucchi
Simeto
S 284
ETNA
A 18
MARE
Collesano
S 120
Petralia Soprana
Nicolosi
Acireale
S 117
S 121
A 19
S 127
CATANIA
ENNA
A 19
Dittaino
S 121
IONIO
S 417
S 114
S 640
S 626
S 194
S 123
Anapo
SIRACUSA
Salso
S 115
Acate o Dirillo
S 514
Valle dell'Anapo
Gela
S 115
Fontane Bianche
RAGUSA
Noto Marina
Vendicari
Sampieri
Marina di Ragusa
Marina di Modica

Services

Concessions

Visitors trying to keep costs down will find information on budget accommodation (*pensioni*, youth hostels, campsites, convents and monasteries) in the **Where to Stay** sections in the various chapters *(also see above)*.

Discounts

By train

The **Carta Club Eurostar** (€77, valid for a year) gives cardholders a 20% discount on first-class travel throughout Italy. This card is valid for the cardholder only and is non-transferrable.

The **Carta Amicotreno** (€50, valid for a year) gives a 50% discount on some local trains and a 20% discount on many medium- and long-distance trains, and is ideal for travellers spending an extended period in Italy, doing most of their travelling by rail. Certain restrictions apply to days of travel. Concessions also apply to a companion travelling with the cardholder.

By air

Several airlines offer budget fares to Rome and other cities in Italy, although the only one which flies directly to Palermo from the UK is Ryanair from London Stansted. Prices vary according to how far in advance the booking is made. Discounts are usually available for those booking on-line.

Virgin Express: www.virgin-express.com; BMI (British Midland): www.flybmi.com; Ryanair: www.ryanair.com; Easyjet: www.easyjet.com

Alitalia has various special offers for passengers buying their ticket one, two or three weeks before departure. The airline also offers special weekend rates for travellers departing on a Saturday and returning on a Sunday of the same weekend *(tipo corto)* and for the same type of ticket, but valid for a month *(tipo lungo)*.

Discounts for young people under the age of 26

By train

The **Carta Verde** (€26, valid for a year) gives young people a 20% discount in both first and second class, on all trains within Italy, including fast Eurocity trains and Eurostar. This card is valid for the cardholder only and is non-transferrable.

By air

Discounted rates exist for young people aged between 12 and 26 (under 26 on the day of departure).

Discounts for senior citizens

By train

For travellers over 60 years of age, the **Carta d'Argento** (€26, valid for a year) offers a 20% discount in first and second class on the Italian section of all routes, including fast Eurocity trains and Eurostar. This card is valid for the cardholder only and is non-transferrable.

By air

Senior citizens aged 60 or over are also eligible for discounts on some airlines, and senior citizens who are at least 65 on the day of travel are entitled to a 10% discount on some tariffs.

Discounts for families and small groups

By train

Families and groups of at least three people and no more than five are entitled to a 20% discount in both first and second class if they are travelling together. Children aged between 4 and 12 travel at half-price of the discounted fare and children under 4 travel free. This discount is available on all trains, including the Italian sections of Eurocity trains and on Eurostar, although it is not valid in July and August, or during the Easter and Christmas holiday periods.

By air

Families qualify for discounted tickets on certain airlines if they fulfil the following conditions: the family must travel together and must comprise at least four people, with a maximum of two adults and a minimum of two children (between the ages of two and eleven). At least one of the adults must be a parent of the children, while the second adult does not necessarily need to be related to the family.

Practical information

Electricity

The voltage is 220ac, 50 cycles per second; the sockets are for two-pin plugs. It is therefore advisable to take an adaptor for hairdryers, shavers, computers etc.

Emergencies

☎ **113:** General emergency services *(soccorso pubblico di emergenza)*; to be called only in cases of real emergency. Calls are free.

☎ **112:** Police *(carabinieri)*; to be called only in cases of real emergency. Calls are free.

☎ **115:** Fire Brigade *(vigili del fuoco)*. Calls are free.

☎ **118:** Emergency Health Services *(emergenza sanitaria)*. Calls are free.

☎ **1515:** Forest Fire Service. Environmental emergencies. Calls are free.

☎ **803 116:** Automobile Club d'Italia Emergency Breakdown Service. Calls are free.

Foreign embassies and consulates in Italy

Australia – Via Alessandria 215, 00198 Rome; ☎ 06 85 27 21; www.australian-embassy.it
Canada – Via G.B. de Rossi 27, 00161 Rome; ☎ 06 44 59 81; rome@dfait-maeci.gc.ca
Ireland – Piazza di Campitelli 3, 00186 Rome; ☎ 06 69 79 121; Fax 06 67 92 354.
UK – Via XX Settembre 80A, Rome; ☎ 06 42 20 00 01; Fax 06 42 20 23 34; www.britain.it
Via Cavour 121, Palermo; ☎ 091 32 64 12; Fax 091 58 42 40.
USA – Via Veneto 119A, 00187 Rome; ☎ 06 46 741; Fax 06 48 82 672; www.usembassy.it
Via Vaccarini 1, 90143 Palermo; ☎ 091 30 58 57; Fax 091 62 56 026.

Money

The unit of currency is the **euro** which is issued in notes (€5, €10, €20, €50, €100, €200 and €500) and in coins (1 cent, 2 cents, 5 cents, 10 cents, 20 cents, 50 cents, €1 and €2).

Banks

Banks are usually open Monday to Friday, 8.30am-1.30pm and 3-4pm. Some branches are open in city centres and shopping centres on Saturday mornings; almost all are closed on Saturday afternoons, Sundays and public holidays. Most hotels will change travellers' cheques. Money can be changed in post offices (except travellers' cheques), money-changing bureaux and at railway stations and airports. Commission is always charged.

Credit cards

Payment by credit card is widespread in shops, hotels and restaurants and also some petrol stations. *The Red Guide Italia* and *The Red Guide Europe* indicate which credit cards are accepted at hotels and restaurants. Money may also be withdrawn from a bank but may incur interest pending repayment.

Newspapers

The main regional newspapers are *La Gazzetta del Sud* (the area around Messina), *La Sicilia* (Catania) and the *Giornale di Sicilia* (Palermo). Foreign newspapers are available in major cities and large towns.

Pharmacies

These are identified by a red and white cross. When closed each will advertise the names of the pharmacy on duty and a list of doctors on call.

Post

Opening hours

Post offices are open 8am-2pm on weekdays, 8.30am-noon on Saturday. Stamps are also sold at tobacconists *(tabacchi)* which display a black *valori bollati* sign outside.

Stamps

Stamps for letters or postcards cost €0.40.
Express service stamps *(posta prioritaria)* cost €0.60.

Shopping

(see also "What to Buy Locally" p 36)

Most shops open from 8am-1pm and 3.30-7.30/8pm. Credit cards are accepted in most stores, with the exception of small food shops.

Telecommunications

The telephone service is organised by TELECOM ITALIA (formerly SIP). Each office has public booths where the customer pays for units used *(scatti)* at the counter after the call. Reduced rates operate after 6.30pm and are even less between 10pm and 8am.

Phonecards

Phonecards *(schede telefoniche)* are sold in denominations of €1, €2.50, €5 and €8 and are supplied by CIT offices and post offices as well as tobacconists (sign bearing a white T on a black background).

Public phones

Telephone boxes may be operated by telephone cards (sold in post offices and tobacconists) and by telephone credit cards. To make a call: lift the receiver, insert payment, await dialling signal, punch in the required number and wait for a response.

Telephoning

When making a call within Italy, the area code (eg 091 for Palermo) is always used, both from outside and within the city you are calling.
For international calls dial 00 plus the following country codes:
61 for Australia
1 for Canada
64 for New Zealand
44 for the UK
1 for the USA

If calling from outside the country, the international code for Italy is 39. Dial the full area code, even when making an international call; for example, when calling Palermo from the UK, dial 00 39 091, followed by the correspondent's number.

USEFUL NUMBERS
(see also "Emergencies", above)
☎ 176: International Directory Enquiries. Provides phone numbers outside of Italy in English and Italian. Note that calls to this number are subject to a charge.
☎ 170: Operator Assisted International Calls. Note that calls to this number are subject to a charge.

TOBACCONISTS

Besides cigarettes and tobacco, *tabacchi* sell postcards and stamps, confectionery, phonecards, public transport tickets, lottery tickets and such like.

D. Hée/MICHELIN

Sightseeing

Information on admission times and charges for museums and monuments is given in the "Selected Sights" section of the guide.
Admission times and charges are liable to alteration without prior notice. Due to fluctuations in the cost of living and the constant change in opening times as well as possible closures for restoration work, the information given in this guide should merely serve as a guideline. Visitors are advised to phone ahead to confirm opening times.
The admission prices indicated are for single adults benefiting from no special concession; reductions for children, students, the over 60s and parties should be requested on site and be endorsed with proof of ID. Special conditions often exist for groups but arrangements should be made in advance. For nationals of European Union member countries many institutions provide free admission to visitors under 18 and over 65 with proof of identification, and a 50% reduction for visitors under 25 years of age.
During **National Heritage Week** (Settimana dei Beni Culturali), which takes place at a different time each year, access to a large number of sights is free of charge. Contact the tourist offices for more detailed information.
When visits to museums, churches or other sites are accompanied by a custodian, it is customary to leave a donation.
In summer, many museums and monuments in Sicily are closed from 1 to 4pm.

SYMBOLS AND ABBREVIATIONS

Sights marked with the symbols ♿ or (♿) offer full or partial access for wheelchairs.

MUSEUMS, ARCHAEOLOGICAL SITES AND GARDENS

Museums are generally closed on Mondays; on other days ticket offices usually shut 30min or 1hr before closing time. As this rule is strictly applied it is almost impossible to enter a museum after this time. Many museums require visitors to leave bags and backpacks in a luggage deposit area at the museum entrance. Taking photos with a flash is usually forbidden.
Archaeological sites generally close 1hr before dusk.

CHURCHES

Churches are usually open 8.30am-noon and 4-6pm, except during services. Exceptions are listed in the Selected Sights section of this guide. Notices outside a number of churches formally request visitors to dress in a manner deemed appropriate when entering a place of worship – this excludes sleeveless and low-cut tops, short miniskirts or skimpy shorts and bare feet.
Visitors are advised to visit churches in the morning, when the natural light provides better illumination of the works of art; also churches are occasionally forced to close in the afternoons due to lack of staff. Works of art are often illuminated by coin-operated lighting.

Ideas for your Visit

Given Sicily's size and rich cultural heritage, visitors are advised to spend at least one week on the island, although a two-week stay would also allow time to explore some of the offshore islands. We have, however, included a few suggestions below for visitors on a shorter break visiting the island for the first time, or who may wish to add a few days' sightseeing to a relaxing beach holiday.

Short breaks (3-4 days)

Highlights of Catania

Whether you arrive by ferry from Messina or at the airport in Catania, one of the highlights of this region is an excursion to **Mount Etna**, combined with a half-day visit to the delightful town of **Taormina**, perhaps ending the day with a brief stop at one of the stunning beaches in the area. You may also like to spend a day visiting **Siracusa** (Ortygia and the archaeological site), followed perhaps by a visit at dusk to **Noto** or **Ragusa Ibla**. Your third day's sightseeing should focus on the Valle dei Templi in **Agrigento,** which can easily be combined with a visit to the magnificent **Villa Imperiale del Casale**, near Piazza Armerina.

Highlights of Palermo

Visitors to the north coast of the island, arriving at **Palermo** airport, should spend their first day in Sicily exploring its capital city. On Day 2, why not head out of the city to admire the mosaic masterpieces in the cathedral at **Monreale**, followed by those in **Cefalù**? An ide[...] the day is to spend a re[...] two on one of the nearby beaches. Possible excursions for Day 3 include a day trip to the Valle dei Templi in **Agrigento**, or to the delightful town of **Erice**, stopping on your way back to Palermo to admire the splendid Doric temple at **Segesta**.

Cloisters, Monreale (detail)

D. Boggini/MICHELIN

The Ionian Coast

In addition to Taormina and its neighbouring seaside resorts, highlights on the Ionian Coast include **Mount Etna**, the **Alcantara Valley**, **Catania** and **Siracusa**. Allow 1hr 30min to travel from Taormina to Siracusa, a distance of some 100km/62mi.

Outskirts of Palermo

Palermo is an excellent base for exploring some of the most fascinating areas of the island. Spend one day exploring **Scopello** and the **Riserva dello Zingaro**, another visiting **Erice** and the **Via del Sale** between Trapani and Marsala, and a third following the suggested tour **inland from Palermo** *(see p 311)*.

A few days in the Mountains

Visitors based on the north coast at **Cefalù** or **Capo d'Orlando** can discover an unusual facet of Sicily by exploring the Alpine landscapes of the **Madonie e Nebrodi** *(see MADONIE E NEBRODI)*.

A week in Sicily

If you are spending a week on the island, you can spend more time exploring the options listed above or choose from some of the tours described below. We have also included a "Highlights of Sicily" tour for first-time visitors.

Highlights of Sicily

The following tour provides a 7-day introduction to the island, with two days spent visiting **Palermo**, **Monreale** and **Cefalù**, one day at **Segesta** and **Erice**, one day at the Valle dei Templi in **Agrigento**, one day visiting the **Villa Imperiale del Casale** and the **Baroque towns** of Ragusa Ibla, Noto and Modica, one day in **Siracusa**, one day visiting **Etna** and **Taormina**... with maybe even some time to relax on the beach at the end of this whirlwind tour!

Touring by Car

The map of **Driving Tours** *(see p 12)* highlights recommended itineraries around the island for those with their own transport. The time spent on each tour will of course vary according to individual interests. The general guidelines provided allow visitors enough time to enjoy the scenery, visit the towns and sights included in the tour and make occasional unscheduled stops.

1 Archaeological Sites and Antiquities

500km/312mi (nine days, including three in Palermo and two in Agrigento) – This tour focuses on the island's most important archaeological sites. After spending a few days in **Palermo**, follow the Golfo di Carini to **Segesta** to admire its splendid Doric temple, and then to **Erice**, a spectacular medieval hill-top village. Return to the junction with the A 29 which you then follow south, stopping at the attractive small town of **Castelvetrano**, and then continuing to the Ancient Greek town of **Selinunte**. From here, take S 115 towards Agrigento, following the coast as far as the ruined city of **Eraclea Minoa** and its stunning beach, before continuing to the world-famous Valle dei Templi in **Agrigento**. Two days in Agrigento will allow you to explore the pleasant historic centre of the town, as well as some of the surrounding area. Returning to Palermo you cross the delightful mountain landscapes of the interior. Just before arriving in the city, take a brief diversion to the right along the A 19 to visit the ruins of the Punic city of **Solunto**.

2 Saltworks and Tuna Fisheries

150km/94mi (eight days, including four in the Egadi Islands) – After spending a few days exploring the **Egadi Islands**, once home to the traditional tuna *mattanza* (a ritual method of catching tuna), return to **Trapani** to spend a little time exploring the town. Continue south along the main road through the **saltpans** (*see VIA DEL SALE*) that lie between Trapani and Marsala. It's worth spending at least half a day here visiting the Ancient Phoenician colony at **Mozia**. After Mozia, head back to the main road and continue to **Marsala** to visit one of the wineries that produce the famous Marsala dessert wine. The town's Baglio Anselmi archaeological museum, housing relics of a Punic ship, is also well worth a visit. Continue southeast to **Mazara del Vallo**, a bustling port with a distinctly North-African feel. Return to Trapani before heading up to **Erice**, a delightful medieval hill-top town in a superb location. You may also like to visit the **Tonnara Bonagia** (tuna fishery) on the coast a few miles from Erice.

Agrigento, Temple of Heracles

M. Guillot/MICHELIN

3 Reach for the Heights

250km/156mi (five days) – This tour explores some of the island's lesser-known sights, driving through the mountains and barren uplands. After visiting **Enna**, the highest provincial capital in Italy at 948m/3 109ft, take S 117 north, skirting past magnificently sited villages such as **Calascibetta** and **Leonforte**. This road takes you into the southern slopes of the Madonie mountains. After a visit to **Nicosia**, a picturesque town at an altitude of 700m/2 296ft, take S 120 west to **Gangi**, where you can wander through the typical narrow medieval streets lined with stone houses. From Gangi, climb to an altitude of 1 147m/3 762ft to **Petralia Soprana**, the highest village in the Madonie. Continue along S 120 to the A 19, following the motorway as far as **Caltanissetta**. A minor road then leads to **Pietraperzia**; from here, pick up S 191 and continue as far as the famous **Villa Imperiale del Casale**, a splendid Roman villa renowned for its magnificent floor mosaics. **Piazza Armerina**, a small medieval town with an impressive cathedral surrounded by Baroque buildings, is located just a few miles from here. S 117 b then continues to wend its way through beautiful scenery as far as Enna, passing the **Lago di Pergusa** a few miles outside the town.

4 Baroque Sicily: Demise and Revival in 1693

350km/219mi (nine days, including three in Siracusa) – This enchanting trip provides an in-depth look at the island's Baroque heritage, including monumental limestone buildings, finely worked gratings and splendid corbels adorned with fantastic and grotesque figures. Start in **Catania**, home to ruins from Ancient times, and then follow the coast as far as **Siracusa** where you can visit the archaeological site, the island of Ortygia and some of the city's splendid museums, finding time perhaps for a boat trip on the **River Ciane**. Leaving Siracusa, follow S 115 to **Noto**, a magnificent Baroque town. The road then continues to Ispica, famous for the nearby **Cava d'Ispica**, a 10km/6mi gorge dotted with troglodyte dwellings and necropoli. Return to S 115 and follow signs to **Scicli**, another famous Baroque town. From here return to **Modica**, renowned for its Baroque architecture and local chocolate delicacies. Not far away stands the town of **Ragusa**, whose lower town (Ibla) is fascinating for its Baroque *palazzi* built according to a medieval layout. From here, S 514 follows the western edges of the Iblei as far as **Grammichele**, a town with a regular plan centred around a hexagonal piazza. The tour then continues to **Caltagirone**, renowned for its ceramics, after which you join S 417 to return to Catania.

5 Mythology and nature

400km/250mi (ten days, including four in the Aeolian Islands) – After spending time in **Catania** take a trip up **Etna** (subject to volcanic conditions), believed by the Ancient Greeks to house the forge worked by the giants of Hephaestus, the god of fire. The tour then follows the eastern side of the volcano as far as **Linguaglossa**. From here take S 284 to **Randazzo**, a small town of black lava streets and buildings. Turn away from Etna, taking S 116 which passes through beautiful mountain landscapes and leads down to **Capo d'Orlando** on the coast. Follow the coast road east, where seaside resorts mingle with archaeological sites such as the Roman villa at **Patti**, the Greek city of **Tyndaris** and the Roman villa of **Terme Vigliatore**. The road then comes to **Milazzo**, the main departure point for the **Aeolian Islands**, which according to Greek mythology were the home of Aeolus, god of the winds. Spend a few days here exploring these beautiful islands before returning to Sicily and visiting **Messina**. Continue along the Ionian coast as far as **Taormina**, the island's most famous sight, renowned primarily for its magnificent Greek theatre commanding breathtaking views of Etna and the coast. Continue along the coast as far as the **Riviera dei Ciclopi** *(see ACIREALE)*; the *Faraglioni dei Ciclopi* off the small port of **Aci Trezza** were said to be the rocks that Polyphemus threw at Ulysses in the *Odyssey*.

M. Guillot/MICHELIN

Climbing Mount Etna

6 Grand Tour of Sicily

850km/530mi (two weeks) – Following in the footsteps of the great travellers of the past, this tour follows the Sicilian coast, visiting the island's most famous cultural and natural sights. After visiting **Palermo** and **Monreale**, head to the splendid Doric temple at **Segesta** and then continue south, following tour 1 as far as **Agrigento**. From here, continue along the coast on S 115 to **Ragusa**, pausing at the archaeological museum in Gela en route. At Ragusa, join tour 4 which you follow as far as **Catania**. Continue to **Etna**, **Linguaglossa**, **Taormina**, **Messina** and the northeast coast, following tour 5 as far as **Capo d'Orlando**. Continue on along the coast as far as **Cefalù**, returning to Palermo after visiting the Baroque villas in **Bagheria**.

Themed Tours

Sicilian wine routes

The Istituto Regionale della Vite e del Vino *(Via Libertà 66, Palermo, ☎ 091 62 78 111, Fax 091 34 78 70)* has created a series of itineraries which explore the major Sicilian vineyards. To obtain a booklet listing details of individual wineries, contact the Istituto or log onto www.infcom.it/irvv

TheAlcamo DOC Route – Alcamo is a white table wine with a dry, fresh palate. This tour wends its way between Castellammare del Golfo, Scopello, Alcamo, Segesta and Calatafimi.

The Marsala and Moscato di Pantelleria Route – Both Moscato di Pantelleria and the more famous Marsala are dessert wines: the Moscato *passito* is a sweet, amber-coloured wine made from *zibibbo* grapes, Marsala a dark, dessert wine *(see MARSALA)*. The Marsala route passes through Erice, Trapani, Marsala, Salemi and Gibellina, while the Moscato route focuses on the island of Pantelleria.

The Insolia Route – The Insolia (or Ansonica) grape variety, present in almost all Sicilian DOC (Dominazione di Origine Controllata) wines, adds a pleasant, fresh palate and floral aromas to the more robust white wines. This tour visits the wine-producing areas of the southern coast stretching from Mazara del Vallo to Agrigento, and then crosses inland to the outskirts of Palermo passing through Sambuca di Sicilia, Santa Margherita Belice and Monreale en route.

The Nero d'Avola and Cerasuolo di Vittoria Route – The Nero d'Avola (or Calabrese) grape variety is the basis of all the best Sicilian DOC red wines. When blended with the frappato grape, Nero d'Avola produces the Cerasuolo di Vittoria, an elegant red wine with warm, harmonious tones. The route heads inland from Cefalù, crossing the island to Ragusa and passing through Castelbuono, Piazza Armerina, Caltagirone, Vittoria, Comiso, Ragusa and Modica.

The Moscato di Noto and Moscato di Siracusa Route – These two *moscati* wines have a sweet and harmonious palate and a delicate floral aroma. This tour explores the extreme southeast corner of Sicily, visiting Siracusa, Noto, Palazzolo Acreide and Pantalica.

The Etna Wine Route – The Etna vineyards produce red, white and rosé wines and were the first in Sicily to receive a DOC label. The Etna Wine Route runs along the Ionian coast from Catania to Taormina, and then turns inland to explore the slopes of Mount Etna.

The Malvasia delle Lipari – Malvasia wine is made according to an ancient method in which the grapes are dried on typical reed mats. This method produces a delicate, fragrant wine. The tour explores the islands in the Aeolian archipelago.

Literary routes

These literary routes *(parco letterario)* have been designed to visit places that have a connection with the life and works of the author to whom they are dedicated. Other projects include themed tours known as "sentimental journeys", led by a guide-cum-storyteller, which often have theatre groups performing as part of the tour. These tours are designed for groups only, but individuals may be able to join a tour if space allows (advance booking recommended). For further information, log onto www.parchiletterari.com/

Parco Letterario Luigi Pirandello – This route links the towns between Agrigento and Porto Empedocle that have a connection with the playwright Pirandello. For further information, contact Il Cerchio, Via Ugo La Malfa a Monte 1, Agrigento; ☎ 0922 40 28 62; Fax 0922 55 40 37; www.parcopirandello.it

Parco Letterario Salvatore Quasimodo – Towns such as Modica (Salvatore Quasimodo's birthplace) and Roccalumera (between Messina and Taormina), whose Saracen tower inspired one of the poet's works, are included on this route. For further information, contact Corso Umberto I, 242 Modica; ☎ 0932 75 38 64.

Parco Letterario Leonardo Sciascia – The route dedicated to Sciascia focuses on Racalmuto, the writer's birthplace, and Caltanissetta, where he studied. For further information, contact the Fondazione Leonardo Sciascia, Viale della Vittoria 3, Racalmuto; ☎ 0922 94 19 93.

Parco Letterario Tomasi di Lampedusa – This route links Palermo, the birthplace of Lampedusa, Santa Margherita Belice, where he spent much of his childhood and adolescence, and Palma di Montechiaro, the family's fief. For further information, contact Vicolo della Neve all'Alloro 2-5 (off Piazza Marina), Palermo; ☎ 091 61 60 796; Fax 091 61 00 618; palermo@parcotomasi.it; Palazzo Ducale, Palma di Montechiaro;

☎ 0922 96 83 99; Fax 0922 96 82 57; Palma di Montechiaro, palma@parcotomasi.it

Parco Letterario Giovanni Verga – This route wends its way between Catania, Aci Castello and Aci Trezza, home to the author Giovanni Verga and many of his fictional characters. For further information, contact Ghenea, Via Provinciale 27, Aci Trezza; ☎ 095 71 16 950; Fax 095 71 17 147.

Parco Letterario Elio Vittorini – The main office is based at Via S. Sebastiano 14, Siracusa; ☎ 0931 48 12 00.

Other Ways of Exploring the Region

Parks and Nature Reserves

Regional Parks

Sicily is home to a total of four Regional Parks. The **Parco delle Madonìe** and **Parco dei Nebrodi** are situated inland between Palermo and Messina, and provide the perfect setting for excursions of varying length and difficulty *(see MADONIE E NEBRODI)*. Another popular area for walking is the **Parco dell'Etna**, which has a number of hiking routes and nature trails (visitors are advised to contact the park authorities for information on conditions on Etna, especially if planning to climb to the craters, and to book a guide to accompany them). The fourth park, the **Parco Fluviale dell'Alcantara**, home to the impressive gorges of the same name *(see p 368)* is located in the same area. For further information, contact the Ente Parco Fluviale dell'Alcantara; ☎ 0942 98 10 38; www.parcoalcantara.it

Regional Nature Reserves

Sicily has a number of regional nature reserves, including:

Cava Grande del Cassibile *(see NOTO)*

M. Magni/MICHELIN

Fiume Ciane e le Saline di Siracusa *(see SIRACUSA)*

Riserva di Fiumefreddo *(see ETNA)*

Foce del Fiume Belice e Dune Limitrofe *(see CASTELVETRANO)*

Riserva Naturale della Foce dell'Irminio, near Marina di Ragusa. For information, contact ☎ 0932 67 51 11 (Provincia Regionale di Ragusa, Viale del Fante 2, 97100 Ragusa)

Riserva delle Macalube di Aragona *(see AGRIGENTO)*

Riserva Naturale Oasi del Simeto *(see ETNA)*

Oasi Faunistica di Vendìcari *(see NOTO)*

Riserva della Valle dell'Anapo *(see PANTALICA)*

Riserva dello Zingaro *(see Golfo di CASTELLAMMARE)*

Riserva Naturale Orientata Monte Pellegrino, run by Rangers d'Italia, Viale Diana, loc. Giusino, Palermo; ☎ 091 67 16 066

For a complete list of parks and reserves, log onto www.parks.it/regione.sicilia/index.html. For information on the above reserves and others in the process of being created, contact the **Assessorato Regionale Territorio e Ambiente**, Via La Malfa 169, Palermo; ☎ 091 75 42 071 and 091 68 90 630, or local **CAI** (Club Alpino Italiano) groups. The main offices of this group in Sicily are located at:

Piazza Scammacca 1, Catania; ☎ 095 71 53 515

Via Natoli 20, Messina; ☎ 090 65 10 126

Via N. Garzilli 59, Palermo; ☎ 091 32 94 07

Via Maestranza 33, Siracusa; ☎ 0931 64 751

WWF Nature Reserves

The World Wildlife Fund manages the following reserves:

Riserva Naturale Orientata Capo Rama, 2km/1.2mi from Terrasini. For information, contact Via delle

Rimembranze, 18, 90049 Terrasini; ☎/Fax 091 86 85 187;
Saline di Trapani e Paceco *(see VIA DEL SALE)*;
Riserva Naturale Integrale del Lago Preola e dei Gorghi Tondi, a few kilometres southeast of Mazara del Vallo. For information, contact Via F. Maccagnone, 2/B, 91026 Mazara del Vallo; ☎ 0923 93 40 55;
Riserva Naturale Orientata di Torre Salsa *(see AGRIGENTO)*;
Riserva Regionale di Isola Bella *(see TAORMINA)*.

For further information, contact WWF Sezione Regionale Sicilia, Via E. Albanese 98, Palermo; ☎ 091 58 30 40; www.wwfsicilia.it/default.asp

Cycling

Several disused railway lines in Sicily have been converted into cycle tracks. The **Agrigento-Castelvetrano** line runs alongside S 115 and passes through Realmonte, Eraclea Minoa and Sciacca. The **Siracusa-Vizzini-Ragusa** line crosses the Iblei mountains, linking Pantalica, Palazzolo Acreide, Monterosso Almo, Vizzini and Chiaramonte Gulfi. The **Noto-Pachino** line runs parallel to S 19, passing through Noto Marina and Vendicari. For further information on cycling in Sicily, contact local tourist offices or the Comitato Regionale della Federazione Ciclistica Italiana, c/o Velodromo Paolo Borsellino, Via Lanza di Scalea, 90146 Palermo; ☎ 091 67 18 715; Fax 091 67 18 711.
Siciclando (www.siciclando.com) organises cycling tours of the island for individuals and groups. For further information, contact the tourist office in Palermo (APT di Palermo), Piazza Castelnuovo 35; ☎ 091 58 38 47 or 091 60 58 351; Fax 091 58 63 38; www.aapit.pa.it

Circumetnea tourist train

The slopes of Mount Etna can be explored on the **Circumetnea** train, which runs around the volcano, starting its journey in Catania and arriving in Riposto some 5hr later. The return trip to Catania is by bus or train operated by Italian State Railways. For further information, contact Ferrovia Circumetnea, Via Caronda 352A, Catania, ☎ 095 54 11 11.

With the children

A good time for families to visit Sicily is undoubtedly during Carnival or over the Easter holidays, when many of the island's towns and villages hold colourful, traditional festivals. *See Events and Festivals on p 39.*
Sights of particular interest for children are marked in the text by the ☺ symbol.
The following sights also hold special appeal for younger visitors:
Museo dei Pupi dell'Opra (puppet museum) in Acireale *(see ACIREALE)*;
Museo del Giocattolo (Via Vittorio Emanuele 201, Catania), with its collection of antique toys. *Open daily except Mon, 9am-7pm. €3.50, children P2. ☎ 095 32 01 11;*
Etnaland-Parco Zoo di Sicilia at Belpasso, at the foot of Etna, with its exciting water park, zoo and prehistory theme park. *Open 9am-3hr before dusk. Closed Wed (except water park), Nov-Mar (zoo), 15 Sep-15 Jun (water park). €19 (children €10); €8.50 (children €5.50), zoo and prehistoric park only. ☎ 095 79 13 333; Fax 095 79 13 334; www.parcozoo.it/*
Centro Studi sulle Tartarughe Marine at Linosa *(see p 220)*;
The **saltpans,** Museo del Sale (salt museum) and windmill in Nubia *(see VIA DEL SALE)*;
Museo Internazionale delle Marionette in Palermo *(see p 304)*.

Ecotourism

Both the WWF and Legambiente run wildlife reserves in Sicily. The WWF has reserves (Centri Recupero Animali Selvatici) at Alcamo, Enna and Messina; a breeding centre for domestic animals in danger of extinction (such as local breeds of hen, goat and donkey) at Alcamo; and marine turtle rescue centres at various locations on the island. Field trips are organised at these centres every year. For further information, contact the Sicilian branch of the WWF (Delegazione Sicilia del WWF) at Via E. Albanese 98, Palermo, ☎ 091 58 30 40. Legambiente (☎ 091 30 16 63) also organises a number of field trips to various wildlife reserves, including one at Lampedusa (for the protection and monitoring of marine turtles) and another at Pantelleria.

Sport and Leisure

Sicily is the ideal destination for outdoor activity enthusiasts, with plentiful opportunities for hiking, horse-riding, scuba-diving, canoeing, sailing, cycling and mountain biking. The *Guida del Turismo alternativo (Sicilia occidentale* and *Sicilia orientale)*, available from bookshops, newsagents, or directly from the Sicilian Tourist Service (☎ 091 54 35 06), is an excellent reference book which is full of active holiday ideas and suggestions (in Italian only).

Pot-holing

The **Federazione Speleologica Regionale Siciliana** is an umbrella organisation for the various pot-holing associations. For further information, call ☎ 0932 62 16 99.

There are some cave-systems classed as natural reserves maintained by the CAI *(for address, see p 33)* and by Legambiente, Comitato Regionale, Via Agrigento 67, Palermo ☎ 091 30 16 63.

The main options are listed below:

Riserva Grotta di Carburangeli at Carini (Province of Palermo). Guided tours of the cave are organised by Legambiente, Corso Umberto I 64, Carini; ☎ 091 86 69 797;

Riserva Grotta di Santa Ninfa (Province of Trapani). Guided tours of the cave are organised by Legambiente, Via S. Anna 101, Santa Ninfa; ☎ 0924 62 376;

Riserva Naturale Grotta Conza (Province of Palermo). Contact CAI Sicilia, Via Roma 443, Palermo; ☎ 091 32 26 89;

Riserva Naturale Monte Conca (Province of Caltanissetta). Contact CAI Sicilia, Corso Pietro Nenni 4, Milena; ☎ 0934 93 32 54;

Riserva Naturale Grotta di Entella at Contessa Entellina (Province of Palermo). Contact CAI Sicilia, Monreale; ☎ 091 84 65 770.

For information on these and other reserves in the process of being created, contact the **Assessorato Regionale Territorio e Ambiente**, Via La Malfa 169, Palermo; ☎ 091 75 42 071 and 091 58 90 630 or local **CAI** offices *(see above)*.

Skiing

The best place for skiing in Sicily is on the slopes of Mount Etna. The two main resorts are at Nicolosi and Piano Provenzana (Linguaglossa), although much of the infrastructure was badly damaged during the most recent eruptions of the volcano. Skiing is also possible at Piano Battaglia (1 600m/ 5 248ft) in the Madonie. For further information, contact local tourist offices.

Scuba-diving

Much of the Sicilian coastline is fringed by fascinating underwater seascapes. The most exotic havens are the islands offshore where the water is particularly clear and the sea-life especially varied. On Ustica, the **Riserva Naturale Marina** *(see USTICA)* organises sea-watching and diving trips, special scuba-diving courses and the opportunity of exploring underwater archaeology and photography. For further information, contact the Federazione Italiana Pesca Sportiva Attività Subacquea, Comitato Regionale Sicilia, Via Terrasanta 93, Palermo; ☎ 091 30 23 02.

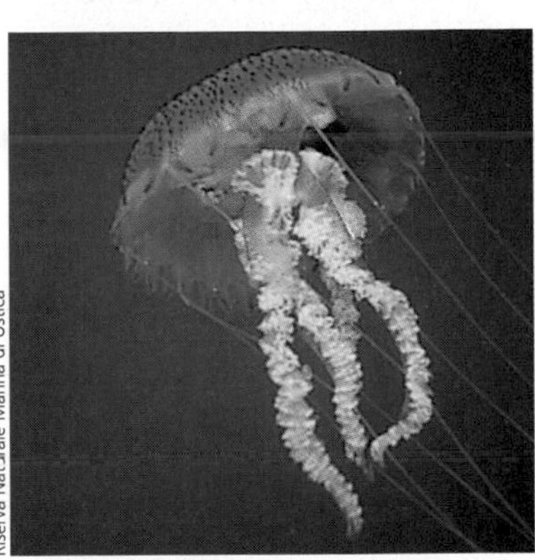

Riserva Naturale Marina di Ustica

Water sports

For details of **yacht charters** in Sicily contact specialist tour operators in your home country or the Federazione Italiana Vela, Via E. Albanese 7, Palermo; ☎ 091 34 28 20.

Information on **canoeing** and **kayaking** is available from the Comitato Regionale Canoa-Cayak, Via Chianchitta 101, Giardini Naxos; ☎/Fax 0942 50 250.

The most popular areas for **windsurfing** are Mondello, Cefalù, Capo d'Orlando, Marinello-Oliveri, Tremestieri (south of Messina), Scaletta, Catania, Portopalo, Marina di Ragusa, Agrigento, Pozziteddu (Capo Granitola, south of Campobello di Mazara) and Lo Stagnone. **Surfing** enthusiasts should make for Mondello, Aspra and Termini Imerese, while the best areas for **kitesurfing** include Marina di Ragusa, Pozzallo and

Scoglitti. The following websites provide further information on the above activities: www.kitesicilia.it (kitesurfing), www.windsurfitalia.da.ru and www.shorebreak.it (windsurfing), and www.fudditu.tk (kitesurfing and windsurfing).

Canyoning

Information on canyoning in Sicily is available from the Associazione Italiana Canyoning, Sezione Sicilia (Signor Diego Leonardi), ☎ 095 70 81 995, www.canyoning.it, and from Etna Canyoning, E. Longo 8, Zafferana Etnea, etnacanyoning@telvia.it

Horse-riding

Several *agriturismi* organise pony trekking and horse-riding around the island. For general information on equestrian activities in Sicily, contact the Federazione Italiana Turismo Equestre, Comitato Regionale, Via Lupis 62, Ragusa; ☎/Fax 0932 25 76 39; www.fiteec-ante.it/index.html

Hang-gliding

Information on hang-gliding in Sicily is available from the Accademia Siciliana Volo Libero, Via degli Astronauti 14 trav. C, Altofonte (PA), ☎ 091 66 40 535.

Golf

Golf courses on the island include the Pìcciolo Golf di Castiglione di Sicilia (CT), near Etna. For further information, contact ☎/Fax 0942 98 62 52.

Spa resorts

Sicily has been famous for its hot springs since Ancient times. The following spa resorts are listed by province:
Agrigento: Terme di **Sciacca** *(see SCIACCA)*; Terme di Acqua Pia, loc. Acque Calde, **Montevago**; ☎ 0925 39 026; Catania: **Acireale** *(see ACIREALE)*, www.terme.acireale.gte.it;
Messina: Fonte di Venere, Viale Stabilimento 85, **Terme Vigliatore**; ☎ 090 97 81 078; Terme di Giuseppe Marino, Via Roma 25; ☎ 0942 71 50 31 and Terme di Granata Cassibile, Via Crispi 1/13; ☎ 0942 71 50 29, both at **Alì Terme**; Terme di **Vulcano** (Aeolian Islands, *see Isole EOLIE*);
Palermo: Terme di **Termini Imerese**, Piazza delle Terme 2; ☎ 091 81 13 557; Trapani: Terme di Gorga, contr. Gorga, **Calatafimi**;
☎ 0924 23 842.

What to Buy Locally

Typical Sicilian souvenirs range from gastronomic specialities to traditional handicrafts.

Food and wine

The area around Trapani and the Egadi Islands (especially Favignana) is well known for its many traditional **tuna** specialities, such as tuna conserved in olive oil and cured tuna, as well as fish roe and smoked swordfish. Pantelleria and Salina produce excellent **capers**, while the **herbs** and **spices** that form such an important part of Sicilian cuisine can be found in markets and grocery stores all over the island – the most common include oregano, wild fennel, pistachios (near Bronte) and Sicilian saffron.

The Palermo region is renowned for its delicious *paste reali* (colourful marzipan delicacies which come in all shapes and sizes), while sweet specialities on the Ionian coast include the local *paste di mandorla* (almond pastries). The famous Sicilian crushed ice *granite* might be difficult to take home, but you could always try your hand at making them yourself by buying packets of almond paste (also used to make almond milk) as souvenirs.
Visitors looking to take **wine** home as gifts are spoilt for choice, particularly in the selection of dessert wines available. The most famous Sicilian sweet wines include Moscato di Noto, Moscato Passito di Pantelleria, Marsala and Malvasia delle Lipari.

Guidorlando/Lara Pessina/MICHELIN

Souvenirs

One of the most typical Sicilian crafts is **ceramic** work. The most important centres are Caltagirone, Santo Stefano di Camastra, Erice and Sciacca. The shops of these small towns display a fine array of vases, statuettes, crockery, ornaments and knick-knacks, as well as traditional containers for Sicilian *mostarda* (a caramel-like substance made from prickly-pear juice) and quince jam.

Apart from ceramics, there are plenty of other natural products and handicrafts which are typical of the island. These include carpets from the area around Erice; natural sponges from Lampedusa; and **papyrus** work (paper and cloth) from the Siracusa region. Finally, mention must be made of the Sicilian puppets and traditional carts, which can be found at antique dealers and in second-hand shops, or, in Palermo, directly from the few remaining craftsmen who still make them.

Books

Sicily has long held a fascination for both Italian authors and writers from abroad. The suggestions below include translated works by famous Sicilian authors, as well as history books, mythology, biography and travel literature. For a wide selection of English and Italian books written about Sicily, log onto www.sicilybooks.it or www.siciliano.it/indexlibri.cfm

Fiction

The Leopard – Giuseppe Lampedusa (Harvill Press 1996)
Little Novels of Sicily – Giovanni Verga, DH Lawrence (Steerforth Press 2000)
Sometimes the Soul: Two Novellas of Sicily – Gioia Timpanelli (WW Norton & Co 1998)
"Cavalleria Rusticana" and Other Stories – Giovanni Verga, H McWilliam (Trans) (Penguin Books 1999)
Short Sicilian Novels – Giovanni Verga (Dedalus Ltd 1994)
The House by the Medlar Tree – Giovanni Verga (University of California Press 1983)
Il Giorno Della Civetta – Leonardo Sciascia, G Slowey (Ed) (St Martin's Press 1998)

Biography

Italian Journey – JW Goethe (Penguin Books 1970)
The Sicilian – M Puzo (Arrow 2000)
The Happy Ant-heap – Norman Lewis (Jonathan Cape 1998)
The Dark Princes of Palermo – Norman Lewis (Jonathan Cape 2000)
I Came, I Saw: an Autobiography – Norman Lewis (Picador 1996)
On Persephone's Island: A Sicilian Journal (Vintage Departures) – Mary Taylor Simeti (Vintage Books 1995)
Sicilian Lives – D Dolci (Writers and Readers 1982)

Reference

The Greek Myths – R Graves (Penguin Books 1984)
Metamorphoses – Ovid, EJ Kenney (Ed), AD Melville (Trans) (Oxford Paperbacks 1998)
Odes – Pindar (Penguin Books 1901)
The Odyssey – Homer, R Fagles (Trans), B Knox (Intro) (Penguin Books 1997)
The Aeneid – Virgil, D West (Trans) (Penguin Books 1991)
The Normans in Sicily – John Julius Norwich (Penguin Books 1992)
The Sicilian Vespers – S Runciman (Cambridge University Press 1992)
The Norman Kingdom of Sicily – D Matthew (Cambridge University Press 1992)
The Golden Honeycomb – V Cronin, W Forman (Harvill Press 1992)
Walking in Sicily – Gillian Price (Cicerone Press 2000)
In Sicily – Norman Lewis (Jonathan Cape 2000)
The Honoured Society – Norman Lewis (Eland Books 1984)

Events and Festivals

This section does not include all the traditional festivals that take place on the island, many of which are held during Carnival and at Easter. For a complete list, contact the APT (tourist information office) in the town or area you plan to visit. *Festivals in towns marked * are also mentioned in the Selected Sights section of the guide.*

Easter festivals

Procession of the dead Christ and Our Lady of Sorrows on Good Friday.	**Alcamo**
Procession of 16 groups of statues.	**Caltanissetta***
Good Friday procession. Easter Sunday morning: Festa dell'Aurora, celebrated since 1860.	**Castelvetrano**
Procession of the Confraternities on Good Friday.	**Enna***
Processione dei Misteri on Good Friday.	**Erice***
Holy Week procession.	**Marsala***
Processione delle Barette on Good Friday.	**Messina***
During Holy Week, the inhabitants walk about in traditional costumes embroidered with gold and silver thread. On Good Friday, choral concert given by the Simenon Kremate choir and the Enkomia procession takes place. On Easter Sunday, white doves are released, sprigs of rosemary are thrown about and red-painted eggs are exchanged.	**Piana degli Albanesi**
Easter Sunday morning: *U n'contru – U ballu di diavula.*	**Prizzi**
Good Friday: *Processione e fiaccolata dei Misteri.*	**Ragusa***
Procession of the Resurrected Christ.	**Scicli***
Processione dei Misteri held on Good Friday afternoon and Saturday morning.	**Trapani***

A. Safina/Lara Pessina/MICHELIN

Processione dei Misteri, Trapani

Other festivals

6 January

Festa della Teofania – Greek-Orthodox Epiphany. — **Piana degli Albanesi**

20 January

Festa di San Sebastiano (St Sebastian). — **Acireale***

First week in February (5 February)

Festa di Sant'Agata. — **Catania***

3 February

Festa dei Pani di San Biagio – Festival of St Blaise held in the Rabato district of the town. Small decorative loaves of bread are baked for the occasion. — **Salemi**

Week of Carnival, culminating in Martedì Grasso (Shrove Tuesday)
Carnival celebrations with processions of allegorical floats. — **Acireale*, Sciacca*, Termini Imerese***

Saturday preceding 19 March
Cavalcata di San Giuseppe. — **Scicli***

19 March
Festa di San Giuseppe (St Joseph's day) – *Cene di San Giuseppe,* special dinners and votive loaves of bread. — **Salemi**

End of May
Festa della Battaglia delle Milizie. — **Scicli***

Last Sunday in May
Re-enactment of the martyrdom of St George. — **Ragusa***

14-15 July
"U fistinu", festival in honour of the city's patron saint, Santa Rosalia. — **Palermo***

24-25 July
Festa di San Giacomo with the *Luminaria.* — **Caltagirone***

2-6 August
Festa di San Salvatore. — **Cefalù***

14 August
Madonna della Luce. Procession of boats. — **Cefalù***

21-24 August
Festa di San Bartolomeo with offshore firework display. — **Lipari***

2 September
Festa della Madonna Odigitria. Festival of Piana's patron saint, with horse races and a parade in traditional costume. — **Piana degli Albanesi**

7-8 September
Madonna della Luce with procession of the two giants Kronos and Mytia. — **Mistretta***

November-January
Exhibition of terracotta Nativity figures. — **Caltagirone***

2 November
Festa dei Morti. — **Palermo***

Cultural events

1-15 February
Sagra del Mandorlo in fiore (Almond-blossom Festival) and International Folklore Festival. — **Agrigento***

M. Magni/MICHELIN

Almond-blossom festival in Agrigento

May-June

Performances of classical drama at the Greek theatre. **Siracusa***

June-December

Orestiadi: theatre, music and film festival. **Gibellina***

July-September

Concerts and performances of classical drama at the Greek theatre. **Segesta***

Taormina Arte: theatre, music, film and dance festival. **Taormina***

Tindari Estate: season of prose readings, music and dance in the Greek theatre. **Tindari***

End of July

Marsala Doc Jazz Festival. **Marsala***

Autumn (although time of year variable)

Festival of sacred music. **Monreale***

Late November to mid-December

Festival di Morgana. **Palermo***

Other traditional events

April-May

Festa del Costume e del Carretto Siciliano. Festival of traditional Sicilian carts and local costume. **Taormina***

25 April

Sagra della Ricotta. **Vizzini**

Third Sunday in May

Primavera Barocca and the *Infiorata.* **Noto***

12-14 August

Palio dei Normanni. **Piazza Armerina***

14 August

Passeggiata dei Giganti **Messina***

Second or third Sunday in October

Sagra della Mostarda. Mostarda is a caramel-like substance made from prickly-pear juice cooked with flour and spices, which is then used to make different types of sweet delicacies. **Militello in Val di Catania**

Glossary
On the road and in town

a destra to the right
a sinistra to the left
aperto open
autostrada motorway
banchina pavement
binario (railway) platform
corso boulevard
discesa descent
dogana customs
fermata (bus-) stop
fiume river
ingresso entrance
lavori in corso men at work
neve snow
passaggio a livello level crossing
passo pass
pericolo danger
piazza, largo square, place
piazzale esplanade
stazione station
stretto narrow
uscita exit, way out
viale avenue
vietato prohibited

Places and things to see

abbazia, convento abbey, monastery
affreschi frescoes
arazzi tapestries
arca monumental tomb
biblioteca library
cappella chapel

casa	house
cascata	waterfall
castello	castle
cena	The Last Supper
chiesa	church
chiostro	cloisters
chiuso	closed
città	town
cortile	courtyard
dintorni	environs
duomo	cathedral
facciata	façade
funivia	cable car
giardini	gardens
gole	gorges
passeggiata	walk, promenade
piano	floor, storey
pinacoteca	picture gallery
pulpito	pulpit
quadro	picture
rivolgersi a	to apply to
rocca	feudal castle
rovine, ruderi	ruins
sagrestia	sacristy
scala	stairway
scavi	excavations
seggiovia	chairlift
spiaggia	beach
tesoro	treasure
torre, torazzo	tower
vista	view

Common words

yes, no	**si, no**
Sir	**Signore**
Madam	**Signora**
Miss	**Signorina**
please	**per favore**
thank you very much	**grazie tante**
excuse me	**mi scusi**
enough	**basta**
good morning	**buon giorno**
goodbye	**arrivederci**
how much?	**quanto?**
where? when?	**dove? quando?**
where is?	**dov'è?**
much, little	**molto, poco**
more, less	**più, meno**
all	**tutto, tutti**
large	**grande**
small	**piccolo**
dear	**caro**

Numbers

0	**zero**
1	**uno**
2	**due**
3	**tre**
4	**quattro**
5	**cinque**
6	**sei**
7	**sette**
8	**otto**
9	**nove**
10	**dieci**
11	**undici**
12	**dodici**
13	**tredici**
14	**quattordici**
15	**quindici**
16	**sedici**
17	**diciassette**
18	**diciotto**
19	**diciannove**
20	**venti**
30	**trenta**
40	**quaranta**
50	**cinquanta**
60	**sessanta**
70	**settanta**
80	**ottanta**
90	**novanta**
100	**cento**
1 000	**mille**
5 000	**cinquemila**
10 000	**diecimila**

Time, days of the week and seasons

1.00	**l'una**
1.15	**l'una e un quarto**
1.30	**un ora e mezzo**
1.45	**l'una e quaranta cinque**
morning	**mattina**
afternoon	**pomeriggio**
evening	**sera**
yesterday	**ieri**
today	**oggi**
tomorrow	**domani**
a week	**una settimana**
Monday	**lunedì**
Tuesday	**martedì**
Wednesday	**mercoledì**
Thursday	**giovedì**
Friday	**venerdì**
Saturday	**sabato**
Sunday	**domenica**
winter	**inverno**
spring	**primavera**
summer	**estate**
autumn/fall	**autunno**

Useful phrases

Do you speak English?
Parla inglese?
I don't understand
Non capisco
Please speak slowly
Parli piano per favore
Where are the toilets?
Dove sono i bagni?
At what time does the train/bus/plane leave?
A che ora parte il treno/l'autobus/l'aereo?
At what time does the train... arrive?
A che ora arriva il treno...?
What does it cost?
Quanto costa?
Where can I buy an English newspaper?
Dove posso comprare un giornale inglese?

Where can I change my money?
Dove posso cambiare i miei soldi?
May I pay with a credit card?
Posso pagare con una carta di credito ?

the road to...?	**la strada per...?**
may one visit?	**Si può visitare?**
what time is it?	**Che ora è?**
I would like	**Desidero/vorrei**

Gastronomic terms

Caffè corretto: *espresso* laced with brandy or *grappa*

Caffè decaffeinato (caffè "Hag"): decaffeinated coffee

Caffè latte: mainly hot milk, with a splash of coffee

Caffè lungo: coffee which is not quite as strong as *espresso*

Caffè macchiato: *espresso* with a splash of milk

Cannelloni: large pasta tubes filled with a meat or other sauce

Cappellini: very thin spaghetti

Cappuccino (or *cappuccio*): coffee topped with frothy milk and a dusting of cocoa

Cassata: ice cream containing chopped nuts and mixed dried fruit (similar to tutti-frutti)

Crema: vanilla (ice cream)

Farfalle: pasta bow-ties

Fettuccine: slightly narrower, Roman version of tagliatelle

Fior di latte: very creamy variety of ice cream

Fusilli: small pasta spirals

Gnocchi: tiny potato dumplings

Lasagne: sheets of pasta arranged in layers with tomato and meat sauce (or other) and cheese sauce, topped with Parmesan and baked

Maccheroni: small pasta tubes

Panino: type of sandwich (bread roll)

Panna: cream; similar to *fior di latte*

Prosciutto: cured ham

Ravioli: little pasta cushions, enclosing meat or spinach

Schiacciata: type of sandwich (on a pizza-type base)

Spaghetti: the great classic

Stracciatella: chocolate chip (ice cream)

Tagliatelle: long narrow pasta ribbons

Tiramisù: coffee-flavoured frozen gateau *(semifreddo)*

Tortellini: small crescent-shaped pasta rolls filled with a meat or cheese stuffing, often served in a clear meat broth

Tramezzino: type of sandwich (on slices of bread)

Zabaglione: dessert made from egg yolks and Marsala wine

Zuppa inglese: trifle

In 1972, the United Nations Educational, Scientific and Cultural Organisation (UNESCO) adopted a Convention for the preservation of cultural and natural sites. To date, more than 150 States Parties have signed this international agreement, which has listed over 600 sites "of outstanding universal value" on the World Heritage List. Each year, a committee of representatives from 21 countries, assisted by technical organisations (ICOMOS – International Council on Monuments and Sites; IUCN – International Union for Conservation of Nature and Natural Resources; ICCROM – International Centre for the Study of the Preservation and Restoration of Cultural Property, the Rome Centre), evaluates the proposals for new sites to be included on the list, which grows longer as new nominations are accepted and more countries sign the Convention. To be considered, a site must be nominated by the country in which it is located. The protected cultural heritage may be monuments (buildings, sculptures, archaeological structures etc) with unique historical, artistic or scientific features; groups of buildings (such as religious communities, ancient cities); or sites (human settlements, examples of exceptional landscapes, cultural landscapes) which are the combined works of man and nature and of exceptional beauty. Natural sites may be a testimony to the stages of the earth's geological history or to the development of human cultures and creative genius or represent significant ongoing ecological processes, contain superlative natural phenomena or provide a habitat for threatened species.

Signatories of the Convention pledge to cooperate to preserve and protect these sites around the world as a common heritage to be shared by all humanity.

Some of the most famous places which the World Heritage Committee has inscribed include: the Great Wall of China (1987); the Egyptian Pyramids (1979); Notre-Dame Cathedral, Paris (1979); the Acropolis, Athens (1987); Venice and its Lagoon (1987); and the Grand Canyon National Park, USA (1979).

UNESCO World Heritage Sites in Italy

Sites in Sicily are marked in bold.

Rock Drawings, Valcamonica
Church and Dominican Convent of Santa Maria delle Grazie, with *The Last Supper* by Leonardo da Vinci, Milan
Historic Centre of Florence
Venice and its Lagoon
Piazza del Duomo, Pisa
Historic Centre of San Gimignano
The Sassi (troglodyte dwellings) of Matera
City of Vicenza and the Palladian Villas of the Veneto
Historic Centre of Siena
Historic Centre of Naples
Crespi d'Adda
The Renaissance City of Ferrara and the Po Delta
Castel del Monte
The Trulli of Alberobello
Early Christian Monuments of Ravenna
Historic Centre of Pienza
18C Royal Palace at Caserta with the Park, the Aqueduct of Vanvitelli and San Leucio Complex
Residences of the Royal House of Savoy, Piedmont
Botanical Garden, Padua
Cathedral, Torre Civica and Piazza Grande, Modena
The Archaeological Sites of Pompeii, Herculaneum and Torre Annunziata
Villa Romana del Casale, Piazza Armerina
Su Nuraxi, Barumini
Portovenere, the Cinque Terre and the Islands (Palmaria, Tino and Tinetto)
The Amalfi Coast
The Archaeological Site of Agrigento
Cilento and Vallo di Diano National Park with the Archaeological Sites of Paestum and Velia and the Certosa di Padula
The Archaeological Site and Patriarchal Basilica of Aquileia
Historic Centre of Urbino
Villa Adriana and Villa d'Este, Tivoli
Verona
The Aeolian Islands
Assisi, the Basilica di San Francesco and other Franciscan sites
Teatro dell'Opera dei Pupi Siciliano (cultural tradition)
Late Baroque Towns of the Val di Noto (southeastern Sicily)
Rome and the Holy See: historic centre of Rome, the properties of the Holy See which enjoy extraterritorial rights, and St Paul Without the Walls.

Insights and Images

An Introduction to the Island

"Climb aboard this triangular ark of stone floating upon the waves of millennia... And keep a smattering of Greek to hand, lest you encounter Aphrodite, the goddess of love, emerging from the sea and eager to exchange a few words..."
Gesualdo Bufalino, *La luce e il lutto (The Light and the Struggle)*

An old legend recounts the story of three nymphs who travel around the world to collect the best produce the world has to offer. Coming across a sea of extraordinary beauty, they interrupt their trip and drop the flowers and fruit they have collected into its waters. From the sea's waters rises the land mass of Sicily, with its three headlands of Capo Peloro, Capo Passero and Capo Lilibeo, the jewel-casket of all the beauty in the world.
This myth attempts to explain the exceptional beauty of the harmoniously shaped triangular island known as Triskeles (three legs) to the Greeks and Triquetra (three peaks) to the Romans. The evocative symbol of the island is the Trinakria, a figure with three legs running around a Medusa's head.
Beauty is certainly the first element that strikes visitors to Sicily, a feature that is ever-present in the island's clear seas, blue sky and grandiose mountains framing the coast. There is nothing subtle about the scenery here: stunning natural landscapes offer bright colours, fragrant scents and unforgettable views. The region has been inhabited by many different peoples over the centuries: the Greeks estab-

lished colonies here that were later developed by the Romans; the Arabs created magnificent buildings and gardens, subsequently converted into splendid palaces by the Normans; and the French and Spanish introduced the severe Gothic and exuberant Baroque styles, visible on the façades of *palazzi* across the island. Sicily was dominated by foreign rulers until 1860, when Garibaldi and his troops landed on the coast near Marsala, paving the way for the unification of Italy. Although an important date for the island, this was just one more chapter in the history of Sicily, which has undergone so many changes over the centuries and yet still remains unchanged at its core.

Three thousand years of tumultuous history have endowed Sicily with its complex character, best expressed through the island's varied and fascinating art. While it is true to say that the art and culture are multi-layered and somewhat difficult to understand, the human and social mosaic here is even more challenging. Media coverage of the island does not help to foster a true image, focusing all too often on Mafia-related crime, and Sicilians are often frustrated by the international portrayal of their homeland, finding themselves torn between unconditional love and inconsolable shame for the island.

And yet Sicily has many facets, as the title *La luce e il lutto* (The Light and the Struggle), a collection of essays by the Sicilian writer Gesualdo Bufalino, suggests. The traditional pictures of Sicily are many – sunshine, blue skies, warm sea, Greek temples, the Mafia and southern Mediterranean vegetation – but visitors willing to look beyond these images will be rewarded by the discovery of a proud, hospitable people and a rich, vibrant culture.

An Island of Contrasts

With its green pastures backed by the sparkling blue of the Mediterranean, prickly pears growing on slopes scorched by volcanic lava, and brilliant white almond blossom dotting the winter landscape, Sicily is truly an island of contrasts.

It is impossible to sum up Sicily in just one image. The seasons bring with them myriad colours and changes to the Sicilian landscape: the yellow broom, mimosa and sweetly scented orange blossom of spring; the red poppies, bougainvillea and green meadows of early summer; and the early autumn ochre-coloured earth burnt dry by the relentless Sicilian sun. On this island of beaches and mountains, it is possible to travel from the heights of magnificent Mount Etna (Sicily's highest peak at over 3 000m/10 000ft and the highest volcano in Europe) to a secluded, sandy bay on the coast in just a few miles. Dramatic, ever-changing and never dull, Sicily's landscapes are truly stunning.

Landscape

Sicily is the largest island of the Mediterranean (25 709km^2/9 926sq mi). It is separated from the Italian peninsula by the Straits of Messina – a mere 3km/1.8mi at the widest point – and from Africa, about 140km/87mi away, by the Sicily Canal. The island is more or less triangular in shape, its long sides fronting onto the Tyrrhenian Sea in the north and the Sicily Canal in the south while the short side fringes the Ionian Sea to the east. Up to the end of the Muslim occupation, the island was divided into three large "valleys" or provinces: the **Val di Mazara** to the west, **Val Demone** to the northeast and the **Val di Noto** in the southeast.

The harbour at Cefalù

B. Morandi/MICHELIN

An island among islands

The region of Sicily includes many minor islands: off the northern coast, in the Tyrrhenian Sea, are the Aeolian or Lipari Islands (northeast) and Ustica (northwest); the Egadi lie to the west, close to the Trapanese Coast; and south, in the Sicily Canal, lie Pantelleria and the Pelagian Islands, including Lampedusa (which is 113km/70mi from Tunisia and 205km/128mi from the Sicilian coast). Added to these is **Ferdinandea Island** (originally claimed by the British as Graham Island and by the French as Ile de

Giulia), a tiny island which surfaced off the coast of Sciacca in 1831, only to sink below the sea again a few months later; it now lies 8m/26ft below sea level.

J. Malburet/MICHELIN

A windmill in the Trapani saltpans

Sandy beaches and rocky cliffs

The Sicilian coastline stretches over some 1 000km/621mi. The northern or Tyrrhenian flank extends from Cape Peloro, near Messina, to Cape Lilibeo in the vicinity of Marsala: here the rocks are uniformly high and protrude jaggedly into the sea. By contrast, the short distance between Trapani and Marsala on the western coast is flat and dotted with saltpans. The southern coast of Sicily remains flat and mainly sandy as far as Capo Passero, the far southwestern spur of the island. Small creeks interrupt the otherwise streamlined profile of the shoreline which accommodates a few of the main resorts like Mazzara del Vallo, Sciacca and Gela, set in the broad bay with the same name between Licata and Marina di Ragusa.

The eastern coast facing onto the Ionian Sea is low-lying at first, shaped into a succession of three broad sweeps: the Gulf of Noto, the Gulf of Augusta and the great Gulf of Catania, which provides Sicily's largest plain with a sea front. North of Catania, the shoreline to Messina consists once more of high cliffs broken by a series of craggy inlets. As Etna's tall black lava flows give way to the Peloritani Mountain limestone (an extension of the Calabrian Apennines), huge steep cliffs plunge down to the sea, endowing the landscape with matchless beauty as at Taormina and Acireale.

Mountains and valleys

The Sicilian land mass is predominantly hilly (62% of the surface area); 24% is mountainous with the remainder (14%) classified as plain or lowland. The highest outcrop is Etna, with an altitude of 3 323m/10 902ft. This mountain typifies the Sicilian landscape, dominating, as it does, the skyline from almost every raised viewpoint on the island. North of Etna, separated from the Alcantara Valley, rise the precipitous heights of Sicily's principal mountain range which run some 200km/124mi parallel to the Tyrrhenian Coast. This chain of peaks comprises, even from a geological point of view, a natural extension of the Calabrian Apennines, hence its name **Appennino Siculo**. These fall into three distinctive sections. The western portion constitutes the **Monti Peloritani** which lie between Messina and Patti; the highest peak is Montagna Grande (1 374m/4 507ft). This relief does not rise to any great altitude: in contrast with a steeply angular and craggy profile, its lower slopes have been eroded by powerful streams heavy with rocks and pebbles discarded along the narrow coastal shelf or plain. The range extends westwards with the **Monti Nebrodi**: these have gentler slopes and rounded, densely wooded summits, which culminate in Monte Soro (1 847m/6 060ft). Next in line, west of the Nebrodi, come the **Madonie**; these do not extend very far but do include several high peaks, such as Carbonara (1 979m/6 491ft), the second highest summit on the island. The high relief is interrupted on the western flank of the Madonie. The vast area between Termini Imerese and the Trapanese consists of a gently undulating landscape of hills and broad valleys. This is rudely broken by three minor massifs – the **Monti Termini Imerese**, **Monti di Palermo** and **Monti di Trapani** – that have geological rather than orographic (physical geography of mountains) affinities with the northern range.

To the south, the high relief gives way to a vast open region of arid upland (often called the solfiferi or solfataras after the high levels of sulphur deposits in the area) which stretches from Marsala to Caltanissetta. The only mountains in the area are the **Sicani Mountains** behind Agrigento and the **Monti Erei** to the east of Caltanissetta. In the southwestern corner of the island are the massive calcareous (limestone) **Monti Iblei**, which rise to 1 000m/3 300ft.

The largest expanse of lowland plain in Sicily is the **Piana di Catania** which extends from the southern lower slopes of Etna to the foothills of the Iblei range. Criss-crossed by large rivers, the plain is renowned for being especially fertile and is intensively farmed (citrus, fruit and market gardening). Other areas of open lowland, although not as extensive, include the plain of Palermo known as the **Conca d'Oro** (golden horn of plenty).

Rivers and lakes

Sicily's lack of water has been a major problem throughout its history. The land here has limited permeability, rainfall is erratic and water distribution is poorly managed. Although numerous, the rivers which run into the Tyrrhenian Sea are short and fast flowing due to the proximity of the river sources to the sea.

The rivers of the southern slopes are more important by far not only because they are sustained by a more extensive system of sunken wells and natural springs but also because they are required to maintain a constant flow of water, however sluggishly, to the waterway. The most important water network of the island comprises the River Gornalunga, River Dittaino, and River Simeto whose waters irrigate the fertile plain of Catania before flowing into the Ionian Sea.

Sicily is almost completely deprived of any natural lakes (the only exception is the Lago di Pergusa); however, there are a number of man-made reservoirs in among the mountains. Frequently punctuating the coastline are many brackish ponds called **bivieri** or **pantani** which form behind the dunes along the shore. A few of these may be observed on the southeastern coast of the island or near Capo Peloro. Many, however, have recently been drained to allow the wider area around them to be cultivated.

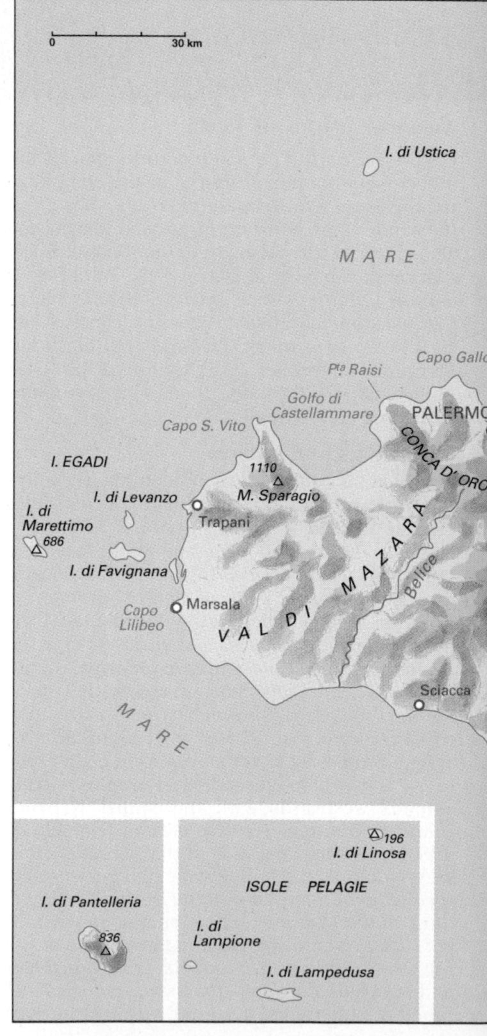

B. Kaufmann/MICHELIN

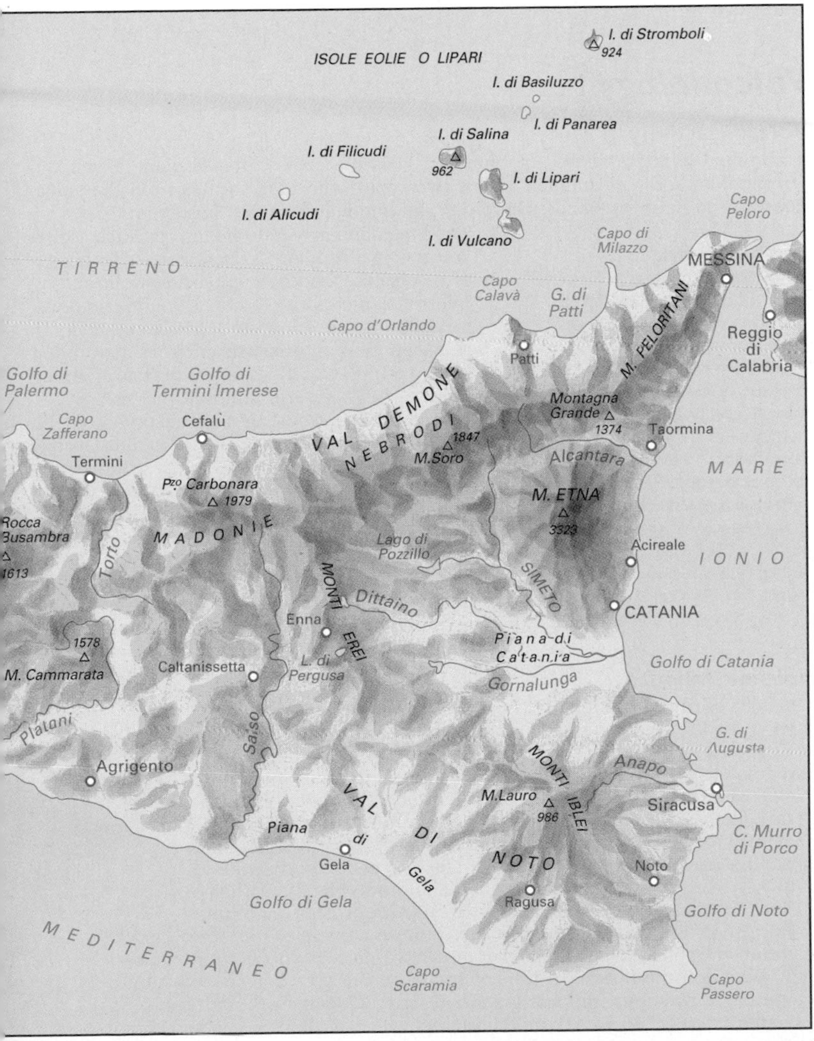

Volcanoes in Sicily

According to mythology, Sicily's underworld was inhabited by Hephaestus, the god of fire, and his team of giants responsible for creating the weapons of the gods. The Ancient Greeks attributed the volcano's rumblings to the noise of the underground anvil and forge, while eruptions from Mount Etna were believed to be sparks from Hephaestus' furnace.

Volcanology

Volcanic activity

Traditionally, there are four types of volcanic explosion: Plinian, Hawaiian, Strombolian and Vulcanian. The last two types take their names from the volcanoes on the Aeolian Islands where the phenomena were first observed.

Zeus and Typhon

In his *Metamorphoses*, Ovid recounts the struggle between Zeus and the giant Typhon (or Typhoeus), in which the god overcomes the giant by crushing him with the island of Sicily: "Because Typhon dared to covet the divine throne, his gigantic limbs were crushed under the vast land mass of Sicily. The giant often fights and struggles to release himself, but his right hand is held down by Peloro, his left by Pachino, his legs are weighed down by Lilibeo and his head by Etna. Typhon lies helpless under this great weight, furiously kicking sand and vomiting flames from his mouth."

The Strombolian phenomenon, peculiar to the volcano on Stromboli, is characterised by phases of persistent, moderate explosions followed by intermittent periods of idleness. Such eruptions, caused by a large build-up of gas being suddenly released like a pressure cooker, have been known to project tall fountains of lava, attaining in some cases several hundred metres.

Vulcanian eruptions, as first observed on the island of Vulcano in 1888, result in outpourings of lava and pyroclastics (solid fragments suspended in clouds of dense gas reaching exceptionally high temperatures), which pour down the sides of the volcano at speeds of up to 300m/330yd per second. This phenomenon is also described as **hydrovolcanic** because the highly explosive effect is caused by an interaction of molten magma with trapped water deep within the earth's crust.

Delicate volcanic flowers

Volcanic fallout

During volcanic eruptions three types of matter are ejected: lava, pyroclastics and gas (including smoke, steam and chemical vapours).

Lava consists of magma, which cools and hardens into complex structures as it flows down the sides of the volcano. Fluid lava collects into smooth flows that fold around the obstacles that snag its course, cooling quickly into glassy smooth stone like obsidian. In contrast to this, viscous lava travels overground with difficulty; heavy scoria causes it to break up into blocks. Both types of lava flow can be seen on the slopes of Mount Etna. Examples of lava tunnels are also in evidence there: these consist of underground conduits of molten lava which form pipe-like outer crusts, while remaining hollow on the inside. In the cooling stage the lava may contract into columnar formations: this phenomenon may be seen in the gorges of the Alcantara and at the Faraglioni dei Ciclopi.

Lara Pessina/MICHELIN

The spectacular volcanic power of Mount Etna

By-products of explosive eruptions are generally classified as **pyroclastics** and are composed of pre-existing rock fragments that are collected from the immediate environment, crystals (solidified particles suspended in the magma/granite) and **juvenile** formations or tuff (consolidated volcanic fragments and solidified magma), which include various types of ash, lapilli and volcanic bombs depending on size. Depending on how the lava cools, the gases in the lapilli and volcanic bombs are released at variable rates and in different quantities. Should the volcanic discharge cool rapidly, it will solidify into a dense formation like obsidian or lava glass; should it cool slowly over a long period of time, trapped gases can bubble out so imparting to the stone a distinctive sponge-like appearance as in pumice and scoria. Great quantities of volcanic vapour are released during eruptions, indeed, sometimes this is the only form of material emitted: both Etna and Vulcano, for example, have intensively active vents or fumeroles through which hot **gases** are expelled. The main constituents of volcanic vapour are aqueous (and highly acidic) compounds of the base elements carbon, hydrogen and sulphur. Fumeroles and thermal springs (therapeutic mud) are the outward effects of magma cooling at depth.

Volcanic areas of Sicily

Aeolian Islands

The volcanic fault of the Aeolian Islands stretches in an arc over some 200km/124mi and comprises eight separate islands (the seven Aeolian Islands plus Ustica) and a large number of submerged volcanoes. **Stromboli** is defined by a series of volcanic outcrops layered one on top of the other over the past 100 000 years. Today the active craters, which vary in number and position, emerge at about 700m/2 300ft up the Sciara del Fuoco. At a distance of 1.5km/1mi off the northeastern coast of Stromboli sits **Strombolicchio**: the outcrop, which stands over 40m/130ft high, is all that remains of the main core of the volcano that erupted during the earliest phase in the island's creation.

Etna

Etna is Europe's largest active volcano, rising to a height of over 3 300m/10 900ft from a base diameter of about 40km/25mi. Volcanic activity started 600 000 years ago following movement between the tectonic plates: this released magma up through the ocean floor into the area now occupied by Aci Castello, and provoked surges of lava which settled in the vicinity of present-day Paternò. During the past 100 000 years, the thrust of subsequent volcanic activity has shifted westwards. The mountain's present profile is largely the result of an explosion about 14 000 years ago in which the Cratere Ellittico (or elliptical crater) came into being. The summit of Etna comprises four active craters (Cratere di Sud-Est, Bocca Nuova, Voragine, Cratere di Nord-Est); in addition there are three principal radial fissures and many (approximately 250) irregular secondary craters, through which the most significant outpourings of lava have been released, even in the most recent times.

H. Le Gac/MICHELIN

Sicily Canal

The Sicily Canal harbours two volcanic islands, Pantelleria and Linosa. The region's volcanic activity is caused by a rift between the continental shelves of Sicily and Tunisia. The most recent signs were registered in 1831 following the emergence of the island of Ferdinandea, currently below sea level, 50km/31mi northeast of Pantelleria, and in 1891, on the seabed approximately 7km/4mi northwest of Pantelleria.

H. Le Gac/MICHELIN

Vegetation

Sicily offers a year-round feast for the senses: January sees the end of winter, with the arrival of delicate white blossom on the almond trees; spring is marked by the flowering of the yellow mimosa trees and bright white, pink and yellow oleander bushes, accompanied by the sweet scent of orange blossom; and as spring turns to summer, it is the purples and scarlets that dominate, with the blossoming of bougainvillea, the large, brightly coloured hibiscus, and the pinkish-red fruit of the exotic prickly pear.

The mild climate enjoyed by the island of Sicily nurtures a fairly typical range of Mediterranean flora, particularly in the coastal regions and low-lying flatlands. The most common species include **myrtle** *(Myrtus)*, **strawberry tree** *(Arbutus)*, **lentisk** *(Pistacia lentiscus)* and **tree spurge** *(Euphorbia dendroides)* – a bush which grows to a height of 1.5m/5ft. In springtime, large stretches of sun-drenched calcareous hillsides are set ablaze by yellow flowering, sweet-smelling broom bushes *(Ginestra cinera)*, the spineless genus which grows to 2m/6.5ft in height, and which was used traditionally to make brooms for sweeping floors. These species alternate with such imports as the evergreen, river-bed loving **oleander** *(Nerium)*; the **carob tree** *(Ceratonia)* that produces toffee-brown bean pods, populating the landscape around Ragusa; the formally erect gum or **eucalyptus** with its weeping branches and aromatic leaves; the tall pyramidal **maritime pine** *(Pinus pinaster)*; and the majestic **stone or umbrella pine** *(Pinus pinea)*. The bastard **olive** *(Olea oleaster)* grows everywhere; interestingly, this spiny shrub produces rather mean, less fleshy fruits than its cultivated cousin even though this wild form was probably the original species grafted by the Syrians to produce the variety cultivated for its fruit and oil.

M. Magni/MICHELIN

Large tracts of land are devoted to **vineyards,** groves of **olive trees** *(Olea)* that assume contorted shapes with age, and **citrus trees** (lemons; sweet, blood and Seville oranges; mandarins), a typical feature of Sicilian gardens (*giardino* is used in Sicily to describe a citrus grove and not an ornamental garden, as elsewhere in Italy).

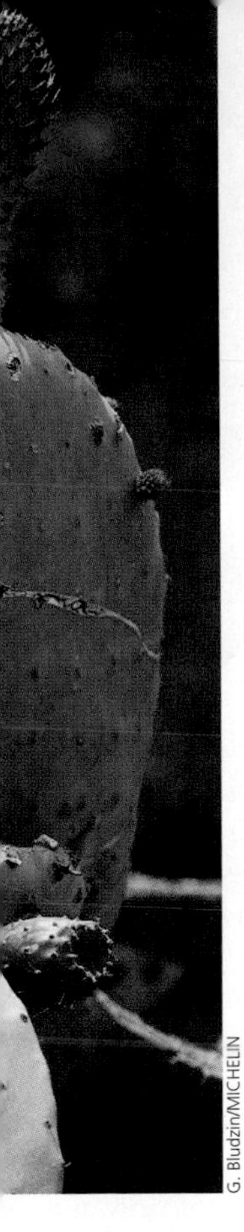

G. Bludzin/MICHELIN

After a long period of vegetation lasting up to 50 years, the agave plant produces a long stem in the shape of a candelabra which can grow to a height of 6-8m/20-26ft. Highly scented flowers blossom along this stem, shortly after which the plant dies. Legend compares the agave plant with a young girl, who having waited years to get married, dies a year after her wedding.

M. Magni/MICHELIN

In the more arid areas thorny plants are common, such as various varieties of thistle (Silybum), **palms** and **dwarf palms** – a perennial typical of the Zingaro area (so much so that it has been chosen as the symbol of the nature reserve). A broad range of succulent plants encompass the huge **agave** or **century plant**, **cactuses** and the ubiquitous **prickly pears** (*Opuntia* – known locally as Fico d'India).

The first signs of spring, heralded by meadows of wild garlic and garishly yellow oxalis at ground level, stir the **almond trees** (especially around Agrigento) into injecting delicate clouds of white blossom into the landscape; next comes the fluffy yellow mimosa and the sweet-smelling, crisp white **orange blossom**, from which bees produce a particularly fragrant honey. Soon the pinks and reds of the **oleanders** and **hibiscus** mark the advent of summer; they are joined by the garishly purple, puce and magenta **bougainvilleas** and the intensely perfumed **jasmine** which blinks open its starry flowers all over the main island – but most especially in Pantelleria and the Aeolian Islands. Through the summer, issuing from the apparently arid stone walls, there tumbles forth a cascade of round-leafed **caper plants** from which the buds are plucked long before the exquisite, pinkish white flowers can flourish.

J. Malburet/MICHELIN

Each region of the island has its local flora, such as the **cork plantations** near Niscemi (inland from Gela), **papyrus** plants along the River Ciane (just outside Siracusa) and the **ash tree manna** grown in the Castelbuono area of the Madonie.

Sicilian Food and Wine

Talk of food in Sicily is like talking about the weather in England – it is fundamental to life itself. Each region has its own dishes and each community will sing the praises of their home-grown vegetables and fragrant herbs which impart flavour, texture and colour to the local cuisine. The island's eternal links with the sea are also clearly evident, with myriad fish dishes featuring prominently in the kitchens of Sicilian homes and restaurants.

Sicilian cuisine relies on an abundance of strongly-flavoured basic ingredients (fennel, for example) which are blended and fused with the ruddiest sun-blushed tomatoes, the most gleaming rich aubergines, delicate courgettes and freshest tuna. The food is a natural extension of the local landscape. It forms an integral part of the gastronomic culture of the Mediterranean, halfway between Greece and North Africa, Spain and Ancient Phoenicia (the Middle East).

Just as the landscapes of the coast and the hinterland are radically different, so their cuisine is quite distinctive. Imagine, therefore, the gastronomy of Sicily as a palette of paints, with strong colours and subtle hints, a blend of flavours and suggestive memories, highly evocative and yet elusive.

Typical Mediterranean cuisine

As with all simple culinary traditions, the most popular single-course meal is often the tastiest. Pasta, prepared with seasonal vegetables and locally made olive oil, is the main staple. *Pasta con le sarde*, originally a Palermo dish using freshly caught sardines, is now common across the whole island; pasta cooked predominantly with vegetables is more typical of the inland areas; more elaborate preparations include types of *pasta al forno* (baked pasta) such as *pasta 'ncaciata* from Messina, and Catania's *pasta alla Norma* (cooked with tomatoes, aubergines and salty ricotta cheese).

However, before pasta was invented, bread was the mainstay of the diet. The many varieties of bread available in Sicily have always been accompanied by what the local area had to offer: oil, oregano and tomatoes resulted in the widespread and very simple *pane cunzato*: this is eaten hot straight out of the oven. The more unusual *pane ca' meusa* is a toasted roll spread with a meat paste, often sold on the streets of Palermo.

The central part of the island is dominated by farming habits and the cuisine consequently uses a great deal of fresh vegetables. The aubergine is an important ingredient and forms the basis of a whole range of delicious dishes, culminating in the glorious *parmigiana* (baked aubergine with ricotta and a touch of tomato sauce, maybe a sprig of basil). The by-products generated by sheep farming play an important role in the hills (providing the fresh and salted cheese known as *ricotta fresca* and *ricotta salata*); meat is usually reserved for special occasions, when *castrato* (literally castrated ram) is roasted. The most common method of cooking meat is on the grill. Pork is also popular.

The eastern flank of the island preserves Greek cooking methods. The west meanwhile is marked by an Arab influence and by courtly practices. The cuisine is more elaborate, refined and full of unexpected contrasts. In an analogy with the landscape, the simple austerity of the Greek temples is replaced here with a sophistication imparted by a *Thousand and One Nights* such as is prevalent in Moorish Palermo.

CANTINE FLORIO

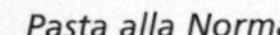

Pasta alla Norma

J. Malburet/MICHELIN

The *caponata di melanzane* is an example of the different approach to vegetables (cooked aubergine, tomato, onion, olives, celery and capers, served cold in a sweet-sour sauce); *falsomagro* (a large roll of meat stuffed with ham, cheese and eggs) or *involtini alla primavera* (rissoles made with breadcrumbs, sultanas, pine nuts, cheese and flavoured with bay leaves and onion) demonstrate the different approach to meat, while *sarde a beccafico* (sardines fried with breadcrumbs, lemon juice and pine nuts) do likewise for fish. The complexity of these dishes had the primary function of displaying wealth.

However, even in the larger towns, a cuisine of popular inspiration is never far away: road-side shops sell food that has just been fried or cooked in the oven, and stalls sell all kinds of dishes around the clock (*sfinciuni* and *panelle* to name but two).

Returning to the historical influences on Sicilian cooking, the Arabs introduced citrus fruits, sugar, cinnamon and saffron, as well as rice to Sicily. Rice is cooked here in various ways that differ, in the main, from the way it is used in making risottos in northern Italy: take *arancine* for instance (delicious deep-fried rice balls filled with meat ragout and peas, or ham and cheese), a sort of symbol of the island's traditional cuisine, and often the first gastronomic encounter on a trip to Sicily.

As you would expect, there is an abundance of fish and hundreds of different ways of cooking it. Tuna has always occupied a prime position, possibly because of the ritual associated with its catch and killing; sardines and anchovies are common everywhere, while *pesce spada* (swordfish) is more common around Messina.

ARANCINE DI RISO (DEEP-FRIED RICE BALLS)

400g/1lb rice, 1/2 small packet of saffron, 150g/6oz minced veal, 1/2 peeled tomato, 100g/4oz shelled peas, six eggs, 75g/3oz fresh *caciocavallo* cheese, 100g/4oz butter, 1/2 onion, 300g/12oz flour, 300g/12oz breadcrumbs. Serves four.

Boil the rice until it has a crunchy, *al dente* texture and then mix it with the saffron, three eggs and half the butter. Leave to cool. Parboil the peas, drain and brown in the remaining butter. In a separate pan, gently fry the chopped onion. Add the meat, peeled tomato, salt and pepper. Cover and cook over a low heat. Once the meat sauce is ready, mix with the peas. To make the *arancini* balls, take some of the rice mixture and make into a shell shape, then pour in some of the meat sauce. Add a slice of cheese and cover with more of the rice, making a ball. Whisk the remaining eggs and add a little salt. Roll the rice ball in the flour, then in the egg mixture and finally the breadcrumbs. Fry in plenty of sunflower oil and serve hot.

Sweet delicacies

Sicily's cake- and pastry-making tradition deserves special attention because it is part of daily life; its fragrance lingers as do the pungent smells of crushed herbs (rosemary, wild fennel, oregano, basil, thyme) which grow in abundance throughout the countryside around the island.

Convent sweetmeats, like the brightly coloured *frutta martorana,* named after the convent in Palermo where they originated, have become popular throughout the island. *Cannoli, cassate, pignoccata, biancomangiare* and the traditional *gelo di mellone* (watermelon jelly) are the most common, but each province has its own particular varieties and surprises.

Then, we cannot forget the exquisite home-made ice cream and *granite* made by real experts, the products of great craftsmanship and culinary pride.

Wines

Sicily's wines used to be regarded as *vini da taglio,* that is, they were used to boost the alcohol content of wines of other areas, but, today, although not all have acquired the fame of the fortified wine of **Marsala**, Sicilian table wines and DOC (denominazione di origine controllata) wines such as Alcamo, Nero d'Avola, Etna Rosso, il Corvo and Regaleali are delights in store for anyone who has not had the opportunity to taste them.

In addition to Marsala, dessert wines made here include Moscato di Noto, Passito di Pantelleria and Malvasia di Lipari. *For a description of wine routes in Sicily, see p 32.*

Gano di Magonza is always depicted with squinting eyes, because a traitor cannot look someone straight in the eye.

Ferraù wears the typical Saracen costume of breeches and carries a shield adorned with the crescent moon.

The beautiful Angelica, loved by both Orlando and Rinaldo, is the daughter of the king of Catai.

R.Corbel/MICHELIN

Sicilian Puppets

"We are puppets, Signor Fifì! Divine spirit enters us and makes us puppets. I'm a puppet, you're a puppet, everyone's a puppet."

Luigi Pirandello, *The Cap with the Jingle Bells*

The fate of puppets and marionettes in Italy took an upward turn in the 16C, when the aristocracy began showing an interest in the puppet shows put on using wire-controlled marionettes. The spread to a wider, paying audience came about in the 18C. But it was not until the mid-19C that the puppet show as we know it today became a genre in itself, complete with shiny armour, swords and agile movements which pay off when it comes to a fight.

Sicilian puppet masters weave their stories around bandits, saints, Shakespearean heroes, not forgetting the vignettes that are strictly of local interest. The favourite source of subject matter is the popular **picaresque stories of chivalry**, from the **Carolingian cycle** in particular. The puppeteers prepare a text that follows the basic lines of the plot, and then set about exaggerating the clashes between the paladins and the infidels because the fight is always the culmination of the show. The puppeteers' arrival was always awaited with great anticipation, most especially by the less fortunate classes, and no-one would dream of missing a single performance. This is why the puppeteers would break up the story into episodes and present them in series that might last several months. Each performance had to include at least one fight (such was the explanation for having to adapt the historical facts). The puppet master also prepared various boards with panels summarising the salient elements of the story. The main events that were relevant for that particular evening were illustrated on the board, and these were changed with each performance. The board, displayed outside the theatre, would act as an advertisement for the evening and also summarise for the public the story so far. In 2001, Sicilian puppet theatre was declared a masterpiece of oral tradition by UNESCO.

Principal characters

As mentioned above, the most famous protagonists were the paladins (courtly peers) of France who, under the leadership of Charlemagne, spent their lives fighting the infidels. The show hinged on predetermined precise values and sentiments: there were "goodies" (the paladins), "baddies" (the infidels) and traitors, such as

King Carlo Magno (Charlemagne), the brave leader of the paladins, can be easily recognised by his crown.

SCALA

Gano di Magonza. The audience participates in the show and takes the side of one character or another: the heroes are challenged, encouraged and applauded; the "baddies" are derided and there is a great roar from the audience every time one of them is killed.

At one time puppet performances were followed so closely that the audience would immediately recognise the different characters. The easiest way to do this is to look at the shields: Orlando's shield is adorned with a cross, while Rinaldo and Bradamante (the latter recognised by her long hair) carry shields bearing the image of a lion.

Orlando and Rinaldo are companions in arms divided by their love for the beautiful Angelica. Orlando is serious, reliable, a scrupulous person, dutiful but unlucky in love. Rinaldo is from a poor background and has learned the art of survival from an early age; he is a cunning, jolly, rebellious womaniser who never misses an opportunity to sneak away if circumstances permit. Like all the paladins, they wear skirts; Orlando has a crossed shield and Rinaldo, and his sister Bradamante, who is also a warrior (but can be distinguished from her brother because of her long hair), have a lion on their shields.

Performance

The show has three main elements: the puppet who acts on stage; the puppet master who remains off-stage and is responsible for handling the puppet and providing the voice-overs of several characters at a time; and the music which emphasises the most dramatic moments, particularly when there is a duel – the sound of clashing swords must be accompanied by the frenzied strains of a mechanical pianola or wind instruments. As stated, the performance must include at least one fight, which is the moment the audience is waiting for. Special additional puppets are used for pulling off special effects: a puppet might lose its head or be torn asunder, only to be magically restored to one piece in the next show, or a witch might need to take on a disguise, turning from a pretty, angelic face to a death mask.

Two traditions

Puppets are made of wood and are jointed with metal hinges (the warriors, at least); their manipulation is controlled by lengths of wire connected to the head and right hand. The embossed armour is usually made of bronze or copper. There are two main schools: one from Palermo and one from Catania which build puppets according to different criteria.

Popular Festivals and Traditions

By combining pagan rites, holy days allowed by the Christian Church and local festivals, the Sicilians ensure that

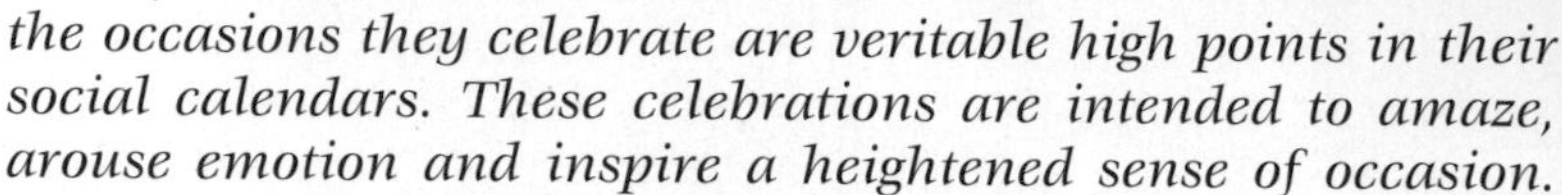

the occasions they celebrate are veritable high points in their social calendars. These celebrations are intended to amaze, arouse emotion and inspire a heightened sense of occasion.

The most important festivals are Easter, Carnival and the celebrations marking the local patron saint's feast day. Other celebrations include secular festivals such as the Palio dei Normanni which commemorates Roger II's delivery of Piazza Armerina; festivals derived from pagan rites, such as the Sagra della Spiga at Gangi with a procession dedicated to the ancient goddess Demeter (Ceres); and festivals linked to a celebration of nature, such as the Sagra del Mandorlo in fiore (celebrating the blossoming of the almond trees) at Agrigento and the Sagra della Ricotta at Vizzini, both of which have their origins in fêting the advent of spring.

Popular Sicilian music

At the very mention of this island's name, anyone with a keen ear for music will call to mind an ancient popular shepherds' dance, the siciliana: this was transcribed in the 17C and 18C in a handful of pieces for instrument and voice.
The songs that brighten the passing of days are the songs called alla carrittera – literally "of the cart-driver", and those sung by the cantastorie – modern equivalents of minstrels who travel from town to town with a guitar and a large board depicting the scenes of the passionate story that is the subject of their song. The most famous is Ciccio Busacca (born Paternò 1926), the singer of the Lament for the Death of Turiddu Carnivali and Train of the Sun, written by Ignazio Buttitta with the collaboration of Dario Fo.

Patron saints

The most spectacular festivals in honour of patron saints are those held in the large towns. In Palermo U fistinu, dedicated to Santa Rosalia, lasts for six whole days: these are six action-packed days of wild celebration with the slow yet triumphant procession of a float bearing the statue of the saint through the crowds. In Catania the citizens direct their hopes and aspirations to St Agatha, whose relics, contained in a precious silver bust of the saint set with enamels and jewels, are processed for three days by the nudi; these men are dressed in simple jute sacks in memory of the fateful night in 1126 when the relics were brought back to the city from Constantinople and the citizens poured into the streets, eagerly jumping out of bed without taking the time to get dressed. In Siracusa eyes of wax, silver and bronze are fixed to the litter of St Lucy in grateful acknowledgement of grace received from the saint, the protector of eyes and eyesight. In Messina the most spectacular festival is held on 15 August, when an enormous statue representing the Assumption of the Virgin Mary is pulled by thousands of willing hands to the cathedral, where it remains for two days guarded by 14 young girls dressed in white. This Festa della Vergine is celebrated alongside the anniversary of the arrival of Count Roger: the sacred mixes with the profane in an inseparable cocktail of religious devotion, high spirits, social occasion and entertainment.

A devil in the festival at Prizzi

N. Reitano/Lara Pessina/MICHELIN

Easter

Easter is certainly the most eagerly awaited festival in Sicily. In almost every town and small village, enormous amounts of effort are invested in preparing for the processions and the celebrations that have changed little through the centuries.

Lara Pessina/MICHELIN

The most poignant elements of the ritual are re-enacted between the Thursday before Easter and Easter Sunday (the discovery of the empty tomb as evidence of the Resurrection), although these can be more protracted, as is the case with the celebrations held at **Trapani**. There, the evenings leading up to the Good Friday grand procession are devoted to the *discese delle Vergini*: at sunset, representatives of each and every *ceto* of the town (associations roughly comparable to the medieval trade guilds) bear on their shoulders the image of their patron Madonna (Madre dei Massari, Madre Pietà del Popolo) and carry her down to the old part of town by candlelight. The men compete to be chosen as bearers. The icon sways along its way, stopping often opposite wayside crosses, shrines and churches, but also outside the houses and workplaces of people who have offered a donation. In so doing, it is almost as though the Madonna is paying homage to the people who worship her. The elegant *palazzi* open their doors and gracious inner courtyards to visitors, to the crowd, and to the band, who at intervals interrupt the silence with a burst of music. On Good Friday, 20 figurative groups are continuously borne aloft round the town over a period of 20 hours: in a meaningful and symbolic succession of day, night and day (from early afternoon on the Friday through the night to Saturday morning) the faithful are reminded of, and share in, the emotional endurance and physical pain suffered by the Madonna and by Christ.

N. Reitano/Lara Pessina/MICHELIN

In **Marsala** the re-enactment of the Passion is assigned to real live men and women who take on individual roles in the different instalments. At **Enna**, the celebrations reach their climax on Good Friday, when hooded members of the confraternities that were instituted originally as trade corporations but which now act as religious organisations, process through the streets to the town centre carrying the two heavy statues of the dead Christ and the Addolorata (Our Lady of Sorrows). The processions make their way independently to the cathedral where they meet and proceed together in an exhausting journey that lasts throughout the night. The whole event is then repeated on the Sunday, but with one fundamental difference. This time, the meeting between the Madonna and the Resurrected Christ takes place in a happy, festive atmosphere.

A rather unusual rite takes place in **Prizzi** on the Sunday morning. It is called the **Uballu di diavula:** devils, dressed in red, with goatskins slung across their shoulders, their faces covered by horrible tin masks, run through the streets of the town rattling iron chains and accompanied by another masked figure, this time dressed in yellow and armed with a wooden crossbow, representing Death. Anyone who gets hit is carried off to the bar (identified as hell) where he pays for a complete round of drinks. These weird-looking figures lurching madly around as if engaged in a hellish dance, jump about uttering threats, trying to avert the Madonna from meeting the Resurrected Christ. The scene repeats itself several times until at last the two angels accompanying the Madonna strike the devils down, and they fall to the ground. Only Death itself cannot be touched, spared partly in recognition of human mortality and partly because Christ has already overcome it. At **Terrasini**, the rite is tinged with the profane, for the festival of **li schietti** – the eligible bachelors – involves the young menhaving to prove their virility by lifting orange trees.

The Legacy of the Past

In the 14C BC, the Mediterranean was crucial to the history of man: in the words of Plato, people flocked to its coasts "like frogs around a pond". Sicily lies in the centre of this sea and consequently became a natural intersection of many cultures and civilisations. The island attracted navigators from the East and over the centuries its coastline was transfigured by myth and poetry.

G. Blot/RMN

The Interior of the Temple of Segesta, *by J*

Pre-Hellenistic Sicily

The Greek historian Dionysius of Halicarnassus tells of how, in Ancient times, expeditions embarked in the East, setting their sails on a course for the Italian peninsula and Sicily. Archaeology provides more concrete proof of this. In fact, evidence of visitations made by the Mycenaeans has been found at Thapsos and Panarea (pottery incised with Linear B script, the Mycenaean syllabic alphabet) – from which it may be assumed that the island acted as a trading post for the Mycenaean fleets.

• **1270-650 BC** – Late Bronze Age: significant finds retrieved from the necropolis at Pantalica (5 000 tombs) and from the one at Cassibile. The arrival of the Greeks seems to have brought with it the use of iron and a higher level of material civilisation.

The Athenian historian Thucydides provides us with information about Ancient Sicily. In addition to telling us about the history of Greek colonisation, he also talks about the indigenous peoples of the island, the **Siculi** and the **Sicani**. The former resided in eastern and central southern Sicily in the area inland from Syracuse, the area around the lake that was sacred to the Palici (Lake Naftia, near modern Palagonia) and the town of Morgantina. The origins of the Siculi, who lived in the western part of the island, should, perhaps, be traced back to the Italian peninsula, given that many pointers indicate an association with the Apennine culture on the mainland. The Sicani seem not to conform with Indo-European people, but rather to be of Iberian origin; the affinity of their name with that of the Siculi has not yet been satisfactorily explained.

The people of the **Elimi**, founders of Erice (Eryx) and Segesta, seem to belong to the ancient family of Mediterranean and pre-Indo-European peoples. Various pieces of evidence suggest contact with the East (like the cult of Aphrodite Ericina) and a rapid Hellenisation of this people (the Doric temple at Segesta).

Phoenicians from Carthage settled at Solunto, Panormus (modern Palermo) and Mozia (Motya) in the northwestern part of the island, where the foundations of Lilybaeum (modern Marsala), an impregnable stronghold and the fulcrum of Carthaginian military power, were later to be laid.

Sikelía: Sicily under the Greeks

• **775 BC** – Establishment of the trading colony of Pithecusa on Ischia; this date heralds the first Hellenistic settlements in mainland Italy.

• **735** – The first Hellenistic settlement, Naxos, is founded in Sicily, a strategic move that would secure control over the trade routes operating through the Straits of Messina. In 734 the Corinthians lay the foundations of Syracuse (Siracusa).
• **730-700** – The Chalcidians found Catana, Leontinoi and Zancle (now Messina); the Megarians found Megara Hyblaea.
• **688** – Colonists from Rhodes and Crete found Gela, the same city that seized Akragas (Agrigento) in 580.
• **598** – Foundation of Camarina.
• **491** – Gelon becomes the tyrant of Gela. In 488, he wins the chariot race at Olympia, thus winning great prestige among the Greeks.
• **480-479** – The Greeks in Sicily face hostility from the Carthaginians and the Etruscans, probably in reaction to the increased threat from Persia against the Greek homeland.
• **485** – Gelon becomes tyrant of Syracuse.
• **480** – Battle of Himera: the Syracusans defeat the Carthaginian onslaught.
• **474** – Hieron, tyrant of Syracuse, wins a decisive naval victory at Cumae over the Etruscans. Catania, on the Ionian coast, is occupied by Dorian colonists and subjugated to the rule of Hieron's son.
• **465** – The tyrant Thrasybulus is expelled and Syracuse is ruled by a moderate democracy.
• **453** – The rebellion of Ducetius results in all the Siculi towns being brought into one confederation. The uprising is quelled in 450.
• **415** – The Athenian fleet, marshalled by Nicias and Alcibiades, sets out to wage war on the enemy, Syracuse.
• **414** – Siege of Syracuse. The Spartan Gylippus comes to the town's rescue.
• **413** – The Athenian hold over Sicily is broken. During the war, Athens loses 50 000 men (including 12 000 ordinary citizens) and more than 200 triremes.
• **409** – The Carthaginians attack and destroy Selinunte and Himera.
• **406** – The general Dionysius I seizes power in Syracuse. Over the ensuing years he secures a vast dominion including a large portion of southern Italy and the Adriatic coast (he conquers Croton and founds Ancona).
• **392** – Peace between the Carthaginians and Dionysius I.

Museo Archeologico di Siracusa/SCALA

Coins

- **367** – Death of Dionysius I.
- **347** – Dionysius II, exiled previously by Dion, a family relative and fellow adherent of Plato, returns to Syracuse.
- **344** – The mother city of Corinth sends 700 soldiers to Syracuse led by Timoleon, who defeats the Carthaginians at the battle of River Crimisus (341).
- **316** – Agathocles, a man of modest origins, heads a revolt against the barons and seizes power in Syracuse.
- **310** – The Carthaginians defeat Agathocles at Ecnomus. Soon after, he lands in Africa at the head of 14 000 men bent on wreaking vengeance on Carthage.
- **289** – Death of Agathocles. In the same year, the Mamertini, mercenaries of Campanian origin, seize Messina.
- **280** – Pyrrhus, king of Epirus in Greece, in Italy. Between 278 and 275, he tries in vain to unite Sicily.
- **269** – Hieron II, formerly one of Pyrrhus' officers, declares himself *basileus* (king) of Syracuse after a victory over the Mamertini.
- **264-241** – First Punic War.

Sicily under the Romans

Ruled by a praetor and two quaestors, Sicily was evidently of prime importance to Rome: the tribute levied has been calculated as around two million *modii*; this was paid according to methods devised by Hieron II (hence the law *lex hieronica*) and probably satisfied one-fifth of the total financial requirement of the city of Rome. Despite suffering two devastating slave rebellions and reeling from the disastrous outcome of Syracuse's revolt – which resulted in the town being sacked – the island continued to be of economic importance. Sicily possessed a good number of large estates, which, in turn, provided the Roman aristocracy with elegant residences; in many cases these villas became centres of literary patronage and recreation for the ennobled Romans.

- **227 BC** – Sicily is made a Roman province.
- **218-201** – Second Punic War. In 211, after a long siege, Consul Marcellus sacks Syracuse which was rebelling against Rome.
- **149-146** – Third Punic War and final destruction of Carthage.
- **138-131** – First slave revolt in Sicily led by the Syrian slave Eunus.
- **104-99** – Second slave revolt led by the slave Trifon.
- **70** – Verres, the praetor in Sicily, is accused by several Sicilian towns of embezzlement. Their legal defence is conducted by Cicero.
- **48** – Battle of Pharsalus: Caesar's troops defeat Pompey's.
- **44** – Pompey's son, Sextus Pompeius, controls Sardinia, Corsica and Sicily with his fleets. In 36 BC he is defeated by Vipsanius Agrippa, one of Octavian's admirals.
- **31** – Battle of Actium: Octavian (later Augustus) becomes sole ruler of Rome.
- **2C AD** – Spread of Christianity on the island.
- **468** – Gaiseric, King of the Vandals in Africa, conquers the island.

Arabic Sicily

The island was also to flourish in the Middle Ages, both on account of its sustained economic importance and because of the cultural dynamism perpetrated by the meeting and exchange of many different and colourful civilisations, as had been the case in Antiquity. In particular, the island was to benefit from almost two centuries of Muslim domination before submitting to Norman rule and becoming the focus of imperial ambitions harboured by the Swabians. The evolution of a magnificent and highly original Arab-Norman style of architecture, the continued flowering of a uniquely Sicilian literary tradition and a predilection for scholarship (it was in Sicily that a selection of Plato's Dialogues were first translated in the 11C) combined to give medieval Sicily an autonomous culture that has proved to be vital to the understanding of European history as a whole.

• **AD 491** – Theodoric's Ostrogoths assume control of the island: its administration is re-organised according to Imperial standards. The Roman Church extends its land holding.
• **535** – Belisarius, a general in Justinian's army, annexes Sicily to the Eastern Roman Empire at the start of the Gothic-Byzantine war. On a cultural level, Sicily, where Greek and Latin were still commonly spoken, draws closer to the Byzantine East.
• **652** – First Arab incursions on the island.
• **663** – For political reasons, the Byzantine basileus, Constans II, takes up residence in Sicily.
• **725** – Iconoclastic crisis: Sicily remains faithful to the cult of images. In 732, the Sicilian Church comes under the Patriarchate of Constantinople.
• **827** – The Arabs land at Mazara. The invaders (mostly Berbers and Persians) conquer Palermo (831) which they then make their capital.
• **842-59** – Messina, Modica, Ragusa and Enna fall: the Byzantine army is put to flight, the last indigenous Christians to resist are quashed. Only the northeastern part of the island resists effectively, with Byzantine assistance.
• **878** – Syracuse, the ancient capital, is taken by storm and destroyed.
• **902** – Fall of Taormina, the last Byzantine stronghold in Sicily.
• **948-1040** – The island is ruled by the Emirs of the Kalbite dynasty. Of Arab origin, they are loyal to the Caliphs of Egypt.

The arrival of the Arabs split the political and economic status quo in Sicily: while a profitable period of collaboration between the indigenous people and invaders in the western part of the island was enjoyed, the area around Syracuse never fully accepted Arab dominion, even if their arrival sealed the demise of the decadent ancient metropolis and of eastern Sicily, where the Greek language and culture still prevailed. The northeastern part of the island, which maintained its Christian solidarity, offered fierce resistance.

Palermo came to symbolise Arab-Sicilian civilisation. It was densely populated (estimated at 300 000 inhabitants) and wealthy, with bands of sprawling suburbs and small farm holdings surrounding the ancient city centre; some 300 mosques and as many *madrasa* (Koranic schools) were instituted. The Emir was advised by an influential assembly (*giama'a*) drawn from members of the local aristocracy. The region of Palermo best epitomised the economic success of Arab domination: land was divided into small plots, thus benefiting the new rulers; intensive and more sophisticated farming methods were imposed (these were often further improved by networks of irrigation channels known as *qanat*, which collected water from the water table, *see p 281*) and new cash crops were introduced such as cotton, flax, sugar cane, rice, citrus fruits, henna, nuts and dates.

Besides the affluence generated by the new materialism, culture flourished, encouraged by links with Islam from around the Mediterranean (Andalucia in the case of literature, the Maghreb and Egypt in the case of science). The perfect expression of this cross-fertilisation is

Linguistic traces of the Arabs in Sicily

Traces of the Arab presence in Sicily can be found in the language of the island, especially in place names. Names of towns and villages that have evolved from Arabic include Calascibetta, Calatafimi, Caltabellotta, Caltagirone, Caltanissetta and Caltavuturo, all of which derive from the word *kalat*, meaning castle; Marsala from *marsa* (port); Mongibello, Gibellina and Gibilmanna from *gebel* (mountain); Modica from *mudiqah* (narrowing in the road); Racalmuto and Regalbuto from *rahal* (hamlet); and Sciacca from *shaqqah* (fissure, referring to the caves at Monte Kronio). The most common Italian words to have derived from Arabic are *albicocca* (apricot), *alcool*, *algebra* (from *al giabr*, meaning transport), *arancia* (orange), *bizzeffe* (galore, from *bizzef*, meaning many), *calibro* (gauge, from *qalib*, the measurement used for shoes), *carciofo* (artichoke), *cifra* (figure) and *zero* (both from *sifr*, meaning empty), *cotone* (cotton), *dogana* (customs), *limone* (lemon), *magazzino* (warehouse), *melanzana* (aubergine), *ragazzo* (boy, from *raqqas*, meaning messenger), *taccuino* (notebook, from *taquim*, meaning proper order), *tazza* (cup), *tariffa* (tariff), *zafferano* (saffron), *zecca* (mint, from *sikka*, meaning coin) and *zucchero* (sugar).

Christ crowning Roger II –
La Martorana, Palermo

(c) Archivi Alinari/Archivio Seat, Firenze

the splendid Arabic literature that emerged from the court at Palermo. Poetry, in particular, was highly regarded and therefore encouraged. Ibn Hamdis, in his melancholy farewell to his beloved Sicily now in Norman hands, wrote: *"a land to which the dove lent its collar, clothed by the peacock from its many-coloured mantle of feathers"*.

• **1061** – The Normans land in Sicily. During the next 30 years, Christianity struggles to reaffirm itself across the island and drive out Islamic culture, which nevertheless continues to prosper until the beginning of the 13C.

Sicily under the Normans

The "men of the north", having set out from their homes in Scandinavia, had settled in what is now Normandy by 911. Subsequently, groups of Norman mercenaries were engaged in the southern Italian peninsula to settle the disputes that raged between the Roman popes, Lombard dukes of Benevento and Salerno, Arabs in Sicily, and Byzantines in Apulia and Calabria. Through the Treaty of Melfi (1059), the Normans not only obtained for themselves the privilege of being recognised as vassals of the Pope, they also secured feudal rights over southern Italy. One mercenary among them belonging to the Altavilla (or Hauteville) family, a certain Robert Guiscard ("the Sly"), having acquired the title of Duke of Apulia, promptly subdued Bari and Salerno. One of his brothers, **Count Roger** (1031-1101), set about conquering Sicily, marching into Palermo in 1072. The last Arab stronghold, Noto, did not capitulate until 1091 when Roger was awarded the coveted title of Papal Legate, making him the direct representative of the Holy See on the island.

• **1130** – **Roger II** (1095-1154) succeeds his father Roger I in 1101; the title of King of Sicily and Duke of Campania is conferred upon him by the anti-Pope Anacletus II; this position is sanctioned nine years later by Innocent II.

Roger II extended his kingdom as far as Tronto, thereby adding Capua, Amalfi and Naples; he maintained his capital at Palermo. Having claimed all rights to the land, Roger proceeded to assign territory to his followers in return for their support. Meanwhile, the feudal system was spreading through Sicily. A key element in the organisation of the Kingdom of Sicily was its complex structure of administration left over from the Byzantine and Arab dominion: in simple terms, the king was assisted by six officials and by magistrates posted throughout the provinces (*iustíciarii* and *connestabuli*). There was also a financial administration (*dohana* in Arabic) and a system of self-government for the Arab community in Palermo, ruled by a *qadi* (judge).

In ecclesiastical circles, special prerogatives were given to the Norman sovereigns nominated as Papal Legates by Pope Urban II: their prime objective was to eradicate Islam and to resist corruption from the (Greco-Byzantine) Eastern Church. Meanwhile, the Arab influence persisted at Roger II's court at Palermo: there, the geographer **al-Idrisi** constructed a large silver planisphere and wrote his geographical treatise which was significantly entitled *Kitab-Rugiar*, or *The Book of Roger*.

• **1147** – Incursions by the Norman fleet in the Byzantine Empire: Corfu, Thessalonika and Thebes are sacked; numerous craftsmen skilled in working with silk are deported to Sicily.

• **1154** – **William I** (1120-66) succeeds his father Roger II. While engaged in conflict with Frederick Barbarossa, he must also confront a rebellion from his barons, which he succeeds in quelling in 1156.

• **1166** – **William II** (1153-89), William I's son, is crowned king. By supporting the Pope and the northern towns in their struggle against Barbarossa, he is also able to wage an attack on the Byzantine Empire now in decline. He is hailed a champion of the Third Crusade against Saladin: in fact, Norman troops were committed to rescuing Tripoli.

He designates his aunt Costanza as his heir; she is betrothed to Henry, the eldest son of Barbarossa; thus the Swabian dynasty can claim legitimate rights to the throne of Sicily.

Swabians and Angevins

- **1186** – The marriage of the future Emperor Henry VI (Barbarossa's son) to Costanza d'Altavilla is celebrated in Milan.
- **1190-97** – Henry VI of Swabia (1165-97) is made Emperor and King of Sicily.
- **1198** – Innocent III is elected Pope. Costanza has her young son Frederick crowned king of Sicily in Palermo Cathedral.
- **1209** – Frederick marries Costanza of Aragon.
- **1214** – Innocent III excommunicates Emperor Otto of Brunswick and nominates Frederick II in his place. Frederick arrives in Germany; he does not return to Sicily until 1220.
- **1228** – Exhorted by Pope Gregory IX, Frederick leaves for the Holy Land, where he reaches a peaceful agreement with the Sultan. In 1229, he is crowned king of Jerusalem.
- **1231** – Frederick II issues the *Constitutions of Melfi*, a code of law designed for a centralised state, that is operational outside the jurisdiction of the feudal lords.
- **1250** – Death of Frederick II.
- **1250-54** – Conradin IV (1228-54) succeeds his father Frederick II and is crowned Emperor despite the rivalry with **Manfred** (1232-66), Frederick's natural son and heir, who was "fair and well-made and of gentle aspect" (*The Divine Comedy*, Purgatory, Canto III).
- **1265** – Pope Clement IV summons the Christian princes to rally against Manfred; the French, led by Charles of Anjou, rise to the call.
- **1266** – Battle of Benevento: Manfred is defeated and killed.
- **1268** – Final defeat of the Ghibellines (supporters of the Empire) at Tagliacozzo; Conradin, the 15-year-old heir of the Swabians, is beheaded in a piazza in Naples. The **Guelphs of Anjou** secure the power to rule southern Italy.

Sicilian Vespers *by Erulo Eruli*

Civica Galleria d'Arte Moderna E. Restivo, Palermo

Sicilian Vespers and the Aragonese (1282-1416)

• **1282** – A revolt against the ruling Angevins by the **Sicilian Vespers** *(see also p 277)* breaks out in Palermo. Corleone and Messina, the seat of the Angevin viceroy at that time, also rise to join the cause. Help in quelling the troubles is required: in the summer of 1282, a delegation of barons and town representatives request assistance from **Peter III of Aragon** (1239-85) who, being married to Costanza, the Swabian daughter of Manfred, believed he had a rightful claim to the crown of Sicily. Furthermore, the powerful Catalan fleet had been patrolling the Mediterranean for some time already, ready to conquer bases in Africa and Italy once the differences between Pisa and Genoa were settled. Peter III was offered the crown of Sicily. At first, there was little resistance, Charles of Anjou withdrew from Messina on 29 September. However, when war broke out in earnest, the Sicilian-Aragonese discovered an able military leader in Roger di Laurìa, a great admiral, who won a decisive victory over the Angevin forces off Naples in June 1283.

• **1285** – Charles dies in 1285, before he is able to return to Sicily.

• **1296** – **Frederick of Aragon** concedes the right for the parliament of the barons to be called at least once a year. During the 14C, Sicily is frequented by foreign merchants: traders from Genoa and England settle in Messina and Trapani. Groups of Greek and Albanian immigrants move to seven townships in Sicily. These communities preserve some aspects of their culture and religion until the 20C. There is also a considerable influx of "Lombards" – people from northern Italy – who settle in Palermo and Corleone.

• **1302** – The war over Sicily is concluded in 1302 with the Peace of Caltabellotta: Frederick of Aragon, Peter's son, is declared King of Trinacria (avoiding use of the name "Sicily") on the condition that, at his death, his kingdom is returned to Robert of Anjou. The pact was broken and the Norman kingdom, once so prosperous and powerful, was divided into two parts. And so the Angevins' attempt to make the Sicilian kingdom the hub of a dominion, in order to extend their influence throughout the Italian peninsula, met with dismal failure.

• **1425-42** – **Alfonso V of Aragon** (1396-1458) intervenes against the Angevins in Naples. The island and the mainland are again united under one king.

The Sicilian Statute

On 15 May 1946, a royal decree promulgated a law on Sicilian autonomy. On 26 February 1948, the Constituent Assembly turns the Statute of Sicily into law, in accordance with provisions under Article 116 of the Italian Constitution listing the specifications and conditions for autonomous rule as granted to five Italian regions. The regional statute provides for a regional council, known as the Parliament, composed of 90 members. The Parliament elects a regional committee *(Giunta Regionale)* and a president from among its members by a majority consensus. The president has the right to sit in with the Council of Ministers in Rome during debates on issues affecting Sicily. The Parliament can approve legislation for the island, its powers, sanctioned by Article 117 of the Italian Constitution, being fairly extensive. Special delegations from the Council of State and the State Audit Court sit permanently in Palermo so as to ensure a certain degree of administrative decentralisation.

Modern Sicily

• **1492** – The Jews are forced to leave Spain; in Sicily also, prosperous communities are expelled from Salemi and Palermo.

• **1497** – The *Tribunale di Sant'Uffizio*, otherwise known as the Spanish Inquisition, is introduced to Sicily.

• **1535** – Emperor Charles V visits Palermo; he is celebrated following his hard-won victories in the Mediterranean over the Barbary pirates of Algeria.

• **1556** – There are 72 barons on the island (by 1810 that number will have increased to 277) who hold the right to a seat in parliament; this institution is considered ancient and is revered by the Sicilians as a symbol of the island's autonomy. It has three *Brazos* or Chambers with one each reserved for the clergy, the barons and military leaders, and for the representatives of towns directly answerable to the king; it only has the power to advise.

• **1570** – The great Christian fleet (comprising galleys from Venice, Spain, the Papal States, the Duchy of Tuscany etc) that will sail into battle at Lepanto in October 1571 and secure its famous victory over the Turks is rallied at Messina. Large numbers of reserve galley crew and oarsmen are recruited from Calabria and Sicily.

• **1624** – Plague ravages Palermo. The miraculous discovery of Santa Rosalia's bones helps, according to popular belief, to assuage the epidemic. Henceforth, the saint is acclaimed a patron of the city.

• **1647** – Revolt in Palermo, coinciding with the insurrection in Naples led by Tommaso di Aniello. The anti-Spanish uprising is spearheaded by two commoners, Nino de la Pelosa and Giuseppe d'Alessi, but the rebellion is quickly suppressed. In 1674, Messina also rises up against the Spanish, with assistance from the king of France. The town is brutally recaptured by the Spanish in 1678.

• **1693** – A terrible earthquake shakes southeastern Sicily.

• **1713** – The Treaty of Utrecht assigns Sicily to Savoy; **Victor Amadeus,** the new king, visits the island.

• **1718-20** – Spain recaptures Sardinia and threatens Naples and Palermo. The Spanish fleet is sunk, however, at Capo Passero, by the British fleet. Sicily is conferred upon the Habsburg emperor who, in return, cedes Sardinia to Savoy.

• **1733** – The Scottish writer Patrick Brydone publishes his *Tour through Sicily and Malta*, an account of his travels in Sicily.

• **1735** – The coronation of **Charles Bourbon** (1716-88) in Palermo heralds the dominion of the Bourbon dynasty in Sicily.

• **1781-86** – Caracciolo is viceroy of the island: a number of reforms are promised with the aim of increasing his powerbase. The Inquisition is abolished.

• **1794** – Leblanc's discovery of how to isolate sodium carbonate revolutionises several industrial processes: the price of sulphur becomes competitive. From 1790, Sicilian citrus fruits are exported on a large scale across Europe. In 1814, English-owned distilleries in Marsala begin producing a sherry-like wine.

• **1806** – British troops are stationed in Sicily to provide protection from the armies of Napoleon Bonaparte. These contribute to the economic prosperity.

• **1812** – With help from Britain's representative in Sicily, Lord Bentinck, reforms are implemented for a more liberal constitution that abolishes feudal rights. Modelled on the British parliamentary system, the constitution comprises two chambers.

• **1816** – Creation of the Kingdom of Two Sicilies: the kingdoms of Naples and Palermo are unified and the Sicilian flag is abolished. At the same time the 1812 constitution is abrogated.

• **1840** – The issue of water and its illegally controlled distribution comes to a head, most especially in the Palermo area, prompted by acute drought conditions. Smuggling and contraband also get out of hand.

• **1847** – An investigation reveals that half of the island's woodland has been destroyed over the past 100 years, resulting in the climate becoming drier.

The "red shirts" disembark at Marsala

Museo del Risorgimento, Roma/SCALA

Francesco Ferrara's *Letter from Malta* is published proposing Sicilian autonomy within a federation of Italian states.

• **1848-49** – Insurrections in Palermo and across Sicily.

• **1860** – In April, there is rioting in Palermo, provoked by agents from the north. The Thousand are sent to Sicily, headed by Garibaldi *(see MARSALA)*. On 21 October, a plebiscite sanctions (432 000 for and 600 against) the island's union with the Kingdom of Italy.

• **1866** – Revolt in Palermo as a result of the acute economic situation. In the end, the Italian fleet bombards the city while 4 000 soldiers quash the riots.

• **1886** – The Jacini report on the state of Italian agriculture reveals that the island is heading towards a food shortage, aggravated by a rise in population. Between 1880 and 1914, about 1.5 million Sicilians leave the island, the majority heading for the United States. This phenomenon favours the repatriation of considerable funds by the émigrés (about 100 million Lire in 1907).

• **1893** – The Notarbartolo scandal surrounding the director of the Banca d'Italia breaks out; he is assassinated after denouncing political and financial malpractice.

ROGER-VIOLLET

• **1894** – A poor harvest, coupled with the inequalities in the distribution of ecclesiastical land, provoke disorder and insurrection rallied by the supporters of the *Fasci di Lavoratori*, an organisation uniting less prosperous farmers (founded in 1889). When the Giolitti government falls, having been reluctant to use force, a government is formed by the Sicilian Francesco Crispi; he posts 50 000 soldiers on the island and imposes martial law.

• **1908** – Serious earthquake in Messina causing over 60 000 fatalities.

• **1911** – Population census: 58% of Sicilians are found to be illiterate.

• **1925** – The Fascist government extends the "battle of wheat" to Sicily, with the intention of making Italy self-sufficient in the production of cereals. **Mori**, nicknamed the "Iron Chief of Police" in reference to his harsh, violent methods against the Mafia, is appointed Chief of Police in Palermo.

Contemporary Sicily

• **1940** – The government's agricultural reforms impeded by the outbreak of war.

• **1943** – Early July sees the beginning of **Operation Husky**, when the first units of the British Eighth Army and the American Seventh Army seize land at Licata and Augusta. The large-scale deployment of men and equipment under Eisenhower's command soon gains control over the four Italian and two German divisions drawn up to defend the island. On 22 July, first Palermo falls, then Messina, from where, to the detriment of their Italian counterparts, the German units succeed in reaching the mainland. On 3 September, at Cassibile, near Siracusa, emissaries of the Badoglio government sign the armistice with the Allied delegations.

• **1947** – In the elections, the separatists, who are demanding the secession of Sicily from the rest of Italy, receive less than 10% of the vote. Many Sicilians dream of the island being annexed to the United States. The separatists seek to take up arms. **Salvatore Giuliano,** in hiding since 1943, is nominated colonel of EVIS (the Voluntary Army for Sicilian Independence). On 1 May 1947 Giuliano's men open fire on a group of demonstrating farmers at Portella delle Ginestre. There are 12 victims and national indignation is high. Giuliano is found dead on 5 July 1950 at Castelvetrano, in mysterious circumstances. The separatists disappear from the political scene with the elections of 1951.

- **1950** – Agricultural reforms are implemented: estates of over 300ha/740 acres are expropriated and divided into numerous land holdings (of 4-5ha/10-12 acres) for distribution among small-scale peasant farmers: a total of some 115 000ha/284 000 acres are reallocated to over 18 000 farmers.
- **1951-75** – A million Sicilians emigrate to northern Italy and Northern Europe.
- **1953** – Crude oil is discovered at Ragusa and Gela; in 1966, 8 million barrels are extracted.
- **1958** – A terrorist bomb shatters the headquarters of the Palermo daily newspaper *L'Ora* following its allusion to the power of the Mafia.
- **1968** – A disastrous earthquake affects the Belice Valley.
- **1973-76** – The Parliamentary Anti-Mafia Commission gets down to work.
- **27 June 1980** – An Italvia DC9 flying from Bologna to Palermo crashes off the coast of Ustica, killing 81 passengers and crew.
- **3 September 1982** – The Palermo Chief of Police, General Carlo Alberto Dalla Chiesa, his wife and a member of his police escort are killed in a terrorist attack.
- **1986** – During the American-Libyan crisis across the Mediterranean basin, the Libyans launch missiles targeted at Lampedusa.
- **1987** – End of the major court case held in Palermo against the Mafia, with 19 people sentenced to life imprisonment.
- **1992** – 12 March: the politician Salvo Lima is murdered in Palermo.

23 May: Giovanni Falcone, Director of Penal Affairs at the Ministry of Justice, is killed by an explosive device placed at a motorway crossing near Capaci.

19 July: in Via D'Amelio in Palermo, a car bomb kills Judge Paolo Borsellino; three policemen and a policewoman also lose their lives.

6 September: the Mafia boss Giovanni Madonìa is arrested.

- **15 January 1993** – The Mafia boss Salvatore Riina, head of the Corleonesi, is arrested in Palermo.
- **13 March 1996** – The dome and some of the nave of the cathedral of Noto collapse.
- **12 May 1997** – The Teatro Massimo in Palermo reopens after 20 years.
- **2001-2002** – Etna continues to make its destructive presence felt, with eruptions destroying the cable car and part of the base station at Rifugio Sapienza on the southern slopes of the volcano, as well as buildings and the pine forest of Piano Provenzana on the northern slopes. In December 2002, part of the Sciara del Fuoco breaks away from the Stromboli volcano, causing an impressive tidal wave.

A moment of reflection in front of Falcone's tree in Via Notarbartolo, Palermo

J.-P. Amet/CORBIS-SYGMA

Frederick II

The Codex Astensis: Frederick II granting privileges to the town of Asti

"This is the light of the great Constance
Who, from the second gale of Swabia,
Produced the third, which was also the last."

Dante Alighieri, *The Divine Comedy, Paradise III (Oxford University Press)*

The life of Frederick II

On 27 January 1186, Costanza d'Altavilla, heiress to the throne of Sicily, married Henry VI of Swabia, son of Frederick I Barbarossa and heir to the Holy Roman Empire, with great pomp and ceremony in Milan. Aged 31, Costanza had long passed the normal age for matrimony and was 11 years older than her young husband. The couple were married for eight years before producing an heir. On 26 December 1194, Costanza went into labour at Jesi and decided to give birth to the infant under a canvas set up in the city's main square, possibly to dispel doubts that may have been cast on her maternity at such an advanced age. In 1197, aged 32, Henry died of a fever caught while out hunting on Mount Etna. His wife died the following year, but before doing so entrusted their son Frederick to Pope Innocent III, who had the child crowned king of Sicily in 1198. For political and dynastic reasons, Frederick had a difficult, lonely childhood in Palermo, where, left to his own devices, he would haunt the poorer districts of the city, mixing with people of all religions and walks of life. It was these cosmopolitan experiences that influenced the future emperor's broad view of life and grand political projects. Back in the court, Frederick's education was worthy of his lineage: he possessed an enquiring mind, loved nature and culture, studied Latin and the natural sciences and deepened his knowledge of the Arab classics and Islamic culture.

In 1215, Pope Innocent III excommunicated Otto IV, Emperor of the Holy Roman Empire, crowning Frederick II emperor in his place. Frederick travelled to Germany and only returned to Sicily in 1220. In 1227, Frederick was excommunicated

SCALA

Frederick II depicted in the Rotolo dell'Exultet, Biblioteca Diocesana di Salerno

The Four Wives of Frederick II

1209: Constance of Aragon, mother of Henry VII, who rebelled against his father. Constance died in 1222.

1225: Isabella of Brienne, heiress to the throne of Jerusalem. She bore Frederick two children: Conrad IV and Margherita. Isabella died in 1228.

1235: Elizabeth of England, sister of Henry III of England and mother of Henry. She died in 1241.

1250: Bianca Lancia. Just before his death, Frederick II married the woman with whom he had enjoyed a relationship for many years. She was the mother of his favourite son, Manfred, of Costanza and, possibly, of Violante.

Archivio Municipale di Asti/SCALA

by Pope Honorius III and in 1229, having completed the "Crusade of the Excommunicants", he declared himself king of Jerusalem. The following year the Pope withdrew the excommunication.

After years of conflict with the Pope and two excommunications, Frederick died in the Castello di Fiorentino on 13 December 1250 and was buried in Palermo Cathedral.

A prodigious talent

Frederick II was a man of many talents. A skilful statesman, commander and legislator, he loved the arts and sciences and was the author of a famous treatise on falconry entitled *De arte venandi cum avibus.* His character combined the medieval holiness of his imperial role and the modernity of an eclecticism and cultural ecumenism that was remarkable for the time. His court was a meeting place for scholars from all fields, including writers, mathematicians, astronomers, doctors and musicians. Frederick was responsible for the foundation of the University of Naples, the development of the Salerno Medical School, where a Chair of Anatomy was created, and the birth of the School of Sicilian Poetry.

It is difficult to draw a fair portrait of the Swabian emperor even if most of the great acclaim with which he is honoured by a large proportion of ancient and modern historians is ignored. Dante affirms Frederick's fame as a man of culture, describing the emperor as "a great logician and scholar". Credited as a lover of wisdom and patron of the arts, Frederick II showed considerable openmindedness in his political dealings. His greatest wish was to be regarded as the "Emperor of recent times", summoned with a mission to restore the golden age of justice on earth. This legendary vision of his own personality and role conflicts violently with the vicious accusations made by the papal curia, which tended to regard Frederick as the Antichrist mentioned in the Bible.

In 1994, the musical "The Cavalier of Intellect", written by Franco Battiato and based on the work of contemporary philosopher Manlio Sgarambro, took to the stage in Palermo Cathedral to celebrate the 800th anniversary of Frederick's birth.

Sicilian School of Poetry

Literature developed in Frederick's court, the *Magna Curia*, as a pursuit for aristocrats and was practised by princes and high officials of the court who regarded poetry as an elegant pastime. For their poetry, the Sicilian poets modelled their subject matter and style on the Provençal troubadour poetry of courtly love: the sort of loving service that man, as a servant, dedicates to a Madonna. The language used is a refined Sicilian stripped of any base vernacular colloquialisms, enriched instead with Latin and Provençal phraseology: an illustrious, strictly literary language that excludes any form of realism and which in turn came to influence Italian lyric poetry as a whole. Among the Sicilian School poets ranked several sovereigns: Frederick II, his sons Henry, Frederick, Manfred and Enzo king of Sardinia, all wrote poetry. Other notable exponents of the genre include the court notary **Giacomo da Lentini**, who is regarded as the inventor of the sonnet, **Pier della Vigna** (mentioned by Dante in Inferno, Canto XIII v 25) and **Cielo d'Alcamo**, author of the famous dialogue-poem *Rosa Fresca Aulentissima*. With the decline of the *Magna Curia*, the Sicilian School's golden age came to an end.

The Ancient Greeks in Sicily

The legendary origins of the Greeks in Sicily date back to the 8C BC. Angry at a failed sacrifice in his honour, Neptune was said to have unleashed his anger against those responsible by causing a shipwreck off the eastern coast of Sicily, the sole survivor of which took refuge in the vast bay that extends between Capo Taormina and Capo Schisò. Struck by the island's beauty, he returned to Greece, where he persuaded others to sail with him to Sicily and found a colony on the island, marking the beginning of the Greeks' presence there.

History and social phenomena

Contacts between Sicily and the Hellenistic world go back to the dawn of Greek civilisation: numerous archaeological artefacts testify to thriving maritime centres along the eastern and southern Sicilian coast trading with Crete and Mycenae from the middle of the 2nd millennium BC. However, this "pre-colonial" presence was strictly limited to the ports of call, for there are no traces of any permanent occupation between the 13C BC and the 8C BC. Colonisation only began when living conditions within Ancient Greece became untenable: famine followed civil war and a

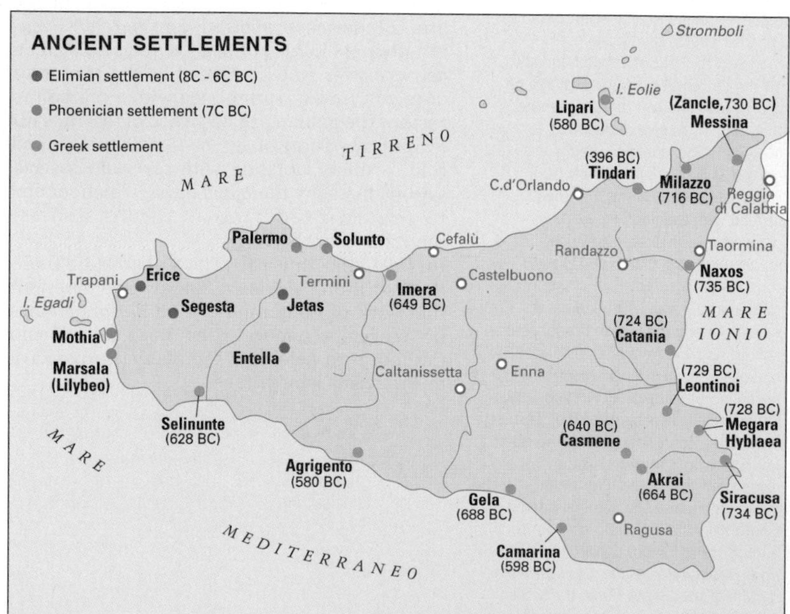

SCALA

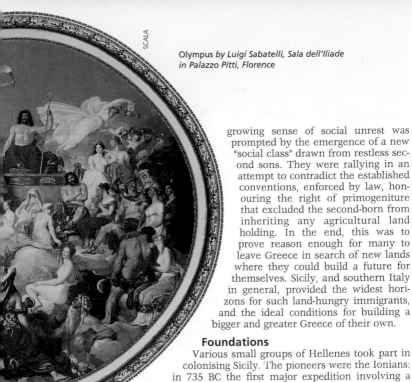

Olympus by Luigi Sabatelli, Sala dell'Iliade in Palazzo Pitti, Florence

growing sense of social unrest was prompted by the emergence of a new "social class" drawn from restless second sons. They were rallying in an attempt to contradict the established conventions, enforced by law, honouring the right of primogeniture that excluded the second-born from inheriting any agricultural land holding. In the end, this was to prove reason enough for many to leave Greece in search of new lands where they could build a future for themselves. Sicily, and southern Italy in general, provided the widest horizons for such land-hungry immigrants, and the ideal conditions for building a bigger and greater Greece of their own.

Foundations

Various small groups of Hellenes took part in colonising Sicily. The pioneers were the Ionians: in 735 BC the first major expedition involving a band of Chalcidians from Euboea led by Theocles, arrived in Sicily; they settled near Capo Schisò and founded Naxos. Settlements were established at Leontinoi, Catane and Zancle (now Messina). Almost simultaneously, a group of Dorians arrived from Corinth and founded Syracuse, present-day Siracusa; meanwhile, colonists from Megara settled at Megara Hyblaea. At the beginning of the 7C BC, Rhodians and Cretans arrived and founded Gela on the south coast of the island. This first phase of expansion involved sites scattered around the island that had abundant supplies of fresh water, and that were easily accessible from the sea and remote enough from any other settlement to allow, in time, for secondary settlements to be developed further inland.

Founders

Each expedition, comprised predominantly but not exclusively of men, was led by an *oikistes* (founder) who, generally, belonged to one of the most renowned families in the city of origin. It is highly probable that, before setting out to found a colony, the *oikistes* would undertake several exploratory voyages during which he would find and choose the most suitable site for settlement. These voyages, however, were always preceded by a journey to Delphi, where the oracle of Apollo Archaghètas *(he who guides)* was consulted as to where the gods wanted the new colony to be founded. The founder-leaders disposed of great power and prestige: charged with transferring the holy flame and the lifeblood of the religious cult from the metropolis to their satellite colonies, their decisions were considered sacred and, when they died, they were honoured almost as if they had been gods. Accompanied by surveyors, engineers and soothsayers that had been recruited before departure, they presided over the construction of the citadel and the public buildings, and the administration of justice. They were also responsible for ensuring fair practice when the draw for plots of land took place, so that nobody should be unjustly favoured. Not all the land available was distributed immediately, however; a proportion was reserved for future colonists.

Colony

The founder would establish the new city's institutions, which were not necessarily identical to those implemented at home. Each colony (*apoikìa* in Greek meaning "new family") was completely independent. Despite Corinth's vain attempts to maintain control over its colonies, they forcefully embraced their autonomy by acting as independent political entities. In this way, Akragas (Agrigento) was able to develop excellent trading relations with Carthage, which officially was hostile to Greece, while Zancle and Reggio blockaded the Straits of Messina and demanded that Greek ships pay harbour taxes. The colonists lost their rights of citizenship in their city of origin and acquired the equivalent status in their new home. Restrictions on religious practices were kept in place, as was the option of "exchanging" citizenship of one city with the resident of another by mutual

B. Kaufmann/MICHELIN

The theatre at Segesta

consent. The colonies were not only independent from their motherland, but also from each other, with each individual city conducting its own political affairs in all but matters arising from an alliance with another, and then only under special circumstances. The cities prospered and grew quickly, thanks to flourishing trade links and fertile territories: a sharp increase in population, partly as a result of the rise in birth rate and partly resulting from the continuous influx of new immigrants, forced the authorities to establish secondary colonies further inland.
Between the 7C BC and the 6C BC, a **second wave of colonisation** swept through Sicily, bringing with it a tendency towards territorial aggregation. The Chalcidians of Zancle occupied Milazzo, affirming their supremacy over the Tyrrhenian coast and the plain of the Mela; they also founded Himera to the west. Catane and Leontinoi claimed influence over territory inland towards Etna, to the valleys of the Simeto and its tributaries. Syracuse founded Akrai and then Kasmenai (Κασμεναι; Casmene), before assuming control over the plateau beyond and monopolising the means of communication with the central states and the plain of the Dirillo, where Camarina was subsequently founded. Megara Hyblaea, hemmed in by Syracuse and Leontinoi, hit upon a safety valve when they founded Selinus (Selinunte), the most westerly of the Greek colonies in Sicily. Towards the mid-6C BC, this precipitated the founding of Heraclea Minoa, a third-generation colony of Megara. In 580 BC, colonists from Cnidus settled in the Aeolian Islands. In the west of Sicily, specific areas of considerable significance – including Lilybaeum (Marsala), Motya and Panormus (Palermo) – were subjugated first by the Phoenicians, later by the Carthaginians.

The Greeks and indigenous populations

Relations with the indigenous peoples were extremely varied. In some cases, the rapport was so peaceable as to inspire commercial and religious exchanges: in effect, the prime Hellenic settlements along the coast barely disturbed the pre-existing communities which, for the most part, were concentrated inland. It was only when the Greeks began to colonise the hinterland that resentment began to grow. Eventually, open conflict led to the systematic extermination of villages as happened during the great revolt by the indigenous population that gripped the eastern part of the island sometime in the mid-5C. With defeat came obligations to pay tributes and, in some cases, enforced conditions of slavery: it is known that in Syracuse, the descendants of the indigenous people (the Cilliri) were constrained to cultivating the land of their overlords (Gamòroi), who were descended from the ancient colonists. The Greek settlers were known as the **Siceliots**; these people, armed and endowed with sophisticated know-how drawn from the superior culture they had brought with them, were rapidly able to impose their civilisation upon Sicily: between the 6C BC and the 5C BC, they managed to completely hellenise the territories they held.

Economy

Prosperity depended not only on the natural fertility of the Sicilian land but on good farming practices: yields from wild plants were improved by grafting, common wheat was adapted for intensive cultivation, almond trees and pomegranates were planted, and animals were bred selectively from fertile stock for best results. The most sophisticated cities set about reclaiming land where possible, most notably at Camarina and Selinus under the direction of Empedocles. Besides their success at arable farming and careful husbandry, the Western Greeks amassed fortunes through commerce with intensive trade links established not only with the motherland, but also with Spain, southern Italy and North Africa. They imported fine ceramics, perfumes and metals against timber, wheat and wool. The upsurge in trade soon made it necessary for the Siceliot cities to introduce their own currencies. The earliest coins are of silver and feature an embossed head whereas the reverse was impressed. At the beginning of the 5C BC, both obverse and reverse was moulded in relief, and two new materials were introduced, namely gold and bronze.

Political evolution

To qualify for citizenship, and thereby participate in the political life of the community, individuals were required to own a piece of land and to claim to have a fixed abode. In reality, many of the Greeks would have earned their living as skilled craftsmen, fishermen, traders and collectors of customs duties. In addition to these, a large number were involved in public works: it has been calculated that at least one-third of the population must have been engaged in building large-scale projects, be it as a woodcutter supplying timber or a painter employed on the decoration. Many more lived from one day to the next without a roof over their heads or permanent employment. In the space of a few years, therefore, the very inequalities that the colonists thought they had escaped by leaving Greece had become issues of contention. The aristocracy, together with the owners of the best land, conferred all the power upon themselves; they repressed the new moneyed classes of businessmen and those who owned no land. To deal with the continual crises provoked by economic rivalry and internal social pressures, some cities tried to correct the balance by replacing the oral legal system of oaths with a written constitution. The first codex, transcribed by **Charondas of Catane** (6C BC), was copied by many other cities, including Athens. It established duties and rights within the family; prescribed punishments for violence and perjury, and the death penalty for anyone entering a political meeting armed, and instituted a sort of citizens' jury, decreeing that a fine – proportional to earnings – be paid by anyone who refused to participate.

Tyrannic rule

The other way of averting economic and social crises was tyranny: this alternative consisted of compromise between patriarchal monarchy as practised effectively in the early Archaic period, and the demagogy of the Classical era of Antiquity. The **tyrant**, who was generally a member of the new moneyed class or the army, invested himself with the bulk of power and delegated the rest to his most loyal supporters. It was precisely during the period of tyranny that Syracuse, first under **Gelon** and then under **Hieron I**, achieved its greatest splendour and managed to impose its authority throughout the island. The other Siceliot cities, in a desperate attempt to resist the aggressor and salvage their independence, were driven to seek assistance from Carthage or Athens, but this was to no avail. Meanwhile, the civil strife continued to split the Greek communities and the Carthaginian threat was growing. After a period of anarchy, **Timoleon**, who had arrived from Corinth to assist the colonies, succeeded in restoring democracy and peace to Sicily. Upon his death, the Greeks began to quarrel once more among themselves and with the Carthaginians: finally, in the second half of the 3C BC the citizens of Messina (Zancle) turned to Rome for help, opening their gates to the Imperial city and so precipitating her conquest of Sicily.

Culture

Legend relates how **Alpheus**, god of the River Alpheus in the Peloponnese, was wandering across the Greek region of Arcadia, when he came across **Arethusa**, one of Artemis' water nymphs. The river god fell in love with the nymph, but as he tried to seize her, she changed into a stream, slipping from him into the Ionian Sea only to re-emerge as a spring in Siracusa. Alpheus pursued Arethusa to Sicily, where his waters mingled with those of the nymph. This myth, diffused among the Greek population of Sicily, was taken to symbolise the transference of the Greek civilisation from the motherland to Sicily. Far from being a marginal colony of Greece, the island in its own right attracted to its shores some of the most illustrious figures in Greek culture. It also succoured others born there who were to become famous throughout the Hellenic world.

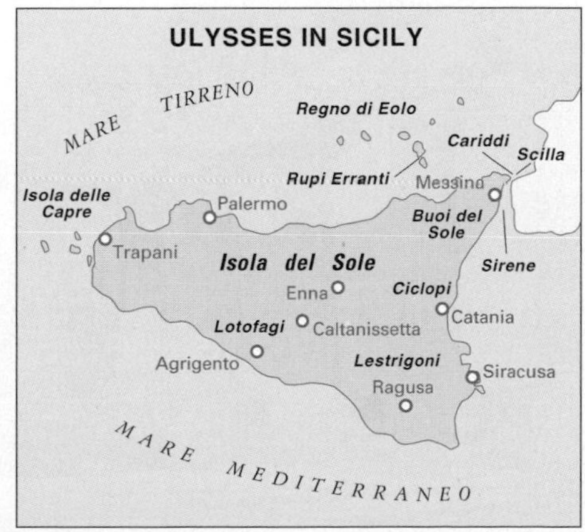

According to some scholars, Greek culture should be indebted to Sicily for one of its fundamental masterpieces, the *Odyssey*. Many of Ulysses' adventures were unequivocally set in the Island of the Sun, the name used by **Homer** to describe Sicily, so obviously that Apollodorus defined the Odyssey as a kind of "journey around Sicily". Many of the places can be identified with Sicily *(see the Ulysees in Sicily map, p 77)*: the Aeolian Islands are the kingdom of Aeolus and the "errant rocks" mentioned by Circe in Book XII are the Faraglioni rocks between Lipari and Vulcano; Scylla and Charybdis personify the impetuous currents in the Straits of Messina; the port at which Ulysses' companions steal the flocks of the Sun is Messina; the Sirens (according to the Sicilian interpretation of the work) waited for sailors in the seas around Capo Peloro; the Cyclops' cave was inside Mount Etna; and the rocks thrown by Polyphemus landed in the sea in front of Aci Trezza. Lastly, the Lestrigoni, the giant cannibals of Book X, lived near Lentini, while the Lotus Eaters (Book IX) lived between Agrigento and Camarina.

Tyrannical patrons

According to Aristotle, comedy in its Classical form was invented by the Megareans of Greece and Sicily. Undoubtedly both **Epicharmus** and **Phormis**, the two earliest identifiable authors of comedies engaged at the court of Gelon, were Sicilian. Interestingly, the tyrants were noted for being generous patrons, summoning to their courts the best poets of the time, who celebrated their hosts in verse in exchange for the hospitality shown to them. Among the illustrious guests of the tyrants of Syracuse, we find the poet **Simonides**, famous as a writer of epigrams and funeral laments, who dedicated many of his verses to Sicily, telling how Hephaestus and Demeter disputed possession of the island because of its fire and abundant wheat harvests. The simultaneous presence of poets of a certain renown also generated bitter rivalries: for years, **Bacchylides** and **Pindar** contested Hieron's favours, as they competed to compose songs of victory exalting his successes with the quadriga at the games. At the height of his achievement, the great tragedian **Aeschylus** was based at the court of Hieron: so, to celebrate the conquest and renaming of the city of Aetna (formerly Catane – later Catania) he arranged performances of *The Women of Etna* (now lost) and *The Persians*. Pindar marked the occasion by composing his Pythian Odes. **Theocritus** (c 300-260 BC), meanwhile, was a native of Syracuse; he is attributed with inventing pastoral poetry.

Philosophy

Two of the most interesting pre-Socratic thinkers were born in Sicily: **Empedocles** came from Agrigento and **Gorgias** from Leontinoi. **Empedocles** (c 500-c 430 BC) is a complex figure, being at the same time a mystic, miracle worker, doctor and student of natural philosophy: the founder, in fact, of a school of medicine which regarded the heart as the seat of life, an idea taken up by Aristotle. He also taught that all matter was composed of four elements (earth, water, air and fire) and that these, regulated by the two universal forces harmony and

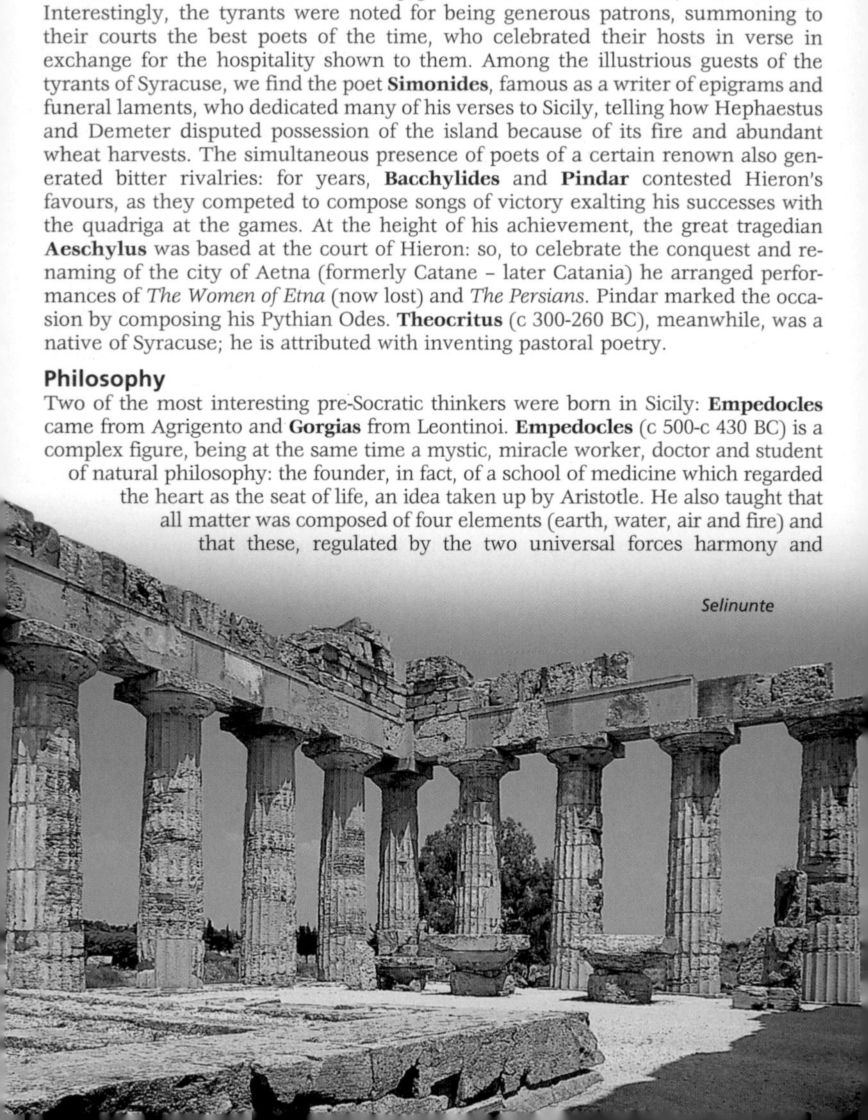

Selinunte

discord (love and hate), had given rise to the whole cosmos. According to legend, he hurled himself to his death by jumping into one of the fiery craters of Mount Etna in the hope of persuading his fellow citizens that he had been summoned by the gods. Gorgias responded to a different cultural climate, one of sophism (false argument), that aimed to satisfy the requirements of the emerging democracy, with particular emphasis on moral and political issues. Gorgias became an orator of considerable renown, especially in Athens where he was acclaimed a "master of wisdom".

The first great philosopher of mathematical harmony was Pythagoras, and he advocated clarity and harmony of dependent parts. The doctrines of Pythagoras were widespread in Sicily, particularly in Agrigento and Catania. The **School of Pythagoras** was established at Croton in the 6C-5C BC as a sort of religious confraternity; in addition to sustaining theories on the arithmetical and geometric structure of the universe, the Pythagoreans exercised considerable influence in political circles by putting forward ideas for an aristocracy drawn from the new classes involved in commerce and trade.

Plato

Museo Pio-Clementino, Roma/SCALA

Sicily was also the setting envisaged by **Plato** for his Utopian state, ruled by philosophers, as contemplated in his Republic. Plato came to Syracuse in 388-387 BC as the guest and friend of Dion, the brother-in-law and son-in-law of Dionysius I; when the tyrant became suspicious of the Athenian, he had him incarcerated as a slave on the island of Aegina. He later returned to Sicily after Dionysius II had succeeded his father; to begin with, Plato appears to have found Dionysius II the better disciple, that is, until Dion was sent into exile and Plato was detained as a prisoner.

Science and history

Archimedes (first half of the 3C BC) was the one person in the Greek world capable of consolidating the theoretical and practical aspects of scientific knowledge at that time. Besides his important discoveries in the fields of mathematics, geometry and naval engineering, his name is associated with the invention of war machines such as were used against the Romans; these weapons of mass destruction managed to deceive the Romans into thinking they were at war with the gods.

Diodorus Siculus, born at Agyrion in the 1C BC, was the author of a universal history of 40 volumes entitled *Biblioteca*. In it he deals with Greek history from the mythical times that lead up to the Trojan War to contemporary times; this still constitutes a valuable source for scholars.

Religion

Religion touched upon everything in the life of a Greek: being but a mere mortal, he or she saw every event, be it of major or minor importance, as a possible manifestation of the divine. In no way, however, was the religion in the least dogmatic. Indeed, on coming into contact with another people, the Greeks were always willing to admit their gods to the Olympic pantheon, or to assimilate them with their own deities. The Greek gods, who personified the forces of nature or some moral quality, were endowed with the physical and psychological attributes of human personality; the main characteristic that defined them as different from humans was their immortality. The Greeks turned to a deity for protection and favour. The cult depended upon prayer, sacrifice and purification. Prayers were usually accompanied by an offering (libations of milk or wine, sweets, cakes or fresh produce). In the event of more demanding requests, an animal might be sacrificed; parts were then burnt on the altar while the rest was divided between the priest and the faithful. However, the most important public ceremonies were those held in celebration of a particular festival, when they would be accompanied with activities that, to the modern mind, have nothing to do with religion: literary and poetry competitions, competitive sporting events or games like the pan-Hellenic games held annually at Olympia and Delphi, in which the Sicilian tyrants also participated on several occasions.

THE GREEK GODS IN SICILY

Acis: god of the river of the same name and lover of Galatea *(see ACIREALE)*.

Aeolus: son of Poseidon, god of the winds and lord of the Aeolian Islands.

Alpheus: god of the river of the same name in the Peloponnese. He fell in love with the water nymph Arethusa and followed her to Sicily *(see SIRACUSA)*.

Aphrodite (Venus): goddess of love and wife of Hephaestus, much worshipped in Erice.

Charybdis: a monster who inhabited the Sicilian shore of the Straits of Messina. Three times a day the monster swallowed huge amounts of water, creating dangerous whirlpools, including one which trapped Ulysses' ship.

Cocalus: Sicilian king who offered refuge to Dedalus; the latter was pursued by Minos after helping Theseus to escape from Minos' labyrinth *(see p 127)*.

Demeter (Ceres): goddess of the harvest, who fought with Hephaestus for control of Sicily.

Eryx: son of Aphrodite and Butes (or Poseidon). He challenged Heracles and was killed by him.

Etna: a Sicilian nymph who intervened in the dispute between Demeter and Hephaestus over the possession of Sicily. One legend recounts that the Palici were born from her union with Hephaestus.

Galatea: a nymph who was loved by the monster Polyphemus and was in love with Acis *(see ACIREALE)*.

Giants: son of Gaia (the Earth) and Uranus, enemies of the Olympic gods, and particularly of Zeus and Athena.

Hades *(Pluto)*: brother of Zeus; lord of the kingdom of the dead. He abducted Demeter's daughter, Proserpina, on the banks of Lake Pergusa.

Helios: god of the sun. He owned a herd of cattle in Sicily, some of which were eaten by Ulysses' companions, thus incurring the wrath of the god.

Hephaestus: god of fire and lord of the volcanoes, in which he worked with his helpers, the Cyclops.

Heracles: a hero during his earthly life and a god after his death. One of his 12 Labours, that of the cattle of Geryon, took place in Sicily.

Palici: twin sons of Zeus and the muse Thalia or, according to another tradition, of Hephaestus and Etna, born in the waters of Lake Naftia, near Palagonia.

Persephone *(Proserpina)*: goddess of the Underworld and wife of Hades.

Typhon: a giant who fought with Zeus and Athena. He escaped by crossing the Sicilian sea, but was then crushed when Zeus hurled the island of Sicily on top of him.

Each part of Greece was especially devoted to a particular deity so when the colonists transferred themselves to new settlements, they took with them the same traditional cults, and their affiliated festivals, espoused by their native land. Of course, these celebrations were in addition to those designated by the new state, which included the annual commemoration of the founding of the city with a great ritual banquet attended, when possible, by the original founders.

Three important figures

Among all the different gods and heroes to be venerated in Sicily, the most significant are **Demeter**, who was regarded as the protector of Sicily, and **Heracles**. Sometimes the Greeks embraced local cults and rites: a case in point are the nymphs who are supposed to have emerged from the hot springs at Termini Imerese; another is that of the **Palici** brothers.

Demeter, the goddess who embodies the earth's fertility, was the object of a cult prevalent especially in Ionian Greece and naturally therefore in Sicily; here, when she assumed the role of mother-protector, she became a more complex deity. Not only did the Greek colonists assimilate the maternal attributes of the earth figure, they adapted her mythological story so as to make it pertinent to the Sicilian soil, rooting it to the place with specific allusions to its topography. It tells of how **Persephone**, daughter of Zeus and Demeter, was gathering flowers near the Lake of

A colossal Heracles in the Museo Archeologico in Naples

Pergusa (the Homeric *Hymn to Demeter* situates its version 19km/12mi from Athens at Eleusis) when Hades (Pluto), the king of the Underworld, saw her, fell in love with her, and carried her off. For nine days, Demeter wandered over Sicily in search of her lost daughter. Near Trapani, she dropped her sickle: this is supposed to be the origin of the sickle-shaped headland behind the town. One night, as she scoured the slopes of Etna by the light of flaming pine trees, she interpreted the sounds made as she passed through the lupins as the ring of their mocking laughter and spurning voices: from that day forth, it is said, lupins lost their sweetness and became bitter. Frustrated at not having found her daughter, Demeter prevented the earth from bringing forth fruit by inflicting a terrible drought: men and animals began to die by the hundreds. This prompted her brother Zeus to intervene by agreeing to demand that Hades release Persephone on condition that she had eaten nothing during her stay in the Underworld. But before she departed from the kingdom of the dead, Hades forced her to eat a few pomegranate seeds as a symbol of fidelity. Thus betrothed to Hades, Persephone was destined to spend a third of the year with him in the Underworld and the remaining months with her mother on earth. In the language of myth, Persephone thus came to stand for the seed that must be planted in the earth for it to grow in spring and summer, yielding up its own ripened seed before winter comes; the story also explains the cycle of seasons and provides hope for times of despair.

The second deity to enjoy a special following in Sicily was **Heracles**. This probably stems from another myth, established before the Greeks arrived on the island, involving a Phoenician deity who shared many elements with the story of the Greek hero. The legend tells of a Heracles that was born out of a union between Zeus and a mortal woman, Alcmena; he too had to undertake 12 labours in order to assuage a dreadful deed and become a god. According to tradition, the first people to attribute divine honours to the hero would seem to be the inhabitants of Sicily. Heracles came to the island in the course of his tenth labour, when he was forced to cross the Straits of Messina in pursuit of a bull belonging to Geryon. Almost every little place on the island claims to have been visited by the hero: Erice was where he wrestled and killed the son of Aphrodite and Butes, the king who shared his name with the town; at Syracuse he is said to have instituted a sacred festival near the Gorge of Cyane; Agiro was the place to honour him as a god; in recognition of this, the hero created a lake outside the city walls and raised two sanctuaries there.

The **Palici** rank among Sicily's own ancient divinities, whom the Greeks later appropriated by adopting them as the twin sons of Zeus and the muse Thalia. The centre of their cult was Naftia, a small lake with bubbling sulphurous waters in the Plain of Catania, near Palagonia. The myth relates how Thalia, fearing the wrath of Hera, hid underground where she gave birth. The subterranean birth of the divine twins henceforth caused the waters of the lake to bubble and steam. Beside the sanctuary dedicated to the Palici, the Greeks pronounced solemn oaths and enacted a kind of ritualistic ordeal in the waters of the lake: if, when they submerged tablets bearing written agreements, the tablets sank, this was interpreted as a sign of perjury, which the Palici punished with blinding. According to another tradition, the Palici were the children of Hephaestus, the god of fire, and Etna, the nymph who intervened in the struggle between the god and Demeter for control of Sicily.

In general, the Siceliots were hugely sensitive to the indigenous cults and were deeply respectful of the cult of the dead and of the chthonic gods of the Underworld. In fact, some gods which were originally completely extraneous to such things, assumed connotations of death and burial in Sicily: Aphrodite (Venus) and Artemis (Diana), for example, in addition to their traditional personalities, were regarded as companions and protectors of the souls of the dead.

Mysteries

Mystery rites were also particularly widespread in Sicily. These special religious doctrines and practices were developed to provide answers to the inexplicable, and to allay worries in the minds of individuals facing death. The Mysteries, to which individuals were admitted by special initiation rites, promised to purify the soul of the initiated and by doing so ensured other-worldly happiness after death. One of the most famous Mystery cults, the Eleusinian Mysteries, revolves around Demeter and Persephone: celebrations in the form of a spring festival were held at the time when seeds should be sown. It is therefore natural that such rites should quickly have been diffused throughout Sicily.

Art

Architecture: civil and military

Archaeological findings seems to suggest that the first military fortifications and examples of civil building in Sicily date from the end of the 6C BC. There are few traces of anything before that time, although it is presumed that military emplacements existed here from the 8C when the various cities began to rival one another before the rise of tyrants.

Fortresses and fortifications – During the domination of the tyrants, the region was reinforced with fortified buildings constructed with materials that varied according to the local geology: in the east, lava was commonly used, as at **Naxos** and **Lipari**. In the absence of suitable stone, walls were built using sun-dried brick with, at the base, a water-resistant foundation layer of broken stones, or a mixture of pebbles and clay.

Although archaeological surveys in Sicily have not yielded many emplacements of major significance, a few forts have survived. These guardian citadels ensured the defence of a city, its roads and other means of access. Maximum protection was provided by their strategic positions beside the city precincts or in their immediate vicinity, sited in as inaccessible a place as possible.

Urban planning – Almost on arrival, the Greek settlers organised the area into a rational system: different sections were designated as places of worship, for public buildings and as residential quarters. Generally Sicilian cities conformed to the precepts for urban planning outlined by **Hippodamus of Miletus**, the 5C BC Greek philosopher and surveyor. The Hippodamian principles consisted of planning a city on a rectangular street plan centred around two axes: the *cardo* (or *stenopos*, in Greek) which ran from north to south, and the *decumanus maximus* (*plateia* in Greek) which bisected it from east to west. The street network was then completed by other smaller streets running parallel to the two axes, forming an orthogonal network. A very precise set of buildings and various areas for particular purposes were then inserted into this plan, such as the *agora*, the main square and the centre of public life, the *pritaneo*, which stood beside the *agora* and was the setting for a range of civic activities, the *ekklesiasterion*, a secular public building reserved for the people's assembly (*ekklesia*), the most famous example of which can be seen at Agrigento, and the *bouleutérion*, where the citizen's council (*boulé*) met. The temples, sometimes built outside the city limits, were often surrounded by other sacred buildings, which in the most monumental structures could include porticoes, votive monuments, gymnasia and theatres. The urban area was usually

The Siceliot house

The Archaic houses were fairly simple affairs: walls marking the confines of the plot were built around the open space in which stood the rectangular sun-dried brick building, erected on a base of dry pebbles. The sloping gable roof was covered with flat tiles. In the courtyard were stored tools and those great terracotta jars in which provisions were kept; it also served as a communal area in which the family gathered, ate and received visitors. The terrace was used for drying fruit, as a place to sit and talk, pray and sleep. Among the foundations, a talisman was hidden, sometimes a bone or a votive object, to ensure the house remained sturdy and solid. Often it was sprinkled with the blood of a young animal, as were the threshold, the architrave and the door-jambs.

In time, the houses became more sophisticated: a raised floor was added complete with a stairway supported by a portico. The largest of the rooms facing onto the portico and connected to the kitchen was the one used for gatherings, for it was here that the men met for their *symposia*.

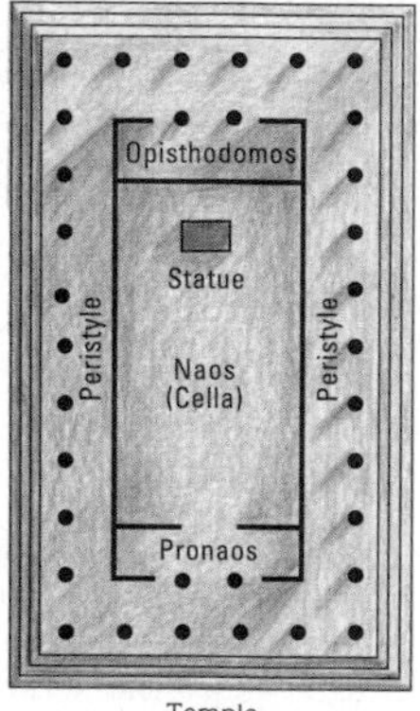

Temple

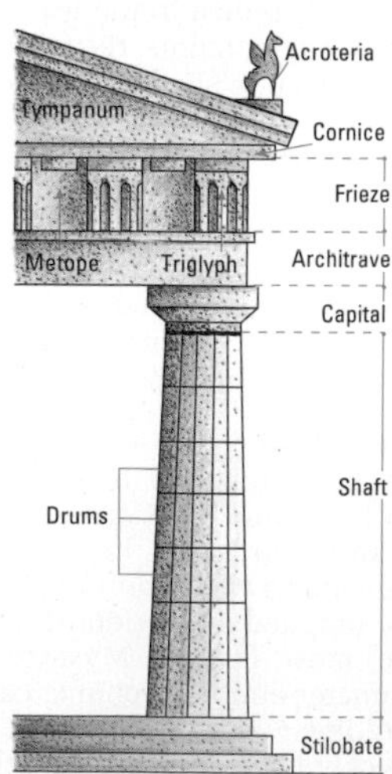

Doric order elevation

fortified with walls; beyond lay the agricultural land, subdivided into family plots, and a specific area destined for use as a burial ground. All the Greek cities and, sometimes even the villages, were supplied with reservoirs for water and aqueducts, the most famous being that built by the architect Phaeax at Akragas (Agrigento), and the extremely complex one at Syracuse.

Architecture: sacred and religious

There are two forms of sacred building: the **temple** and the theatre. Usually located outside the city itself, these buildings were designed to be visible from a distance, hence the reason for their situation in the landscape, orientated so as to enjoy a splendid view.

Temples – From the 8C BC, Greek colonists came to Sicily bringing with them their own cults and gods, transforming the island into what is now regarded as one of the most extraordinary open-air museums of Doric temples, of the "severe style". The heart of the building comprised the **naos** *(cella),* an oblong chamber which housed a statue of the god; temples normally faced east, so that the statue could be illuminated by the rising sun, the source of all life. Before the *naos* was the **pronaos** (a kind of ante-chamber), while behind stood the **opisthodomos** which served as a treasury. A **peristyle** or colonnade surrounded the building.

The temple was founded on a stepped base; onto the last step **(stylobate)** were erected the **columns** which rose to support the **architrave**. The building was covered by a sloping roof.

First conceived in the Peloponnese, the **Doric style** spread to mainland Greece and consequently to its colonies, including Sicily, where some of the most splendid expressions of this style can be seen. The Doric order, which combines majesty with sobriety, comprises a base-less column shaft indented with 20 vertical grooves or flutes (as from the 5C) that sits directly on the stylobate. The entablature consists of a plain architrave, the upper section of which comprises a frieze articulated by **metopes** (generally panels sculpted with shallow relief) and **triglyphs** (rectangular projections ornamented with two deep vertical grooves in the centre flanked by a narrower one at each edge).

In the 6C BC, almost all the temples built in Sicily were peripteral (that is, surrounded by a line of columns) and hexastyle (6-columned front elevation); although some examples have more than six front columns, such as Temple G at Selinunte.

As a result of its simplicity of structure and perfect harmony of proportion the temple was long considered to be the architectural prototype of ideal beauty. When building designers became aware of the tendency of the human eye to perceive emphatic architectural accents as distorted, they decided to correct the optical illusion: the central section of the architrave, which otherwise appeared to sag slightly, was fractionally raised, making it in effect imperceptibly concave; to restore an impression of perfect balance, the outer columns of the façades were slightly inclined inwards, thereby countering the natural tendency to lean outwards. Finally, in particularly large buildings (such as the Temple of Concord at Agrigento and the temples at Selinunte and Segesta), as the rows of columns would otherwise appear exaggeratedly narrow at the top, to compensate for this optical illusion the columns were cut with a very slight central swelling about two-thirds of the way up the shaft.

When compared with the architecture of mainland Greece, the temples of Magna Graecia and Sicily are more monumental, pay more attention to spatial effect and show a particular taste for abundant decoration. Sculptures, often having a didactic purpose, crown the prominent features, in some cases those elements with no structural function – on the **tympanum** of a pediment, for example, or above the **metopes** of the architrave and on the edges of roofs.

Theatres – Beside most of the Greek sanctuaries there was a theatre where Dionysian celebrations were held (in honour of Dionysus, the god of wine) with hymns called "dithyrambs" from which, later, Greek tragedy was derived.

Built first of wood and then, from the 4C BC, in stone, a theatre would comprise a **cavea** *(koilon)* – a series of tiered ledges arranged in a semicircle, the first row being reserved for priests and dignitaries. Access was from the base by means of side entrances *(parodos)*; one passage *(diazoma)* led through to the central section, another up to the top rows of seating. The **orchestra** consisted of a circular area where the chorus and actors, wearing masks corresponding to their roles, took their places around the altar of Dionysus. Behind the orchestra stood the

proscenium, a construction similar to a portico which served as backdrop scenery, and the *skéné* which at once fulfilled three functions, namely stage scenery, backstage and a storage area. During the Hellenistic period, the *skéné* came to be reserved for actors. Given that these complexes are generally set in the most splendid landscape, on the slope of a hill or a mountain, the natural scenery (particularly spectacular at Taormina and Segesta) provided the perfect background for productions. The *skéné*, almost always raised onto a platform, dominated the circular orchestra, where sacrifices were also sometimes made.

Sculpture

According to authors such as Diodorus Siculus (1C BC historian) and Pausanias (Greek traveller of the 2C AD), Sicily had established an artistic heritage even before she was colonised. In any case, it is difficult to formulate a Sicilian style before the arrival of the Greek settlers given the full extent of artistic exchange between Sicily and Greece, particularly in the south of the island which at that time was occupied by the Sicani. During colonisation, indigenous artistic taste and aesthetics were affected by Greek influences, leading to the gradual erosion and eventual extinction of a purely "Sicilian" style.

B. Kaufmann/MICHELIN

The white marble Ephebus of Motya, now on display in the Joseph Whitaker Museum near where it was found, clearly demonstrates the evolution of the Ionic style: this 1.81m/5.93ft youth is dressed in a long tunic of soft, figure-hugging linen, which flatters the muscular body of the athlete.

In such a way, the island succumbed to the three chronological phases used to define the evolution of Greek art: the Archaic, Classic and Hellenistic eras.

The scarcity of marble and the particular Sicilian taste for pictorial and chiaroscuro effects resulted in the predominant use of limestone and sandstone as raw materials. Clay was widely used in the pediments and acroteri of the temples, as well as for votive statues.

Archaic (8C-5C BC) – This phase coincides with the production of the first large, rather wooden, hieratic figures which, in the 6C BC, gave rise to two distinctive forms: the *kouros* – the young male nude, and the *koré* – the young female equivalent, though modestly dressed in a tunic.

The statue of the **Ephebus of Agrigento** is one excellent example of late Archaic sculpture: it suggests the sculptor was striving to conform to a predetermined aesthetic type, although its basic sense of balance has yet to be perfected (the right leg appears extremely rigid while the outstretched arms seem set too far away from the body).

As far as Archaic sculptural ornament used to adorn temples is concerned, two examples are to be found in Sicily: the polychrome winged **Gorgon** that once ornamented the pediment of the Athenaion in Syracuse, and the six **metopes of Selinunte**, now displayed in the archaeological museum at Palermo.

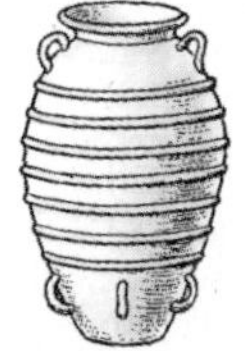

Pithos: used for storing grain

Amphora: had the dual purpose of storing and transporting oil and wine

Pelike: container for oil

Crater: container for wine

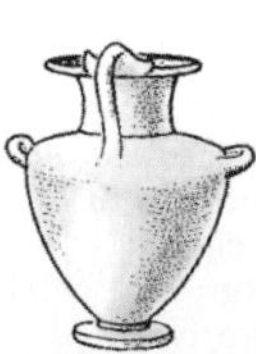

Hydria: container for water. The two side handles were used to lift the container, the larger handle for pouring

The discovery of the bronze ram at Castello Maniace (on display at the Palermo Archaeological Museum) betrays the major impact of Greek aesthetics, notably their canons of beauty, on a city such as Syracuse.

Classic (5C-3C BC) – The Ionic style of sculpture, which appeared in Sicily from the 6C BC onwards, is characterised by a better portrayal of individual features, and a greater sense of realism and sensitivity, now free of the severe rigidity of the earlier phase, as shown in the famous Ephebus of Motya.

Hellenistic (3C-1C BC) – During this phase sculpture becomes yet more expressive and Oriental: deities are portrayed with more realism, with human rather than ideal features and in a less formal state of dress (Aphrodite, the goddess of beauty and love, is often shown in a pleated, flowing shift nonchalantly revealing her glorious nudity). Sculpture from this period is highly expressive in terms of emotion, as well as physical strength and movement.

The terracotta **theatrical masks** in the Archaeological Museum on Lipari (over 250 examples) are fascinating in the great range and subtlety of expression they portray, influenced in the main by Greek tragedy which became widespread in Sicily from the 3C BC.

Painting and pottery

Painting was considered by the Greeks to be the most noble and eloquent form of artistic expression, described by the poet Simonides (5C BC) as "mute poetry". Unfortunately, examples of this art form are rare because of the fragile nature of the pigments used to make the paints and their vulnerability to weather conditions. Large easel paintings, extolled by original sources, can be partially reconstructed from vase paintings, which often took the former as their model.

Styles – Vases with **black figures** on a red or pale yellow background date from the Archaic and the beginning of the Classic phase. The detailing of the figures was obtained by simply scratching away the black paint with a steel-tipped instrument. The most common subject matter was scenes drawn from mythology or from everyday life; sometimes purely geometric or abstract motifs were used as decorations, most especially on the early vases.

Red-figure vases appear in southern Italy towards the latter half of the 5C BC, earlier than in Greece where this style became prevalent from 480 BC. In this case, the black paint used hitherto for delineating the figures, is used exclusively as a background to the decoration, with the figures drawn in a brick red colour with touches of black and white. This inverted technique, allowing greater freedom of artistic expression, was a revolutionary discovery for artists; their designs acquired softer lines and contours than those obtained with a sharp steel point. The choice of subjects, however, does not change a great deal. Among the most beautiful examples of imported Attic vases are the magnificent two-handled craters from Agrigento (5C BC).

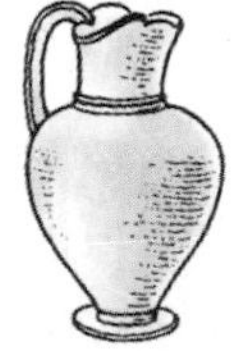

Oinochoe: a jug for wine

Kantharos: a tall goblet

Kylix: a drinking cup

Rhyton: a cup shaped like a horn or an animal's head, with a small hole in the bottom to allow liquid to pour into the mouth

Lekythos: a vase for ointment

Architecture

Thermal baths

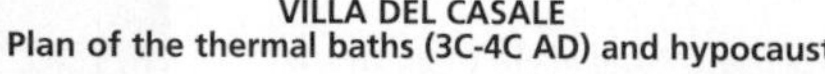

VILLA DEL CASALE
Plan of the thermal baths (3C-4C AD) and hypocaust

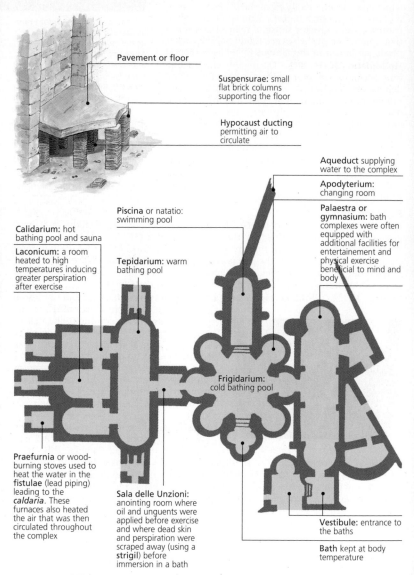

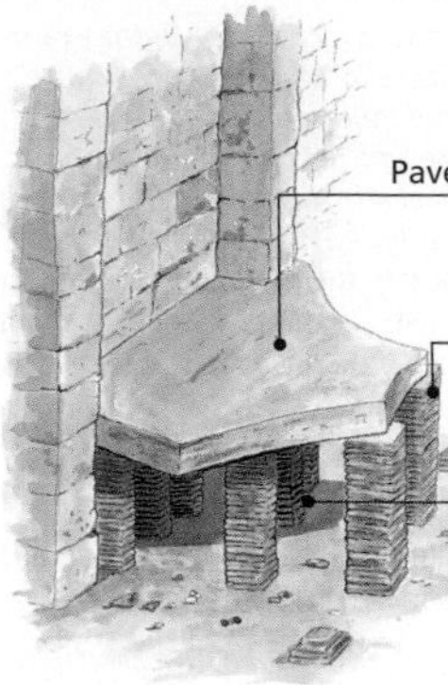

Pavement or floor
Suspensurae: small flat brick columns supporting the floor
Hypocaust ducting permitting air to circulate

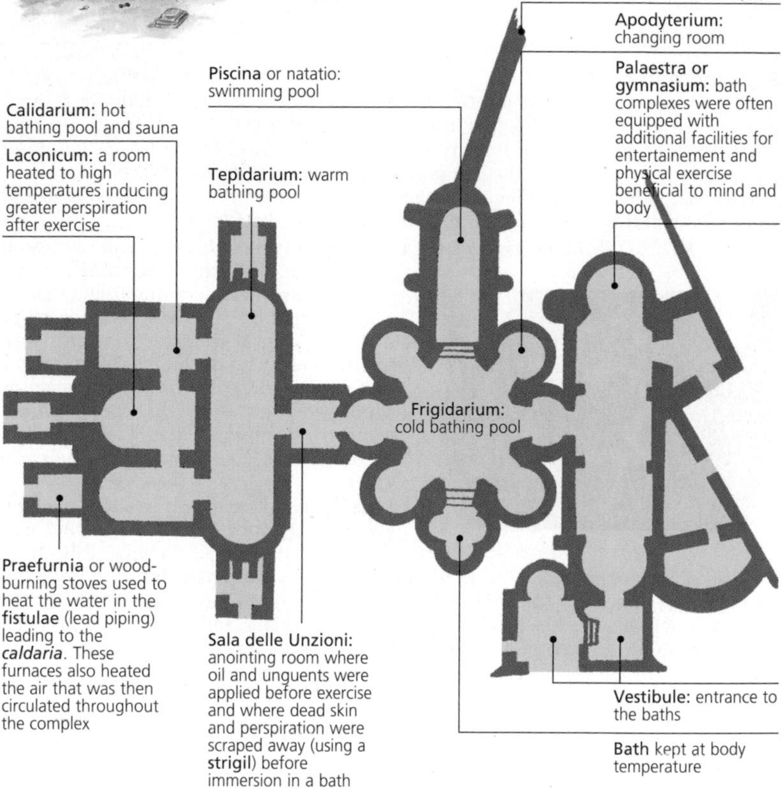

Aqueduct supplying water to the complex
Apodyterium: changing room
Palaestra or gymnasium: bath complexes were often equipped with additional facilities for entertainement and physical exercise beneficial to mind and body
Piscina or natatio: swimming pool
Calidarium: hot bathing pool and sauna
Laconicum: a room heated to high temperatures inducing greater perspiration after exercise
Tepidarium: warm bathing pool
Frigidarium: cold bathing pool
Praefurnia or wood-burning stoves used to heat the water in the fistulae (lead piping) leading to the caldaria. These furnaces also heated the air that was then circulated throughout the complex
Sala delle Unzioni: anointing room where oil and unguents were applied before exercise and where dead skin and perspiration were scraped away (using a strigil) before immersion in a bath
Vestibule: entrance to the baths
Bath kept at body temperature

Tibuli: ducting through which hot air was circulated by convection up the walls

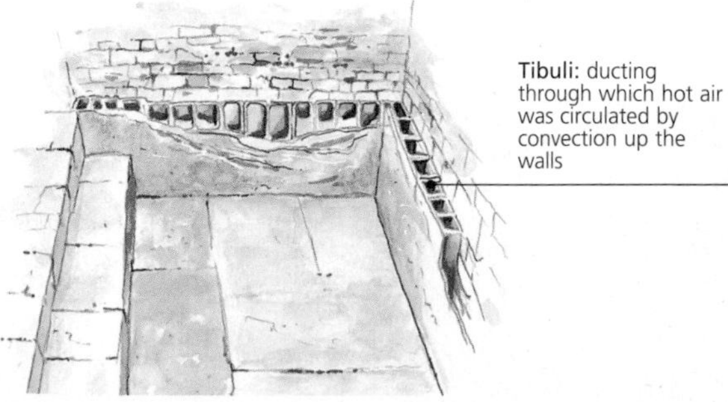

R. Corbel/MICHELIN

Religious architecture

RAGUSA IBLA – Duomo di San Giorgio (18C)

Latin cross floor plan with transepts

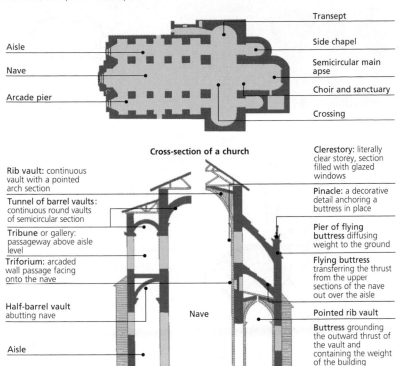

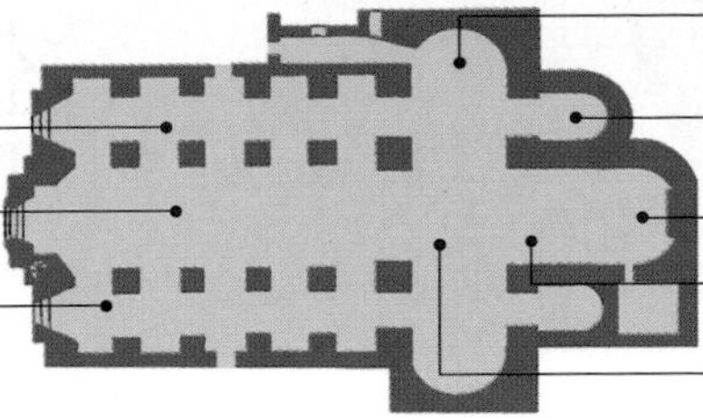

Transept
Side chapel
Semicircular main apse
Choir and sanctuary
Crossing
Aisle
Nave
Arcade pier

Cross-section of a church

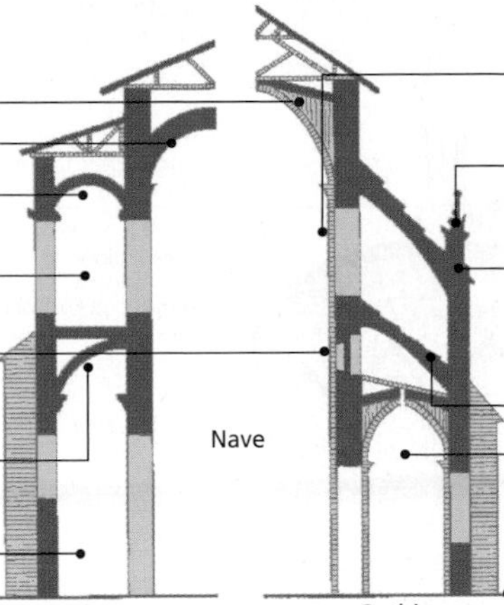

Rib vault: continuous vault with a pointed arch section
Tunnel of barrel vaults: continuous round vaults of semicircular section
Tribune or gallery: passageway above aisle level
Triforium: arcaded wall passage facing onto the nave
Half-barrel vault abutting nave
Aisle
Nave
Clerestory: literally clear storey, section filled with glazed windows
Pinacle: a decorative detail anchoring a buttress in place
Pier of flying buttress diffusing weight to the ground
Flying buttress transferring the thrust from the upper sections of the nave out over the aisle
Pointed rib vault
Buttress grounding the outward thrust of the vault and containing the weight of the building
Romanesque
Gothic

NICOSIA – Cattedrale di San Nicolò: main doorway (14C)

Corinthian capital modelled on prototypes from Antiquity, comprising an inverted concave cone encircled with acanthus leaves
Column: engaged or free standing, sometimes in a stone of contrasting colour or texture
Pier or door jamb
Statues: Allegories of the four Virtues – of which three survive: Prudence, Justice and Temperance
Archivolt: comprising a series of arched mouldings decorated with carved detailing (geometric or figurative elements)
Pedestal ornamented with volutes and at the centre a decorative head.
Door panel

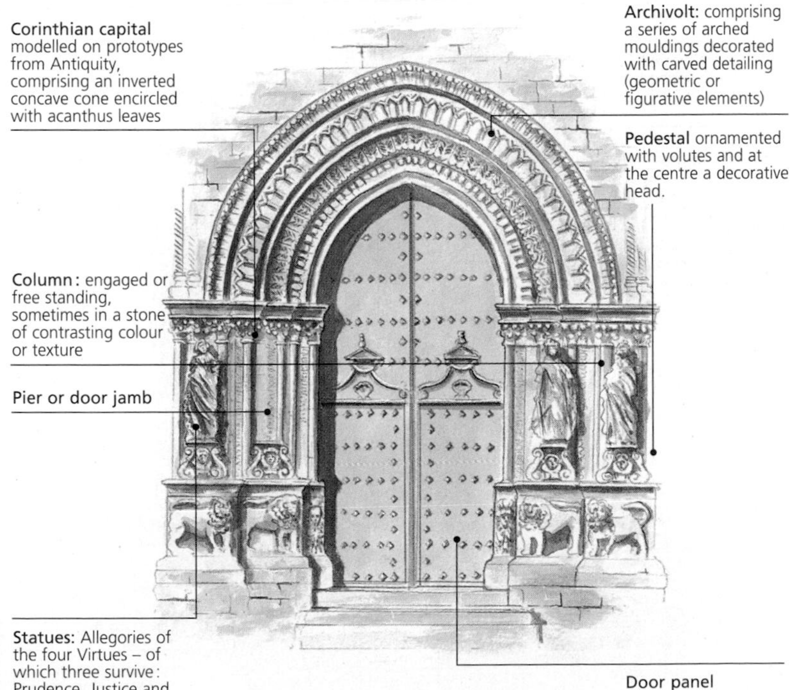

R. Corbel/MICHELIN

PALERMO – Cappella Palatina: ceiling detail (12C)

Muqarnas ceiling: complicated geometric plasterwork of interconnected stars and crosses elongated into stalactites

Stalactite decoration: a gay profusion of stucco pendants

Honeycombed plasterwork decorated with narrative scenes

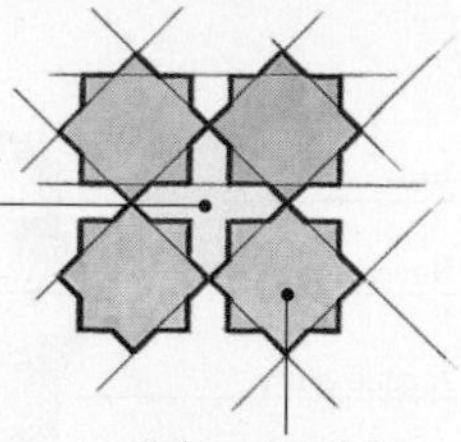

Schematic drawing illustrating the basis of Moorish decorative elements using the eight-pointed star

Cross

Eight-pointed star obtained by overlaying one square with another

MONREALE – Cathedral apse exterior detail (12C)

Interlaced pointed blind arches textured with zigzag decoration

Rose-window: each with a different geometric configuration

Applied arch

Column

CEFALÙ – Front elevation of cathedral (12C-13C)

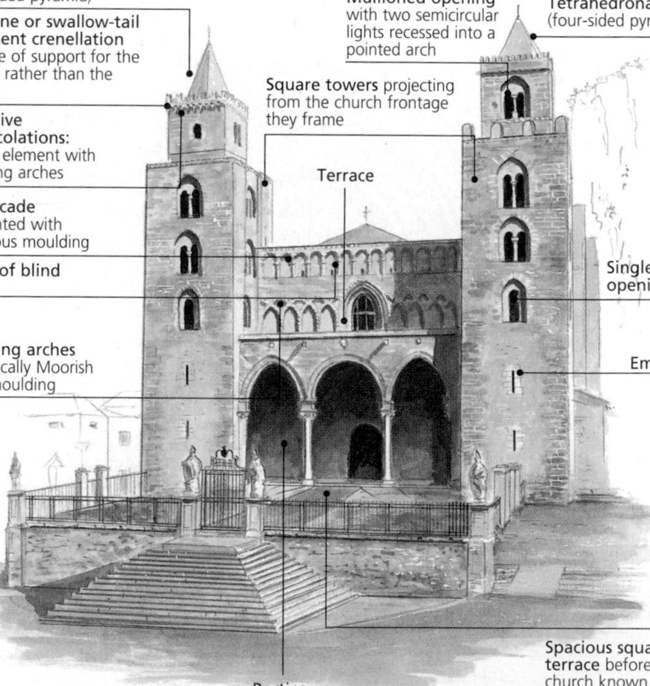

Octahedronal spire (eight-sided pyramid)

Ghibelline or swallow-tail battlement crenellation indicative of support for the Emperor rather than the Church

Decorative machiocolations: Moorish element with interlacing arches

Blind arcade ornamented with continuous moulding

Gallery of blind arches

Interlacing arches with typically Moorish zigzag moulding

Mullioned opening with two semicircular lights recessed into a pointed arch

Tetrahedronal spire (four-sided pyramid)

Square towers projecting from the church frontage they frame

Terrace

Single-light opening

Embrasure

Spacious square terrace before the church known as the *Turniale*

Portico

R. Corbel/MICHELIN

RAGUSA IBLA – Palazzo Cosentini: balcony (18C)

Wrought-iron balcony with pot-bellied balustrade
Brackets carved with figurative elements
Grotesques: masks of fantastical beasts and monsters
String-course horizontal moulding separating floor levels

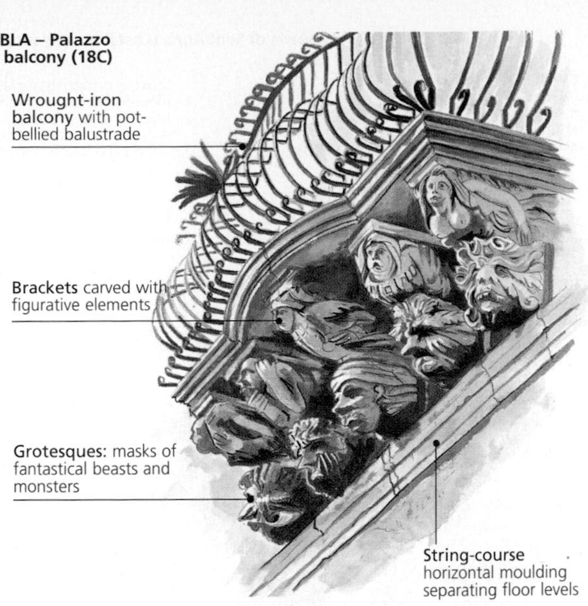

RAGUSA – Baroque cathedral of San Giovanni (18C)

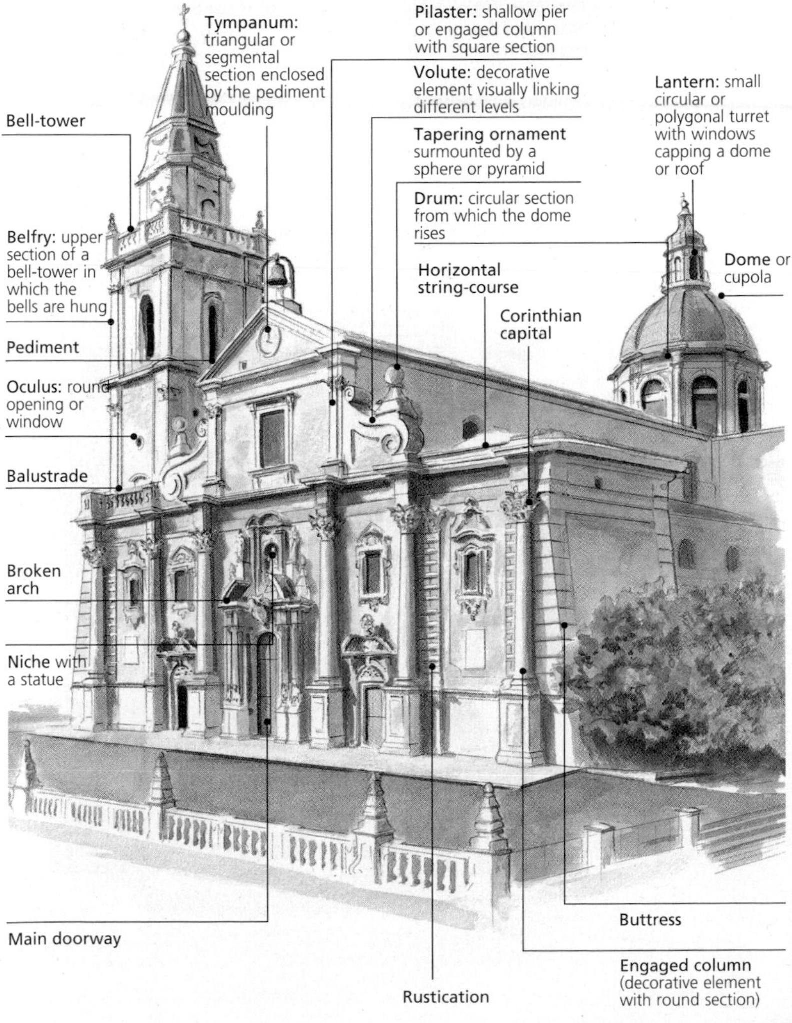

Bell-tower
Tympanum: triangular or segmental section enclosed by the pediment moulding
Pilaster: shallow pier or engaged column with square section
Volute: decorative element visually linking different levels
Tapering ornament surmounted by a sphere or pyramid
Drum: circular section from which the dome rises
Lantern: small circular or polygonal turret with windows capping a dome or roof
Belfry: upper section of a bell-tower in which the bells are hung
Horizontal string-course
Dome or cupola
Corinthian capital
Pediment
Oculus: round opening or window
Balustrade
Broken arch
Niche with a statue
Main doorway
Buttress
Engaged column (decorative element with round section)
Rustication

R. Corbel/MICHELIN

CASTELBUONO – Cappella di Sant'Anna (Castello dei Ventimiglia) (1683)

Putto: the angelic spirit represented as a Cupied-like infant, from the Latin *putus* – little man: sometimes an allegory of opulence and ease
Cornice
Frieze
Stucco: ornamental plasterwork, carved or moulded in low or high relief comprising figurative, geometric, architectural elements. A highly popular form of applied decoration during the late Mannerist to Baroque periods
Tabernacle with a grille: receptacle for Eucharistic elements
Chancel: section of the church comprising the **choir** – reserved for choristers and furnished with wooden stalls, very often ornamented with carving and intarsia work, and the **sanctuary** – the area around the high altar
Heavy drapery
Basket or depressed arch
Main or high altar
Side altar

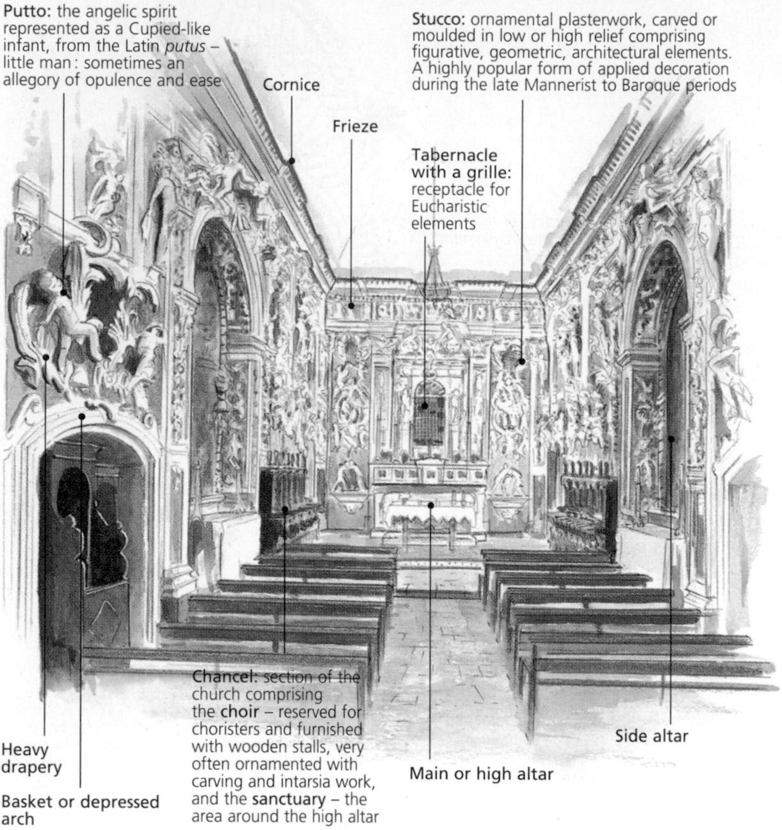

COMISO – Chiesa dei Cappuccini: high altar (17C-18C)

Altarpiece: large central painting surrounded by six smaller panels
Niche
Tabernacle: ornate wooden receptacle, inlaid with walnut, olive and cypress
Altarfront
R. Corbel/MICHELIN

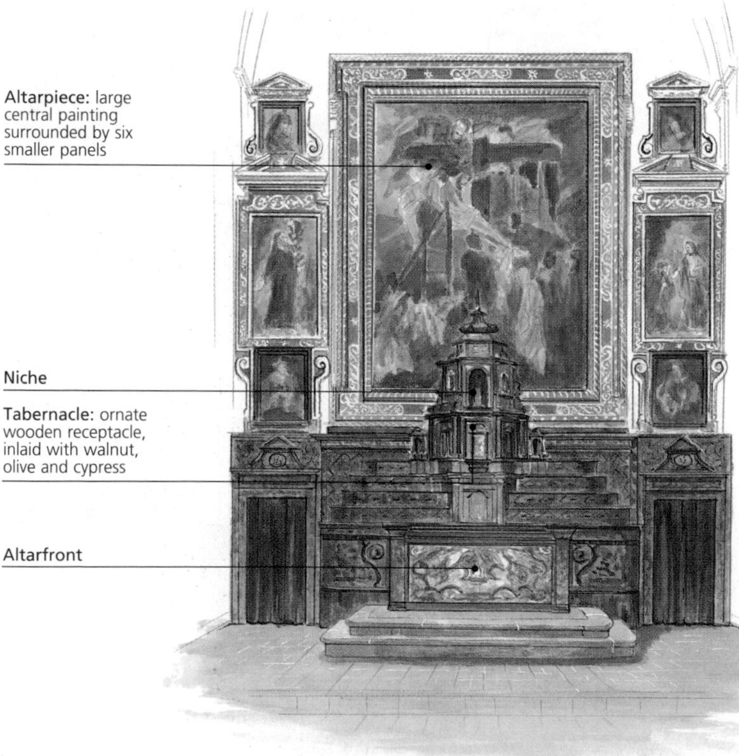

Civil and military buildings

Sicilian stronghold or *baglio*

Complex of buildings arranged around a central courtyard, including living quarters and workshops. In some cases the complex includes a small private chapel. Fortifications are integrated for defensive purposes. Examples located in rural positions were often used as grain depositories and for storing farm equipment; those located by the sea were inhabited by fishing communities (especially tuna fishermen) and included areas reserved for processing the fish and for repairing boats. At Marsala these *bagli* served as wineries (hence by implication, an actual cellar). Today most of these complexes have been transformed into museums or hotels.

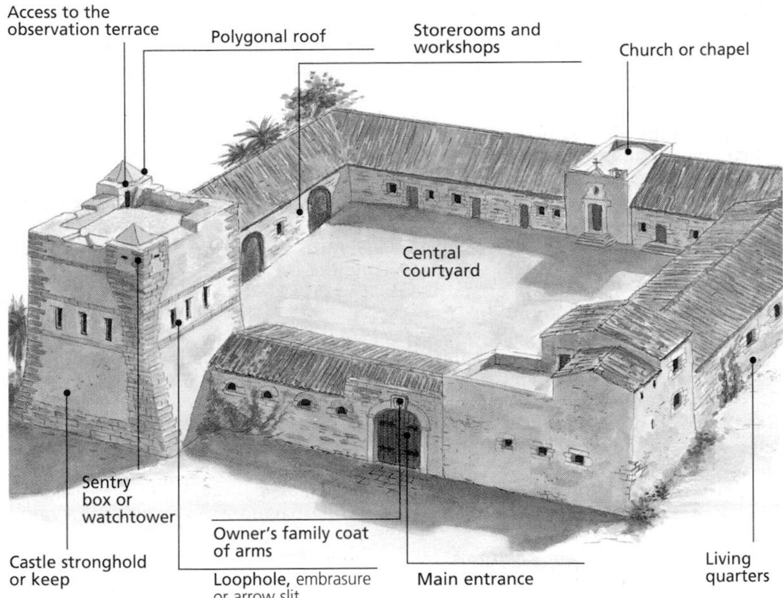

CATANIA – Castello Ursino (1239-50)

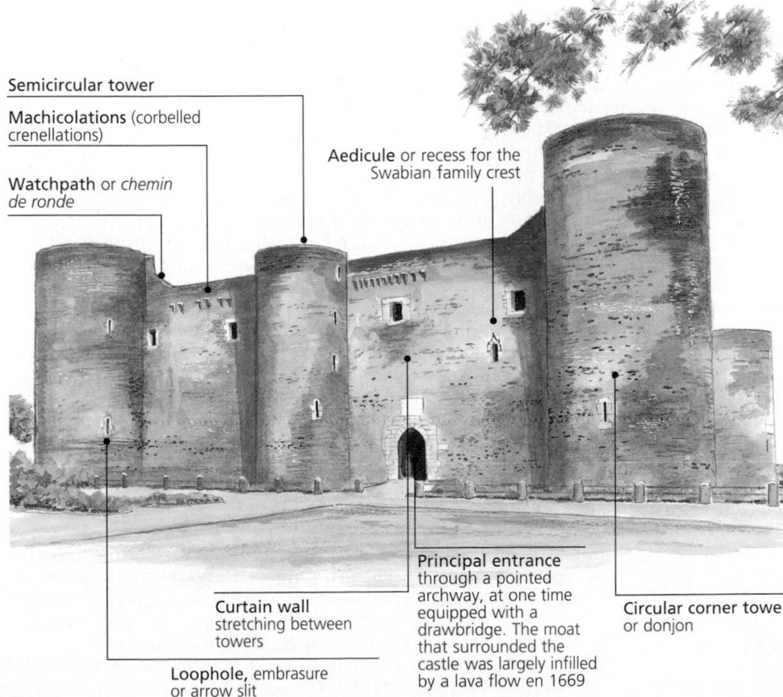

R. Corbel/MICHELIN

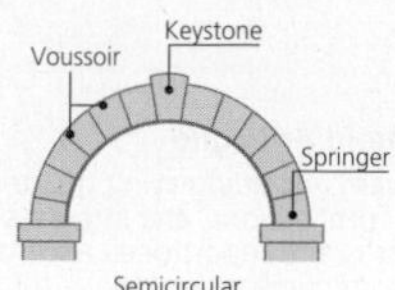

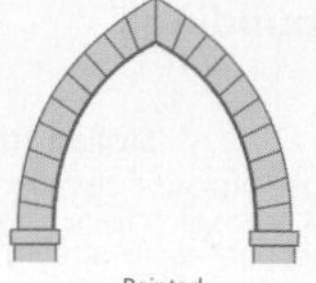

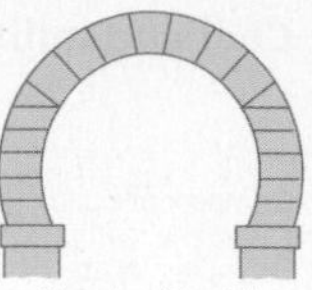

Glossary of Architecture

Altarpiece (or ancona): a large painting or sculpture adorning an altar.
Ambulatory: extension of the aisles around the chancel for processional purposes.
Antefix: a carved ornament at the end of the eaves of a roof to hide the joint between the tiles.
Antependium: a covering hung over the front of an altar.
Apse: semicircular or polygonal end of a church behind the altar; the outer section is known as the chevet.
Apsidiole: small chapel opening onto the ambulatory of a Romanesque or Gothic church.
Architrave: the lowermost horizontal division of a Classical entablature sitting directly on the column capital and supporting the frieze.
Archivolt: arch moulding over an arcade or upper section of a doorway.
Arcosolium: tomb found in numerous catacombs, which was built in the wall and surmounted by a niche.
Atlas figure or telamon: a sculptured figure of a man used as a column (the female equivalent is called a caryatid). In Sicily, the most famous are the telamons of the Temple of Olympian Zeus at Agrigento.
Bay: any of a number of principal divisions or spatial units of a building (or part of a building like an aisle of a church) contained within two or four vertical supports (piers, columns, pilasters).
Bouleuterion: meeting place for the town council *(boulé)*.
Buttress: external support of a wall, which counterbalances the thrust of the vaults and arches.
Capital: the upper end of a column, pillar or pier crowning the shaft and taking the weight of the entablature or architrave. There are three Classical orders: Doric *(see illustration in the section on Greek Art)*; Ionic, with a scroll-like ornament – the Composite has the Ionic scrolls and acanthus leaf ornament; and the Corinthian, ringed with burgeoning acanthus leaves, especially popular in the 16C and 17C for Baroque buildings. The abacus sits between the capital and the architrave; the structure beneath the abacus is the echinus.
Cardo: one of the main axes of the town plan as recommended by the Classical surveyor Hippodamus of Miletus, normally orientated north-south; the Greek equivalent is the stenopos.
Cathedra: high-backed throne in Gothic style.
Chiaramonte: architectural style characterised by two- or three-light windows surmounted by arches with tracery or polychrome geometric decoration
Ciborium: a canopy (baldaquin) over an altar.
Corbel (or truss): triangular bracket, usually made of wood, supporting a roof.
Counter-façade: internal wall of church façade.
Cross (church plan): churches are usually built either in the plan of a Greek cross, with four arms of equal length, or a Latin cross, with one arm longer than the other three.
Crypt: underground chamber or vault usually beneath a church, often used as a mortuary, burial place or for displaying holy relics. Sometimes it was a small chapel or church in its own right.
Decumanus: a major thoroughfare bisecting a Classical town plan, running on a complementary axis to the cardo, orientated east-west; the Greek equivalent is the plateia.
Dosseret: supplementary capital in the shape of the base of an upturned pyramid, often decorated, set above a column capital to receive the thrust of the arch.
Ekklesiasterion: meeting place for popular assemblies *(ekklesia)*.
Entablature: in certain buildings, the section at the top of a colonnade consisting of three parts: the architrave (flat section resting on the capitals of a colonnade), the frieze (decorated with carvings) and the cornice (projecting top section).
Exedra: section in the back of Roman basilicas containing seats; by extension, curved niche or semicircular recess outside.
Fresco: wall painting applied to wet plaster.

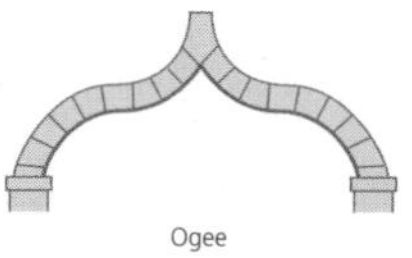
Ogee

Ghimberga: a triangular Gothic pediment adorning a portal.
Hypocaust: underground heating system used in Antiquity, whereby floors were raised on a series of small brick columns, enabling hot air to circulate underneath.
Intrados: inner surface of an arch or vault.
Jamb or pier: pillar flanking a doorway or window and supporting the arch above.

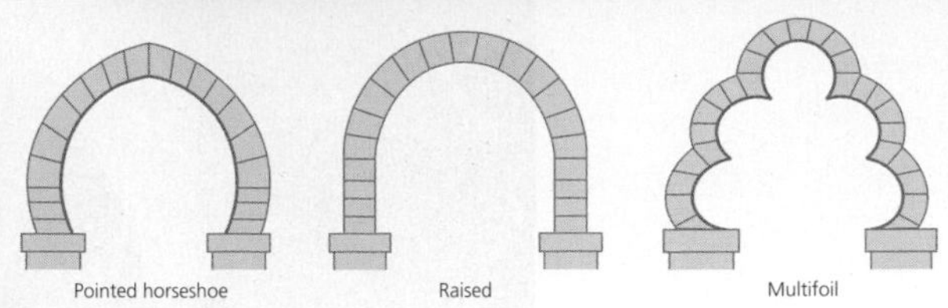
Pointed horseshoe Raised Multifoil

Keep: the tower stronghold of a castle, usually situated in the centre of a well protected area.
Keystone: topmost stone in an arch or vault.
Lantern: turret with windows on top of a dome.
Lesene (or Lombard strips): decorative band of pilasters joined at the top by an arched frieze.
Matroneo: the gallery reserved for women in palaeo-Christian and Romanesque churches.
Merlon: part of a crowning parapet between two crenellations. There are two types of merlons: Ghibelline (swallow-tailed), symbolising civil, Imperial power, and Guelf (rectangular), symbolising religious, Papal power.
Modillion: small console supporting a cornice.
Moulding: an ornamental shaped band which projects from the wall.
Ogive: pointed arch.
Opus signinum: floor covering obtained by mixing fragments of terracotta and other small pieces of rubble with lime. It is sometimes decorated with marble or stone cobbles.
Overhang: overhanging or corbelled upper storey.
Ovolo moulding: egg-shaped ornament incorporated into the entablature.
Palazzo: Italian for town house or square building (housing commercial offices, for example) subtly different in connotation to the word "palace". In the Renaissance, the ground floor was usually reserved for storage or commercial activities, the first floor or *piano nobile* comprised the main apartments, and the second floor *(alto piano)* was allocated to children and domestic staff.
Pantocrator: a hieratic figure of Christ with his hand raised in blessing, often depicted in the apse of palaeo-Christian churches.
Pendentive: the spherical triangular panel that provides the transition from a square or polygonal base (at a crossing) to a circular dome.
Peristyle: the range of columns surrounding a Classical building or courtyard.
Pilaster strip: structural column partially set into a wall.
Pluteus: decorated balustrade made from various materials, separating the chancel from the rest of the church.
Polyptych: a painted or carved work consisting of more than three folding leaves or panels (diptych: 2 panels; triptych: 3 panels).
Predella: base of an altarpiece, divided into small panels.
Pulpit: an elevated dais from which sermons were preached in the nave of a church.
Pyx: cylindrical box made of ivory or glazed copper for jewels or the Eucharistic host.
Raceme: ornamental vine motif with tendrils, leaves and stylised fruits.
Relief: high relief *(altorilievo)* is a sculptural term describing the modelled forms that project from the background by at least half their depth (halfway between shallow relief and sculpture in the round). Low relief *(bassorilievo)* projects only very slightly from the background (also known as bas relief).
Retable: large and ornate altarpiece divided into several painted or carved panels, especially common in Spain after the 14C.
Rib: a projecting moulding or band on the underside of a dome or vault, which may be structural or ornamental.
Rustication: facing of a building that exaggeratedly replicates dressed stonework, raised or otherwise from the mortar joints. Rustication was used in the Renaissance to consolidate the impression of impregnability on the ground floor of a *palazzo*.
Splay: a surface of a wall that forms an oblique angle to the main surface of a doorway or window opening.
Squinch: alternative to a pendentive comprising a compound number of miniature strainer arches, often intricately decorated with Moorish plasterwork.
Tambour: a circular or polygonal structure supporting a dome.
Trompe l'oeil: two-dimensional painted decoration giving the three-dimensional illusion of relief and perspective.
Vault: an arched structure of stone or brick forming a ceiling or roof over a hall, room, bay or other wholly or partly enclosed space. Barrel vault – A vault having a semicircular cross section. Groin vault (or cross vault) – Formed by the perpendicular intersection of two vaults. Bowl-shaped vault – A spherical vault enclosing a semicircular apse.

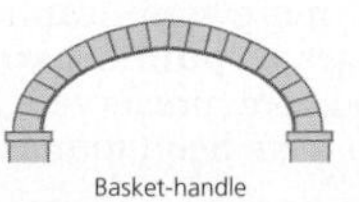
Basket-handle

Vaulting cell: one of the four segments of the cross vault.
Window cross: a stone or wooden post which divides the opening of a window or door. The vertical posts are known as mullions.

Rampant

Art

From the period of Greek colonisation to the present day, Sicilian creativity has never been idle. The complex history of this island, fashioned and formed by a number of foreign peoples and cultures, isolated by the sea, in part explains the unique and varied nature of Sicilian artistic expression over the centuries.

Interior of the Martorana, Palermo

Roman art

Vestiges from Roman times are fewer and less impressive than those from the Greek period, largely because the Romans showed comparatively little interest in Sicily by comparison with their other colonies. Once the threat of a potential Carthaginian invasion had receded, the island lost its strategic importance and became prized exclusively as a "Roman granary", thereby enabling the enriched native land owners to build splendid villas by the sea – as the ruins of such villas as the one at Patti, near Tyndaris, testify. Not until the end of the 3C AD, during the reign of Diocletian, did Sicily become one of the regions most sought after by the Roman aristocracy who set about acquiring large tracts of land on the island. During seven centuries of Roman occupation (3C BC-5C AD), Rome did not endow Sicily with any prestigious monuments other than the odd functional public building (amphitheatres, public baths), although they did lay the foundations for a comprehensive road system built for military and commercial use. Several urban public areas (the fora, for example) have yet to be excavated.

Architecture

Unlike the Greeks, the Romans knew about cement and how to use it effectively. They erected walls, vaults and columns using casements filled with small bricks, and then poured concrete into them. Finishing touches were added in the form of marble facings (or high-quality stone) or, for the interiors, ably applied stucco so as to suggest splendid stone walls.

Civil architecture – During this period, **Greek theatres**, like the ones at **Taormina** and **Catania**, underwent considerable transformation: the circular orchestra (reserved for the chorus) was reduced to a semicircle, while a stage wall was added for the machinery required to create special effects. The theatre provided a venue both for circus entertainment and combat with wild animals; to protect the spectators, a wall was constructed along the bottom of the cavea (part of which can still be seen at Taormina). Those Roman monuments that may be of special interest include the amphitheatre at **Siracusa** built for extravagant gladiatorial combats and fights pitched against wild animals; that at Catania; the odeons at Taormina and Catania, and, finally, the Naumachie of Taormina (now badly damaged) which consists of a large-scale brick-built gymnasium (122m/400ft long) ornamented with niches. Besides these complexes dedicated to sport and entertainment, the Romans left nothing of value in terms of civic architecture: the fine basilica at Tyndaris suggests that the Romans introduced the art of vaulting to Sicily (for it was unknown to the Greek civil engineers), and more significantly, to settlements removed from the major urban centres. Vestiges of **public baths complexes** (terme), largely dating from the Imperial period, are preserved at Catania, Taormina, Comiso, Solunto and Tindari; traces of fora have been found at Taormina, Catania, Siracusa and Tindari.

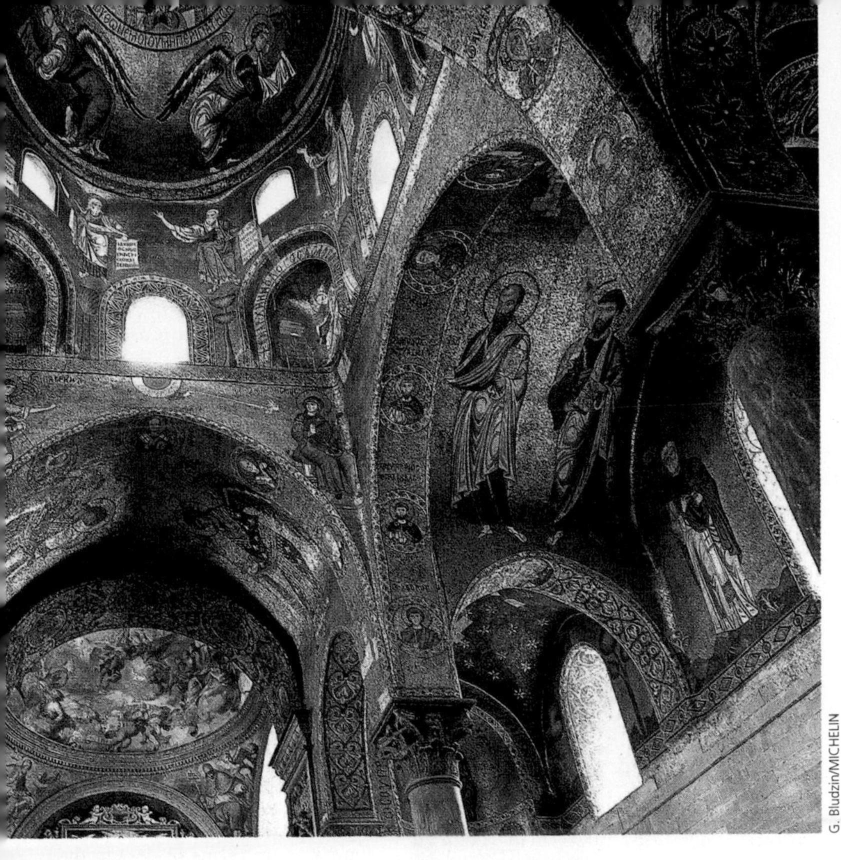

Domestic architecture – The Romano-Sicilian house closely resembles its Hellenistic counterpart. The town house graced with a peristyle was introduced towards the close of the 3C-2C BC (Morgantina); only at Marsala and Agrigento have houses with an atrium and a peristyle courtyard (a model first conceived in Campania) been discovered. The most elegant homes, however, are to be found among the country villas, the most typical example being the magnificent **Villa Imperiale del Casale** near Piazza Armerina. Here, the existence of its private bath facilities would indicate that this was indeed a highly sophisticated and luxurious house; it is particularly renowned for its splendid floor mosaics.

Byzantine art

Archaeological excavation undertaken in Palermo and Siracusa has uncovered complete cemeteries on the outskirts of the urban area dating from late Antiquity, when the Romans imposed Christianity on Sicily. The **catacombs** that preserve traces of painted decoration, most particularly those at Siracusa (4C-5C AD), provide the earliest examples of Christian art in Sicily. As in all the palaeo-Christian world, Sicily was gradually coerced into erecting churches, modelled on the Roman **prototype basilica**: this consisted of a simple rectangular building, articulated by columns into three aisles, with a central nave terminated by a single apse. The other, more striking solution, was to incorporate a church around a pagan Antique temple – as with the Temple of Concord at Agrigento and the Temple of Athena at Siracusa: to achieve this, the walls of the cella were cut away to make arcades and the outer colonnade was infilled with masonry.

In AD 535, as a result of the Byzantine conquest, links between the Church of Sicily and the Exarchate of Ravenna were reinforced: in 751 when Ravenna fell to the Lombards, this allegiance was transferred to Constantinople. Interestingly enough, the rift dividing the Roman and Byzantine Churches as a result of Pope Gregory II's opposition to Emperor Leo III's Iconoclast movement in 725-26 had serious repercussions in Sicily. The ban on the cult of holy icons imposed by the Byzantine Emperor prompted crowds of refugees to seek asylum in Sicily where the icon continued to be venerated. Whole monastic communities and numerous groups of skilled craftsmen found sanctuary in Sicily and set about applying their trades, notably in the art of mosaic.

This prosperous period gave rise to the building of numerous shrines (including the ones at Cava d'Ispica and Pantalica) and the institution of troglodyte settlements hewn into the bedrock (almost all now destroyed). It also resulted in the

building of small, centrally planned, square (typically Byzantine) churches, consisting of three curved walls or exedras enclosing a spatial cube contained by a dome, and fronted by a flat façade with an entrance (west facing). A few examples survive in the eastern part of the island, north and east of Etna *(Castiglione di Sicilia – see p 369)*, in the vicinity of Noto and around Siracusa.
Other monuments erected in Byzantine times were completely transformed, dismembered or converted to another use through the ensuing centuries.

Arabo-Norman art

Arab occupation

The Muslim conquest began in 827 in the area of Trapani. During their two and a half centuries of sovereignty, the Arabs transformed the appearance of Sicily, transposing their power base from Siracusa to Palermo, altering the countryside by instigating the use of irrigation and a range of new crops from the east, and, most particularly, by introducing architectural forms that, hitherto, had been unknown on the island. They were prolific builders and sensitive planners, ever conscious of a building's relationship with its natural setting: palaces, mosques and minarets were placed among gardens and fountains. In terms of design, their acute sense of line and elegance was applied to sophisticated decorative schemes: human figures gave way to geometric and arabesque forms, house interiors were transformed with coloured ceramic tiles, while ceilings were encrusted with rich honeycomb stalactite plaster decoration *(muqarnas)*.

G. Bludzin/MICHELIN

The story of Samson, Monreale Cathedral cloisters

Alas, no important monument survives intact from the Arab occupation. Indeed, most of their splendid buildings disappeared with the arrival of the Normans, who appropriated them for their own use, rebuilding and redecorating them, and in so doing, stripping them of their original integrity. A few examples of Arab craftsmanship survive, as do a number of intricate networks of irregular streets tucked away in the urban fabric of such cities as Palermo.

Norman eclecticism

The Arabo-Norman style combines elements from Islamic, Romanesque (introduced by Franco-Norman Benedictine monks) and Byzantine art. Much of its wealth is rooted in the ardent wish harboured by the Norman sovereigns of emulating the splendour of Byzantium, a city they yearned to conquer. The new Sicilian master builders set about channelling all their creative power to erect monuments of incomparable beauty. From the end of the 11C and throughout the whole of the following century, large churches were conceived by architect-monks mainly from the Benedictine and Augustinian orders, whether Greek, French or Latin (from mainland Italy). Designs were modelled on Classical prototypes: a transept was incorporated in a basilica giving it a Latin- or Greek- cross plan, towers were erected to house bells, a doorway was inserted in the front elevation, the presbytery was often crowned with a dome. At the same time, these edifices were given the latest contemporary decoration: Byzantine mosaics laid by Orthodox (Greek) artists and Moorish features (horseshoe arches, arabesque and honeycomb ornament). The result made for a curious mixture of buildings in which these three styles were blended to make something quite unique.

Byzantine influence – The Eastern elements incorporated into religious architecture include the square centralised plan, adapted in turn to the Greek cross, roofed with intersecting barrel vaults (Church of the Martorana, San Nicolò at Mazara del Vallo, or Santissima Trinità di Delia at Castelvetrano). Elsewhere, the intersection is vaulted with the typical Sicilian Byzantine dome rising from a polygonal drum.

Cloisters, Monreale Cathedral

Even the capitals reflect an Arabo-Norman style adapted from the Byzantine, by incorporating a dosseret between the capital and the impost of the arch (Monreale Cathedral).

The reason for the lack of any Byzantine figurative representations of the human form in sculpture is threefold: firstly, the Christians wished to distance themselves from pagan statuary; secondly, the Iconoclastic movement forbade the veneration of anything that might be construed as an idol; and, lastly, because of the Islamic influence. The techniques used were also adapted; stone was no longer worked just on the surface but in the round, using small drills to make tiny holes and intricate fretwork effects that resembled stone lace.

The richest and most effective medium used by the Byzantine artists was the mosaic. This they applied to immense areas, animating them with figures and decorative motifs, upgrading the art form to monumental proportions. Apart from the Martorana which fully conforms to Byzantine canons, the iconography and presentation of subject matter were adapted in Sicilian churches. At Cefalù, Monreale and the Cappella Palatina in Palermo, Christ Pantocrator fills the top of the vault above the apse; in Greek Byzantine churches, He would always have been placed in the dome. Finally, the Norman kings had themselves depicted in areas traditionally reserved for saints, with the symbols of the basilei (Byzantine emperors), as a way of asserting their power.

Islamic influence – The Arabs brought with them new building methods and decorative know-how that enabled them to create veritable masterpieces. In architecture, they introduced the stilted arch (an arch resting on imposts treated as downward continuations of the archivolt), as well as what may perhaps be the most evocative import, the horse-shoe (or Moorish) arch: the upper part of this arch is semicircular, although it can be pointed at its apex, but comes in at the base to form a horseshoe shape. The interior of Arab buildings were often encrusted with stalactite plasterwork decoration called **muqarnas**; this in turn was painted, carved and textured into overhanging honeycombs. The interior decoration of Monreale Cathedral, the Palatine Chapel, the Zisa and Cuba *palazzi* are splendid testimonies to the influence of Islam. The characteristically Arab predilection for elaborate ornamentation can also be discerned in other forms of decoration: the serrated edge to the cornice with merlons of San Cataldo in Palermo provides an elegant base from which spring the three pink domes. The Arabs also brought an alternative view of proportion and volume as indicated by the squat domes of San Giovanni degli Eremiti.

Romanesque influence – The most typical elements provided by the Romanesque style is the Latin-cross plan and the façade framed by massive towers, features that were devised by the Benedictine monks, most notably at Cluny, for the buildings they planned on a massive and monumental scale. On the whole, the religious buildings did not allocate much space to Norman sculpture, which manifests itself exclusively in terms of geometric motifs on small arches and other decorative details – like strips of small leaves and ovolo moulding – applied to the dosserets of capitals. Their inclination towards stylisation touched representations of animals and plants which are reduced to simple palmettes or rather thin, flat, rigid-looking flowerless species (reeds and rushes). A handful of monuments, including the cloisters at Monreale, preserve some most splendid figurative capitals relating historical and biblical scenes, founded in the Romanesque tradition.

Arabo-Norman creativity

Although many buildings from this period conform to a clearly defined influence, some combinations of styles end up becoming models and prototypes for other art forms promoted during the rule of the Altavilla (de Hauteville) dynasty.

Religious buildings – The undisputed masterpiece of this Sicilian Norman School is the Palatine Chapel (Cappella Palatina) in Palermo. Here elements of Romanesque art – an extended plan comprising nave and side aisles and narrow windows through which suffused light is allowed to permeate – are married with the Moorish love for sumptuous decoration (notable in the ceiling), calligraphy (various Arabic inscriptions) and structural design (pointed arches), and merged with the monumental splendour of Byzantine art (dome pendentives, gold-background mosaics, marble wall facing, and inlaid floors). The chapel demonstrates how the centrally planned Byzantine choir is superimposed onto the wooden-vaulted Latin basilica nave (set at a lower level). This came to be used as a new prototype and was used subsequently at Monreale.

Secular buildings – Besides the odd large castle built in strategic positions as at Palermo, Castellammare and Messina, the Norman kings built themselves various summer or pleasure palaces for rest and recreation purposes. At the end of the Altavilla (de Hauteville) rule, there were nine such residences in Sicily; today only the **Zisa** and **Cuba** *palazzi* in Palermo survive. These splendid houses are surrounded by large gardens ornamented with expanses of water. The interior space was divided into two main areas: the iwan (a room with three exedras) and an open courtyard containing one or more fountains and surrounded by porticoes. The first of these two distinctive areas originated in Abbasid Persia, the second in Fatimid Egypt. Together, they appear in Sicily sometime in the 12C, imported via the Maghreb (North Africa), which at that time extended as far as the coasts of modern Tunisia, and was under Sicilian rule. The decoration is also largely drawn from Islamic art: the floors are laid with marble or brick in a herringbone pattern, the walls are faced with mosaic (more the influence of Byzantine craftsmen, but incorporating Moorish motifs) and finally, the ceilings and arches are encrusted with carved and painted muqarnas.

Gothic art

For two centuries between the 13C and the 15C, Sicily suffered a long period of political instability under a succession of sovereigns: the Swabians (1189-1266), Angevins (1266-82), and the House of Aragon. Common to them all was the way in which they came to appreciate the Gothic style on a grand scale – which was not the case in the mainland peninsula.

Swabian military constructions – Henry VI, and more particularly **Frederick II** who enjoyed a longer reign (1208-50), preserved the numerous religious and civil buildings erected by the Normans. They impressed their mark on the landscape by building fortresses designed by northern master masons. The Gothic style was introduced to Sicily in the 13C in the form of fortified architecture. From this era date the castles at Siracusa (Castello Maniace), Catania (Castello Ursino) and Augusta, as do the fortifications of the castle at Enna (strategic centre of the island occupied since Byzantine times) from which there survive eight imposing towers. These buildings conform to a highly geometric ground plan (square centrepiece defended with angle, and sometimes lateral, towers), doorways and windows set into pointed arches, austerely bare walls pierced with embrasures, that rise to battlements and, finally, quadripartite vaulted casemates.

14C: Chiaramonte style – The great feudal dynasties in power during the 14C, most especially the Chiaramonte, demonstrated a real talent for the construction of town houses and churches. The Palermo residence, Palazzo Chiaramonte, provided a model for future *palazzi*: the façade is extremely refined, the windows set into decorative pointed arches are unique and quite wonderful, the roof line is crested with merlons. The Chiaramonte style is characterised by two- or three-light windows surmounted by arches with tracery or polychrome geometric decoration. The Chiaramonte, who maintained their supremacy throughout the 14C as the royal power base declined, sponsored many new buildings and restored others: from Mussomeli to Racalmuto, Montechiaro to Favara, they are responsible for at least 10 castles and *palazzi*.

15C: Catalan Gothic – The reason why the Catalan Gothic flourished so easily in Sicily rests in the importance wielded by the Spanish viceroys from the late 14C, under the rule of the House of Aragon. There were delays in the Gothic style being introduced to Sicily, especially if compared with the rest of Europe where the Flamboyant Gothic style was reaching its peak. When it did travel care of the Catalan-Aragonese federation (which since the 13C had become one of the most powerful forces in the Mediterranean), it was a more sober form of Gothic characterised by elongated forms, a marked tendency towards breadth of space over height (particularly in the religious context), and ample windows alternating with bare flat wall surfaces. Typical examples include the Palazzo Santo Stefano and Palazzo Corvaja at Taormina and the main doorway of Palermo Cathedral.

Towards the end of the 15C, **Matteo Carnelivari** probably best epitomises the new influence, incorporating Catalan features in and among the Byzantine, Arab and Norman elements that were prevalent in the established vernacular style. Carnelivari is responsible for designing Palazzo Abatellis and Palazzo Ajutamicristo, and probably the Church of Santa Maria della Catena in Palermo.

Sculpture and painting – Only artists that were foreign to Sicily achieved any renown in these two fields at this time: sculptors were summoned from Tuscany, particularly from Pisa. **Nino Pisano** completed a graceful Annunziata that was true to his style for the cathedral in Trapani, a place that attracted a large number of sculptors to its marble quarries from the 14C. Bonaiuto Pisano carved the eagle which stands above the gateway of Palazzo Sclafani in Palermo.

In painting, **Antonio Veneziano** (trained in Venice, worked in Florence), Gera da Pisa, and various Spanish artists such as **Guerau Janer** also worked in Sicily for a time. Towards the end of the 15C, some of these painters became so successful that they decided to settle permanently in Sicily, among them **Nicolò di Maggio** (from Siena) who worked particularly in Palermo.

Renaissance and Mannerism

As a result of the strong influence of the Spanish Gothic style favoured by the Aragonese court, the Renaissance and Mannerism which spread from Italy to the rest of Europe did not have a great impact on Sicily. It fell to artists trained by the great Tuscan masters to introduce the principles of the Renaissance to Sicily.

Painting – In the 15C, Sicily started to show an interest in the new Renaissance movement, prompted by the work of **Antonello da Messina**. Although his life and career have long been something of a mystery, there is no doubt that this artist is the most famous Sicilian painter. He was born in Messina in 1430; in 1450, he was in Naples, possibly engaged as a pupil to the workshop of Colantonio. There he would most certainly have come into contact with Flemish painting. In 1475-76 Antonello was in Venice where he must have encountered Giovanni Bellini and Piero della Francesca. Antonello's supreme reputation, however, is founded on the fact that he mastered and diffused widely the exacting oil-painting techniques used by the Van Eycks. His mature style combines the detail so typical of Flemish art with the breadth of form upheld by the Italian Schools. Indeed, his works all conform to being static in composition, exploring texture, and demonstrating an almost perfect tonal unity in terms of colour: his works found in Sicily include an Annunciation in Palazzo Bellomo in Siracusa, a Polyptych of St Gregory in the Museo Regionale in Messina, and the Portrait of an Unknown Man in the Museo Mandralisca in Cefalù. These are among the most notable works of the Renaissance to be preserved in Sicily.

During the first half of the 16C, the painters **Cesare da Sesto**, **Polidoro da Caravaggio** and Vincenzo da Pavia played their part in spreading the Mannerist style prevalent in Tuscany and Rome. **Simone de Wobreck** meanwhile, who lived in Sicily until 1557, introduced the basic elements of Flemish Mannerism.

Sculpture – In the second half of the 15C, sculpture was completely revitalised by a range of Italian artists, notably Francesco Laurana and Domenico Gagini.

The sculptor and engraver Francesco **Laurana** spent five years in Sicily (1466-71) during which time he worked at the Cappella Mastrantonio in the Church of San Francesco and produced the bust of

Portrait of an Unknown Man *by Antonello da Messina*

Museo Mandralisca, Cefalù/SCALA

G. Bludzin/MICHELIN

Eleonora of Aragon in Palazzo Abatellis in Palermo. Other paintings include a Madonna and Child in the Church of the Crocifisso in Noto, another in the Church of the Immacolata in Palazzolo Acreide and a third in the museum at Messina.

Domenico Gagini, who was born into a family of Italian sculptors and architects from Lake Lugano, moved south and settled in Sicily. There he practised his art in association with his son **Antonello** who was born in Palermo in 1478. Their workshop flourished in the capital, producing works that satisfied the contemporary predilection for elegant, refined forms in Carrara marble rather than travertine. Domenico's style and technique were later continued by his descendants (including his son Giandomenico), sculptors and goldsmiths who achieved fame up to the mid-17C. Numerous Sicilian churches preserve splendid statues executed by the Gagini, although their very proliferation has aroused accusations of their work being repetitive and therefore considered of a lesser value.

Mannerism exercised its influence on sculpture in the 16C largely thanks to such artists as the Florentine **Angelo Montorsoli** (1505-63) who was working in Messina around 1547-57. The fact that he had collaborated with Michelangelo in Florence and Rome gave Montorsoli a certain cachet and his work demonstrates a shift from the Renaissance style to a Michelangelesque Mannerism. The works that survive include the Fontana di Orione (1547-50) in Messina which is regarded as one of the greatest masterpieces of the 16C.

Baroque

During the 16C the Spanish authorities asserted their influence in the arts. They imposed the values promoted by the Counter-Reformation (resulting from the Council of Trent 1545), before choosing to sponsor an elaborate, exuberant form of the Baroque that was more typically Spanish than Italian.

Counter-Reformation – Sicily soon succumbed to the power and influence of the Society of Jesus (later known as the Jesuits), founded in 1540 by the Spaniard St Ignatius Loyola (1491-1556). Modelled on the Chiesa del Gesù in Rome, the **Jesuit** churches in Sicily were designed with the same features. The one broad nave is devoid of any element that might restrict the congregation's view of the main altar and obstruct or deflect the words of the preacher from reaching each and every one of the faithful. The solemnity, authority, opulence and luminosity of the internal space is in keeping with the exterior: the main body of the church, so tall and wide, is screened by a central bay; the lateral chapels which open directly off the nave are screened by a lower bay. The bare surfaces that lent a dignity to the Renaissance buildings are here textured with features that vary in weight and depth: engaged columns at ground level give way to superficial pilasters above as sharp contrasts effectively dissolve into lightness (the Church of Sant'Ignazio all'Olivella in Palermo is a good example of this style). The painting of the **Counter-Reformation** revives a predilection for those images that had been rejected by Protestantism, subjects such as the Virgin Mary, the dogma of the Eucharist and the veneration of saints. Painting follows the examples of Michelangelo and Raphael, although in Sicily the practitioners of this style who were active in Palermo, like Vincenzo degli Azani, are few and lesser known.

Politics and style – The Baroque which in Spain reached its apogee in the second half of the 17C, was quickly assimilated by the Sicilians, for they had enjoyed and appreciated the opulent use of marble and gilding since Arab and Byzantine tastes

G. Bludzin/MICHELIN

had prevailed in previous centuries. This movement placed great importance on detail, producing finely worked wrought-iron railings and gates, balcony brackets carved with the most original grotesques, and imaginative designs interpreted in polychrome panels of *pietra dura*.

At the beginning of the 17C, the Spanish viceroy's administration launched an ambitious building programme involving the founding of some 100 new towns in an attempt to underpin their plans for reorganising and then developing their extensive territories. The earthquake of 1669, followed by a more devastating one in 1693, destroyed almost all the southeastern part of the island. The rebuilding of the towns was immediately initiated under the combined direction of the local authorities, the aristocracy, town planners (Fra' Michele la Ferla, Fra' Angelo Italia) and architects (Vaccarini, Ittar, Vermexio, Palma and Gagliardi). The earthquake laid bare a great expanse of land stretching from Catania to Siracusa, damaging Avola, Noto, Scicli, Modica, Ragusa, Vittoria, Lentini and Grammichele. As a result, Sicilian Baroque is concentrated in this part of the island and around Palermo (Bagheria, Trapani), being the seat of power.

Architecture – The majority of the Baroque architects had trained in Rome. They therefore modelled their ideas on Roman interpretations of the Baroque, sometimes exaggerating their iconographic forms, volumes and subject matter for sculptural effect. The delicate relationship between the fragility of life and the forces of nature was translated into an art form that by now was far removed from any quest for beauty. The grotesque, excess, death, suffering and even ugliness (decrepitude of old age, poverty and physical deformity) underlie the expressions of exuberance that ornament every surface at this time.

Giovanni Battista Vaccarini (1702-69) served his apprenticeship in Rome under Carlo Fontana, through whom he came to understand the ingenious creativity of the tormented architect Borromini; on his return to Sicily around 1730, Vaccarini settled in Catania and devoted the next 30 years of his life to rebuilding the city. His undoubted masterpiece is the Church of St Agatha which is elliptical in shape and has a façade inspired by Borromini's oval Church of San Carlo alle Quattro Fontane in Rome.

G. Bludzin/MICHELIN

Even **Palermo** bristles with buildings modelled on prototypes in Rome. Most of these were built by one of the city's most highly regarded architects **Giacomo Amato** (1643-1732), who came from Palermo and was trained in Rome. He uses decorative elements borrowed from 16C Roman architecture: characteristic examples include the Church of Santa Teresa alla Kalsa (1686), the Church of the Pietà which rises through two imposing storeys articulated with columns (1689), the Church of the Santissimo Salvatore with its oval dome, as well as numerous private *palazzi*. The monument that best epitomises the urban Baroque style in Palermo is the Quattro Canti junction faced with four interacting building façades and fountains.

Noto, which had to be completely rebuilt following the 1693 earthquake, exemplifies the harmonious homogeneity of the Baroque style in the urban context in Sicily, largely as a result of being conceived as a vast theatre. The author of this exceptional ensemble is presumed to be the enigmatic **Rosario Gagliardi**, about whom little is known other than his date of birth (Siracusa 1680) and death (Noto 1726). This man, the greatest Baroque architect of Sicily, exerted his considerable impact on this small area around Noto and its two neighbouring towns: Ragusa and Modica. In **Ragusa**, he is responsible for the churches of San Giuseppe and San Giorgio; in **Modica**, he designed the magnificent Church of San Giorgio with its distinctive slender bell tower.

The most evocative Sicilian Baroque villas are to be found at **Bagheria**, a few kilometres from Palermo. One of the most remarkable of these refined residential buildings, endowed with luxuriously furnished halls and gardens populated with statuary, is the Villa Palagonia which is famous for its wildly extravagant interior decoration. The villa became a symbol of the absurd, renowned throughout Europe during the Age of Enlightenment, long before Goethe's famous visit in 1787 *(see BAGHERIA)*.

Sculpture and applied decoration – Baroque sculpture and decoration is characterised by rich ornamentation. Altarpieces are provided with carved marble panels and contained among twisted columns; cornices and pediments are crested with figures of angels. Ranking high among his many fellow artist-craftsmen, **Giacomo Serpotta** (1652-1732) excelled at using marble, stucco and polychrome decoration. After training in Rome, Serpotta returned to his home town Palermo to work on an equestrian statue of Charles II of Spain before embarking on a long career there as a decorator specialising in stucco. The Oratory of San Lorenzo, the Oratory of Santa Cita and the Oratory of the Rosary at San Domenico are encrusted throughout with figures and swirling curlicues in bold relief, executed with an exquisite attention to detail. The other church interiors on which Serpotta worked include La Gancia, and Il Carmine; later in life, he was engaged on the decoration of the Church of San Francesco d'Assisi and that of Sant'Agostino (with pupils) which contains a number of narrative panels in shallow relief that illustrate a rare degree of virtuosity. While Serpotta is regarded as the greatest exponent of Sicilian Baroque sculpture, he is also considered to be a precursor of the characteristic forms of Rococo.

Baroque painting – Baroque painters were predominantly engaged in experimenting with perspective and trompe l'oeil, constructing complex compositions on diagonal axes around swirling gestures. Their most common forms of subject matter were narrative scenes from the Bible or mythology. The most representative adherent of this movement was **Caravaggio**. Michelangelo Merisi (1573-1610), known as Caravaggio after the town where he was born near Bergamo, began his career in Rome alongside Cavaliere d'Arpino in 1588. Implicated in various incidents provoked by his tempestuous temperament, Caravaggio was forced to flee the city in 1605, making for Naples, Malta and then Sicily. Venturing to the extremes of every artistic convention, Caravaggio perfected a highly personal style using low-life figures to animate his pictures and heightening the dramatic element of the narrative with bold contrasts of light and shadow, the technique known as "chiaroscuro". In the course of his visit to Sicily, he executed a number of important works, notably the Burial of St Lucy (1609, in Palazzo Bellomo in Siracusa), The Adoration of the Shepherds and The Resurrection of Lazarus (in the museum in Messina). These paintings fired the imagination of many subsequent artists, namely Alfonso Rodriguez (1578-1648) and **Pietro Novelli** (1603-47). Novelli was also influenced by the Dutch painter **Anthony Van Dyck** who, during a sojourn in Palermo in 1624, painted The Madonna of the Rosary for the oratory in the Church of San Domenico.

18C to the present day

Neo-Classicism – The Classical revival started in the mid-18C and was succoured by the reigning passion for Ancient Greek and Roman architecture following the discovery and archaeological excavation of Herculaneum, Pompeii and

San Giorgio di Modica

G. Biudzin/MICHELIN

Paestum. In the graphic arts, this movement was translated into depictions of Romantic ruins and topographical views that met with great success. One of the most successful of the neo-Classical sculptors was **Ignazio Marabitti** (Palermo 1719-97) who trained in Rome under Filippo della Valle. Works by this artist include the altarpiece of St Ignatius commissioned for the Church of Sant'Agata al Collegio in Caltanissetta. In Palermo, the native-born **Venanzio Marvuglia** (1729-1814) met with moderate success: a pupil of Vanvitelli in Rome, he was responsible for enlarging the Church of San Martino delle Scale, the Oratory of Sant'Ignazio dell'Olivella (Palermo) and the villa for the Prince of Belmonte. Marvuglia's predominantly Classical style is sometimes touched with the exotic, as the Chinese pavilion in the park of La Favorita in Palermo testifies.

Naturalism – Although sharing with many other contemporary Italian artists a keenness to portray reality, the sculptor **Domenico Trentacoste** (born Palermo 1859, died Florence 1933) still cannot be regarded as a true exponent of Naturalism. Fascinated first by 15C exponents, Trentacoste then turned to the Naturalism of Rodin, whom he encountered in Paris in around 1880, before gradually directing his interest to popular painting, mythological subjects, portraiture and nude painting (*Little Faun* in the Galleria E. Restivo in Palermo).

Ettore Ximenes (born Palermo 1855, died Rome 1926) trained first in Palermo then in Naples under Domenico Morelli.

Stile Liberty – The Art Nouveau style appeared in Italy at the turn of the 20C by which time it was well established in the rest of Europe. Its main impact was on the decorative arts; its most distinctive feature, the serpentine line, insinuated itself into figurative depictions, wrought-iron work, and furniture. Its best exponent in Sicily is the architect **Ernesto Basile** (born Palermo, 1857-1932), son of **Giovanni Basile** (designer of the Teatro Massimo in Palermo), who turned to the Art Nouveau style after studying forms of Arabo-Norman and Renaissance design. Examples of his work from this period include the decoration of Villa Igiea (now a hotel), notably the wonderful floral decoration of the dining room, Caffè Ferraglia in Rome, and various villas in Palermo such as Villino Florio *(see p 302)*. He also worked on designing soft furnishings, fabrics and furniture.

The **Villa Malfitano** in Palermo, once owned by the Whitakers, a prominent English family, epitomises the success and effectiveness of the Stile Liberty in Sicily.

Contemporary art – Although Sicily has not given rise to an international movement, it can claim to have nurtured several interesting personalities.

The painter **Fausto Pirandello** (1889-1975), the son of the famous writer, was mainly interested in Cubist painting (Braque in particular) before later finding a balance between the abstract and figurative.

The neo-Realist painter **Renato Guttuso** (1912-87) studied classics in Palermo before moving to Rome and then Milan. There he affirmed his political position as clearly anti-Fascist. During these years he turned to Realist art. His paintings are characterised by a perspective which has been flattened and by form that has been refracted into geometric shapes in a way that is reminiscent of Picasso, yet his choice of subject always reflects his social predicament. From 1958 onwards, Guttuso was influenced by Expressionism. The result is a new painting style: the realism that pervaded his subject matter is now imbued with emotion, movement is suggested by the use of strong colour and boldly decisive line.

Among the contemporary Sicilian artists, mention should be made of various sculptors. **Pietro Consagra**, who comes from Mazara del Vallo (b 1920), studied in Palermo before going to Rome where he came into contact with abstract art. His works show how he experiments with different materials, how he hones down the thickness of material to produce the finest end result.

The sculptor **Emilio Greco** (b Catania 1913, d Rome 1995) centred his work on Classical form, ever in quest of that elusive harmony and equilibrium, drawing his inspiration from Greek, Etruscan, Roman and Renaissance art. One of his favourite subjects was the female body; other concepts and ideas explored are associated with religion (the bronze doors of Orvieto Cathedral and the monument to Pope John XXIII for St Peter's in Rome).

Finally, **Salvatore Fiume** (1915-97), also known as Giocondo, was active in various media including sculpture, film and painting. His paintings, which reflect a diverse source of inspiration, range from ideal depictions of nature to flat portrayals of real and everyday life (depictions of women in a market). Pertinent influences evident in his work include the various cultures and civilisations that history has imprinted on Sicily. In later life, Fiume also devoted himself to religious art, undertaking the illustration of biblical texts for the Catholic publisher Edizioni Paoline.

The Grand Tour

Without Sicily, Italy leaves no image in the soul: it is the key to everything.

Italian Journey, JW von Goethe

It was during the reign of the English Queen Elizabeth I (1533-1603) that the concept of a "Grand Tour" of the Continent first became popular. The medieval style pilgrimages that were undertaken by noblemen had been decried by the likes of Erasmus. Now, excursions were to be undertaken for education and pleasure *(utilitas et verits)*: Venice, Milan, Verona, Florence and Rome, of course, were the compulsory ports of call; but after Elizabeth I's excommunication and aggressive actions against Spain, Protestant travellers would have been wary of journeying south to Naples and Sicily, then under the dominion of the Spaniards and their Catholic Inquisition. Slowly the Papacy endeavoured to woo the English. Aristocrats sojourned at leisure in Italy; Inigo Jones (1573-1652) reported on the delights of Classical and Palladian architecture. Finally, after the Restoration (1660) of Charles II, the frontiers were opened once more.

The **Age of Sensibility** exalted Italy as the cradle of civilisation. Instructive journeys were therefore undertaken by young intellectuals to complete their education. This involved travelling to the Continent, visiting places and cities endowed with a rich artistic heritage and cultural fervour, and coming into contact with everything that might enrich a man's spirit and intellect. Richard Boyle, then Lord Burlington (1684-1753), and Robert Adam (1728-92) followed in the wake of Jones to study the original Antique monuments.

As the **Age of Reason** dawned, still Rome and its academic institutions attracted ambitious young artists to study, muse and acquaint themselves with life without responsibility. After the Seven Years War (1756-63) the Grand Tour became institutionalised: now not only the British **(Sir William Hamilton**, **Gavin Hamilton**, **Benjamin West)** came, but also the French, the Germans and the Dutch. Visitors extended their tours to Naples and the south following the exciting discovery and excavation of Pompeii (1740s) and the neighbouring Herculaneum (1750s). This provided a genuine and "scientific" view of Roman life buried intact beneath layers of volcanic debris since the eruption of Vesuvius in AD 79, as had been described by Pliny the Younger. Scholars and tourists alike extended their travels to take in Paestum (documented by two other Englishmen, **John Berkenhout** and **Thomas Major**, in 1767-68). Beforc long, Sicily was also included in the itinerary. But these discoveries not only encouraged interest in things Roman relevant to neo-Classicism and the Greek Revival, they also precipitated an ever greater fascination for the latent power of volcanoes. This is encapsulated by Sir William Hamilton (Plenipotentiary at the Court of Naples 1764-1800) in his book *Observations on Mount Vesuvius, Mount Etna and other Volcanos* (1773).

Napoleon's invasion of Italy (1796) interrupted all forms of travel across the Continent, and when peace was restored the grandness of the tours evaporated. After 1815, Thomas Cook began operating his package tours; foreign visitors urged the Italians to rise up against their Austrian occupiers; yet all the while, Italy provided a safe haven for those fleeing trouble at home, most especially those young and of a Romantic disposition (Byron, Shelley, Browning).

Englishmen abroad

The first English traveller to compile a journal of his travels abroad is Sir **Thomas Hoby** (1530-66) who set out from England in June 1549 and travelled to Padua, Florence, Rome, Naples, Calabria and Sicily.

Taormina 1876 *by WJ Ferguson (1849-86), private collection*

John Dryden junior travelled in the Mediterranean in the early 18C (*A Voyage to Sicily and Malta* was published in 1776). In 1770, the Scotsman **Patrick Brydone** visited the island: his impressions are contained in the entertaining letters that form his *Journey to Sicily and Malta* (published 1773), which library records prove to be the most popular book of the late 18C. The first thing that strikes him is the port of Messina, a harbour enclosed by a sickle-shaped tongue of land protecting it from all the winds. Here reality combines immediately with myth, in which the terrible monsters of Scylla and Charybdis lurk in the underground caves on either side of the Straits of Messina. The luxuriant vegetation also catches the traveller's eye, alongside the more everyday crops of vines, olives and wheat, which alternate with flowers, bushes and prickly pears. Ever present in the background stands the menacing form of Etna, smouldering benignly – the ultimate "curiousity" in this southern region. Then Taormina, and the first leap into the Classical past, and Etna looms up again, a sleeping giant, but ever vigilant and ready to prove its great power: *"in the centre...we could just see the summit of the mountain raising its proud head, vomiting clouds of smoke"*.
For travellers, Etna acts as a powerful magnet: the very antithesis of the peace and serenity of the past inspired by the Greek ruins of Girgenti (Agrigento). It symbolised life in the form of fire and heat, an uncontrollable, unpredictable phenomenon. The fact that it is visible from a long way off seems almost to endow it with the inevitability of something that man cannot control, like life and death. Brydone journeys on towards the larger towns on the island: Catania, Siracusa and the *"beautiful, elegant"* Palermo, to which pages and pages of description are devoted.
In Brydone's footsteps followed **Henry Swinburne**, urged on by the other writer's *"lies"* and *"nonsensical froth"*; he published his travels in four volumes entitled *Travels in the Two Sicilies in the Years 1777, 1778, 1779 and 1780*. These, along with the Brydone account, were soon translated into French and German. **Johann Wolfgang von Goethe** (1749-1832) used Brydone and JH Von Riedesel's *Reise* (1771) when he undertook his Italian journey, writing his own *Italienische Reise* (1786-88).
As descriptions were penned, draughtsmen and painters flocked to the island eager to depict the natural landscape, the topography of the cities and views, the ruins and the people. Towards the end of the century, Sicily became the key destination for anyone undertaking the Grand Tour: it was the gateway of things Classical, but also a natural treasure trove of rare features that could not be found elsewhere.

Travelling diary

The diary was the traveller's faithful companion. In it he would transcribe his impressions, musings, pleasures and discomforts (Goethe's descriptions of seasickness, for example) in an informal letter to himself or a close friend. What is remarkable is how perceptive these observations are, touching upon technical and scientific details, curious facts, encounters, and images of a Sicily that has changed profoundly since. Yet the portraits of the Sicilians, their kindness and hospitality are true for all time.

Literature

Sicilian literature has evolved in a curious way: nowhere has dialect been used as a literary language for such a long time and in such an uncompromising way as on this island. This is so much the case that it has given rise to two linguistically different parallel streams, often present in the same author: one form being written in Italian, the other in the Sicilian dialect.

The Sicilian School of Poetry's golden age came to an end with the decline of the Magna Curia of Frederick II *(see p 310)*. During the 14C-15C, poetry was modelled on Tuscan literature; then it gradually faded, overshadowed by a more popular genre in local dialect.

Humanism and the Renaissance

The discovery of Classical texts, in particular the understanding of Ancient Greek which underpinned the emergence of Humanism, resounded strongly in Sicily. Noto, Palermo, Siracusa, Catania and Messina became leading cultural centres, with Messina instituting a school for Greek which achieved international acclaim largely thanks to the teachings of **Costantino Lascaris**.

The 16C saw a resurgence in the use of Sicilian: this period also saw the consolidation of local patriotism and pride, marked by the publication of the first Sicilian-Latin dictionaries and grammar primer for the regional dialect.

17C-18C

In keeping with the general mood of the Baroque, the 17C witnessed an upsurge of interest and development in the theatre, largely generated by the tragedies of **Ortensio Scammacca** and by comedies written both in Italian and in dialect.

In the course of the 18C, the Age of Enlightenment made its presence felt in Sicily, as expressed in the *History of Sicily* written by the abbot **G Battista Caruso** (1673-1724) and the *History of Sicilian Literature* edited by **Antonio Mongitore** (1663-1743). Philosophical reflection inspired various other literary genres: Cartesian thought was voiced by **Tommaso Campailla** (1668-1740), who wrote a philosophical poem entitled *Adamo, ovvero il mondo é creato* (Adam, or How the World was Created); Leibniz meanwhile was exalted by **Tommaso Natale** in his work *La filosofia Leibniziana (The Philosophy of Leibniz)*. The precepts of Rousseau on the Noble Savage and the relationship between morality and the environment were promoted in poetry by the greatest poet of the century, **Giovanni Meli** (1740-1815), in his bucolic contemplations *La bucolica* and philosophical satires clearly influenced by the Enlightenment *L'origini du lu munnu, Don Chisciotti e Sanciu Panza*.

19C

Romanticism encouraged the writing of lengthy histories and research into the origins of regional culture and tradition: Michele Amari (1806-89) initiated a new period of history criticism with his *La guerra del Vespro siciliano (War of the Sicilian Vespers)* and *Storia dei Musulmani di Sicilia (History of the Muslims in Sicily)*, while Giuseppe Pitré (1841-1916) can claim the merit for having begun to study folklore, and in so doing, raising the life and traditions of the Sicilian people to a level worthy of historical consideration *(see p 73)*.

Realism was formulated as a reaction to Romanticism. It advocated that inspiration for art should come from the concrete reality of the natural world, and became widespread in Sicily towards the close of the 19C. Early foundations were laid by the Positivist poetry of **Mario Rapisardi** (1844-1912); reinforcements came from the accomplished theorist **Luigi Capuana** (1839-1915), according to whom a work of art should embrace a sense of real life and examine the contemporary world and the laws of nature so as to document human life. His masterpieces – *Giacinta* and *Il Marchese di Roccaverdina* – reflect these values; furthermore they portray reality in an impersonal way. Even **Giovanni Verga** (1830-1922), after the late-Romantic tone of his earliest

Luigi Pirandello

work, shows a move towards Realist poetry. His masterpiece – *I Malavoglia* – intended as the first part of a cycle of novels entitled *I vinti (The Conquered)*, was followed by just one sequel *(Mastro Don Gesualdo)*. The main theme of the work by Verga concentrates on the description of the real Sicily, with the destiny of the humble folk portrayed objectively yet compassionately. He uses a sombre writing style and a language which, when compared to the Italian mainstream, succeeds in mimicking the cadences and rhythms of the spoken vernacular. Other adherents of the Realist School include **Federico de Roberto** (1861-1927) – author of *I Viceré (The Viceroys)* and *L'Illusione (The illusion)* – and the poets **Giuseppe Aurelio Costanzo** (1843-1913) and **Giovanni Alfredo Cesareo** (1861-1937).

20C

Modern Italian literature is indebted to Sicily for one of its greatest protagonists: the 1934 Nobel Prize winner **Luigi Pirandello** (1867-1946). His early work as a poet and novelist lies in the Realist vein. Later works explore the theme of isolation, painting the individual at sea in a society that is foreign to him *(Il fu Mattia Pascal, Novelle per un anno)*. Pirandello's portrait of this human condition relative to a person's environment found its most poignant expression on the stage; there he experimented with form and content. Pirandello's masterpieces include *Liolà, Pensaci Giacomino! (Think about it, Giacomino), Così é (se vi pare) – That's How It Is (If You Like)* and *Sei personaggi in cerca di autore (Six Characters in Search of an Author)*.

Another figure that is central to the history of Italian culture is the philosopher **Giovanni Gentile** (1875-1944) who, as Minister for Education in the Fascist government, promoted the reform of the Italian education system. On the opposing political front, **Concetto Marchesi** (1878-1957) published studies on the history of Latin literature which are still regarded as classics today.

The decadence of the Sicilian aristocracy during the Risorgimento is poignantly, if bitterly, portrayed in *Il Gattopardo (The Leopard)*, the novel by Prince **Giuseppe Tomasi di Lampedusa** (1896-1957), published posthumously. The satirical and grotesque storyteller **Vitaliano Brancati** attacked myths of eroticism and sexual conceit in his novels (*Don Giovanni in Sicilia, Il bell'Antonio* and *Paolo il Caldo*). **Elio Vittorini** (1908-66) played a fundamental role in spreading awareness of contemporary American literature and in revitalising the Italian narrative tradition in the neo-Realist convention *(Conversazione in Sicilia, Uomini e no)*. The rough-and-ready style more often associated with police enquiries animates the novels of **Leonardo Sciascia** (1921-89), which include *Il giorno della civetta (The Day of the Owl), Todo modo,* and *Candido ovvero un sogno fatto in Sicilia (Candido, or a Sicilian Dream)*. **Gesualdo Bufalino** (1920-96) is a literary personality in his own right: having emerged at the age of 60 with the Baroque and Expressionist *Diceria dell'untore*, he was immediately acclaimed by critics and the public alike following the publication of his books of prose, poetry, memoirs and criticism *(Argo il cieco, Il Guerrin Meschino)*. The baroque prose of **Vincenzo Consolo** (b 1933) is full of precise reflections on history. The detective novels of **Andrea Camilleri** (1925), based on the fictitious character of police superintendent Montalbano, have enjoyed great success both in Italy and abroad; Camilleri's novels are infused with a strong Sicilian atmosphere and characterised by the use of extremely original language which uses Sicilian expressions and vocabulary and is very musical in tone.

As far as poetry is concerned, **Salvatore Quasimodo** (1901-68), awarded the Nobel Prize for Literature in 1959, occupies a position of prime importance: his later work sought to draw attention to political and social issues *(Ed é subito sera, La terra impareggiabile, Dare e avere)*. Less well known, but nevertheless of interest, is the metaphorical poetry of **Lucio Piccolo** (1903-69), cousin of Tomasi di Lampedusa and author of *Canti Barocchi and Plumelia*. A great sense of social commitment is voiced in the poetry of **Ignazio Buttitta** (1899-1997), who demonstrated once again that dialect was the best vehicle for expressing the thoughts and emotions of the Sicilian people *(Lu pani si chiama pani, La peddi nova)*.

Cinema

Many famous directors have attempted to create a portrait of Sicily on film. This complex, stunningly beautiful island is a land of contradictions, inhabited by a proud, hospitable people who, despite a certain reserve, are happy to extend warmth and generosity in equal measure, and where the conspiracy of silence known as "omertà" exists alongside an equally ardent will to fight this silence. Transcribing all these characteristic traits into art is no simple task.

Philippe Noiret and Massimo Troisi in "Il postino" ("The postman")

The first great masterpieces were based on the classics: **Luchino Visconti** turned to Verga to make such films as **La Terra Trema** *(The Ground Trembles)* in 1948 based on his book *I Malavoglia*, and to Tomasi di Lampedusa for **Il Gattopardo** *(The Leopard)* in 1963 from the book of the same name. His determination to capture reality in all its different guises, while peppering it with the local colour and poetry that such a major artistic undertaking demands, prompted Visconti firstly to select his main cast from among amateur actors living in a typical community such as Aci Trezza who spoke in dialect. Secondly, he chose a historical epic that was respected and established in its own right, set in the magnificent, yet already decadent Palermo of the late 19C, illuminated by the sparkling performances of Claudia Cardinale, Burt Lancaster, and Alain Delon.

In the same vein, the sad and agonising story related in **Stromboli terra di Dio** (1949), depicts a strong portrait of a woman filmed against a background of untamed nature, directed by **Roberto Rossellini** and starring Ingrid Bergmann.

Films about the Mafia are a case apart. Since the making of the film-cum-denunciations – **In nome della legge** *(In the Name of the Law)* directed by Pietro Germi (1949) and **Salvatore Giuliano** directed by Francesco Rosi (1961) – the subject matter and circumstances were quickly exploited and transformed into a genre of its own, which for Italian viewers compares well with the popular Spaghetti Western elsewhere. This in turn generated a veritable industry of Mafia family epics with the inevitable shoot-outs, clashes, and use of broad Sicilian dialect. These films were distributed all over the world, giving a somewhat negative impression of Sicily. However, also belonging to this genre are films of social importance, such as **I cento passi** *(One hundred steps)* directed by Tullio Giordana (best screenplay in the 2000

"The Leopard" by Visconti

Cat's Collection

Venice Film Festival), which skilfully recounts the story of the journalist Peppino Impastato, who was killed in 1978 after many years fighting the Mafia.
A very different Sicily is also shown on the cinema screen: a Sicily that is mournful but veined with humour emerges in the magnificent tales retold in **Kaos** *(Chaos)*, made in 1984 by the **Taviani brothers**, based on novels by Pirandello (brilliant performances by Franco Franchi and Ciccio Ingrassia in *La Giara*). A poetic view of Sicily is portrayed in Michael Radford's **Il Postino** *(The Postman)* made in 1994 and starring Massimo Troisi, and in Giuseppe Tornatore's **Nuovo Cinema Paradiso** (1989), which received an Oscar for Best Foreign Film in 1990.

Other films set in Sicily

L'Avventura by Michelangelo Antonioni (1960).
Divorzio all'italiana by Pietro Germi (1962). A superb performance by Marcello Mastroianni in a film which met with international acclaim.
Il Mafioso by Alberto Lattuada (1962). A story of great cruelty, starring a masterful Alberto Sordi.
A ciascuno il suo by Elio Petri (1967). Based on Sciascia's novel of the same name, this film tells the story of an academic captured by the Mafia.
Il giorno della civetta by Damiano Damiani (1968). Based on Sciascia's novel of the same name.
The Godfather by Francis Ford Coppola (1972). The first of the famous trilogy.
Cadaveri eccellenti by Francesco Rosi (1976). Obscure political plots are uncovered in this film.
Il prefetto di ferro by Pasquale Squitieri (1977). The story of Chief Inspector Mori, based on Petacco's novel of the same name.
Il siciliano by Michael Cimino (1987). The story of the bandit Giuliano, based on Mario Puzo's novel.
Mery per sempre by Marco Risi (1989), set in Palermo Prison, and its sequel *Ragazzi fuori* (1990).
Dimenticare Palermo by Francesco Rosi (1990). A New York mayoral candidate is kidnapped by the Mafia during a visit to Palermo.
Porte aperte by Gianni Amelio (1990). Based on a novel by Sciascia and inspired by a real-life event, this film explores the themes of crime and punishment.
Johnny Stecchino by Roberto Benigni (1991). Comedy about a naïve bus driver mistaken for a Mafia boss.
Il giudice ragazzino by Alessandro di Robiland (1993). The last days of the Assistant Public Prosecutor Livatino, killed by the Mafia in 1990.
Lo zio di Brooklyn by Ciprì and Maresco (1995). The first feature film by these two controversial directors, set in the Palermo suburbs.
La lupa by Gabriele Lavia (1997). Based on the play by Verga.
La fame e la sete by Antonio Albanese (1999). Triplets are reunited at their father's funeral.
Sicilia! by Danièle Huillet and Jean-Marie Straub (1999). Based on *Conversazione in Sicilia* by Elio Vittorini, this black-and-white film relates the story of a man who returns to Sicily in search of his childhood.
I giudici by Ricky Tognazzi (1999). The story of Giovanni Falcone and Paolo Borsellino.
Malèna by Giuseppe Tornatore (2000). A young boy in provincial Sicily falls in love with the enticing Monica Bellucci at the beginning of the Second World War.
Placido Rizzotto by Pasquale Scimeca (2000). Another Mafia film, telling the story of the trade unionist Placido Rizzotto, killed in Corleone in 1948.
Prime luci dell'alba by Lucio Gaudino (2000). Family problems force the main character of this film to examine his beliefs, behaviour and relationship with Sicily.
Angela by Roberta Torre (2002). An intense, passionate film, quite unlike the early work of this director, which examines the life of a woman in the Mafia.

Caccamo

B. Kaufmann/MICHELIN

Selected Sights

Acireale

This elegant and lively Baroque town is centred around Piazza Duomo, a delightful square dotted with numerous cafés and "gelaterie" serving the excellent ice cream for which Acireale is justifiably famous. Renowned since Antiquity for its sulphurous waters, the town is better known nowadays for its Carnival, characterised by processions of allegorical floats, masked revellers and dances in the piazza.

Location

Population: 51 838. Michelin map 565 O 27 – Catania. Acireale is accessible via the A 18 motorway (Acireale exit) or along S 114 coast road. The historic centre and Piazza Duomo are clearly signposted. A number of car parks (fee) are located around Piazza Duomo. Corso Umberto 179; ☎ 095 60 45 21; www.acirealeturismo.it

Neighbouring sights are described in the following chapters: CATANIA; ETNA; GIARDINI NAXOS; TAORMINA.

Background

Acis and Galatea – The sea nymph Galatea, daughter of Nereus, fell in love with the shepherd Acis, son of the god Pan. Unfortunately, she also caught the eye of Polyphemus, the gigantic Cyclops and arch enemy of Odysseus (Ulysses). As the nymph continued to reject him, so his jealousy and hatred were aroused, until finally the monstrous creature from the caves of Mount Etna set out to kill the young shepherd boy. Zeus, moved to pity by the pain suffered by the young nereid, transformed her lover into a river (the modern Akis) which, by flowing towards the sea, the realm from where Galatea had come, enabled the two lovers to be together for ever more.

A popular legend tells of how the dismembered body of Acis became separated into nine parts and was scattered in areas which later became known as the nine Aci: Aci Bonaccorsi, Aci Castello, Aci Catena, Aci Platani, Acireale, Aci San Filippo, Aci Sant'Antonio, Aci Santa Lucia and Aci Trezza.

This particular stretch of coastline is also known as the **Riviera dei Ciclopi** (Cyclops' Coast).

Walking About

The main hub of the town is Piazza Duomo, from which emanates the principal artery – Corso Umberto I to the north and Via Settimo, then Via Vittorio Emanuele to the south – lined by fine buildings, shops and *gelaterie.*

Directory

Taking a Break

Local delicacies can be enjoyed at any of the pastry shops and ice cream parlours in the town centre. Specialities include simple or combined-flavour crushed ice drinks known as *granite* (try the coffee and almond flavour), often accompanied by a brioche; almond milk; and ice cream served with cream, fresh or dried fruit, or melted chocolate. If you want the perfect reminder of Sicily, buy a packet of almond paste to take home.

Festivals

Festa di San Sebastiano – On 20 January, St Sebastian's float is taken out of the church dedicated to him and carried through the streets of the small town.

Carnevale – This is one of the most famous carnivals in Sicily, with a magnificent parade of brightly coloured floats.

Puppet Theatre

Acireale is renowned for its puppets, which are slightly smaller and lighter than those made in Catania *(see p 58)*. The Acireale puppet tradition is kept alive by two companies: the **Centro Servizi Spettacoli E. Macrì** *(Via Galatea 89; ☎ 095 60 62 72)* and **Turi Grasso**. The latter runs the **Museo dei Pupi dell'Opra** *(Via Nazionale per Catania 193-195, Capomulini)* which displays a collection of traditional puppets typical of the Aci area. These illustrate the high skill and craftsmanship involved in the making of the figures, the intricacy of their costumes and the individuality of the different painted faces. The museum also has a small theatre. (♿) *Open summer, Wed, Sat-Sun and public hols, 9am-noon and 5-8pm; otherwise Wed, Sat-Sun and public hols, 9am-noon and 3-6pm. €2.50. ☎ 095 76 48 035. For information on shows, contact the museum.*

Piazza Duomo★★

At one time the piazza was called Piazza del Cinque d'Oro (Square of the Golden Five), a reference to playing cards reflecting the arrangement of a platform surrounded by four small flower-beds that occupied the square. It was here that musical and theatrical events were performed at one time. The finely proportioned open space is enclosed by Baroque buildings: the **Duomo**, the **Basilica dei Santi Pietro e Paolo** (17C-18C) with its fine façade marked by a single campanile, and the **Palazzo Comunale** (1659) graced with elegant wrought-iron **balconies**★ supported on richly decorated brackets bearing masks and gargoyles. Slightly back, at the beginning of Via Davì, sits the 17C **Palazzo Modò** which has two splendid balconies with brackets again decorated with grotesques; the façade still bears the name of the theatre, the Eldorado, that occupied the premises in the early 20C, crowned with a large mask.

Ice cream

The invention of sherbet, a mixture of fruit pulp, honey and snow, is often attributed to the Chinese; the recipe was introduced to the West by the Arabs and so to Sicily, an important Arab stronghold in the Mediterranean, where it has been known since Antiquity.
Indeed, the name sherbet or sorbet is derived from the Arabic ***sharba*** or ***sciarbat*** (a cold drink concocted from snow flavoured with essences). Furthermore, an 11C tract on Arab cuisine has a section devoted to ice cream. Nowadays, Sicily is particularly associated with a number of ice cream varieties: notably home-made *tartufo*, which consists of a chocolate ball concealing a cream core; ***brioches*** (the classic round type) filled with ice cream; ***cassata*** (the kind made during the summer with ***ricotta*** cheese, a typical Sicilian sweet) and the two-flavoured ***mattonella*** (ice brick).

Duomo

The cathedral is dedicated to the Annunciation and Santa Venera. Its two-tone neo-Gothic façade was designed by GBF Basile (1825-91), the architect of the Teatro Massimo in Palermo and father of the more famous Ernesto Basile, master of the Liberty style. Standing between two campanili with majolica spires, the front is ornamented by a fine 17C portal. Inside, the most interesting feature is between the transept and the chancel, frescoed by P Vasta. The right transept, its floor dominated by a 19C sundial by W Sertorius and F Peters, harbours the Baroque chapel of Santa Venera.

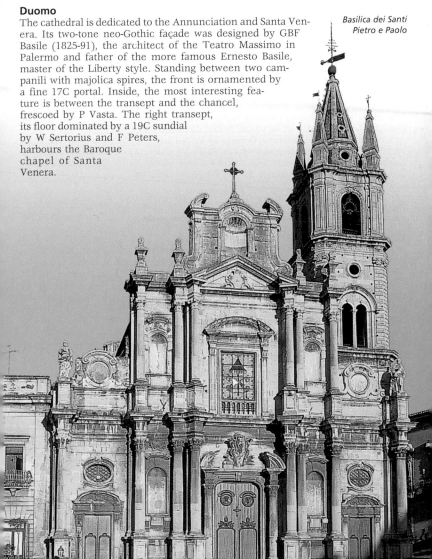

Basilica dei Santi Pietro e Paolo

From Piazza Duomo take Via Settimo, then Via Vittorio Emanuele.

Basilica di San Sebastiano

A statue-topped balustrade crowns the **Baroque façade★**, which consists of a harmonious combination of columns, pilasters, niches and volutes, drawn together within a frieze of angels bearing a continuous garland at the first cornice level. Inside, the transept and chancel contain frescoes by P Vasta depicting episodes from the life of St Sebastian, the patron saint of the town to whom the church is dedicated.

From Piazza Duomo take Via Cavour (in front of the square).

Piazza San Domenico

The fine Baroque façade of **San Domenico** dominates one side of the tiny piazza which is also overlooked by **Palazzo Musmeci** (17C) with its elegant wrought-iron balconies and Rococo windows.

A little further on, along the road on the right when facing San Domenico, is the **Biblioteca Zelantea**, the town library, annexed with an **art gallery**. Here reside the plaster model for the statue of Acis and Galatea (now in the gardens of the Villa Comunale) by Rosario Anastasi, and the bust of **Julius Caesar** known as the Busto di Acireale (1C BC). Closed for restoration at the time of going to press. For information, call ☎ 095 76 34 516.

From Piazza Duomo continue to the end of Corso Umberto I.

Villa Belvedere

The lovely, peaceful gardens, complete with a panoramic terrace, provide a magnificent **view★** of Mount Etna and the sea. It is here that the statue of **Acis and Galatea** is to be found. The platform at the entrance, on the left, is a reproduction of the one that used to ornament Piazza Duomo.

Terme di Santa Venera

To the south of the town, entrance off S 114. The neo-Classical baths complex dates back to 1873, built at the request of Baron Agostino Pennisi di Floristella (whose castle can still be seen behind the baths, near the old railway station). Acireale quickly became a renowned spa town, whose visitors included Wagner and the royal family. The baths of Santa Caterina, which opened in 1987, are known for their radioactive, sulphurous water with traces of sodium bromide – these waters are used in combination with volcanic clay for mud therapy treatments.

The baths are fed with sulphurous water which is channelled from a spring about 3km/2mi inland, south of Acireale, in the district of Reitana. There, the remains of the **Roman Baths of Santa Venera al Pozzo** have been discovered: including two barrel-vaulted rooms which are presumed to have served as **tepidarium** and **caldarium**. *Open daily except Sun and public hols, 9am-noon by appointment (at least two days in advance). No charge. ☎ 095 60 12 50; www.terme.acireale.gte.it*

Excursions

Grotta del Presepe di Santa Maria della Neve

From S 114 to Messina, turn right at the traffic lights by the Villa Belvedere towards Santa Maria la Scala. The church of Santa Maria della Neve is immediately on your left. Open Sun, 9am-noon. For information, call ☎ 095 60 56 33.

The Grotto of the Crib, adjacent to the church, is a winding lava ravine which, until the 18C, was used as a refuge by bandits and fishermen, before being transformed to represent the cave of the Nativity at Bethlehem. In 1752, a crib was arranged here comprising 32 life-size figures with wax faces, dressed in sumptuous clothes (most especially the Magi).

Follow the same road as far as the coast.

Santa Maria della Scala

This picturesque village overlooking the sea, which grew up around the 17C parish church, has an attractive little harbour.

Tour

OTHER ACI IN THE AREA

Approximately 15km/9mi.

Aci Catena

Aci Catena, along with Aci San Filippo, is almost a natural extension of Acireale. The little town, which owes its name to the cult of the *Madonna della Catena* (Madonna of the Chain), centres on the charming square, Piano Umberto, on which stands the attractive late-19C and early-20C town hall and a number of other noble residences. Similar *palazzi* grace the neighbouring Via IV Novembre and Via Matrice where the 18C church and Palazzo Riggio (adjacent), sadly now in ruins, are to be found.

B. Kaufmann/MICHELIN

The harbour, Aci Trezza

Aci San Filippo

At the heart of the little town stands the church, ornamented with a fine 18C façade and, to one side, a campanile with a stone lava base.

From Aci San Filippo return to S 114 and continue towards Catania.

Aci Trezza

This small fishing town is dominated, on the seaward side, by the **Rocks of the Cyclops★** (Faraglioni dei Ciclopi), a treacherous pointed mass of black lava rising up from the crystal-clear waters. The Odyssey relates that these were the rocks hurled by Polyphemus against Ulysses, who had blinded him by thrusting a flaming stake into his only eye; the hero then escaped with his companions by clinging to the bellies of rams belonging to the Cyclops.

Next to these rocks sits the **island of Lachea**, now a biology research station run by the University of Catania.

Continue along S 114.

Aci Castello

This small seaside town is situated on a stretch of coastline dotted with lemon trees (hence the name **Riviera dei Limoni**, as the Riviera dei Ciclopi is also known), agaves and palm trees.

Castle★ – The Norman fortress, built of black lava, stands tall on a rocky spur surrounded by sea, a striking landmark even from the road. This place has been fortified since Roman times when it accommodated the Rocca Saturnia (Saturnia Fortress). Under the Bourbons (1787), the castle was used as a prison.

From the top there is a marvellous **view★** of the **Faraglioni dei Ciclopi** and the island of **Lachea**. The castle houses a small **museum** with an educational slant, containing mineral specimens and archaeological artefacts. *Open May-Sep, 9am-1pm and 4.30-8pm; Oct-Apr, 9am-1pm and 3-5pm.*

Giovanni Verga

The little harbour of Aci Trezza, bathed in sunshine and dotted with multicoloured boats hauled up onto the beach, seems inhabited by the ghosts of fictitious characters created by the Italian author Verga. How easy to imagine Maruzzi and the other members of the Malavoglia family waiting here anxiously on the shore, ceaselessly searching the horizon, alas in vain, for the *Provvidenza* with its cargo of lupins. How appropriate, therefore, that Aci Trezza should have been used by Luchino Visconti in 1948 to shoot his film *La Terra Trema (The Ground Trembles)*, based as it was on Verga's novel I *Malavoglia*. An organisation based in Aci Trezza organises tours to the **Parco Letterario Giovanni Verga** (a route that links places mentioned in the works of Verga, which winds between Catania, Aci Castello and Aci Trezza), as well as boat trips entitled *"In the footsteps of the Provvidenza" (see p 33).*

Agrigento★★★

As the road winds its way to Agrigento, the almond trees gradually become more numerous. When in flower (January and February), their blossom appears like little clouds of white against the green fields and the bare earth of the hillsides. For visitors approaching Agrigento from the coast, the unattractive sight of unbridled construction suddenly gives way to a glorious view, particularly if arriving at sunset when the houses along the crest of the hill are coloured with pastel hues. The Temple of Heracles dominates the foreground from on high and the rich gold tufa of the town's Ancient remains are magnificently illuminated by the last rays of evening sunlight. *Although Agrigento is best known for its archaeological site, it is also worth exploring the historic city centre, which has a wealth of impressive buildings and monuments.*

Location

Population: 55 446. Michelin map 565 P 22, including a city map. The archaeological site is situated in the lower part of Agrigento, facing the sea, while the modern urban centre is perched on the slope of the hill behind the site, well hidden from the unattractive rash of modern construction. The archaeological area has two car parks: one in the temple area, the other near the archaeological museum. In the city centre, visitors can park in Piazza Vittorio Emanuele, east of the old town, which is crossed by a busy shopping street, Via Atenea. Because of the hot summers in Agrigento, and the many flights of steps in the historical centre, visitors are advised to plan their visits for early morning or late afternoon, when the warm tufa stone takes on an attractive golden hue.

Via Cesare Battisti 15; ☏ 0922 20 454; Fax 0922 20 246 or Viale della Vittoria 255; ☏ 0922 40 13 52; Fax 0922 25 185; www.agrigentoweb.it

Neighbouring sights are described in the following chapters: CALTANISSETTA; GELA; LAMPEDUSA; SCIACCA.

The temple of the Dioscuri

B. Kaufmann/MICHELIN

Background

Story of Akragas – The **site**★★ upon which Agrigento was constructed has been inhabited since prehistoric times, but it was not until about 580 BC that a group of people from Gela, originally from Rhodes and Crete, decided to found Akragas, taking its name from one of the two rivers which confine the city. Under the tyrant **Phalaris** (570-554 BC), the city was fortified and organised politically. It is to him that the ancients attribute the idea of using a hollow bronze bull as an instrument of torture for his enemies. These unfortunate victims were imprisoned in the belly of the animal and roasted alive; the screams of the condemned emanating from the animal were likened to the lowing of a cow. Hated by his people, Phalaris was publicly stoned to death.

Directory

Transport

Visitors arriving by air will land at either Falcone-Borsellino airport in Palermo (approximately 150km/93mi from Agrigento) or at Fontanarossa airport in Catania (approximately 160km/100mi). Bus services operate between Agrigento and the other main cities in Sicily, as well as to Porto Empedocle (the port for ferries to Lampedusa); the bus terminal is situated in Piazza Rosselli. For train enthusiasts, the only enjoyable option is the Palermo-Agrigento service (approx. 2hr). Agrigento Centrale railway station (not to be confused with Agrigento Bassa) is in Piazza Marconi. This square is also the departure point for shuttle buses to the archaeological area and the beaches in San Leone.

Where to Eat

• ***For all budgets***

Kókalos – *Via Cavaleri Magazzeni 3, Agrigento (Valle dei Templi) – ☎ 0922 60 64 27 – www.ristorante-kokalos.com – Booking recommended – €15/40.* This rustic restaurant, ideally placed for the archaeological site, serves pizzas and typical regional dishes. It also has a well-stocked wine bar.

Leon d'Oro – *Via Emporium 102, San Leone – 7km/4mi S of Agrigento – ☎ 0922 41 44 00 – Closed Mon – – €20/33 + 15% service.* Situated in the seaside resort of San Leone, this renowned family-run restaurant also has an excellent wine list, as one of the owners is a professional sommelier. Local dishes and fresh fish are served in two warmly decorated rooms.

Trattoria dei Templi – *Via Panoramica dei Templi 15, Agrigento – ☎ 0922 40 31 10 – Closed Sun (Jul-Aug), Fri (Sep-Jun) and 10-20 Jan – – €24/37.* After an interesting day exploring the archaeological site, why not stop in this friendly trattoria where traditional Sicilian fish dishes are served in pleasant rustic surroundings.

Kalo's – *Piazza San Calogero, Agrigento – ☎ 0922 26 389 – Closed Sun and at lunchtime Nov-Jan – €30/45.* This simple, well-kept restaurant is situated on the first floor of a building in the city centre, nor far from the station. Meat and fish dishes, plus daily specials.

Where to Stay

Alternative accommodation options to Agrigento include San Leone, a seaside resort 7km/4mi from the city with a wide choice of hotels and restaurants, and Villaggio Mosè, 4km/2.5mi east of the Valley of the Temples, on S 115.

• ***Budget***

Camping Nettuno – *Via Lacco Ameno 3, San Leone – 7km/4mi S of Agrigento – ☎ 0922 41 62 68 – Fax 0922 41 69 83 – www.geocites.com/campingnettuno €7.* After a day wandering through the atmospheric Valley of the Temples, this campsite is an inexpensive but pleasant outdoor option.

Hotel Akragas – *Viale Emporium 16/18, San Leone – 4km/2.5mi S of Agrigento – ☎ 0922 41 40 82 – Fax 0922 41 42 62 – hotel.akragas@libero.it – – 15 rooms. €37/68.* This family-run hotel in San Leone bears the old name of Agrigento. The hotel offers simple, well-appointed rooms and a renowned restaurant serving traditional Sicilian cuisine.

Fattoria Mosè – *Via Pascal 4, Villaggio Mosè – 4km/2.5mi SE of Agrigento on S 115 – ☎ 0922 60 61 115 – Fax 0922 60 61 115 – agnello@asinform.it – Closed Nov-Feb – 24 rooms. €31/72.* Not far from the sea and the Valley of the Temples, this farm has a number of comfortable houses for rent, all equipped with a kitchen area and an outdoor sitting area. There is a room in the restored olive mill available for business visitors.

• ***Moderate***

Oasi 2000 Bed & Breakfast – *Via Atenea 45 (first floor), Agrigento – ☎ 0922 27 645 – Fax 178 22 61 714 – oasi2000ag@libero.it – – 5 rooms. €77/130.* This comfortable family guesthouse in the city centre has a small reception area with attractive wooden fittings, a breakfast room and six attractive bedrooms decorated with antique furniture and parquet floors. Bed and breakfast accommodation with hotel-style comfort!

• ***Expensive***

Hotel Villa Athena – *Via dei Templi 33, Agrigento – ☎ 0922 59 62 88 – Fax 0922 40 21 80 – villaathena@athenahotels.com – – 40 rooms. €130/205 – Restaurant €34/56.* This restored 18C villa is situated in a charming location, surrounded by a delightful garden of citrus trees. The hotel has spacious, comfortable rooms, a terrace for meals outside in the summer and a magnificent view of the Temple of Concord.

Local Specialities

The Benedictine nuns of the **Abbazia di Santo Spirito**, in Via S. Spirito *(see Walking About)*, make exquisite almond sweetmeats and the famous *cuscusu* (its name recalls the more typical semolina dish using coarsely ground wheat, which is steamed and served with fish to make the Trapani variety of couscous) – a semolina pudding served in small bowls, sweetened with chocolate and pistachio nuts, and decorated with candied fruit *(available by advance order only)*.

Shows

Stoai – *Via Cavaleri Magazzeni 1, Valle dei Templi – ☎ 0922 60 66 23 – Fax 0922 60 83 53, www.lestoai.it, info@lestoai.it* The atmosphere of the former covered market where stalls once stood opposite each other among the arcades of the agora survives in this multimedia environment, which hosts the *Mostra-mercato dell'artigianato artistico* as well as a theatre show *(by reservation only; €13)*.

FESTIVALS

Sagra del Mandorlo in Fiore – This almond blossom festival is the highlight of the year in Agrigento. It takes place during the first ten days of February, at the same time as the International Folklore Festival, which is attended by groups from all around the world.

Festa di San Calogero – The Feast of San Calogero is celebrated from the first to the second Sunday in July.

The city reached its golden age under the tyrant **Theron** (488-472 BC): military might (he defeated the Carthaginians several times) enforced a rule which, among other things, forbade the people from making human sacrifices. Economic stability, coupled with political strength, favoured a flowering of the arts: the Temple of Zeus was built, literature and the performing arts flourished.

The philosopher Empedocles (c 492-c 432 BC) advocated a moderate form of democracy which lasted for some time. In 406 BC, Akragas suffered a crushing defeat at the hands of the Carthaginians, who all but destroyed it. It was rebuilt in the second half of the 4C BC by **Timoleon**, a mercenary general from Corinth engaged in the fight against the Carthaginians in Sicily. It was at this time that the Greco-Roman quarter was built, the remains of which give some idea of the town's reformed urban planning. In 210 BC, Akragas was besieged by the Romans, who conquered the city and changed its name to Agrigentum.

Vicissitudes of Girgenti – With the fall of the Roman Empire, the city passed first to the Byzantines, then into Arab hands (9C). They built a new town centre higher up (at the heart of the modern town), calling it **Girgenti** – a name which lasted until 1927, when its Latin name was restored – which became the capital of the Berber kingdom. In 1087, the town was conquered by the Normans, prompting a new phase of prosperity and power which also enabled it to repel the frequent attacks of the Saracens.

It was during the reign of Roger the Norman that the churches of San Nicola, Santa Maria dei Greci and San Biagio were built.

After a turbulent period which resulted in a gradual decline in the population of the town, Girgenti enjoyed a change in fortune, most notably in the 18C when the town centre was shifted from Via Duomo to Via Atenea. In 1860, the inhabitants, dissatisfied like the rest of the island with Bourbon misrule, enthusiastically supported Garibaldi's mission. During the Second World War, Agrigento suffered a number of air raids.

Two famous sons – Agrigento has nurtured famous personalities both in Antiquity and in more recent times. Among the most renowned are the philosopher **Empedocles** (5C BC), who died, according to legend, by leaping into the crater of Etna attempting to prove his divine powers (and, as if in confirmation of this, Etna is supposed to have thrown back his shoes, which had turned to bronze). In the 20C, the greatest figure with which the town is associated is **Luigi Pirandello**, the playwright and novelist born in the small village of Caos *(see Il Caos, p 125)* below the town, where his ashes are interred. Pirandello enthusiasts should visit the **Biblioteca Luigi Pirandello** at 120 Via Regione Sicilia, which also contains a vast selection of works by other Sicilian authors.

Special Features

LA VALLE DEI TEMPLI*** (VALLEY OF THE TEMPLES)

Tour: half a day. Archaeological site: open 8.30am-dusk (the site often stays open until 11pm in summer). Museo Archeologico: open 9am-1.30pm and 2-6pm; closed Mon, and the afternoon of Sun and public hols. Antiquaria: open 9am-1pm; closed Mon, and the afternoon of Sun and public hols. €4.50 archaeological site; €6 combined ticket with the Museo Archeologico and Antiquaria; €5 combined ticket with the Antiquaria. ☎ 0922 49 73 41 (archaeological site); ☎ 0922 40 15 65 (Museo Archeologico); ☎ 0925 28 989 (Antiquaria).

The monuments in the Valley of the Temples are grouped in two areas: the first (the lower agora, to the south) includes the temples, the Giardino della Kolymbetra, the antiquaria and the palaeo-Christian necropolises; the second (the upper agora, to the north) comprises the archaeological museum, the Chiesa di San Nicola, the Oratorio di Falaride and the Greco-Roman quarter. To walk from one area to the other, visitors can either follow the very busy main road or the quiet road within the park. Car parks are located near the Temple of Zeus and the archaeological museum. Ticket offices can be found at the entrances to both areas of the site.

The description below starts with the archaeological site around the Temple of Zeus. However, visitors with plenty of time to explore the site are advised to begin their visit at the Antiquarium di Villa Aurea, which provides a comprehensive introduction to the Valley of the Temples site.

The Greek form of the names of the divinities has been used to describe the temples, with the Latin equivalents given in brackets.

Stretched out along the ridge, inappropriately called the "valley", and nestling in the area to the south of it, are a series of temples which were all erected in the course of a century (5C BC), as a testimony to the prosperity of the city at that time. Having been set ablaze by the Carthaginians in 406 BC, the buildings were restored by the Romans (1C BC) respecting their original Doric style. Their subsequent state of disrepair has been put down either to seismic activity or the destructive fury of the Christians backed by an edict of the Emperor of the Eastern Empire, Theodosius (4C). The only one to survive intact is the Temple of Concord which, in the 6C, was converted into a Christian church. During the Middle Ages, masonry was removed to help construct other buildings. In particular, the Temple of Zeus, known locally as the Giant's Quarry, provided material for the church of San Nicola and the 18C part of the jetty at Porto Empedocle.

All the buildings face east, respecting the Classical criterion (both Greek and Roman) that the entrance to the cella (Holy of Holies) where the statue of the god was housed should be illuminated by the rays of the rising sun, the source and blood of life. On the whole, the temples are Doric and conform to the hexastyle format (that is, with six columns at the front), the exception being the Temple of Zeus, which had seven engaged columns articulating the wall that encloses the building.

Built of limestone tufa, the temples provide a particularly impressive sight at dawn, and even more so at sunset when they are turned a warm shade of gold.

Sacrificial altar

Just beyond the entrance, on the right, slightly set back, are the remains of an enormous altar, used for large-scale sacrifices. As many as 100 oxen could be sacrificed at one time. The Italian word *ecatombe*, used today to mean a disaster, actually comes from the Greek words meaning to kill 100 – *hecatòn* – oxen – *bôus*.

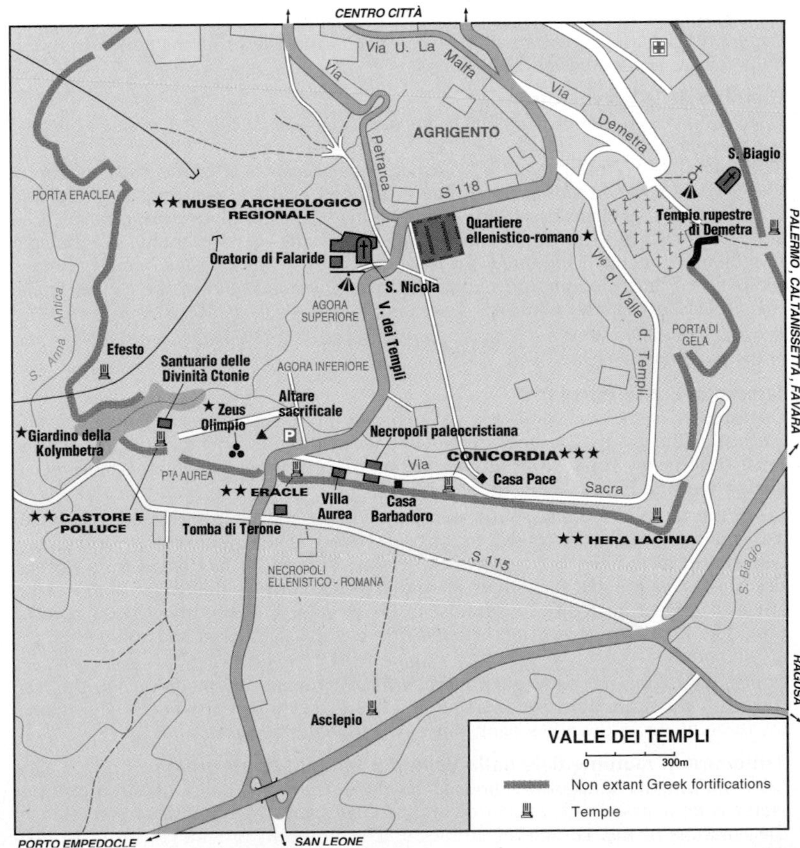

Tempio di Zeus Olimpico (Giove)★

> **Sicilian gardens**
> For visitors from outside Sicily, the term garden is misleading: the garden here is planted with citrus trees rather than flower-beds and ornamental plants, creating an area that is both productive and pleasantly aesthetic.

Having been razed to the ground, the Temple of Zeus (Jupiter) was re-erected following the victory of the people of Agrigentum (allied with the Syracusans) over the Carthaginians at Himera (in about 480 BC) as a gesture of thanks to Zeus. It was one of the largest temples built in ancient times, being 113m/371ft long by 36m/118ft wide, and is thought never to have been completed. The entablature was supported by half-columns 20m/66ft high, which probably alternated with giant male caryatids (atlantes or **telamons**), an example of which can be seen in the local archaeological museum *(see below)*. A reproduction of an atlantes is displayed in the middle of the temple, giving some idea of scale proportional to the vast building. Instead of the more usual open colonnade, this temple is surrounded by a continuous screen wall sealing off the spaces between the columns which, inside, become square pilasters.

Some blocks still bear the marks made for lifting them into place: these are deep U-shaped incisions through which a rope was threaded and then, attached to a kind of crane, could be used to lift or haul the blocks one upon another.

Tempio di Castore e Polluce o dei Dioscuri★★

The Temple of Castor and Pollux or of the Dioscuri is the veritable symbol of Agrigento. Built during the last decades of the 5C BC, it is dedicated to the twins born from the union of Leda and Zeus while transformed into a swan.

Four columns and part of the entablature are all that remain of the temple, which was reconstructed in the 19C. Under one edge of the cornice is a rosette, one of the typical decorative motifs used.

On the right are the remains of what was probably a sanctuary dedicated to the Chthonic Deities (the gods of the underworld): Persephone (Proserpina), queen of the underworld, and her mother, Demeter (Ceres), the goddess of corn and fertility and patroness of agriculture. On the site are a **square altar**, probably used for sacrificing piglets, and another, **round one**, with a sacred well in the centre. This is probably where the rite of the Thesmophoria, a festival held in honour of Demeter, was celebrated by married women.

In the distance, last on the imaginary line linking all the temples of the valley, is the **Temple of Hephaistus** (Vulcan), of which little remains. According to legend, the god of fire and the arts had a forge under Etna where he fashioned thunderbolts for Zeus, assisted by the Cyclops.

Giardino della Kolymbetra★

Open daily except Mon, 9.30am-1hr before dusk. Closed 7-31 Jan. €2. ☎ 335 12 29 042 (mobile phone).

This 5-ha/12-acre "basin", dug by Carthaginian prisoners after the Battle of Imera and used as a fish-breeding pond, has developed over the centuries into a fertile grove of fruit and citrus trees. After years of neglect, the Kolymbetra, now restored and managed by the Italian Foundation for the Environment (Fondo per l'Ambiente Italiano), is planted out with olive trees, prickly pear, poplar, willow, mulberry, orange, lemon and mandarin trees. Paths laid out in the garden make this a pleasant area for a stroll.

Retrace your steps, leave the fenced area and follow Via dei Templi, on the other side of the road, on the right.

Tempio di Eracle (Ercole)★★

Conforming to the Archaic Doric style, the Temple of Heracles (Hercules) is the earliest of the group. The remains enable us to imagine how elegant this temple must have been. Today, a line of eight tapering columns stands erect, re-erected during the first half of the last century.

From the temple, looking south, can be seen the mistakenly named **Tomba di Terone** (*also visible from the Caltagirone road*). The monument, erroneously believed to have been the tomb of the tyrant Theron, in fact dates from Roman times and was erected in honour of soldiers killed during the Second Punic War. Made of tufa, it is slightly pyramidal in shape and probably once had a pointed roof. The high base supports a second order with false doors and Ionic columns at the corners.

Continuing along the path, deep **ruts** in the paving can be made out on the left: these are generally interpreted as having been caused by cartwheels. The reason for them being so deep has been put down to water erosion.

Antiquarium multimediale della Valle dei Templi (Villa Aurea)

This multimedia museum is housed in the former residence of Sir Alexander Hardcastle, a passionate patron of archaeology, who financed the re-erection of the columns of the Temple of Heracles. The museum provides historical, topo-

B. Kaufmann/MICHELIN

Tempio della Concordia

graphical and mythological information relating to the archaeological site and greatly enhances any visit to the Valley of the Temples.

Necropoli paleocristiana

The palaeo-Christian necropolis is situated beneath the road, dug into the bed rock, not far from the ancient walls of the city. There are various types of ancient tomb: loculi (cells or chambers for corpse or urn) and arcosolia (arched cavities like niches), as often found in catacombs.

Before the Temple of Concord there is another group of tombs on the right.

Tempio della Concordia★★★

The Temple of Concord is one of the best-preserved temples surviving from Antiquity, thereby providing an insight into the elegance and majestic symmetry of other such buildings. The reason it has survived intact is due to its transformation into a church in the 6C AD. Inside the colonnade, the original arches through the cella walls of the Classical temple can still be made out.

It is thought to have been built in about 430 BC, but it is not known to which god it was dedicated. The name Concord comes from a Latin inscription found in the vicinity. The temple is a typical example of the architectural refinement in temple building known as "optical correction": the columns are tapered (becoming narrower at the top so as to appear taller) and have a very slight convex curve at about two-thirds of the height of the column in order to counteract the illusion of concavity; those columns at the ends of the façade are also slightly inclined towards the central axis, avoiding the effect of divergence. This allows the observer standing at a certain distance from the temple to see a perfectly straight image. The frieze consists of standard Classical features: alternating triglyphs and metopes, without further low-relief ornamentation. The pediment is also devoid of decoration.

Antiquarium di Agrigento Paleocristiana e Bizantina (Casa Pace)

Turn back through the town, stopping perhaps to consult the various information boards set among the ruins that may be of interest: one in particular explains how the Temple of Concord was transformed into a basilica.

Antiquarium Iconografico della Collina dei Templi (Casa Barbadoro)

In this modern but sympathetically designed building are collected together a series of drawings, engravings and prints of the Valley of the Temples as seen in the past by travellers undertaking the Grand Tour. *Closed at the time of going to press.*

Tempio di Hera Lacinia (Giunone)★★

The Temple of Hera Lacinia (Juno) is situated at the top of the hill and is traditionally dedicated to the protector of matrimony and childbirth. The name *Lacinia* derives from an erroneous association with the sanctuary of the same name situated on the Lacinian promontory near Crotone.

The temple preserves its colonnade (albeit not in perfect condition), which was partially re-erected in the early 1900s. Inside, the columns of the *pronaos* and *opisthodomos* and the wall of the *cella* can still be seen. Built in about the mid-5C

BC, it was set ablaze by the Carthaginians in 406 BC (evidence of burning is still visible on the walls of the *cella*).

To the east is the altar of the temple while, at the back of the building (beside the steps), there is a cistern.

From the Antiquarium di Casa Pace a small road leads up the Collina di San Nicola, crossing fields of prickly pear, pistachio and olive trees. As you approach the top of the hill, continue straight on towards a group of ruins, passing under a bridge. The path leads to the Greco-Roman Quarter (entry ticket required).

Greco-Roman Quarter★

This extensive urban complex contains the vestiges of houses in which survive fragments of ancient pavements laid with stone tesserae *(protected by roofing and plexiglass)* bearing geometric or figurative motifs. The network of streets follows the standard rules advocated by the Greek town planner Hippodamus of Miletus of having broad parallel avenues *(decumani)* bisected at right angles by secondary roads *(cardini)*.

Chiesa di San Nicola

Open 10am-12.30pm. Donation welcome.

Built of tufa, the Church of St Nicholas was erected in the 13C by Cistercian monks in a transitional Romanesque to Gothic style. The stone blocks used were taken from the Giant's Quarry, as the ruined Temple of Zeus was known providing, as it did, an almost inexhaustible easy source of building material. The façade is dominated by two imposing reinforcing buttresses (added in the 16C), which flank a beautiful pointed-arched doorway.

The interior is enclosed within a single barrel-vaulted nave. Four chapels open off the south side. The second contains the famous **sarcophagus of Hippolytus and Phaedra**★ (3C AD) with which Goethe was particularly smitten. Inspired by Greek prototypes, all four sides are sculpted in high relief, the compositions are animated by clean flowing lines and the figures are endowed with delicate features set in gentle expressions. The subject treated is the tragic story of Phaedra's unrequited love for her stepson Hippolytus, who is banished from the kingdom and killed by crazed horses under the shameful (and unfounded) accusation that he had tried to seduce her.

Above the altar is a fine 15C wooden crucifix, nicknamed *il Signore della Nave* (Lord of the Ship), which inspired Pirandello's short story of the same name included in his anthology entitled *Novelle per un Anno*.

From the terrace before the church, there is a beautiful **view**★ over the Valley of the Temples.

Oratorio di Falaride

According to legend, the oratory occupies the site of the palace built by the tyrant Phalaris, hence its name. The present monument was probably a small Greco-Roman temple, converted in Norman times.

Next to the oratory are the remains of an Ekklesiasterion, a small amphitheatre used for political meetings (from the Greek *ekklesia* – meeting), identified as an ancient agora (market place or place of assembly).

Museo Archeologico Regionale★★

Partially housed in the old monastery of San Nicola, the museum contains finds from the province of Agrigento. *Panels provide information on the most important exhibits.*

Pre-Greek conquest – Among the prize exhibits is a fine two-handled cup with a very tall base, decorated with geometric patterns; its shape may stem from the custom of eating seated on the ground with the cup at chest level. Others of note include a small, elegant Mycenaean amphora, the mould of a **patera** with six animals (oxen) in relief, and two signet rings, again bearing animals. The most interesting, meanwhile, is a **dinos** (sacrificial vase) depicting the triskelos (literally "three legs"), the symbol of Sicily.

Colonisation – The superb collection of **Attic vases**★ *(Room 3, exhibited in two parallel corridors)* consists mainly of black-figure and red-figure ware, including the *cratere di Dionisio* (or cup of Bacchus): the god of wine, dressed in flowing robes, holds a sprig of ivy in his hand, and has a leopard-skin draped over his arm. Among the other

Telamons and Atlantes (or Atlas figures)

These imposing giants from Agrigento, more often referred to as atlantes, are sometimes called Telamons (*Telamone* in Italian) after the Latin word derived by the Romans from the Greek, *Telamo(n)* which indicated their function: to carry or bear the structure. Their supporting role is accentuated by their position, with arms bent back to balance the weight upon their shoulders. The more common term alludes to the mythological figure Atlas, the giant and leader of the Titans who struggled against the gods of Olympus and was condemned by Zeus to support the weight of the sky on his head. When the earth was discovered to be spherical, he was often shown bearing the terrestrial globe on his shoulders.

vessels, look for a *krater* with a white background, depicting the proud figure of Perseus on the point of liberating Andromeda from her chains.

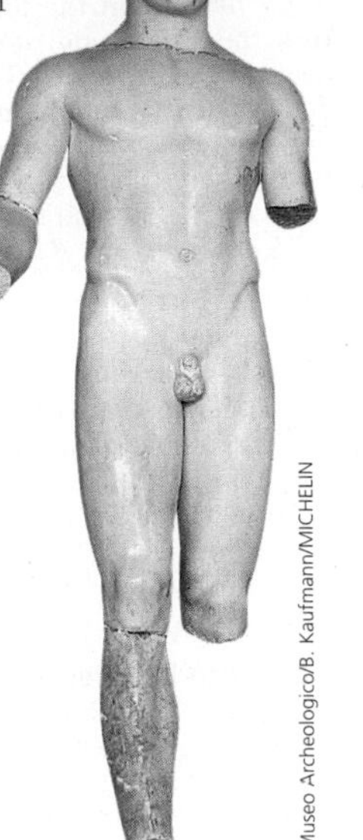
The Ephebus of Agrigento

Museo Archeologico/B. Kaufmann/MICHELIN

This section also contains a large number of votive statues, theatrical masks, moulds and other terracotta figures found during the excavations of the temples. A lower level of this section is filled by the massive figure of **Atlas★** from the Temple of Zeus, the only one to survive of the original 38 male caryatids which once adorned the building. On the left, in a case, are the heads of another three such powerful figures, one of which has well-preserved facial features.

The ***Ephebus of Agrigento★★*** *(Room 10)* consists of a marble statue of a young man (5C BC), found in a cistern near the Temple of Demeter, which was transferred during the Norman period to the Church of San Biagio *(see below)*. It is thought to represent a young man from Agrigento who won various events at the Olympic games, and was thus destined to be subjected to heroic status.

Other archaeological finds – Artefacts retrieved from various other sites in the province include sarcophagi, prehistoric remains and the magnificent krater from **Gela★★** (Room 15), attributed to the Painter of the Niobids. The upper half depicts a centauromachia (battle between Centaurs and Lapiths) while the lower section shows scenes from battles between the Greeks and the Amazons.

Visitors may wish to finish their tour of Ancient Agrigento with a visit to the Chiesa di San Biagio and the Tempio di Asclepio, both of which are situated some distance from the other Ancient monuments.

Chiesa di San Biagio

There is space to park in front of the cemetery. The church is on the left, and can be reached by a path. The Norman church, erected in the 13C, stands on the remains of a **Greek temple** dedicated to Demeter. Just below the church, there is another more rudimentary **temple** to her (Tempio rupestre di Demetra) although inaccessible, which bears witness to the popularity of the cult of the goddess in ancient Sicily.

Tempio di Asclepio (Esculapio)

Just beyond the Tomb of Theron, on the road to Caltanissetta. Look out for a sign (although obscured) on the right. The ruins of this 5C BC temple are to be found in the middle of the countryside. It was dedicated to Asclepius (Aesculapius), the Greek god of medicine and son of Apollo – who it was believed had the power to heal the sick through dreams. The interior, it is thought, harboured a beautiful statue of the god by the Greek sculptor Myron.

Walking About

The broad **Viale della Vittoria**, shaded by trees, provides beautiful views of the Valley of the Temples and leads to a square in front of the station. On the right stands the 16C **Church of San Calogero**, dedicated to a saint who is particularly venerated in this area. The façade has a fine doorway with a pointed arch.

A little further on is Piazza Aldo Moro, where the lovely **Via Atenea** begins. Along this thoroughfare are to be found: on the right **Palazzo Celauro** (best admired from the street of the same name) where Goethe stayed when on his Grand Tour and, on the left, the Franciscan Church of the Immacolata (Blessed Virgin), altered in the 18C. To the right of the church, beyond the gate, can be seen the façade of the 14C **Conventino Chiaramontano**, so called because of the style of the portal between the two-light windows.

Return to Via Atenea and continue to Piazza del Purgatorio, which is overlooked by the splendid façade of **San Lorenzo★** (18C), its golden ochre tufa contrasting dramatically with the whiteness of the doorway, ornamented with twisted columns. The **interior** contains stuccoes by Serpotta and a painting by Guido Reni. *Open Mon-Sat, 10am-1pm and 5-8pm; Sun and public hols by appointment. €1.50. ☎ 0922 40 18 10; www.sanlore.it*

Nearby, level with Via Bac Bac, stands San Giuseppe, a **church** dedicated to St Joseph.

In Piazza Pirandello is the town hall, formerly a Dominican monastery (17C) and an adjacent church with a fine Baroque façade overlooking an elegant flight of steps. Set back, on the left side of the church, is the bell tower.

From Via Atenea, take Via porcello, follow the steps up Salita di Santo Spirito.

Abbazia di Santo Spirito★

The church and its dependent convent date from the 13C. Sadly, the state of the buildings is gradually deteriorating. The church façade has a fine Gothic doorway with a rose window above. The Baroque interior consists of a single nave. On the walls are four high **reliefs** attributed to Giacomo Serpotta: *The Nativity* and *The Adoration of the Magi* on the right, *The Flight into Egypt* and *The Presentation of Jesus at the Temple* on the left. To the right of the façade is a doorway into the **cloisters**, leading under two of the great buttresses supporting the church. The beautiful **entrance★** to the chapterhouse of the monastery consists of an elegant doorway through a pointed arch, flanked by highly decorative Arabo-Norman two-light windows. The monastery is also home to the **Museo di Santo Spirito**, housing a collection of everyday objects relating to rural life, and works by Francesco Lojacono from Palermo (1841-1915). *Open Mon-Fri, 8am-1pm and 3-6pm; Sat-Sun, 9am-1pm. €1.50. ☎ 0922 59 03 71.*

Via San Girolamo

This street is lined with elegant *palazzi*: of note in passing is the façade of the 19C **Palazzo del Campo-Lazzarini** at n° 14 (opposite Santa Maria del Soccorso) and that of the 18C **Palazzo Barone Celauro** at n° 86, which has two rows of small balconies gracing the windows which are articulated with semicircular and triangular pediments.

Taking a Break

Before leaving the Abbazia di Santo Spirito, make sure you try the excellent confectionery made by the nuns here *(ring the bell to the right of the cloisters; also see Directory).*

Biblioteca Lucchesiana

Open Fri, 9am-1.30pm by appointment. No charge. ☎ 0922 22 217.

The library founded in 1765 by Bishop Lucchesi Palli contains more than 45 000 ancient books and manuscripts. The central hall, dominated by a statue of the bishop, is lined with beautiful wooden shelving. Books on profane subjects are kept to the left of the statue, while religious texts are on the right. This division is echoed by the two sculpted wooden figures behind the statue: on the left is a woman meditating, on the right, a woman holding a mirror, symbolising the search for truth in the inner self.

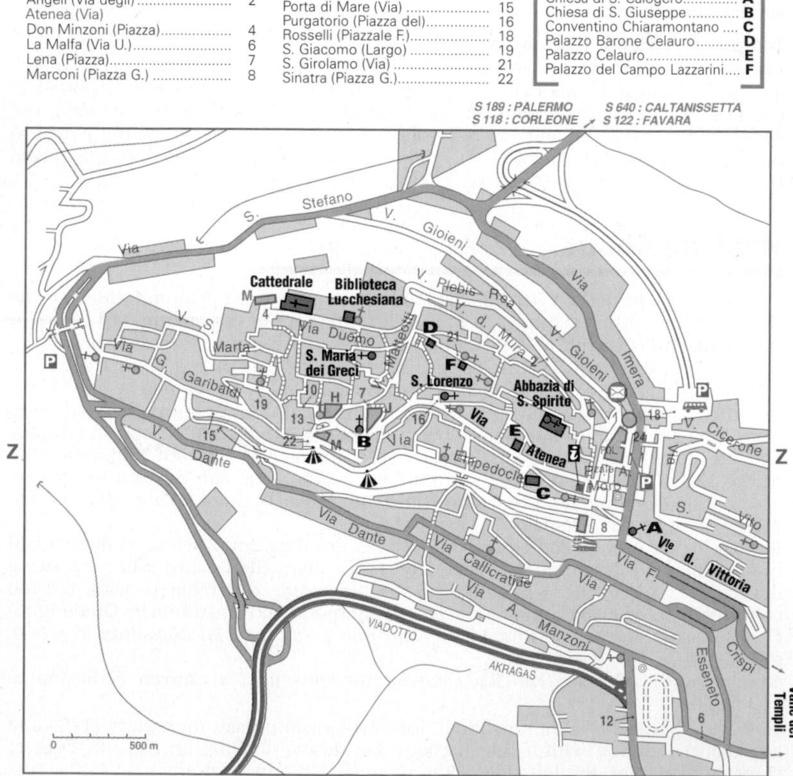

Cathedral

The side of the cathedral facing onto Via del Duomo still bears traces of the Noman original (notably the 11C windows). The main church was rebuilt in the 13C-14C, and remodelled in the 17C; it was then restored after a landslide in 1966. A broad double stairway leads up to the main door, marked by a tympanum, flanked by pairs of pilasters. On the right stands the unfinished bell tower (1470), which on the south side is articulated with four blind arches in the shape of an inverted ship's keel, and a series of pointed arches above.
Inside★, the nave has a beautiful **wooden ceiling★** with tie-beams decorated with figures of the saints, painted in the 16C. The section beyond the triumphal arch is coffered (18C); the great two-headed eagle in the centre is the symbol of the Royal House of Aragon. The Baroque exuberance of the choir, with its angels and golden garlands, contrasts dramatically with the sobriety of the nave.

Santa Maria dei Greci

Closed for restoration work at the time of going to press. The 14C church dedicated to St Mary of the Greeks was built upon the foundations of a temple dedicated to Athena (5C BC), remains of which can still be seen inside the church. The church celebrated mass according to the Greek-Orthodox liturgy.

Tours

FROM PIRANDELLO TO MINOS ALONG STUNNING BEACHES

90km/56mi round trip from Agrigento – allow one day.
From Agrigento, head 6km/4mi W on the Porto Empedocle road (S 115). Turn left after Morandi viaduct.

Il Caos

In the Villaseta district. (♿) *Open Apr-Nov, 9am-1pm and 2-7pm; Jan-Mar, 9am-1pm and 2-6pm. €2. ☎ 0922 51 18 26; www.regione.sicilia.it*
This village, on the outskirts of Agrigento, was the birthplace of **Luigi Pirandello**, whose **house** stands alone and silent in the middle of the countryside. The first floor of the writer's house is open to the public. A short film documents the most salient moments of his life and career, including the Nobel Prize award ceremony and his funeral. Pirandello last visited the house in 1934, but by then it had been sold and he saw it only from a distance. The rooms contain written and illustrative material pertaining to the writer and Marta Abba, the actress to whom he became very close in the latter period of his life, pictures of stage performances, hand-written documents, editions of his plays and novels, as well as a Greek *krater* dating from the 5C BC in which Pirandello's ashes were once kept. The Parco Letterario Luigi Pirandello *(see p 32)* is dedicated to the writer.
A small path to the right of the house leads to the **pine tree** (damaged in the storm of November 1997) at the foot of which are buried Pirandello's ashes. Beyond, lies the sea.
Continue along S 115 to Sciacca. From Porto Empedocle, follow signs to Madison Hotel.

Scala dei Turchi★★

Turn left into the Discesa Maiata (the Scala dei Turchi is signposted), which leads along the beach to the rock (10min on foot). Alternatively, follow the road for a further 300m/330yd until you come to an electricity transformer hut on the left. A small path to the left of the hut leads down to the sea. Arriving from Realmonte, the rock is visible once you have passed the Madison Hotel. This impressive white rock (made of marl, a mixture of clay and limestone smoothed by erosion) is shaped into a number of

RITORNO (LA VIA)

A solitary house set amid my native
countryside: up here, on this plateau
of blue clay, to which the submissive
bitter African sea sends a fervour of foam,
I see you always, from afar,
if I think of that moment in which my life
opened up minutely to the immense, vain world:
this, this, I say, was where I set out along the path of life.

Luigi Pirandello
in *Zampogna*, Rome 1901

M. Guillot/MICHELIN

Pirandello's Pine before the storm

steps which slope gently towards the sea and is a popular place for sunbathing in summer. The other side of the "steps" *(scala)* has been more obviously shaped by the wind and the sea, forming a series of narrow, winding, wave-like formations. The name of the rock refers to the local legend which recounts how Saracen pirates once scaled the rock after having anchored their ships in the bay.

Continue along S 115 as far as Siculiana Marina, then follow the road to Montallegro for approximately 2km/1.2mi.

Riserva Naturale Orientata di Torre Salsa

This World Wildlife Fund reserve covers a wide variety of habitats (dunes, cliffs, marshland and Mediterranean maquis) inhabited by porcupines, crows, birds of prey, waders and sea birds. The reserve also has a delightful beach of fine sand, made all the more spectacular by the intense blue of the Mediterranean. *The reserve is closed from Nov to Feb. For guided tours, contact the WWF, ☎ 0922 81 82 20; Fax 0922 81 79 95; www.riservewwfsicilia.it*

Eraclea Minoa

The remains of the Greek city Heraclea Minoa enjoy a magnificent **situation**★★ on the edge of a lonely hill with a fine view of the sea, at the beginning of Capo Bianco. At its feet, the coast opens out into a broad bay, lined with a long **beach**★★ of the whitest sand extending up to a handsome glade of pine trees behind *(from S 115 follow signs to Montallegro-Bovo Marina and Montallegro Marina; a small road on the right leads to the sea).* Before the excavations, note on the right, the white "dunes" of marl sculpted by the wind, echoing the cliff on the east side of the promontory.

The city was probably founded in the 6C BC by Greek colonists from Selinus (now Selinunte). Sometime in the 3C BC, the town passed into the hands of the Romans; thereafter it embarked upon a series of wars and was gradually abandoned. By the 1C BC it was deserted.

A concerted effort to undertake a thorough excavation of the area began in 1950: this has uncovered the **remains** of dwellings made of rough bricks, some still containing fragments of mosaic and, most excitingly, a **theatre** built of a very friable stone. This, inevitably, is not well preserved. The complete layout of the *cavea* in relation to the horseshoe-shaped orchestra pit is easy to determine.

A small **antiquarium** collects together various objects found for the most part in the necropoli. *Open 9am-1hr before dusk. €2. ☎ 0922 84 60 05.*

TOWARDS MONTI SICANI

175km/109mi round trip from Agrigento – allow one day.

This tour wends its way up through **magnificent scenery**★★ from the Agrigento coast to the slopes of Monti Sicani, offering delightful views of hills, woods, mountains and meadows. In the spring, the area is an explosion of red poppies and yellow broom.

Take S 189 to Palermo and exit at Aragona.

Vulcanelli di Macalube★

At the entrance to Aragona, follow signs to Macalube. Turn left at the roundabout, then left again at the next junction and follow the tarmacked road that ends in a clearing. Park here and then follow the middle path that heads up to the top of a small hill (on the right). For information, contact Legambiente-Uffici della Riserva, Via Salvatore La Rosa 53, Aragona; ☎/Fax 0922 69 92 10; macalube@tin.it

The spectacular Scala dei Turchi

M. Magni/MICHELIN

Minos, Daedalus and Cocalus

Minos, who was married to Pasiphaë, reigned over Crete and the islands of the Aegean, instituting their constitution and founding their naval supremacy. The Cretan Bull was sent by the god of the sea Poseidon for sacrifice. It was so magnificent a creature that Minos decided to spare it by substituting another at the sacrifice. This so angered Poseidon that he inspired Pasiphaë with an unnatural passion for the bull. Pasiphaë requested that Daedelus construct her a hollow cow that would allow her to hide inside; from her coupling with the Cretan Bull, the Minotaur was born. The Labyrinth was built by Daedelus in order to conceal and contain the monstrous creature with a human body and a bull's head to whom Minos insisted on sacrificing seven Athenian youths and seven maidens every ninth year. On discovering Daedelus' treachery, Minos imprisoned him and his son Icarus in the Labyrinth; they were released by Pasiphaë whereupon Daedelus set about making wings to help him escape to Sicily. When the third tribute was due, Theseus volunteered himself; on his arrival in Crete, Minos' daughter Ariadne fell in love with the Athenian hero; she gave him a sword with which to kill the monster and a ball of silk to help him retrace his way out of the impenetrable maze.

The ancient settlement was probably called Minoa, linking it to Minos, who, according to more recent traditions, is reputed to have followed Daedalus to Sicily to punish him for revealing the secret of the labyrinth to Ariadne and her accomplice Theseus. Daedalus is said to have taken refuge with Cocalus, the king of Sicily, who killed Minos in order to protect his guest. In fact, the kingdom of Cocalus was situated on the banks of the River Platani, with a capital called Camico, now identified by some as being the modern Sant'Angelo Muxaro, by others as Caltabellotta.

This hill is dotted with mud cones, known as *vulcanelli* (literally, small volcanoes) because of the cold, whiteish slime that they expel. This process is a sedimentary, gaseous volcanic phenomenon in which the pressure of methane bubbles forces a mixture of clay sediments and water to the surface.

Return to Aragona and take the road to Sant'Angelo Muxaro.

Sant'Angelo Muxaro

Sant'Angelo clings to its craggy mountainside overlooking the surrounding countryside. It has been alleged that this was the capital of the ancient kingdom of Cocalus, that mythical king who is said to have received Daedalus on his flight from Minos *(see p 127)*. The 18C front elevation of the Chiesa Matrice is divided into three sections by strongly accented pilaster strips framing the three doorways, and rectangular windows above.

Festivals

If you find yourself in this region over the Easter period, make sure you stop at **San Biagio Platani**, where the *Festa degli Archi di Pasqua (Festival of the Easter Arches)* is celebrated. The inhabitants of the town, divided into two brotherhoods, erect spectacular reed arches decorated with citrus fruit, dates and various types of bread, which are then exhibited along Corso Umberto I.

Grotta del Principe – *By the side of the road, just outside town. Leave the car on the verge so that it does not obstruct the traffic. Although the distance is short, the going is rough.* The Prince's Cavern is a proto-historic tomb (9C BC) consisting of two circular chambers. The first, the larger of the two with a domed ceiling, comprised the atrium for the actual burial chamber.

Take the road to Alessandria della Rocca.

The road winds its way uphill through delightful rolling countryside.

Bivona

At the centre of Bivona stands a lovely **Arabo-Norman archway**, all that remains of the former Chiesa Matrice. A little further on, **Palazzo Marchese Greco** preserves its fine, albeit damaged, façade ornamented with wrought-iron balconies and elegant Baroque stonework. The cornices of the windows are decorated with bunches of grapes and other varieties of fruit.

From Bivona take the road to Santo Stefano Quisquina, then continue to Castronuovo di Sicilia.

The road (*attractive, but in poor condition*) skirting the **Lago di Fanaco** passes through beautiful **mountain scenery★** of meadows, thick woodland, flowers and rocky outcrops.

Castronuovo di Sicilia

The picturesque small hamlet comprises a number of houses neatly built with carefully dressed stone. The little piazza is overlooked by the Chiesa Madre della Santissima Trinità (1404) and its fine bell tower. From the centre, an attractive paved street leads up to the Chiesa di San Vitale and the castle ruins. A **viewpoint★** at the top of the village offers a magnificent panorama of the surrounding countryside.

From here, the tour heads along S 189 to Agrigento before turning left to Mussomeli. Alternatively, visitors can follow the tour described on p 128.

Mussomeli

Mussomeli crams itself onto the bare hillside, in a place high enough to enjoy a scenic position. The houses jostle one with another, separated only by very narrow streets, apparently cowering below the watchful gaze of the **Castello Manfredonico** which perches on its lonely rock outcrop. Fort and rock are completely fused with man-made sections merely complementing those provided by nature.

The centre of the town is marked by the tall front elevation of the Chiesa Matrice (altered in the 17C) which peeps over the rooftops. Some way below stands the 16C white limestone Santuario della Madonna dei Miracoli with its attractively arranged doorway set between two spiral columns and broken pediment.

Head back along S 189 to Agrigento. At Comitini you can either carry on to Agrigento or join the tour described below.

THE HILLS AROUND NARO

90km/56mi, starting and finishing in Agrigento – allow one day.

Take S 640, then turn right towards Favara.

Favara

A town of Arab origin, Favara reached its apogee under the powerful Chiaramonte family (13C-14C) who oversaw the building of the massive castle. Piazza dei Vespri is dominated by the imposing façade of the 18C Chiesa Madre, its tall dome resting gently on a ring of arches.

Return to S 640. After 7km/4mi, turn left to Racalmuto.

Racalmuto

Racalmuto was once an important centre for sulphur extraction. In the centre of the town stand the remains of the **Chiaramonte castle,** marked by two large towers.

Follow signs to Canicattì. Just before the village, take the turn-off to the right to Naro.

Leonardo Sciascia

Racalmuto is known as the birthplace of **Leonardo Sciascia (1921-89)**, the Sicilian writer and astute commentator who spent much of his life here and who is buried in the town's small cemetery. Much of Sciascia's inspiration came from this harsh, dry and sun-scorched landscape, and from the toil of living and working here. In works such as *The Day of the Owl and To Each His Own*, the writer is constantly exploring themes which have their roots in Sicily and Sicilian identity. A **literary park** in Racalmuto *(see p 32)* is dedicated to the writer.

Naro★

The many Baroque buildings in Naro (some of which now have a rather neglected appearance) testify to the prosperous history of the town, which was probably founded by the Greeks.

The historical centre – Via Dante, the town's central axis which runs into Viale Umberto to the east, is lined with elegant Baroque buildings. At the western end of the street, Piazza Padre Favara is overlooked by the Chiesa di San Agostino and its adjacent Augustinian monastery, a powerful influence in the 18C. On the left-hand side of Via Dante stands the **Chiesa di San Nicolò di Bari**, preceded by a flight of steps and with a fine early Sicilian Baroque façade (17C-18C).

Another church, the **Chiesa Madre**, is immediately visible on the left. This church, built in the 17C by the Jesuits, became the town's main one when the Duomo began to crumble (1867). At the same time, many of the furnishings and works of art were transferred here from the abandoned cathedral, including the carved wooden sacristy furniture with spiral columns intertwined with vines and ornamental half busts (1725). To the left of the entrance is a lovely font from 1424.

A right turn after the Chiesa Madre leads into the attractive **Piazza Garibaldi**, enclosed on all sides by gracious buildings. Among the most notable of these is the **façade★** of the **Chiesa di San Francesco**, founded in the 13C but restored four centuries later. The adjacent former Franciscan monastery has attractive cloisters overlooked by municipal offices.

From Piazza Garibaldi take Corso Vittorio Emanuele and turn left into Via Cannizzaro.

The Chiesa di Santa Caterina, which was built in 1366 and altered in the 18C, has subsequently been restored to its original appearance. A bold linearity pervades the interior arrangement, relieved in part by a highly decorative Chiaramonte archway.

Returning to Via Dante, pass the elaborate Baroque façade of the **Chiesa del Santissimo Salvatore** on your left.

From Piazza Cavour turn left into Via Archeologica.

The **Norman Duomo** (12C-13C) stands impressively on the right-hand side of the street. All that now remains is a sad ruin, although fragments of the beautiful Chiaramonte doorway do still grace the main front. The bulky silhouette of the **castle** can be seen further along the street. This is built in the Chiaramonte style out of irregularly shaped blocks of tuff (consolidated volcanic ash); the only relief is provided on one side of the square tower, by two blind arches and by a fine entrance way.

Retrace your steps to Piazza Cavour and walk to the end of Viale Umberto I.

B. Kaufmann/MICHELIN

Santissimo Salvatore, doorway detail

Santuario di San Calogero – *Piazza Roma.* From this church there are lovely **views** over the Valle del Paradiso. The church, built in the 16C, was completely remodelled during the Baroque period. Inside, standing against the wall of the stairway down to the crypt, is a remarkable **Wounded Christ★** in pink marble, its dark veins suggestive of the blood being shed.

The crypt is built around the cave where San Calogero, the patron saint of Naro, is supposed to have lived. The black statue of the saint by the altar is the one carried in procession on 18 June, the saint's feast day.

Catacombe paleocristiane – *In the contrada Canale, just south of the town.* This rural catacomb comprises several passageways lined with niches and shallow hollows containing a sparse number of grave goods. The main underground chamber or hypogeum is the Grotta delle Meraviglie (Cave of Marvels), which extends some 20m/66ft.

Castellazzo di Camastra – 2km/1.2mi S along the road to Palma. This small ruined castle is perched on an isolated rocky outcrop. The foundations are provided by great blocks of stone cut from the bed rock; according to local folklore, this is where Cocalus might have lived while ruling over his mythical kingdom, hence the popular epithet **Reggia di Cocalo** (Palace of Cocalus) given to the castle *(see p 32).*

Follow S 410 as far as Palma di Montechiaro.

Palma di Montechiaro

The town was founded in 1637 by the twins Carlo and Giulio Tomasi, one of whose descendants, **Giuseppe Tomasi di Lampedusa** (1896-1957) wrote the famous novel *The Leopard,* which was published posthumously in 1958. This book, on which Luchino Visconti based his magnificent film, retells the decline of an aristocratic family from Palermo between 1860, the year in which Garibaldi's Thousand landed in Sicily, and 1910. The title recalls the heraldic coat of arms and the pride of the main character, Prince Fabrizio di Salina, played in the film by Burt Lancaster.

> **Taking a Break**
> Make sure that you try the delicious confectionery made by the nuns of the Benedictine convent next to Palazzo Tomasi.

Tomasi di Lampedusa visited Palma late in his life, after he had started writing his masterpiece, and soon fell in love with the area. Palma, along with Palermo and Santa Margherita di Belice, is now part of the **Parco Letterario Giuseppe Tomasi di Lampedusa** *(see p 127).*

Standing at the top of a long flight of steps, the **Chiesa Madre** has a broad Baroque **façade★**, built in white limestone, and is framed by two bell towers with attractive onion domes.

Set to one side of the great stairway up to the church is **Palazzo Tomasi**. The building is often referred to as the "palace of the holy duke", in reference to Giulio Tomasi's nickname. The duke had a strong religious vocation and converted the palace into a monastery.

Castello di Montechiaro – *8km/5mi SW along the road to Marina di Palma, then right towards Capreria.* Crouched high upon a rocky crag above the sea (magnificent **view★** of the coast), the 14C castle has a rather bleak and proud quality about it. In 1863, the name of the castle was incorporated into the name of the nearby town of Palma.

Head back to S 115 to return to Agrigento.

Ville di **Bagheria**

Bagheria is a city of splendid Baroque villas (over 20 in all), many of which have sadly been neglected or abandoned. However, the few that are visible and open to the public are delightful, recalling the wealth of the Palermo aristocracy who built their summer homes here in the 17C and 18C. As well as its famous villas, Bagheria is renowned as the birthplace of well-known Sicilian personalities such as the painter Renato Guttuso, the poet Ignazio Butitta and the director Giuseppe Tornatore, who captured his childhood in the city in the film Nuovo Cinema Paradiso.

Location

Population: 54 164. Michelin map 565 22M – Palermo. Bagheria, situated approximately 15km/9mi from Palermo, can be reached along the A19 motorway (Bagheria exit), along S 113 or by train (the railway station is located close to Villa Cattolica). For easy access to the monuments described below, it is best to enter the town along S 113, which leads into Corso Butera and then the main street, Corso Umberto.

Neighbouring sights are described in the following chapters: CEFALÙ; MONREALE; PALERMO; SOLUNTO; TERMINI IMERESE.

Worth a Visit

Villa Palagonìa★

The entrance is at the rear of the villa which faces onto the small Piazza Garibaldi, at the end of the main street of the town, the fine Corso Umberto I. Open Apr-Oct, 9am-1pm and 4-7pm; Nov-Mar, 9am-1pm and 3.15-5.15pm. €2.50. ☎ 091 93 20 88; www.villapalagonia.it

This most celebrated of Bagheria villas, built in 1715, is an elegant building of unusual shape: the façade is concave, almost as if to welcome the visitor, while the rear is convex. Goethe considered the building a monstrosity, with its unusual structure and decorative features. The house was constructed by Prince Gravina's father, but it was the prince's idea to add the exuberant **sculptural decoration★** along the top of the wall in front of the façade. This arrangement, consisting of about 60 crude and often monstrous tufa statues, has provoked various esoteric interpretations. They include mythological figures, ladies, gentlemen, musicians, soldiers, dragons and grotesque beasts with threatening expressions, creating a surreal atmosphere. What is especially peculiar is that the statues are placed facing in towards the villa and not, as was usual, towards the outside world with the idea of keeping evil spirits at bay.

The result provides an insight into the mind and spirit of the prince, who aimed to surprise, if not frighten, his guests. This eccentricity runs through the villa's reception rooms. The great oval entrance hall, painted with *trompe l'oeil* frescoes illustrating four of the twelve Labours of Heracles, leads into the Hall of Mirrors,

A few of the fantastical figures

M. Magni/MICHELIN

an appropriate name given its ceiling encrusted with mirrors set at different angles, so as to distort the reflection of anyone entering the room, projecting it through a kaleidoscope of images multiplied a hundredfold to infinity or reduced to nothing with each step taken (today, sadly, this magical effect is barely discernible). The upper part of the hall is ornamented with a trompe l'oeil, a balustrade enclosing a series of inquisitive animals and birds; caught occasionally by a mirror in the ceiling, the creatures are reflected as though they exist under an open sky. The illusion is reinforced further by other decorative effects as panels of real marble are set alongside others of painted paper under glass: the real may be differentiated from the unreal from a few feet away.

Villa Butera

This stands at the southern end of Corso Butera. The villa was built in the second-half of the 17C by Prince Branciforti di Raccuia. Although now in a sad state of repair, the villa preserves on its eastern side (which can be seen by going around the left side of the building) an imposing tufa doorway to the piano nobile betraying Spanish influence: a drape held in place by ribbons and festoons of fruit and flowers bears an inscription in Spanish.

Villa Cattolica

Via Consolare 9 (S 113). From the motorway, cross Bagheria following the signs to Aspra. ♿ Open May-Sep, daily except Mon, 10am-8pm; Oct-Apr, daily except Mon, 9am-7pm. Closed national hols. €4. ☎ 091 90 54 38.

This massive, square building, built in 1736 by Giuseppe Bonanni Filangeri, Prince of Cattolica, houses the **Civica Galleria d'Arte Moderna e Contemporanea Renato Guttuso**, a modern art gallery which exhibits works by Guttoso and other artists close to him. Most of the works were donated by Guttoso to his native town in 1973. The villa gardens harbour a Camera dello Scirocco (*see p* 295) and the **tomb** of the painter, designed by his friend, Giacomo Manzù.

Caltagirone★

Visitors arriving in Caltagirone cannot fail to notice the outward signs of a thriving industry now synonymous with the name of the place: brightly painted ceramics not only fill shop windows with a profusion of vases, plates and other household goods, they decorate the bridges, balustrades, frontages and balconies. This bears witness to an art which, in this area, is as old as the origins of the town itself.

Location

Population: 39 145. Michelin map 565 P 25 – Catania. Caltagirone is divided into an upper and lower town. Most of the monuments of major interest are found in the upper town, which is best explored on foot. Vehicles can be left in the car parks situated along the ringroads to the east and west of the town. ℹ *Palazzo Libertini; ☎ 0933 53 809; Fax 0933 54 610; and Via Duomo 7; ☎ 0933 34 191; www.comune.caltagirone.ct.it/turismo2.htm*

Neighbouring sights are described in the following chapters: CATANIA; COMISO; GELA; PIAZZA ARMERINA; RAGUSA; VILLA IMPERIALE DEL CASALE.

Background

CITY OF EARTHENWARE POTTERIES

The reason behind it all rests in the inexhaustible deposits of clay in the area. The ease with which this raw material can be extracted has underpinned the success of the terracotta potteries, in manufacturing tableware especially, for distribution throughout the region. This soon became one of the town's main activities. Local shapes gave way to Greek influences (as trade increased), production improved, becoming more efficient and more precise with the introduction of the wheel (by the Cretans in about 1000 BC). The critical turning point, however, was the arrival of the Arabs (9C), for with them practices were changed irrevocably. They introduced Eastern designs and, more importantly, introduced glazing techniques: a useful and innovative development which even rendered objects impermeable to water. The art became more sophisticated as exquisite geometric patterning and stylised decoration were modelled on plants and animals. The dominant colours were blue, green and yellow. The significance of the Arab contribution is honoured in the town's name which, according to the most intriguing hypothesis, might be derived from the Moorish for *castle* or *fortress of vases*.

With the advent of Spanish domination, tastes and demands changed. The painted decoration was predominantly monochrome (blue or brown) and comprised organic designs or the coats of arms of some noble family or religious

Scala di Santa Maria del Monte

order. The town enjoyed a period of notable prosperity thanks also to the area's other industries: honey production, which generated particularly high yields here, meant that apiculturists soon ranked among the potters' most assiduous customers. The *cannatari* (from the word cannate meaning jug) were supplemented by quartari (amphorae with a capacity of 1.25 litres equal to a quartare, a quarter of a barrel). The artisans organised themselves into confraternities which, in turn, helped build workshops in quite a large area south of the town but still within the town walls. In addition to ceramic table- and kitchenwares, Caltagirone established its reputation for making tiles and ornamental plaques for domes, floors, church and *palazzo* façades. Among the great artists to work here during the 16C and 17C, the Gagini brothers and Natale Bonajuti are perhaps the most renowned. The main decorative elements are the same as those featured on domestic wares: geometric, floral and stylised motifs, such as the small Persian palm leaf transcribed from Tuscan designs (Montelupo). In the 17C, decorative medallions filled with figurative vignettes or effigies of saints (typical in products from all over Sicily) became popular; a century later, moulded relief was applied to vases with elaborate volutes and polychrome decoration.

With the 19C there began a period of decline, arrested in part by the production of figurines, often used in Nativity cribs. In the second half of the century, this art-form reached new heights of excellence in the hands of such experts as Bongiovanni and Vaccaro.

The art of clay-working – The techniques used for creating articles from clay have remained unchanged for centuries. The ductile clay mixture is worked wet, by hand, using a potter's wheel, or is turned into a liquid and cast in a mould. The object is then left to dry and placed in an oven at a very high temperature. Once the object is fired it is ready for use.

There are a number of different techniques for decorating ceramics. These may include a final working of the clay (carvings, graffito designs or mouldings made with stones, shells or other objects on the unbaked article) or the use of colour which, depending on the type of technique and paint used, can be applied at different stages of manufacture (before or after firing, following a second firing, or cold).

Clay-working techniques allow a range of different articles to be produced, depending on the mixture, techniques and type of baking used. The most simple product is the porous reddish terracotta, typical of objects made in Antiquity. The first maiolica (terracotta decorated with enamel) appeared in the 16C.

Porcelain is produced from a different type of clay, a white paste known as kaolin, and usually has a glazed finish. Opaque porcelain is known as biscuit porcelain. It is interesting to note that the name ceramic comes from the Greek word for clay, κεραμοζ (keramos).

Walking About

Via Roma, Caltagirone's main street, bisects the town, cutting its way to the famous steps up to Santa Maria del Monte, and continuing on up to the church entrance. Its way is lined with some of the town's most interesting buildings, many with maiolica decoration. Near its start, on the left, begins the elegant balustraded enclosure of the Villa Comunale (a public garden) and the Teatrino (housing the Ceramics Museum).

Directory

Where to Eat

• For all budgets

CALTAGIRONE

La Scala – *Scala di S. Maria del Monte 8, Caltagirone –* ☎ *0933 57 781 –* ▤ *– €20/37.* This restaurant is housed in a fine 18C building to the right of the famous steps leading up to Santa Maria del Monte. The restaurant serves a good selection of regional dishes.

CHIARAMONTE GULFI

Majore – *Via Martiri Ungheresi 12, Chiaramonte Gulfi –* ☎ *0932 92 80 19 – majoreristorante@tin.it – Closed Mon and in Aug –* ▤ *– €12/17.* This hundred-year-old restaurant only serves dishes made from pork, as a sign on the wall testifies ("qui si magnifica il porco"). The food here is beautifully presented and reasonably priced.

MILITELLO IN VAL DI CATANIA

U' Trappitu – *Via Principe Branciforte 125, Militello in Val di Catania –* ☎ *095 81 14 47 – Closed Mon –* ▤ *– €18.08.* This trattoria is housed in an old oil mill (*trappitu* in the Sicilian dialect) dating from 1927. The building has been carefully restored and retains many of its original features, with oil presses and millstones adding to the restaurant decor.

PALAZZOLO ACREIDE

Valentino – *Via Galeno, on the corner of Ronco Pisacane 125, Palazzolo Acreide –* ☎ *0931 88 18 40. €25/29.* This pleasant restaurant is situated in the centre of an attractive small town, whose origins date back to the Ancient Greeks. Both the atmosphere and the food served here are simple in style, with the emphasis on regional cuisine.

Where to Stay

CALTAGIRONE

• Budget

Albergo La Scala 2 – *Piazza Umberto I 1, Caltagirone –* ☎ *0933 51 552 – 6 rooms. €25/55.* The owners of the La Scala restaurant in the main square have a number of simple, but well-kept rooms without private bathrooms.

• Moderate

Pomara – *Via Vittorio Veneto 84, San Michele di Ganzaria – 14km/9mi NW of Caltagirone on S 124 –* ☎ *0933 97 69 76 – Fax 0933 97 70 90 – info@hotelpomara.com –* ▣ ♨ ▤ *– 40 rooms. €59/77.50* ☕. This hotel is in a perfect location for visitors looking for a rural retreat within easy distance of a town. Situated between Caltagirone and Piazza Armerina, the family-run hotel has spacious rooms and classical decor.

VIZZINI

• Budget

Agriturismo A Cunziria – *Contrada Masera, Vizzini –* ☎ *0933 96 55 07 – Fax 0933 96 60 87 – www.cunziria.com – Closed Mon –* ♨ ▤ *– 14 rooms. €34/56* ☕ *– Restaurant €14/21.* This *agriturismo,* situated close to the village of the same name, includes a restaurant housed in former troglodyte dwellings. Accommodation is provided in simple wooden chalets amid a landscape of prickly pears and sweet-scented orange trees.

Shopping

Glazed earthenware is on sale in countless shops in the town centre and on either side of the Scala di Santa Maria del Monte. In general, the further up the steps you climb, the lower the prices. For an overview of what is produced locally, head for the **Mostra Mercato Permanente** in Via Vittorio Emanuele, where representative examples of work by all the town's craftsmen are on display.

Festivals

La Luminaria – Festa di San Giacomo – This festival in honour of San Giacomo, the patron saint of the town, is the highlight of the summer in Caltagirone. On the 24 and 25 July, the steps of Santa Maria del Monte are decorated with thousands of small oil lamps known as *coppi*, which are arranged in different designs each year.

Festa del Presepe – The art of the *figurinai* – sculptors who created small terracotta statues for traditional Nativity cribs (*presepe* in Italian) – flourished in Caltagirone until the end of the 18C. This old tradition is celebrated from November to January, with exhibitions of different kinds of cribs held throughout the town.

Villa Comunale★

This rather wonderful garden was designed in the late 19C by GB Basile, modelled on English gardens. The edge along Via Roma is marked by an ornamental balustrade topped with vases with disturbingly devilish faces; these alternate with bright green pine cones and maiolica lamp standards. The garden is threaded by a series of shaded pathways which open out into secluded spaces ornamented by ceramic sculptures, figures and fountains. The most impressive open area is graced with a delightful **bandstand** decorated with Moorish-looking elements and glazed panels of maiolica.

Beyond the Museo della Ceramica on the right-hand side of Via Roma *(see Worth a Visit)*, is the splendid 18C balcony-cum-terrace of **Casa Ventimiglia**, which is named after the local artist responsible for its maiolica decoration. Beyond the **Tondo Vecchio**, the curved stone and brick building, sits the remarkable façade (on the right) of **San Francesco d'Assisi**; this overlooks the maiolica bridge, also named after St Francis, which carries the road into the very heart of the town. Beyond the little Church of **Sant'Agata**, the seat of the ceramicists' confraternity, stands an austere prison block built under Bourbon rule.

M. Magni/MICHELIN

Bandstand

Carcere Borbonico

The prison, an imposing square sandstone building, has been greatly improved by recent restoration. It was designed in the late 18C by the Sicilian architect Natale Bonajuto and used as a prison for about a century. It now houses the town's small municipal museum *(see Worth a Visit)*, thereby allowing access to its interior.

Piazza Umberto I

The most prominent building to face onto the square is the **Duomo di San Giuliano**, a great Baroque edifice that has been subjected to much remodelling, the most drastic involving the replacement of the whole front in the early 1900s. It comes into view from the steps below Santa Maria del Monte, at the foot of which, on the left, stands **Palazzo Senatorio** with the courtyard, **Corte Capitaniale**, behind, a fine example of early civic architecture (1601) by one of the Gaginis.

To the right, a stairway leads up to the **Chiesa del Gesù**, which is home to a Deposition by Filippo Paladini *(third chapel on the left)*. Behind it nestles the **Chiesa di Santa Chiara** with its elegant façade attributed to **Rosario Gagliardi** (18C) and, beyond again, the early 20C Officina Elettrica, the façade of which was designed by **Ernesto Basile**.

Return to Piazza Umberto I.

Scala di Santa Maria del Monte★

This long flight of steps acts as a conjunction between the old town (at the top), which in the 17C accommodated the seat of religious authority, and the new town, where the municipal administrative offices were in fact located. On either side of this axis lie the old quarters of San Giorgio and San Giacomo; among their narrow streets, both conceal some fine buildings *(see below)*. The 142 lava stair treads are complemented by highly decorative multicoloured maiolica tile uprights bearing various combinations of geometric and organic designs inspired by the animal kingdom, echoing Moorish, Norman, Spanish, Baroque or some other more contemporary influence. Once a year, the stairway is brought to life by a multitude of flickering little coloured candles which pick out a kaleidoscope of ever-changing patterns: swirls, volutes, plant tendrils, female figures and the recurring emblem of the town, an eagle emblazoned with a crossed shield. This fabulous spectacle, when thousands of little candles wrapped in red, yellow or green paper are placed on the steps and lit, takes place on the nights of San Giacomo, 24 and 25 July. Presiding from the top of the steps, sits **Santa Maria del Monte**, formerly the town's main church and headquarters of the religious authorities. The high altar is graced with the *Conadomini Madonna, a 13C painting on panel. For opening times, contact the parish priest, ☎ 0933 21 712.*

San Giorgio and San Giacomo quarters

Via L Sturzo, leading off to the right from the foot of the steps, has a number of fine buildings including **Palazzo della Magnolia** (n° 74), which is ornamented with exuberant and elaborate terracotta decoration by Enrico Vella. Just beyond the *palazzo* are two 19C churches: San Domenico and **Santissimo Salvatore**. The latter contains the mausoleum of the politician Don Luigi Sturzo, and a *Madonna and Child* by **Antonello Gagini**. At the far end of Via Sturzo stands the **Chiesa di**

San Giorgio (11C-13C); home to the panel painting of the ***Mystery of the Trinity****, attributed to the Flemish artist Rogier van der Weyden.

The logical extension of Via Sturzo, on the opposite side of the steps, is Via Vittorio Emanuele. This leads to the **Basilica di San Giacomo**, dedicated to the town's patron saint, in which a Gagini silver casket containing the relics of the saint is preserved.

ON THE EDGE OF TOWN

A stroll through the typical back streets of the old quarters on the periphery of town will reveal various unexpected surprises, like the neo-Gothic façade of the Chiesa di San Pietro (in the district of the same name, to the southeast), complete with maiolica decoration.

Chiesa dei Cappuccini

Open 9am-noon and 3.30-7pm. €2. ☎ 0933 21 753; www.cappuccinicaltagirone.it-homepage.com

The Capuchin church on the eastern edge of the town contains a lovely altarpiece by Filippo Paladini which depicts the Hodegetria Madonna (an icon representing the Virgin as a Guide or Instructress pointing to the Way of Redemption, said to have been painted by St Luke) being carried on the shoulders of Basilian monks from the East (Jerusalem) to the West (Constantinople). On the left side of the nave, is a *Deposition* by Fra' Semplice da Verona which has an interesting play of perspective. Additional paintings are displayed in the local art gallery next to the church, with art works drawn from the 16C to the present day. From here, there is access to the crypt where an unusual arrangement of figures re-enact different scenes from the life of Christ; one after the other, the different tableaux are illuminated and provided with a short commentary. The figures, all made by different local artisans, date from the 1990s.

Worth a Visit

Museo della Ceramica

Via Giardino Pubblico. (♿) Open 9am-6.30pm. €2.50. ☎ 0933 21 680; www.regione.sicilia.it/beniculturali

The **Teatrino**, an unusual 18C building decorated with maiolica tiles, houses this interesting museum which relates the history of the local ceramic industry from prehistoric times to the beginning of the 20C. The diffusion and importance of moulded clay is exemplified by an elegant 5C BC **krater*** bearing a potter working at his wheel being watched by a young apprentice.

The 17C is particularly well represented, with albarello jars (apothecaries' jars) painted in shades of yellow, blue and green, and amphorae and vases with medallions depicting religious or profane subjects.

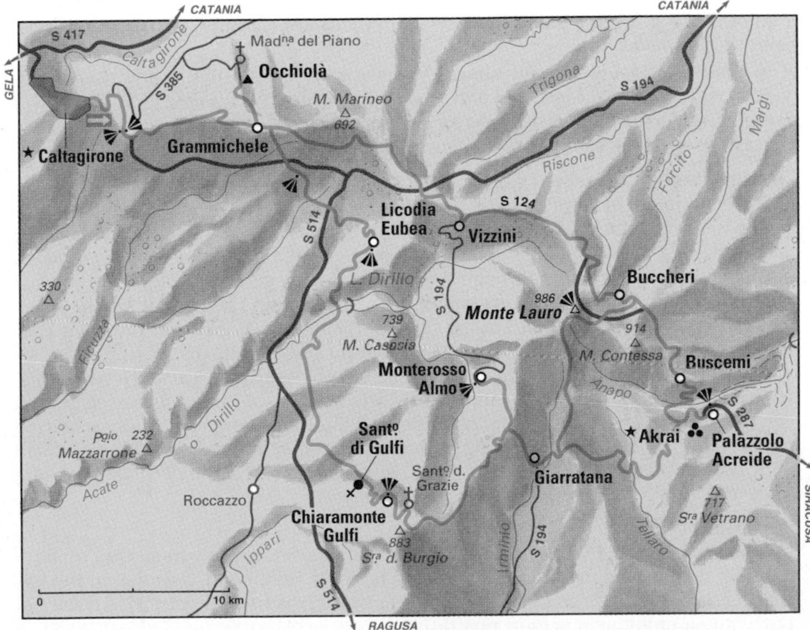

The geometric town plan of Grammichele

Museo Civico

Via Roma 10. Open 9.30am-1.30pm (2.30pm Sun) and 4-7pm. Closed Mon, Wed and Thu afternoons. No charge. ☎ *0933 41 212; www.comune.caltagirone.ct.it*

The displays on the second floor of this museum comprise a permanent exhibition of contemporary work in maiolica. One room displays the gilded wood and silver litter of San Giacomo (late 16C), which continued to be used in processions on 25 July until 1966: note the caryatids' delicate facial features. The third room is devoted to the Vaccaro family: two generations of painters active during the 19C; Mario's *Little Girl Praying* is especially evocative.

The first floor accommodates the municipal art gallery containing works by Sicilian painters.

Tours

GLI IBLEI*

The round trip of approx 160km/100mi can be completed over two days, starting at Caltagirone and overnighting in Vizzini. From Caltagirone follow signs to Ragusa and Grammichele along S 124.

The southeastern corner of Sicily is dominated by the Iblei mountains, posted here almost as if to defend the area around Ragusa. The little mountain villages perched on the ridges or scattered among the woods and valleys have retained their rural aspect, in close harmony with the land that has sustained them for centuries.

Follow S 124 as far as a junction where both roads are signposted to Grammichele; take the left-hand fork.

The road provides wonderful **views**** over the vast plain that is intensely cultivated with cereal crops. Beyond the hills which, according to Tomasi di Lampedusa, evoke *un mare bruscamente pietrificato* (a suddenly petrified sea), looms the dark majestic form of Mount Etna.

Grammichele

The development of Grammichele can be traced back to 1693 when a terrible earthquake shattered the southeastern section of Sicily. The new town was laid out according to a highly singular and regular plan centred around a hexagonal piazza and six radial axes passing through the centre of each side. A series of orthogonal streets are then arranged in concentric hexagons around the central space.

The buildings overlooking the piazza include the Chiesa Madre and the town hall; the latter, in turn, houses the municipal **museum** (*first floor*) which brings together various archaeological artefacts recovered from the nearby area of Terravecchia, where the ancient town of Occhiolà was situated before being destroyed by the earthquake and abandoned. The inhabitants of Occhiolà were eventually rehoused in the new town of Grammichele, named after the saint traditionally associated with protection from earthquakes. *Open 9am-1pm and 4-7.30pm (3-6.30pm Tue and Thu). €1.50.* ☎ *0933 85 92 09.*

Occhiolà

Occhiolà is situated about 3km/1.8mi from Grammichele along the road to Catania, near a road-maintenance building before a tight bend. A stone on the left bearing an inscription marks the beginning of the road to the site where the old town stood, enjoying a **scenic position**.

From Grammichele, the road up to Licodia Eubea (11km/7mi) provides a series of wonderful views★★ over the plain below.

Licodia Eubea

This hamlet, occupying a panoramic situation at the head of the valley of the River Dirillo, was probably built upon the ancient ruins of Euboia, which was founded by the colonists of Leontinoi in about the 7C BC. It comprises several 18C churches and **Palazzo Vassallo** *(Via Mugnos, at the end of Via Umberto, on the right)*, a formal Baroque building with a doorway flanked by columns and a balcony with brackets bearing masks and volutes.

From the ruins of the medieval castle extends a sweeping **view★** over the valley below and the artificial lake formed by the Dirillo.

Retrace your steps to the turn-off for the Lago di Licodia (or Dirillo) and head towards the lake.

Follow the old road to Chiaramonte Gulfi for approximately 10km/6mi through a lovely stretch of **mountain scenery★**. A little further on, the **Lago Dirillo** dam comes into view on the left.

Near a bend, just before a road-maintenance casa cantoniera (on the right), turn left (the road to the right leads to Vittoria and Chiaramonte Gulfi).

Santuario di Gulfi

Before the 1693 earthquake, a village occupied the broad site where the lonely sanctuary of Gulfi now stands, isolated. The sanctuary was built in the 18C on the spot where, it is said, the yoked oxen transporting a statue of the Madonna "emerged from the sea" (found on the shore near Camarina) knelt down. The story is illustrated inside by four painted medallions, which also relate how the statue of the Salvatore (Saviour) came to be found and taken to the Church of the Saviour in Chiaramonte.

Continue along the road for approximately 4km/2.5mi.

Chiaramonte Gulfi

The Greek town of Akrillai, renamed Gulfi by the Arabs, was razed to the ground in 1296 and immediately rebuilt by Manfred Chiaramonte, after whom it was renamed.

Although much of the fabric was destroyed by the 1693 earthquake, the hamlet preserves its medieval organisation. The Arco dell'Annunziata, an ancient gateway to the old town, is the only fragment to survive from the Chiaramonte era (14C). Among the principal Baroque buildings, look out for San Giovanni (at the top of the hill) and the **Chiesa Madre**. The main street, Corso Umberto I, is lined with 18C and 19C *palazzi;* and at its western extremity, stands the Villa Comunale (town hall), from where a magnificent **view** opens out over the valley.

In the higher part of town, sits the Santuario delle Grazie surrounded by pine trees (picnic facilities) and an all-encompassing **view★** over Chiaramonte and Etna. The legend that touches upon this little sanctuary relates how the local people offered up their prayers to the Madonna for salvation from the plague in 1576, whereupon a spring of clear water emerged from the ground on this very spot.

The road to Monterosso Almo (20km/12.5mi) snakes its way among gentle slopes covered with cultivated fields enclosed by **drystone walls**, an ever-present feature of the Iblei landscape. These transfer geometric figures onto the green fields, endowing the scenery with a sense of order and distorted perspective. At times, even the road is delineated by drystone walling.

The Iblei landscape, with its typical drystone walls

G. Bludzin/MICHELIN

Drystone walling

An ever-present reminder of human impact on the rural landscape are the ribbons of drystone walling that extend in all directions: small, low-lying yet resistant courses of stone, no more than a metre high, enclose the cultivated fields. Interestingly, the very nature of these walls reflects the geological formation of the Iblei. For, just as with the bed rock, the surface layer of limestone is impermeable: where this layer is damaged by erosion or fracture, water will penetrate through the underlying layers causing them to crumble and disintegrate into lumps; in the most extreme cases, this can produce whole canyons. The broken lumps of rock litter the ground, requiring farmers to remove them before they can sow their fields: the walls are conceived as a way of re-using the stones so laboriously gathered which, instead of being heaped in a pile, are employed as building materials. However, this is no haphazard pastime but a skilled art learned from master-craftsmen known in the vernacular as *mastri ri mura a siccu*. The walls segregate different land holdings and enable flocks to graze unsupervised; they also support terraced land.

Monterosso Almo

The Church of **San Giovanni★** lends its name to the piazza onto which it faces: together they provide a focal point for the upper part of the little town, which depends entirely upon agriculture. The front elevation of the church, attributed to **Vincenzo Sinatra**, rises through columns to culminate in a bell tower. Inside, it is ornamented with friezes of stucco picked out against pastel backgrounds. The nave ceiling is punctuated with shallow relief medallions containing scenes from the life of St John.

In the lower part of the town (in the wake of the 1693 earthquake, Monterosso – like Ragusa and Modica – was divided into two parts), stands a church to rival San Giovanni, this time honouring **Sant'Antonio** (also known as Santuario di Maria Santissima Addolorata). The same square is graced with the neo-Gothic **Chiesa Madre**, and the elegant Palazzo Zacco.

Follow S 194 for 7km/4mi.

Giarratana

Three monuments constitute the artistic heritage of this hamlet: the late-Renaissance Chiesa Madre, and two Baroque churches dedicated to San Bartolomeo and Sant'Antonio Abate.

An onion festival, the Sagra della Cipolla, is held annually in August in Giarratana.

From Giarratana it is possible to either continue to Palazzolo or shorten the tour by turning left to Buccheri and following the road that leads to the top of **Monte Lauro**. The road (10km/6mi) that winds its way up the mountain through intense patches of colour provided by red valerian (Centranthus ruber), dark green carobs and pines, provides glorious **views★** over the high plateau.

To get to Palazzolo from Giarratana, follow the main road for 14km/9mi, then turn right towards the site of Ancient Akrai.

Akrai★

(♿) Open Apr-Oct, 9am-6pm; Nov-Mar, 9am-3pm. €2. ☎ *0931 48 11 11.*

The small theatre at Akrai

The strategically located Ancient town of Akrai was founded in 664 BC as a defensive outpost of Syracuse. At the top of the hill where the acropolis used to lie, all that is visible of the small **Greek theatre** built of white stone is the floor of the orchestra, and this actually dates from Roman times. To the right lay the ***bouleuterion***, a stepped meeting-area, connected to the theatre by a narrow passage leading straight into the *cavea*. Near to the gate that seals off the excavation area on this side, may be seen a section of the old *plateia* (main road running from east to west) paved with large slabs of lava stone.
Two former Greek quarries next to the theatre were converted by the Christians for use as catacombs and troglodyte dwellings. Near the entrance to the **Intagliatella**, the narrower of the two quarries, on the right, there is a low relief of a heroic figure participating in a banquet (*right*) and offering up a sacrifice (*left*). Excavation of the area along the fence has uncovered vestiges of a residential quarter and a circular building, probably a temple built in Roman times.
The track that skirts around the edge of the archaeological site provides a lovely **view★** over the surrounding valley.

I Santoni – *1km/0.6mi from the archaeological site.* Tucked away in a small valley nearby, 12 rock-hewn figures dating from the 3C BC testify to the existence in Sicily of a cult of Oriental origin. The main sculpture represents the **goddess Cybele** (Demeter), seated between two lions, or standing surrounded by smaller figures. N° II, one of the best-preserved, represents the Dioscuri – Castor and Pollux on horseback on either side. N° VIII shows the goddess seated.

Palazzolo Acreide

Palazzolo was largely rebuilt in the 18C and so has many Baroque buildings lining its main thoroughfares: Corso Vittorio Emanuele and Via Carlo Alberto, which intersect at Piazza del Popolo. The square is dominated by the majestic façade of **San Sebastiano** raised up a flight of steps. At the western end of the *corso* stands the **Chiesa dell'Immacolata** with its convex frontage, in which is preserved a most delicate *Madonna and Child* by **Francesco Laurana**. Via Carlo Alberto passes between a series of palazzi with wonderful Baroque details. One of the streets off to the right (Via Machiavelli) leads to the **Casa-Museo dell'etnologo Antonino Uccello** – a *palazzo* once owned by Baron Ferla and later turned into a house-museum by another owner, the ethnologist Antonio Uccello. On the ground floor is displayed an oil-press *(third room)* and the Casa del Massaro: the house of the baron's most trusted man, furnished with everyday objects. *Open 9am-1pm and 3.30-7pm. No charge. ☎ 0931 88 14 99.*
At the end of the street, turn right onto Piazza Umberto I where the Church of **San Paolo** is situated. The striking frontage, possibly designed by **Vincenzo Sinatra**, rises through three tiers of rounded arches and columns capped with Corinthian capitals. The top storey comprises the bell tower.
Follow Via dell'Annunziata out of the piazza to the church of the same name; its façade, which remains incomplete, has an interesting **doorway★** flanked with spiral columns. Return along Via dell'Annunziata and turn left down Via Garibaldi to take a look at **Palazzo Iudica** (at n°s 123-131) and its amazingly long balcony supported by brackets carved with monsters, fantastical figures, masks and other such elements so typical of the Baroque period.
The road to Buscemi *(9km/5.5mi)* provides a succession of wonderful **views★**.

Seeds and Diamonds

One of the most commonly recurring elements in the Iblei landscape is the **carob tree**, a large evergreen growing, often in isolation, in the middle of a field. The broad growth of characteristically shiny dark green leaves provides deep shade. Its beans, which can be used as a thickener or as an alternative to coffee when ground into powder, or as animal feed, once had a nobler use: the fact that their weight is always consistent, meant that they came to be used as units of measurement for precious stones; the term "carat" derives from the Arabic name for the carob, *Qirat*.

Buscemi

This little farming hamlet accommodates an unusual and intriguingly interesting museum dedicated to rural craftsmanship: **I Luoghi del Lavoro Contadino★**. The various venues, eight in all, are scattered throughout the town: each is dedicated to recapturing the life and work of the Iblei mountain people. These include the blacksmith's forge, the oil press (where some of the scenes of the film *La Lupa* by Gabriele Lavia were shot), a farmstead, the houses of a farm labourer *(lo Jurnataru)*, cobbler and carpenter, and a wine press to which the grapes were brought; a room attached to this last venue contains a small film library. Despite possible problems of language, the archive films showing the various activities in times past are most engaging. The tour finishes with the watermill (Mulino ad acqua Santa Lucia), situated in the valley of mills *(valle dei mulini)* at Palazzolo Acreide. The mill now houses a small museum, **the Museo della Maccina del Grano**. *Open 9am-1pm. €4 for the "Luoghi del Lavoro Contadino", €2.50 for the mill and minibus there (reservation necessary). ☎ 0931 87 85 28; www.museobuscemi.org*

A wander through the streets will also reveal a number of Baroque monuments, including the lovely façade of the Chiesa Madre, the curvilinear elevation of Sant'Antonio da Padova e San Sebastiano, as well as various other hidden corners of town, notably the farmers' quarter populated with low stone houses.

Immediately after rejoining the main road, a glance up at the rock face below the town will provide a view of the tombs excavated by the Siculi (12C-13C BC).

After 6km/4mi, the road reaches Buccheri.

Buccheri

Perched at a height of 820m/2 689ft, this hamlet boasts a church dedicated to Mary Magdalen with a lovely façade (18C) articulated by two tiers of columns and pilasters, and another dedicated to St Anthony Abbot with a front elevation that rises in one sweep to a tall tower, exaggerated by a long, steep staircase up to the door.

Continue to Vizzini.

> **Tours**
>
> The cry "Hanno ammazzato compare Turiddu" can be heard at the end of Cavalleria Rusticana, a Tuscan opera set in Sicily, very much inspired by the sunshine isle as seen and interpreted by Mascagni when placing Verga's novel in the opera house. For those familiar with these acclaimed works of Italian literature, an exploration of Vizzini might begin at the hostelry where Turiddo and Alfio challenge each other to a duel, or at the church of Santa Teresa where the friends go to pray (in the opera), or even the houses of Gnà Lola and Santuzza, and la Cunzirìa, the old tanners' district outside town, where the two friends fight. A careful search will also uncover the house and noble *palazzi* around which the story of Mastro Don Gesualdo unfurls. Themed guided tours are organised by the Pro Loco at Via Lombarda 8, ☎ 0933 96 59 05.

Vizzini

Vizzini was used by the novelist **Giovanni Verga** as a backdrop for several of his books, including *La Lupa (The She-Wolf)*, *La Cavalleria Rusticana* (on which Mascagni based his famous opera), and *The Story of Mastro Don Gesualdo*.

Vizzini has grown up around Piazza Umberto I, where the Palazzo Verga and the Palazzo Municipale are located. Alongside the town hall rises a flight of steps, the **Salita Marineo**, decorated with maiolica tiles featuring geometric and floral designs arranged around a central medallion painted with views of buildings in Vizzini. This scheme, completed in 1996, echoes a similar stairway to Santa Maria del Monte at Caltagirone (*see CALTAGIRONE*).

The Chiesa Madre preserves a Norman-Gothic doorway (*right side*), a lonely vestige of the original church that survived the earthquake of 1693 which destroyed much of the town and provided an incentive for major rebuilding. The town's Baroque constructions include the beautiful frontage of **San Sebastiano**.

The church of **Santa Maria di Gesù** contains a *Madonna and Child* by **Antonello Gagini**. *To visit the church, contact Signore Giovanni Torturice a few days in advance, ☎ 335 13 81 727 (mobile) or 0933 96 11 09.*

From Vizzini, either take the old road to Caltagirone and Grammichele (S 214 for 30km/19mi), or follow the tour described below.

Vizzini: Ricotta Festival

G. Iacono/Lara Pessina/MICHELIN

BEYOND THE NORTHERN SLOPES OF THE IBLEI

Tour:100km/62mi from Caltagirone or 75km/47mi from the end of the tour described above (Vizzini) – allow one day.

See above for the Caltagirone-Grammichele section of the tour.

After Grammichele, follow S 124 for approximately 10km/6mi as far as the turn-off to the left for Militello in Val di Catania (25km/15mi E of Grammichele).

Militello in Val di Catania

The Baroque town of Militello is largely indebted to Joan of Austria (1573-1630), Charles V's granddaughter, for its prosperity: when she married Francesco Branciforte, she came to the place with her predilection for sophisticated culture and her taste for beautiful things. Militello was transformed into an aristocratic court and enjoyed living its period of glory to the full. As a result, the streets of the old town centre bristle with a multitude of fine Baroque buildings.

Start your visit in Piazza del Municipio, home to the **Monastero Benedettino** (1614-41), an imposing Benedictine monastery (now used as the town hall), which has a highly decorative frontage. The main **façade** of the **church** next door is ornamented with rusticated window surrounds, a common feature peculiar to the Militello style of Baroque. Inside, it contains Sebastiano Conca's painting of *The Last Communion of St Benedict* (third chapel on the left) and a fine set of carved wooden choir stalls depicting the Mysteries and scenes from the life of St Benedict (1734). *Open Mon-Fri, 4.30-7pm; Sat, 5-7pm; Sun and public hols, 9.30-10.30am. No charge.*

Continue along Via Umberto, past the 18C Palazzo Reforgiato, to Piazza Vittorio Emanuele.

Museo di San Nicolò – *Open summer, daily except Tue, 9am-1pm and 5-8pm; otherwise, daily except Tue, 9am-1pm and 4-7pm. €2.50. ☎ 095 81 12 51.*

The museum is housed in the undercrofts of the Chiesa Madre, built in 1721. The objects displayed are **fabulously arranged★** so as to enhance their beauty and heighten their impact. These include a fine collection of 17C and 18C religious vestments, prized treasures from the town's various other churches – notably the silver plate from Santa Maria alla Catena, as well as the jewellery, votive and liturgical objects from Sant'Agata. The last rooms are devoted to pictures: an altarpiece *Annunciation* by Francesco Franzetto (1552), a strongly lit Caravaggesque *Attack on San Carlo Borromeo* by the Tuscan painter Filippo Paladini (1612), and a gentle treatment of the *Immacolata* by Vaccaro.

The Church of **Santa Maria alla Catena** on Piazza Vittorio Emanuele was rebuilt in 1652. Its fine **interior★** is encrusted with lovely **stuccowork** by artists from Acireale; this represents in the upper tier, scenes from the Joyful Mysteries, while the lower tier harbours various Sicilian saints surrounded by cherubs, festoons and cornucopias. The overall effect is completed by an elegant coffered wooden ceiling from 1661.

Turn left onto Via Umberto. Beyond the attractively concave façade of the Chiesa del Santissimo Sacramento al Circolo, lies Piazza Maria Santissima della Stella.

Maria Santissima della Stella – *Treasury open by appointment only. ☎ 095 65 53 29.*

This church, with its fine doorway and spiral columns, was erected between 1722 and 1741. Inside, it preserves a magnificent glazed terracotta **Nativity altarpiece★** (1487) by the early Renaissance Florentine master **Andrea della Robbia**. The **Treasury** contains a fine late-15C altarpiece with scenes from the life of St Peter by the Maestro della Croce of Piazza Armerina, and the *Portrait of Pietro Speciale,* a shallow relief by **Francesco Laurana**.

Palazzo Majorana, one of the few buildings dating from the 16C, extends along the same side of the square beside the church. Note its heavily rusticated cornerstones bearing carved lions.

At the far end of the palazzo, turn left, then immediately right for Santa Maria la Vetere up ahead.

Chiesa di Santa Maria la Vetere – Most of the church collapsed following the earthquake of 1693, leaving only the wall of the south aisle intact. Above the front entrance with its 16C porch, sits a lunette enclosing shallow reliefs. The overall **impact★** is heightened by the splendid position of the church, nestling in its green valley, right on the edge of town.

Pass back through the town gate and turn immediately left for the Chiesa dei Santissimi Angeli Custodi.

The **Chiesa dei Santissimi Angeli Custodi** contains a wonderful maiolica **floor★** laid with tiles from Caltagirone (1785). *Closed for restoration at the time of going to press. ☎ 095 65 53 29.*

Return the way you have come and turn left so as to skirt around the ruins of the Branciforte castle (comprising a round tower and sections of wall), pass through the town gate – Porta della Terra – and reach the piazza beyond.

At the centre of what once constituted the castle courtyard sits a fountain: **Fontana della Ninfa Zizza**, built in 1607 to commemorate the opening of Militello's first aqueduct, sponsored by Branciforte.

> **TAKING A BREAK**
>
> The seasonal specialities in the sweets line associated with Militello range from the cassatelline – made with ground almonds, chocolate and cinnamon; the mastrazzuoli – Christmas titbits made with almonds, cinnamon and vermouth; to the mostarda – concocted from semolina or wine must, boiled with prickly-pear extract (available around the second or third Sunday in October, for the Sagra della Mostarda).

Continue on to Scordia (11km/7mi NE).

Scordia

Scordia is built on a rectilinear town plan, arranged around the palazzo of the Branciforte family, the lords of the town during the 17C. The main square, Piazza Umberto, is enclosed by noble *palazzi* and a church with a lofty front elevation, dedicated to San Rocco.

The 18C **Santa Maria Maggiore** has an interesting façade incorporating a bell tower.

Continue on to Palagonia (12km/7.5mi NW).

S 385 picks its way through **rolling landscape★** past the lush groves of lemon and orange trees for which the area is famous, and the small rocky hills known as Coste to the south.

Palagonia

For the Siculi, Palagonia was important in both political and religious terms: according to local legend, it was from the bubbling sulphurous waters of the **Laghetto di Naftia** that their gods, the **Palici**, were born and it is to them that they dedicated the temple built on the edge of the lake. Nowadays, the lake is masked from view by installations for collecting the natural gas for industrial purposes. The name Palagonìa is strongly associated with the superb blood oranges that are grown in this area.

Eremo di Santa Febronia

Follow S 385 from Palagonia towards Catania; take the right fork signposted for Contrada Croce. After 4.5km/3mi, as the road curves to the right, look out for a track on the left barricaded by a metal barrier. The hermitage is a 15min walk up the track. The evocative little hermitage is named after Santa Febronia, known locally as a' *Santuzza*, because her relics are brought here each year in a great procession from nearby Palagonia. The small retreat, carved out of the rock, is Byzantine in date (7C). Inside, the apse contains a fine, albeit damaged, fresco of Christ flanked by the Madonna and an angel.

Take S 385 to Caltagirone. After 8km/5mi, turn left to Mineo.

Mineo

The place where the writer Luigi Capuana (1839-1915) was born has its origins in Antiquity, especially since it has been identified as the ancient town of Mene, founded by Ducetius, the king of the Siculi. The town's main gateway, Porta Adinolfo, is 18C; beside it sits the Jesuit College; while beyond lies the main square and the **Chiesa del Collegio**. Via Umberto I leads into Piazza Agrippina, where a 15C church (apses) with the same name is to be found. At the top of the town, next to the Church of Santa Maria, lie the ruins of a castle. From here, a wonderful view extends over the whole valley.

Retrace your steps to S 385, from where the views on the return journey to Caltagirone (25km/15mi) are particularly impressive.

Caltanissetta

Situated at the very heart of Sicily, surrounded by gently rolling hills and wide valleys dotted with sulphur and rock salt mines, Caltanissetta extends across a plateau 568m/1 863ft above sea level, offering magnificent views of the outlying countryside.

Location

Population: 62 274. Michelin map 565 O 24. Caltanissetta is a difficult town for motorists, as a result of poor signposts and frequent road works. Visitors are best advised to leave their car in the nearest car park and explore the narrow streets of the town on foot. ℹ *Viale Conte Testasecca 21; ☎ 0934 21 089; Fax 0934 21 239.* *Neighbouring sights are described in the following chapters: AGRIGENTO; ENNA; PIAZZA ARMERINA; VILLA IMPERIALE DEL CASALE.*

Background

Caltanissetta started out as a small Greek town, before succumbing to the same fate endured by the rest of Sicily, passing from one domination to another. It enjoyed its greatest prosperity in the early 1900s when the extraction of local sulphur deposits was at its height, an activity which soon became the prime industry. Caltanissetta established itself as the leading exporter of sulphur, responsible for as much as four-fifths of world production. Fierce competition from America, however, soon threatened Caltanissetta's pre-eminence, forcing all the sulphur mines in the area to close.

Directory

Where to Eat

• For all budgets

Legumerie le Fontanelle – *Via Pietro Leone 45, contrada Fontanelle – 2km/1.2mi NW of Caltanissetta – ☎ 0934 59 24 37 – €17/22.* This small restaurant is part of a farm riding centre. With its rural-style decor, rustic feel and simple local dishes featuring meat and vegetables, it has the atmosphere of a typical trattoria.

Duomo – *Piazza Garibaldi 3, Caltanissetta – ☎ 0934 58 23 31 – Closed Sun, Mon lunchtime and in Aug – ▤ – Booking recommended – €20.50/26.* This simply decorated restaurant situated near the Duomo has a wide selection of dishes, with the emphasis on delicious, innovative regional cuisine.

Where to Stay

• Budget

Hotel Plaza – *Via Gaetani 5, Caltanissetta – ☎ 0934 58 38 77 – Fax 0934 58 38 77 – www.hotelplazacaltanissetta.it – ▤ – 33 rooms. €49/70 ☕.* After a day's sightseeing in Caltanissetta and its surrounding area, enjoy a relaxing stay in this pleasant hotel located in the centre of town. The rooms here are spacious and comfortable, with modern furnishings.

Festivals

The town is notorious for its extravagant celebrations of **Holy Week**: when, on the Thursday evening, groups of 19C statues arranged in tableaux representing scenes from the Mysteries of the Passion (the Deposition composition is particularly powerful), made by Neapolitan craftsmen, are processed through the streets; on Good Friday, the statue of a Black Christ is carried in procession across town. Outside Holy Week, these figures are kept in the **Chiesa di Pio X** in Via Colajanni.

Walking About

The historic town centre clusters around **Piazza Garibaldi** at the junction of the town's two main thoroughfares, Corso Umberto and Corso Vittorio Emanuele. Grouped around the square are the town hall (in the former Carmelite convent), the cathedral, the **Chiesa di San Sebastiano** with its Baroque frontage which, like Sant'Agata (at the end of Corso Umberto) and Santa Croce (at the end of Corso Vittorio Emanuele), is painted dark red, in marked contrast with the natural stone colour of the other architecture. In the centre sits the **Fontana del Tritone** (1956) by the local sculptor Michele Tripisciano, based on a 19C model. The bronze sculpture consists of a sea-horse being held back by a triton while under threat from two winged monsters.

Beyond the town hall in Salita Matteotti, stands the 17C **Palazzo Moncada**, which although never completed, has a façade with intriguing carved corbels in the form of human and animal figures.

Cathedral

The cathedral was erected in the late 16C. Its interior frescoes are by the Flemish painter Guglielmo Borremans (1720). The alternation of painted panels and stucco decoration combine to produce a dramatic impact. The 17C wooden figure of St Michael (1615) is by the Sicilian sculptor Stefano Li Volsi *(chapel to the right of the choir)*. The wonderful gilded wooden organ in the choir was built in 1601.

Sant'Agata al Collegio

The 17C church has a composite front elevation fashioned in natural stone, red plasterwork and marble (doorway); inside, it contains elaborate inlaid polychrome marble decoration, and a beautiful marble altarpiece by **Ignazio Marabitti**.

In front of the church stands a statue of Umberto I.

To the east of Piazza Garibaldi stretches the Quartiere degli Angeli which preserves its medieval layout. At its centre stands **San Domenico**, a church with a fine Baroque façade with undulating panels. The painting inside of the *Madonna of the Rosary* is by Filippo Paladini. *Open 4-5.30pm. ☎ 0934 25 104.*

Further along Via degli Angeli, the remains of the Saracen castle of Pietrarossa, perched on a rock, comes into view. Below, at the foot of the rock, stand the derelict ruins of Santa Maria degli Angeli (13C) with the church's lovely doorway.

Worth a Visit

Museo Archeologico

Via Napoleone Colajanni 1 (near the railway station). Open 9am-1pm and 3.30-7.30pm. Closed last Mon in the month. €2. ☎ 0934 50 42 40.

The museum gathers together artefacts recovered from around Caltanissetta and highlights the indigenous pre-Hellenistic civilisation and the impact made by Greek influences. Finds from the Greek necropolis at **Gibil-Gabib** include an unusual small clay cask from the 4C BC, later used as a funerary urn; other exhibits, such as a *strigil* (the tool used by athletes to scrape away oil, sweat and dead skin as illustrated in a mosaic at Villa Imperiale del Casale, *see p 384*), were discovered at the Greek necropolis at **Vassallaggi**. Among the objects found in the Greek settlement of Sabucina, note the small-scale terracotta model of a **temple★**; the votive object dating from the 6C BC; two large basins (one on a high pedestal) for holding drink or oil; and the *krater* bearing a painting of the god Hephaestus, seated in his forge, hammering out hot iron (6C-5C BC). From the site at **Dessueri** there is a fine set of "teapots" used for boiling opium (indigenous culture, 13C BC) and an Attic *kylix* showing Heracles armed with a club, evidence of the hero's enduring popularity in Sicily. The last room contains a series of particularly sophisticated early artefacts from the local pre-Hellenistic cultures: note the refined geometric decoration and the stylised relief of the bull's head that appear on many of the clay pieces, and the two bronze statuettes with their arms outstretched (7C-6C BC) in the centre of the room. At the back, a bronze **shin-guard** and **helmet** dating from the Corinthian period (6C BC) are displayed.

Excursions

Abbazia di Santo Spirito

*3km/2mi NE on S 122 to Enna.*The abbey founded by Roger I (11C) and consecrated in 1153, is Romanesque in style. It has three typically Norman apses ornamented by decorative blind arcading. Inside, it has a wonderful 15C wooden crucifix and a deep early Romanesque baptismal font for the total immersion of infants, decorated with stylised palmettes.

ARCHAEOLOGICAL SITES AROUND CALTANISSETTA

The archaeological excavations undertaken (and still in progress) in the Province of Caltanissetta are open to the public, even if they are difficult to find and rarely visited by tourists. Indeed, they remain the preserve of impassioned enthusiasts.

Sabucina

Signposted off the main Enna road, 12km/7mi E of Caltanissetta. Here, traces of an early hut settlement (12C BC) have been brought to light, together with elements from the subsequent phase (7C BC) in the local civilisation. A section of wall dating from the 5C or 4C BC has also been found.

Vassallaggi

From Caltanissetta, take S 640 towards San Cataldo. Follow to the junction with Serradifalco signed to the left and San Cataldo to the right: the sign (pointing right) for the excavations is wrong; the correct direction is straight on. After a few metres, a small tarred road branches right, passing through a gate which is usually open (information panel); follow the road until it degenerates into a dirt track (farm on the left). A green fence on the left delineates the excavated site. The dig has so far uncovered an ancient settlement. The area includes a sacred precinct dedicated to gods of the underworld, surrounded by some 50 or so dependent buildings for use by officiators of the cult.

Gibil-Gabel

6km/4mi S of Caltanissetta. This site preserves the ruins of an ancient Sicani town and its necropolis.

Capo d'Orlando

This pleasant small town is one of the most popular seaside resorts along this stretch of coastline, with beautiful sandy and pebble beaches, including the delightful Lido San Gregorio, to the east of the town.

Location

Population: 12 755. Michelin map 565 26M – Messina Capo d'Orlando is a good base for trips to the Nebrodi, while little more than 60km/37mi separate it from Randazzo, on the slopes of Mount Etna. In summer, daily excursions are organised to the Aeolian Islands. *Via Piave 71 A/B, ☎ 0941 91 27 84.*

Neighbouring sights are described in the following chapters: CEFALÙ; Isole EOLIE; ETNA; MADONIE E NEBRODI; MILAZZO; Golfo di PATTI.

Walking About

The centre of the town falls between Via Piave which is lined by smart shops, and the promenade which runs parallel, along the beautiful beach.
At the very tip of the promontory, up a flight of steps, is a purpose-built **viewpoint★** overlooking the ruins of the castle of Orlando and the 17C **Santuario di Maria Santissima di Capo d'Orlando**, to which pilgrims flock each year (22 October).

The Legend of Capo d'Orlando

The history of Capo d'Orlando is intertwined with the legend of its foundation at the time of the Trojan War by Agathyrsus, the son of Aeolus. The legend also relates how the ancient settlement of Agathyrnis came to be renamed Capo d'Orlando by Charlemagne, who passing through these lands on a pilgrimage to the Holy Land, decided to call the place after his heroic paladin.
In 1299, the town watched the naval battle between James and Frederick of Aragon over the throne of Sicily.

Tours

ALONG THE COAST FROM CAPO D'ORLANDO TO CAPO CALAVÀ

Approximately 20km/12.5mi along S 113 in the direction of Messina.
Following the coast beyond the cape towards San Gregorio, the road offers beautiful **views★** of the beach and the deep blue sea, its surface broken here and there by rocks and small seaside resorts.

Terme di Bagnoli

Open Apr-Sep, 9am-7pm; Oct-Mar, 9am-2pm. No charge. ☎ 0941 95 54 01.
On the outskirts of Capo d'Orlando at San Gregorio, in the district of Bagnoli, the remains of a bathing complex attached to a Roman villa dating from the Imperial period have been found. They include the **frigidarium** (marked 1-2-3), the

Directory

Where to Eat

• *For all budgets*

Trattoria La Tettoia – *Contrada Certari 80, Capo d'Orlando – 2.5km/1.5mi S of Capo d'Orlando on S 116 – ☎ 0941 90 21 46 – Closed Mon (except Jul-Sep) and 15-30 Oct –* ⊠ *– €16/21.* This family-run trattoria has everything you need for a pleasant meal out: a friendly, informal atmosphere; genuine regional cuisine; and a panoramic terrace for eating outside in the summer.

Il Gabbiano – *Via Trazzera Marina 146, Capo d'Orlando – ☎ 0941 90 20 66 – ristorantegabbiano@virgilio.it – Closed Tue –* ⊠ *– €18/23.* Unanimously considered to be the best pizzeria in the area, this simple, well-run restaurant also has a spacious veranda. Don't miss the house specialities, which are based on traditional local dishes.

Bontempo "Il ristorante" – *Via Fiumara 38, Naso – From S 113 to Milazzo, turn right to Sinagra just before Ponte Naso. – ☎ 0941 96 11 88 – info@bontempoilristorante.com – Closed Mon – €28/36.* This restaurant is housed in a modern, white building surrounded by greenery, 10km/6mi to the southeast of Capo d'Orlando. It has three spacious dining rooms and serves a range of local dishes.

Where to Stay

• *Budget*

Nuovo Hotel Faro – *Via Libertà 7, Capo d'Orlando – ☎ 0941 90 24 66 – Fax 0941 91 14 61 – nuovo.hotelfaro@tiscali.it –* ⊠ *– 30 rooms. €26/68 ☕ €3.* As its name suggests (*faro* is lighthouse in Italian), this family-run hotel is situated near the lighthouse. The communal areas of the hotel are simple but pleasant, and although the bedrooms are not the most modern, they are clean and well kept. What is more, the beach is only a stone's throw away.

• *Moderate*

Hotel La Tartaruga – *Lido San Gregorio, Capo d'Orlando – 2km/1.2mi E of Capo d'Orlando – ☎ 0941 95 50 12 – Fax 0941 95 50 56 – info@hoteltartaruga.it – Closed Mon (restaurant) and in Nov – 53 rooms. €65/100 ☕.* Situated in the heart of the tourist area of the town, 2km/1.2mi from Capo d'Orlando, this hotel is situated in an imposing building overlooking the beach. The rooms here are comfortable and modern in style and the adjoining restaurant is renowned for its fresh fish dishes.

Festivals

Vita e paesaggio di Capo d'Orlando – Since 1955, the town has hosted a summer competition, backed by the Messina painter Giuseppe Migneco, on the theme of the life and countryside of Capo d'Orlando whereby successful artists from Italy and abroad are commissioned to come and paint; some of the works, once the prize has been awarded, are acquired by the municipal art gallery.

Capo d'Orlando in blues – For information on this summer festival of Blues music, contact the Cross Road Club/Associazione Siciliana Musica Blues, Via Consolare Antica 623, Capo d'Orlando; ☎ 0941 95 72 35.

tepidarium (marked 4) and the **caldarium** (marked 5 and 6). Clearly visible are the **suspensurae** which would have served to heat the various rooms. In rooms 4, 5 and 6 are fragments of mosaics with geometric decorations.

Fondazione „Famiglia Piccolo di Calanovella"

Il Gran Visir by Casimiro Piccolo

Villa Piccolo di Calanovella

Marked by the 109km/68mi distance marker on S 113 between Messina and Palermo. (♿) Open mid-Jun to mid-Sep, 9am-noon and 5-7.30pm; otherwise, 9am-noon and 4-6pm. Closed national hols. €3. ☎ 0941 95 70 29; www.fondazionepiccolo.it

In keeping with the wishes of the last members of the Piccolo family, a museum-foundation was set up in the late 19C villa where they had lived since the 1930s. The Piccolos were an artistic family: in particular there was Lucio (who died in 1969), an acclaimed poet, and Casimiro, an enthusiastic painter and photographer, and a scholar of the occult. They were often visited by their cousin **Giuseppe di Lampedusa**, attracted as he was by the peace and quiet of the villa where he wrote a large part of his masterpiece *(The Leopard)*; in the room he once used is one of his letters to the Piccolo family, as is the bed in which he slept, ornamented with a beautiful ivory and mother-of-pearl bedhead depicting the Baptism of John (made by Trapani craftsmen in the 17C). Elsewhere in the villa are displayed porcelain from China, ceramics from Faenza and Capodimonte (notably a 10C Hispano-Moresque vase), dinner services, antique weapons, some Caltagirone 17C-18C ceramic water-bottles, and a fascinating series of fantastical **watercolours★** by Casimiro Piccolo, who enjoyed painting imaginary scenes from a fairy-tale world suffused with light and populated with amiable gnomes, elves, fairies and butterflies.
Before leaving, it is well worth taking a stroll under the pergolas in the villa gardens and seeking out the **canine graveyard** for the family pets.

Brolo

A flourishing port until the late 17C and now a seaside resort, the town has a fine medieval castle *(private)* built by the Lancia family in the 15C. Above the main archway is the family coat of arms, with the three pears of the Barony of Piràino.
Beyond Brolo, turn right at the next junction for Piràino.

Piràino

Stretched out along the spine of a hill enjoying a strategic position, Piràino retains much of its medieval form, scattered with religious buildings. Its legendary origins (supposed, as it is, to have been founded by the Cyclops Piracmon – Arges in Homer – one of the three Ministers of Vulcan) are probably rooted in the discovery of large bones in several caves nearby, erroneously believed to have belonged to the Cyclops.
All the **churches** are strung along the main street of the town. *Open Jun-Aug, 10am-noon and 6-8pm; Sep-May, 10am-noon only. When churches are closed, contact the tourist office for the key, ☎ 0941 58 14 07.*
The **Chiesa del Rosario**, the easternmost, dedicated to the Madonna of the Rosary, while retaining its 16C campanile, was rebuilt in 1635. Inside, it has a fine coffered wooden **ceiling** set with Byzantine-Norman rosettes, and an unusual wooden **high altar** painted with floral motifs (first half of the 17C) decorated with wooden medallions representing the Mysteries of the Rosary. The wooden figures in the centre of the altar represent the Madonna with saints.
Further along is the **Chiesa della Catena**, erected in the latter half of the 17C, where the first elections were held after the Unification of Italy. It contains some fine Byzantine-type **frescoes** from another church, the Chiesa della Badia.
Beyond is Piazza del Baglio, named after the complex of low-level workers' houses and workshops arranged around the **Palazzo Ducale**, built by the Lancia family (15C-16C).

Proceeding westwards, the way leads up to the highest part of the town which is marked by the beautifully preserved **Torre Saracena** or Torrazza (10C), from the terrace of which extends a magnificent **view★** across the rooftops nestling below and beyond to Capo d'Orlando. The tower was part of a defensive system which would have transmitted signals from the 16C **Torre delle Ciavole** on the coast, via the **Guardiola** situated to the north of the town, to the Torrazza.

On the western edge of town is **Santa Caterina d'Alessandria**, the church dedicated to St Catherine of Alexandria, built in the 16C but altered in the 17C. Inside, the wooden altar is decorated with floral motifs. A low relief to the right of the altar depicts St Catherine of Alexandria overcoming the infidel.

Turn back towards the coast.

Note, on your left, the **Torre delle Ciavole** *(see above).*

Continue to the small seaside resort of **Gioiosa Marea** *and follow the signs for San Filippo Armo and San Leonardo (about 9km/5.5mi) to Gioiosa Guardia.*

Rovine di Gioiosa Guardia

The ruins of this medieval town, abandoned by its inhabitants in the 18C for Gioiosa Marea, are situated at 800m/2 625ft above sealevel surrounded by romantic landscape. The idyllic serenity of the place is enhanced by the splendid **view★** over the surrounding countryside.

Return to the coast.

A little further on is **Capo Calavà**, a spectacular rocky spur.

Carini

A winding road leads to this delightful town, set on a hill overlooking its own bay, and overlooked in its turn by the elegant silhouette of its castle. The medieval town, haunted by the tragic spirit of Baronessa Laura di Carini and her lover, clusters around the foot of the castle.

Location

Population: 24 907. Michelin map 565 21M - Palermo. Carini, situated slightly inland from the bay of the same name, lies some 20km/12.5mi from Palermo. Good bus services operate between the two towns.

Neighbouring sights are described in the following chapters: Golfo di CASTELLAMMARE; MONREALE; PALERMO.

Historical Notes

Carini claims to have legendary origins. Allegedly, it was founded by Daedalus who called it Hyccara in memory of his son Icarus; history then records how the town came to be destroyed by the Athenians in 415 BC, rebuilt by the Phoenicians and, after the Roman conquest, became a stipendiary town of the Empire. With time came changes in fortune: the town was assimilated into the feudal holdings of the most powerful Chiaramonte dynasty, before passing to the Moncada (14C) and, finally in the 15C to the La Grua-Talamanca, in whose hands it remains today.

Walking About

Corso Umberto I, Carini's main street, begins just beyond a belvedere presenting sweeping views over the coast. From here, a horseshoe-shaped flight of shallow steps makes its way up past the town's medieval water fountain, to a 12C archway and beyond to the old part of the town, threaded by narrow streets, and the castle.

Castle – *Open 9am-1pm and 3-7pm. No charge. ☎ 091 86 11 341 or 091 86 11 339.*

The ancient Norman fortress-cum-castle, the famous setting for the tragic episode involving **Baronessa di Carini**, has been radically remodelled over the centuries, most especially since it has been owned by the La Grua-Talamanca family.

On the ground floor is the **Salone delle Derrate** (Victuals Hall), later transformed into a library, with its two elegant 15C stone arches springing from a single solid pier. On the floor above, the **Salone delle Feste** has a wonderful 15C coffered wooden **ceiling**, heavy with typical Catalan Gothic decorative pendentives. The square tower beyond is lit by a two-light window; above, the roof beams rest on a series of corbels, decorated with a profusion of organic elements, that alternate with machicolations.

Return to Corso Umberto I.

Opposite the fountain stands the **Chiesa di San Vincenzo**. The space within is bisected by a wrought-iron grille (segregating the area reserved for the nuns from the adjacent convent) and decorated with white and gold neo-Classical stucco festoons, cherubs and grotesques.

Corso Umberto I opens out into **Piazza del Duomo**, overlooked by two churches: San Vito on the right and the Chiesa Madre on the left.

Chiesa Madre

Open by appointment, 9am-1pm and 3-7pm (same admission times for other churches in the town). ☎ *091 86 11 341 or 091 86 11 339.*

Although subjected to considerable alteration in the 18C, the church preserves on its right side a loggia and a series of interesting maiolica panels depicting the *Crucifixion, Assumption, St Rosalia* and *St Vitus* (1715). **Inside**, the church houses a prized *Adoration of the Magi* by Alessandro Allori (1578), an eminent Tuscan painter who came to prominence at the Medici court; in the chapel dedicated to the Crucifixion sits an exquisite 17C wooden Crucified Christ with a crown of silver on cross of agate, set above a grandiose altar flanked by expressive stucco statues by Procopio Serpotta.

> **A TALE OF LOVE AND TRAGEDY**
>
> 1563: Laura Lanza, the beautiful young daughter of the Count of Mussomeli, although betrothed to Don Vincenzo La Grua, falls in love with Ludovico Vernagallo, who reciprocates her love. Despite every effort by the girl's father to put an end to the affair, nothing will quell the passion of the two young lovers. Finding an accomplice in her nurse, the girl devises a plan with her lover, enabling them to marry in secret and run away together. The appointed day arrives: 4 December. Laura and Ludovico pronounce their vows of reciprocal fidelity before a chaplain, when Laura's enraged father bursts in on the scene. The two clandestine lovers are put to death, thereby salvaging the family's honour. The story is hushed up, no-one is punished, yet with time, the incident was assimilated into the colourful anthology of romance popularly celebrated in ballad and song.

Oratorio del Santissimo Sacramento

The oratory beside the Chiesa Madre dates from the mid-16C. Its interior is a glorious profusion of **stucco decoration**★★ (18C) by the Trapani artist Vincenzo Messina, populated by life-size allegories (Faith, Charity, Strength and Penitence on the left; Hope, Justice, Divine Grace and the Roman Catholic Church on the right) and a crowd of smaller figures leaning on parapets below the windows, or engaged in scenes from the Mysteries of the Eucharist. Elsewhere, surfaces are encrusted with other Serpotta-like elements: cherubs, garlands of flowers and fruit, heraldic coats of arms and grotesques. The ceiling is frescoed with the Triumph of Faith.

Chiesa di Santa Maria degli Angeli

Behind the Chiesa Madre, in Via Curreri. This church once belonged to the Capuchin monastery; a ring of side chapels radiate from the nave, each one embellished with intricate intarsia. Pride of place in the elaborate Rococo chapel of the Crucifixion, among the various small reliquaries, is a lovely wooden **Crucifix** by the Capuchin Fra' Benedetto Valenza (1737), who also worked on the overall decor.

Chiesa degli Agonizzanti

Via Roma. This church, completed in 1643, is richly decorated inside with white and gold **stucco**★: playful cherubs, eagles, garlands of flowers and fruit encircle frescoed panels depicting the scenes from the life of the Virgin, culminating in the ceiling *(Apotheosis of the Virgin)*. Halfway along the sidewalls, two small stucco scenes below the frescoes represent the Death of Joseph and the Madonna.

Excursions

Terrasini

15km/9mi W. The seaside resort overlooks the sea, closed in behind by a lofty red **cliff**★ which intermittently shelters little beaches and delightful little rocky creeks.

Museo Civico – Terrasini harbours an interesting local **museum**, although its presentation does not do justice to the quality of its collections. These comprise three departments, the most significant being the **natural history** section *(Via Cala Rossa, 8)*. This

The red cliffs at Terrasini

M. Magni/MICHELIN

comprises, among other things, the rich Orlando collection of birds with species ranging from crows, nocturnal birds, storks, raptors, and species approaching extinction or considered rare like the griffon vulture, golden eagle and capercaillie.

The **archaeological** department *(next to the town hall in Piazza Falcone e Borsellino)* displays marine artefacts retrieved from wrecks found off Terrasini – mainly fragments of amphorae from the 3C BC and objects from a 1C AD Roman ship.

The **ethnological** section *(Via C.A. Dalla Chiesa, 42)* contains the excellent **Museo del Carretto Siciliano★**, which houses some truly remarkable examples of Sicilian carts from Palermo and Trapani. *The museum is in the process of moving at the time of going to press. For information, call ☎ 091 86 82 652.*

EVENTS

Festa di li schietti

The Saturday before Easter, all the eligible young men (schietti) of the town go out and cut a bitter-orange tree (melangolo). They trim and tidy the top into a round shape and decorate it with coloured ribbons and bells of all shapes and sizes (ciancianieddi). The dressed result, which must weigh at least 50kg/110lb, is then carried into the town ready for the Sunday morning, when each tree is blessed in the piazza before the main church. After the service and urged on by the local populace, each young man carries his tree to the house of his chosen love; there he must demonstrate his strength by balancing the tree on the palm of his hand for as long as possible.

This local festival has lost much of its importance today. Once it constituted a veritable test of virility: if the young man should fail to lift his heavy offering or, indeed, should fail to hold it up long enough, the engagement might, literally, be broken off.

Golfo di Castellammare★★

This magnificent bay is characterised by gentle hills punctuated by harsh mountain ranges and is dominated to the west by the impressive bulk of Monte Còfano, which overlooks the promontory of Capo San Vito. In addition to the stunning coastal scenery and well-known resorts dotted along the coast, this region is also of cultural interest with its many castles, tuna fisheries, fortified buildings and archaeological sites, all set against a landscape which is both agricultural and popular with tourists.

Location

Michelin map 565 2N 0 – Trapani. The Golfo di Castellammare stretches from Capo San Vito to Capo Rama. A scenic road follows the coast as far as Scopello, then heads inland at the Riserva dello Zingaro to rejoin the coast at Capo San Vito. **i** *Via Savoia 57, San Vito lo Capo; ☎ 0923 97 24 64; Fax 0923 97 43 00.*

Neighbouring sights are described in the following chapters: CARINI; ERICE; MONREALE; PALERMO; SEGESTA.

Worth a Visit

Castellammare del Golfo

Set in the beautiful bay of the same name, this town, now a popular seaside resort, was once the main port and principal trading post for the ancient cities of Segesta and Erice. In the centre of the town stands the **medieval castle** which gave it its name.

After Castellammare del Golfo, the road winds its way up a bare mountainside providing glorious **views★** *(car park)* of the town and its harbour.

Scopello

The road leads onwards to Scopello, a small hamlet on the sea dominated by its 18C *baglio* (a large, fortified building – *see Insights and Images*) which faces onto the central piazza. After a bend in the road, a dirt road on the right leads down to the old tuna fishery (can be reached on foot).

La Tonnara – The tuna fishery, now disused, testifies to an activity that once flourished in the fish-rich waters off this coast. Out of season, the place takes on an atmosphere all of its own. Silence reigns among the abandoned buildings; the only sound is the irregular rhythm of the waves. Time seems to stand still like the main buildings where the cruel rituals of killing tuna *(la metanza)* were enacted. The net weights sit impassively aside.

Directory

Tours

Boat trips to the Riserva dello Zingaro – Two boats offer trips from San Vito Lo Capo: the *Leonardo da Vinci* (☎ 0924 34 222) and the *Nautilus* (☎ 0347 57 66 391). The latter has a glass bottom, which allows visitors to admire the colourful underwater life without the need for a snorkel and mask.

Where to Eat

• For all budgets

CASTELLAMMARE DEL GOLFO

Al Madarig – *Piazza Petrolo 7, Castellammare del Golfo – ☎ 0924 33 533 – almadarig@tin.it – ☒ – €18/32. 33 rooms. €77/98 ☕ €6.* This atmospheric restaurant facing the sea is housed in some of the carefully restored old warehouses around the port. The restaurant serves local cuisine on tables outside during the summer and also has a number of simple, spacious guest rooms.

SAN VITO LO CAPO

Gnà Sara – *Via Duca degli Abruzzi 8, San Vito Lo Capo – ☎ 0923 97 21 00 – www.gnasara.com – Closed Mon (except Jun-Sep) and in Nov – €20/34.* Situated in a street parallel to the town's main thoroughfare, this restaurant is renowned for its generous portions of good quality fish. Meals are served on comfortable tables with linen tablecloths either in the rustic dining room or on the summer veranda.

Da Alfredo – *Contrada Valanga 3, San Vito Lo Capo – 1km/6mi S of San Vito Lo Capo – ☎ 0923 97 23 66 – Closed Mon (except mid-Jun to Sep) and 20 Oct-20 Nov – €22/38.* A splendid terrace-cum-garden, delightful shady arbour and traditional Sicilian cuisine are the main features of this pleasant restaurant.

SCOPELLO

Il Baglio – *Via Baglio Isonzo 4, Scopello – ☎ 0924 54 12 00 – Closed Mon and Nov-Feb – €20/28.* This restaurant, housed in the 13C Baglio Isonzo, has an attractive courtyard with wooden tables, as well as a smart interior dining room. The menu includes traditional fish dishes and pizza cooked in a wood oven.

Where to Stay

CASTELLAMMARE DEL GOLFO

• Moderate

Arabesque Agriturismo – *Loc. Manostalla, Balestrate – 10km/6mi E of Castellammare; take the Balestrate exit on A 29. – ☎ 091 87 87 755 – Fax 091 89 87 663 – agriturismoarabesque@tin.it – ⛱ €43/88 ☕.* This beautiful guesthouse is situated among vineyards and olive trees, just 2km/1.2mi from the coast. Facilties include a swimming pool, children's games, boules and table tennis. Mountain bikes are also available to explore the surrounding countryside.

Hotel Punta Nord Est – *Viale Leonardo da Vinci 57, Castellammare del Golfo – ☎ 0924 30 511 – Fax 0924 30 713 – puntanordest@tiscalinet.it – P ☒ – 58 rooms. €70/84 ☕ €7.* This hotel on the seafront has private access to a small beach. The interior is tastefully decorated in pale colours and the rooms are well appointed, light and spacious.

SAN VITO LO CAPO

• Budget

El Bahira Campeggio – *Località Salinella, Bahira – 4km/2.5mi S of San Vito Lo Capo – ☎ 0923 97 25 77 – info@elbahira.it – ☒ €10.* This campsite offers a good range of sports and leisure facilities. The site is divided into separate sections for tents, camper vans and caravans, and also has chalets and small apartments for rent.

La Pineta Campeggio – *Via Del Secco 88, San Vito Lo Capo – ☎ 0923 97 28 18 – Fax 0923 97 40 70 – lapineta@camping.it – Closed Nov €29.* As well as providing plentiful space for tents under the shade of its pine trees, this campsite has around 40 rooms available for rent on site.

• Moderate

Halimeda – *Via Generale Arimondi 100, San Vito Lo Capo – ☎ 0923 97 23 99 – Fax 0923 97 23 99 – info@hotelhalimeda.com – ☒ ♿ – 9 rooms. €52/78 ☕ €50.* This small hotel has been recently renovated in a highly original style by its young, dynamic management team. Despite their simplicity, the rooms have lots of character. An attractive veranda roof-garden is also open to guests.

L'Agave – *Via Nino Bixio 35, San Vito Lo Capo – ☎ 0923 62 10 88 –* lagavevito@libero.it *Closed Nov – ☒ – 10 rooms. €65/90 ☕ €4.* Although this small hotel has only 10 rooms, plans are underway to extend its capacity. Enjoy a quiet, relaxing stay in this modern establishment with its good service and facilities.

Al Tair Hotel – *Via Duca degli Abruzzi 83, San Vito Lo Capo – ☎ 0923 97 25 33 – Fax 0923 62 11 98 – hotel_al-TAIR@libero.it – Closed Nov-Feb – P ☒ ♿ – 9 rooms. €65/98 ☕.* A recently opened hotel with a very pleasant atmosphere. The decor has made good use of different types of marble and the stylish bedrooms are decorated with Tunisian tables and furnishings. Breakfast is served in the small garden at the back of the hotel.

SCOPELLO

• Moderate

Tranchina – *Via A. Diaz 7, Scopello – ☎ 0924 54 10 99 – Fax 0924 54 10 99 – 10 rooms. €50/75 ☕.* Right in the heart of the town, this friendly, well-maintained family-run hotel has 10 individually decorated rooms adorned with wooden furniture. Excellent cuisine.

Festivals

Festa di Maria Santissima del Soccorso – The festival of the patron saint of Castellammare del Golfo is celebrated from 19 to 21 August with a procession to the sea, during which thousands of small candles are floated on the water.

Couscous Fest – In September every year, a festival celebrating Mediterranean food and wine is held at San Vito Lo Capo, along with concerts of ethnic music and other cultural events. For further information, log onto

M. Guillot/MICHELIN

Old tuna fishery

In the summer, on the other hand, the place bustles with sun-seekers and bathers. From here there is a wonderful view of the large monolithic rocks *(i faraglioni)*, that recall their more famous cousins off the island of Capri.

Riserva Naturale dello Zingaro★

The nature reserve between Scopello and San Vito lo Capo can be accessed from either of these two places. For information on admission times and prices, call ☎ 0924 35 093 or 800 11 66 16 (toll-free number); www.riservazingaro.it

This, the first nature reserve to be designated in Sicily, measures some 7km/4mi in length and covers approximately 1 650ha/4 076 acres. The main track follows the coastline high above the sea offering spectacular **views★** down over the successive creeks, bays, beaches (many of which are accessible), sheer cliffs and rocky headlands: these, seen together, provide a gloriously unspoilt area of Sicily. The wonderful, lush, Mediterranean vegetation (some 700 species) occasionally allows patches of red bedrock to show through. This provides a striking contrast of warm colour, offset by the deep green fronds of dwarf palms and the softer shades of green added by the shiny laurel bushes, matt agave spikes, tender asphodels and succulent prickly-pears; a further accent is provided by the garishly yellow flowering oxalis (also known as wood sorrel, Bermuda buttercup or Cape sorrel). Other equally attractive paths meander their way inland: as the scenery alters, so the vegetation changes until, at last, tumbling capers and flowering ash predominate.

The reserve maintains a number of nooks and crannies that provide sheltered burrows and nesting sites for a variety of animals (including small predators) and, more particularly, birds (with 39 different species documented including Peregrine falcons, Bonelli's eagles and kestrels).

The Zingaro Nature Reserve also preserves ancient vestiges of early man's presence in the area through the centuries: evidence of Neolithic and Mesolithic settlements have been uncovered near the Grotta dell'Uzzo, while vestiges of rural settlements, consisting of some 20 well-preserved houses, have been found at Baglio Cusenza; others have been found at la Tonnarella dell'Uzzo.

As there is no coast road from Scopello to San Vito lo Capo, you will need to retrace your steps for a couple of kilometres before turning right towards Castelluzzo.

After Castelluzzo the road offers splendid **views★** of the Golfo del Còfano. To the left, note one of the many 16C watchtowers that punctuate this area; the road then continues past an attractive, characteristically cube-like, little chapel dedicated to **Santa Crescenzia** (16C).

San Vito lo Capo⌂⌂

San Vito is a well-known seaside resort, noted in particular for its beautiful coastline. This opens out into a bay lined with wonderful beaches lapped by limpid water that seems tinged with ranges of blues and greens, from aquamarine to navy.

The small whitewashed town, which developed in the 18C, clusters around the **Chiesa Madre**, which is square and massive in profile, a constant reminder of its early beginnings as a Saracen fortress. Inside, it used to preserve a small church

J. Malburet/MICHELIN

dedicated to San Vito (erected over the site where the saint is supposed to have lived) but this became too small to accommodate the many pilgrims, and so it was enlarged until it actually incorporated the very building which once harboured it.

Capo San Vito e Golfo del Còfano

Leaving San Vito to the east and heading beyond the Punta di Solanto, a scenic road provides views to the left of the old and now abandoned tuna fishery **(Tonnara del Secco)**, and continues as far as the solitary **Torre dell'Impiso** *(visible on the return trip)*. The Riserva dello Zingaro starts at the end of the road.

Return to San Vito and take the road to Castelluzzo. Once past Castelluzzo, turn right to Custonaci and head up the hill on the road to the right.

Monte Còfano – The towering limestone peak and the bay that surrounds it, now a nature reserve, make for a magnificent **sight★** as the steep pinky-red cliffs extending skywards are mirrored in the crystal calm sea. A number of quarries can be seen gouged into the rocky flank. From these are extracted the marble known as *Perlato di Sicilia,* a startlingly white stone by comparison with the other brownish natural rock of the area. Not far from the quarries *(follow the signs)* nestles the grotto known as the **Grotta Mangiapane** (in the vicinity of Scurati). Inside, it shelters a tiny rural hamlet, complete with chapel and cobbled street. The endearing charm of this abandoned village, with its vaguely Mexican air (especially because of the square, mud-coloured houses), is especially poignant at Christmas, when it provides a setting for a captivating enactment of the Christmas story.

Excursions

Alcamo

About 11km/6.5mi S of Castellammare del Golfo. The name of the town is suggestive of the 13C poet **Cielo d'Alcamo**, author of a well-known work entitled *Rosa Fresca Aulentissima (The Fresh Fragrant Rose)*, one of the earliest texts to be written in Italian. One glance at the landscape, populated with vineyards, is likely to prompt more basic – though no less pleasant – associations with the local dry white wine which bears the town's name.

The town's churches contain works by members of the **Gagini** family (16C) and by Giacomo Serpotta, one of the Sicilian masters of the Baroque. The main works are to be found in Santa Oliva, San Francesco d'Assisi, San Salvatore and the imposing **Chiesa Madre**, the principal church, which has a fine 15C chapel. Overlooking Piazza Repubblica, which has been laid out with gardens, is the **Castello dei Conti di Modica**. The castle, built for the Counts of Modica in the 14C, is rhomboid in shape and has two rectangular and two round towers. Gothic two-light windows pierce the northern side.

Castelvetrano

The attraction of the nearby archaeological site overshadows interest in this small farming town, which is primarily concerned with the cultivation of vines and olive trees. The *comune* itself is more commonly known as Castelvetrano-Selinunte.

Location

Population: 30 160. Michelin map 565 2N 0 – Trapani. The first sight of the town, situated some 10km/6mi from Selinunte and the coast, is the large, square glass hospital, beyond which extends the old town. 🅸 *Piazza Generale Cascino;* ☎ *0924 90 91 28.*

Neighbouring sights are described in the following chapters: MAZARA DEL VALLO; SCIACCA; Antica città di SELINUNTE.

Walking About

The focal centre of Castelvetrano hinges on two adjacent squares, **Piazza Umberto I** and **Piazza Garibaldi**, and it is in this part of the town that the main monuments are to be found.

Piazza Garibaldi

The square is lined with fine buildings such as the town's main church and the **Chiesa del Purgatorio** (now an auditorium), the latter an elegant conglomeration of elaborate detail (classical friezes, false balcony, statues nestling in niches, volutes) drawn from a transitional late Mannerist-Baroque style. Next in line sits the 19C **Teatro Selinus**, which preserves its original stage.

Chiesa Madre

The town's principal church dates, in its present form, from the 16C. The front elevation rises through two storeys; a pair of pilasters ornamented with garlands flank the entrance at ground level, the upper section is pierced by a rosewindow. Swallow-tailed merlons run the length of the side walls.

The internal space is arranged according to a composite Latin-cross/basilica plan typical of Norman churches: the nave is flanked by aisles with two transepts, the second terminating in apses (a square-ended one between two round ones). The glorious **stucco decoration★** adorning the triumphal arch is attributed to **Gaspare Serpotta** (17C, father of the more famous Giacomo): a host of angels bearing festoons and garlands interplay with others brandishing musical instruments. The same elements are applied to the transept arch, although here the decoration is more restrained.

The central ridge of the vaulted ceiling is painted with allegorical figures, inscribed with two dates: 1564 and 1570.

Piazza Umberto I

This delightful little piazza lies to the left of the church, providing a clear view of the bell tower, which is hidden from the front. Gracing the square is a fine little fountain, the **Fontana della Ninfa**, named after the nymph nestling in a niche near the top, erected in the 17C in celebration of the restitution of an aqueduct.

In the nearby Piazza Regina Margherita, overlooking a pleasant municipal garden, is the stark façade of **San Domenico** (15C) which, at one time, was attached to a convent (now a secondary school) from which it preserves the cloisters *(entrance to the right of the church)*; on the opposite side sits the 16C Church of **San Giovanni** complete with its massive bell tower.

Worth a Visit

Museo Selinuntino

Via Garibaldi. Open Apr-Oct, 9.30am-1.30pm and 3.30-7.30pm; Nov-Mar, 9.30am-1.30pm and 2.30-6.30pm. €2.50. ☎ *0924 90 49 32.*

The 16C *palazzo*, once home to the Majo family, now accommodates a museum for artefacts recovered from Selinunte. The well-presented displays are arranged around the prize exhibit: an elegant bronze statue of a young man (c 460 BC) which is famously known as the **Ephebus of Selinunte★**.

In a side niche nestles a lovely *Madonna and Child* by **Francesco Laurana** and his workshop, from the Church of the Annunziata. The museum continues on the first floor with displays of religious objects and three shallow reliefs by the contemporary artist Giuseppe Lo Sciuto.

Excursions

Santa Trinità di Delia

Santa Trinità di Delia★

4km/2.4mi W: follow directions from Piazza Umberto I. The church is part of the Baglio Trinità farm complex. Contact Signore Stefano Saporito for the key. ☎ 0924 90 42 31.

This enchanting Arabo-Norman church (12C) conforms to a Greek-cross plan with three apses projecting on one side; it is capped by a pink dome. The exterior walls are pierced by single-light windows screened with perforated stone panels, inset into articulated surrounds. Inside, the dome hovers above pendentives – a typically Moorish element – supported by four marble columns with Corinthian capitals. The apses are ornamented with delicate little columns. Resting here and in the crypt are various tombs (19C) of the Saporito family, a powerful local dynasty.

A few metres from the church, on the opposite side of the road, extends the **Trinità forestry estate**, a lush area of eucalyptus, palm trees and pines. This ideal spot for a picnic looks out onto an attractive **man-made lake**.

Riserva Naturale Foce del Fiume Belice e Dune Limitrofe

12km/7.5mi S, between Marinella di Selinunte and Porto Palo di Menfi. For guided tours, contact Via Vivaldi 100, Marinella di Selinunte, ☎ 0924 46 042.

The dunes sculpted by the wind make this natural reserve at the mouth of the River Belice particularly evocative. The marsh-like terrain attracts a number of species of birds to the area, as well as the Caretta-Caretta turtle *(see p 221)*.

Where to Stay

Baglio San Vincenzo – Via Leopardi 11, Contrada San Vincenzo, Menfi, 10km/6mi NE of Porto Palo di Menfi – ☎ 339 24 26 103 – Fax 0925 71 123 – www.bagliosanvincenzo.it – Closed 15 Jan-15 Feb – 13 rooms. €62/129 ☕ – Restaurant €20/25. The surrounding Sicilian countryside and the rural traditions still practised here make this a truly delightful place to stay. Accommodation is in a beautifully restored 17C building, where guests can buy oil and wine produced on the property.

Catania★

Over the centuries Catania has been affected by frequent volcanic eruptions, earthquakes and war. The city is overshadowed by Mount Etna, the volcano which has often betrayed the trust of the local people, sending forth great flows of lava, on one occasion down into the town itself. Reminders of the mountain, besides the physical presence of its towering profile on the horizon, appear in every sombre-looking monument, house and doorway detail which, when it is not made of lava stone, is of plaster painted to look like lava. The colours of the city are predominantly black and white, and these are used in combination to maximum effect and can also be seen in the small elephant, the symbol of the city, in Piazza Duomo. The home of the composer **Vincenzo Bellini** and the writer Giovanni **Verga**, Catania is also an elegant and busy town, with a popular horse fair and a growing high-tech industry; some now refer to the area as Etna Valley in reference to Silicon Valley in California.

Location

Population: 336 222. Michelin map 565 O 27, including a map of the town. When the town planner William Light was designing the city of Adelaide in 1836, he adopted the layout of the historic centre of Catania, which he had visited a few years previously. Fortunately, the chaotic traffic conditions in Catania were less easy to export: visitors arriving in Catania by car would do well to leave their vehicle as soon as possible and to explore the pleasant city centre in a more relaxed manner on foot. Catania is one of the hottest cities in Italy, with summer temperatures

Directory

Transport

Getting to Catania – For visitors arriving by **air**, Fontanarossa airport is situated 7km/4.5mi to the south of Catania (☎ 095 72 39 111). The airport is served by a number of airlines which operate services to all the major Italian cities. The Alibus links the airport with the city centre and the railway station (departures every 20min from 5pm to midnight); the ticket is the same price as on the city buses.

The bus terminal is located in Piazza Giovanni XXIII; bus companies operate services between Catania and other major cities in Sicily. Catania has good train connections with Messina (2hr) and Siracusa (1hr 30min); the service to and from Palermo (just over 3hr) is less frequent. The main railway station is also situated in Piazza Giovanni XXIII.

City buses – These are operated by AMT (Azienda Municipale Trasporti), Via Plebiscito 747; ☎ 095 73 60 111; www.amt.ct.it A ticket costs €0.80 and is valid for 90min; a day pass costs €2.

Sightseeing

By bus – The circular bus route n° 410 provides tourists with a round tour of the main sights and points of interest. Services run by appointment only. For further information, contact ☎ 095 73 60 111; Fax 095 31 06 16.

Guided tours – Catania's tourist office (APT di Catania) organises themed tours at 9am from Friday to Sunday, starting in Largo Paisiello. Themes include Literature and Cinema, Homage to Vincenzo Bellini, From the Birth of the City to the Baroque Period, and Sacred Itineraries. For information and reservations, call ☎ 095 73 06 238; Fax 095 31 64 07; www.turismo.catania.it

Where to Eat

• *For all budgets*

For a quick bite at midday, take your pick from one of the many bars in the centre selling sandwiches or one-course lunches *(see Taking a Break below)*, or make for one of the little trattorias near the fish market (behind Piazza Duomo). The following list offers a few suggestions for dinner:

Cantine del Cugno Mezzano – *Via Museo Biscari 8, Catania – ☎ 095 71 58 710 – cantinecugno @tin.it – Closed Sun, Mon at lunchtime, 10-28 Aug, and lunchtime 15 May-15 Oct – €21/32.* This young, fashionable restaurant, housed in an 18C *palazzo* in the centre of Catania, serves fine, modern cuisine accompanied by a good selection of wine. The decor is rustic, with large wooden tables.

La Lampara – *Via Pasubio 49, Catania – ☎ 095 38 32 37 – Closed Wed – ☐ – €25/31.* A simple, family-run restaurant, where the son is the chef and the father the maître-d'. The cuisine here is traditional, based on fresh fish and seafood specialities.

Metrò – *Via Crociferi 76, Catania – ☎ 095 32 20 98 – Closed Sat at lunchtime, Sun, Easter, 1 May and 25 Dec – €26.* This modern restaurant-cum-wine bar situated near Villa Ceremi serves regional dishes accompanied by a good wine list. A pleasant outdoor setting for the summer months.

La Siciliana – *Viale Marco Polo 52/A, Catania – ☎ 095 37 64 00 – lasiciliana@tiscalinet.it – Closed Sun evening, evenings of public hols and Mon – ☐ – Booking recommended – €26/37 + 15% service.* This renowned local restaurant is well worth a visit for its traditional Sicilian cuisine served in a rustic setting. Don't miss the chance to eat outdoors in the summer.

Where to Stay

• *Budget*

Jonio Campeggio – *Via Villini a Mare 2, Catania – From Corso Italia take Via Messina – ☎ 095 49 11 39 – Fax 095 49 22 77 – jonio@camping.it – €16.50.* This campsite, offering a relaxed alternative to the town's more traditional hotels, has bungalows for rent in addition to pitches for tents.

Villaggio Turistico Europeo – *Viale Kennedy 91 – 6km/4mi S of Catania on S 114 – ☎ 095 59 10 26 – Fax 095 59 19 11 – www.villaggioeuropeo.it – Closed 10 Oct-20 Apr €20.50.* This campsite, in a tranquil, rural setting by the sea, enjoys an ideal location a few miles from Catania. Easy access to the city. Tent pitches and bungalows available.

Agorà Hostel – *Piazza Currò 6, Catania – ☎ 095 72 33 010 – Fax 095 72 33 010 – agorahost@hotmail.com – ☐ – €17/45 ☐.* This reasonably priced hostel is situated in a 19C building fronting an old square close to the fish market. Two double rooms, rooms with bunk beds and a number of communal areas.

Bed & Breakfast Casa Mia – *Via D'Annunzio 48 (second floor, with lift), Catania – ☎ 095 44 56 82 – Fax 095 50 99 79 – casamia48@tin.it – 6 rooms €34/54 ☐ €4.* This bed and breakfast establishment in the centre of Catania has six well-appointed rooms with wrought-iron beds and dark wooden furniture, as well as an attractive lounge with comfortable armchairs and sofas. Pleasant accommodation at a reasonable price.

• *Moderate*

Hotel La Vecchia Palma – *Via Etnea 668, Catania – ☎ 095 43 20 25 – Fax 095 43 11 07 – info@lavecchiapalma.it – ☐ – 11 rooms €60/90 ☐.* This family-run, Art Nouveau-style hotel has spacious, comfortable rooms which offer modern facilities, while at the same time retaining their original decor. Guests are made to feel at home by the friendly management.

Il Gelso Bianco – *Misterbianco – 8km/5mi SW of Catania on the Catania-Palermo A19 motorway – ☎ 095 71 81 159 – info@gelso*

bianco.it – ▦ – *91 rooms. €82/134* ▭. Conveniently situated near the motorway to Palermo, this hotel is suitable for business clients, conference delegates and tourists. A lovely garden and swimming pool in the summer months.

Taking a Break

Al Caprice – *Via Etnea 28-34, Catania* – ☎ *095 32 05 55. Closed Mon.* This old-style café, situated in the city centre not far from the cathedral, is perhaps the most typical in Catania with its pleasant old-world atmosphere. A good selection of pastries, cakes, drinks, coffee and hot meals.

Caffè-Pasticceria Savia – *Via Etnea 302-304, Catania* – ☎ *095 31 69 19. Closed Mon.* Opened in 1897 opposite the entrance to Villa Bellini, this café is popular with locals and tourists alike who come here to sample the wide range of sweet and savoury snacks on offer.

Chiosco Vezzosi – *Piazza Vittorio Emanuele, Catania.* This *chiosco* (kiosk) serves a range of healthy and refreshing snacks, such as inexpensive fresh fruit salads and freshly squeezed juices made from fruit such as lemons, melons and peaches. The perfect antidote to Sicily's hot summer temperatures.

Enoteca Regionale di Sicilia – *Viale Africa 31, Catania* – ☎ *095 74 62 210 – Open 8.30am-1pm and 4.30-8pm. Closed Mon.* The full force of the Sicilian sun can be tasted in the island's wines, many of which can be sampled at this wine bar. A good selection of wines and an interesting wine tasting.

Focacceria Turi Finocchiaro – *Via Euplio Reina 13, Catania* – ☎ *095 71 53 573 – Open from 7pm. Closed Wed.* This establishment has been serving excellent, home-made Sicilian cuisine such as meat from the rotisserie and delicious fish and seafood dishes since 1900. Tables inside and out. A real gastronomic treat.

Pasticceria Spinella – *Via Etnea 300, Catania* – ☎ *095 32 72 47.* This pastry shop opposite the Villa Bellini opened in 1930 and has since developed into one of the best-known *pasticcerie* in Catania. The elegant atmosphere, excellent service and high-quality produce ensure that this remains one of the busiest cafés in town.

Shopping

Tertulia – *Via Michele Rapisardi 1-3, Catania* – ☎ *095 71 52 603.* This modern bookshop-cum-café offers book lovers a relaxed atmosphere in which to enjoy a coffee and a leisurely browse. Good selection of books.

Shows

Le Ciminiere – *Viale Africa 2 (at the Eastern end of Via Umberto I), Catania* – ☎ *095 73 49 911.* The town's old sulphur refinery, abandoned after the Second World War, has been transformed into a venue for cultural events, such as art exhibitions, music concerts and theatre shows. There are also plans to house a puppet theatre, the Teatro Stabile dell'Opera dei Pupi, in the building.

Festivals

Festa di Sant' Agata – During the Festival of St Agatha, from 3 to 5 February, the bust and reliquary of this patron saint of Catania are paraded through the city to scenes of great jubilation.

often exceeding 40°C/104°F, and is therefore best visited early in the morning or later in the evening. **ℹ** *Via Cimarosa 10;* ☎ *095 73 06 211; Fax 095 34 71 21; www.turismo.catania.it*

Neighbouring sights are described in the following chapters: ACIREALE; CALTAGIRONE; ETNA; GIARDINI NAXOS; SIRACUSA; TAORMINA. Catania is the departure point for the "Circular Tour of Etna" described on p 206.

Background

Katane, founded by Greek colonists around 724 BC, flourished during the Roman period, as many of the Ancient monuments whichhave survived to this day testify. The saddest century in the city's history must surely be the 17C when lava flowed into the streets (1669) from holes in the volcano that opened near Nicolosi, and, a little more than 20 years later, a terrible earthquake destroyed most of the buildings (1693). This also marked the rebirth of a new city laid out according to a more modern urban plan with wide streets, piazzas and monuments. The main force behind the change was the architect **Giovanni Battista Vaccarini** (1702-68).

The Liotru of Catania

Locals refer to the elephant in Piazza Duomo as the **Liotru**, which is local dialect for **Eliodoro**, the name of a learned 8C necromancer from Catania, who, it was said, used to ride the elephant after bringing it to life; over the centuries, the magician's name has been adopted for the elephant itself. However, there may be more than a legendary link between the city and elephants, as during prehistoric times Sicily was inhabited by dwarf elephants, the memory of which is preserved in mythology. The Cyclops in the Homeric legend may well have developed from an imaginative interpretation of the elephant's face, in which the animal's trunk was replaced by a single eye. Models of two dwarf elephants found in Sicily are exhibited at the Museo Archeologico Paolo Orsi in Siracusa.

U'liotru by Vaccarini. The fountain was inspired by the Fontana della Minerva in Rome

For obvious reasons, therefore, Catania was predominantly rebuilt in a homogeneous style, so much so that the last vestiges of its more ancient past disappeared from view beneath an all-enveloping Baroque cloak: the theatre, odeon and amphitheatre from Antiquity are all hidden behind or beneath 18C *palazzi*.

Walking About

PIAZZA DEL DUOMO★

This square is the centre of town and is surrounded by an elegant Baroque ensemble designed by Vaccarini. In the middle stands the **Fontana dell'Elefante**, the symbol of Catania. On the south side of the square, offset by the Chierici and Pardo *palazzi* behind, sits the more delicate Fontana dell'Amenano.

The most prominent ensemble is provided by the Duomo façade, flanked to the right by the Bishop's Palace and Porta Uzeda and, to the left, by the attractive front of the Badia di Sant'Agata, slightly set back. The north side of the square is almost completely taken up by the elegant front elevation of the **Palazzo Senatorio** or **Palazzo degli Elefanti** (now the townhall), designed by GB Vaccarini. In the courtyard stand two senatorial carriages and a late-19C cart.

Fontana dell'Elefante

This fountain, recalling Bellini's famous obelisk-bearing monument in Piazza Minerva in Rome, is the symbol of Catania and was conceived by Vaccarini in 1735. The lava elephant standing on a high stone platform dates from the Roman period and bears on its back an Ancient Egyptian obelisk covered with hieroglyphics celebrating the cult of Isis (the Mother goddess, sister, wife and saviour of Osiris, who became the centre of a popular Greco-Roman mystery cult), as well as the emblem of St Agatha

Duomo★

Open 7am-noon and 4-7pm. ☎ *095 32 00 44.* The cathedral is dedicated to St Agatha, the patron saint of the city; it was erected in the late 11C by the Norman king Roger I, and rebuilt after the earthquake of 1693. The **façade★** is considered to be one of Vaccarini's masterpieces. Further along Via Vittorio Emanuele II, the tall Norman lava apses can be admired from the courtyard of the Bishop's Palace. Its solid outward appearance, relieved in part by the tall, single, narrow, slit-like openings, underlines the fact that the Duomo was conceived as a fortified church.

The north side is graced with a fine 16C portal ornamented with an entablature with cherubs.

The remains of Roman baths, the **Terme Achilliane** *(accessible through a trapdoor)*, can be seen to the right of the entrance outside the church. *The baths are closed at the time of going to press.*

Interior – Restoration of the floor has revealed several column bases from the original Norman church.

Against the second pilaster on the right, in the nave, stands the funerary monument of Bellini who died at his home in Puteaux, near Paris, where he was originally buried.

The transepts both contain chapels, segregated from the crossing by a glorious Renaissance archway. The chapel to the right, dedicated to the Madonna, contains the sarcophagus of Constanza, wife of Frederick III of Aragon, who died in 1363.

The southern chapel is dedicated to St Agatha: this, although Renaissance in spirit, is encrusted with gilded stucco decoration that verges on the exaggerated. The especially elaborate Spanish doorway leads through to the reliquary and treasury of the saint. On the right wall, the fine funerary monument belongs to Ferdinandez de Acuña (1495), the figure depicted on his knees. The 16C carved choir stalls illustrate scenes from the life of St Agatha.

U'liotru by Vaccarini. The fountain was inspired by the Fontana della Minerva in Rome

J. Malburet/MICHELIN

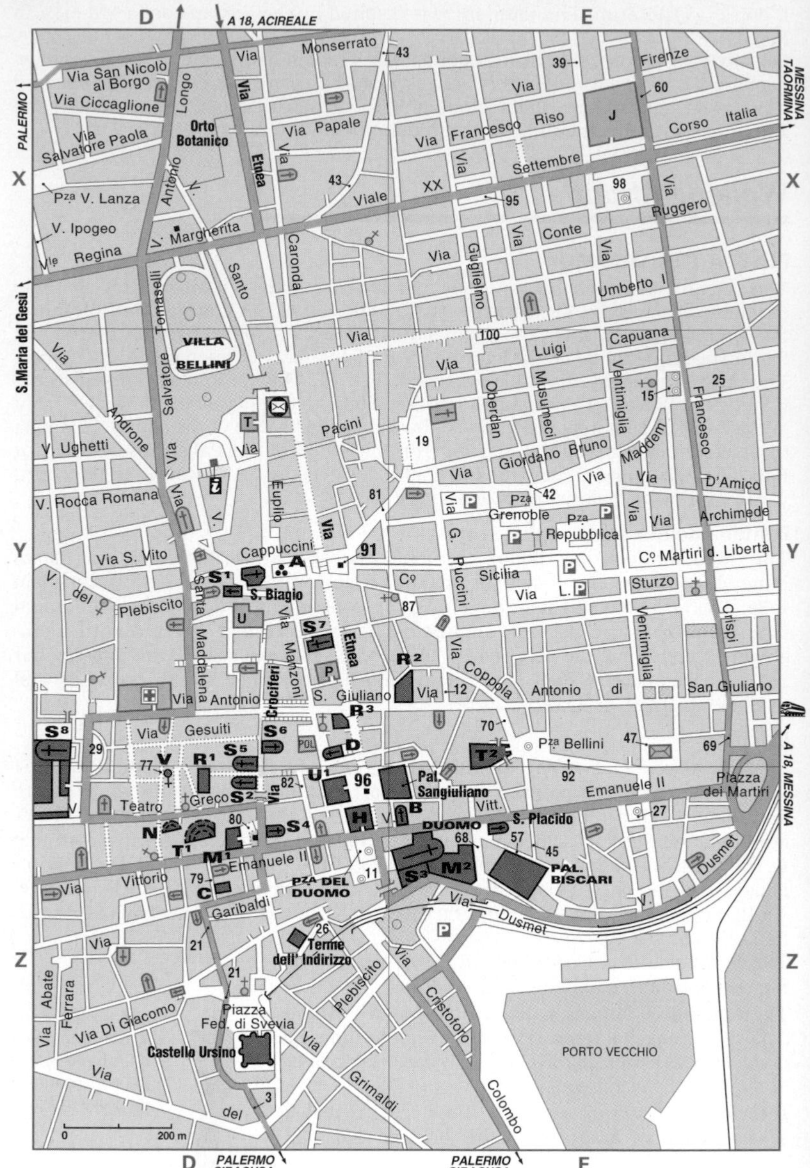

The sacristy has a large fresco (badly damaged, alas) showing a fairly accurate topographical view of Catania before 1669, with Etna on the skyline spewing lava which, lower down, is shown on the point of invading the city.

To the right of the Duomo, the Seminario houses the Museo Diocesano di Catania *(see Worth a Visit)*.

Badia di Sant'Agata★

The church beside the Duomo contributes to the overall splendour of the piazza. The serpentine lines of the **façade★** are contained by a cornice that emphasises the ground level with, at the centre, a triangular pediment. This is another example of Vaccarini's mastery in design.

Fontana dell'Amenano

The fountain is named after the river that supplies it on its way past a few of the principal monuments from the Roman period (the theatre and baths or Terme della Rotonda). Locally, the fountain is called "Acqua a lenzuolo" by the people of Catania because of the way the water cascades down from the top basin, resembling a continuous fine veil. The open area behind is Piazza Alonzo di Benedetto, where a bustling and picturesque **fish market** takes place each morning. The covered section, in times past, housed the military guard for the **Porta Carlo V**, which in the 16C used to be part of the city's fortifications. Its main frontage can still be seen from Piazza Pardo.

CATANIA

Street	Grid	No.
Angelo Custode (Via)	DZ	3
Androne (Via)	DY	
Archimede (Via)	EY	
Bellini (Piazza)	EY	
Benedetto (Piazza A. d.)	DZ	11
Biondi (Via)	EY	12
Bovio (Piazza G.)	EY	15
Bruno (Via G.)	EY	
Cappuccini (Via)	DY	
Capuana (Via L.)	EY	
Caronda (Via)	DX	
Carlo Alberto (Piazza)	EY	19
Castello Ursino (Via)	DZ	21
Ciccaglione (Via)	DX	
Colombo (Via C.)	DEZ	
Conte di Torino (Via)	EY	25
Conte Ruggero (Via)	EX	
Coppola (Via)	EY	
Crispi (Via F.)	EXY	
Crociferi (Via)	DYZ	
Currò (Piazza)	DZ	26
Cutelli (Piazza)	EZ	27
D'Amico (Via)	EY	
Dante (Piazza)	DY	29
Duomo (Piazza d.)	DZ	
Dusmet (Via)	EZ	
Etnea (Via)	DXY	
Ferrara (Via A.)	DZ	
Firenze (Via)	EX	
Garibaldi (Via)	DZ	
Gesuiti (Via)	DY	
Giacomo (Via d.)	DZ	
Giuffrida (Via V.)	EX	39
Grenoble (Piazza)	EY	
Grimaldi (Via)	DEZ	
Guardie (Piazza d.)	EY	42
Imbriani (Via M. R.)	DEX	43
Ipogeo (Via)	DX	
Italia (Corso)	EX	
Landolina (Via)	EZ	45
Lanza (Piazza V.)	DX	
Longo (Via A.)	DX	
Lupo (Piazza P.)	EY	47
Maddem (Via)	EY	
Manzoni (Via)	DY	
Martiri (Piazza d.)	EZ	
Martiri della Libertà (Corso)	EY	
Monserrato (Via)	DX	
Museo Biscari (Via)	EZ	57
Musumeci (via)	EXY	
Oberdan (Via G.)	EXY	
Orlando (Via Vitt. E.)	EX	60
Pacini (Via)	DY	
Paola (Via S.)	DX	
Papale (Via)	DX	
Plebiscito (Via d.)	DY	
Porticello (Via)	EZ	68
Puccini (Via G.)	EY	
Rabbordone (Via)	EY	69
Rapisardi (Via M.)	EY	70
Regina Margherita (Viale)	DX	
Repubblica (Piazza)	EY	
Riso (Via F.)	EX	
Rocca Romana (Via)	DY	
Rotonda (Via d.)	DYZ	77
S. Anna (Via)	DZ	79
S. Eupilio (Via)	DXY	
S. Francesco d'Assisi (Piazza)	DZ	80
S. Gaetano alle Grotte (Via)	DEY	81
S. Giuliano (Via A. d.)	DEY	
S. Giuseppe al Duomo (Via)	DZ	82
S. Maddalena (Via)	DY	
S. Nicolò al Borgo (Via)	DX	
S. Vito (Via)	DY	
Sicilia (Corso)	DEY	
Spirito Santo (Piazza)	EY	87
Stesicoro (Piazza)	DY	91
Sturzo (Via)	EY	
Svevia (Piazza F. d.)	DZ	
Teatro Greco (Via)	DZ	
Teatro Massimo (Via)	EYZ	92
Tomaselli (Via S.)	DXY	
Trento (Piazza)	EX	95
Ughetti (Via)	DY	
Umberto I (Via)	DEX	
Università (Piazza d.)	DZ	96
Ventimiglia (Via)	EXY	
Verga (Piazza)	EX	98
Vittorio Emanuele II (Via)	DEZ	
Vittorio Emanuele III (Piazza)	EY	100
XX Settembre (Viale)	DEX	

Sight	Grid	Key
Anfiteatro	DY	A
Badia di S. Agata	EZ	B
Casa di Verga	DZ	C
Castello Ursino	DZ	
Collegiata	DY	D
Duomo	EZ	
Museo Belliniano	DZ	M1
Museo Diocesano	EZ	M2
Museo Emilio Greco	DZ	M1
Odeon	DZ	N
Orto Botanico	DX	
Palazzo Asmundo	DZ	R1
Palazzo Biscari	EZ	
Palazzo Manganelli	EY	R2
Palazzo S. Demetrio	DY	R3
Palazzo Sangiuliano	DEZ	
Palazzo Senatorio o degli Elefanti	DZ	H
S. Agata al Carcere	DY	S1
S. Benedetto	DZ	S2
S. Biagio	DY	
S. Francesco	DZ	S4
S. Francesco Borgia	DYZ	S5
S. Giuliano	DY	S6
S. Michele Arcangelo	DY	S7
S. Nicolò l'Arena	DY	S8
S. Placido	EZ	
Seminario Arcivescovile	EZ	S3
Teatro Antico	DZ	T1
Teatro Bellini	EY	T2
Terme dell'Indirizzo	DZ	
Terme della Rotonda	DZ	V
Università	DZ	U1
Villa Bellini	DXY	

Back in Piazza Benedetto, down by the side of Palazzo Chierici, stands the Fontana dei Sette Canali.

THE SURROUNDING QUARTER

In the stretch of Via Vittorio Emanuele II behind the Duomo nestle a number of important sights. A small square on the rightharbours the lovely church of **San Placido** with its gently undulating façade by **Stefano Ittar** (1769). Opposite the right side of the church (Via Museo Biscari) sits the former convent on which it depended, although little of the original remains besides the remnants of a doorway and a few windows. The courtyard *(access from Via Landolina)* preserves remains of the 15C **Palazzo Platamone**, given to the monastery by the family of the same name in the 15C. Original features include a decorative balcony in coloured stone, adorned by a series of pointed arches. The courtyard is now used as a venue for concerts and theatre performances.

Palazzo Biscari★

This is the finest civic building in the city. It was erected after the earthquake of 1693, but reached its greatest splendour about 60 years later thanks to Ignazio Biscari, a man of eclectic interests, and an impassioned lover of art, literature and archaeology. It was he who promoted many of the excavations in the area and pushed for a museum of archaeology to be set up in this building *(see Worth a Visit)*.

The south wing, in particular, is lavishly **decorated★★**: figures and volutes, cherubs and racemes fill the window frames along the long terrace, relieving the sombreness of the dark façade.

VIA CROCIFERI★

Begin at Piazza San Francesco with its monumental church dedicated to St Francis, and turn down the lovely Via Crociferi.

Via Crociferi is regarded as Catania's Baroque street *par excellence*. The magnificent buildings ranged elegantly along either side, particularly in the first section, impart a graciousness that is quite unique. Through the gateway, **Arco di San Benedetto**, are the Badia Grande and its diminutive Badia Piccola. On the left are aligned two churches dedicated to **San Benedetto** and **San Francesco Borgia**; between the two runs a narrow street with **Palazzo Asmundo** at the far end.

Further along Via Crociferi on the left, stands a former Jesuit residence that now accommodates the Istituto d'Arte. The first courtyard, attributed to Vaccarini, is graced with a fine two-tiered portico: the same bay elevation has also been used in the University courtyard in Piazza dell'Università. It also has a striking black and white cobbled pavement.

The elegant, curvilinear **façade★** of **San Giuliano** on the right was probably designed by Vaccarini. The internal space is arranged to a Greek-cross-cum-octagonal plan. Above the elaborate altar of agate and other semi-precious stones sits a 14C painted wooden Crucifix.

Elaborate ornamentation on Palazzo Biscari

Turn left into Via dei Gesuiti.

San Nicolò l'Arena

The Benedictine Order, one of the richest and most powerful in the city, built a grandiose monastery (16C-17C) and an imposing **church** alongside, although the façade was never completed. Inside the huge and bare church, there is a lovely 18C organ case behind the altar. The meridian line was laid into the transept floor in 1841; this catches the sunlight precisely at 13 minutes past midday (at one time, this occurred dead on noon).

Monastery★ – The present building dates from the 18C. The eye-catching doorway on the left of the church provides access to the courtyard, from where the east and south sides of the building, designed by Antonino Amato, may be admired. The opulent **decoration** recalls that of the contemporary Palazzo Biscari *(see above)*. The first cloisters surround a small neo-Gothic arcaded inner courtyard decorated with maiolica. The monastery now accommodates the University's Faculty of Arts; from the original have been preserved the fine oval refectory, now transformed into the main lecturehall, and library along with the magnificent **Sala Vaccarini** that has extraordinarily large oval windows and an attractive 18C Neapolitan maiolica floor.

Return to Via Crociferi.

The street terminates at the gates of Villa Cerami, now the seat of the Faculty of Jurisprudence.

Head towards Corso Vittorio Emanuele. You may wish to continue the tour with visits to the Museo Belliniano, Museo Emilio Greco, Teatro Antico and Casa di Verga (see Worth a Visit).

VIA ETNEA★

This straight, 3km/1.8mi long thoroughfare is lined with Catania's best shops and boutiques, and runs through Piazza del Duomo *(see above)*, Piazza dell'Università, Piazza Stesicoro, before arriving at last in front of Villa Bellini, Catania's lovely public gardens.

Piazza dell'Università

The square piazza is surrounded on all sides by elegant *palazzi*. On the right stands Vaccarini's **Palazzo Sangiuliano**; on the left, the **University** arranged around an attractive courtyard surrounded by a portico with a loggia above. In the evening, the piazza is illuminated by four splendid lamps (1957) produced by a sculptor from Catania.

Further down the street rises the lovely concave frontage of the **Collegiata** (Santa Maria della Consolazione) designed by **Stefano Ittar** (18C). A short distance beyond, on the left, comes the gracious **Palazzo San Demetrio** (17C-18C) with its elaborate doorway and corbels.

On the right, along Via Antonio di S. Giuliano, stands the richly decorated **Palazzo Manganelli**. This *palazzo* was used as the setting for some of the scenes in Luchino Visconti's film *The Leopard*, based on the famous novel by Tomasi di Lampedusa.

Returning to Via Etnea, just inside the entrance to the next church, the 18C **San Michele Arcangelo**, a double marble staircase climbs up to two Baroque stoups with angels drawing aside a marble drape to reveal the basin while the rest conceals the supporting ledge.

Piazza Stesicoro

The ruin in the middle of the square is all that survives of an enormous **Roman amphitheatre** (105m/344ft x 125m/410ft) that might have accommodated 15 000 spectators, and whose arena was the second biggest in the Empire after the Colosseum. Most of the area it once occupied lies hidden beneath the piazza and the surrounding Baroque buildings. *To visit, contact the Ancient Theatre in advance,* ☎ *095 74 72 111.*

St Agatha

Agatha was a wealthy, Christian noblewomen from Catania who lived in the city during the 3C. A victim of religious persecution and the unwelcome attentions of the Consul Quilianus, she was thrown into prison and tortured (her breasts were cut off) with red-hot pokers and coals. She died on 5 February 251. The following year, the saint's veil was said to have saved Catania from a flow of lava, after which Agatha became the city's patron saint. During the festival in her honour, celebrated on 3-5 February, the city's streets are thronged with noisy and colourful crowds, bearing witness to her continuing popularity. She is even remembered in one of the local specialities, the *minni di Sant' Agata* (*minni* is Sicilian dialect for breasts); these small cakes covered with frosted icing and topped with a cherry recall the martyrdom of the saint.

San Biagio (Sant'Agata alla Fornace)

Open Mon-Sat, 5-7pm; Sun and public hols, 9am-1pm. ☎ *095 71 59 360.*
The actual 18C building stands upon the foundations of a chapel dedicated to the patron saint of Catania, who was martyred here. In Roman times, the town's limekilns were concentrated in this area. A chapel within the church *(at the far end on the right)* preserves the *carcara* (kiln or furnace) in which Agatha is meant to have met her death (other sources say she died in prison).

According to popular tradition, the Church of **Sant'Agata in Carcere**, behind Piazza Stesicoro, was built on the site of a Roman jail where the saint was imprisoned in 251. It has a fine Romanesque doorway. The wild olive tree growing next to the church was planted on the spot where another had sprouted after Agatha had stopped there on her way into the prison.

Villa Bellini*

The large, luxuriant park is thick with exotic plants. From the top of the hill (where a kiosk stands), there is a beautiful view over the city and out towards Mount Etna.

Santa Maria del Gesù

Although built in 1465, this church has undergone considerable alterations. From the original there survives the Cappella Paternò complete with Renaissance archway surmounted by a lunette, inset with a Pietà by **Antonello Gagini**. He is also the author of the Madonna and Child *(second altar on the right).*

Worth a Visit

Palazzo Biscari*

Via Museo Biscari. For a description of the exterior, see Walking About. Guided tours only (20min) by appointment, Mon-Sat, 9.30am-12.30pm and 4-7pm. €5. ☎ *095 32 18 18.*
The entrance to the *palazzo (Via Museo Biscari)* is through an elaborate portal that leads into a courtyard with a fine stairway. The first floor accommodates the main reception rooms. At the far end, there is a splendid room with frescoes by Sebastiano Lo Monaco, complemented with stuccowork, gilded mouldings and mirrors. The centre of the ceiling opens out into an oval dome, complete with gallery, behind which musicians once played: this was conceived in this way to suggest that the music was descending from the heavens. The fresco depicts the triumph of the family being celebrated by a council of the gods. A pretty spiral staircase situated in the gallery next to thehall provides access to the little platform. From the gallery, an admirable view extends over the terrace on the south side of the building.

Teatro Antico and Odeon*

Corso Vittorio Emanuele II 260. Open 9am-12.30pm and 3-7pm. €2. ☎ *095 74 72 111.*
The present layout of the theatre dates from the Roman era. It is quite possible, however, that it occupies the site of an older Greek structure, as suggested by the natural slope of the hill and a number of contemporary documents (notably a speech by Alcibiades addressing the people of Catania during the Peloponnese War). It is built of lava stone, and would have had tiers of seats made of white limestone or marble (for the more important citizens) for a capacity audience of

7 000 spectators. The *cavea* is supported on three vaulted inter-connected passageways; these also provide access to the auditorium by means of *vomitoria*, flights of steps that enabled large numbers of people to come and go quickly.
As far back as Norman times, the theatre was despoiled of its marble slabs for re-use in building the cathedral, while houses and a street were built within the theatre structure; arches from the street can still be seen to this day.
Beside the theatre stands an **odeon**, although this is later in date. It served as a more intimate context for musical shows, poetry readings and orations. At the back of the auditorium runs a series of galleries: their exact purpose is not known.
The visit finishes in the small **antiquarium**, which exhibits a collection of materials and fragments discovered during excavation work.

Casa di Verga

Via Sant'Anna 8. Open Tue-Sat, 9am-1.30pm (also 3-6pm Wed). Closed public hols. €2. ☎ 095 71 50 598.
The little house where the writer **Giovanni Verga** (1840-1922) spent many years of his life is preserved much as he left it; some items of furniture from his home in Milan have been added (especially to the last rooms). His study provides the opportunity of browsing through the author's "literary passions" and identifying his favourite writers such as Capuana, D'Annunzio and Deledda.

Catania during the Roman period

Visitors particularly interested in Roman remains can request to be taken by a theatre custodian to visit the **Terme della Rotonda** *(Via della Rotonda)*; little survives of these baths, however, other than a single circular domed chamber that was converted into a church in Byzantine times (6C). Access may also be arranged to the **Terme dell'Indirizzo** *(Piazza Currò)*, a more extensive baths complex comprising at least 10 domed rooms. Here the wood-stoked burner that provided heating is clearly visible as are sections of rectangular hot-air ducting. *Guided tours run by the staff of the Ancient Theatre; contact the theatre in advance, ☎ 095 74 72 111.*

Castello Ursino

Piazza Federico di Svevia. Open Tue-Sat, 9am-1pm and 3-6pm; Sun and public hols, 9am-1pm. ☎ 095 34 58 30.
Frederick II of Swabia erected this austere, solid-looking castle on the seafront in the 13C; the reason why today the sea lies so far away is explained by the great river of lava that flowed down here in 1669, pushing the water offshore. The castle is supposedly named after a Roman consul (Arsinius), or possibly after the Orsini, an offshoot of the famous Roman family that fled to these parts in the Middle Ages seeking refuge after siding with the Ghibelline sympathisers (supporting the Emperor rather than the Church).
The castle is square in plan; it has a large round tower at each corner and two additional towers halfway along two sides.

Pinacoteca – The local art gallery assembles a collection of paintings, principally by southern Italian artists, that range from the 15C to the 19C.
Notable works include a polyptych with the *Virgin Enthroned with St Anthony and St Francis* by **Antonello de Saliba** (15C), a pupil of Antonello da Messina: see how delicately the features of the Madonna are rendered. Among the pictures influenced by Caravaggio's strong use of chiaroscuro and theatrical gesture for dramatic effect, look out for the expressive *St Christopher* by **Pietro Novelli**. There are two beautiful studies by **Michele Rapisardi**, an artist from Catania who came to

A composer of genius

The creator of *La sonnambula, Norma* and *I puritani* was a Romantic composer, who dedicated himself to his works with "the passion that is so characteristic of genius, convinced that a large part of success depends on the choice of an interesting theme, warm expressive tones and a contrast of passions". He is commemorated in Catania's opera house, the **Teatro Bellini**, inaugurated with a production of his *Norma* in 1890. The acoustics of its beautiful auditorium are among the best in the world.

Lara Pessina/MICHELIN

prominence in the 19C: one prefigured his depiction of the Sicilian Vespers, the other work is a sketched *Head of the Mad Ophelia* – a haunting image of a woman's hypnotic stare addressed accusingly towards the spectator. Examples by another Catanese artist, Giuseppe Sciuti, include a *Widow* – an expression of infinite sadness. Before leaving, cast an eye over the *Pastorello Malato (The Ailing Shepherd-boy)*, a delicate watercolour by Guzzone, and the vivid paintings by Lorenzo Loiacono.

Museo Belliniano

Piazza S. Francesco 3. Open daily, 9am-1pm (also 3-6pm Tue, Thu and Sat). Closed public hols. No charge. ☎ 095 71 50 535.

The house where **Vincenzo Bellini** (1801-35) was born now comprises a museum for displaying relevant documents, mementoes and portraits of the composer, together with a harpsichord and a spinet that once belonged to his grandfather. The last room contains various autographed original scores.

Museo Diocesano

Piazza Duomo. Open daily except Mon, 9am-12.30pm and 4-7.30pm. €4.20. ☎ 095 28 16 35; www.museodiocesicatania.it

The Diocesan Museum houses a collection of paintings, ornaments and vestments belonging to the cathedral and the diocese, as well as the **Vara di Sant'Agata** – the float used to carry the saint's bust and reliquary during processions. A panoramic terrace accessed from the museum has fine views of Porta Uzeda.

Museo Emilio Greco

Piazza S. Francesco d'Assisi 3. Open daily, 9am-1pm (also 3-6pm Tue and Thu). Closed public hols. No charge. ☎ 095 31 76 54.

This archive-cum-museum houses the complete **graphic output★** of the native-born artist Emilio Greco (1913-95), who achieved particular fame as a sculptor. The subjects, for the most part female heads and nudes, illustrate his perceptive predilection for Hellenistic art, notably for its graceful lines and elegant forms.

Orto Botanico

Entrance in Via Longo. (♿) Open daily except Sun, 8.30am-1.30pm. Closed national hols. No charge. ☎ 800 90 11 42; www.dipbot.unict.it

The botanical gardens were laid out in the 1950s with various indigenous as well as exotic varieties, notably examples of *Dracaena Draco* and *Euphorbia Brachiata*.

Cefalù★★

Colonised by the Greeks, the Ancient town of Kephaloidion (meaning "head") developed into a delightful fishing village and then a bustling town, which is very popular with modern visitors. Attractions here include the town's magnificent natural setting, its splendid cathedral and a plethora of restaurants and bars.

Location

Population: 14 006. Michelin map 565 24M – Palermo. Arriving from Palermo, visitors catch their first **sight★★** of the town from a distance, with the impressive bulk of the cathedral set against the Rocca. Cefalù is an excellent base for excursions into the Madonie. *Corso Ruggero 77; ☎ 0921 42 10 50; Fax 0921 42 23 88; www.cefalu-tour.pa.it/*

Neighbouring sights are described in the following chapters: BAGHERIA; CAPO D'ORLANDO; MADONIE E NEBRODI; PALERMO; SOLUNTO; TERMINI IMERESE.

Cefalù is the departure point for a tour through the Madonie (see MADONIE E NEBRODI).

Special Feature

Duomo★★

Open 8am-noon and 3.30-7pm (5pm winter). ☎ 0921 92 20 21.
The gold-coloured cathedral, a Romanesque jewel set back behind a series of palm trees, appears to merge with the limestone hillside called La Rocca behind. It was built by the Norman **King Roger II** between 1131 and 1240 following a vow he made when on the point of being shipwrecked when returning from Naples. It is also more evidently Norman than its counterpart in Palermo, notably in the Moorish style of façade framed by towers and, at the east end, its tall central apse flanked by two smaller ones. The façade, completed in 1204, is divided into two storeys by the portico which was rebuilt in the 15C by the Lombard architect Ambrogio da Como. The upper section is beautifully ornamented with blind arcading. The twin towers, built on a square plan, rise through levels with single- and two-light openings to culminate in crenellations. The central doorway, known as the **King's Gate** (Porta dei Re), served at one time as the main entrance.

H. Champollion/MICHELIN

Interior – The church, with a Latin-cross floor plan, consists of a single nave flanked by aisles, subdivided by columns with fine **capitals★** carved in the Sicilian Arabo-Norman style.

The fabulous **mosaics★★** (1148), executed in a spectacular array of colours (emerald green in particular) on a gold background, adorn the chancel. The eye is immediately attracted to the huge majestic image of the **Christ Pantocrator** gazing down from the apse, his right hand raised in benediction, his left holding a sacred scroll inscribed with text from St John's Gospel (Chapter 8, verse 12) in Greek on the left and in Latin on the right: "I am the light of the world: he who followeth me shall not walk in darkness, but shall have the light of life."

Below, on three different levels, the Virgin, attended by four Archangels and the twelve Apostles, is imbued with sensitivity and gentleness of a kind far removed from the more typical wooden face-on portrayals normally associated with Byzantine art. The side walls of the choir are covered with more mosaics dating from the late 13C, depicting Prophets, saints and patriarchs; the angels in the vault date from the same period.

To the right of the choir, note the old bishop's throne and, on the left, the royal marble and mosaic throne *(under restoration at the time of going to press).*

The three aisles and the transept have all been modified over the centuries and are still being restored today. The stained-glass windows designed by Michele Canzoneri depict biblical themes and date from the 1990s; they bathe the interior of the church in evocative coloured light.

In the cloisters, whichhave been closed for years, there are columns and capitals in the same style as the ones at Monreale.

Walking About

Piazza del Duomo, which stretches out below the cathedral, is enclosed with ranges of splendid *palazzi*: Palazzo Piraino (on the corner of Corso Ruggero) with its late 16C portal, the medieval Palazzo Maria with a Gothic portal, possibly once a royal residence and, to the left of the cathedral, the 17C Palazzo Vescovile or Bishop's Palace.

Directory

Transport

For visitors arriving by car, the motorway exit leads easily to Via Roma, where you can park the car and head towards Via Matteotti and Corso Ruggero on foot. Cefalù can also be reached from Palermo by bus (the bus terminal is in front of the railway station) or by train, which takes just over 1hr. Train connections are less frequent from Messina and the journey takes approximately 3hr. The railway station is about 10min walk from Corso Ruggero, following Via Aldo Moro and Via Matteotti. Boats leave Cefalù for the Aeolian islands (approx. 90min); for further information, contact Aliscafi SNAV, Corso Ruggero 82, ☎ 0921 42 15 95.

Where to Eat

• ***For all budgets***

La Botte – *Via Veterani 6, Cefalù – ☎ 0921 42 43 15 – Closed Mon and in Jan – €22/38.* This centrally located, family-run trattoria serves fresh, traditional Sicilian cuisine in a simple, rustic atmosphere.

Porticciolo – *Via C.O. di Bordonaro 66, Cefalù – ☎ 0921 92 19 81 – al.porticciolo@libero.it – Closed Wed – – Booking recommended – €23/30.* In the heart of the small town, this pleasant, well-run restaurant is decorated in traditional style, with colourful furnishings. It serves fish and seafood, as well as pizza, the local speciality.

Where to Stay

• ***Expensive***

Hotel Baia del Capitano – *S 113, Località Mazzaforno, 5km/3mi E of Cefalù on S 113 – ☎ 0921 42 00 03 – Fax 0921 42 01 63 – baiadelcapitano@kefa.it – Closed in Jan and Feb – – 48 rooms. €90/135 €7.75.* This attractive, recently restored hotel offers guests spacious rooms, a swimming pool, access to a delightful cliff and a quiet location surrounded by Mediterranean vegetation.

Taking a Break

Bar del Molo – *Piazza Marina 4-5, Cefalù – ☎ 0921 42 23 39.* This popular bar with a splendid terrace enjoys lovely views of the surrounding area. A pleasant option for an ice cream, sandwich or fresh salad.

Bar Duomo – *Piazza Duomo 19, Cefalù – ☎ 0921 42 11 64.* Situated close to the town's magnificent cathedral, this bar is well known for its excellent ice cream.

Pasticceria-Gelateria Pietro Serio – *Via Giuseppe Giglio 29 (at the intersection with Via A. Moro, the continuation of Via Matteotti), Cefalù – ☎ 0921 42 22 93. Open 7am-1pm and 3-10pm. Closed Wed.* This recommended pasticceria serves a range of cakes, pastries and traditional confectionery.

Going Out

Le Petit Tonneau – *Via V. Emanuele 49, Cefalù – ☎ 0921 42 14 47 – Open in summer, 9am-midnight; in winter, 9am-1pm and 3.30-8pm.* This excellent rustic-style wine bar overlooking the marina in the medieval heart of Cefalù has a pleasant balcony on which to enjoy a wide selection of Sicilian and Italian wines and liqueurs.

Shows

Teatro dei Pupi a Cefalù – *Corso Ruggero 92, Cefalù – ☎ 0921 92 38 82 – Shows at 6pm and 9pm. Closed Fri.* The Girolamo Cuticchio puppet company from Palermo recounts the extraordinary exploits of Orlando, Rinaldo and Carlo Magno (Charlemagne) in the setting of this splendid theatre in Cefalù.

Shopping

A Lumera – *Corso Ruggero 180, Cefalù – ☎ 0921 92 18 01 – Open in summer, 9am-1pm and 2-10pm; in winter, 9am-1pm and 4-8pm.* This shop sells a range of traditional Sicilian ceramics, famed for their quality and beauty. The excellent and varied selection includes the shop's own range of ceramics, as well as items from Sciacca, Caltagirone and Santo Stefano di Camastra.

Festivals

Festa di San Salvatore – The festival of Cefalù's patron saint is held from 2 to 6 August and includes the *'nntinna 'a mari*. During this competition volunteers crawl along a horizontal pole suspended above the water to reach the statue of the Saviour (5pm on 6 August).

Madonna della Luce – On 14 August a procession of boats makes its way from Kalura to the old harbour and back.

Corso Ruggero

Cefalù's main street, lined with a wide range of boutiques, overlies the ancient Roman *decumanus* which bisects the town on a north-south axis. The two resulting halves are quite different with their own particular character: to the west lies the medieval quarter, a labyrinth of narrow streets dotted with steps, arches and narrow passageways; to the east, a network of regular streets at right angles. The difference can probably be attributed to the two different social classes that lived in the two quarters: the western half was occupied by the common people, the easternhalf by the clergy and the nobility.

From Piazza Duomo, take the road to the left. Further along on the left, stands the **Chiesa del Purgatorio** (formerly Santo Stefano Protomartire), its front graced by an elegant double staircase leading up to a Baroque doorway. Just inside is the sarcop hagus of Baron Mandralisca. *For information on admission times, call ☎ 0921 92 20 21.*

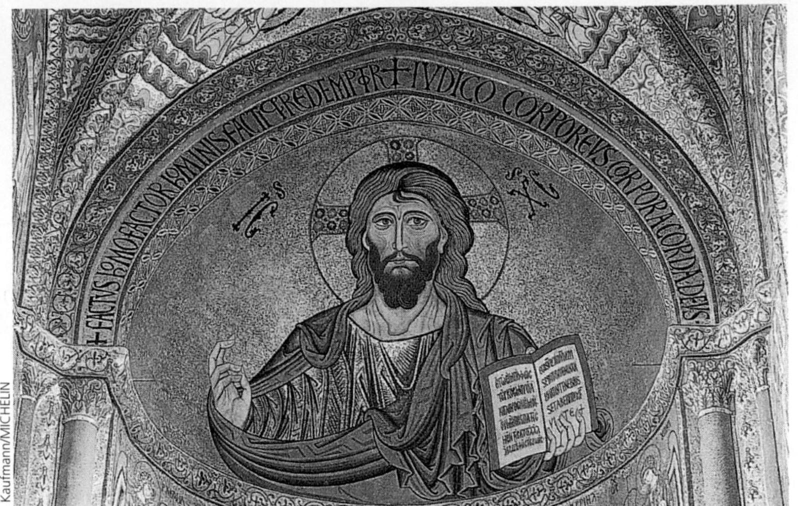

B. Kaufmann/MICHELIN

Christ Pantocrator in the apse

Osterio Magno★ – On the right of the *corso* stands the residence of King Roger, later the property of the Ventimiglia family, comprising two parts dating from different periods. The older, two-coloured part of lava and gold-coloured stone faces onto Via Amendola and has two elegant **two-light windows**; it dates from the 13C. The adjoining square tower, on the corner of Corso Ruggero, built in the 14C, has a fine three-light window set into an elaborate Chiaramonte-style arch. The palace, now completely restored, is used for temporary exhibitions.

Corso Ruggero leads into **Piazza Garibaldi**, site of one of the four gateways of the town. Facing the piazza is the Baroque Church of **Santa Maria alla Catena** (Saint Mary of the Chain), the bell tower of which incorporates remains from the ancient megalithic town walls.

From Piazza Garibaldi, take Via Spinuzza and then Via Vittorio Emanuele.

A little further along on the left is the medieval **wash house**, known by the locals as *u ciumi* – meaning the river – which was used by the town's womenfolk until comparatively recently. The end of the road leads into Piazza Marina; a little before the piazza, note **Porta Pescara** on the left. This is the only surviving medieval gateway of the original four that once provided access to the town: it is currently used to display a collection of fishing equipment.

Turn right into Via Ortolano di Bordonaro. Towards the end of the road, a street to the left leads into Piazza Crispi where the **Chiesa della Idria** (Church of the Hydria) stands, flanked by the Bastion of Cape Marchiafava from where the view encompasses a large stretch of the coastline.

Retrace your steps and continue as far as Via Porpora, where there is a **tower** with a postern (an opening which allowed only one person to pass at a time) and the ancient remains of massive fortifications. Behind Via Giudecca the ruins of ancient fortifications can still be seen.

Return to Piazza Duomo and take the picturesque **Via Mandralisca**, leading to the museum of the same name *(see Worth a Visit)*. Set into the paving (towards the beginning of the street before Piazza del Duomo) is the Cefalù coat of arms: three fishes with a loaf of bread, all symbols of Christianity, while also referring to the town's economic resources.

CHRISTIAN SYMBOLS

The Greek word for fish, *Ichths*, is composed of the initial letters of the Greek words *Iesoûs Christòs Theoû Hyiòs Soter*, which translates as "Jesus Christ, Son of God, Saviour". This is why the image of a fish is often used as a symbol of Christ.

Worth a Visit

Museo Mandralisca

Via Mandralisca 13. Open Apr-Sep, 9am-12.30pm and 3.30-7pm; Oct-Mar, 9am-12.30pm and 3.30-6pm. €4. ☎ 0921 42 15 47; www.museomandralisca.it

The museum was founded at the request of one of Cefalù's most generous benefactors, Baron Enrico Piraino di Mandralisca, a 19C art collector who bequeathed his art treasures and extensive library (more than 6 000 books, including many from the 16C) to the town. The museum houses a collection of coins and medals; a series of paintings including **Antonello da Messina**'s wonderful ***Portrait of an Unknown Man***★ from c 1470; archaeological artefacts, notably some from Lipari including an unusual bell-shaped *krater* (Antique vessel used to mix wine with water) depicting a tuna seller (4C BC); a changing selection of molluscs taken from an extensive collection of some 2 000; and a variety of objets d'art, including a Chinese puzzle in ivory.

Excursion

La Rocca

20min to the Temple of Diana; another 40min to the top. A path leads uphill from Corso Ruggero and Via dei Saraceni to the top of the outcrop. The first part of the route leads past ancient crenellated walls before rising steeply: particularly tiring in the midday heat of summer, it is best tackled in the early morning or at dusk. From such height, the magnificent **view**★★ pans across from Capo d'Orlando to Palermo; below, to the east, the town is protected by the promontory marked by a lookout tower, the Torre Caldura, only the ruins of which survive. On a good day the Aeolian Islands are quite clearly visible. Finds on this rocky outcrop confirm it to have accommodated the earliest settlements in the area, with evidence from different periods in history including the ruins of an Ancient Greek megalithic building, popularly called the **Temple of Diana**. On the top are the remains of a 12C-13C castle, recently restored.

Tour

EXCURSION INLAND

60km/37mi. From Cefalù, follow signs to the Santuario di Gibilmanna, 12km/7mi along an attractive scenic road.

Santuario di Gibilmanna

Open 8am-1pm and 3-7pm (5.30pm winter). ☎ *0921 42 18 35.* The **sanctuary**, dedicated to the Madonna, is perched high on the Pizzo San Angelo 800m/2 600ft above sea level, surrounded by oak and chestnut woods: its name refers to its position (from the Arabic *Jebel*, a mountain) and the old tradition, now obsolete, of making manna *(see p 225)*. Of ancient origins – the monastery is supposed to have been one of the six earliest Benedictine communities of coenobites founded at the behest of Gregory the Great in the 6C – it passed into the hands of the Capuchin Friars Minor in 1535. The present building is the result of numerous remodellings, especially in the Baroque period. The façade was rebuilt in 1907. The shrine is the object of a devout pilgrimage on 8 September, the festival of the Madonna. Inside the chapel of the Madonna (1625) is an 11C Byzantine fresco of a Madonna and Child, from an earlier Benedictine building, and a statue of the Virgin, probably the work of Antonello Gagini, set into an ornate Baroque altar.

The building adjacent to the monastery, once used as a stable and guest rooms, has been converted into an interesting **museum** dedicated to the life and culture of the Capuchin Friars of the Demone Valley. On display are sacred vestments (17C-18C), paintings, tools (the community was completely self-sufficient), and objects worked from base materials such as wood, tin and wax, as was the custom for this order. Of particular interest are a polyptych by Fra' Feliciano (at the time he was Domenico Guargena), a 16C alabaster rosary belonging to Fra' Giuliano da Placia and a small 18C reed organ.

Down in the catacombs there are rare reliquaries in painted tin or wood made by the friars.

Return to the road and continue for a further 10km/6mi.

Isnello

This little holiday resort, the starting-point for many walks into the surrounding area, stands in a spectacular **position**★ clinging to the rock in the middle of a gorge surrounded by high limestone walls. Its narrow streetshave a typical medieval layout.

Take the road back towards the sanctuary; at the junction (signposted to Piano delle Fate), turn left to continue along the panoramic road. This leads through two small villages, **Gratteri**, the centre of which preserves a medieval feel, and **Lascari**, before continuing on down to the coast and Cefalù.

Comiso

This little town, which was thrown into the limelight in the 1980s with front-page reports of a controversial American missile base being built there (and subsequently dismantled in the 1990s), boasts several notable 18C buildings.

Location

Population: 29 080. Michelin map 565 Q 25 – Ragusa. Comiso stands on the lower western slopes of the Iblei. As a result, many of the streets in the town are quite steep, with some houses having external staircases to enable easier access.

Neighbouring sights are described in the following chapters: CALTAGIRONE; GELA; Cava d'ISPICA; MODICA; NOTO; RAGUSA.

Walking About

Piazza Fonte di Diana

The central square of the town is graced with a neo-Classical **fountain** dedicated to the goddess Diana; this flows with water which would have supplied the public baths in Roman times. Archaeological excavations carried out in the little street directly opposite the fountain, connecting the square to Piazza delle Erbe, have revealed parts of the **Ancient baths**: an octagonal *caldarium*, and a nymphaeum with a black and white mosaic featuring Neptune surrounded by nereids (2C AD).

Piazza delle Erbe

The main building overlooking the square is the town's principal church, dedicated to **Santa Maria delle Stelle**. Its front elevation rises through three tiers of Doric, Ionic and Corinthian pilasters. The square also harbours the neo-Classical **covered market** (1871): this houses the **Museo Civico di Storia Naturale** with its collection of cetaceans (whales and other such mammals) and sea turtles, and the **Biblioteca di Bufalino**, a library endowed by the author (who died in 1966) for his native town and refuge. *Open daily except Sun, 8am-1pm. Closed national hols. ☎ 0932 86 40 38.*

Gesualdo Bufalino

The elaborate and expressive writing of Gesualdo Bufalino, born in Comiso in 1920, first came to public attention in 1981, with the publication of the author's first novel, *Diceria dell'untore*, which was awarded the Premio Campiello. An intense period of literary activity followed until 1996, when the writer was killed in a car accident. Some of Bufalino's best works include the collection of poetry *L'amaro miele*, and the novels *Argo il cieco owero i sogni della memoria* and *Le menzogne della notte*.

Chiesa dell'Annunziata

The elegant neo-Classical front elevation of this church, raised high above an unusual flight of steps, comprises two levels linked by a single element: the palm leaf. The airy light interior, ornamented with white, blue and gold stucco decoration, contains two paintings by Salvatore Fiume *(in the chancel).*

Chiesa di San Francesco (dell'Immacolata)

This Renaissance church contains the great **Naselli Chapel**; this rises from a square ground plan, through pendentives, to an octagon from which springs a ribbed dome. Against the wall stands the funerary monument of Baldassare Naselli, surmounted by a small shrine, both by the Gagini. At the back of the church, there is a lovely 17C gallery, painted with baskets of fruit and flowers.

Piazza San Biagio

The square is graced with the **Chiesa di San Biagio**, a Byzantine church (buttresses) that was rebuilt in the 18C, and the **Castello Aragonese** which was converted into a baronial residence by the Naselli family.

Chiesa dei Cappuccini

In the southern part of the town. Open 9-10am. ☎ 0932 72 25 21.

The building dates from 1616. Inside, there is a fine intarsia (inlaid wood) **altar★** and a little statue of the Madonna full of delicacy (18C). The mortuary chapel preserves the mummified remains of various religious and illustrious men, like a miniature of the Capuchin Catacombs in Palermo *(see Index)*.

Excursions

Vittoria

6km/3.6mi W. The town which was founded in the 17C at the wishes of Countess Vittoria Colonna, after whom it is named, was partly spared by the 1693 earthquake. The town appears neat and orderly, organised into straight, perpendicular streets, through which are scattered elegant Liberty style *palazzi*. The heart of the town centres around Piazza del Popolo, where **Santa Maria delle Grazie** with its harmoniously curvilinear façade and the neo-Classical municipal theatre are situated. In Via Cancellieri, leading off the piazza, are a number of fine buildings: note the Liberty-style **Palazzo Carfì-Manfré** (n° 71) and the Venetian Gothic **Palazzo Traìna** (n°s 108-116).

Via Cavour provides access to the town's main church and the museum. **San Giovanni Battista** (1695) has a distinctively linear front with three entrances and two small lateral domes. The interior is richly decorated with neo-Classical stucco friezes picked out in white, pale and dark blue and gold; the chapel to the left of the altar has Serpotta-style stucco ornament. The **Museo Civico** is accommodated in the countess's castle which was completed in 1785 on much earlier foundations. The well-restored rooms continue to reflect the fact that they were used as a prison until 1950. The small museum collects together old machinery for producing special theatrical effects (wind and hail-producing apparatus), a selection of traditional farming tools, and various ornithological specimens. *Open Tue-Sat, 9am-1pm and 4-7.30pm; Sun, 9am-1pm only. No charge.* ☎ *0932 72 25 21.*

The First World War **concentration camp** located just outside the town centre in Via Garibaldi was used primarily for Hungarian soldiers (who lived there on excellent terms with the local people); one of the dormitory blocks now contains a museum **(Museo Storico Italo-Ungherese)** for documents, artefacts and photographs. Further information is provided on display panels which also provide an insight into the current relations between Italy (and, in particular, this little town) and Hungary. *Open daily except Sun, 8.30am-1pm. Closed public hols. No charge.* ☎ *0932 86 59 94.*

GUIDED TOURS

Tours of the historic centre of Vittoria take place every Saturday morning. These are organised by the town council and take in the town's main monuments, including the picturesque local market. Tours leave at 9am from piazza del Popolo, in front of the tourist bus stop. For further information, contact ☎ 0932 86 40 38 (Signor Lo Piano).

Acate

Approx 15km/9mi NW. In the past the little town was called Biscari; its modern name probably comes from the word for agate, a semi-precious stone commonly found locally. For generations, it formed part of the feudal holdings of the princes of Paterno-Castello, hence the presence of such a massive residence in the town centre. It is also worth seeking out the town's main church (Chiesa Madre) and San Vincenzo which claims to preserve the martyred saint's relics.

Isole Egadi★

The ancient Aegates, the islands of goats referred to in the "Odyssey", form a mini-archipelago off Trapani and are blessed with lovely coastlines immersed in glorious crystal-clear water.

Location

Population: 4 382. Michelin map 565 M-1N 8-19 – Trapani. Favignana, the largest of the three islands and the most accessible, is popular with holidaymakers. Levanzo, the smallest island, and Marettimo, the most inaccessible, have fewer traditional tourist facilities, and appeal to visitors looking for a simpler vacation, surrounded by peaceful natural landscapes. ℹ *Favignana Largo Marina 14;* ☎ *0923 92 21 21 and Piazza Madrice 8;* ☎ *0923 92 16 47; www.egadiweb.it/index.htm. These tourist offices also provide information on Levanzo and Marettimo.*

Background

The islands, which are known to have been inhabited since prehistoric times (indeed, it is thought that Levanzo and Favignana formed part of the main island of Sicily in Palaeolithic times), witnessed a very important event in

Directory

Transport

Several hydrofoil and ferry services (especially during the summer) operate every day out of Trapani and Marsala (20-60min by hydrofoil and 1hr-2hr 45min by ferry). For information contact: **Siremar** (Gruppo Tirrenia), ☎ 199 123 199 (from Italian land lines) or 081 31 72 999 (from mobile phones or abroad); www.gruppotirrenia.it/siremar/html/home/mainframeset.htm; or **Ustica Lines**, Via Amm. Staiti 23, Trapani, ☎ 0923 22 200, info@usticalines.it, www.usticalines.it

In the summer, **Ustica Lines** operates a return hydrofoil service between Trapani-Favignana-Levanzo-Ustica-Naples. The Favignana-Naples crossing takes approximately 6hr.

For transport on the islands, see Sport and Leisure below.

Sightseeing

The Pro Loco of Favignana (Piazza Madrice 8, ☎ 0923 92 16 47) arranges guided tours of the tuna fishery and other excursions that change annually.

Where to Eat

• *For all budgets*

FAVIGNANA

La Bettola – *Via Nicotera 47, Favignana – ☎ 0923 92 19 88 – www.isoleegadi.it/labettola/ – Closed Thu (winter) and Jan – ⊄ – €20.50/23.50.* This typical trattoria serves traditional Egadian cuisine using fresh, local ingredients. The ambience is simple and typical of the islands.

MARETTIMO

Il Timone – *Via Garibaldi 18, Marettimo – ☎ 0923 92 31 42 – www.marettimonline.it/mangiare.html – Closed mid-Oct to Mar – ⊄ – Booking recommended – €15/25.* Situated down a narrow typical street in Marettimo, this simple restaurant, with its striking blue and white decor, serves delicious fresh fish and hand-made pasta. Perfect for visitors looking for genuine Sicilian cuisine.

Where to Stay

In addition to several traditional hotels, a number of **rooms** are also available for rent (apply to the Pro Loco for names and addresses).

FAVIGNANA

• *Budget*

Camping Villaggio Egad – *Contrada Arena, Favignana – ☎ 0923 92 15 55 – Fax 0923 92 15 67 – www.egadi.com/egad/ – Closed Oct-Apr. €19.* This beautiful campsite just one kilometre from the centre of Favignana is surrounded by pine, eucalyptus, acacia and oleander. A number of small apartments with modern bathrooms and kitchens are also available for rent.

• *Moderate*

Egadi Hotel – *Via Colombo 17, Favignana – ☎ 0923 92 12 32 – Fax 0923 92 12 32 – Closed Oct to mid-May – ▣ – 12 rooms. €44/78 ☕.* Now under new management, this hotel is one of the best known and most popular on the island. The staff here are friendly and helpful and the rooms simple, attractive and well maintained.

L'Oasi Albergo – *Contrada Camaro 32, Favignana – ☎ 0923 92 16 35 – Fax 0923 92 16 35 – diamonik@libero.it – Closed Oct-Easter – P – 25 rooms. €50/82 ☕.* This family-run hotel is located in a peaceful setting within close proximity to the town centre. The recently renovated rooms are comfortable and well-appointed and are arranged around an attractive garden with tropical plants, pine trees and other Mediterranean vegetation.

Aegusa Hotel – *Via Garibaldi 11/17, Favignana – ☎ 0923 92 24 30 – Fax 0923 92 24 40 – aegusa@cinet.it – Closed Jan and Feb – ▣ – 28 rooms. €100/135 ☕ – Restaurant €24/32.* The Aegusa hotel has bright, airy rooms furnished with simple wicker furniture and a pleasant holiday atmosphere. The restaurant, set in a pleasant garden-courtyard, offers a reasonably priced menu, with a wide selection of fish dishes and traditional cuisine.

Shopping

The most popular local specialities available on Favignana are of the edible kind: *bottarga* (dried tuna roe) and *bresaola* (cured or smoked) tuna and swordfish.

A. Safina/Lara Pessina/MICHELIN

Sport and Leisure

Mopeds and bicycles – The two most convenient ways of exploring the island are by bicycle or moped: cycling is especially popular because the island is so flat, thus requiring no great effort. To hire one, make your way into town; any of the shops will be happy to assist.

Diving and snorkelling – Visitors who like to explore the underwater scene will find a profusion of flora and fauna. The best areas for diving and snorkelling are Punta Marsala, Secca del Toro, the submerged cave between Cala Rotonda and Scoglio Corrente, and the rocks off Punta Fanfalo and Punta Ferro.

Antiquity: for it was in these waters that the treaty sealing an end to the First Punic War (241 BC) was signed, whereby Carthage assigned Sicily to the Roman Empire.
After changing hands many times over the centuries, the islands were sold in 1640 to the Pallavicino-Rusconi family from Genoa, in whose possession they remained until 1874, when they were acquired by the Florio family.

Spending time on the islands

FAVIGNANA★

The island is often referred to as *La Farfalla* on account of its shape, which has been likened to a butterfly fluttering over the blue sea. Its proper name is, in fact, derived from *favonio*, the prevalent local wind, although in Antiquity, it was known as Aegusa. In more recent times, the fortunes of the island have been inextricably linked with the Florio family *(see MARSALA)* after they invested in a tuna fishery here, down by the harbour, where a prominent tower still marks the skyline. In times past, tuna fishing, and the **mattanza** (the traditional, but cruel ritual of killing the tuna trapped in the nets known as the *camera della morte*) comprised the principal means of earning a livelihood on the island.
Favignana covers an area of about $20km^2$/8sq mi. The west "wing" is dominated by **Montagna Grossa** which, despite its name, rises to a mere 302m/991ft. The eastern part of the island, on the other hand, is flatter and harbours the island's main town.
The jagged coastline is interrupted, here and there, with short stretches of sandy beach.

Cave di tufo – Beside tuna fishing, tufa quarrying at one time provided the island with a second principal source of employment and income. Once cut, the blocks were transported elsewhere in Sicily and exported to North Africa. These quarries, a characteristic feature of the island's eastern flank, give the landscape an disturbing quality, as if great chunks had been bitten out of the hillside by some large square-jawed monster, leaving great, gaping, rectangular, stepped cavities. These are often overgrown with bushes, sometimes – alas – used as rubbish tips, or otherwise – luckily – transformed into secret small gardens, sheltered from the marauding winds. Near the sea, along the east coast, some of the old quarries have been partly flooded by waves let in by a landslip. Where it penetrates, the sea leaves small geometric pools of water. The most spectacular quarries are those grouped around Scalo Cavallo, Cala Rossa and Bue Marino *(see below: Bathing and beaches)*.

Favignana città

The main town of the island, indeed of the archipelago, is built around a small port that nestles in a large bay. On the skyline, perched up on its very own hill, sits the **Fort of Santa Caterina** *(now under military control)* which began life as an ancient Saracen warning station; this was rebuilt by the Norman King Roger II, and subsequently enlarged before serving as a prison under Bourbon rule (1794-1860).

LA MATTANZA

The complex and ritual method of catching tuna follows – or rather used to follow – very precise rules, timings and strictly disciplined practices established by the **Rais**, the head of the tuna fishermen and, at one time, also the head of the village: a sort of shaman who specified when it should begin and what procedure should be followed. The methods by which the tuna used to be hunted and killed date back to ancient times, indeed possibly even to the Phoenicians, although it was not until the islands came under Arab domination that the most fundamental elements of the "rite" that underpinned more recent fishing practices were firmly established. For the *mattanza* was a ritual in its own right, complete with propitiatory songs (the *scialome*), concluding in a cruel struggle with these powerful creatures at very close quarters. The outcome, however, was a foregone conclusion and rarely, if ever, in the tuna's favour.
In late spring, the tuna collect in great shoals off the west coast of Sicily where the conditions are conducive to breeding. The fishing boats would put out to sea to lay the nets in a long corridor which the tuna were forced to follow. The last nets were dropped like barriers to form antechambers that would prevent too many fish from being gathered in a single unit, thus averting the risk of the nets being torn and the fish escaping. Beyond these antechambers was laid the *camera della morte*, an enclosure provided by tougher netting and often closed along the bottom. When an appropriate number of fish were deemed to be trapped in the chamber, the Rais ordered the *mattanza* to begin, and so the killing of the fish was initiated: what was cruel was that, by now, the fish were exhausted after trying vainly to find a means of escape, and panicked after being injured by inevitably knocking into other tuna, crowded together as they were. One by one they were speared or hooked and heaved aboard.
The term *mattanza* comes from the Spanish word *matar*, to kill, which derives from the Latin *mactare*, meaning to glorify, or immolate.

Down by the seafront, Favignana boasts two buildings endowed by the **Florio** family, a wealthy dynasty involved in the production and export of Marsala wine before it developed any financial interests in tuna fishing. These comprise the **Palazzo Florio**, built in 1876, which is set back from the harbour and, at the opposite end of the bay on the right, the great **tonnara** or tuna fishery, now abandoned (plans are afoot to completely redevelop the old buildings to provide a multipurpose complex with a variety of facilities). *For information, contact the tourist office, ☎ 0923 92 16 47.*

The little town centres around two piazzas: Piazza Europa and Piazza Madrice which are linked by the main street, where the evening "constitution" or *passeggiata* (stroll) is enacted each evening. On the northeastern edge of town lies the district of San Nicola (behind the cemetery) which preserves vestiges of the past: there is no access to this area, however, as long as it remains private property.

Bathing and beaches★

There are two main beaches: a small sandy bay south of the town in **Cala Azzurra** and, still in the southern part but a little west of Cala Azzurra, the broad beach called the **Lido Burrone**. For those without their own means of transport, there is an hourly bus service. The rocky bays are more exciting and thrilling, notably **Cala Rossa**★ and **Cala del Bue Marino** nearby. What makes these spots especially unusual is the fact that they were once tufa quarries; deep in the grottoes where the roof has not fallen in, is a network of long, dark and mysterious passages that can be explored by torchlight.

The other half of the island harbours such lovely bays as the **Cala Rotonda**, **Cala Grande** and Punta Ferro, which doubles as a popular area for diving.

The caves

The west side of the mountain slopes down into the sea, forming a number of evocative caves and grottoes. Each summer morning, when the sea is becalmed, the local harbour fishermen vie with each other to whisk visitors off to see the most picturesque: Grotta Azzurra (so called because of the colour of the water), Grotta dei Sospiri (The Grotto of Sighs which sounds its laments in winter), and Grotta degli Innamorati (Lovers' Grotto), so named because of two identical rocks standing side by side deep against the back wall.

Levanzo

LEVANZO★

Tiny Levanzo (pronounced with an emphasis on the first syllable) has a surface area of 6km²/2sq mi, and bristles with hills. The tallest, Pizzo del Monaco (278m/912ft), tumbles its jaggedly rocky skirts down into the sea; the most beautiful part is a section of the southwest coast.

Only one road bisects the island from south to north, making it a veritable haven of peace and serenity, beloved by nature-lovers and those who seek solitude and rhythms set by the breaking waves or by the sound of one's own feet on the stones. The northern part of the island consists of a succession of sheer drops, rocky outcrops and secluded little creeks. Between Levanzo and the coast of Sicily lie two minute islets, **Maraone** and **Formica** (on which there are the remains of an old tuna fishery).

Cala Dogana

The only hamlet on Levanzo overlooks a bay of the clearest water on the south side of the island. From here, a well-kept path snakes its way to the bays that open out along the southwestern coast, each tightly embracing its very own miniature pebbled beach, as far as the Faraglione (a large rock).

Grotta del Genovese★

Accessible on foot (approx 2hr there and back), by jeep and then on foot along a steep slope, or by sea. To visit the cave, contact Signore Castiglione, Via Calvario, Levanzo. ☎ 0923 92 40 32, 0360 63 92 61 or 339 74 18 800 (mobile).

Discovered in 1949, this excavated hollow in the side of a tall cliff bears traces of prehistoric man. Vestiges of wall-painting have been identified as dating from the Upper Palaeolithic era, while the incised drawings may be from the Neolithic period. The *graffiti* drawings, completed at a time when the island was still attached to the island of Sicily, represent bison and a **deer★★** of the most pleasing proportions, elegance and foreshortening. The charcoal and animal fat paintings represent early attempts at fishing (both tuna and dolphins are discernible), animal husbandry (a woman leads a cow with a halter) and ritual images of men dancing and women with wide hips. These paintings are comparable with the Franco-Cantabrian cave paintings of Lascaux in southwest France *(see The Green Guide Dordogne Berry Limousin)* and Altamira in Spain *(see The Green Guide Spain)*.

MARETTIMO★

A steep rocky mountain with great limestone cliffs plunging down into the sea define this, the most remote island of the Egadi group. It welcomes only the more curious visitors, who arrive at its tiny harbour knowing that there are no hotels there. The only accommodation available is that offered by local fishermen and consists of rented rooms *(for addresses, contact the Pro Loco in Favignana)*.

At the foot of the mountain nestles the hamlet of Marettimo, a compact collection of square white houses and terraces collected together around the miniature harbour. Behind the Scalo Nuovo (the main landing stage) stands the Scalo Vecchio reserved for the local fishermen. To one side, extends **Punta Troia**, topped with ruins of a Spanish castle (17C) that served as a prison until 1844. A series of rugged paths (manageable even astride a donkey) lead inland uphill to higher ground where Mother Nature, remote and wild, can provide companionship in contemplating the glorious views out over the sea.

Boat trip around the island★★

Down in the harbour, many a local fisherman will volunteer himself and his boat to provide excursions to the numerous caves that hide among the precipitous cliffs along the coast. The most striking include the **Grotta del Cammello**, in which shelters a small pebble beach, **Grotta del Tuono** (Cave of Thunder), Grotta Perciata and, most notable of all, the **Grotta del Presepio**, likened to a Nativity scene because of the rocks it contains, fashioned and crafted by the wind and the waves.

Enna★

Occupying a magnificent position★★ on a plateau 948m/3 109ft above sea level, Enna is known as the belvedere of Sicily; it is also the highest provincial capital in Italy.

As the road winds gradually upwards to the town, beautiful views pan out across the valley to Calascibetta, the town perched on the concave slopes of the hill opposite.

Location

Population: 28 401. Michelin map 565 O 24. Enna is situated at an altitude of approximately 1 000m/3 000ft, and is approached for the last few hundred metres via a narrow winding road. Visitors are advised to park in the upper town and to bring a sweater or jacket as the temperature here is generally cooler than on the coast.

ℹ Via Roma 413; ☎ 0935 52 82 28; Fax 095 52 82 29.

Neighbouring sights are described in the following chapters: CALTANISSETTA; PIAZZA ARMERINA; VILLA IMPERIALE DEL CASALE.

Background

Historical notes – The origins of Enna date back to prehistoric times. Its elevated position, so easily defensible, made it especially desirable. It was probably inhabited by the Sicani, who exploited the strategic potential of the site to defend themselves from the threat of Siculi advances. There subsequently developed a Greek, and then later, a Roman town; in 135 BC it was here that the First Slave War erupted, prompted by the Syrian slave Euno, before spreading across the island and lasting for seven long years.

After being reconquered by the Romans, it fell in the 6C, only to be absorbed into the Byzantine dominion (as did all the rest of Sicily), when it was quick to reassume its defensive role pending the threat of siege by the Arabs. It capitulated only in the 9C. The name Henna, probably of Greek origin (from *en naien*: to live inside) was retained by the Romans who prefixed it with the Latin word for fortress, making it *Castrum Hennae*; with the advent of the Arabs, the name was transformed into *Kasrlànna* (*Qasr Yânnah* or *Qasr Yani*), which was eventually vulgarised to Castrogiovanni. Enter the Normans, who made it the political and cultural stronghold of their kingdom, and they were followed by the Swabians, the Angevins and the Aragonese. It was here that Frederick II of Aragon took the title of King of Trinacria (the ancient name for Sicily) in 1314, and convocated parliament in 1324. Subsequently, the town followed the vicissitudes of the rest of the island, rebelling against the Bourbons and supporting Garibaldi. In 1927, the ancient name of Enna was restored under Mussolini.

Mythology – In ancient times, the cult of **Demeter** (Ceres to the Romans), earth mother and goddess of fertility, was especially important here, possibly because of the extensive cultivation of wheat that continues to characterise this area. Furthermore, according to the Greek myths, it was on the shores of Lake Pergusa, *(see section entitled Natural History, Archaeology and Sulphurous Deposits below)* which is not far from here, that Demeter's daughter Persephone (Proserpina) was abducted by Hades, the god of the Underworld; built at the highest point above Enna, in the place known as the belvedere, there used to be a temple dedicated to Demeter.

Directory

For additional suggestions, see Piazza Armerina: Directory.

Where to Eat

• For all budgets

Tiffany – *Via Roma 467, Enna – ☎ 0935 50 13 68 – Closed Thu – ⊠ – €12,91/25,82.* This small, reasonably priced restaurant, considered one of the best pizzerias in the centre of Enna, has a particularly warm and friendly atmosphere.

Centrale – *Piazza VI Dicembre 9, Enna – ☎ 0935 50 09 63 –* ristcentrale@yahoo.it *Closed Sat (except Thu-Sep) – ⊠ – €19/31.* As the name suggests, this family-run restaurant is situated right in the heart of the town, and offers a good choice of local fish and meat dishes, served in a simply decorated dining room with high ceilings.

Where to Stay

• Moderate

Sicilia – *Piazza Colaianni 7, Enna – ☎ 0935 50 08 50 – Fax 0935 50 04 88 – ⊠ – 76 rooms. €57/91 ☕ €5.* The Sicilia is a modern hotel in the heart of this attractive town which caters for both tourists and business visitors. The roomshave been recently renovated and the communal areas are spacious and attractive. A comfortable hotel with good service.

Taking a Break

Bar del Duomo – *Piazza Mazzini 1, Enna – ☎ 0935 24 205.* This popular bar, located just in front of the cathedral, serves a good selection of typical Sicilian cakes, savoury specialities and excellent ice cream.

Caffè Roma – *Via Roma 312, Enna – ☎ 0935 50 12 12 – Open 8am-11pm. Closed Tue.* The Caffè Roma was founded in 1921 and has long been a firm favourite with locals. Rustic decor and exposed stone provide the backdrop for some excellent sweet and savoury specialities. Well worth a visit!

Festivals

Settimana Santa – During the traditional Holy Week festival the confraternities of Enna take part in a procession through the town *(see box below)*.

Walking About

TOWN CENTRE

With its plethora of churches, Enna has a great deal to offer the visitor. The axis of the town is marked by the **Via Roma** which starts near the Castello di Lombardia and, after a sharp turn, leads down the hill to the Torre di Federico *(both buildigs are described below)*. It is along this principal thoroughfare that most of the monuments and points of interest are to be found.

Castello di Lombardi★★

Open mid-Apr to mid-Oct, 8am-8pm; otherwise, 9am-1pm and 3-5pm. No charge. ☎ 0935 40 347.

Situated uppermost on the plateau, the **castle** looks out over the town and the valley, including the Rocca di Cerere (Fortress of Ceres) where, it is thought, a temple dedicated to the fertility goddess was built.

This site has been fortified since earliest times because of its strategic position. Under Norman dominion, the castle was reinforced. It was made habitable by Frederick II of Aragon, who added a number of rooms that rendered it suitable for court life. Indeed, he intended it as his summer residence: it was here that he was crowned King of Trinacria and, in 1324, convocated the Sicilian parliament. The name of the castle dates from this same period, linked to the presence of a garrison of Lombard soldiers posted there to defend it. The ground plan of the castle, which is roughly pentagonal, hugs the tortuous lie of the land. Of the original 20 towers, only six survive (some only in part). The most interesting and complete is the one called *La Pisana* or *Torre delle Aquile* (The Pisan Tower or Tower of the Eagles), topped by Guelph crenellations. From the top, a breathtaking **view★★★** stretches over the best part of the Sicilian mountain ranges, Mount Etna and Calascibetta.

Enclosed within the walls are three courtyards: the one named after St Nicholas is used as an open-air theatre; the one named after Mary Magdalen was where the supplies were kept during times of siege; the Courtyard of St Martin, at the heart of the royal apartments, gives access to the Pisan Tower.

Just outside the castle precincts, in the direction of the Fortress of Ceres, stands the statue of **Euno**, a memorial to the slave who began the Slave War *(see also introduction to the chapter)*.

Rocca di Cerere

From the top of the hill, where the Fortress of Ceres – a temple dedicated to the fertility goddess – once stood, extends an all-encompassing **view★★** including Calascibetta opposite, and Enna itself.

The Confraternities

One peculiarity of the residents of Enna is the fact that they are divided into confraternities, each having its "spiritual *contrada* or quarter". Every confraternity has its own hierarchy of officers, church and traditional costume, all of which are fiercely and proudly defended by its adherents. The most important popular event is the **Processione della Settimana Santa**, a week-long festival beginning on Palm Sunday when the Collegio dei Rettori (a council of governors) processes to the Duomo to begin celebrations in adoration of the Holy Eucharist. In turn, delegations from each confraternity leave their own churches and converge on the cathedral, followed by bands playing funeral marches. At noon on the Wednesday of Holy Week, the church bells are removed and the *troccola*, a special mechanical instrument made of wood, is sounded. The real and proper procession takes place on the evening of Good Friday: hundreds of representatives from the various confraternities, hooded and cloaked in mantles of different colours, process through the streets bearing first the Dead Christ, followed by Our Lady of Sorrows, on their shoulders. On Easter Sunday, the two statues are carried back to their respective churches.

J. Malburet/MICHELIN

Duomo

Although largely rebuilt in the Baroque style in the 16C and 17C, the cathedral has retained its Gothic apses (best admired inside, especially in the left apse).

The cathedral front, preceded by a dramatic staircase, rises above a portico to a bell tower through the three Classical orders: Doric (the portico has an entablature with metopes and triglyphs, as found in the temples of Antiquity), Ionic and Corinthian. The 16C south door, named after San Martino, has a marble relief panel depicting St Martin and the Pauper; this balances the Porta Santa, adjacent, which is Gothic. The **interior★** is divided into nave and aisles by columns of black basalt, each with finely sculpted bases and capitals (note, in particular, the reliefs incorporating allegorical creatures, *putti*, serpents and two-headed gargoyles on the second column on the right and the corresponding column on the left, which are considered to be by **Giandomenico Gagini**). The 16C woodwork is especially fine. The coffered **ceiling★** is finely inlaid, and graced at the end of each beam by unusual winged figures. At the end of the aisles, the organ loft and choir gallery, although in far from pristine condition, have elegant inlaid and painted wooden balustrading, and niches containing statues of Christ and the twelve Apostles. Behind the high altar, the wooden choir stalls are further decorated with scenes from the Old and New Testaments redolent with didacticism; this is echoed in the door panels of the sacristy cupboard or *casciarizzo* which illustrate scenes from the life of Christ. Above the altar hangs a fine 15C Christ on the Cross with, on the reverse, a painting of the Resurrection: this is called the Christ of the Three Faces because Christ's expression appears to alter depending on the angle from which the painting is contemplated.

San Michele Arcangelo

Erected in 1658, probably on the site of an old mosque, the church of the Archangel Michael has a square façade and is built on an elliptical plan with radiating side chapels.

Follow Via Polizzi out of the square and turn right into Via del Salvatore to the church dedicated to the Holy Saviour **(San Salvatore)**, an old Basilian church remodelled in the 16C, and recently restored.

Continue to Piazza Colajanni, which is bordered by fine buildings, including the **Palazzo Pollicarini** and the Church of Santa Chiara.

Santa Chiara

For information on admission times, call ☎ 0935 26 119.

The Church of St Clare, now a memorial to fallen soldiers, has a single nave. The tiled floor is set with two panels: *The Triumph of Christianity over Islam* and *The Advent of Steam Navigation.*

Further along Via Roma is **San Giuseppe**, with its lovely (though rather dilapidated) Baroque façade, complete with bell tower.

From Piazza Coppola, turn left into Via Candrilli.

Campanile di San Giovanni Battista

The elegant bell tower of John the Baptist, articulated by large ogive arches at ground level, a decorative three-light Gothic window above and round-headed arches in the upper storey, is all that remains of the church of the same name.

Return to Via Roma.

San Giovanni

Originally built in the Romanesque style, the Church of St John has been remodelled, decorated with stucco and completely restored in 1967. Inside there is an unusual font: the base is Roman, the central section is a Byzantine capital made of red marble, the carved basin is medieval (14C).

San Marco

This church, dating from the 17C, was erected on the site of an old synagogue, in what was Enna's Jewish quarter. **Inside**, the spacious hall church is decorated with fine stuccoes of cherubs, garlands of flowers, fruit and shells by Gabriele de Blanco da Licodia (1705). It is also worth noting the inlaid wooden women's gallery, reserved for nuns attending functions.

Almost directly opposite the belvedere in Piazza Francesco Crispi, there extends a fabulous **view★** of Calascibetta, Lake Nicoletti and the Lombardy Castle on the right. The fountain ornamenting the garden is graced with a bronze copy of Bernini's *Rape of Persephone.*

Further along is a monumental church dedicated to St Francis **(San Francesco)**. Right on the bend of the road is another, San Cataldo, with a square façade. Via Roma continues to Piazza Neglia, onto which faces the **Chiesa delle Anime Sante** (All Souls) – with a fine Baroque limestone doorway – and the 15C **San Tomaso**, with its lovely gallery and campanile pierced by single openings, intended and used (around the 10C) as a watchtower.

Continue along Via Roma.

Torre di Federico★

At one time, Enna might have been called the city of towers. Their proliferation is explained by the defensive and strategic role of the town. Many have disappeared, many have been incorporated into churches as bell towers; only a few survive as free-standing towers today. A case in point is the octagonal tower named after Frederick II of Swabia, which occupies pride of place in a small public park.

This tour can be continued through the Fundrisi Quarter.

FREDERICK'S TOWERS

Frederick II, the Swabian King of Sicily, gave a considerable boost to civic building in the south of Italy. This architecture is characterised by rigorous geometry: buildings rise from a square base, imitating the form of the Roman *castrum*, also employed in the Islamic world, with cylindrical or square towers at the corners and one cylindrical or polygonal tower in the centre *(see the castle at Augusta or Maniace Castle at Siracusa)*. Through time, the *octagonal* ground plan was evolved and applied to the one here, at Enna. This choice of plan is in accordance with the mind of medieval man, fascinated as he was by precise geometry and the symbolic significance of such forms. The square – symbolising the Earth and humankind – contrasts with the circle, which symbolised the divine and the heavens. At that time, the octagon represented mediation, the fusion of the two opposing "rudiments".

ENNA

Anfiteatro (Via) .... CY 3
Arcangelo Ghisleri (Piazza) .... BY 4
Aspromonte (Via) .... BY 6
Bovio (Piazza G.) .... BY 7
Candurra (Via) .... BY
Catalano (Via O.) .... BY 9
Catania (Via) .... ABY
Catena (Via) .... AY 10
Catenanuova (Via) .... AY 12
Cavalieri di Vitt. Veneto (Via) .... BZ 13
Cerere Arsa (Via) .... BCY
Chiaramonte Francesco (Via) .... BY 15
Cittadella (Via d.) .... CY 16
Colajanni (Piazza N.) .... BY 18
Colombaia (Via) .... ABY 19
Coppola (Piazza M.) .... BY 21
Diaz (Viale A.) .... AYZ
Donna Nuova (Via) .... BY
Duomo (Piazza) .... CY
Europa (Piazza) .... BZ
Fontana Grande (Via) .... BY 22
Garibaldi (Piazza G.) .... BY 24
Gervazi (Via T. G.) .... AY 25

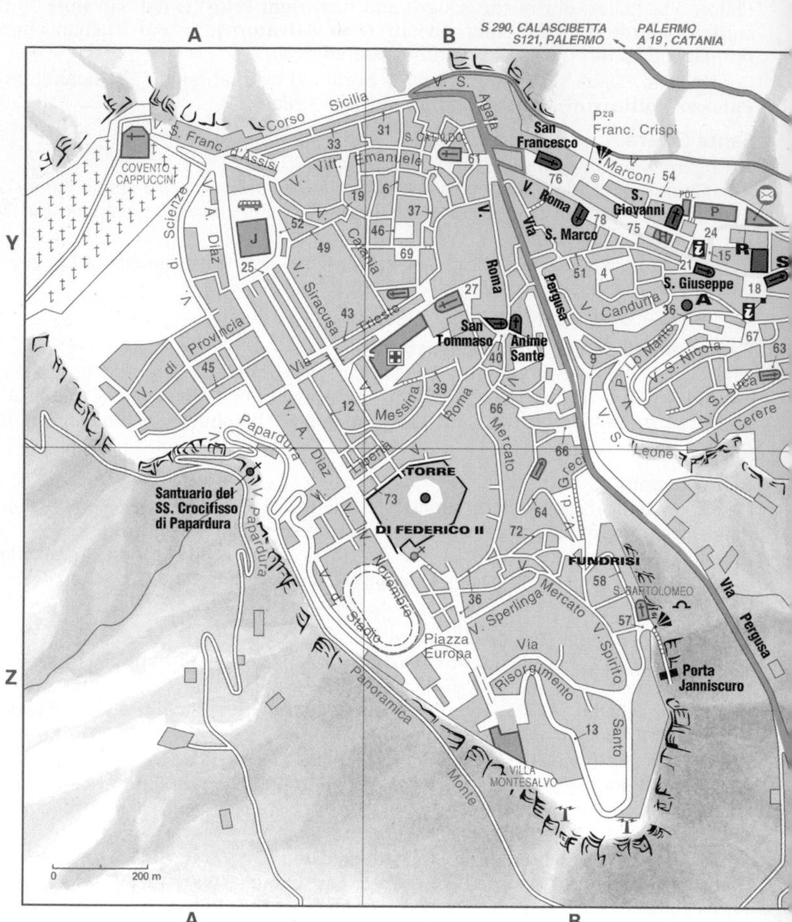

QUARTIERE FUNDRISI

About halfway along Via Mercato. The Fundrisi Quarter was established on the southwestern end of the Enna plateau when, in 1396, King Martin of Aragon quelled the revolt on the island and razed several of the small towns in the vicinity of Castrogiovanni, as it was then, to the ground. The inhabitants of the town called Fundrò were transferred here and, over the centuries, constituted a separate community independent of the main town. A walk through the narrow streets of this part of the town, all up and down, among the typical single-storey houses with their distinctive galleries (especially along Via San Bartolomeo), is particularly recommended. From here or Piazzetta San Bartolomeo, which takes its name from the church that presides over the scene, extend various **prospects**★ across the northeastern part of the town. A short way below the piazza, stands **Porta Janniscuru**, the only gate to survive of the five that once served the city, and, adjacent to this, the Grotta della Guardiola (literally translated as the Cave of the Guardroom) which is thought to have been the site of a cult long before the foundation of the town. Continuing on an axis with Via Mercato, Via Spirito Santo leads to the church which gives it its name, enjoying a splendid position, perched on a rocky spur over a vertical drop.

Giovanni XXIII (Piazza) **BY** 27
Greci (Via d.) **BZ**
Kennedy (Piazza) **AY** 28
La Paglia (Via G.) **CY** 30
Libertà (Via) **ABZ**
Lo Manto (Via P.) **BY**
Lombardia (Via) **CY**
Longo (Via) **BY** 31
Manzoni (Via A.) **AY** 33
Mazzini (Piazza G.) **CY** 34
Mercato (Via) **BYZ**
Messina (Via) **ABY**
Montesalvo (Via) **BZ** 36
Mulino a Vento (Via) **BY** 37
Muse (Via d.) **BY** 39
Neglia (Piazza F. P.) **BY** 40
Ospedale (Via U.) **BY** 42
Panoramica Casina Bianca **CY**
Panoramica Lombardia **CYZ**
Panoramica Monte **ABZ**
Papardura (Via) **AYZ**
Pergusa (Via) **BYZ**
Piazza Armerina (Via) **AY** 45
Pirandello (Via L.) **BY** 46
Polizzi (Via S.) **CY** 48
Provincia (Viale d.) **AY**
Raccordo (Via) **AY** 49
Repentite (Via) **BY** 51
Regione Siciliana (Via) **AY** 52
Repubblica (Piazza d.) **BY** 54
Rinascita (Via d.) **CYZ**
Risorgimento (Via) **BZ**
Roma (Via) **BCY**
S. Agata (Via) **BY**
S. Agostino (Piazza) **BY** 55
S. Bartolomeo (Piazza) **BZ** 57
S. Bartolomeo (Via) **BZ** 58
S. Biagio (Via) **CY** 60
S. Cataldo (Piazza) **BY** 61
S. Francesco d'Assisi (Via) **AY**
S. Giorgio (Piazza) **BY** 63
S. Leonardo (Via) **BYZ** 64
S. Leone (Via) **BY**
S. Luca (Via) **BCY**
S. Matteo (Via) **BY** 66
S. Nicola (Via) **BY**
S. Pietro (Via) **CY**
S. Sofia (Piazza) **BY** 67
Salvatore (Via) **CY** 69
Savarese Nino (Viale) **CY** 70
Savoca (Viale P. e C.) **CY**
Scienze (Via d.) **AY**
Sicilia (Corso) **ABY**
Siracusa (Via) **AY**
Sperlinga (Via) **BZ**
Spirito Santo (Via) **BZ**
Stadio (Via d.) **ABZ**
Studio (Via) **BZ** 72
Torre di Federico (Via) **BZ** 73
Trieste (Via) **ABY**
Umberto I (Piazza) **BY** 75
Valverde (Via) **CY**
Vittorio Emanuele (Piazza) **BY** 76
Vittorio Emanuele (Via) **ABY**
IV Novembre (Viale) **ABZ**
VI Dicembre (Piazza) **BY** 78

Anime Sante **BY**
Campanile di S. Giovanni Battista **BY A**
Castello di Lombardia **CY**
Duomo **CY**
Fundrisi **BZ**
Museo Alessi **CY M1**
Museo Archeologico Varisano **CY M2**
Palazzo Pollicarini **BY R**
Porta Janniscuro **BZ**
Rocca di Cerere **CY**
S. Chiara **BY S**
S. Francesco **BY**
S. Giovanni **BY**
S. Giuseppe **BY**
S. Marco **BY**
S. Michele Arcangelo **CY**
S. Tommaso **BY**
SS. Salvatore **CY**
Santuario del SS. Crocifisso di Papardura **AZ**
Torre di Federico II **BZ**

Worth a Visit

Museo Alessi

Entrance at the back of the Duomo. Open 8am-8pm. Closed 1 Jan, 1 May and 25 Dec. €2.50. ☎ *0935 50 31 65.*

In 1862, the museum was created to house the collections of Canon Alessi, which include 17C and 18C sacred vestments embroidered with gold thread and coral *(in the basement)*, and a selection of **paintings** *(on the upper floor)*, notably a gentle *Madonna and Child* by an unknown 15C Flemish painter, a 16C *Pietà* with the symbols of the Passion, and two panels with John the Baptist and St John the Evangelist from a 16C polyptych attributed to Il Panormita. Displayed on the first floor is a canvas by Giuseppe Salerno (known locally as the Lame Man of Gangi) depicting the *Madonna delle Grazie*, together with the glorious **treasures** from the Chiesa Madre. The latter consists of sacred relics, a fabulous Madonna's **crown★** exquisitely enamelled and engraved with narrative scenes relating the life of Christ (17C), a magnificent 17C **pelican jewel★** – symbol of the Sacrifice of the Resurrection for Eternal Life – and the monumental **processional monstrance★** engraved with the graceful spires of a Gothic cathedral, a work of supreme quality attributed to Paolo Gili (1536-38).

On the second floor is exhibited a collection of Greek, Roman and Byzantine **coins**; an assortment of archaeological finds ranging from prehistoric times to the Late Middle Ages; not forgetting a series of interesting **Egyptian funerary figurines**, found among grave goods recovered in Sicily, having been placed in tombs, it is thought, much in the way they were by the Ancient Egyptians. These *ushebti* figurines (literally translated as "those who answer the call") were interred to execute the earthly labours of the deceased.

Museo Archeologico Varisano

Piazza Mazzini. Open 8am-7.30pm. €2. ☎ 0935 52 81 00.

On display are the archaeological finds, mainly in terracotta, recovered from the necropoli at Calascibetta, Capodarso, Pergusa, Cozzo Matrice and Rossomanno.

Santuario del SS Crocifisso di Papardura

Take Via Libertà after the crossroads with Viale Diaz; turn right down a minor road marked with the Stations of the Cross. Closed for restoration at the time of going to press. For information, call ☎ 0935 37 626.

The Sanctuary of the Holy Crucifix of Papardura incorporates the cave where, in 1659, an image of the Crucifix was found painted on a stone slab. This has been attributed as the work of Basilian monks and can now be seen on the high altar. Inside, the fine **stuccoes** initiated in 1696 by Giuseppe and Giacomo Serpotta, were completed in 1699 by another artist, who also executed the statues of the Apostles. Note also the high altar silver **façade★** made by a craftsman from Messina (17C); the wooden 19C coffered ceiling and the side altar façades of tooled, painted leather.

Tours

AMONG THE HILLS NORTH OF ENNA

85km/53mi, plus 55km/34mi back to Enna – allow one day. Leave Enna as indicated on the plan and follow directions for Calascibetta, 4km/2.5mi N.

This tour runs through the gently rolling hills that separate Enna from Catania, passing old hill-top villages and providing stunning **panoramic views★** of the surrounding countryside.

Calascibetta

Benefiting from a glorious **setting★** which consists of a natural amphitheatre nestling in a rocky hollow on the side of a hill, this little town was probably founded during the Arab occupation. The **Chiesa Madre**, founded in the 14C, was completely rebuilt in the 17C following an earthquake; remains of the former building form the foundations of the present church, and can be seen below the north aisle. Inside, the nave is divided from its aisles by stone columns which rise from bases bearing carvings of monstrous figures to support the arcades of pointed arches. To the left of the entrance is a fine 16C font.

The **Norman tower** (11C), standing beside the ruined church of San Pietro, is ornamented with a shallow relief in stone. From the piazza on the left extends a marvellous **view★★**, with Enna on the right (where the castle and belvedere can be seen quite clearly) and the Lago di Pergusa below.

Leaving the town in the direction of Villapriolo, the road passes the rock-cut tombs of the **necropolis of Realmese** (4C BC).

The spectacular setting of Calascibetta

B. Kaufmann/MICHELIN

Return to the crossroads and take the left turning (S 121) for Leonforte (20km/12mi NE of Calascibetta).

Leonforte

The town perches on a hump enjoying a superb **position★**. The monumental silhouette of Palazzo Branciforte is discernible from a distance, a powerful reminder of the fact that the town was founded in the 17C by Nicola Placido Branciforte. The *palazzo*, dating from 1611, runs the whole length of one side of the enormous piazza of the same name. Of particular interest is the lovely fountain or **Granfonte** (1651) built by the Branciforte family: of gold-coloured stone it comprises 24 spouts, a series of small pointed arches crowned with a pediment bearing the family coat of arms.

Turn back down the same road, and at the fork, turn left for Assoro (6km/4mi E of Leonforte).

Assoro

At a height of 850m/2 800ft, the town is grouped around the little Piazza Umberto I, which is attractively paved, has a fountain in the centre and a lovely **belvedere-terrace★**. Beyond the elegant archway linking Palazzo Valguarnera to the town's main church, is another little square with viewing terrace, which opens out before the Chiesa Madre, or **Basilica di San Leone**. The church, founded in 1186, has been subjected to major alterations: first in the late 14C and again in the 18C. It consists of a nave and aisles and has a doorway on the south side. The north porch was adapted in 1693 so as to accommodate the Capella dell'Oratorio del Purgatorio and given an elegant Baroque doorway. The **interior★**, enclosed by a fine ribbed vault, is particularly attractive on account of its compactness and profuse gilded Baroque **stucco decoration**. The spiral columns were in fact embellished with their climbing plant ornament in the 18C, at the same time as the pelican *(right)* and the phoenix *(left)* were added above the apses. These emblems allude to the Sacrifice of the Crucifixion and the Resurrection of Christ: the first represents the bird which, according to myth, plucked flesh from its own breast to feed its young, while the second fabulous creature, having burnt itself to ashes on an altar fire, re-emerged rejuvenated.

The main body of the church has a fine **wooden tie-beam ceiling**, painted and ornamented with arabesques (1490); the attractive wrought-iron chapel **gates** (15C) are also worthy of note.

To visit the church, contact the parish priest on ☎ 0935 66 72 78.

Beyond the town, follow the road past San Giorgio which intersects S 121 again at Nissoria. Turn right towards Agira (17km/10mi E of Assoro).

Agira

Spread over the slopes of Monte Teja, at a height of 650m/2 130ft, the town is overshadowed by the silhouette of the **castle**, which towers above it. Built under Swabian rule, this defensive outpost appears to have played an active role in various struggles between the Angevins and the Aragonese and, later, between the Aragonese and the Chiaramonte. From the ruins, there is a beautiful **view★** over Lago di Pozzillo.

Town and monastery

The story of Agira, home of the ancient historian Diodorus Siculus (90-20 BC), echoes the pattern in fortune of the Basilian monastery of San Filippo, which was founded by a Syrian monk some time between the 5C and 6C AD, and which quickly rose to become an important centre of culture and religion. It came to particular prominence when, during the Norman occupation, the resident community was joined by a group of monks from Jerusalem who were forced into exile by the wrath of Saladin. The monastery also prospered on account of the enormous income generated by its immense holdings throughout Europe. In 1537, Emperor Charles V conceded the title of *città demaniale* upon Agira, providing it with a special "royal" status complete with privileges that included the right to administrate its own civil and penal justice system. The town's decline began in 1625 when King Philip IV of Spain, in a desperate effort to boost the dwindling finances of the monarchy, decided to sell the town to Genoese merchants: faced with the threat of losing their freedom, the citizens of Agira offered to raise the enormous sum required themselves.

Abbazia San Filippo – *Open 7.30-11.30am and 4-7pm. ☎ 0935 69 10 08.* This abbey is the town's most important religious building. It dates in its present form from the late 18C and early 19C (the front was completely rebuilt in 1928). **Inside**, it is decorated with gilded stuccowork; among the works of art is a dramatic wooden Crucifix by Fra' Umile da Petralia *(over the high altar)*, wooden choir stalls depicting scenes from the life of St Philip by Nicola Bagnasco (1818-22), three 15C polyptych panels representing the Madonna in Majesty with Saints, as well as paintings by Olivio Sozzi and Giuseppe Velasquez.

Continue along S 121 for 14km/9mi.

Regalbuto

Coming from Agira, the visitor is welcomed by the fine Baroque pink stone façade of **Santa Maria La Croce** (1744), graced with columns crowned by an elegant pediment. Turning left into Via Ingrassia, immediately on the left-hand side is the Jesuit school and, just beyond it, the Liberty-style **Palazzo Compagnini**. A little further, the town's main square provides a broad open space before the **Chiesa Madre** (1760), from which to survey the monumental Baroque façades of the church dedicated to St Basil assembled from a miscellany of features, articulated by pilasters.

From S 121, a narrow road winds its twisted way to Centùripe (21km/13mi SE of Regalbuto).

Centùripe

This little town, which today seems rather off the beaten track, was at one time in the distant past a strategic outpost on the main route between the plain of Catania and the mountains inland. This explains why, particularly in Roman times, Centùripe enjoyed considerable economic prosperity (in 70 BC, Cicero described it as one of the most prosperous towns in Sicily). And it is from the Roman era that Centùripe retains its most monumental remains. The **Tempio degli Augustali** (1C-2C AD) is a rectangular building raised above a colonnaded street onto which it faced (alongside the new archaeological museum). The two monumental tombs with towers are known as *la Dogana* (with only the upper floor visible) and the "the castle of Conradin". Down a cobbled side street on the far northwestern side of the town, in the *contrada* of Bagni, sit the ruins of what must once have been a spectacular **nymphaeum** hanging above the ravine of the river, with fountains designed to delight visitors approaching the town. A brick wall containing five niches, the remains of a cistern in which water was collected, and parts of the aqueduct are also visible.

Finally, the vast majority of artefacts recovered from the 8C BC to the Middle Ages are displayed in the **Museo Archeologico** (Via SS Crocifisso), including the statues from the Tempio degli Augustali representing various emperors and members of their families. Highlights are a fine head of the Emperor Hadrian which, given its size, must have belonged to a statue at least 4m high; two splendid **funerary urns**★ belonging to the Scribonii family (almost certainly imported from Rome); locally produced pottery (3C-1C BC), and an impressive collection of theatrical masks. *Open daily except Mon, 9am-7pm. Closed on national hols. €2.50. ☎ 0935 73 079 or 0935 91 94 40.*

To return to Enna from Centùripe, continue in the direction of Catenanuova and take the motorway (55km/34mi).

NATURAL HISTORY, ARCHAEOLOGY AND SULPHUR

Approximately 130km/81mi – allow one day. Leave Enna as indicated on the plan and follow directions for Pergusa (9km/5.5mi S).

The shores of **Lago di Pergusa**, now disfigured by a motor-racing track, provided the backdrop for a mythical story: the abduction of **Persephone** by Hades.

At the next junction, turn left, signposted for Valguarnera (18km/11mi SE of Pergusa).

Parco minerario Floristella-Grottacalda

Flagged along the roadside. Operational as a sulphur mine until 1984, the park's main attraction, which may not immediately be evident, lies in the way it documents an important area of activity that affected the lives and destinies of large numbers of Sicilians, particularly of those living in the provinces of Enna and Caltanissetta.

A dirt track leads to a large open area and the *palazzina* Pennisi, a small building erected by the barons of Floristella, who were the long-standing owners of the mine since workings began around 1750. Behind the building, all the aspects of the site and industrial archaeology can be seen. On the left stands Hoisting Shaft N° 1 (bricks and mortar) and a ventilation shaft (metal), which were in use until 1972. The small white hillocks are the *calcheroni*, round pits lined with inert

Persephone and Hades

Legend describes how the daughter of Demeter and Zeus was once playing here with her companions the ocean nymphs, when her eye was caught by a particularly beautiful narcissus. As she reached out to pick it, the earth gave way, forming a great abyss from which, with due majesty, **Hades** and his immortal horses emerged. The god forced her to mount his golden chariot before disappearing with her, near Syracuse, by the Cyane Fountain *(see SIRACUSA)*, down into the Underworld. Her distraught mother, hearing her daughter's piercing cries, set about searching for her. After wandering relentlessly, she finally succeeded in discovering where the girl had been taken and arranged to see her. Before allowing his bride to see Demeter, Hades (or Pluto, as he is also known) made her eat some pomegranate seeds, thus binding her to him for the winter months.

material in which, using spontaneous combustion, the sulphur was separated from its slag of impurities. After 1860, the *calcheroni* were replaced by domed Gill furnaces in groups of two, three or four, connected by small channels. This made it possible to use the heat generated from the sulphur dioxide fumes produced by the combustion in the furnaces, as a catalyst in breaking down the sulphur material in the next furnace. Opposite the *calcheroni* is a sort of gallery with arcades and narrow slits, from which the molten sulphur would flow down to the collection point. There it was allowed to solidify in wooden trapezoidal moulds so as to produce 50-60kg/110-130lb blocks. On the far right is the oldest section of the mine, where the shaft-steps used by miners and *carusi* – the young boys employed to carry the ore up to the surface in wooden structures on their backs – can still be seen.

Valguarnera

This small town, associated until only a few years ago with sulphur mining, has a 17C church with an overpowering Baroque front made of limestone.

Return in the direction of Piazza Armerina (18km/11mi S of Valguarnera). The road winds through a beautiful **valley**★ with gently sloping hills, covered, in springtime, with a veil of emerald green.

Piazza Armerina *See PIAZZA ARMERINA.*

Imperial Villa of Casale★★★ *See Villa Imperiale del CASALE.*

Proceed along S 191 towards Caltanissetta to the fork signposted on the left for Barrafranca (21km/13mi W of Piazza Armerina).

Barrafranca

At one time called Convicino (its current name dates from the 16C), Barrafranca simply consists of a collection of ochre-coloured houses clustered on the gentle slopes of a hill. The entrance into the town is along Via Vittorio Emanuele which is flanked on either side by elegant town houses, including Palazzo Satariano and Palazzo Mattina. The **Chiesa Madre** (18C) has a bare brick façade and a bell tower crowned with a small dome covered with polychrome tiles. The **Benedictine Monastery** in Piazza Messina is now virtually in ruins; just beyond it stand a large, eye-catching 18C building which once accommodated small shops **(i Putieddi)** and the **Chiesa della Maria Santissima della Stella**, marked by its tall campanile topped with a maiolica spire.

Return to the town's main street, Corso Garibaldi, which leads into Piazza dell'Itria; taking pride of place here is the 16C church of the same name with its façade and bell tower of brick.

From here it is possible to continue towards Pietraperzia (10km/6mi) or make a detour (14km/9mi) via Mazzarino.

Mazzarino

This medieval hamlet largely developed as a result of the Branciforte family. The main features are collected along the main street Corso Vittorio Emanuele. Alongside the Chiesa Madre sits Palazzo Branciforti (17C) and the contemporary Carmelite church. Just outside the little town, perched on top of a small hill lie the ruins of the **castle** with its solid, impenetrable round keep. No doubt the castle was built on the site of a Norman-Byzantine fortress, was enlarged and reinforced with fortifications during the Norman occupation in the course of the 14C before being converted into a major residence for its aristocratic owners towards the close of the 15C.

Take S 191 to Barrafranca and continue as far as Pietraperzia.

Pietraperzia

Here, too, the dominant colour of the stone is ochre. The ruins of the Norman castle overlook the valley of the River Salso. On entering the town, you see in Piazza Matteotti the 16C Chiesa del Rosario and, opposite, the fine neo-Gothic Palazzo Tortorici. The **Chiesa Madre** (19C) has a square façade crowned with a squat pediment. Inside, hanging above the main altar, is the lovely *Madonna and Child* painted by Filippo Paladini. *For information on admission times, call ☎ 0943 40 16 83.*

Also of interest in passing is the **Palazzo del Governatore** (17C) with its elegant square balcony ornamented with brackets provided by grotesque figures.

From Pietraperzia the road continues to Caltanissetta (approximately 15km/9mi).

Caltanissetta *See CALTANISSETTA.*

From Caltanissetta, return to Enna via S 117bis, a road providing fine views over the countryside (33km/20mi).

Isole Eolie★★★

The blue of the sea off the northeastern coast of Sicily is dotted with a archipelago of seven islands. The sea is clear and warm; the water's cobalt blue transparency gives way to ever greater limpidity the shallower it gets; the rocky shoreline nurtures a rich variety of aquatic flora and fauna: sea anemones, sponges, shellfish, seaweed, crustaceans and molluscs as well as countless species of fish, making it a paradise for bathers, snorkellers, divers and spear-gun fishing enthusiasts alike.

Location

Population: 12 625. Michelin map 565 K-L 25-27 – Messina. The islands in the archipelago vary in character: the two most remote islands, **Filicudi** and **Alicudi, are wild** and untamed; Salina is secluded and isolated; Lipari and Panarea are busy and popular with tourists; and **Vulcano** and **Stromboli** are active volcanoes which never cease to impress visitors with their explosions of fire and volcanic stone. *Lipari: Corso Vittorio Emanuele 202; ☎ 090 98 80 095; Vulcano: Via Levante, (Jul-Sep); ☎ 090 98 52 028.*

Background

The Greek myths ascribe the islands to **Aeolus**, the son of Poseidon, whom Zeus made guardian of the winds; they suggest that it was here that the god ruled over an island encircled by walls of bronze (Lipari?), and that the hero **Odysseus** (Ulysses) sheltered temporarily during his travels and met the monster Polyphemus with his companions, the legendary smiths employed by the god of fire after whom the island of Vulcano is named.

The history of these islands is lost in the mists of time, when tectonic plates moved to create a great chasm in the Tyrrhenian Sea, thereby releasing a mass of molten magma that hardened into a great volcanic outcrop, some 1 000m-3 000m (3 000ft-10 000ft) from the ocean floor, of which only a minute proportion emerges above the water. According to the most recent theories, this happened during the Pleistocene Era, just under a million years ago. The first islands to be formed were Panarea, Filicudi and Alicudi. The youngest are those which continue to be active today: Vulcano and Stromboli. Each successive eruption over the millennia has resulted in a variety of different phenomena: this ranges from the formation of pumice, a material so light that it will float on water, to the great streams of black obsidian, a glassy and friable material with edges so sharp as to be used by ancient peoples to make razor-like cutting tools.

The islands' resident population, which in places is sparse and liable to be cut off from the rest of the world for several months at a time, subsists on fishing, farming (especially vines and harvesting of capers for salting), quarrying pumice (as on Lipari, although this is a dying trade), and most particularly, albeit for a short season, from tourism.

T. Spagnone/Lara Pessina/MICHELIN

Directory

Transport

The Aeolian islands are linked to the mainland by hydrofoil *(aliscafo)* and ferry *(traghetto)*, which incur inversely proportional costs and times. On average, the hydrofoil (foot-passengers only) costs twice as much as the ferry and takes half the time. The closest port on the main island of Sicily, which as might be expected runs the most frequent sailings, is Milazzo; buses run directly from the port to the main towns in Sicily.

Ferries run regularly from **Milazzo** (1hr 30min-4hr) and are operated by Siremar; the same agency also runs a hydrofoil service (40min-2hr 45min). SNAV also operates a daily hydrofoil service from **Messina**, **Reggio Calabria**, Palermo (Jun-Sep), and **Cefalù** (Jun-Sep only; not daily). Ferries (14hr; twice a week) and hydrofoils (4hr, Jun-Sep) also leave from Naples. The former are operated by Siremar and the latter by SNAV. For information and reservations, contact:

Siremar (Gruppo Tirrenia); ☎ 199 123 199 (from Italy) or 081 31 72 999 (from mobile phones and abroad); www.gruppotirrenia.it/siremar/html/home/mainframeset.htm

SNAV, Stazione Marittima, Napoli; ☎ 081 42 85 111, mergelli@tin.it, www.snav.it/

For information on additional services, contact **N.G.I.**, Via dei Mille 26, Milazzo; ☎ 090 92 84 091; www.cormorano.net/ngi/

Sightseeing

SNAV and **Siremar** operate regular services between the islands. Departure times are usually posted up at the port; for further information, contact the operating companies (*see above*).

Taranto Navigazione runs mini-cruises during the day and night, with departures from Milazzo, Capo d'Orlando, Patti and Vulcano. For further information, contact Tar.Nav., Via dei Mille 40, Milazzo; ☎ 090 92 23 617, 0348 30 05 839 (mobile phone); www.minicrociere.com

Boat trips – The most congenial and easiest way to explore the islands by far is by rubber dinghy. However, given the exorbitant cost of hiring one, there is always the option of joining one of the organised excursions by boat from Lipari or Vulcano (from the other islands, the boats are smaller and the services less frequent) which go to Stromboli (even at night, when the "Strombolian explosions" can be watched from the sea). Excursions also leave from Filicudi and Alicudi, Panarea and Salina.

The trips usually take in all the islands, making the most interesting approaches from the sea to include a view of caves, rock formations, bays and beaches; they sometimes include stops for swimming and for brief visits to the main towns. Excursions can last a whole day (departing around 9am and returning between 5pm and 7pm) or half a day (departing early afternoon and returning late in the evening as for the Stromboli evening trip).

The following companies operate services from Lipari: Viking, Vico Himera 3, ☎ 090 98 12 584; Compagnia di Navigazione G La Cava, Via Vittorio Emanuele 124, ☎ 090 98 11 242; Pignatoro Shipping, Via Prof Carnevale 29, ☎ 090 98 11 417 or 0368 67 59 75; Regina dei Mari, Marina Corta, ☎ 090 98 22 237 or 0339 74 86 560; Motoveliero Sigismondo, Via San Vincenzo-Canneto, ☎ 0338 21 10 229.

On land – The best way to explore the islands is to rent a bicycle or moped. Contact the tourist office for further information.

Excursions on Stromboli – Visitors to the volcano are charged a tax of €3 and must be accompanied by a guide. Contact the CAI-AGAI guide office at Porto di Scari and Piazza San Vincenzo, Stromboli; ☎/Fax 090 98 62 11 or 090 98 62 63, 0368 66 49 18 or 0330 96 53 67 (mobile phone). Visitors are advised to ensure that the guide booked is a qualified mountain guide.

Useful Information

Banking facilities – Banks are available on Lipari, Vulcano (in Porto di Levante) and Salina (in Malfa). Visitors should note that the only cashpoint facilities in the Aeolian Islands are on Lipari, in Corso Vittorio Emanuele, and that credit cards are NOT universally accepted.

Post offices – Corso Vittorio Emanuele 207, Lipari; Via Risorgimento 130, Santa Maria di Salina; Via Roma, Stromboli.

G. Bludzin/MICHELIN

Where to Eat

LIPARI

• *Budget*

La Ginestra – *Loc. Pianoconte, 5km/3mi NW of Lipari – ☎ 090 98 22 285 – €23/38.* Situated inland, this traditional restaurant serves typical fish dishes and regional cuisine. Fish and *antipasti* are displayed in the dining room and meals are generally served on the shady, covered terrace.

• Moderate

Filippino – *Piazza Municipio, Lipari – ☎ 090 98 11 002 – filippino@netnet.it – Closed Mon (except Jun-Sep), 16 Nov-15 Dec – – €32/46 + 12% service.* This long-established restaurant is renowned throughout Sicily for its locally caught fish, prepared according to traditional recipes. The restaurant has a relaxed and informal atmospere, friendly, efficient service and a delightful view of Piazza della Rocca.

E Pulera – *Via Isa Conti, Lipari – ☎ 090 98 11 158 – Closed lunchtime and Nov-Mar – Booking recommended – €33/47 + 12% service.* E Pulera has a beautiful garden in which guests can dine in the open air. In July and August, typical Aeolian dishes are accompanied by traditional music and folk dancing.

SALINA

• Moderate

Da Franco – *Via Belvedere 8, Loc. Santa Marina Salina, Salina – ☎ 090 98 43 287 – Closed 1-20 Dec – – €31/43.* This typical, simple restaurant is easy to find in the upper part of the village. Its delightful terrace and veranda with wonderful views of the surrounding countryside is the setting for cuisine that relies heavily on the sea. Definitely worth a visit!

STROMBOLI

• Moderate

Punta Lena – *Via Marina, Loc. Ficogrande, Stromboli – ☎ 090 98 62 04 – Closed Nov-Mar – €35/48.* The Punta Lena is renowned for its high-quality fresh fish and delicious seafood specialities served under an arbour with magnificent sea views.

VULCANO

• Budget

Don Piricuddu – *Via Lentia 33, Vulcano – ☎ 090 98 52 424 – www.donpiricuddu.it – Closed Tue, 26 Oct-Easter – Booking recommended – €18/30.* This restaurant has a friendly atmosphere and efficient service. Fresh fish dishes are served either in the dining room or on a long terrace overlooking one of the main roads in the village.

Il Diavolo dei Polli – *Loc. Cardo, Vulcano – ☎ 090 98 53 034 – Closed in Nov – Booking recommended – €19/25.* Open throughout the year, this family-run establishment has a spacious dining room adorned with decorative plates and maritime paintings. The restaurant serves specialities from the Aeolian interior, which are beautifully presented and served with great attention to detail.

Where to Stay

In addition to traditional hotels, more moderately priced accommodation is available in **rented rooms and flats** (contact the tourist office for a detailed list).

ALICUDI E FILICUDI

• Moderate

Hotel Ericusa – *Via Regina Elena, Alicudi – ☎ 090 98 89 902 – Fax 090 98 89 671 – www.alicudihotel.it – Closed Oct-May – 20 rooms. €55/110.* The only restaurant and accommodation option on the island, this small, simple hotel is situated right on the beach. Ideal for visitors in search of sun, sea and solitude, the rooms at the Ericusa each have their own private entrance. The restaurant serves freshly caught fish, accompanied by simple salads or local vegetables.

Hotel La Canna – *Contrada Rosa, Filicudi – ☎ 090 98 89 956 – Fax 090 98 89 966 – vianast@tin.it – Closed in Nov – – 8 double rooms. €120 – €7.50.* This typical hotel, built in keeping with its surrounding environment, enjoys an excellent location overlooking the port and the sea. The two rooms with small terraces offer the perfect romantic hideaway for newly-weds. Facilities here include an attractive pool and sun terrace.

LIPARI

• Budget

Baia Unci Campeggio – *Via Marina Garibaldi, Loc. Canneto, Lipari – ☎ 090 98 11 909 – Fax 090 98 11 715 – baiaunci@tin.it – Closed mid-Oct to mid-Mar – €11.* For visitors who enjoy the outdoors, this campsite is ideally placed by the sea, in one of Lipari's delightful bays. Fully equipped with modern facilities, the campsite also has a beach where deckchairs, parasols and boats are available for rent.

• Moderate

Hotel Poseidon – *Via Ausonia 7, Lipari – ☎ 090 98 12 876 – Fax 090 98 80 252 – info@hotelposeidonlipari.com – Closed Nov-Feb – – 18 rooms. €73/124.* This centrally located hotel is built in typical Mediterranean style with vivid blue and white tones. The fully equipped rooms are spotlessly clean, with modern, practical furnishings. Polite, attentive service and a pleasant sun terrace.

Hotel Oriente – *Via Marconi 35, Lipari – ☎ 090 98 11 493 – Fax 090 98 80 198 – hoteloriente@netnet.it – Closed Nov-Easter – – 32 rooms. €77/129.* This small, family-run hotel in the town centre has simple rooms surrounded by a pleasant garden. The owner's interest in ethnography is reflected in his large collection of traditional Aeolian artefacts.

• Expensive

Villa Augustus – *Via Ausonia 16, Lipari – ☎ 090 98 11 232 – Fax 090 98 12 233 – villaaugustus@tin.it – Closed Nov-Feb – – 34 rooms. €90/134 €11.* Hidden among the alleyways of the historical centre, this hotel is situated in an old patrician villa, with a pleasant reception area, spacious lounge and well-appointed rooms. Breakfast is served on an attractive patio decorated with plants and flowers.

SALINA

• Budget

Tre Pini Campeggio – *Via Rotabile 1, Loc. Leni, Salina – ☎ 090 98 09 155 – Fax 090 98 09 052 – info@tre-pini.com – Closed Nov-Mar €11.* This campsite is located on the southern side of the island, among olive groves which provide welcome shade for tents and caravans. The site also has bungalows for rent.

• ***Expensive***

Hotel Santa Isabel – *Via Scalo 12, Malfa, Salina – 4.5km/3mi NE of Pollara beach – ☎ 090 98 44 018 – Fax 090 98 44 362 – Closed Nov-Mar – 10 rooms. €72/144 ☕ – Restaurant. €21/30.* The Santa Isabel enjoys a delightful panoramic location, with an attractive terrace overlooking the beach and the inviting crystal-clear waters of the Mediterranean. The rooms are spacious, each with its own small lounge area and mezzanine. The restaurant serves a varied choice of fish dishes and local cuisine.

STROMBOLI

• ***Expensive***

Locanda del Barbablù – *Via Vittorio Emanuele 17/19, Stromboli – ☎ 090 98 61 18 – Fax 090 98 63 23 – info@barbablu.it – Closed at lunchtime (Nov-Feb) – 6 rooms. €117/180 ☕ – Restaurant. €30/50.* This inn has six pleasant rooms, decorated in a successful fusion of modern, *arte povera* and period styles. The daily menu offers a wide selection of typical dishes.

VULCANO

• ***Budget***

Campeggio Togo Togo – *Via Porto Levante, Vulcano – ☎ 090 98 52 303 – Fax 090 98 52 128 – info@campingtogotogo.it – Closed Oct-Mar – €16.* The perfect compromise for visitors who are on a tight budget but don't want to miss out on the splendours of Vulcano. The bungalows, tents and pitches available for rent here enjoy a delightful setting either among trees or by the sea, lined by black sandy beaches.

• ***Moderate***

Hotel Conti – *Loc. Porto Ponente, Vulcano – ☎ 090 98 52 012 – Fax 090 98 80 150 – conti@netnet.it – Closed 21 Oct-Apr – 67 rooms. €92/130 ☕* – This Mediterranean-style hotel is situated near the thermal baths. Housed in a number of different buildings, the rooms are simply furnished and all have their own private entrance. A stone's throw from the famous black sandy beaches.

• ***Expensive***

Hotel Orsa Maggiore – *Via Porto Ponente, Vulcano – ☎ 090 98 52 018 – Fax 090 98 52 415 – orsa-maggiore@usa.net – Closed Nov-Mar – – 25 rooms. €65/150 ☕.* A delightful garden and refreshing swimming pool are two of the highlights of this recently renovated white hotel. Situated near the port, the hotel has comfortable communal areas and simple, but well-maintained rooms. The hotel restaurant specialises in fish dishes.

Shopping

The famous Malvasia delle Lipari is a strong, sweet, golden wine made from grapes that have been left to wither on the vine before being picked. Its smooth, aromatic flavour makes it an excellent dessert wine. There are various types of Malvasia available. The DOC-endorsed variety, produced only on the islands, must bear the words "Malvasia delle Lipari" in full on the label.

Recreation

Diving – As long as the sea continues to provide endless hours of fascination, the main sport has to be sub-aqua diving. For beginners and those without equipment of their own, contact the Diving Center La Gorgonia (☎ 090 98 12 060; mobile 0360 86 34 55) on Lipari.

Mud therapy on Vulcano – This special mud treatment is recommended for people with rheumatic ailments and dermatological conditions (greasy skin, acne, psoriasis). It is NOT recommended for expectant mothers or people suffering from tumour-related diseases or with fevers, heart conditions, osteoporosis, gastro-intestinal upsets, diabetes and hyperthyroidism. Recommendations: short immersions (never more than 20min at a time), in the coolest hours of the day, followed by a hot shower. Do not apply to the eyes. In the event of mud getting into the eyes, rinse liberally with fresh water. For any ailments resulting from mud baths, consult a doctor.

Festivals

Festa di San Bartolomeo – The festival of St Bartholomew is held on Lipari from 21-24 August, finishing at Marina Corta with a magnificent display of fireworks set off from the sea.

Worth a Visit

LIPARI*

This is the largest and most densely populated of the Aeolian Islands. Its physical relief, with its areas of gentle lowland, has prompted a number of towns to spring up both along the coast and inland.

Inhabited since Antiquity, when it was famous for its obsidian, the island has enjoyed several periods of great prosperity, interrupted by frequent incursions and attacks: among the most famous is the one launched by the Turk **Kaireddin Barbarossa** who, in 1544, landed at **Porto delle Genti** (a small hamlet near Lipari) before razing the town, killing or deporting the population as slaves to Africa.

The main moorings on the island are in the town of Lipari, which is served by two ports: Marina Corta is used by the hydrofoils and by smaller craft, whereas the ferries moor at Marina Lunga.

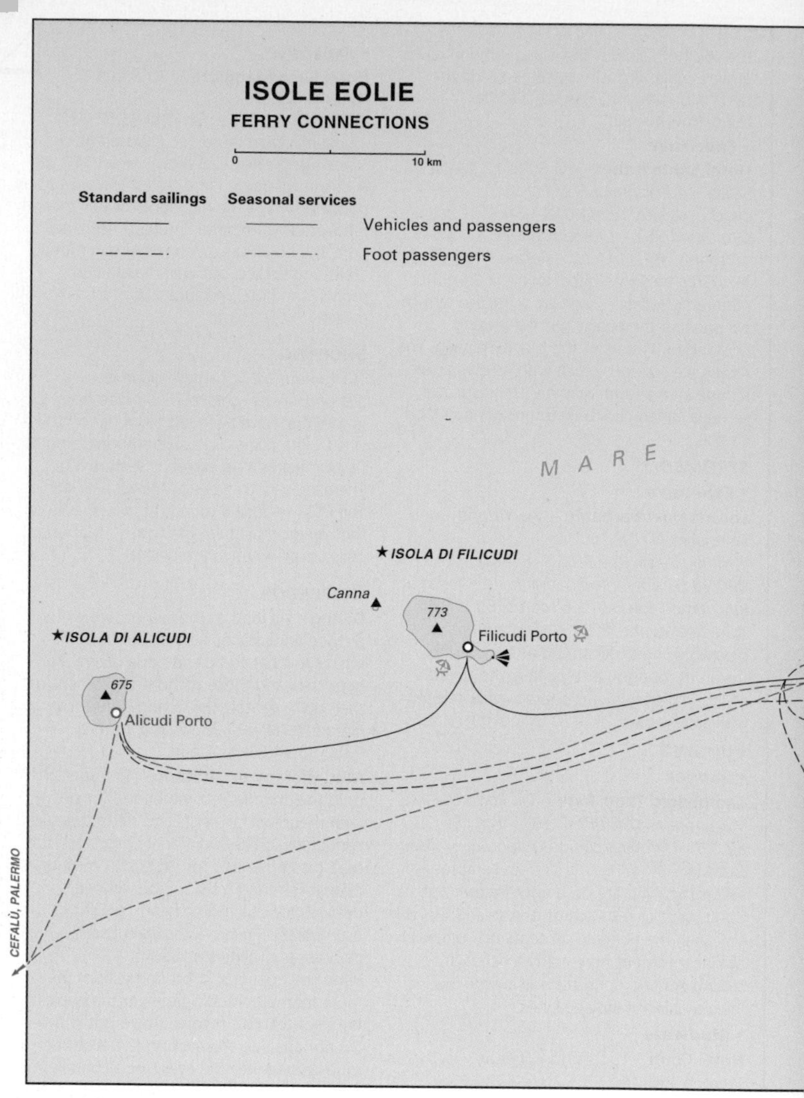

From here it is easy to get to the island's other towns: Canneto, Acquacalda, Quattropiani and Pianoconte. The best way to explore the island is by private vehicle or with a hired moped.

Città di Lipari★

Lipari is also the name of the main town on the island. Approaching it by sea, the top of the town may be glimpsed from a distance, with its fortified citadel and, behind, the former Franciscan monastery which now accommodates the town hall (visible when moored at Marina Lunga). Far below at its feet sit two bays. **Marina Corta** is watched over by a little church dedicated to the souls in Purgatory – **'Anime del Purgatorio'** (once isolated on a rock, but now linked to the mainland), and by the 17C **Chiesa di San Giuseppe** (which stands on the south side of the bay); **Marina Lunga** is the larger of the two inlets. The lower part of town or *città bassa*, with its very own Corso Vittorio Emanuele lined with small shops and restaurants, provides the perfect context for the traditional *passeggiata* or early evening stroll.

Taking a Break

Pasticceria Subba – Corso Vittorio Emanuele 92, Lipari; ☎ 090 98 11352. Since 1930, this *pasticceria* has been making fabulous cakes and pastries, such as *cannoli* (filled with ricotta cheese), *cassate* (brimming with candied fruit), *pasta paradiso* (almond cake with fine strips of citron peel), *nacatuli* (puff pastry made with Malvasia wine filled with almond paste and mandarin juice), as well as delicious ice cream.

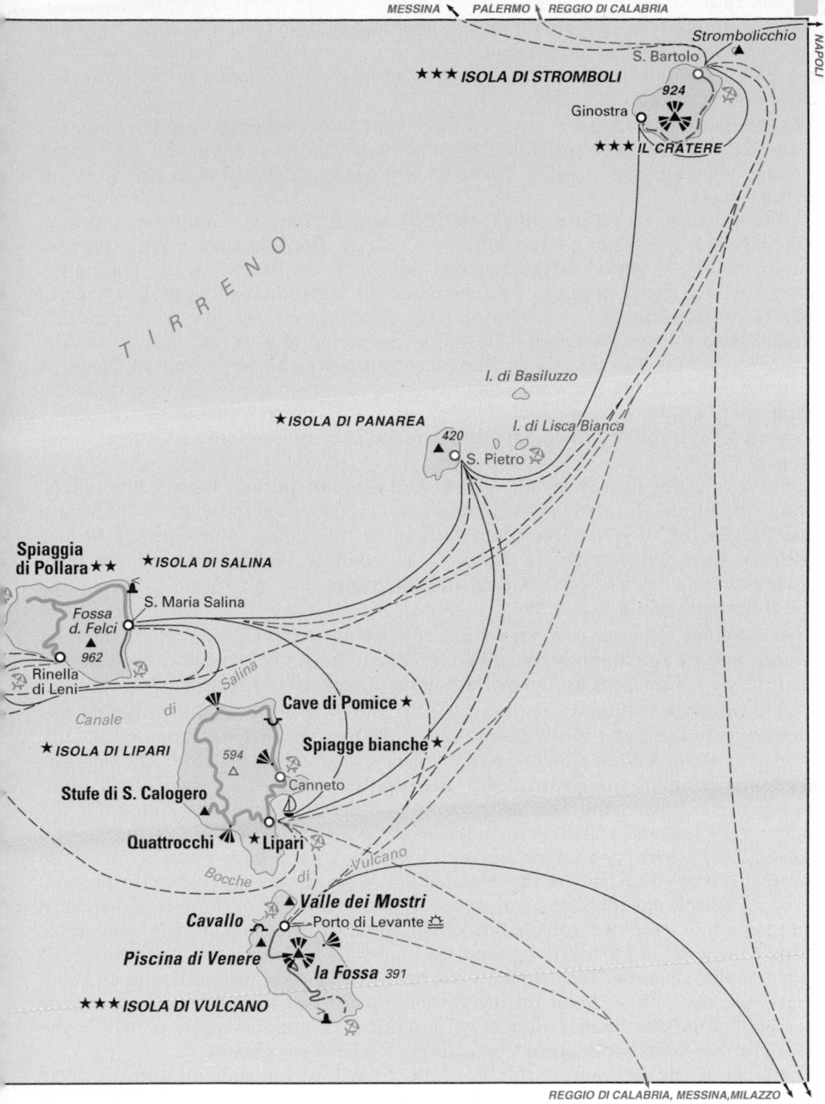

Castle★ – *Head up to the castle from Piazza Mazzini.* The citadel was constructed on a Greek acropolis before being surrounded by walls (13C); it was reinforced by Emperor Charles V (16C) after the town was sacked by Barbarossa *(see Insights and Images).*

It is best approached from Piazza Mazzini, by the most ancient route: beyond the Spanish fortifications and the Greek tower (4C BC) with its great medieval portcullis (12C-13C) lies the heart of the citadel. On the right is a church, Santa Caterina, with beyond it, an **archaeological area** which has been excavated to reveal superimposed layers of dwellings (huts), buildings and roads from various periods spanning the Bronze Age (Capo Graziano culture) through to Hellenistic and Ancient Roman times. Behind sits the **Chiesetta dell'Addolorata** and the 18C **Chiesa dell'Immacolata**. To the left of these, in the centre, stands the cathedral dedicated to the patron saint of the Aeolian Islands, **San Bartolomeo**: medieval in plan, it was rebuilt under Spanish rule; the façade is 19C. The adjacent cloisters are Norman. The flight of steps opposite the cathedral was inserted at the beginning of this century; in order to build it, some of the ancient walls had to be demolished.

Museo Archeologico Eoliano★★ – *Via del Castello. (♿) Open 9am-1.30pm and 3-7pm. €4. ☎ 090 98 80 174; www.regione.sicilia.it*

The collections are housed in several different buildings and are displayed in sections relating the history of the islands from prehistoric to Classical times. There are also special displays devoted to marine archaeology and vulcanology. Most of the artefacts have been recovered from excavations since 1949.

At the entrance to each room are two different types of information panel: the more detailed one is intended for use by those wishing to complete a thorough tour of the museum; the other (red) one provides the basic facts pertaining to the successive development of cultures.

The **prehistory of Lipari** is outlined in a room dedicated entirely to obsidian, the glass-like volcanic stone which has been so prized for its strength and razor-sharp cutting edge; although fragile, it was widely used and exported in Antiquity for making tools.

The Capo Graziano culture (1800-1400 BC), which takes its name from a site on Filicudi, and the ensuing Capo Milazzese culture from Panarea mark a particularly prosperous period for the islands *(Rooms V and VI)* when the population increased and goods began to be exchanged on a commercial basis. Evidence of this is provided by the presence of large Mycenean vases that were probably traded here for raw materials. The following period (13C-9C BC), known as the Ausonian period after the people who (according to the ancient historian Diodorus Siculus) arrived from the Italian mainland, is classified according to various criteria: there are many one-handled bowls with horn-shaped appendages (probably to ward off evil spirits) which, later on, evolved into stylised forms of animal heads *(Rooms VII-IX)*.

Room X onwards deals with the **Greek and Roman period**. Having been abandoned for a time, the acropolis at Lipari was then colonised by people from Knidos and Rhodes (6C BC). Note the interesting lid of the *bothros* (votive pit) of Aeolus, with its stone lion-cum-handle *(Room X)*. The cult of Aeolus seems to have been shared by both established residents and colonisers. The other glass cases contain the "offerings" found in the pit.

The buildings opposite contain rooms devoted to the prehistory of the smaller islands and to **vulcanology** *(building on the left)*; here the geological evolution of the islands is explained by means of boards, diagrams and scale models.

The chronological displays continue in the building north of the cathedral *(the numbering of the rooms has been inverted in the first three rooms: Room XVIII leads through to Room XVII and then Room XVI before continuing with Room XIX etc)*. The **reconstruction of the Bronze Age necropolis★** (12C BC) is particularly interesting: this compares burial after cremation (12C BC) – when urns containing the ashes were covered with bowls and placed inside small pits dug in the ground *(Room XVII)* – with inhumation burials (14C BC) – when large *pithoi* or jars (containing the curled-up body of the dead person) were simply interred in the ground. Trading vessels encountering storms at sea often came in to shore to find shelter; on their route were two notable black spots renowned as being highly dangerous: Capo Graziano (on Filicudi) and the area known as Le Formiche (the Ants, which consists of treacherous rocks hidden just below the surface just off Panarea). From these two places have been retrieved the shipwrecked cargo of some 20 trading vessels comprising large numbers of amphorae of various types, of which the museum has a vast **collection★** *(see Marine Archaeology section)*.

The grave goods dating from the 6C-4C BC from Lipari include an unusual array of rather coarsely modelled clay figurines *(Room XXI)*, of particular interest in that they re-enact different domestic tasks: a mother washes a child, a woman is intent on making soup in a bowl, while another grinds grain with a mortar, on the edge of which perches a cat. Among the fine examples of **red-figure ware★**, made in Sicily or mainland Italy, there is one depicting a highly unusual scene (360 BC): a naked acrobat balances in a handstand before Dionysus and two comic actors with exaggerated features. Behind the group, in two panels, are painted the portraits of two additional actors. The same case contains three vases by the **"painter of Adrastus"** (king of Argos): the third one bears a very dramatic scene in which, under the portico of the palace of Argos, Tydeus confronts Polynices, the son of Oedipus, who was exiled from Thebes.

The cult of Dionysus, god not only of wine but also of the theatre and celestial bliss (for those who were initiated into his mysteries), explains the inclusion among the grave goods recovered from votive pits of **statuettes of actors** and **theatrical masks**; the museum has an extremely rich, varied and early **collection★★** of such objects *(Room XXIII)* which is quite unique.

The last section of the museum is essentially devoted to Lipari's history in the Hellenistic and Roman periods (from which there is a considerable quantity of moulded oil lamps stamped with different kinds of decoration). It also displays various artefacts (particularly ceramics) relating to the Norman, Spanish, Renaissance and Baroque periods.

Parco Archeologico – *On the far side of the citadel on the right.* In the archaeological gardens are aligned numerous ancient sarcophagi. From the terrace there is a lovely **view★** over the little Church of the Lost Souls, jutting out into the sea opposite Marina Corta, and Vulcano on the horizon.

Tour of the island

Boat trips★★ leaving from Marina Corta offer visitors the chance to admire the indented coastline of the southwestern corner of the island.

The island can also be explored by **car**, setting out from Lipari town in the direction of Canneto, to the north (27km/17mi round trip).

Canneto – This small town set back from the great sweep of coast is a favourite spot from where to set out for the **white beaches★**, visible from Canneto, that are accessible by a footpath. The brilliance of the white sand, and, in particular, of the clear sea is due to the high content of pumice dust *(see below)*. From the harbour of Canneto, it is possible to visit the pumice quarries near Porticello. *To get to the white beaches and quarries by boat, contact the fishermen at the harbour. Boat trip there and back: €5 per person; the return time should be arranged directly with the fisherman. The trip can also be made by bus from Canneto and Marina Piccola; ask to be dropped by the only factory still in operation (5min by foot).*

Cave di Pomice a Porticello★ – This lovely bay is lined by a mass of pumice quarries and workshops; all, save the last and most northern, are now abandoned. Waste resulting from the extraction and working of the stone accumulates naturally along the shore in mounds of very fine white sand, which hardens with time. On the beach lie small fragments of black obsidian. The **scene★★** is strangely compelling: the sea is of the palest tinges of blue, as clear as glass (revealing the pumice-lined seabed), old wooden jetties once used for loading pumice onto boats now stand still and empty. One of the bathers' favourite pastimes is to climb the white mounds and cover themselves with pumice dust to smooth their skin. The keenest can then emulate the children in the scene from *Chaos* (the film directed by the Taviani brothers), who hurled themselves down the mounds, roly-poly fashion, straight into the sea (however, the sea is now about a metre away).

At sunset, the **view★** from the road is dramatic as the white pumice pyramids in **Campo Bianco** catch the last sunlight of the day: for a split second, the scene might evoke some alpine context among tall snow-covered slopes. A little further on is the **Fossa delle Rocche Rosse** where the island's most impressive flow of obsidian can be admired.

Beyond **Acquacalda** is Puntazze, from where a wonderful **view★★** opens out over five of the islands: from left to right, Alicudi, Filicudi, Salina, Panarea and Stromboli.

Stufe di San Calogero – *Turn right immediately after Pianoconte.* The waters of these hot springs have been famous for their therapeutic properties since Antiquity. Among the ancient ruins (alongside a modern spa which, alas, is closed) is a **domed chamber**. Since recent studies have revealed it to be from the Mycenean period, it may be considered the oldest thermal complex, and indeed the only Ancient Greek building still in use today, even if it only provides people with "DIY" therapy requiring them to splash themselves with water that springs from the ground at a temperature of 60°C.

Pumice

White and sponge-like, light enough to float on water, pumice stone is used in pharmaceutical processes, cosmetics (it has delicately abrasive properties), buildings (to make earthquake-proof breeze-blocks) and most recently for stone-washed jeans and denim. The pumice from Lipari is of particularly high quality.

Quattrocchi – This viewpoint offers the most spectacular **panoramas★★★** in the archipelago, with Punta di Jacopo and then Punta del Perciato in the foreground. Behind sit treacherous crags of rock known locally as *faraglioni*, while the profile of Vulcano interrupts the skyline.

As Lipari looms back into the picture, a fine **view★** opens out onto the town.

VULCANO★★★

It was on this island, with a surface area of 21km/8sq mi, that Ancient Greek mythology placed the forge of Hephaestus, the god of fire who worked as a blacksmith with the assistance of the Cyclops. But it was the Roman name of the god (Vulcan) that became synonymous with the island and, indeed, with vulcanology: the scientific study of volcanoes.

The very existence of the island results from the fusion of four volcanoes: the largest and most dominant peak, **Vulcano della Fossa**, is a 391m/1 282ft mountain of reddish rock; it is also the most active. Beside it sits the diminutive Vulcanello (123m/403ft) which erupted on the north side in 183 BC, to form a round peninsula. The peculiar way in which these volcanoes be have, spewing acid lava and setting off a series of explosions until the plug is catapulted skywards, thereby releasing large incandescent masses of molten rock, has been classified as **Vulcanian** *(see Insights and Images: Volcanoes in Sicily)*.

Although the last eruption occurred in 1890, Vulcano has never ceased to betray signs of its activity; even today, such phenomena as fumaroles, jets of steam above and below sea level, and sulphurous mud highly prized for its therapeutic properties, continue to be very much in evidence. The shoreline, so jagged in places as to resemble tentacles plunging into the sea, the range in colour of the rock from red to yellow ochre, and the desolate, lonely scenery endow the island with a strangely unnerving yet outstanding beauty.

> **Taking a Break**
> **Bar Ritrovo Remigio –** Via Vulcano 1, Porto Levante, Vulcano, ☎ 090 98 52 085. This café offers an enticing selection of typical specialities such as cannoli, cassate and granite, as well as delicious profiteroles.

Porto di Levante e Porto di Ponente

The main town of the island nestles midway between these two ports, and borrows both their names. A small place full of little shops, it is furnished with contemporary sculptures made of lava (*Hephaestus and Pandora's box* at the harbour, *Aeolus at Rest* in the main square).

Ascent to the crater★★★

Allow 2hr. From end of main road leading out of Levante. The way to the crater is to be found at the far end of the road from Porto di Levante. As the track gently climbs up the mountainside in a series of broad zig-zags, it provides fabulous **views★★★** of the archipelago: in the foreground is the Vulcanello peninsula, Lipari lies opposite, on the left is Salina – recognisable by its two humps – while in the distance sits Filicudi (on a clear day Alicudi may also be visible); off to the right, surrounded by its flock of islets, sits Panarea, with Stromboli some way beyond. About halfway up to the top is an area of compacted red earth, cut with deep regular furrows, suggestive of some Martian landscape. The higher the path climbs, the stronger the smell of sulphur, accompanied by the occasional cloud of steam. At the top, the **sight★★★** is unforgettable: the Cratere della Fossa's huge bowl stretches out below, its southern rim blurred by clouds of boiling sulphurous vapours released from cracks in the crust with a whistle that seems to emanate from deep within the earth; the rock is stained yellow ochre and red by the fumes that condense into the most delicate crystals while still hot. These are the fumaroles.

A **tour of the crater★★★** *(about 30min)* permits an exploration of the southern part of the island and, from the highest point, enjoyment of one of the most stunning **views★★★** of the archipelago.

Beaches★

There are two beaches near the main town: black beaches **(spiagge nere)** – so called because of the dark lava sand – line the lovely bay of Porto di Ponente, although these tend to become very crowded; the other **(spiaggia delle Fumarole)** is unusual in that its waters, heated by bubbles of sulphurous steam, can reach very high temperatures *(beware of being scalded).*

On the opposite side of the island is the remote, and therefore less frequented, **spiaggia del Gelso** (Mulberry Beach) which is accessible by sea, by bus from Porto del Levante *(check timetables as services are highly restricted)*, or by car along the road from Porto Levante to Vulcano Piano which forks for Gelso and Capo Grillo.

Fumarole on Vulcano

M. Andreini/Lara Pessina/MICHELIN

Grotta del Cavallo e la piscina di Venere

Departures by boat from the black beaches. The boat skirts around Vulcanello, with its so-called Valley of Monsters *(see below)*, before circumnavigating the most jagged part of the coast on the way to this glorious grotto named after the sea horses that once lived here. On the left is Venus' Pool, a shallow pool of the clearest water, an idyllic place for an unforgettable swim. *(Those who wish to stay for a few hours can go with one of the early boat trips, which run fairly regularly throughout the day, and return on one of the later ones; check with the fisherman.)*

I fanghi★

Mud is one of Vulcano's specialities. Leaving the port on the right, behind a rock of incredible colours ranging through every shade of yellow to red, there is a natural pool containing sulphurous mud renowned for its therapeutic properties.

La Valle dei Mostri

On Vulcanello. A trip at dawn or sunset is particularly recommended when the evocative shapes of the rocks, caught by the sun's rays, are at their most impressive. The Valley of Monsters consists of a downward slope of black sand dotted here and there with blocks of lava that have cooled into weird forms and intriguing profiles suggestive of prehistoric animals, monsters and wild beasts (including a bear reared up on its hind legs, and a crouching lion).

Capo Grillo

Approx 10km/6mi from Porto Levante. The local road to Vulcano Piano and beyond to the cape, offers a variety of prospects of Lipari and the great crater. From the promontory, there is a splendid **view★** of the archipelago.

STROMBOLI★★★

The island-volcano possesses a sombre, disquieting beauty all of its own: its coastline of steep crags emerging from the sea are forbidding. The almost total lack of roads, the untamed scenery and, more particularly, the volcano which methodically makes its presence felt with outbursts of fire and brimstone, have both a strange and awesome power of attraction.

In Rossellini's film *Stromboli, terra di Dio* (Stromboli, Land of God – 1950), which highlighted the difficulties of living in such a place, the volcano plays the main role while the island is portrayed as the most fascinating and atmospheric of all the Aeolian isles.

There are two villages on the island: on the northeastern slopes, surrounded by a green mantle that stretches to the north as far as San Bartolo, stand the small square white houses of **San Vincenzo** (where the landing stage is located); on the southwestern side is **Ginostra**, which consists of a huddle of about 30 houses clinging to the rock, in desperate isolation (there are no roads, just a mule-track which winds along the side of the hill), but accessible by sea (although not all year around) by means of the smallest port in the world. The arid, precipitous northern flank which separates the two villages is the most impressive, scarred as it is by the *Sciara del Fuoco* – down which the burning lava flows each time the volcano decides to erupt. On 30 December 2002, new vents opened in the volcano as a result of intense volcanic activity and a huge section of the mountain fell away from the *Sciara del Fuoco* flank into the sea, causing a tidal wave which engulfed boats and houses, fortunately without any loss of life.

Opposite San Vincenzo is the tiny islet of **Strombolicchio**, a single spur of rock topped by a lighthouse, bestowed by nature with a strange profile in which a horse's head may be perceived.

The crater★★★

The hike up to the crater of Stromboli makes for a unique and fascinating experience, as it provides the opportunity to wonder at the phenomenal workings of Mother Nature. The route itself is beautiful, opening up unforgettable

The ascent to the crater

To watch the eruptions at night is particularly exciting: we therefore recommend hiking up the mountain in the late afternoon and returning in the evening (don't forget to take a torch) or the following morning. Allow three hours for the climb up and two hours for the descent; it is not particularly taxing, but is not recommended for those who suffer from heart problems, asthma or vertigo and should not be undertaken by the faint-hearted, especially in rare cases of bad weather. **Qualified guides** are available on Stromboli; they offer guided walks of the island and afternoon or evening excursions to the crater.

For the ascent, the following hiking equipment is recommended: walking boots (or sturdy trainers), an electric torch, wind cheater, water (according to the weather), a pair of long trousers, a spare T-shirt and, if opting to stay the night, a good sleeping-bag and a jumper to wear at the top where the temperature can drop quite dramatically.

This excursion can be completed all year round. The best time is late spring when the weather is mild and temperatures are not too high; however, a night excursion during the summer months is also highly recommended.

views★★ in all directions, before emerging at the top of one of the very few active volcanoes in the world. The crater comprises five vents. A certain feeling of restlessness pervades the place. This atmosphere is charged and heightened by what is going on some few hundred metres away, as with each successive explosion, incandescent stones are thrust skywards: a spectacle which more than compensates for the steep and somewhat arduous climb.

Ascent – *5hr round trip.* From the ferry jetty at San Vincenzo, head for the centre of the village and follow the tarred road to San Bartolo. Before long, the typical white houses dwindle to none and a mule-track begins *(follow the signs)*, at first paved with slabs of lava and then, after a few bends, degenerating into a well-worn footpath. After 20min, it reaches an observation point called Punta Labronzo (refreshments available; good view of the craters); beyond this point, the real climb begins. From here, the path heads straight for the summit, picking its way through the lush vegetation; ascending at a moderate incline, swinging first right then left, to its end at a ledge *(be careful)*, which provides a magnificent **view★★** of the Sciara del Fuoco – the great black slope down which chunks of lava make their way from the crater to the sea. The footpath is reduced to a steep track cut deeply into the side of the mountain. This veritable trench, excavated by water erosion, leads to a reddish lava section where care should be taken in the awkward scramble upwards. After the next easy bit, a fine view opens out to the left, taking in the town and Strombolicchio, now almost 700m/2 300ft below. At this point, the path climbs up onto a broad, steep and sandy ridge to the summit. Level with the craters, safely tucked away behind low semicircular walls, are the first viewing points from where the eruptions may be observed at leisure. At this altitude, the craters appear between intermittent clouds of vapour; a final stretch of ridge leads to the highest point and the observation point closest to the crater vents. On a day blessed with a favourable light wind, the view from here can be truly exceptional, providing an unforgettable **experience★★★**: one after another, the startling explosions shoot matter high into the air, tingeing the night's blackness with red.

Evening boat trip★★★

The easiest way of encapsulating an overall picture of this island and all its different aspects is, possibly, by means of a nocturnal excursion. Under normal conditions the rocky Sciara del Fuoco *(see above)* makes for an impressive sight; at night the impact is exaggerated a hundredfold as the volcanic eruptions, with incredible regularity, thrust fountains of luminous stones up into the black night sky in nature's most magnificent firework display (in daylight, the emissions merely look grey).

SALINA★

Recognisable from its distinctive two-humped profile (hence Didyme, its name in Antiquity, meaning twins), this remote and lonely island offers visitors the perfect place for a quiet holiday at one with nature. At one time it comprised six volcanoes, since when four have disappeared. It derives its name from the salt works (a small lake) – now abandoned – at Lingua, a small town situated on the south coast. Today, the island is renowned for two specialities: capers which are gathered locally, and the famous wine Malvasia delle Lipari, made from the island's grapes.

There are two landing stages: **Santa Maria Salina** and the smaller **Rinella di Leni** (where there is also a campsite which gets extremely crowded during the second and third week of August).

Possible trips inland

By car or moped (available from small car-hire firms on the island). Ask the local inhabitants for information. There is also a local bus service: timetables are displayed at the port of Santa Maria Salina.

A panoramic road offering many **views★** of the jagged coastline links the harbour with the island's other hamlets. From the main town, **Santa Maria Salina**, the road heads northwards, past Capo Faro, on its way to **Malfa**. The coast road climbs above Punta del Perciato, a beautiful natural arc visible only from the sea or from the beach a little further on at **Pollara**, which is considered to be one of the most attractive and atmospheric stretches of coast on the island. Before going down to the beach, take a peep through the vegetation for a glimpse of the house *(private)* where parts of the film *Il Postino* (The Postman) were made: it was here that the meetings between Neruda (Philippe Noiret) and the postman (Massimo Troisi) took place.

Spiaggia di Pollara★★

There are two paths down to this beautiful bay: one leads to a small anchorage enclosed by its own miniature shoreline of rocks; the other provides access to a broad beach overshadowed by a striking white semicircular cliff wall, a desolate remnant of a crater.

M. Magni/MICHELIN

The cliffs at Pollara

On the way back to Malfa, the road forks inland to **Valdichiesa**, where a popular pilgrimage site – the sanctuary dedicated to the Madonna del Terzito – is located, and **Rinella di Leni**.

Fossa delle Felci★

Nestling inside the dormant crater of the taller of Salina's two mountains is a beautiful fern wood (known as Fossa delle Felci). This protected nature reserve is accessible on foot *(about 2hr)* by a path from the Santuario della Madonna del Terzito in Valdichiesa. A second track runs from Santa Maria Salina.

PANAREA★

The smallest Aeolian Island rises to its highest point with **Punta del Corvo** (420m/1 378ft high), the western flank of which plunges almost vertically down into the sea. The gentler slopes on the eastern side accommodate Panarea's small resident community before terminating in a tall black lava coastline, skirted by small pebbled beaches. In the southeast, around **Punta Milazzese**, lie the remains of a prehistoric village set high above the bay of Cala Junco.

All around the island are scattered a collection of small islets and rocks, including the dreaded Formiche which, lying hidden just below the surface, have been the cause of so many shipwrecks since Antiquity.

FILICUDI★

Steep slopes and a rocky coastline, for the most part of basalt, determine the nature of this small island, which consists of a group of craters: the highest being the **Fossa delle Felci** (773m/2 535ft). An estimated population of 250 souls reside, in the main, in three hamlets.

From the island's landing stage at **Filicudi Porto**, it is simple to reach the **prehistoric village** situated on the promontory of **Capo Graziano** *(about 40min there and back)*; this contains the remains of about 25 roughly oval huts. The settlement dates from the Bronze Age and was transferred from its original site closer to the shore, so that it could be better defended against potential attack *(see also the Archaeological Museum at Lipari, where the finds from this site are displayed)*. From here, there is a beautiful **view★** of the bay, the summit of Fossa delle Felci and Alicudi (in the distance on the left).

If approaching by sea, a stop to visit the huge cave called **Grotta del Bue Marino** is a must. The tall volcanic chimney-stack formation which lies not so far offshore is known as **la Canna** (stick or cane) on account of its shape.

ALICUDI★

Alicudi is the most isolated of the Aeolian Islands: it consists of a round cone covered with heather (hence its ancient name, Ericusa), inhabited by no more than 140 people; to all intents and purposes, it has remained unchanged since the dawn of time. A single village groups together the handful of pastel-coloured houses scattered at the foot of the mountain; this rises up to the **Filo d'Arpa** (literally, Harp String) which provides a magnificent view *(the footpath snakes its way from Chiesa di San Bartolo up through the cultivated terraces. About 1hr 45min to the top and back, at a brisk pace)*.

Erice★★★

Erice occupies a memorable site★★★ at a height of 751m/2 463ft, perched on the mountain of the same name, covering a triangular plateau with a glorious view over the sea. Enclosed within defensible bastions and walls, the town is a veritable labyrinth of little cobbled streets and passages wide enough to accommodate only one person at a time.

Erice, like Janus, is two faced: there is the bright, sunny face that smiles during the long, hot summer days, when light floods its tiny streets and distant views extend over the valley and far out to sea; there is also the mask of winter when, shrouded in mist, the town seems to hark back to its mythical origins, leaving the visitor with a feeling of unease and the impression of a place removed from time and reality. Its enveloping medieval atmosphere, cool mountain air, beautiful pine woods and pervading silence, combined with its rich local craft traditions, make Erice a highly popular destination for tourists.

Directory

Transport

A.S.T. **buses** (☎ 0923 23 222) run between Trapani (Piazza Malta) and Erice. Journey time is approx 30-60min.

Where to Eat

• *For all budgets*

Belvedere San Nicola – *Contrada San Nicola, Erice – ☎ 0923 86 01 24 – www.pippocatalano.it – €20/32. 10 rooms. €50/72* ☕. This restaurant, situated close to the old town walls, enjoys beautiful views of Trapani and the sea from its large terrace. For guests wishing to stay overnight, the restaurant also offers 10 comfortable rooms.

Monte San Giuliano – *Vicolo San Rocco 7, Erice – ☎ 0923 86 95 95 – ristorante@montesangiuliano.it – Closed Mon, 7-25 Jan and 5-23 Nov – Booking recommended – €23/33.* This fine restaurant in the heart of Erice specialises in local cuisine. Meals are served either in pleasant, rustic dining rooms or under an arbour in a cool inner courtyard.

Where to Stay

The only options for budget accommodation in Erice are the youth hostel *(see below)* and the hostels run by religious orders (addresses available from the tourist office).

• *Budget*

Ostello per la Gioventù – *Viale delle Pinete, Erice – ☎ 0923 86 91 44 – Closed Nov – 52 beds €10* ☕. If you want to stay in this splendid old town but are on a tight budget, then the youth hostel is a good option. Open from July to September, it has space for up to 100 guests.

Azienda Agricola Pizzolungo – *Contrada S. Cusumano, Erice Casa Santa – ☎ 0923 56 37 10 – Fax 0923 56 97 80 – fraadr@tin.it – – Apartments. €40.* A rustic and romantic atmosphere awaits guests at this 19C farmhouse, which is surrounded by a luxuriant garden and is only a few metres from the sea. Enjoy a cool dip in an old stone basin filled with spring water. The hotel has 2-, 4- and 6-bedded apartments, each equipped with a kitchen. An ideal base for a relaxing stay.

• *Moderate*

Hotel La Pineta – *Viale N. Nasi, Erice – ☎ 0923 86 97 83 – Fax 0923 86 97 86 – P – 23 rooms. €85/115* ☕ The hotel's attractive stone bungalows, many of which have small terraces, have been built in the tranquil surroundings of a cool pine forest. Comfortable accommodation decorated with modern furnishings.

VALDERICE

• *Moderate*

Hotel Baglio Santacroce – *2km/1.2mi E of Valderice on S 187 (Km 12) – ☎ 0923 89 11 11 – Fax 0923 89 11 92 – bagliosantacroce@libero.it – P – 24 rooms. €58/96* ☕ *– Restaurant. €18/23.* This 17C farmhouse has been transformed into a delightful small hotel in a bucolic setting with magnificent views of the Golfo di Cornino. The rooms are quite small, but are embellished with typical wood beam ceilings and attractive tiled floors.

Taking a Break

Maria Grammatico – *Via Vittorio Emanuele 14 – ☎ 0923 86 93 90 – Via Guarnotta 1 – ☎ 0923 86 97 77, Erice.* Signora Maria's 15 years spent in a convent served as a fine introduction to the secrets of delicious "convent" pastries. Her specialities include almond and marzipan cakes, *buccellati* (stuffed with dried figs, almonds, walnuts and sultanas), *genovesi*, and orange and chocolate *palline*.

Festivals

Good Friday – 18C wooden figures are borne aloft in procession through the town during the traditional Good Friday Processione dei Misteri.

Settimana di Musica Medievale e Rinascimentale – Concerts are held in Erice's churches during the Medieval and Renaissance Music Festival which takes place annually at the end of July.

Location

Population: 30 787. Michelin map 565 19M – Trapani. On fine days, the two roads that climb up to the town offer magnificent **views★★** across the plain and out to sea; the road to the north, overlooking Monte Cofano, is the easier of the two. Once in Erice, visitors are advised to leave their vehicle in the car park near Porta Trapani. *ℹ Viale Conte Pepoli 11; ☎ 0923 86 93 88; Fax 0923 86 95 44.*

Neighbouring sights are described in the following chapters: MARSALA; SEGESTA; TRAPANI; VIA DEL SALE.

Background

Between myth and legend – The history of Erice is lost among local folklore and superstition. The name is the one given by Eryx, the mythical hero and king of the Elimi, to the mountain upon which the temple to his mother, Venus Erycina (later associated with the cult of Aphrodite), was built. The origins of the town are also linked with **Aeneas**, who also had a claim on the Elimian king's mother. In Virgil's narrative, Aeneas came ashore at the foot of the mountain to perform the funeral of his father Anchises. Having lost several ships in a fire, he was forced to abandon there a number of his companions, who set about founding the town.
Another major mythological figure associated with Erice is **Heracles**. The hero is alleged to have landed in this part of Sicily on his way back to Greece,having stolen the cattle of Geryon (one of the legendary Twelve Labours); during his sojourn he was forced to kill the Elimian king after he tried to steal the cattle from him. Notwithstanding this, Heracles decided to leave the rule of the kingdom in the-hands of the Elimi, with the warning that one of his descendants, Dorieus, would later take over as ruler.
In Antiquity, Erice was famous for its temple where, in succession, the Phoenicians worshipped Astarte, the Greeks venerated Aphrodite, and the Romans celebrated Venus. Mount Eryx served as a point of reference for sailors who, in time, adopted Venus as their protector. At night, a large fire would be lit within the sacred precinct and used as a guiding beacon. Venus Erycina became so famous that a temple was dedicated to her in Rome; meanwhile, her cult spread throughout the Mediterranean.

Walking About

It is advisable to park at Porta di Trapani.
The little town takes the shape of a perfect equilateral triangle, whose symbolism has provoked mystery and endless argument; it is bounded by the Castello di Venere (southeastern axis) and the Chiesa Madre (southwestern side). Exactly in the centre of the triangle is the Church of St Peter with its adjacent monastery that now houses the E Majorana Centre for Culture and Science. An intricate maze of narrow streets, each cobbled with rectangular stones, provides unexpected glimpses of churches and monasteries, of which there are over 60, scattered through the town.

Chiesa Matrice★

The town's main church is situated near **Porta di Trapani**, one of the entrances to the town. Built in the 14C, principally using stone from the Temple of Venus, its massive form and merlon-topped walls suggest it was intended as a church-fortress. The façade is graced with a fine rose window (replicating the original), that is now partly concealed by the Gothic porch that was added a century later. Inside, fashioned in neo-Gothic style, sits a fine marble altarpiece from the Renaissance.

Bell tower – The lonely tower to the left of the church was originally intended as a watchtower. The first level has simple narrow slits, while the upper section is graced with fine two-light Chiaramonte-style windows. The top is crenellated with Ghibelline merlons.

R. Mattes/MICHELIN

ERICE

Addolorata (Viale d.) ... AZ 3
Cordici (Via) ... ABZ 4
Giudaica (Via) ... ABZ 6
Guarnotti (Via G. F.) ... BZ 9
Guarrasi (Via) ... ABZ 10
Rabata (Via) ... AZ 12
S. Cataldo (Piazza) ... BZ 13
S. Cataldo (Via) ... BZ 15
S. Domenico (Piazza) ... BZ 16
S. Giuliano (Piazza) ... BZ 18
Salerno (Via Gen. G.) ... ABZ 19
Umberto I (Piazza) ... AZ 21
Vittorio Emanuele (Via) ... AZ

Museo Cordici ... AZ M
Torre Campanaria ... AZ R

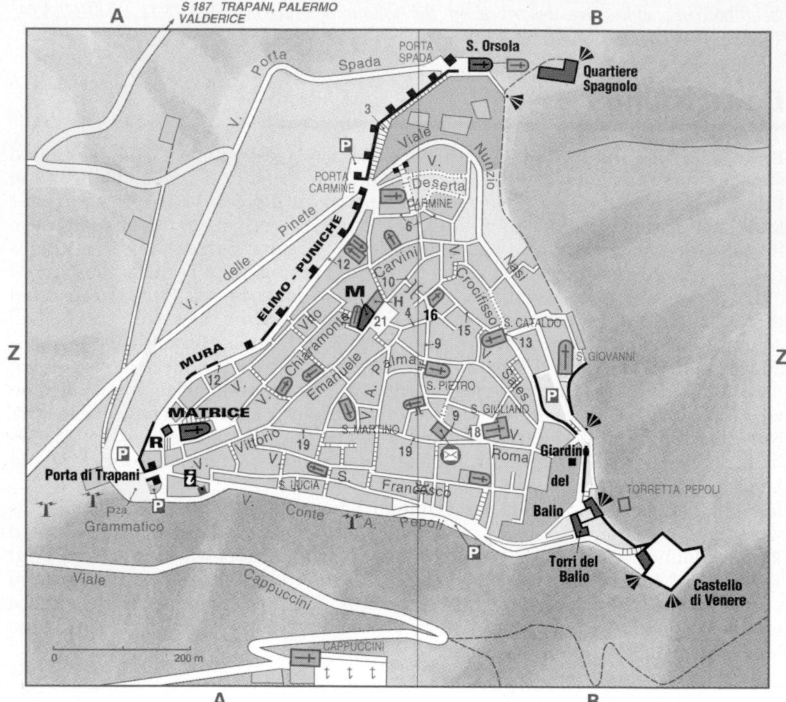

The town hall on Piazza Umberto I houses the Museo Cordici *(see Worth a Visit)*. A little further along, on the right of the piazza, is Via Cordici which leads into the picturesque **Piazza San Domenico**, lined on one side by a street of the same name and on the other by elegant *palazzi*.

Elimo-Punic Walls*

A mighty wall was built by the Elimini (8C-6C BC) around the northeastern flank of the town – the only section open to possible attack. Massive blocks characterise the lowest and most ancient stone courses which were built up through successive ages with smaller components. The skyline was punctuated with lookout towers, steep stairways provided access to the *chemin-de-ronde*, while small openings allowed residents to come and go freely and supplies to be imported. The best-preserved stretch of walls runs along Via dell'Addolorata, from Porta Carmine to Porta Spada.

Santa Orsola

This church, built in 1413, preserves its original Gothic rib-vaulting down the nave. It is here that the 18C Mystery figures are kept when not being processed around the town on Good Friday before the Easter celebrations.

Quartiere Spagnolo

From the top of the so-called Spanish Quarter building, initiated in the 17C but never completed, there is a marvellous view over the bay of Monte Cofano and the area beyond, and down towards the tuna fishery at Bonagìa.

Giardino del Balio

The lovely public gardens are arranged around the Castello di Venere and the Torri di Balio which were built by the Normans as a forward defence for the castle. The towers and gardens are named after the Norman governor (Baiulo) who once lived on this site.

The glorious **view***** embraces Monte Cofano, Trapani, the Egadi Islands and, on a particularly clear day, Pantelleria and, possibly, Cap Bon some 170km/106mi away in Tunisia.

Castello di Venere

The 12C Venus' Castle is appended to the very tip of the mountain, looking out over the sea and the plain below; although the present building is Norman, the site itself has a more ancient history. Indeed, it was once occupied by a temple dedicated to Venus Erycina, who became completely associated with Aphrodite especially after a temple was dedicated to her in Rome (217 BC) when she gained popularity. By the time the Normans were in occupation the temple was in ruins, and so it was decided that the area should be cleared to make way for a fortress surrounded by great walls: the complex was designed to exploit the strategic nature of the site and have the added protection of forward defences in the form of towers **(Torri del Balio)** that would once have been accessible from the castle by a drawbridge. Its defensibility was further emphasised by the machicolations above the entrance; note the coat of arms of Charles V of Spain and the rather attractive two-light window.

This provides a perfect **viewpoint★★★** from which to survey Trapani and the Egadi Islands to the southwest and, to the north, the towers, the Pepoli turret *(down below)*, San Giovanni, Monte Cofano, the coast around Bonagia and, if the weather is fine, the island of Ustica.

Worth a Visit

Museo Cordici

Piazza Umberto I. Open Mon-Fri, 8.30am-1.30pm (also 2.30-5.30pm Mon and Thu). Closed last Wed in Aug and national hols. No charge. ☎ 0923 86 00 48.

Accommodated inside the town hall is the local museum which collects together various archaeological finds, statuary and paintings. Notable exhibits include Antonello Gagini's sculpture of the *Annunciation* (1525) and, on the first floor, beyond the library containing manuscripts and early books, a small marble **head of a woman**, modelled on a Greek original.

Excursion

Tonnara di Bonagìa

Approx 13km/8mi N. Drive down to Valderice and continue towards Tonnara (from the main Valderice road, turn left at the supermarket). At Bonagìa, follow signs for the Tonnara (tuna fishery) while looking out for its distinctive tower. The tuna fishery *(which now accommodates an attractive hotel complex)*, set up in the 17C, was once a simple self-contained village: clustered around a large central courtyard were the fishermen's houses, facilities for cleaning and processing the tuna, the boathouse, the Saracen tower, built for defensive purposes, and a small chapel where the tuna fishermen used to assemble before going out to sea.

The Saracen tower now houses the **Museo della Tonnara**, a small museum displaying the tools and equipment required in building and repairing boats, fishing and the initial stages of sorting and processing the fish. On the second floor, a scale model shows the long corridors of net that the tuna had to enter before reaching the last chamber made of very strong twine, known as the *camera della morte* (death chamber). It was here that the cruel *mattanza* (the kill or slaughter) took place *(see p 172)*. *To visit the tuna fishery, contact the Hotel Tonnara a few days in advance. No charge. ☎ 0923 43 11 11.*

Etna★★★

Mount Etna is also known as **Mongibello**, a name derived from the erroneous interpretation of the Arab word "gebel" meaning mountain, which, prefixed by the Italian word, translates as "Mount Mountain". Etna is Sicily's tallest peak and although capped with snow for much of the winter, it is one of Europe's most famous active volcanoes. Its actual height is regularly modified by each eruption; it currently stands at 3 323m/10 902ft above sea-level. Formed by a series of active craters, Etna is one of the highlights of a visit to Sicily. In addition to the evocative spectacle of the volcano itself, visitors are attracted here by the varied excursions and activities available: hiking, cycling, skiing, horse-riding, or following the circular tour of Etna, either by car or by bus. The area also has an interesting artistic and cultural heritage, as well as a rich culinary tradition, which includes specialities such as wine from Etna, pistachio nuts from Bronte, orange blossom honey from Zafferana Etnea, strawberries from Maletto, and the typical crushed ice drinks known as "granite", which are often accompanied by warm, fresh brioches.

Location

Michelin map 565 N-O 26-27 – Catania. Etna can be explored from the southern or northern slopes of the volcano. The two routes offer contrasting views and landscapes: the route up the southern side to Rifugio Sapienza passes through a barren, black and desert-like environment, while that on the northern side via Piano Provenzana winds its way through a lush larch forest. ℹ *Catania: APT, Via Cimarosa 10, ☎ 095 73 06 211, Fax 095 34 71 21, www.turismo.catania.it; Nicolosi: Azienda di Soggiorno e Turismo, Via Garibaldi 63, ☎ 095 91 15 05; Linguaglossa: Pro Loco, Piazza Annunziata 7, ☎ 095 64 30 94; Zafferana Etnea, Pro Loco, Piazza Luigi Sturzo 3, ☎ 095 70 82 825.*

Neighbouring sights are described in the following chapters: ACIREALE; CAPO D'ORLANDO; CATANIA; GIARDINI NAXOS; TAORMINA.

H. Champollion/MICHELIN

Background

The volcano and its story – Etna evolved as a result of submarine eruptions during the Quaternary Era (c 500 000 years ago), at the same time that the plain of Catania was formed, originally as a broad bay. Etna is known to have erupted regularly during Antiquity, as documented at least 135 times. In the Middle Ages, eruptions were recorded in 1329 and 1381; they disseminated terror among the people of the region. It was in 1669, however, that the most cataclysmic disaster occurred and a great river of lava, expelled from a lower vent which developed at an altitude of around 850m/2 800ft not far from Nicolosi, flowed down to the sea, devastating part of Catania along its route.

In the first half of the 20C, the most violent eruptions took place in 1910 leading to 23 additional craters being formed; in 1917 a fountain of lava spurted 800m/2 500ft into the air from its base; in 1923 outpourings of molten lava stayed hot for more than 18 months after the eruption; and in 1928, a lava flow destroyed the village of Mascali. In the second half of the 20C, a number of eruptions took place. The most recent were in 1992, when the village of Zafferana Etnea was threatened; in 2001, when the southeastern crater erupted, sweeping away the cable car arrival area and base-station and four of its pylons and reaching as far as the boundary of Rifugio Sapienza; and in 2002, which badly affected Rifugio Sapienza, buildings in Piano Provenzana and part of the pine forest along the Mareneve road.

The black lava around the craters dates from recent eruptions as compared with the older grey lava on which lichens are beginning to grow. The presence of both and, sometimes, their distressing effects (blocked roads and ruined buildings) are evidence of the volcano's constant activity.

On the slope of the central crater at around the 3 000m mark, in the vicinity of Torre del Filosofo where a refuge was destroyed by lava in 1971, there are four craters: the southeastern crater that began suppurating in 1978, the immense **central crater**, the northeastern crater at the highest point, which has been dormant since 1971, and the Bocca Nuova (literally the 'New Mouth') which, in recent times, has been the most active.

For more detailed information about volcanic activity on Etna, see Insights and Images: Volcanoes in Sicily.

M.Magni/MICHELIN

The lunar landscape of the Crateri Silvestri

National Park – The protected area designated a National Park in 1987 covers some 59 000ha/145 730 acres. The mountain consists of an enormous black cone, visible from a distance of up to 250km/155mi away. The extremely fertile lower slopes are heavily cultivated with dense groves of oranges, mandarins, lemons, olives, agaves and prickly pears, as well as bananas, eucalyptus, palm trees, maritime (parasol) pines, and vines from which the excellent red, rosé and white *Etna* wines are produced. Probably the most common of the wild plants is *Euphorbia dendroides* (tree spurge). Above 500m/1 640ft, plantations of hazelnuts, almonds, pistachio and chestnuts give way to oaks, beeches, birches and pines, especially around Linguaglossa *(see below)*. The landscape at this altitude is also characterised by a local variety of broom.

At 2 100m/6 900ft, the desolate landscape sustains desert-like plants like *Astragalus aetnensis* (a local variety of milk-vetch), a small prickly bush often found alongside colourful endemic varieties of violet, groundsel and other flowers which populate the slopes of secondary craters. Higher up, snow and, for a long time after an eruption, hot lava prevent any type of macroscopic vegetation from growing: this comprises the "volcanic desert".

The protected areas of Etna also harbour a large variety of small mammals (porcupine, fox, wild cat, weasel, marten and dormouse), birds (kestrel, buzzard, chaffinch, woodpecker and hoopoe), a few reptiles, including the asp viper, and a large variety of butterflies, including the Eastern orange tip *(Anthocharis damone*, which is more commonly known in Italy as the *Aurora dell'Etna)*.

Special Features

THE VOLCANO

As the volcano is still active, the landscape on Etna is constantly changing. Visitors on a tight schedule are advised to contact the local tourist office to find out which of the two sides of the mountain is currently the most interesting. The delightful village of **Zafferana Etnea** is a good base for trips to either side of the volcano; because of its altitude of 600m/1 950ft, it has the advantage of offering magnificent views of the coast from Acireale to Taormina.

South side★★★

Four-wheel drive excursions operate daily (weather permitting) from the week before Easter to the end of Oct, 9am-4pm. Duration: approximately 2hr there and back. €38, including guide. For further information, contact Funivia dell'Etna, Piazza V. Emanuele 45, Nicolosi; ☎ 095 91 11 58 or 095 91 41 41.

Ascent of Etna

The ascent of Etna was difficult, but the view from the top was worth all the effort: *"no imagination in the world has had the courage to depict such a marvellous sight. There is nowhere on the surface of the globe that can combine so many striking, sublimely beautiful details ...The summit ...is situated on the edge of a bottomless chasm, as old as the world itself, and it often erupts cascades of fire, thrusting up incandescent stones with a roar that shakes the whole island."*

From *Journey to Sicily and Malta* by Patrick Brydone (1773)

Directory

Where to Eat

• For all budgets

RANDAZZO

Trattoria Veneziano – *Via Romano 8, Randazzo – ☎ 095 79 91 353 – Closed Sun evening and Mon –* ▣ *– €16/27.* This elegant, friendly restaurant, situated in the centre of the delightful village of Randazzo, serves a selection of regional dishes, with special emphasis on the local mushrooms which are plentiful in this area.

TRECASTAGNI

Villa Taverna – *Corso Colombo 42, Trecastagni – ☎ 095 78 06 458 – Closed Mon, at lunchtime during the week and evenings on Sun and public hols –* ▣ *– €19/26.* Go back in time in this highly original restaurant, where the decor evokes a typical district of the old town of Catania. Typical Sicilian cuisine.

Where to Stay

NICOLOSI

• Budget

Ostello Etna – *Via della Quercia 7, Nicolosi – ☎ 095 79 14 686 – Fax 095 79 14 701 – www.ostellionline.org/ostello.php?idostello44 4 –* ▣. The Ostello Etna is located in the village of Nicolosi, perched on the slopes of the volcano and surrounded by typical volcanic landscapes. Entrance to the Museo Vulcanologico, housed inside the hostel, is included in the price of your stay here.

• Moderate

Hotel Corsaro – *Loc. Piazza Cantoniera, Etna Sud, Nicolosi – ☎ 095 91 41 22 – Fax 095 78 01 024 – info@hotelcorsaro.it – Closed 15 Nov-24 Dec – 20 rooms. €50/80* ▣. If you'd like a contrast to Sicily's coastal scenery, then this comfortable hotel situated at an altitude of 2 000m/6 560ft is the perfect choice. Popular with skiers and walkers, the hotel has 20 pleasant rooms and a restaurant serving local cuisine.

RANDAZZO

• Budget

Agriturismo L'Antica Vigna – *Loc. Monteguardi, 3km/1.8mi E of Randazzo on S 284 – ☎ 095 92 40 03 – Fax 095 92 33 24 –* ▣ ▣ *– 10 rooms. €34/68* ▣ *– Restaurant. €19/24.* This farmhouse is perfect for those looking for a tranquil stay in beautiful scenery. Surrounded by vineyards and olive groves at the foot of Mount Etna, the family-run *agriturismo* is simple in style and serves regional dishes made from organic home-grown produce.

TRECASTAGNI

• Budget

Bed & Breakfast Il Vigneto – *Via Zappalà 1, Trecastagni – ☎ 095 78 01 029 – maferli@tiscalinet.it –* ▣ *– 3 rooms. €35/55* ▣. Surrounded by greenery, this large villa offers bed and breakfast accommodation in three period-style rooms with antique furniture. The villa also has an attractive lounge and a kitchen where breakfast is taken. Minimum stay of two nights.

ZAFFERANA ETNEA

• Expensive

Hotel Airone – *Via Cassone 67, Zafferana Etnea – ☎ 095 70 81 819 – Fax 095 70 82 142 – airone@mail-gte.it – Closed 2 Nov-15 Dec –* ▣ ▣ ▣ *– 60 rooms. €100/150* ▣ *– Restaurant. €23/30.* An elegant and friendly mountain hotel with modern, comfortable rooms and magnificent views extending as far as the coast. Famous guests at the hotel, which was founded in the 1930s, have included the Italian writer Vitaliano Brancati.

Excursions

ASCENT TO THE SUMMIT OF THE VOLCANO

Practical information – Unpredictable and ongoing eruptions of the volcano undermine any permanent tourist amenity infrastructure (roads, ski runs, ropeways, refuges); favourite or recommended itineraries, therefore, should be considered as temporary and subject to being closed at short notice following any recent eruption. At the start of the season (normally in May), shorter walks that stop well below the top are organised. Only when there is no snow, or, if there is, after the snowplough has cleared the roads through the highest sections, is it possible to reach 3 000m/10 000ft. The best time of the year for hiking on Etna is normally high summer, especially in the early morning. Whether aiming for high *(see below)* or low altitudes, it is important to remember that temperatures can plummet here. It is therefore advisable to carry a thick sweater, a wind-cheater and appropriate footwear (preferably hiking boots suitable for walking through snow higher up). Those without suitable attire can, however, hire jackets and boots locally.

It is also advisable to have sunglasses and sunscreen to hand, for the sunlight can be dazzling when reflected off the snow and the ultra-violet can be deceptively powerful in the clear mountain air.

WALKING

Opportunities abound when it comes to walking in the park, with facilities for both short and long excursions (the longest and most complex being the **Grande Traversata Etnea** which involves five days of trekking, with daily 12-15km (7-9mi) hikes), and marked nature trails.

TOURING

For the less agile, an excellent way to see the volcano is the **circular tour of Etna**, either by car *(see below)* or train: this latter option uses the section of railway that starts at Catania, goes around the mountain, and stops at Riposto (approximately 5hr); onward services to Catania are by bus or train. *For information, apply to the Ferrovia Circumetnea, Via Caronia 352/A, Catania; (☎ 095 54 11 11).*

From **Nicolosi*** and **Zafferana Etnea** two beautiful roads wind their way up to **Rifugio Sapienza** (1 910m/6 262ft), the starting-point for all expeditions to the crater. The **route**★★ lies through a strangely unnerving landscape, dominated by black lava and relieved occasionally by a white patch of snow or pink and yellow bursts of flower in spring. Arriving from Zafferana, just before the refuge, a sign points to the **Crateri Silvestri**, craters formed in 1892 which can be reached by a short walk through a spectacular lunar landscape.

TREKKING

Hiking, downhill skiing trips and visits to the extraordinary **volcanic caves** dotted around Etna are organised on request by local mountain guides. *For further information, contact the Gruppo Guide Alpine Etna Sud, Via Etnea 49, Nicolosi; ☎ 095 79 14 755 and, for the northern side of the volcano, S.T.A.R., Via Santangelo Fulci 40, Catania; ☎ 095 37 13 33, or Albergo Le Betulle at Piano Provenzana, Linguaglossa; ☎ 095 64 34 30.*

The ascent up to 1 923m/6 307ft can be made by cable car from Rifugio Sapienza, then on foot *(2hr)* or by four-wheel drive vehicle with a guide. Following the 2001-02 eruptions, which seriously damaged parts of the cable car, the only options for reaching the summit are currently by Funivia dell'Etna four-wheel drive vehicles which depart from Rifugio Sapienza and reach an altitude of approximately 2 700m/8 850ft, or on foot (*allow 4hr for the ascent*). From the 2 700m/8 850ft point, the ascent is by foot, although for safety reasons visitors are strongly advised to keep away from the central vent.

The **Valle del Bove**, a vast sunken area (hence the description as a valley) enclosed by 1 000m/3 300ft high walls of lava, split with great crevasses and chasms, extends to the southeast of the central crater. This area is prone to violent eruptions, some of which are highly dangerous, precipitating flows of lava that on occasion have reached the towns below. *At the time of going to press the Valle del Bove can be reached on foot (1hr there and back from the arrival area for four-wheel drive vehicles). The walk is fairly strenuous and walking boots are essential. Ask local guides for precise directions to the path.*

North side★★★

Four-wheel drive excursions with a guide operate May-Oct, 9am-4pm (weather permitting), from Piano Provenzana. Duration: approximately 2hr there and back. €35, including a guide. To book a trip and arrange a time, contact S.T.A.R. a few days in advance. ☎ 095 37 13 33.

The guided ascent to the craters can be made either on foot or by four-wheel drive. Visitors can leave their car at Piano Provenzana, which was badly affected by the eruption in 2002.

A spectacular route leads up to an altitude of 3 000m/9 840ft. A new observatory has been built here, replacing the one destroyed by lava during the eruption of 1971 (lasting 69 days), which affected both the south slope (wiping out both the observatory and ropeway) and the eastern slope, where the lava flow threatened some of the towns below (Fornazzo and Milo), before stopping about 7km/4mi short of the sea. From the observatory, at 2 750m/9 020ft, there is a magnificent **view**★★. The minibus can then transport the more intrepid to 3 000m/9 840ft before abandoning them to the final leg and those awesome puffing vents, on foot. What is spine-chilling is that, at a whim, these craters can spare the surrounding area or cover it with spewing hot fire. The route may vary according to the latest outward signs given by the volcano.

On the downward return journey, there is an opportunity to stop at 2 400m/7 900ft and examine the craters that were the cause of the 1809 eruption.

Tours

FROM THE COAST TO THE SOUTHERN SLOPES 1

45km/28mi drive starting from Acireale: allow half a day (excluding the ascent to the summit).

There are various ways of approaching the southern slopes of the volcano, the bleaker side, where concretions of black lava form a lunar-like **landscape**★★. All along the edge runs a ring of little towns which all have one feature in common: dark lava stone paves the streets, ornaments the doorways and windows of the houses, fashions awesome black masks with exaggerated menace, and articulates the lines of the churches.

Acireale‡ *See ACIREALE.*

Aci Sant'Antonio

Several of the town's most important monuments are collected around Piazza Maggiore, most notably the Duomo with its imposing façade, rebuilt after the terrible earthquake of 1693. Opposite stands the 16C church of San Michele Arcangelo.

At the far end of the town's main street, Via Vittorio Emanuele, which leads out from the piazza, stands what remains of the Riggio family *palazzo*.

Viagrande

The centre of the village is paved with huge slabs of lava. The front elevation of the 18C Chiesa Madre is of the same dark stone, used here to emphasise the strong verticals of the doorways and windows above.

Trecastagni

According to some sources, the name of this little town (which translates literally as "three chestnuts") actually derives from *tre casti agni* (short for *agnelli*), a reference to the three chaste lambs that are worshipped here: Alfio, Filadelfio and Cirino. A festival in their honour is annually celebrated on 9 and 10 May, the highlight coming with the **procession of the wax effigies**, some immensely heavy, borne by strong bare-chested *ignudi* through the streets to the **Santuario di Sant'Alfio** on the outskirts of town.

Via Vittorio Emanuele, lined by fine buildings, leads to the foot of **Chiesa Madre di San Nicola** with its great central campanile. The façade towers above a steep flight of steps that is flanked on the right by a recess which rises to become a series of asymmetrical ramps above. The terrace at the top provides marvellous views over the plain below.

Pedara

Piazza Don Diego is graced with the Duomo which has an unusual spire covered in brightly coloured maiolica tiles.

Nicolosi* *See above*

For further information on the ascent to the crater, see Special Features.

THE NORTHEAST FLANK 2

60km/37mi drive starting from Linguaglossa: allow half a day (excluding the ascent to the summit).

Linguaglossa*

The name Linguaglossa derives from the ancient term "Linguagrossa", referring to a "grossa lingua di lava" (a big tongue of lava); the name was later distorted accidentally. This is a reference perhaps to its vulnerable "red-hot" position on the slopes of Etna down which incandescent lava has flowed perilously on several occasions.

The **Chiesa Madre**, built of sandstone and lava, is situated on the central piazza. Inside, it is furnished with lovely **wooden choir stalls★** (1728) depicting scenes from the life of Christ.

The scenic **Mareneve** road leads through a wonderful larch and pine wood (affected by the eruption in 2002) to **Piano Provenzana** *(for further information on the ascent to the crater, see Special Features).*

Eastern approach★

From Piano Provenzana, the Mareneve road skirts the eastern side of the summit before dropping back downhill. On the lower slopes of the east side of Etna, many farming villages have rallied to exploit the fertile volcanic soil by cultivating vines and citrus fruits.

Near **Fornazzo**, just before the road meets the more major Linguaglossa to Zafferana Etnea road, it passes the incredible lava flow which managed to spare the little **Cappella del Sacro Cuore** *(on the left)* in 1979, although lava did flow right up to one of the walls and even slightly penetrated the chapel. Regarded as having been preserved by sacred intervention, the chapel attracts people from far and wide who come here to give thanks, bearing *ex-voto* offerings.

From Fornazzo, a road down to the left leads to Sant'Alfio.

Sant'Alfio

This tiny village has a monumental 17C **church**, remodelled in the 19C, with an unusual lava façade incorporating a campanile. From the terrace before the church, there is a splendid **view★** of the Ionian Coast.

Sant'Alfio's main attraction, however, is a famous giant chestnut tree known as the **castagno dei 100 cavalli★** *(on the main road to Linguaglossa).* This fabulous specimen, over 2 000 years old, comprises three distinct trunks with a combined circumference of 60m/196ft. Its name derives from a legend relating how Queen Joan (whether it refers to Joan of Aragon, Queen of Castile, or Joan of Anjou, Queen of Naples, is not clear) sheltered under its branches one night during a storm with her entourage of 100 knights. *Open Sat-Sun, 10am-12.30pm and 3.30-6.30pm; for visits midweek, contact the tourist office on ☎ 095 96 87 72. The tourist office also organises guided tours. Donations welcome.*

Go back in the direction of Fornazzo and continue towards Milo.

Milo

This small farming community tenaciously survives, as it has over the years, against all odds given the unpredictable, blind advances of lava which have so far spared it: indeed, on many occasions, the lava has come to within a few metres (1950, 1971, 1979) before, at the last minute, changing direction.

Continue in the direction of Zafferana Etnea as far as Trecastagni and Nicolosi, then continue along the southern slope or towards Catania.

CIRCULAR TOUR OF ETNA 3

155km/97mi round trip, starting in Catania – allow one day.

The road runs around the circumference of Mount Etna providing a kaleidoscope of different views of the volcano, while passing through various picturesque little villages.

This tour is also possible by train *(see Directory). The directions given below refer to touring by car.*

Catania★ *See CATANIA.*

Leave Catania along Viale Regina Margherita or Via Vittorio Emanuele and take S 121 (6km/4mi).

Misterbianco

The imposing 18C church dedicated to **Santa Maria delle Grazie** rises tall above the town rooftops, its elegant façade visible from miles away. In the south apse, nestles a ***Madonna and Child*** attributed to **Antonello Gagini**. *Open by prior arrangement only, 8am-noon and 3-8pm.* ☏ *095 30 14 83.*

Continue along S 121 for 11km/7mi.

Paternò

In 1072, **Roger II** built a castle here on top of a crag. Its square form is relieved on one side by a series of two-light windows: a line of four smaller ones with one larger opening above. The black lava stone provides a strong contrast for highlighting the white stone ornamental features. Clustered around the castle are the main religious buildings: the Chiesa Madre founded in Norman times and rebuilt in the 14C, and San Francesco. Below these developed the town's other buildings, predominantly in the 17C.

After 7km/4mi, turn right off S 121.

Santa Maria di Licodia

At the heart of this little town is Piazza Umberto; this slightly raised square stretches before a former Benedictine monastery (now the town hall) and the Chiesa del Crocifisso. Down the left side of the church stands its attractive **bell tower** (12C-14C) built in stone of two colours.

Continue to Adrano (8km/5mi).

Adrano

This is one of the oldest settlements on the slopes of Mount Etna (the earliest traces found date from Neolithic times), founded, it is alleged, by the tyrant Dionysius I in the 5C BC under the name of Adranon. Evidence of the massive walls built of squared blocks of lava are still clearly visible *(follow Via Catania and turn right at the yellow sign).*

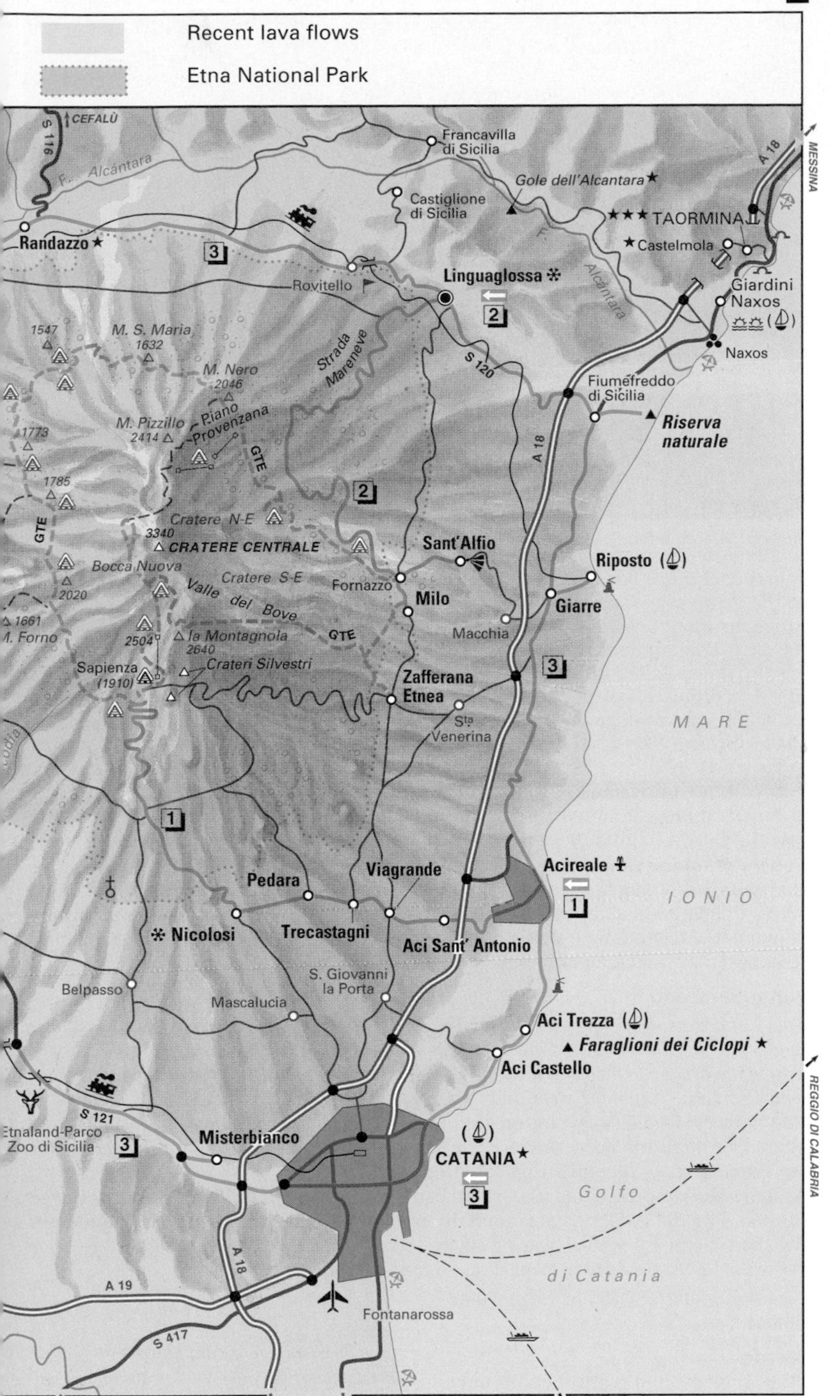

The **castle** was built during the Norman occupation and still overlooks the centrally placed Piazza Umberto. This unmistakable square edifice of dark lava stone owes its form to the Swabian era; inside, it contains three museums.

The **Museo Etnoantrolpologico** collects objects made by local craftsmen.

Over three floors, the **Museo Archeologico Regionale** displays artefacts relating to the history of the area (and from other parts of eastern Sicily) dating from Neolithic times until the Byzantine period. Of particular note *(on the second floor)*, there is the *banchettante* (which translates as the banqueting guest), an early bronze figurine of Samian workmanship (second half of the 6C BC) which probably

M.Magni/MICHELIN

Adrano: Saracen bridge

adorned a bronze bowl or chest; the terracotta bust of a female Siculian deity found in the Primosole district (5C BC), a clay Locrian female bust (5C BC), a clay figurative group of Eros and Psyche, and a splendid **Attic vase★** with small columns (5C BC). The top floor is devoted to the **picture gallery** showing paintings on canvas (by the so-called Zoppo di Gangi, Filippo Paladino and Vito D'Anna), glass and metal; sculptures in wood, alabaster and bronze dating from the early 17C to the early 20C; and a series of contemporary works by artists from Adrano and beyond. *Open Tue-Sat, 9am-1pm and 3-6pm; Sun and public hols, 9am-1pm. No charge. ☎ 095 76 98 849.*

The piazza extends eastwards into the delightful garden of the Villa Comunale, onto which face the imposing elevation of the **Church and Monastery of Santa Lucia**. The 18C church façade, in two colours of stone, is by Stefano Ittar.

Centrale Solare Eurelios – This experimental power plant lies a few kilometres from Adrano. Following a brief period of trial and experimentation from 1981 to 1987, tests were halted (it succeeded in generating 1 mW). Currently, attempts are being made to generate electric power with solar energy using photovoltaic panels (composed of silicon cells).

Ponte Saraceno

The Saracen bridge is located outside the town, beside the River Simeto. Leave by the road south of Adrano and follow signs for Bronte. A sign at a crossroads indicates the way to the bridge: to the right and left, the road is tarred; straight on leads to a dirt track which continues on to the river and the bridge.

The Saracen bridge was first erected by the Romans, rebuilt under Roger II and altered through the successive centuries. The pointed arches spanning the water are articulated with contrasting coloured stone.

A short walk north along the river bank leads to the amazing **Simeto Gorge** formed, like the gorges of Alcàntara, by a lava flow (this time from Etna) and then polished clean by water bearing away great blocks of basalt. *A visitor centre is located on S 114 near Ponte Primosole, heading towards Siracusa.*

Continue along S 284 for 15km/9mi to Bronte.

Bronte

Pride of place in the centre of this town, which is famous for its pistachios, is given to the Collegio Capizzi, a prestigious 18C boarding-school housed in a fine *palazzo*.

Museo della Civiltà Contadina – *Follow signs to La Cascina hotel-restaurant and cross the hotel car park to the museum. Guided tours only, 9.30am-1pm and 3-5pm. Closed national hols. €2. ☎ 095 69 16 35 or 328 40 08 626 (mobile).*

The centrepiece of this attractive farmhouse is the paper mill built by the Arabs sometime before the 11C. The museum also houses an interesting collection of

Etna's pistachio industry

The pistachio tree, which exists in both masculine and feminine varieties, grows to a height of around 4-5m/13-16ft. The male trees are usually planted upwind so that they pollinate the female trees. The trees grow very slowly and produce fruit every other year. Once picked, the pistachio nuts are removed from their husks and left to dry for about a week. The nuts are used in both sweet and savoury recipes.

items relating to rural life and provides a pleasant environment for a stroll, with its many fruit trees and farmyard animals. Before leaving, visitors are able to buy some of the excellent pistachios grown on the property.

Follow signs from Bronte to the Castello di Nelson. The castle is situated by the entrance to the village of Maniace.

Castello di Nelson★

Open Apr-Sep, daily except Mon, 9am-1pm and 3-7pm; Oct-Mar, daily except Mon, 9am-1pm and 2-4.30pm. Closed 20 Jan and last Sun in May. Guided tours available (45min). €2.50. ☎ 095 69 00 18.

The Benedictine Abbey, founded in the 12C at the behest of Queen Margaret, wife of William the Bad, was situated on an important route of communication into the Sicilian hinterland. This prosperous monastery underwent various modifications before finally being handed over by Ferdinand III to the British naval hero Admiral Nelson in 1799 as a token of thanks for his assistance in suppressing anti-Bourbon rebellions in Naples. Although Nelson never visited the building, his descendants lived there until 1981 and transformed it into a magnificent private residence. The adjacent abbey **chapel** is graced with an elegant doorway ornamented with figurative capitals. Inside, it houses a Byzantine icon, which is more popularly believed to be the original one carried by the Byzantine *condottiere* George Maniakes who inflicted a crushing defeat on the Saracens in this area in 1040. Remains of the small church built to house the icon can be seen in the abbey's barn. The main house, surrounded by a park (4ha/10 acres) and an attractive garden, has a number of beautifully furnished rooms.

Continue along S 284 for 20km/12mi.

Randazzo★

This small town, situated on the slopes of Mount Etna, is so close to the volcano that only by a miracle has it never been threatened by a flow of molten lava. Randazzo could be called the black town, black because of the lava used not only to pave its streets and highlight arches above doorways and windows but also as the main building material for the principal monuments in its attractive historical centre, built around the main street, Corso Umberto.

The walk begins at the northeastern end of Corso Umberto.

The 13C **Chiesa di Santa Maria** has undergone considerable modifications through the centuries. What survives from the original is the plan, the characteristic tall Norman **apses★** ornamented with blind arcading, and the south wall pierced by its two- and three-light windows. The neo-Gothic façade and bell tower are 19C. The black lava building stone contrasts effectively with the white window and door surrounds. The sacristy, which stands proud of the main church, once accommodated an ecclesiastical tribunal.

Turn right into Piazza Roma.

A street to the left leads to Piazza San Nicolò. The church after which the square is named was erected in 1594, and has a front elevation articulated by dark lava stone; the campanile dates from 1783. The other buildings overlooking the square include Palazzo Clarentano (1508) graced with decorative two-light openings sepa-

A window made from lava stone

G. Bludzin/MICHELIN

rated by slender columns, and the 14C Church of Santa Maria della Volta. To the right of it opens the delightful **Via degli Archi** ornamented, as its name suggests, with a series of arches. Via Polizzi, on the right, leads from the piazza to **Casa Spitaleri**, with its fine lava doorway.

Turn down Via Duca degli Abruzzi.

An intersection from the right leads into Via Agonia: this street is so called because, it is said, condemned prisoners were led along here from their castle-prison to the Timpa, in front of San Martino, to face their executioners. Look out for the one house that conforms to the 14C archetype, with a single large open space on the ground floor and two square rooms above on the first floor *(only visible from the outside).*

Via Duca degli Abruzzi leads back into Corso Umberto.

An archway on the right marks the old entrance to the **Palazzo Reale**. Only part of the façade, a lovely two-coloured string-course and a pair of two-light windows now remain from this elegant country town residence: before the *palazzo* was destroyed in the earthquake of 1693, it accommodated such famous guests as Joan of England, the wife of the Norman King William II, Costanza of Aragon (the town was chosen as the summer residence of the Spanish court) and, in 1535, Emperor Charles V.

Continue to **Chiesa di San Martino** *(closed noon-4pm)*, founded in the 13C and rebuilt in the 17C. The fine **campanile★** (13C-14C) is battlemented at roof level, with a tall octagonal spire pointing skywards. Lower down, it is ornamented with elegant single openings, emphasised by deep polychrome strips, and decorative, pointed three-light windows.

Inside, the church preserves two Madonnas by followers of the Gagini and a polyptych attributed to Antonello de Saliba – a pupil of Antonello da Messina.

Across from the church lie the ruins of the castle-prison. This began life in the 13C as a fortified tower set into the city walls that extended around the medieval citadel. **Porta di San Martino**, just beyond, constitutes one of the entrances to it.

Either continue along S 120 or take the quiet road that runs parallel to it by going back towards Bronte for 4km/2.5mi and then following signs to Linguaglossa.

Linguaglossa* *See above, in the section devoted to the northeastern slope of Etna.*

Pass through Fiumefreddo di Sicilia (11km/7mi) and head for the coast, taking the turning for Marina di Cottone.

Riserva Naturale di Fiumefreddo

Visitor centre near Masseria Belfiore in Via Marina, Fiumefreddo. (♿) Open May-Sep, daily except Mon, 9am-6pm; Oct-Apr, daily except Mon, 8.30am-4.30pm. No charge. ☎ 095 64 62 77.

The River Fiumefreddo rushes down from the northeastern slopes of Etna, swollen with snow melt which has permeated through the volcanic rock and reached the high water-table, an impermeable layer of clay, to be channelled across the plain. Essentially, the river rises from two springs, both 10-12m (33-39ft) deep, known as Testa dell'Acqua and Le Quadare (*paioli* in Sicilian dialect). It is well worth arranging a visit to the springs when the sun is at its height; this allows the depth and clarity of the water to be appreciated in full. The pH of the water in the river, which never exceeds temperatures of 10-15°C even in summer and flows remarkably slowly, provides the right conditions for an unusual range of water-loving plants more often associated with Central Europe (certain members of the Ranunculus family) or Africa, as with papyrus. Other species include the white willow, aquatic iris, European aspen and horsetail. The springs also attract a variety of birds on migration: herons, oystercatchers, golden orioles, and many species of duck.

Beside the nature reserve stands the 18C **Castello degli Schiavi** *(private, not open to the public)*, designed by the architects Vaccarini and Ittar.

Continue for 10km/6mi along S 114 to Catania.

Giarre

The little town was once part of the feudal estate belonging to the Mascali, having been bestowed upon the Bishop of Catania by **Roger II** in 1124. Its name, however, is taken from the jars in which the tithes on the harvest due to the bishop were collected. The **Duomo** is an imposing neo-Classical building with twin square-set bell towers. The town's main axis is Via Callipoli which is lined with elegant shops and noble town houses including the Liberty-style **Palazzo Bonaventura** (n° 170); at n° 154, **Palazzo Quattrocchi** is ornamented with Moorish designs.

From Giarre, head for the coast in the direction of Riposto.

Riposto

It was to Riposto that the tithes from the Mascali estates were brought pending their onward shipment by sea. The town itself developed around a colony of people from Messina (hence the popularity of the cult of the Madonna of the Letter) who established their warehouses here before it became an important depot for wine destined for the export market in the 19C. Indeed, the vestiges of a number of commercial buildings survive from the 1800s.

The charming **Santuario della Madonna della Lettera** with its face turned towards the sea, was built in 1710, although a church probably existed on the site in Norman times. Four excavations undertaken beneath the sanctuary have revealed the existence of crypts containing funerary chambers dating from the palaeo-Christian period, coins from the Arabo-Norman era and architectural remains from Aragonese times. The painting of the ***Madonna and Child*** on the 18C altar is of uncertain date. The choir has an interesting set of recently carved wooden stalls and an unusual Baroque lamp set with mother-of-pearl, probably made locally. *Open by appointment only at least three days in advance, Mon-Sat, 9.30-11.30am and 4-6pm; Sun and public hols, 10-11am. Closed the week before 15 Aug. ☎ 095 93 35 27 or 095 93 11 87.*

Return to Giarre and head along S 114 for 13km/8mi.

Acireale‡ *See ACIREALE.*

Aci Trezza *See ACIREALE.*

Aci Castello *See ACIREALE.*

Gela

The plains surrounding Gela, which hosted the landings by American troops in July 1943, are some of the most fertile areas of Sicily. Pockets of crude oil are being exploited here to supply a refinery and a petrochemical plant, which, in turn, are helping to improve the local economy of the area. Sadly, the same cannot be said of their effect on the appearance of the town, whose major interest lies in its illustrious past.

Location

Population: 77 702. Michelin map 565 P 24 – Caltanissetta. As a result of pollution from the oil refinery and its hotchpotch of unfinished or poorly maintained buildings, modern Gela has little in the way of tourist attractions. Its most important sight is the archaeological museum, situated in the eastern side of the city. **ℹ** *Via Bresmes Navarra G. 48; ☎ 0933 91 37 88.*

Neighbouring sights are described in the following chapters: AGRIGENTO; CALTAGIRONE; COMISO.

Background

Historical notes – The colony of Gela was founded by colonists from Rhodes and Crete towards the end of the 7C BC. The town prospered and expanded westwards, leading to the eventual foundation of Agrigentum, which soon surpassed it in importance. Gela reached its height during the rule of two tyrants: Hippocrates and Gelon. The latter in fact decided halfway through his reign to move to Syracuse. Over the ensuing period, the city gradually lost its political might but none of its cultural importance. Indeed, it was here in Gela that Aeschylus decided to spend the last years of his life.

Following each successive attack, the town was rebuilt; finally, in 1230, Gela was completely reconstructed by Frederick II.

A fatal case of mistaken identity – Aeschylus, the tragic poet who spent part of his life in Athens and part in Sicily, died at Gela. According to legend his death was caused by a tortoise which was dropped onto his bald head by an eagle that mistook it for a rock (eagles drop tortoises onto rocks so as to split the shell, thus enabling them to be eaten).

Worth a Visit

THE GREEK CITY

Museo Archeologico★

At the east end of the town in Corso Vittorio Emanuele. (♿) Open 9am-1pm and 3-6.30pm. Closed last Mon in the month. ☎ 0933 91 26 26.

The collections are beautifully presented in chronological order and by category, thereby displaying the locally found artefacts to best possible effect. Prefacing the exhibition is a *kylix* inscribed with the name of the city's founder, Antiphemus.

The fine array of **antefixes** come from the acropolis area; some bear the features of gorgons, others the sneering traits of sileni or satyrs (6C-5C BC). Among the artefacts recovered from the wreck of a 5C BC ship with a valuable cargo, there is a delicate *askos* with a silenus and a maenad. The upper-floor displays relate to the sanctuaries outside Gela and to other sites in the area. The various iron agricultural implements, including a rake, were found in a votive pit near the temple precincts at Bitalemi. The last room *(on the ground floor)* gathers together a fine selection of **Archaic and Attic vases** from the necropoli at Navarra and Nocera and their collections.

Acropolis

Alongside the museum. The *plateia* (equivalent to the Roman *decumanus* or main street) divides the town neatly into two halves: to the south lie the sacred precincts with two temples (a single standing column survives from Temple C, built in the 5C BC to celebrate the victory at Himera); to the north lie the residential quarters, complete with shops.

Fortifications★★

West of the town, in the district of Capo Soprano. (♿) Open 9am-1hr before dusk. €2. ☎ 0933 93 09 75.

Excavation has revealed some well-preserved fragments of the Greek fortifications. A stretch of wall, some 300m/330yd long, dates from the period between the 4C and 3C BC when Timoleon restored democracy and decided to rebuild the town after it had been razed to the ground by the Carthaginians (in 405 BC).

The wall consists of two courses: the lower, older section consists of well-appointed, regular, meticulously dressed, square blocks of sandstone.

The need to raise the wall came about following a major build-up of sand c 310 BC; extra height was achieved by using crudely made bricks of sun-dried clay to build a merloned *chemin-de-ronde* on the outermost side, parts of which are still visible. Although extremely fragile, this section was preserved by being covered by encroaching sand. Today, it is protected with plexiglass.

Complesso termale

A short distance from the fortifications, near an almshouse. For information, call ☎ 0933 91 26 26.

The two rooms of this baths complex date from Hellenistic times. The first is divided into two areas: one containing a series of small tubs arranged in a circle, the other set in a horseshoe shape. The second room would have been the *hypocaust* (with under-floor heating), used at times as a sauna. The baths were largely destroyed by fire some time towards the end of the 3C BC.

Excursion

Licata

31km/19mi W. At the heart of the little town is Piazza Progresso and from this radiate Via Roma and Corso Vittorio Emanuele, the two main streets along which the town's principal 18C monuments are aligned.

On Via Roma are the church and cloisters of San Domenico and Chiesa del Carmine. Corso Vittorio Emanuele, meanwhile, claims Palazzo Frangipane with its fanciful brackets shaped like monsters and some other fantastic creatures, and the churches of San Francesco and the Chiesa Madre dedicated to Santa Maria la Nova.

Giardini Naxos

The beach which saw the first Greek colonists land in Sicily 2 700 years ago is now invaded each year by thousands of tourists attracted here by its delightful location, the exceptionally mild climate and the splendid backdrop of nearby Taormina. In addition to its attractive seaside resorts, the area is also renowned for the rich archaeological remains of its Greek city.

Location

Population: 9 128. Michelin map 565 2N 7 – Messina. Giardini Naxos stands behind a popular sandy beach which runs along the coast from Capo Taormina to Capo Schisò. The archaeological site extends from behind the port area, close to the Giardini Naxos exit on the A 18 motorway. The town is just 5km/3mi from Taormina and is linked to the city by frequent bus services (departures every 30min to Taormina station in Via Pirandello).

Lungomare Tysandros 54; ☎ 0942 51 010; www.aast-giardini.naxos.it

Neighbouring sights are described in the following chapters: ACIREALE; ETNA; MESSINA; TAORMINA.

G. Bludzin/MICHELIN

The beach, with the snow-capped volcano in the background

Background

Capo Schisò is a promontory formed originally as a consequence of a great lava flow. It was here that the first Chalcidian colonisers, led by Theocles, founded Naxos in 735 BC, making it the oldest Greek colony in Sicily, or so it is commonly claimed. The name is borrowed from the Cycladic island where, according to legend, Dionysus met and then married Ariadne after she was abandoned by Theseus. In 729 BC Theocles founded the two colonies Catane and Leontinoi, which lie further south.

From the 5C BC, the domination of Naxos became a prime objective for aspiring empire-builders, notably Hippocrates of Gela and, later, Hieron of Syracuse who, in 476, evicted the inhabitants of Naxos and deported them to Leontinoi. Eventually, the support offered by Naxos to the Athenian expedition against Syracuse (415 BC) led to the demise of the city: in 403 BC, Dionysius the Great razed it to the ground, leaving the exiled survivors to found Tauromenion.

Directory

For additional suggestions, see Taormina: Directory.

Where to Eat

Sea Sound – *Via Jannuzzo 37/A, Giardini Naxos – ☎ 0942 54 330 – Closed Nov-Apr – €25/38.* This sea-facing restaurant serves delicious fish dishes on a delightful terrace surrounded by greenery.

Where to Stay

• *Budget*

Hotel La Riva – *Via Tysandros 52, Giardini Naxos – ☎ 0942 51 329 – Fax 0942 51 329 – hotellariva@hotellariva.com – Closed Nov – 38 rooms. €53/68 ☕ €10.* A charming family-run *pensione* on the seafront, with 38 rooms furnished in original Sicilian style and a dining room on the fourth floor offering superb sea views.

Agriturismo Villa Antonella – *Via Fondaco d'Accorso, Trappitello, 2km/1.2mi W of Giardini on S 185 – ☎ 0942 65 41 31 – Fax 0942 65 41 31 – villantonella@villantonella.com – Closed Oct-Apr (open Sat-Sun only) – ⊭ – 10 rooms. €35/70 ☕.* This modern family-run *agriturismo* guesthouse is attractively situated among fruit and citrus trees and has 10 simple but well-maintained rooms. The service here is both friendly and efficient.

• *Moderate*

Hotel Arathena Rocks – *Via Calcide Eubea 55, Giardini Naxos – ☎ 0942 51 349 – Fax 0942 51 690 – reservation@hotelarathena.com – Closed 27 Oct-11 Apr – P 🏊 – 49 rooms. €54/94.* Facilities at this quiet, elegant hotel in an isolated location include a beautiful garden and swimming pool overlooking the sea.

The modern town developed into an important seaside resort in the 1950s. For a long time the "garden town" merely served as a sheltered anchorage for nearby Taormina; the epithet originated from the cotton and sugar-cane plantations which, through the ages, were replaced by citrus orchards which provided the main source of income. The town is now a popular resort and one of the largest tourist centres in Sicily.

Worth a Visit

Naxos

Access to the site is from Via Stracina, the continuation of Via Naxos, or, during opening hours, via the museum in Via Schisò. (♿) Open 9am-1hr before dusk. €2. ☎ 0942 51 001.
The town founded in the 4C BC followed the same boundaries as those of the older town (7C-6C BC): all but the old city walls and the **temenos** (sacred precinct) were removed and replaced by a regular orthogonal (right-angled) street plan as advocated by the 5C BC architect-urban planner Hippodamus of Miletus *(see p 82)*, with three **plateiai** (principal avenues – **decumani** in Latin – A, B, and C, oriented on an east-west axis) intersected at right angles by an indeterminate number of **stenopoi** (minor roads or **cardini**).

On entering the site from Via Stracina, follow the path along the boundary walls of the ancient city. On the southwest side, these incorporate the walls of the **temenos** which enclose what are now the ruins of a large temple (B) from the late 6C BC. The site is scattered with various heaps of stones which date from the same period and which appear to be the remains of several small altars. Nearby sit two kilns: the larger rectangular chamber would have been used for firing architectural elements in terracotta, while the smaller round one served in the production of vases and votive objects.

Skirt around the kilns and leave the sacred precinct by its northern entrance (traces of which are still visible) to emerge onto plateia B. Follow this broad avenue some distance while surveying the urban plan of the new city. At stenopos 6, turn left towards the museum: on the left, level with stenopos 11, are the remains of a small temple from the 7C BC.

Archaeological museum

Via Schisò. Open 9am-1hr bfore dusk. €2. ☎ 0942 51 001.
Situated alongside a small Bourbon keep, the museum houses artefacts from the excavations. The ground floor contains pottery which testifies to the existence of settlements on Capo Schisò from Neolithic times and throughout the Bronze Age, before the arrival of the Greeks. A fabulous range of broken **cymae** (decorative roof ornaments) painted with animated elements in different colours and drip-mouldings for channelling rain water, possibly from Temple B (early 6C BC), are displayed on the ground and first floors. Also on the upper level are arranged various examples of votive objects for hanging on the wall in the shape of a female breast or face; antefixes (decorative end-pieces) with silenus masks, testifying to the cult of Dionysus; a fine altar; a lovely **figurine of a veiled goddess** (probably Hera); a delicately contrived **statuette of Aphrodite Hippias**; a collection of objects from a **surgeon's tomb**, including small ointment jars, a strigil, a specillum (used by doctors to examine wounds); and a beautiful glass dish. There is also a fine 4C BC Thracian bronze helmet and a miniature bust of Athena (5C-6C AD) used as a weight for scales.

Inside the keep are displayed various objects found at sea: anchor shafts, amphorae and grindstones.

Gibellina

Completely destroyed by the earthquake which struck the Valle del Belice in 1968, Gibellina Nuova has been rebuilt as an embodiment of a highly unusual concept: to design the town as a kind of permanent museum with sculptures scattered through the streets and among the buildings which, in turn, could be seen as individual works of art. Contemporary artists such as Arnoldo Pomodoro, Consagra, Cascella and Isgrò (to name but a few) were commissioned to realise this unusual dream; this led to the installation of some 50 works of art, including the imposing Star at the entrance to the town by Pietro Consagra, Quaroni's Piazza del Municipio with its musical tower, and his great white spherical Chiesa Madre, which dominates the landscape from miles around.

Location

Population: 4 784. Michelin map 565 2N 0 – Trapani. Along S 119 linking Castelvetrano (11km/7mi to the south) with Alcamo, Gibellina Nuova is situated just a few kilometres from the A29 motorway, which runs from Palermo to Mazara del Vallo.
Piazza XV Gennaio 1968 n° 1; ☎ 0924 67877.
Neighbouring sights are described in the following chapters: CASTELVETRANO; SEGESTA.

B. Kaufmann/MICHELIN

Consagra's Star

Tour

THE RUINS OF THE 1968 EARTHQUAKE

On the afternoon of 14 January 1968, eastern Sicily was struck by a series of earth tremors which developed into a full-blown earthquake during the terrible night that followed. The earthquake, 40km/25mi beneath the Valle del Belice, measured IX on the Mercalli scale (roughly 6-7 on the Richter scale), tearing buildings from their foundations, opening fissures in the ground and destroying underground cavities. Many of the villages in the Belice region were completely destroyed, and Gibellina, Salaparuta and Poggioreale were all rebuilt away from their original locations.

60km/38mi – allow at least half a day.

From Gibellina, take S 188 heading south. Turn left onto S 119 and follow signs to Ruderi di Gibellina.

Ruderi di Gibellina

The ruins are still visible, although many have been petrified into a work of art called ***Cretto** (Crack)* by **Alberto Burri**, in which the artist has covered much of what used to line the streets of the old town in a gentle concrete blanket furrowed by cracks.

> **Festival**
> In summer, the Orestiadi music, film and drama festival is held in the ruins of Gibellina.

Return to Santa Ninfa and take S 188 to Partanna.

Partanna

This small town was also badly affected by the same earthquake of 1968. Its distinguishing feature, a battlemented castle, was rebuilt in the 17C by the princes of Graffeo (or Grifeo) on the foundations of an earlier, Norman, construction. The flat area behind the castle provides a splendid **view★** of the valley. Unfortunately, the churches have been reduced to ghostly shells by the earthquake: all that remains of San Francesco along Via Vittorio Emanuele is a lonely bell tower (16C-17C) while, higher up, the church of the Madonna delle Grazie preserves its original tower.

Take S 188 to Salemi.

Salemi

The small town of Salemi enjoys a lovely position surrounded by the vineyards that are so typical a feature of the Trapani region. The older parts of Salemi bear the indelible imprint of Arab influences; the narrow cobbled streets wind their way to the top of the hill crowned with the inevitable castle. Salemi was inadvertently blessed with a moment of unexpected glory when, after Garibaldi landed in Sicily, it was declared the first capital of Italy.

In 1968, the town was badly damaged by the earthquake.

Castello Normanno – The Norman castle was erected at the wishes of Roger d'Altavilla on the foundations of a fortress: the castle has two square towers and one high round one.

On its right stand the remains of the **Chiesa Madre**, destroyed as a result of the earthquake of 1968.

Turn down Via D'Aguirre and along past the church.

Chiesa e Collegio dei Gesuiti – The rather elegant façade of the church is Baroque, complete with a portal flanked with spiral columns of tufa. The Collegio, meanwhile, accommodates the **Museo Civico** which contains various religious works of art rescued from the churches destroyed in the earthquake in 1968: a particular highlight is the lovely *Madonna della Candelora* (Candlemas) by Domenico Gagini. Beyond the last room of the museum sits an 18C chapel that replicates the Casa Santa of Loreto. *Open 9am-1pm and 3-7pm. No charge. ☎ 0924 98 23 76.*

Further downhill, lies the picturesque **Rabato** quarter complete with all its Moorish flavour. The outside streets provide wonderful **views★** of the valley. Here, on 3 February each year, the residents distribute tiny, very elaborate and strangely shaped loaves of bread for the feast day of San Biago. Bread also plays its part in the celebrations of St Joseph's day (19 March), when special large votive loaves are baked in the shape of angels, garlands, flowers, animals and work-tools so as to represent every aspect of daily life.

Take S 188A north, then follow S 113 to Calatafimi.

Calatafimi

This little town was once well defended by its **Castello Eufemio**, a Byzantine fortress that was rebuilt in the 13C and now lies in ruins. From here, a fine **view★** stretches over the valley and town.

On the hill opposite stands the **Pianto Romano**, a monument commemorating the followers of Garibaldi who died in action (Calatafimi was the scene of an important battle). From there, a marvellous **view★★** extends back over Calatafimi, the surrounding hills, and the sea beyond.

Every five years, during the first three days of May, the Festival of the Holy Crucifix **(Festa del Santissimo Crocefisso)** is held: an important procession takes place through the streets with representations from all the various town "corporations". The Massari delegation can be distinguished by its float decorated with bread.

From Calatafimi, it is possible to continue to Segesta (4km/2.5mi).

Cava d'Ispica★

Situated between the *comuni* of Ispica and Modica, this great fissure some 13km/8mi long, is stacked with abandoned troglodyte dwellings, small sanctuaries and necropoli. The earliest signs of human occupation in the area date from Neolithic times. The hollows studding the walls of the gorge are natural phenomena in karst rock; they came subsequently to be modified and adapted by humans according to their requirements.

Location

Michelin map 565 Q 26 – The gorge comprises two parts: the first, between Modica and Ispica, consists of a fenced section which is open to the public, and an area to the north, which is less accessible and best visited on a guided tour; the second part of the gorge, known as the Parco della Forza, is located in Ispica and is mainly visited on organised tours.

Neighbouring sights are described in the following chapters: COMISO; MODICA; NOTO; RAGUSA.

Worth a Visit

Cava d'Ispica

From S 115 follow signs to Cava d'Ispica. Tours leave from the Ufficio della Sovrintendenza. Open Apr-Oct, 9am-8pm; Nov-Mar, 9am-1.15pm. €2. Guided tours available. ☎ 0932 77 16 67.

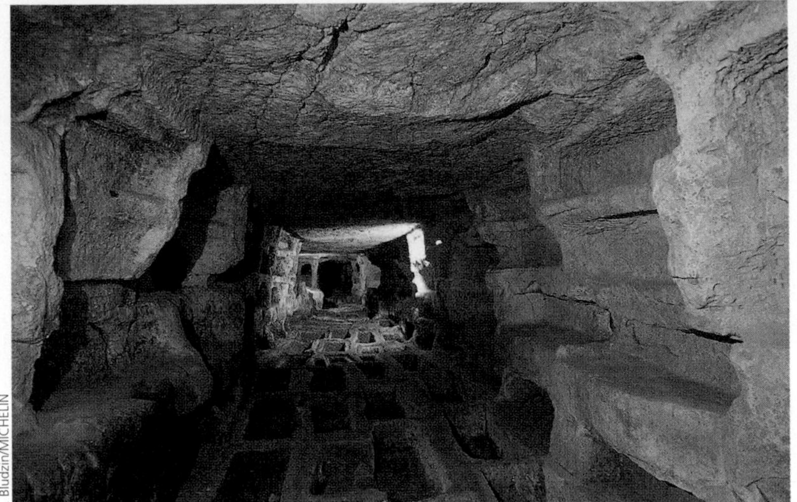
G. Bludzin/MICHELIN

La Larderia

The actual Cava d'Ispica contains the **Larderia**★ (from the word *ardeia* – with abundant water) which consists of a palaeo-Christian catacomb (4C-5C) lined with an impressive number of burial chambers (464). The original entrance was at one time located at the opposite end of the corridor that is now used, off which branches the "main nave" extending 35.6m/117ft. The two lateral passageways were added later.

The tour follows the contours of a rock wall. Beyond the Church of Santa Maria (high up in the cliff on the left) and the Camposanto or Holy Ground, are located the **Grotte Cadute** which comprise a residential complex on several levels. Holes in the ceiling and steps cut in the walls below enabled the residents to move from one level to another with the aid of poles and ropes that could be pulled up in times of danger.

Opposite the entrance to the fenced area, on the far side of the main road, another road leads to the **rock-hewn Church of San Nicola** and the **Spezieria**, a little church perched on a sharp rocky outcrop. The name, corrupted from the local dialect, is linked to the mythical existence of a monk-cum-apothecary who prepared herbal remedies. The church interior is subdivided into two parts: a nave and a misaligned chancel with three apses.

Return to the car and drive up the main road to the first turning on the left.

Baravitalla – On the plateau, now scattered with drystone walls, stand the ruins of the Byzantine Church of **San Pancrati** *(on the left, fenced off)*. It was beside here that vestiges of a small settlement were recovered. A little further on, a path leads left to an area with other points of interest *(difficult to find without a guide)*: the **Tomb with decorative pilasters** has a double front entrance, and the **Grotta dei Santi** consists of a rectangular chamber containing fragments of fresco along the walls *(the haloes of the figures depicted can just be discerned)*.

Back on the main road, continue towards Cava d'Ispica, before looking and finding *(if accompanied by a guide)* the **Grotta della Signora** which shelters a spring considered sacred since ancient times. The walls bear traces of graffiti dating from the prehistoric or palaeo-Christian eras (swastikas and crosses).

Meanwhile, in the opposite direction further towards Ispica, the central part of the gorge conceals the "**Castello**", an enchanting residential complex several storeys high that was abandoned only in the 1950s (very difficult to find: consult a local guide for detailed directions).

Parco della Forza

Located at Ispica, 13km/8mi SE of Cava d'Ispica. For information on admission times, call ☎ 0932 77 16 67. Closed Sun and public hols. €2.

This, one of the earliest areas of settlement, has been occupied since Neolithic times and was abandoned in the 1950s *(very difficult to find: consult a local guide for directions)*. During the Middle Ages, the plateau above the gorge was fortified with a citadel. This was raised around the so-called **Palazzo Marchionale**, the basic layout of which may still be made out. Some rooms preserve fragments of the original floor covered with painted, fired lime tiles. The small fortress also contained several churches including the **Annunziata** which has 26 graves inlaid into its floor.

The cave known as the **Scuderia**, so called because it accommodated stables in medieval times, bears traces of graffiti horses. An idea of just how considerable this settlement was may be gleaned from the known number of people residing there: before the earthquake in 1693, approximately 2 000 people lived within the precincts of the actual citadel, while an additional 5 500 people inhabited the nearby gorges.
Perhaps the most striking feature is the **Centoscale**, an extremely long underground stairway (consisting of 240 steps cut into the rock) which descends 60m/200ft at an angle of 45° into the side of the hill to emerge on a level with the valley floor, below the river bed. It is not known when exactly the passage was made; its function was to ensure a water supply even in times of drought. A total of 100 slaves (hence the name) were positioned along the length of the stairway to collect the water as it filtered down from the river bed (at its deepest point, the passageway was 20m/65ft below water level); having been collected it was passed up in buckets to the surface.

Outside the actual park stands **Santa Maria della Cava**, a little rock-hewn church containing the fragments of fresco in successive layers *(for access, permission must be sought from the custodians).*

Excursions

Ispica

13km/8mi SE of Cava d'Ispica. The hub of the little town is **Piazza Regina Margherita**, where the Chiesa Madre, San Bartolomeo and Palazzo Bruno (1910) with its distinctive angular tower are situated. Corso Umberto I, running behind the church, passes between a series of fine buildings before leading to the Liberty-style jewel of the town: **Palazzo Bruno di Belmonte** (now the town hall) designed by **Ernesto Basile**. Almost opposite stands the lovely **covered market**, now used to host events organised by the local council. Other additional buildings of quality lie beyond it, notably at n° 76 and n° 82.
Return to Piazza Regina Margherita and turn down Via XX Settembre to the church of **Santa Maria Maggiore**. The elegant semicircular arcade before the church was conceived by **Vincenzo Sinatra** as an effective **complement★** to the church. Inside, the church contains a fine cycle of **frescoes★** painted by the Catania artist Olivio Sozzi (1763) who was clearly influenced by the Rococo. The large central panel depicts scenes from the Old and New Testaments: Adam and Eve, Judith with the head of Holofernes, Moses *(below)*, the Apostles with St Peter *(centre)* and Christ holding the Eucharist *(above)*. The chapel in the left transept contains a canopy with an unusual carved wooden figure of Christ at the Column. This statue, the head bowed in an expression of defeat as if Christ is succumbing to the pain of His wounds, is carried in procession annually during the Maundy Thursday (Thursday before Easter) celebrations.
In the opposite direction, Corso Garibaldi leads to the elegant **Chiesa dell'Annunziata** which is decorated internally by G Gianforma with 18C stuccoes depicting stories from the Bible.

Lampedusa★

The island of Lampedusa consists of a flat limestone platform which culminates, at the northern end, in a series of dramatic cliffs★★. The south coast, on the other hand, is jaggedly rugged as headlands alternate with small, precipitous creeks sheltering sandy beaches. Closer to Africa than Italy (forming a part, in fact, of the African continental shelf), Lampedusa is surrounded by a spectacular sea★★ that ranges in colour from a transparent turquoise to emerald green and blue.

Location

Population: 5 938. Michelin map 565 U 19 – Agrigento. The port is situated in the southeastern section of Lampedusa, an area that is also home to the island's beaches and hotels; the north of the island is mountainous and rocky and is best explored by boat. Most of the roads are located to the east of the island, although one road heads west inland from the town of Lampedusa to Capo Ponente. The Riserva Naturale Isola di Lampedusa covers much of the southeastern section of the coast between Cala Greca and the Vallone dell'Acqua, and includes the Isola dei Conigli. *Via Vittorio Emanuele 89; ☎ 0922 97 13 90.*

Background

The islands of the "high sea" – The archipelago of the **Isole Pelagie★**, approximately 200km/125mi south of Agrigento between the island of Malta and Tunisia, comprises the large island of **Lampedusa** (surface area of 33km²/12.7sq mi) and the two small islands **Linosa** and **Lampione**. The inhabitants of Lampedusa have little experience of agriculture: the interior of the island is white and yellow, stony and arid, like a miniature desert. Instead they depend on fishing for a livelihood, as the large fleet anchored offshore in the well-sheltered bays will testify. A few finds confirm that the island was inhabited as early as the Bronze Age. In 1843, the island belonged to the illustrious Lampedusa family (of which Giuseppe, author of *The Leopard*, is the most famous member) when it was acquired by King Ferdinand II; he had a prison built on the island and sent a handful of people to reside there.

G. Bludzin/MICHELIN

Isola dei Conigli

Marine underworld – Fabulously beautiful scenery awaits to be discovered by anyone prepared to don mask and fins for an expedition underwater to explore the island's rocky coastline: brightly coloured rainbow wrasse, scorpion fish, blenies (lurking in small crevasses in the rock), starfish, slender needlefish, octopus, sea cucumbers, sea hares and sponges. The sea floor is a jigsaw of rocky and white sandy patches. At intervals these are suddenly monopolised by dark green underwater meadows of *Poseidonia oceanica*, the seaweed nicknamed "the lung of the Mediterranean", which efficiently oxygenates the water and sustains large colonies of fish.
Divers ready and equipped for more prolonged ventures underwater will discover abundant groves of living coral, sponges and madrepores populated with colourful parrot fish and, off Capo Grecale (at a depth of 50m/165ft), lobsters.

Directory

Transport

The simplest way to get to the islands is by air: flights operate from Palermo (approximately 1hr), with additional services during the summer months from the main Italian cities.
There is also a hydrofoil service during the summer months from Lampedusa to Linosa (1hr). For further information call ☎ 0922 97 00 03 (Agenzia Marittima Strazzera).
Overnight ferry services operate from Agrigento (Porto Empedocle) to Linosa (6hr) and Lampedusa (8hr). For further information contact Siremar at Porto Empedocle, ☎ 0922 63 66 83 or ☎ 0922 63 66 85.

Where to Eat

Lampedusa has a wide choice of small restaurants and trattorias all serving a wonderful variety of fresh fish. The *cuscus di pesce* (often made with grouper), a local speciality based on a Tunisian dish, is particularly recommended.

• ***For all budgets***

Al Gallo D'Oro – *Via Ludovico Ariosto 2, Lampedusa* – ☎ *0922 97 12 97* – *Closed Dec-Feb* – *€20/30*. This restaurant is renowned for its fresh fish and good value for money. The decor is rustic, with a wooden gallery and exposed beams, and numerous prints and paintings on the walls. Meals are served outside in summer.

Da Nicola – *Via Ponente, Lampedusa* – ☎ *0922 97 12 39* – *Closed Thu (in winter)* – *Booking recommended* – *€21/26*. For excellent seafood and home cooking typical of Lampedusa, this family-run restaurant is well worth a visit. Meals are served in a simple rustic dining room decorated with small paintings.

Lipadusa – *Via Bonfiglio 6, Lampedusa* – ☎ *0922 97 16 91 – Closed at lunchtime, Nov-Easter* – ▨ – *€25/34.* This friendly, family-run restaurant in the town centre serves regional cuisine with an understandable emphasis on fresh fish. The decor is simple and well maintained.

Where to Stay

Various types of apartment (book well in advance for the summer months) are available to rent, in addition to the usual array of expensive traditional hotels. For further information, contact the tourist office.

• ***Budget***

Campeggio La Roccia – *Via Madonna, Cala Greca, Lampedusa* – ☎ *0922 97 00 55 – Fax 0922 97 33 77 – laroccia@iol.it* – ⊭ *€13.* Located right on the seafront, this campsite offers a wide selection of accommodation options: bungalows, mobile homes and caravans, as well as large shady pitches for tents. Facilities include a restaurant and supermarket, and, of course, the beach!

I Dammusi di Borgo Cala Creta – *Contrada Cala Creta, Lampedusa* – ☎ *0922 97 03 94 – Fax 0922 97 05 90 – calacreta@lampedusa.to* – ⊭ *€44/65* ☕. The traditional *dammusi* (typical white-domed buildings with stone walls) offers a picturesque alternative to staying in a hotel. The complex also includes small white villas which are rented out by the week.

• ***Expensive***

Cavalluccio Marino – *3, Contrada Cala Croce* – ☎ *0922 97 00 53 – Fax 0922 97 00 53 – hotelcavallucciomarino@cavallucciomarino.com – Closed Nov-Easter* – ⊭ 🅿 ▨ – *10 rooms, half board only. €105.* This small, elegant family-run hotel, situated near one of the island's most attractive bays, offers guests a choice of 10 comfortable, well-maintained rooms. Fresh fish is caught daily by the hotel owner, Signor Pietro.

Shopping

Natural **sponges** are collected from all around Lampedusa making them one of the most popular purchases available to visitors: a word of advice – the whiter sponges, although more attractive, have been treated with bleach making them less durable; the slightly brown sponges, on the other hand, last longer.

The locally grown produce available on Linosa includes lentils and miniature tomatoes; reed baskets are also on sale in the town centre.

Turtle Conservation

The Pelagie – notably Lampedusa's bay of Isola dei Conigli with its long stretch of sand – have been chosen by the loggerhead turtles as suitable sites for laying their eggs. A special conservation-cum-education centre, **Centro Recupero, Marcaggio e Tutela delle Tartarughe Marine**, has been set up on Lampedusa to monitor and protect the turtle population, with a programme involving local children under the supervision of Dr Daniela Freggi. The number to call should a turtle be found in distress, or for volunteers to participate in local monitoring, is: ☎ 0338-219 85 33 (mobile).

On **Linosa**, the black (and therefore warm) sands of Cala Pozzolana di Ponente seem to favour the birth of female turtles. It has been established that the sex of a turtle is determined by the temperature of the sand: below 30°C males will predominate, temperatures in excess of 30°C favour females. By the beach the Associazione Hydrosphera runs its **Centro Studi sulle Tartarughe Marine**: this displays information concerning the life cycle of the turtles, complete with illustrations provided by enthusiastic volunteers. The centre also has a small "Casualty department" for turtles found sick and exhausted or brought in by fishermen who have inadvertently caught them on a hook. The two centres (on Lampedusa and Linosa) are part of an Italian project run by the Department of Animal and Human Biology of La Sapienza University in Rome. *(♿) Open mid-Jun to mid-Sep, 10am-noon and 4.30-7pm.* ☎ *0922 97 20 76.*

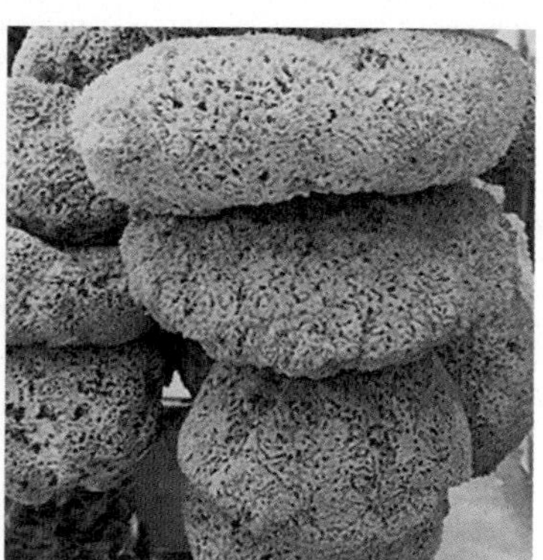
M. Magni/MICHELIN

Worth a Visit

Lampedusa ⌂

The town shares its name with the island land mass. Apart from the odd house scattered here and there, this is the only urban conurbation as such, and it hinges on Via Roma. The main street comes to life in the morning at breakfast time, and again in the evening at sunset until late into the night. It hosts a cluster of small shops and cafés from which tables and chairs tumble out onto the pavement. In summer these bars proffer low-key entertainment (sessions of karaoke or live music).

A boat trip around the island*

In summer, many a boat owner will tout for business down in the harbour, happy to take visitors out and round the island for a reasonable sum. Excursions usually take a whole day, departing at about 10am and returning at approximately 5pm, touring the island in a clockwise direction.

The low, jagged coastline is laced with little creeks and inlets including the one known as **la Tabaccara****: this lovely bay washed with the most stunningly turquoise sea is only accessible by boat. The next in line is the **Baia dell'Isola del Coniglio***** *(see below)* before the headland Capo Ponente, the most westerly point of the island. Here, the landscape suddenly changes: the **coastline**** of the island's north flank consists of a single great tall cliff plunging straight down into the sea, indented here and there by a number of intriguing caves and grottoes. Eventually, the island contours open out into the **Baia della Madonnina*** (so called because of the shape of one of the rocks above it), and various impressive rocks. These are known as the **Scogli del Sacramento** and they guard the mouth of a deep cave with the same name and the one alongside it called **Grotta del Faraglione**.

The northeastern tip of the island, Capo Grecale, is capped with a lighthouse that swings its beam across some 60 nautical miles (110km) offshore. Immediately after Cala Pisana, by the Grotta del Teschio (Cave of the Skull) is a 10-15m/30-50ft long beach, accessible down a path on the right.

Exploring the island on land

The circular coast road is not asphalted all the way around the island; it is therefore recommended that mopeds or small four-wheel drive vehicles be hired for the day. From the town of Lampedusa, head east towards the airport.

The dirt track that runs parallel to the runway skirts round many of the creeks and small rocky bays on the south coast. Beyond Cala Pisana the track continues out to the tip of Capo Grecale where the lighthouse is situated; from this lofty position, the fine **view*** pans in either direction along the coast and down to the sea stirring dizzily below. The road then links up with another that runs along the south side of the island. Turn right towards the telecommunications signalling station.

Albero del Sole – These steep cliffs are the highest point on Lampedusa (133m/436ft). The small round building contains a wooden crucifix. From the other side of the stone wall *(be careful, as it conceals a horrendous drop)*, there is a dramatic **view**** of the **Faraglione** – or Scoglio a Vela (shrouded rock) as it is also called – and the cliffs plunging steeply down into the sea. One way of enjoying the view without fear of falling is to lie flat on the ground, not too near the edge.

Return back the same way and fork right along the partially asphalted road, that runs past a tree plantation on the right. At the far end of the enclosure wall, continue along the vague dirt track leading to a small iron cross. The headland on the right provides a glorious **view**** of the **Scoglio del Sacramento*** *(right)*. In the distance on the left, can be seen the little island of Lampione.

Return to the main road and head south towards the bay around Isola dei Conigli (Rabbit Island).

Baia dell'Isola dei Conigli*** – In this broad bay, petticoated with white cliffs and the most beautiful beach on the island, sits a little islet. It could almost be a corner of the Caribbean: the whitest sand slopes gently down to the water's edge, delicate clear tints of turquoise and emerald green stretch out to sea. Annually, a colony of loggerhead turtles makes its way up the beach to lay its eggs. Today, this exciting event is threatened by the ever larger numbers of spectators who linger here until sunset (turtles lay their eggs at night, but their extreme shyness means that the slightest disturbance will frighten them away).

This is also the only place in Italy inhabited by an unusual species of stripy lizard of the Large Psammodromus *(Psammadromus algirus)* variety, more usually found in North Africa (Tunisia, Algeria and Morocco).

Loggerhead turtle (Caretta caretta)

This is the most common species of sea turtle in the Mediterranean. This wonderful sea creature is a docile, solitary being other than during the mating season; they live in temperate waters all year round except for when the females must haul themselves up onto dry land to lay their eggs, every two or three years. The mother-to-be chooses a sandy beach undisturbed by lights or noise. With enormous effort, she heaves herself up from the water's edge (awkwardly deprived of all her natural dignity, agility and grace when in water) and, using her hind flippers, she digs a deep hole (40-75cm/16-30in deep) in the sand. There she passively lays her eggs before covering them with sand. Her task now over, she turns round and shuffles back to the sea, abandoning the eggs to their fate. Hatching takes place six to eight weeks later. The baby turtles emerge from the sand and instinctively make their way down the beach towards the sea, a threatening and dangerous world at least until they grow to any size. Only a few will survive to adulthood. In fact, even before they hatch, the eggs easily fall prey to birds and man. As newly hatched turtles, their greatest threat comes in the shape of fish, greedy for their tender meat. This is why it is important to protect and safeguard both the sites where the eggs are laid (thus eliminating or reducing the risks prior to hatching) and the seas the turtles inhabit. People should respect a few fundamental rules, notably disposing of their plastic bags with care: in the water, these take on the appearance of a tasty jellyfish for a turtle, and the mistake can cost it its life.

G. Bludzin/MICHELIN

Madonna del Porto Salvo – This small, ancient shrine of uncertain date is surrounded by a pretty garden full of flowers.

LINOSA*

The untamed beauty of Linosa resides in the blackness of its volcanic rock, and its three great lofty cones pitched dramatically against the blue sky. This island has evolved in different stages, and this is strikingly evident. The volcanoes, now extinct, leave the visitor with a lasting, if haunting, impression.

The only town, huddled around the little harbour, consists of a collection of houses attractively painted in pastel shades with strongly accented coloured corners, doors and windows. From here, there exist a variety of possible excursions on foot into the mountains, or by boat around the coast. The few resident inhabitants of this peaceful islet who once depended on rearing cattle, now eke out a living from tourism.

The tallest peak is Monte Vulcano (186m/610ft), a volcano, as its name suggests, though now extinct. The interior of the island, predominantly desert-like, still supports a few areas of cultivation (notably the Fossa del Cappellano which is particularly well sheltered from the wind).

Fringed with a jagged lava coastline, Linosa is considered to be a veritable paradise by scuba-divers and snorkelling enthusiasts *(underwater fauna and flora are described above under Lampedusa)*.

The land-based fauna of Linosa includes large colonies of Maltese wall lizards and **Cory's shearwaters** – the seabirds that shatter the quiet summer nights with their plaintive cries. Loggerhead turtles still come up the black beach in Cala Pozzolana to lay their eggs.

A number of footpaths, popular among keen walkers, lead to the summits of the island's three main peaks: **Monte Rosso** – the crater of which shelters various garden allotments, **Monte Nero** and **Monte Vulcano**. From the top of Monte Vulcano, when the *libeccio* wind blows, it is possible to make out cars as they move along the roads of Lampedusa.

Boat trip round the island**

Excursions by boat can be arranged down at the harbour. The boat sets out from the harbour leaving Monte Nero, Monte Bandiera and Monte Vulcano behind it. It skirts the **Fili**, a group of rocks surrounding a sort of natural swimming-pool, enclosed on the landward side by sheer walls of **rock*** polished and moulded by the rain and wind into wave-like forms. The restless sea and a handful of clumps of caper plants complete the landscape. Beyond the Faraglioni rocks that stand guard outside the "natural pool" or Piscina Naturale *(also accessible on foot)*, the lighthouse comes into view. This stretch of coastline is particularly jagged. Just before the circular trip draws to its conclusion, the boat steams across **Cala Pozzolana****; this shelters the only beach on the island backed by an amazing wall of incredible colour ranging from sulphur yellow through to rust red. The hydrofoils from Lampedusa moor here.

LAMPIONE

Occupied only by a lighthouse, this small island rises vertically from a depth of 60m/196ft or so as a series of sheer cliffs. The deep and therefore unpolluted sea provides ideal conditions for scuba divers to venture out for a glimpse of groupers, lobsters, yellow and pink coral and the occasional grey shark.

Madonie e Nebrodi★

With its gently rolling hills, wooded landscapes, rivers, mountain streams and white snow-capped peaks, the alpine scenery of the Madonie e Nebrodi is in many ways more typical of the Dolomites than Sicily. Visitors to this magnificent region will discover another side to Italy's largest island, providing a striking contrast to its more typical Mediterranean landscapes.

Location

Michelin map 565 M-2N 3-24-25 – Messina, Palermo. The gently undulating hills of the Madonie, which dominate the coast between Cefalù and Castel di Tusa, are replaced to the north by the wilder scenery of Piano Battaglia and Battaglietta, the Pizzo Carbonara (1 979m/6 491ft, the highest peak in the range) and the Serre di Quecella; the latter are often referred to as the "Sicilian Alps" on account of their resemblance to the Dolomites. The Nebrodi, which extend between Santo Stefano di Camastra and Capo d'Orlando, culminate in Monte Soro, near San Fratello, at a height of 1 847m/6 060ft.

ℹ ***Madonie**: Corso Paolo Agliata 16, Petralia Sottana, ☎ 0921 68 08 40 and 0921 68 40 11; Contr. Farchio, Isnello, ☎ 0921 66 27 95 and 0921 66 27 37; www.parks.it/parco.madonie/*

ℹ ***Nebrodi**: Via Ruggero Orlando 126, Caronia, ☎ 0921 33 32 11; Via Ugo Foscolo 1, Alcara Li Fusi, ☎ 0941 79 39 04; Strada Nazionale, Cesarò, ☎ 095 77 32 061; www.parks.it/parco.nebrodi/*

Neighbouring sights are described in the following chapters: CAPO D'ORLANDO; CEFALÙ; NICOSIA.

Background

Sicilian Apennines – The Sicilian Apennines form a natural extension in geological terms to the Calabrian Apennines. The range comprises the **Monti Peloritani** (above Messina) together with the **Nebrodi** and **Madonie** mountains: these are entirely consistent in terms of the landscape, flora and fauna. The two latter areas have been designated national parks so as to preserve the natural heritage.

The valleys accommodate rivers and mountain streams that flow through gorges cut by erosion: one of the most spectacular is the **Gole di Pollina**, near Borrello. The vegetation varies with altitude: the coastal strip, up to 600-800m (2 000-2 600ft), is covered with oaks (cork, holm) and scrubby shrubs typical of the Mediterranean maquis (tree spurge, myrtle, *Pistacia lentiscus*, wild olive, strawberry tree/arbutus, juniper); above, at 1 200-1 400m (4 000-4 600ft), grow various species of oak; over 1 400m/4 600ft, the slopes are covered with glorious beech woods. Between Vallone Madonna degli Angeli and Manca li Pini (northern side of Monte Scalone), grow 25 Nebrodi spruce, the only examples of this endemic, and now rare, species (one other stands by the ruined castle at Polizzi). One of the most interesting places for plants is Piano Pomo where the giant holly grows: a few, thought to be over 300 years old, reach over 14m/46ft in height and have a circumference of 4m/13ft.

G. Bludzin/MICHELIN

The area has a variety of indigenous birds and animals, although the increased presence of humans (and increased hunting and poaching) has virtually annihilated many of the larger species (red and fallow deer, wolf, lammergeier and griffon vulture). Those still found, however, include porcupines, wild cats, foxes, martens and some 150 or so species of bird such as hoopoes, buzzards, kestrels, red kites, peregrine falcons, ravens, golden eagles and grey herons. Among the area's most interesting groups of residents are the many (70 or more) species of butterfly, many of which are brightly coloured.

Directory

Sightseeing

Parco delle Madonie – The Madonie Park was founded in 1989 and encompasses 39 679ha/98 007 acres. Its roughly rectangular perimeter also contains four categories of reserve designated special, general, protected and controlled according to different guidelines. For detailed information, illustrated material and advice on excursions (by car or on foot), contact the Ente Parco at Petralia Sottana or Isnello *(see Location)*.

Parco dei Nebrodi – The Nebrodi Park, designated a nature reserve in 1993, covers a large area, touching upon several local districts or *comuni*. Its 85 687ha/211 647 acres are divided into four categories consistent with the level of conservation implemented: special, general, protected and controlled. The park authority (Ente Parco) provides a number of information centres which dispense advice and guidance about footpaths and nature trails *(see Location)*. The office at Cesarò organises free guided walks of different grades and duration, especially in summer: book first by phone.

Where to Eat

• *For all budgets*

CASTELBUONO

Vecchio Palmento – *Via Failla 2, Castelbuono – ☎ 0921 72 099 – Closed Mon – €15/25.* This simple, family-run restaurant has a number of dining rooms, as well as a delightful garden (unfortunately by the road) where meals are served in the summer. The menu features a number of typical Madonie specialities.

Nangalarruni – *Via delle Confraternite 5, Castelbuono – ☎ 0921 67 14 28 – Closed Wed and for 2 weeks in Nov – €20/34.* This typical local restaurant serves delicious regional cuisine. The main dining room, dating from the mid-18C, is an attractive blend of exposed brickwork, old wooden beams and bottles lined up on shelves and around the chimney piece.

Romitaggio – *Loc. San Guglielmo, 5km/3mi S of Castelbuono – ☎ 0921 67 13 23 – Closed Wed and 15 Jun-15 Jul – ⊭ – €22/27.* Housed in a former 14C monastery, this restaurant has retained the simple, rustic style of its original building. Traditional local cuisine is served in a pleasant inner courtyard in the summer months.

GALATI MAMERTINO

Antica Filanda – *Contrada Parrazzi, Galati Mamertino – ☎ 0941 43 47 15 – Closed Wed and 15 Jan-15 Feb – ⊭ – €23/27.* Genuine regional specialities are the order of the day in this friendly, rural style trattoria offering excellent value for money.

SAN MARCO D'ALUNZIO

La Fornace – *Via Cappuccini 115, San Marco D'Alunzio – ☎ 0941 79 72 97 – info@lafornaceristorante.it – Closed Mon (in winter) – €10/22.* A popular address for gourmets who are more concerned with the quality of the cuisine than the elegance of their surroundings. This restaurant is renowned for its *maccheroni al ragù* and char-grilled meat.

Where to Stay

SANT'AGATA DI MILITELLO

• *Budget*

Villa Nicetta – *Contrada Nicetta, Acquedolci, 6km/4mi SW of Sant'Agata di Militello – ☎ 0941 72 61 42 – Fax 0941 72 61 42 – ⊭ – 10 rooms. €31/62* ☕. This old house dating from 1700 is surrounded by old barns, olive presses and other farm buildings, now transformed into tastefully decorated accommodation for guests. The perfect base for a relaxing holiday, with horse-riding and mountain biking available.

CASTELBUONO

• *Budget*

Hotel Milocca – *Contrada Piano Castagna, 7km/4.5mi SW of Castelbuono – ☎ 0921 67 19 44 – Fax 0921 67 14 37 – albergomilocca@libero.it – P 🏊 – 54 rooms. €41/62* ☕. A narrow road leads through holm oak woods to this isolated hotel which enjoys magnificent views of the Aeolian Islands and where each room has its own individual style. Local cuisine is to the fore in the restaurant.

• *Moderate*

Agriturismo Masseria Rocca di Gonato – *Località Eremo di Liccia, 8km/5mi S of Castelbuono – ☎ 0921 67 26 16 – roccadigonato@hotmail.com – Closed Tue – ⊭ 11 rooms, half board. €57 – Restaurant. €19.* This typical mountain *agriturismo* enjoys an isolated location with panoramic views within the Parco delle Madonie. The spacious rooms are furnished with basic creature comforts and the restaurant serves local cuisine, including meat produced on the farm.

CASTEL DI TUSA

• *Expensive*

Albergo Atelier sul Mare – *Via Cesare Battisti 4, Castel di Tusa – ☎ 0921 33 42 95 – Fax 0921 33 42 83 – ateliersulmare@interfree.it – 40 rooms. €75/160* ☕. This hotel-cum-museum provides an original approach to art, with guests rooms decorated by artists of international renown. *For further information, see p 235.*

GANGI

• *Budget*

Villa Rainò – *Contrada Rainò, Gangi – ☎ 0921 64 46 80 – Fax 0921 64 49 00 – villaraino@citiesonline.it – Closed Jul – – 15 rooms. €50/60 ☕ – Restaurant. €19.* Access to this delightful hotel is via a rather awkward descent along a narrow road. The effort is well worth it, as the hotel has 15 tastefully decorated rooms and a restaurant serving typical regional cuisine.

• *Moderate*

Tenuta Agrituristica Gangivecchio – *Contrada Gangi Vecchio, 4km/2.5mi from Gangi – ☎ 0921 68 91 91 – Fax 0921 68 91 91 – paolotornabene@interfree.it – Closed Jul – 9 rooms. €45/90 ☕.* This 14C Benedictine monastery was purchased by an aristocratic family at the beginning of the 18C and converted into a hotel in 1978. Guest rooms are housed in the main building, as well as in the converted stables. A delightful guesthouse with a fascinating history.

SAN MAURO CASTELVERDE

• *Moderate*

Agriturismo Flugy Ravetto – *Contrada Ogliastro, San Mauro Castelverde – ☎ 0921 67 41 28 – aziendeflugyravetto@aziendeflugyravetto.com – Closed Tue – – 6 apartments, half board. €62 ☕ – Restaurant. €19.50.* The former fief of Ogliastro and Parrinello, now owned by Baronessa Flugy, is located on a gentle hill. The family property now has six comfortable apartments for rent, with a swimming pool and play area for children. The perfect setting for a relaxing stay.

Festivals

Museo domestico – As part of the Fiumara d'arte project *(see below)*, a large canvas painted by dozens of artists is laid along the streets of participating villages, which vary from year to year. The event usually takes place in June. *For further information, contact the Atelier sul Mare, ☎ 0921 33 42 95; www.nebro.net/ateliersulmare/index.html*

Madonna della Luce – Annually, on 7 and 8 September, Mistretta celebrates its *Madonna of Light* festival when a Madonna is borne aloft in solemn procession, escorted by two giant figures representing Mythia and Kronos (the legendary founders of Mistretta). At one time, an ugly, deformed dwarf – *i figghiu ri gesanti* – also took part, but this was discontinued because, it is said, he frightened the young women in early stages of pregnancy.

Tours

The itineraries proposed below follow **scenic routes★★** which, depending on the direction in which they are followed, provide a completely different set of views.

THE HEART OF THE MADONIE 1

160km/100mi round trip starting from Cefalù – allow one day.

Cefalù★★ *See CEFALÙ.*

Take the road out of Cefalù along the coast eastwards, enjoying the views of the look out tower on the promontory. A signpost a little further on indicates the road, right, for Castelbuono *(22km/14mi)*.

Castelbuono

This charming town grew up in the 14C around the **castle** built by the **Ventimiglia** family, a massive square construction with square towers, which has undergone many alterations over the years. At the very heart of the town is Piazza Margherita, which is overlooked by the Church of Madrice Vecchia and the old **Banca di Corte**. This currently accommodates the local **Museo Civico**, pending its relocation to the castle as soon as restoration work is completed. Its collections include treasures

Taking a Break

Extra Bar Fiasconaro – Piazza Margherita 10, Castelbuono, ☎ 0921 67 12 31. This bar sells the most delicious *panettone* (traditional Christmas cake), *colomba* (dove-shaped Easter cake) and, in summer, *ciambelle* (almond doughnuts). Also available if ordered in advance is the local speciality, *testa di turco* ("Turk's head"), made from bread dough stuffed with pork, ricotta cheese, eggs, cocoa and cinnamon.

Shopping

Manna – Small, whitish, slightly sweet stalactites hanging from ash trees, manna is an exudation from these trees which, when dried, is collected and used as a sweetener and a laxative. Although once one of the town's sources of income, it is now more of a curiosity sought by tourists, who can find it at the tobacconist's at the end of Corso Umberto I (virtually in Piazza Margherita).

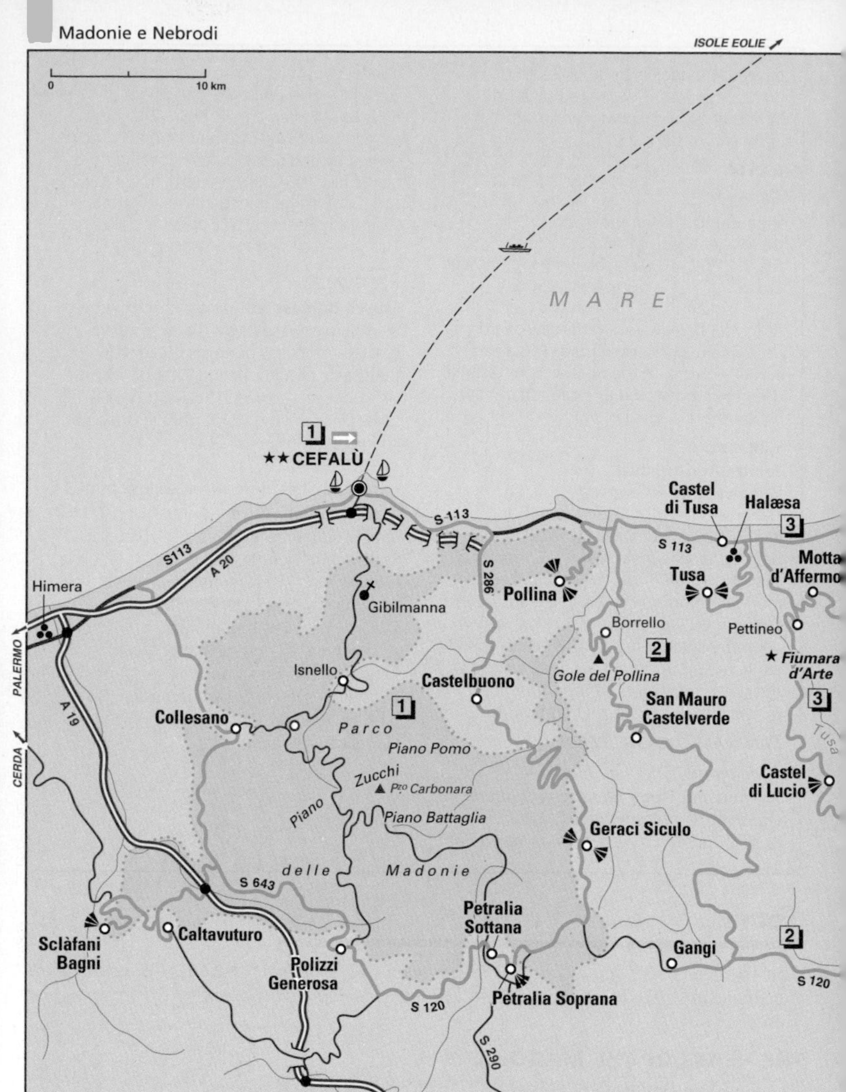

and furnishings from the Cappella Palatina *(see below)* and a fine selection of contemporary paintings, mainly by Italian artists. *Open summer, 9am-1pm and 4-8pm; otherwise, 9am-1pm and 4-7pm. Closed Mon afternoon. €5. ☎ 0921 67 34 67.*

Madrice Vecchia – Built in the 14C on the ruins of a pagan temple, the church has a Renaissance portico, added in the 16C, and a splendid central portal in the Catalan style. On the left side rises a campanile with a fine Romanesque two-arched bell opening, culminating in an octagonal spire covered with maiolica tiles. The interior, originally built as a nave with flanking aisles, was enlarged in the late 15C to its present plan with four aisles. It preserves several rare works of art, the most remarkable, above the high altar, being a splendid **polyptych★** depicting *The Coronation of the Virgin*, attributed to Pietro Ruzzolone (or possibly Antonello del Saliba). Note, in the bottom right, the unusual figure of a saint wearing spectacles. To the right is a statue of the *Madonna delle Grazie* by **Antonello Gagini**. Below the north aisle, the fresco of the *Sposalizio delle Vergini* (Betrothal of the Virgins) shows a strong Sienese influence in the elegant features and the symmetry of the composition.

A few of the columns separating the aisles are painted with frescoes; among these is the figure of St Catherine of Alexandria, characterised by her poise and delicate features. The crypt is entirely decorated with 17C frescoes depicting episodes from the Passion, Death and Resurrection of Christ.

Take Via Sant'Anna up to the castle.

Through the Gothic arch appears the massive form of the **castle** with a square tower at each of its four corners. The **Cappella Palatina**, on the second floor of

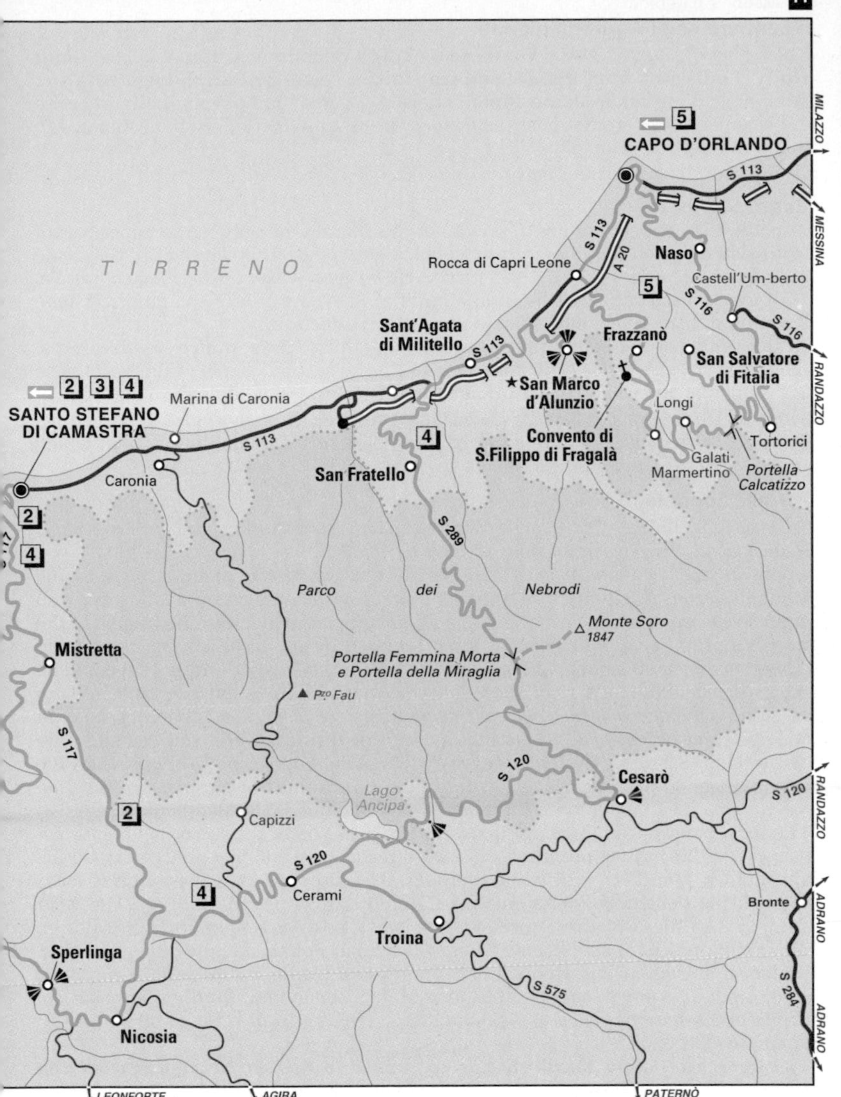

the **castle,** is decorated with some enchanting **stuccowork★** picked out from a gold-leaf background, attributed to Giuseppe Serpotta (1683), the brother of the more famous Giacomo. *Open summer, 9am-1pm and 5-8pm; otherwise, 9am-1pm and 4-7pm. Closed Mon afternoon. No charge.*

Via Roma leads off from Piazza Margherita.

Museo Francesco Minà-Palumbo – *Via Roma. Open summer, 9am-1pm and 5-8pm; otherwise, 9am-1pm and 4-7pm. Closed Mon afternoon. No charge. ☎ 0921 67 65 96.* Currently housed in the precincts of a former Benedictine convent, the **museum** evolved from the passion for botany of **Francesco Minà-Palumbo**, a doctor living in the 19C. The result is a lifetime's assemblage of conscientious and systematic collection, classification and representation on paper of the botanical species, reptiles and insects of the nearby Madonie mountains, some of which are now extinct.

A little further on is the church of **San Francesco** together with its extension, the **Mausoleo dei Ventimiglia**, a late medieval octagonal structure known as **la Madrice Nuova**, which contains a fine *Deposition from the Cross* by Giuseppe Velasco, and Baroque altars with spiral columns by Vincenzo Messina. In Corso Umberto I is the **Fontana di Venere Ciprea** (reconstructed in 1614), with Andromeda *(at the top),* Venus and Cupid in the central niche and four bas-reliefs depicting the myth of Artemis (Diana) and Actaeon.

Leave Castelbuono and follow signs for San Guglielmo and Rifugio Sempria, where the car can be left.

Il Sentiero degli Agrifogli giganti

3.5km/2mi – allow 2hr 30min. For those seeking a ramble away from it all, the **Giant Holly Trail** leads from **Piano Sempria** along a beautiful path through woods of holm and young oak to **Piano Pomo** where a congregation of giant holly trees are to be found; these are not bushes but huge trees 15m/50ft tall, some estimated to be more than 300 years old.

The road continues onwards towards Geraci Siculo 22km/14mi.

Geraci Siculo

A medieval quality continues to prevail in this hamlet, notably in the upper part of town riddled with a maze of narrow cobbled streets. All that survives of the castle built for the Marchesi Ventimiglia *(accessible by road – turn right by the entrance to the town)* is a sad ruin and the little church of Sant'Anna, once the family chapel. From here, marvellous **views**★ extend in every direction.

At the centre of the community stands the Gothic **Chiesa Madre**, its nave separated from its side aisles by a stone arcade. In the second chapel of the north aisle is a Madonna and Child by **Antonello Gagini**, commissioned by the Ventimiglia.

The road from Geraci to Petralia *(14km/9mi)* proceeds through a glorious, sweeping, open landscape with lovely **views**★ of the mountains, the high outcrop on which Enna is perched, and Mount Etna.

Petralia Soprana

To visit the Chiesa Madre and other churches, contact the local police (Polizia Municipale) a few days in advance. ☎ 0921 64 10 88.

Upper Petralia stands at 1 147m/3 762ft, making it the highest town in the Madonie. From its situation, it appears to survey the surrounding landscape and open space, enjoying the unforgettable all-encompassing views. The origins of the town seem to go back to Petra, a town founded by the Sicani which they could defend from enemy attack. In feel, however, it remains rooted firmly in the Middle Ages, thanks to the local regulation dictating that all houses must be built in natural stone. The narrow streets weave between austere *palazzi* and churches, all built of local stone, occasionally opening out into picturesque little squares and onto breathtaking scenery. The **Belvedere** (by Piazza del Popolo) probably provides the best vantage point from which to survey the **panorama**★★ that takes in Enna *(on the far left)*, Resuttano, Monte Cammarata and Madonna dall'Alto *(on the right)*.

The focal point of the town is **Piazza del Popolo** where the town hall is located, occupying the former premises of a Dominican convent that retains its Gothic appearance, complete with pointed arches. The street to the Chiesa Madre leads through the delightful Piazza Quattro Cannoli past its stone fountain. The right flank of the **Chiesa Madre**, preceded by a lovely portico, is open for all to admire. The **view** from here extends over Piano Battaglia, Polizzi, Mount Etna and Enna. **Inside**, it shelters a fine wooden crucifix by **Frà Umile da Petralia** *(right of the altar)* and a lovely wooden altar carved by Bencivinni in the Cappella del Santissimo Sacramento *(left of the main altar)*. The rear wall is taken up by an 18C organ case.

The Church of **Santa Maria di Loreto** stands on the site of a former Saracen fortress. Its convex front elevation, framed between two bell towers, was designed by the Serpotta brothers. The large altarpiece inside, depicting the Madonna and Child, is attributed to Giacomo Mancini (15C). From behind the church extends a splendid **panorama**★★★ with views of Mount Etna.

Another church, dedicated to the Great Redeemer **(Santissimo Salvatore)** conforms to an elliptical plan and has an 18C decoration. It contains a wooden figure of St Joseph by Quattrocchi and, in the sacristy, two works by **Giuseppe Salerno** *(see p 232)*: *St Catherine of Alexandria* and the *Madonna with a Cat*; both pictures show an intimacy and gentleness that is unusual for this painter.

Petralia Sottana

Despite its name, Lower Petralia is perched on a rocky spur 1 000m/3 300ft above sea-level, in a lovely position overlooking the valley of the River Imera. Corso Paolo Agliata, where the headquarters of the Madonie Park Authority (Ente Parco delle Madonie) are located, leads past the church of **Santa Maria della Fontana** with its lovely 15C doorway. Further along the same street stands **San Francesco**, with its fine bell tower rising from a pointed arch; inside, it contains a number of paintings by Giuseppe Salerno. *To visit the church, contact the parish priest.*

As the street curves round to the right, the eye is drawn to the bell tower-cum-archway of the Chiesa della Misericordia inlaid with a meridian line. A little further on lies Piazza Umberto I and the **Chiesa Madre** (17C), an imposing building overlooking the valley. The internal space is articulated into nave and flanking aisles by a series of monolithic stone columns. There are various paintings by **Giuseppe Salerno** *(see p)* here including a *Triumph of the Eucharist (first altar on the left)* and *The Five Wounds of Our Lord* (once erroneously thought to be a *Deposition*). In the chapel to the right of the high altar is preserved a picture of the *Nativity*: the delicate rendering of the Christ Child is by **Antonello Gagini**.

G. Bludzin/MICHELIN

Petralia Sottana

Continue on through the bell tower-cum-archway, uphill to the 16C **Chiesa della Trinità** (sometimes called la Badia). A fine Gothic doorway leads through into the church which gives pride of place to a large 23-panel **marble altarpiece**★ by **Giandomenico Gagini**. The central section shows the Mystery of Easter; this is surrounded by the Trinity *(above)*, the Crucifixion, the Resurrection and the Ascension. The lateral panels *(top left to bottom right)* relate incidents from the life of Christ. At the end of the nave, on the right, stands a fine 18C organ. *To visit the church, contact the parish priest.*

Excursion on foot – *Allow 3hr 30min to the top.* On the northern edge of Petralia, a track worn by pilgrims leads up to the **Santuario della Madonna dell'Alto** (1 819m/5 966ft). This houses a painting of the Virgin and Child from 1471.

Proceed to Polizzi Generosa (20km/12mi).

Polizzi Generosa

Like the other preceding hilltop towns, Polizzi enjoys a splendid **situation**★, sitting on a limestone spur dominating the northern and southern slopes of the Imera Valley. The most suggestively Romantic view may be glimpsed on crisp mornings when low cloud *(la maretta)* collects around the foot of the mountains, shrouding the base in shadow while the tops, caught in the sunshine, appear to float on the mist.

Despite the town's elusive origins, it seems to have played an active role in ejecting the Arab invader: **Roger II** had a castle built and prepared defences against an attack from the infidels. Later, Frederick II was so impressed by the warmth of hospitality extended to him on his visit that he bestowed the title of *Generosa* on the little town.

A good place from which to begin a tour of the town is the main piazza, marked by the ruins of the castle on the highest point (917m/3 008ft). Also located on the piazza is the Palazzo Notarbartolo (16C) which houses the **Museo Ambientalistico Madonita**. This natural history collection is presented as a series of reconstructed natural habitats (note that the preserved animals died of natural causes or were retrieved from poachers): the flora and fauna are displayed in tableaux that range from the water in the bottom of the valley (the river as it was 30-40 years ago) to the highest peaks in the Madonie range; intermediate stages include woodland, beech forest (1 300m/4 250ft-1 800m/5 900ft) and the fauna that thrives at the lower and higher altitudes, including vultures (notably the griffon vulture which disappeared in the 1920s) and golden eagles. ♿ *Open summer, 9am-1pm, afternoons by appointment; for admission times at other times of year, call* ☎ *0921 64 94 78. €4; www.mam.pa.it*

Via Roma leads downhill past Palazzo Gagliardo (16C-17C) and, opposite, the **Chiesa Madre**, which although largely dating from the 19C, still preserves a number of earlier features from the 14C-15C (portico and pointed arch). Inside, it contains a number of works of art: a Flemish triptych *(presbytery)* and a lovely *Madonna of the Rosary* by **Giuseppe Salerno** – one of the two Zoppi di Gangi *(see p 232)*. *Closed for restoration at the time of going to press.*

Beyond lies Piazza Umberto I. From here, Via Garibaldi leads to San Girolamo with its fine Baroque doorway before finally terminating at Piazza XXVII Maggio. This square offers a dramatic **view**★★★ that pans across the highest peaks of the

Madonie: in the centre is the northern valley of the River Himera (along which the motorway runs today); to the left, sits Rocca di Caltavuturo, Monte Calogero (right in the middle, in the far distance) and Monte Cammarata; the far right is marked by the Dolomite-like profile of Quacella, followed by Monte Mufara and Pizzo Carbonara. Almost directly opposite extends the lower section of the Massicio dei Cervi, known as the *Padella* (meaning a frying pan). According to local tradition, this is where a secret entrance leads into a cave full of treasure, the whereabouts of which may only be revealed during Easter Mass. Below lies the Valle dei Noccioleti.

Taking a Break

Pasticceria al Castello – *Piazza Castello 10, Polizzi Generosa* – ☎ *0921 68 85 28.* This *pasticceria* produces excellent pastries and cakes including the typical *sfoglio polizzano*, a type of local millefeuille made with *fromage frais*, sugar, chocolate and cinnamon, which is traditionally eaten during the third week of July as part of the **Sagra dello sfoglio**.

Continue on down to the coast along S 643 for approximately 15km/9mi; at the fork, turn left towards Caltavuturo (25km/15mi from Polizzi).

The road runs through a delightful, varied **landscape★** of bare tracts of mountain alternating with gentle green slopes and steep limestone escarpments.

Caltavuturo

Clinging to the foot of the Rocca di Sciara, the "Fortress of the Vulture" – derived from the Arabic (*qalaat*, fortress) and the Sicilian vernacular (*vuturo*, vulture) – preserves a few prized 16C works of art in the **Chiesa Madre**. These include an attractive *Madonna of the Rosary surrounded by the Mysteries,* executed by followers of Pietro Novelli and, at the back of the church, a fine Baroque organ by Raffaele della Valle.

Leave Caltavuturo by S 120 towards Cerda; at the fork, turn left for Sclàfani Bagni (10km/6mi).

Sclàfani Bagni

Crouched on the edge of a rocky crag in a wonderful **position★**, the little hamlet retains a certain medieval quality. The entrance is boldly marked by the **Porta Soprana**, a gate comprising a pointed arch surmounted by the Sclàfani family coat of arms. On the left sits the *castelletto*, probably conceived as a defensive tower. Just beyond stands the **Chiesa Madre,** graced with a decorative Gothic doorway (15C). Inside, it contains a painting entitled *L'Agonizzante* by the Zoppo di Gangi **Giuseppe Salerno** *(see p 232)*, and a sarcophagus carved with a bacchanal from the ancient city of Himera *(see TERMINI IMERESE)*. The organ *(under restoration)* at the back of the church is by Raffaele della Valle (1615).

Up to the right of the church may be seen a tower, the last vestige of the 14C fortifications. From here, a wonderful **view★★** extends across to the Madonie mountains, over the sea below Himera and Caltavuturo.

Return to S 643, following it to Collesano (30km/19mi).

Collesano

The heart of this small holiday resort preserves its original medieval fabric. Its most interesting building is the **Chiesa Madre**, theatrically placed up a great flight of steps. The façade betrays nothing of the marvellous works of art – paintings and sculptures – it conceals within. Above the nave hangs an enormous *Crucifixion*, painted in 1550. A protective case in the south aisle contains a 17C sedan chair. Among the many paintings, look out for *St Catherine* (1596) in one of the first bays in the south aisle, completed by Giuseppe Alvino who was also known as *Il Sozzo* (which literally translates as the Soak!), and more particularly, for works by Zoppo di Gangi **Gaspare Vazzano** *(see p 232)*, such as the wonderful great canvas of **Santa Maria degli Angeli★** *(north aisle)* and the **cycle of frescoes★** in the chancel illustrating scenes from the lives of Christ *(ceiling)* and of St Peter and St Paul *(left and right walls respectively)*. The elegant tabernacle in the south aisle is the work of Donatello Gagini (1489).

The way up to Piazza Gallo, in the oldest part of town, leads past the ruins of the castle, from where a splendid view opens out over the valley bottom and the coast beyond.

From Collesano, turn down towards the coast signposted for Cefalù (17km/10.5mi).

BETWEEN THE MADONIE AND THE NEBRODI 2

180km/112mi round trip starting from Santo Stefano di Camastra – allow one full day.

Santo Stefano di Camastra

Santo Stefano is famous for its hand-painted ceramics and so it comes as no surprise that its streets are lined with a myriad of small shops offering locally made pots, vases, plates and ceramic trinkets to suit every taste and requirement. Its most interesting buildings include **Palazzo Sergio**, which once belonged to the Duke of Camastra, and which now houses the **Museo della Ceramica**. Pride of place in the museum is given to S Lorenzini's *Andare (Departing)* on the right of the entrance. This comprises a group of five warriors gradually "sinking" into the ground. Several rooms in the *palazzo* preserve their original **tiled floors★**, frescoed ceilings and 18C furnishings. *(♿) Open 9am-1pm and 3-8pm. Closed 25 Dec. €2.50. ☎ 0921 33 10 62.*

Outside the town (beyond the Ceramics Institute), lies the **Cimitero Vecchio**: a cemetery that was used for two years only, between 1878 and 1880, and which contains a number of graves ornamented with maiolica.

The road from Santo Stefano to Mistretta *(14km/9mi)* provides magnificent **views** of the valley.

Mistretta

This small hamlet, located 950m/3 000ft above sea-level, is one of the departure points for excursions into the Nebrodi mountains and comprises a collection of simple stone houses grouped around the ruins of a feudal castle: the best vantage point from which to enjoy the view. A second glance will reveal a clutch of striking buildings including the Church of **San Giovanni** (1530) which is graced with an elegant double stairway and a bell tower with openings at the top.

The front elevation of the 16C **Chiesa Madre**, dedicated to St Lucy (the popular saint martyred in Syracuse), lacks its second bell tower (the left side being incomplete): one can but wonder whether it might have had two bell openings like its counterpart on the right. Although partly rebuilt in the 17C, it preserves from the original a fine marble doorway *(right side)*. Inside, a chapel dedicated to the Madonna shelters a *Madonna of Miracles* attributed to Giorgio da Milano; a larger side chapel honouring St Lucy contains a fine altarpiece by **Antonello Gagini** with statues of St Lucy, St Peter and St Paul (1552). The elegant choir stalls behind the main altar are 17C, the organ is 18C.

At the top of the town stands the Renaissance Church of **Santa Caterina**.

From Mistretta, continue along S 117 as far as the junction with the Troina/Nicosia road, then turn right to Nicosia (30km/19mi).

Nicosia *See NICOSIA.*

8km/5mi further on, the road reaches Sperlinga, a little town overlooked by its castle, backed up against a vertical cliff face.

Sperlinga

The compact hamlet stretches along the side of a spur of rock shaped like an upturned ship's keel. It seems to have started life as a troglodyte community contemporary with the Sicani; several cave dwellings are open to view below the town. At the highest point, overlooking the other rooftops, stands the strategically placed **castle-fortress** firmly rooted to the bedrock to which it clings. On the way up to the castle entrance, there are two spacious caves that were once furnished as stables; today they house a small ethno-anthropological museum. Through the first gateway stands a second archway, this time consisting of a pointed arch with an inscription above extolling the virtue of the town: *Quod Siculis placuit, sola Sperlinga negavit* ("That which pleased the Sicilians was only rejected by Sperlinga"). The significance of such a proclamation must be sought in history for, in 1282, at the height of the War of the Sicilian Vespers, a band of Frenchmen sought refuge in the castle: instead of being treated as hostages, they were shown kindness and understanding by the town residents. Elsewhere, the episode caused a great outcry.

The castle is built on several levels. The caves excavated from the rock *(to the left of the entrance)* were used for stabling animals, as prison cells and forges and probably for making weapons. At the front is the prince's reception room. Opposite, on

Sperlinga: the castle

Guidorlando/Lara Pessina/MICHELIN

a single level, lies the chapel and the residential quarters: the undercrofts in this section of the castle served as granaries. Centrally placed between the two wings, a steep staircase cut into the bedrock climbs up to the lookout tower: from here the **view★★** pans 360° over the Gangi plateau with the Madonie range behind, the Nebrodi to the north, Mount Etna to the east and the Erei mountains to the west. To the right stretches the long undulating ridge that runs from Monte Grafagna to San Martino, and links up with the Nebrodi mountain chain. *Open 9am-1pm and 4.30-7pm.* ☎ *0935 64 31 98.*

A beautiful scenic road snakes its way towards Gangi, the largest town in the Madonie *(20km/12.5mi).*

Gangi

At one time, Gangi was identified with the ancient Engyum, a Greek town founded by colonists from **Minoa**; the town that survives today has largely evolved since the 14C. Gangi is scattered over the crest of Monte Marone, its picturesque narrow streets lined with stone-built houses which preserve its somewhat medieval character.

Guided Tours

The Gangi Pro Loco organises guided tours of the town. Those interested should book at least a week in advance. For information, contact Corso Umberto I 1; ☎ 0921 50 20 17 (9am-1pm and 3-7pm; closed Mon); www.comune.gangi.pa.it

Città alta – The tree-lined Viale delle Rimembranze, commemorating every soldier killed in the Second World War, leads to the entrance to the higher town. The most obvious point of reference in **Piazza San Paolo** is the simple stone front of the church (16C) dedicated to St Paul, with its fine entrance ornamented with shallow relief decoration. The later Chiesa della Badia (18C) has a similar, bare stone, front elevation. **Corso Umberto I** passes a number of harmonious *palazzi*, including the 19C **Palazzo Mocciaro**, on its way into the centre of town.

The imposing **Palazzo Bongiorno★** was built in the 18C for the ennobled Bongiorno family, one of the wealthiest in the area. Its most endearing feature is the elegant *trompe l'oeil* **frescoes★** in the rooms on the piano nobile. These are by Gaspare Fumagalli, a painter from Rome who was active in Palermo around the mid-18C, and comprise a series of allegorical subjects, both sacred and profane *(Modesty, The Triumph of Christianity, Time)* set within an elaborate framework of architectural elements, ornamented with masks, volutes and medallions containing pastoral landscapes. *Open daily except Mon, 8.30am-1pm and 3.30-7pm. No charge.* ☎ *0921 50 20 17; www.comune.gangi.pa.it*

The town's main square is the **Piazza del Popolo**, overshadowed by the **Torre Ventimiglia★**. This tower was erected in the 13C as a watchtower; in the 15C it came into the possession of the Knights of Malta; it was transformed into a bell tower in the 17C when the Chiesa Madre was built. It is Norman Gothic in style and has a pointed arcade portico along the street side, with attractive three-light, double-arch windows above.

In a corner of the piazza is a small grotto with a fountain, the Fontana del Leone (1931).

The **Chiesa Madrice**, the town's main church, was erected in the 17C on the foundations of an older oratory; inside, are several significant works of art. The eye is immediately drawn to the huge canvas occupying the left side of the chancel. This depicts ***The Last Judgement★*** (1629), the main masterpiece of Giuseppe Salerno, which is modelled on Michelangelo's Sistine Chapel in Rome *(see The Green Guide Rome)*, among others: common elements include the standing figure of Christ, the skin of St Bartholomew, a self-portrait of the artist, and the figure of Charon, the devil's ferryman. The level beneath is divided into two: to the left, stand the Elect with the Archangel Michael; to the right, are shown the Damned, with the jaws of

The Popular Epithet: Zoppo di Gangi

The last work of **Gaspare Vazzano** (or Bazzano), a cycle of frescoes in the Chiesa Madre at Collesano, is clearly signed "Zoppo di Gangi". Vazzano was born in Gangi in the latter part of the 16C and, despite being trained as a painter in Palermo, always gravitated towards the towns of the Madonie mountains in search of work. The other painter with whom he shares his nickname (which translates as "The Lame Man of Gangi") was a contemporary, also from Gangi, **Giuseppe Salerno**. It remains difficult to ascertain the relationship enjoyed by the two artists, despite a recent theory suggesting that Salerno collaborated with Vazzano, at least during his early career as a painter. The common pseudonym might possibly be explained as an act of homage by the pupil, who was a few years younger than Vazzano. The two painters fit into the same artistic movement, yet their styles are quite different. Vazzano's use of tonal colour, gentle facial expression and softer line endow his paintings with a certain sentimentality that contrasts sharply with Salerno's bolder style achieved by a strong use of line and precise draughtsmanship. His intention is to produce a cruder kind of work that dogmatically embodies a concept, a message or a doctrine. These different personalities and distinctive means of artistic expression are the hallmarks of two Sicilian painters who have each left an important legacy to their native land.

Leviathan. Each of the Damned embodies one of the capital sins, its name emblazoned upon a label, sometimes written in Sicilian. The Damned include various religious figures, but there is no priest, as it was a priest who commissioned the work.

The church also contains a number of fine wooden sculptures by Quattrocchi, among them a **San Gaetano★** *(at the far end of the south aisle)*.

From the church forecourt, there is a fine view of the lower part of Gangi including the Torre Saracena on the left and the Capuchin Monastery.

The natural continuation of Corso Umberto I, Corso Fedele Vitale, is lined with "Roman shops" **(botteghe romane)** that date from the 16C – so called because they have next to the doorway a window and counter through which goods are sold.

A little further up the street, Palazzo Sgadari houses the local **museum** with displays of archaeological artefacts from Monte Alburchia. *Open daily except Mon, 8.20am-1pm and 3.30-7.30pm. No charge. ☎ 0921 68 99 07; www.comune.gangi.pa.it*

At the far end sits the square mass of **Castello dei Ventimiglia**.

Città bassa – Return to Piazza del Popolo so as to turn down Via Madrice (stepped) and find the **Chiesa del Santissimo Salvatore**. This contains a wooden Crucifix by Fra' Umile da Petralia and a painting by Giuseppe Salerno entitled *On the Road to Calvary*, which reflects the influence of Raphael's *Spasimo di Sicilia* commissioned for the Chiesa dello Spasimo in Palermo.

A little further down hill stands the **Chiesa di Santa Maria di Gesù**, which originally comprised a Benedictine Hospice (15C). The bell tower, dating from the same period, is relieved by single and two-arch openings. The façade of the church has an attractive doorway ornamented with shallow reliefs. Inside, there are several works by Quattrocchi, most notably a wooden group representing *The Annunciation*.

Santuario dello Spirito Santo – *About 1.5km/1mi S of Gangi on the Casalgiordano road.* A popular local story relates how, in the 16C, a deaf mute labourer was working in the fields when he came across an image of Christ painted on a rock, and miraculously began to speak. On the very spot the miracle occurred, a sanctuary was built; this continues to attract pilgrims from far and wide. Today, the image on the rock is masked by the painting behind the altar by Vazzano.

From Gangi, it is possible to continue along S 120 to link up with itinerary 1, *extending it with a drive to Petralia Sottana (15km/9mi).*

Alternatively, if proceeding with itinerary 2, *make your way back for about 3km/2mi to the fork and turn left towards San Mauro Castelverde (approximately 30km/19mi from Gangi).*

San Mauro Castelverde

On a clear day, this ideally situated little hamlet enjoys a range of bird's-eye **views★★** from its own hilltop across to the Aeolian Islands and the Nebrodi and Madonie mountain ranges (visible from Piano San Giorgio in the higher part of the town).

The centre is typically medieval in feel and layout. The church, **Santa Maria dei Franchi** (13C), and its 18C bell tower are surrounded by tortuous narrow streets like a beetle caught in a web. Inside, it contains a Madonna by **Domenico Gagini** and a font by **Antonello Gagini**. *To visit the church, contact the Ufficio Relazioni del Comune a few days in advance. ☎ 0921 67 40 83.*

Follow the road to Borrello. After Borrello Alto, follow signs to Gangi-San Mauro (left). After approximately 1km/0.6mi, a signpost on the right indicates the Case Tiberio U' Miricu.

Le Gole di Pollina

Follow the small road to a fork, then turn left. The asphalt peters out at this point and it is best to park and proceed on foot. A little further on, follow the paved road on the right to the flight of over 400 steps leading to the gorge.

The gorge is particularly impressive in summer when the lack of water makes the river bed accessible, allowing visitors to walk in between the overhanging cliff faces.

Head back to Borrello and continue down towards the coast: at the fork, turn left, following the coast road. Turn right along the road signposted for Pollina.

Pollina

The hilltop town of Pollina is in a perfect **position★** to enjoy picture-postcard **views★** of the coast below. The **Chiesa Madre** (16C) sitting at the heart of a complicated network of medieval streets, preserves within various prized works of art including an attractive and engaging **Nativity★** by **Antonello Gagini**. In the Middle Ages, the top of the town was marked by a castle: today only a square tower remains. Alongside, a theatre has recently been built according to ancient Greek and Roman prototypes, complete with spectacular **panoramic views★★** over the mountain landscape and the sea; a winding road leads from the theatre all the way to the coast.

Continue back down towards the coast and Cefalù. Signs on the right indicate the way to Tusa and thereby to the archaeological site of Halaesa which lies before the village itself.

Halaesa

The remains of Halaesa are to be found just beyond the chapel of Santa Maria di Palate. The little town was originally founded by the Siculi in the 5C BC; later it passed first into Greek then Roman hands, before being completely destroyed by the Arabs. **Excavations** have revealed the precincts of a Roman forum complete with its associated sanctuaries, a patrician family house and sections of bastions along the enclosure walls from the Greek era; opposite, a temple is supposed to have stood, occupying a strategic position above the River Tusa. Another temple was located at the top of the hill *(closed to the public). Open 9am-2hr before dusk. €2. ☎ 0921 33 45 31.*

Tusa

8km/5mi S of Halaesa. This little town, which enjoys a fabulous position high on the brow of a hill, was probably founded by the people who managed to escape Halaesa as it was being ransacked and razed by the Arabs. The upper part of the town preserves its medieval appearance. Access to it is through the main gateway. This is where the most interesting churches are to be found, including the **Chiesa Madre** with its entrance set in a decorative pointed arch. Inside, a delicate marble *Annunciation* from the Renaissance (1525) ornaments the altar; the wooden choir stalls carved with dragons, cherubs and masks are 17C; the *Madonna and Child* is by followers of Gagini. Alongside the church rises a free-standing bell tower. Nestling among the other narrow streets is the little stone Church of San Nicola with its distinctive tile-topped campanile.

Return to the coast road. At this point you can either continue the tour by following the itinerary described below, or return to Santo Stefano di Camastra (9km/5.5mi).

LA FIUMARA D'ARTE★ 3

80km/50mi, starting at Santo Stefano di Camastra – allow at least half a day.

Fiumara d'Arte literally translates as River of Art (*fiumara* means 'a broad river'). An appropriate name, given that it consists of an unusual attempt at exhibiting contemporary sculpture in a kind of open-air museum, following the course of the River Tusa. The project was the brainchild of Antonio Presti, who also founded the *Atelier sul mare* hotel-cum-museum *(see below)*. Not only does the initiative take best advantage of the natural landscape to arrive at a symbiosis of art and nature, it provides interested visitors to the area an opportunity of exploring and appreciating in a highly original way a series of secluded and little-known places off the beaten track. The scheme, which was initiated only a few years ago and continues to evolve, has already secured the cooperation of a number of contemporary artists from both Italy and abroad.

From Santo Stefano di Camastra, follow S 113 towards Palermo.

The first gigantic sculpture looms into sight on the right, standing on the beach of Villa Marigi. Tano Festa's *Monument to a Dead Poet* (1990) is conceived as a type of window looking out to sea and to infinity; like the two elements (sea and sky) that surround it, it is blue.

Continue a few kilometres along S 113, then turn left to Pettineo.

On the right, set in the middle of the almost permanently dry river bed, stands the second work: Pietro Consagra's *Matter could have not existed* (1986), consisting of two reinforced concrete sections on two levels, one white, the other black, creating a type of complex line. The **scenic road★** climbs up into the Nebrodi mountains providing **good views★** over the landscape. Before long, evidence of humankind dwindles and disappears, giving way in its stead to the overriding presence of nature. All along the sides of the road, the olive trees are contorted into forms resembling tortured, imprisoned souls; these make way for a sun-drenched landscape ablaze with startlingly yellow bushes of flowering broom. **Pettineo** crouches on the top of a small hill. Beyond it on the left, just before Castel di Lucio, stands a work by Paolo Schiavocampo entitled *A Curve Thrown After Time (1990)*, shrouded in silence. At last **Castel di Lucio** comes into view; a sign on the left points to Italo Lanfredini's *Ariadne's Labyrinth* (1990) standing lonely on a hill *(as the road turns in a hairpin bend to the left, keep straight on)*. This windswept cement and clay maze enclosed on all sides by a succession of towering mountains enjoys a fabulous **location★**. At the Carabinieri station in Castel di Lucio, note Piero Dorazio and Graziano Marini's ***Arethusa*** (1990), made from polychrome ceramic panels.

Back down on the main road, follow the winding road to **Mistretta** *(see above)* to view one of the last artistic creations: *The Ceramic Wall* (1993), a work to which some 40 artists contributed.

The Hidden work of Art

One other work deserves a mention: ***The Room of the Golden Boat*** by Hidetoshi Nagasawa shelters within a cave on the bed of the River Romei *(near Mistretta)*. Inside, the rock is entirely faced with plates of polished steel – most disorientating. Somewhere within the enclosed space, a pink marble tree has been "planted" in the ground, on which the shell of an overturned boat has been built, and covered in gold leaf. This work, however, is not intended to be seen: the reason for its existence lies in the fact that it exists at all. As such, we are encouraged not to go and see it, but merely to imagine it.

After Mistretta, a road forks left towards **Motta d'Affermo**, where Antonio Di Palma's blue wave entitled *Mediterranean Energy* (1990) dominates the landscape. Head back down towards the sea to the *Atelier sul Mare* hotel in **Castel di Tusa**.

Atelier sul Mare – *Via Cesare Battisti 4, Castel di Tusa. Guided tours of the art rooms, 11am-noon. €3. ☎ 0921 33 42 95, www.ateliersulmare.com.* In this hotel-cum-museum Antonio Presti, among the prime instigators and promoters of the Fiumara project, has made several rooms available to artists and allowed them to transform them into works of art in their own right. The idea is to create an interaction between the existing work, which with time becomes inert and part of the everyday furnishing, and the artist who during his/her stay will contemplate and inwardly digest the decor before responding with his/her personal touch. The predominant theme is water – the sea, treated as a fundamental element and purifier of life, the return to man's basic origins and hence to humankind's very existence. Each artist interprets this idea in different ways. Every guest is given the choice of the passionate red of *Power* (by Maurizio Machetti), the white of the absorbing *Nest* (by Paolo Icaro), the minimalist *Mystery for the Moon* (by Hidetoshi Nagasawa), the deeply reflective *Denial of the Sea* (by Fabrizio Plessi), or the complicated and crooked *Room of the Prophet*, to name but a few. *For further information, see Directory.*

A DAY IN THE NEBRODI MOUNTAINS 4

Approx 200km/125mi – allow one day

This circuit may also be undertaken from Sant'Agata Militello, although it is worth doing it in an anti-clockwise direction so as to enjoy the best views of Mount Etna, notably those savoured from Lago Ancipa. For the first part of the tour, from Santo Stefano di Camastra to Mistretta (14km/9mi), see itinerary 2.

From Mistretta follow S 117 to the Nicosia/Troina fork, then turn left to Troina.

Troina

A medieval citadel perched high above the town's rooftops shelters Troina's main church: sadly, only the bell tower survives from the original Norman building (11C), built in blocks of sandstone spanning the road.

From Troina, return towards Cerami so as to turn right down to Lago Ancipa (approximately 8km/5mi from Troina).

Lago Ancipa

This man-made lake, formed when the great San Teodoro dam (120m/394ft) was built, lies in a glorious stretch of countryside. The road skirts the lake before leading on to Cesarò *(25km/16mi)*. Although narrow and badly rutted in places, it picks its way scenically through woods and along open valleys, providing unforgettable **views**★★ of Mount Etna.

Cesarò

The town is overshadowed by the volcano. Just outside the hamlet, follow the signs for Cristo sul Monte from where a wonderful but haunting **view**★★ extends across to Mount Etna.

S 289 twists and turns up to the narrow pass, Portella della Miraglia and Portella della Femmina Morta, through the mountain scenery and extensive beech woods. At the top of the pass, a dirt track leads up to the summit of **Monte Soro**, the highest peak in the Nebrodi mountains (1 847m/6 058ft).

Continue along the scenic road to San Fratello (35km/22mi from Cesarò).

San Fratello

This town, founded by a group of Lombard settlers, was partly destroyed by a landslide in the 18C. San Fratello is linked by name to the *sanfratellani*, a fine breed of horse, examples of which may be spotted roaming freely on the edge of town. The San Francesco monastery preserves 16C cloisters with fragments of fresco.

On the north side of the hamlet, by the cemetery, a track provides access to a Norman church, the **Chiesa Normanna dei Santi Alfio, Filadelfio e Cirino** (11C-12C). A marvellous **view★★** extends over the surrounding landscape from the area behind the church. *Open Mon-Fri, 9am-1pm; Sat-Sun and public hols, by appointment only. ☎ 0941 79 40 30.*

From San Fratello, follow the road back to the coast and turn right for Sant'Agata di Militello (18km/11mi).

Sant'Agata di Militello

This comparatively recent resort has been developed along the seafront with access to a long stretch of beach. The main buildings, the Castello dei Principi Gallego and the adjacent 18C Chiesa dell'Addolorata, are both located on Piazza Crispi. The town has a small natural history museum dedicated to the inland mountain region, the **Museo Etnoantropologico dei Nebrodi** *(Via Cosenz). Open Mon-Fri, 9am-noon and 3-6pm; Sat, by appointment only. No charge. ☎ 0941 72 23 08.*

Sant'Agata is a good place to stay as it is conveniently situated close enough to the mountains for short excursions to escape the summer heat, and within easy range of other coastal sights like Capo d'Orlando to the east, Halaesa and Tusa to the west.

From Sant'Agata follow S 113 to Capo d'Orlando, then turn right to San Marco d'Alunzio (10km/6mi).

San Marco d'Alunzio★

This delightful small town, spectacularly situated 550m/1 800ft above sea level and just 9km/6mi from the coast, enjoys **magnificent views★★** of Cefalù and the Aeolian Islands. Each phase in Sicilian history has left its mark here, with the site occupied by the Greeks and becoming *Municipium Aluntinorum* under the Romans. It was renamed San Marco dei Normanni in memory of the first town conquered by the Normans in Calabria. The local red marble, extracted from nearby quarries, can be seen in many of the buildings in the town.

> **FESTIVAL**
>
> **Processione dei babbaluti** – On the last Friday in March, in celebration of the Passion, the wooden cross of Aracoeli is borne aloft through the town by hooded men singing and praying, known as the *"babbaluti"*.

Before entering the heart of the town itself, isolated on the left of the road stands the Church of **San Marco**. This was built on the foundations of a **temple** dedicated to Heracles (4C BC), of which only a few blocks of tufa stone remain. The church, which is open to the sky, preserves its stone walls and a re-erected doorway.

San Teodoro (or Badia piccola) – San Teodoro was built in the 16C on the site of a Byzantine chapel. It is built on a Greek-cross plan with each square arm enclosed by a little dome. The interior is ornamented with magnificent Serpotta-style **stuccowork★** depicting *Judith and Holofernes, Manna falling from Heaven in the Desert (at the sides of the altar)*, scenes from the parable of the prodigal son; saints and the four Theological Virtues grace the pilasters that rise up to the vault. A number of Hellenistic cisterns and the remains of paving dating from the 2C-3C AD can be seen in the churchyard and in front of the neighbouring museum.

Monastero delle Monache Benedettine – *(♿) Open 9am-1pm and 3-7pm. Closed 1 Jan, Easter and 25 Dec. €1.60. ☎ 0941 79 77 19; www.comune.sanmarcodalunzio.me.it*

Next to San Teodoro, the former Benedictine convent built in 1545 has recently been renovated so as to accommodate a **museum** dedicated to Byzantine-Norman art. On the ground floor, interesting 11C **frescoes★** have been uncovered. Those on the right are very well preserved: the Madonna in the vault has beautifully delicate hands; in the tier below (separated by a clear boundary symbolising the separation of heaven and earth), the four Doctors of the Orthodox Church – St John Chrysostom, St Gregory of Nazianzus, St Basil the Great and St Athanasius – are shown against a bright blue background. Frescoes from other churches in the region are also displayed on the ground floor, while objects discovered in local necropoli can be seen on the first floor.

In the Chiesa di San Giuseppe is the Parish Museum **(Museo Parrocchiale)** whose collections comprise sacred furnishings, wooden reliquaries, a wooden polychrome Madonna, a charming wooden figure representing Mary Magdalene (17C) and a painting of the Deposition (18C). *For information, call ☎ 0941 79 70 45.*

The main street, Via Aluntina, runs through the **historical centre** of San Marco past the Chiesa Madre dedicated to **San Nicolò**, which has an austere façade relieved in part by three doorways in red Alunzio marble, also in profusion inside.

Shopping

La Tela di Penelope – *Via Aluntina 40, San Marco d'Alunzio.* This shop sells a delightful range of handcrafted woven textiles produced on old restored looms. Well worth a visit.

In Piazza Sant'Agostino some way ahead stands **Santa Maria delle Grazie**, which preserves the Filangeri funeral monument by Domenico Gagini (1481) with its fine reclining figure exuding gentle serenity.

Note the 18C **Church of San Basilio** with its arcade of pointed arches on the right, and then continue on to the 17C **Church of Ara Coeli**, graced with a lovely doorway flanked by fluted columns and ornamented with volutes and floral elements. Inside, contained within the **Cappella del Santissimo Crocefisso**, encrusted with fine **stuccowork★** by Serpotta depicting saints, lively cherubs, angels and festoons of fruit, is an expressive 17C Spanish wooden **Crucifix★**. *For information, call ☎ 0941 79 70 45.*

San Salvatore – San Salvatore is also known as the **Badia Grande**, going back to the time it used to adjoin an important Benedictine convent; now alone, it stands in ruins not far from the football pitch. Its elegant **doorway★** made of Alunzio marble is ornamented with columns, angels and cherubs. **Inside**, visitors are greeted by a band of serenading angels playing trumpets, various allegorical figures, playful cherubs bearing heavy drapes, scrolls and garlands of flowers; the exuberant **stucco decoration★** culminates in sumptuous drapery hanging from the wooden canopy over the tabernacle.

Leave San Marco and head back to S 113. Turn left to Santo Stefano di Camastra.

Look out for signs along the road to **Caronia** (*4km/2.5mi inland*) where one of the Parco dei Nebrodi visitor centres is situated *(see p 224)*.

THE EASTERN NEBRODI 5

Approximately 85km/53mi – allow at least half a day.

This itinerary snakes its way inland from Capo d'Orlando on the eastern slopes of the Nebrodi Mountains.

Leave Capo d'Orlando by the coastal road towards Sant'Agata Militello. At Rocca di Capri Leone, turn left towards Frazzanò (17km/11mi S of Capo d'Orlando).

Frazzanò

According to tradition, the town was founded in the 9C AD by people fleeing the Arab invasions. The **Chiesa Madre della Santissima Annunziata** (18C) has a fine Baroque façade ornamented with giant pilasters and an elegant portal with spiral columns, flanked by niches containing statues.

The **Chiesa di San Lorenzo** has a plainer façade relieved by a fine portal with spiral columns and a flurry of sculptural motifs including plant fronds, cherubs and volutes. Inside, there is a fine wooden statue of the church's patron, St Lawrence (1620).

Proceed to the next right turning, signposted for the Convento di San Filippo di Fragalà (4km/2.5mi S of Frazzanò towards Longi).

Convento di San Filippo di Fragalà

The Basilian church, which has recently been restored, was built by Roger I d'Altavilla in the 11C, very probably among the ruins of an earlier monastery dating from the 5C. It is worth pausing to view the exterior of the abbey complex from below: note the three apses in the Arabo-Norman style, articulated by brick pilasters, and the octagonal drum over the intersection of the transepts. The church is T-shaped in plan and inside, particularly in the central apse, there are traces of Byzantine-style frescoes.

The adjoining monastic buildings are also open to the public.

The road continues to Portella Calcatizzo. Beyond the town, turn left at the fork towards San Salvatore di Fitalia (approximately 20km/12mi from San Filippo di Fragalà).

San Salvatore di Fitalia

Perched high among the Nebrodi Mountains, this small town has a fine church (1515) dedicated to **San Salvatore**. The exterior is somewhat severe, but the interior comes as a surprise; recent restoration has uncovered the 16C structure of the building with its nave separated from the aisles by sandstone columns supporting pointed arches. The fine **capitals** are sculpted with the plant and anthropomorphic motifs so typical of medieval decorative schemes. The capital of the first column on the right, bearing the name of the stonemason who carved it, features a highly unusual mermaid with a forked tail. In the right aisle hangs Antonello Gagini's gentle *Madonna of the Snow* (1521) and, on the high altar, a highly prized **wooden statue of Salvator Mundi★** (Saviour of the World, 1603) at the moment of the Transfiguration.

Museo Siciliano delle Tradizioni Religiose – ♿ *Open Mon-Fri, 9am-1pm; Sat-Sun and public hols, by appointment only. No charge.* ☎ *0941 48 61 72.*

The fascinating **museum of religious practices** documents local popular cults with displays of simple objects, such as amulets against the evil eye, votive objects including a series of anatomical replicas made of wax originally from the Santuario di San Calogero (18C-19C); the *pillole* (meaning pills) consist of tiny squares of paper that were designed to be swallowed by the faithful while they recited prayers requesting divine intervention in the cure of disease or other malady and sheet music used by ballad-singers and terracotta whistles bearing figurative images sold on saints' days. An unusual 17C "priest toy" comprises a doll dressed as a priest complete with all the necessary holy vestments (sadly the liturgical objects have been stolen), reminiscent of the one described in Manzoni's 19C novel *Promessi Sposi (The Betrothed)* belonging to the nun from Monza since childhood. The collection also includes a series of engravings and lithographs of sacred images (17C-20C), special dress worn by the confraternities in sacred processions, various examples of devotional statuary in wood, plaster and terracotta, and small figures for Nativity cribs (19C).

Return to Portella Calcatizzo and Tortorici, then head towards Castell'Umberto. From here, follow S 116 to Naso (28km/17mi from San Salvatore di Fitalia).

Naso

This small town, situated at an altitude of 500m/1 640ft, enjoys superb views of the Aeolian Islands. Founded by the Normans, it was subsequently controlled by the Cardona family before becoming a lordship of the powerful Ventimiglia family.

The central Piazza Garibaldi, with its magnificent **view** of Etna, runs into Piazza Dante and Piazza Roma. The **Chiesa Madre** on Piazza Roma is worthy of note for its *Madonna and Child* painted in Gagini style and housed in the Baroque Cappella del Rosario (*left aisle*).

Follow the right side of the Chiesa Madre into Via degli Angeli.

This street leads to the Chiesa di **San Cono**, founded in the 15C and restored two centuries later. An interesting crypt housing the relics of the church's patron saint can be seen in the catacombs here.

Return to Piazza Roma and take Corso Umberto.

After Piazza Parisi, turn right into Via Belvedere to enjoy another spectacular **view★★** of Etna and the Aeolian Islands.

Follow Via Convento past a small well to the Convento dei Minori Osservanti and the neighbouring Chiesa di **Santa Maria del Gesù.** Inside the church, note the splendid funerary monument of Artale Cardona, in Gothic-Renaissance style.

The route back into town along Via Cibo passes the **Chiesa del Salvatore**. This church is adorned with an attractive Baroque façade with a double bell tower and a parvis in locally fired brick.

Continue along S 116 for another 15km/9mi as far as Capo d'Orlando.

From Naso, visitors can continue to Randazzo (approximately 55km/34mi) to link up with the circular tour of Etna *(see p 206)*.

Marsala

The name Marsala recalls one of the most important events in the unification of Italy as well as conjuring up images of a sweet dessert wine, originally marketed by a British merchant and now enjoyed across the globe. With its ethnic diversity (including a large Tunisian population), its harbour and web of narrow streets, Marsala has a distinctly North African flavour.

Location

Population: 80 818. Michelin map 565 1N 9 – Trapani. Marsala sits on the westernmost tip of Sicily, closer to Africa than to the rest of Europe. Situated on the headland of Capo Lilibeo (also known as Capo Boeo), behind the Lungomare Boeo and Piazza Vittoria, its historical centre is a maze of narrow streets best explored on foot. From Piazza Vittoria, Via XI Maggio leads to Piazza della Repubblica *(see Walking About)*. Marsala is a good base for excursions to the surrounding area. **ℹ** *Via XI Maggio 100;* ☎ *0923 71 40 97.*

Neighbouring sights are described in the following chapters: ERICE; MAZARA DEL VALLO; MOZIA; TRAPANI; VIA DEL SALE.

Background

Marsala is situated on the headland which continues to bear the town's ancient name, Lilybaeum (from *Lily* meaning water and *beum* referring to the Eubei, its pre-Phoenician inhabitants). The settlement is presumed to have been founded in 397 BC by the Phoenicians who fled from Motya following their defeat by the Syracusans. Its name in current use probably derives from the Arabic *Marsah el Ali*, meaning port of Ali, which would indicate that it has been a maritime town of considerable importance since its early history. Later, the harbour witnessed one of the most momentous events in the history of Sicily: the landing of Garibaldi's Thousand in Sicily.

Grazie ... mille – Early May 1860: accompanied by 1 000 volunteers dressed in red shirts, **Garibaldi** set sail from Quarto (near Genoa) bound for Sicily. Their mission was to overthrow the Bourbon government and liberate the Kingdom of the Two Sicilies. On 11 May, the two ships – the *Lombardo* and the *Piemonte* – moored at Marsala. The Mille (one thousand) made their way inland, winning their first battle at Calatafimi: this opened up the way to Palermo. As the campaign progressed, the band was swollen by new volunteers so that by the time they reached the Straits of Messina, their number exceeded 20 000. In less than two months, Sicily had been liberated from Bourbon government. The expedition continued to sweep through the rest of the kingdom until, following a plebiscite, the island was admitted on 21 October to the nucleus of northern states (Piedmont, Lombardy, Liguria, Emilia Romagna, Tuscany and Sardinia) that later were to unify to form the Kingdom of Italy.

Directory

Where to Eat

Divino Rosso – *Via XI Maggio (Largo A. di Girolamo), Marsala – ☎ 0923 71 17 70 – Closed Mon and in Nov – Booking recommended – €22/44.* This restaurant-cum-wine bar, situated in the historical centre of Marsala, serves typical Sicilian cuisine and excellent fresh fish dishes. In summer, the tables outside on the main street are shaded beneath large parasols.

Where to Stay

Tenuta Volpara – *Contrada Digerbato, 9km/5.5mi E of Marsala – ☎ 0923 98 45 88 – Fax 0923 98 46 67, volpara@delfinobeach.it – ⊠ – 18 rooms. €50/72 ☐ €5. – Restaurant €16/41.* Situated in the countryside outside Marsala, this farm guesthouse offers genuine Sicilian hospitality. The restaurant specialises in local cuisine, including a special warm ricotta cheese with whey, known as *zabbina*, which, in accordance with old Sicilian tradition, is served at breakfast.

Festivals

Settimana Santa – Marsala becomes progressively more animated in the period leading up to Easter: celebrations begin with a Maundy Thursday procession (the eve of Good Friday) when the Stations of the Cross are re-enacted in the streets of the town centre by local men and women in the different roles involved in the Passion. In the evening, the Crucifixion and Resurrection are also re-enacted.

Marsala Doc Jazz Festival – This International Jazz Festival takes place every year in July.

Special Features

MARSALA WINE

History – In 1770, a violent storm forced a British ship to take shelter in the harbour of Marsala. A certain merchant by the name of **John Woodhouse** disembarked and went into town to sample the Marsala wine in one of the humble taverns. Although more accustomed to the liqueur wines of Spain and Portugal, his palate immediately detected their similarity, prompting him to risk despatching a considerable consignment of wine (blended with alcohol so as to better withstand the journey) to his native land to sound out the market. The response being positive, the merchant set up his own company in Marsala. A little later, a second English merchant landed in town: **Ben Ingham**, a great connoisseur of fortified wines. With his intervention, the quality of the wine was gradually improved using carefully selected blends of different, improved, grape varieties. His business passed into thehands of his nephews, the **Whitakers** (*see p 305*). In 1833, the entrepreneur **Vincenzo Florio**, a Calabrese by birth and Palermitano by adoption, bought up great swathes of land between the two largest established Marsala producers and set to making his own vintage with an even more specialised range of grapes. At the end of the 19C, several more wine-growers joined the competition, including Pellegrino (1880). After the turn of the century, Florio bought out Ingham and Woodhouse, and retained the two labels. Florio in turn succumbed to a takeover by a conglomeration of other producers; again the famous, well-established, labels continued to be made and marketed.

The wine – Marsala is registered as a DOC wine (a State-designated label of controlled quality); this means that production is restricted to an exclusive area around Trapani, and a collection of additional vineyards in the provinces of Agrigento and Palermo. Only grape varieties with a high natural sugar content are used to make Marsala: these, once pressed, are left to ferment, and/or caramelise, before being blended with ethyl alcohol to produce the different types and flavours of Marsala.
Relative to the sugar content, Marsala may be categorised as dry, semi-dry or sweet. Its main denomination, however, is relative to the length of time it is left to mature: Marsala Fine (1 year), Superiore (2 years), Superiore Riserva (4 years), Vergine (5 years) and Vergine Riserva (10 years). Dry Marsala is usually served as a refreshing aperitif (below 10°C) while the sweeter forms are drunk as a dessert wine (no more than 18°C).

Wine producers

Florio – *Via Florio. Open by appointment only. Book five days in advance in summer and 10 days in advance the rest of the year. Guided tours Jul-Sep, Mon-Thu, 11am and 3.30pm, Fri, 11am; Oct-Jun, Mon-Thu, 9-11am and 3-4pm, Fri, 9-11am. Closed public hols and Aug. No charge. ☎ 0923 78 11 11; Fax 0923 98 23 80; www.cantineflorio.com*
A tour of this long-established winery provides the opportunity of comparing old techniques and installations with the new. The huge wine cellars *(cantine)* themselves are somewhat close and stuffy: the environment is carefully maintained at a constant temperature of 18°C by means of tufa walls (insulation), a tiled roof (aeration) and sand on the floor (temperature control and humidity). Perhaps the most interesting part of the process, however, is the explanation relating to the **Soleras Method** by which the wine is conditioned through the pyramid arrangement of oak barrels. This practice, imported from Spain, is used to age the wine: the young wine is added at the top, this is then allowed to percolate gently down through the interconnected barrels as the older, matured vintage is drawn off from the bottom tier of casks. This ensures that the wine is perfectly blended and remains of a consistent high quality.
The winery also has a small museum where the requisite equipment and tools are displayed.

CANTINE FLORIO

Pellegrino – *Via del Fante 39. (♿) Open Mon-Fri, 9am-noon and 3-5.30pm; Sat, 9am-12.30pm. Closed public hols. ☎ 0923 71 99 11; www. carlopellegrino.it*
This is another of the large producers: besides Marsala they also make Passito and Moscato di Pantelleria. Five wonderful **Sicilian carts** decorated in the 19C with historical scenes are to be admired at the entrance. Another memento of times past is the grille which once segregated the bottles on which customs duties were to be levied, subject to inspection.

Marco De Bartoli – *292 Contrada Samperi. Open by appointment only. For information, call ☎ 0923 96 20 93; Fax 0923 96 29 10.*
This producer, situated in the Samperi district, is responsible for one of the best Marsalas, achieved by traditional methods.

In addition to the numerous Marsala wine producers, the **Cantina Sperimentale Istituto Regionale della Vite e del Vino** is open to the public, and allows visitors to sample a number of experimental wines. *Via Trapani 218, Istituto Tecnico Agrario A Damiani. Visits and tastings by appointment only. For further information, contact ☎ 091 62 78 111; www.vitaevino.it*

Walking About

The centre of Marsala radiates from **Piazza della Repubblica**, where the Chiesa Madre and Palazzo Senatorio, completed in the 18C and known as the Loggia, are located.

Chiesa Madre – The main church with its tufa front decked with statues was built during the Norman occupation, but extensively remodelled in the 18C. Inside, it contains a number of works by the Gagini, most notably a fine icon by **Antonello Gagini** and Berrettaro *(north apse)*, and a delicate Madonna by **Domenico Gagini** from 1490 *(south transept)*. Above this hangs a good Renaissance painting by Antonello Riggio depicting the Presentation of the Virgin at the Temple.

The main thoroughfare leading from Piazza della Repubblica is Corso XI Maggio, the old *Decumanus Maximus* of the Roman town, lined as ever with splendid buildings. Perpendicular to the principal axis, **Via Garibaldi** leads southwards to **Porta Garibaldi** on the edge of town, running past the town hall, a former Spanish military barracks, on the way. The area behind is brought noisily to life each morning by a bustling fish market. The 17C Chiesa del Collegio and a series of fine 18C buildings line Via Rapisardi, the northern extension of Via Garibaldi.

The building behind the Chiesa Madre houses the Museo degli Arazzi *(see Worth a Visit below)*.

Worth a Visit

Museo degli Arazzi

Entrance in Via Garraffa. For information, call ☎ 0923 71 29 03.

The collection comprises eight large 16C Flemish **tapestries★** relating scenes from the war waged by the Emperor Titus against the Jews. Vivid colours and a strong sense of composition determine the central panel as well as the borders of flowers, fruit and allegorical figures. The sixth tapestry, illustrating a violent fight, manages to convey a great sense of movement and action.

Museo Archeologico di Baglio Anselmi

Lungomare Boeo (turn left at the end of Viale Vittorio Veneto and follow the road along the headland). ♿ Open daily, 9am-2pm (also 4-7pm Wed, Sat-Sun and public hols). €4. ☎ 0923 95 25 35; www. regione.sicilia.it/beniculturali

This archaeological museum is accommodated inside a former wine warehouse designed by Basile. Pride of place is given to the remains of a **Punic ship★** (3C BC) recovered in 1969 near the island of Motya. This was probably a *liburna*, a type of fast warship (35m/115ft long) used and lost at the end of the First Punic War, in the Battle of the Egadi (241 BC). The detailed analysis of these fragments has provided valuable information on the shipbuilding methods practised by the Phoenicians using prefabricated units marked with letters. Furthermore, the metal alloy nails used for assembling the hold have proved to be quite remarkable: after more than 2 000 years under water, they show no sign whatsoever of deterioration. The museum also displays important artefacts relating to the historic evolution of Marsala and its surrounding area from prehistoric times to the Middle Ages. Among the most interesting displays are those devoted to Motya and to various examples of finely crafted Hellenistic **jewellery** found off Capo Boeo.

Insula di Capo Boeo

At the end of Viale Vittorio Veneto, turn right and follow the headland. ♿ Open daily except Sun and public hols, 8am-1pm and 2-7pm. No charge. ☎ 0923 95 25 35 or 0923 80 81 11.

Porta Garibaldi

B. Kaufmann/MICHELIN

Right on the tip of the headland are situated the remains of three Roman *insulae* (blocks of buildings). Almost the whole of one is taken up by a large **villa**, built in Imperial times (3C BC), complete with its own private set of baths. Fragments of the mosaic floors are still in evidence, as are a number of the small pillars *(suspensurae)* used to support the floor, thereby enabling hot air to circulate through the cavity. The access roads to the area were paved with white stone from Trapani.

A little further on stands the Church of **San Giovanni al Boeo**, built around the Sibyl of Lilybaeum's legendary grotto. *Guided tours only. Contact the tourist office to make a reservation. ☎ 0923 71 40 97.*

Mazara del Vallo

The settlement founded by the Phoenicians at the mouth of the River Mazara became an important harbour in Antiquity on account of its protected position and its proximity to Africa. The trading post that so flourished under the Ancient Greeks, however, reached its apotheosis under Arab and then Norman dominion. The cosmopolitan range of people of different origins who have been attracted to this town through the ages, not least from nearby North Africa, is still much in evidence today, constituting a considerable proportion of the local population. As in times past, Mazara continues to be regarded as one of the most important deep-sea fishing towns in Italy, accounting for 20% of the national catch.

Location

Population: 51 869. Michelin map 565 O 19 – Trapani. The heart of the town is centred on the harbour and the shipping canal of the River Mazara, where the town's fishing industry is based. The main monuments of the town lie to the east of the harbour, behind Lungomare Mazzini. ℹ *Piazza S. Veneranda 2; ☎ 0923 94 17 27.*

Neighbouring sights are described in the following chapters: CASTELVETRANO; MARSALA; Antica città di SELINUNTE.

Walking About

Harbour and shipping canal

The heart of the town is the harbour; this throbs with life early in the morning when the fishing fleet returns with its catch. The quays bustle with activity as refrigerated trucks manoeuvre into place; the harbour echoes with the sounds of fishermen, merchants, packers and drivers who see to the offloading, processing, packaging and despatching of the fish. Meanwhile, the fishermen go about preparing their boats, moored to the jetty, sorting and folding the nets, stacking up the lobster-pots and stowing the cages in readiness for the next expedition. Overlooking the scene with benign approval, set back from the actual harbour front, is the Norman church, San Nicolò Regale.

San Nicolò Regale

Open daily except Sun and public hols, 9am-1pm. No charge. ☎ 0923 90 94 31.

This evocative building erected under William I, has a square plan with the three apses contained by a bulbous dome characteristic of Arabo-Norman architecture. The skyline is edged with rounded battlements.

Below the floor inside, fragments of mosaic have been discovered: these, from palaeo-Christian times, probably form part of a Roman floor.

Among the streets behind sits **Piazza Plebiscito**, graced with the elegant façade of **Sant'Ignazio** (18C), and the former **Jesuit College** (17C) with its lovely doorway. This currently accommodates the municipal library, small local **museum** and the Sala Consagra *(see Worth a Visit below)*.

Where to Eat

Del Pescatore – *Via Castelvetrano 191, Mazara del Vallo – ☎ 0923 94 75 80 – Closed Mon – 💳 – €30/53 + 10% service.* As its name suggests, this restaurant specialises in fish and seafood, prepared with a strong Sicilian influence. Del Pescatore's wine cellar is renowned for its wide selection.

Cathedral

The main building dates from the 11C although this was subjected to considerable remodelling in the 17C. The façade, completed in 1906, is ornamented with a decorative doorway and a 16C shallow relief panel depicting Roger I, on horseback, felling a Moor.

H. Champollion/MICHELIN

Roger I felling a Moor

Interior★ – The overall somewhat theatrical effect is achieved by interspersing a few genuine elements of gilded stucco decoration among frescoed *trompe l'oeil* stucco volutes, curlicues and little cherubs. The most complex group is in the central apse where a large drape richly embroidered with gold "stitching" is suspended and drawn aside by angels, to reveal the **Transfiguration★**. The whole composition by Antonello Gagini sits upon a majestic Renaissance altar. In the first chapel on the right is an ancient ciborium, which may have been used, according to the inscription, at the christening of Frederick II's son. The Chapel of the Crucifix, also right of centre, takes its name from the fine painted wooden Crucifix (13C) in the adjoining room.
Set into the floor is a glass plate that provides a view of the ancient foundations. Elsewhere, the church contains a number of Roman sarcophagi.

Piazza della Repubblica

This pleasing piazza laid out in the Baroque period acts as the focal point for the old town. The statue (1771) in the centre is by **Ignazio Marabitti** and represents San Vito, the patron saint of Mazara. On all sides rise a harmonious collection of *palazzi* from the 18C: at the far end sits the cathedral overshadowed by an elegant Baroque campanile, along the left side stands the Bishop's Palace and, to the right, extends the **Seminario dei Chierici** complete with its lovely neo-Classical portico and round-headed arched loggia. The former seminary now houses a small **Museo Diocesano** *(see Worth a Visit below)*.

Lungomare Mazzini

South of Piazza della Repubblica. The seafront is flanked by gardens shaded by magnolias and palm trees, making it a perfect place for the habitual Italian *passeggiata* or "constitutional". At its eastern end, Piazza Makara contains all that remains of the Norman castle (11C), namely a pointed gateway.

Worth a Visit

Museo Civico and Sala Consagra

Piazza Plebisicito 2. Open daily 8.30am-1.30pm (also 3.15-5.45pm, Tue and Fri). No charge. ☎ 0923 67 11 11.
This small museum contains artefacts from various periods, predominantly from the Neolithic to late Byzantine Eras. The separate **Sala Consagra** is devoted to Pietro Consagra, a contemporary artist born in Mazara: it contains etchings, acquatints and relief panels together with small-scale models of his best-known sculptures.
The museum also maintains a large reserve collection of paintings for which permanent exhibition space has yet to be found.

Museo Diocesano

Entrance at Via dell'Orologio 3. (♿) Open Tue-Sat, 9am-1pm. Closed public hols. €2. ☎ 0923 90 94 31.
The most important section of this collection, comprising silverware, church furnishings and vestments dating from the 14C-19C, contains items which belong to the cathedral treasury.

Messina

The construction of a bridge over the Straits of Messina, the subject of much debate over the past 40 years, could become reality within the next decade, thus lessening Sicily's special island appeal. However, at present the bridge is no more than an idea and Messina, separated by just 5km/3mi of sea from the Italian peninsula, remains strongly connected to its port, which acts as the disembarkation point for visitors arriving from the mainland.

Location

Population: 257 302. Michelin map 565 28M, including a city map. Messina is a modern city which grew up behind the sickle-shaped port that gave the town its name in ancient times. Most of the monuments that survived the terrible earthquake of 1908 and the bombing raids of the Second World War are grouped behind the central port area. To reach the historical centre from the motorway, take the Messina-Boccetta Porto exit and follow Viale Boccetta as far as Corso Garibaldi, which runs parallel to the seafront. *Via Calabria isol. 301 bis; ☏ 090 67 42 36; Fax 090 67 42 71 and Piazza Cairoli 45; ☏ 090 29 35 292; Fax 090 69 47 80; www.azienturismomessina.it*

Neighbouring sights are described in the following chapters: Isole EOLIE; GIARDINI NAXOS; MILAZZO; TAORMINA.

Background

Founded as a Greek colony in the 8C BC, Messina was originally given the name of **Zancle** after the sickle-like shape of its harbour. The history of the town is therefore inextricably linked to the sea and to the straits that bear its name. According to tradition, sailors have long claimed that the straits are guarded by two monsters, Scylla and Charybdis. **Scylla** was the daughter of Phorcys and Hecate (Greek goddess associated with the underworld and with night; she later assumed the role of queen of the ghosts and magic,haunting crossroads attended by hell-hounds, protectress of enchanters and witches. In art she is represented in triple form looking down three roads). She was loved by Poseidon and this aroused the jealousy of his wife Amphitrite who, using magic herbs, turned Scylla into a monster that devoured mariners who sailed too close to her cave under a cliff on the Calabrian side of the strait. She is said to have had 12 feet and six heads. It was she who flung herself at Odusseus' ship, catching and devouring six of his sailors. On the Sicilian side of the strait, under another rock, lived **Charybdis**, who used to drink the sea water and regurgitate it three times every day; when trapped by this whirlpool, the sailors often fell prey to Scylla (*Odyssey*, Book XII, v 234-259).

Strategically situated as far as commerce was concerned, Messina acted as a trading post for the interchange of goods and people, and therefore artistic trends and ideas. From this dynamic and stimulating context emerged such figures as the 15C painter Antonello da Messina.

In more recent times, the town has suffered the effects of devastating earthquakes, most notably in 1783 and in 1908, when 90% of the town was destroyed, leaving more than 60 000 victims. During the Second World War, the town was subjected to several intensive bombing raids.

G. Bludzin/MICHELIN

Directory

Transport

From mainland Italy – Messina handles the principal ferry services from mainland Italy. Ferries run from Reggio Calabria (45min, Stazione Ferrovie Stato, ☎ 0965 86 35 25) and Villa San Giovanni (20min, Caronte Shipping, Via Marina 30, ☎ 0965 75 14 13 and Ferrovie dello Stato, Piazza Stazione, ☎ 0965 75 60 99). For hydrofoil services (20min), contact SNAV, Stazione Marittima, Reggio Calabria, ☎ 0965 29 568.

For visitors arriving by air, the nearest airports are in Reggio di Calabria and Catania.

From within Sicily – Messina is linked by train with Palermo (3hr), Taormina (1hr), Catania (approximately 2hr) and Siracusa (3hr). A number of bus companies operate services to Palermo, Taormina, Catania, Capo d'Orlando, Patti and Tindari.

Connections with the Aeolian islands – Trains (approximately 40min) and buses run from Messina to Milazzo, from where ferries cross to the Aeolian islands. Alternatively, daily hydrofoil services are operated by Aliscafi SNAV from Messina (1hr 20min), Via San Raineri 22, ☎ 090 36 21 14, Fax 090 71 73 58.

Where to Eat

• ***For all budgets***

Don Nino – *Viale Europa 39, Isolato 59, Messina* – ☎ *090 69 42 95* – *€13/18.* Take some dried cod, tomatoes, potatoes, olives, capers, pine nuts, sultanas, onion, garlic, oil, celery and carrot, mix them all together and you have *ghiotta di pesce stocco*, one of the specialities of Messina cuisine and Don Nino in particular. *Buon appetito!*

Casa Savoia – *Via XXVII Luglio 36/38, Messina* – ☎ *090 29 34 865* – *info@ristorantecasasavoia.it* – ▤ – *€20/37.* Built on the spot where the "Regio Teatro Savoia" once stood, this family-run restaurant comes highly recommended for those visitors wanting to sample local Messina cuisine.

Le Due Sorelle – *Piazza Municipio 4, Messina* – ☎ *090 44 720* – *Closed Sat-Sun at lunchtime and in Aug. Booking recommended* – *€28/37.* This pleasant restaurant in the heart of the historical centre serves a range of local home-made dishes. Fish takes centre stage in the evening, although you will still find other traditional Messina dishes on the menu.

Where to Stay

• ***Moderate***

Villa Morgana – *Via C. Pompea 237, Ganzirri, 5km/3mi N of Messina along the coast road* – ☎ *090 32 55 75* – *Fax 090 32 55 75* – *villamorgana@tin.it* – P – *14 rooms. €46.50/77.50* ☕. Guests will immediately feel at home in this hotel housed in a private villa, surrounded by a large, well-tended garden. Situated on the coast road a few kilometres from Messina, the hotel has an attractive lounge and comfortable, well-appointed rooms.

Taking a Break

Pasticceria Irrera – *Piazza Cairoli 12, Messina* – ☎ *090 67 38 23; www.irrera.it/.* Founded in 1910, this pastry shop is one of the best in Messina. Local delicacies include *pignolata* (a typical Messina speciality made with twists of fried puff pastry with lemon or chocolate icing) and *torrone fondente* (a sweet delicacy stuffed with candied fruit and almonds).

Pasticceria F. Gordelli – *Via Ghibellina 86 (the road running parallel to Via Cesare Battisti), Messina* – ☎ *090 66 29 22.* Another excellent *pasticceria* in which to sample some of the city's renowned cakes and pastries.

Festivals

Venerdì Santo – The *Processione delle Barette*, a procession of wooden sculptures which follow the Stations of the Cross, takes place on Good Friday.

Passeggiata dei Giganti – On 14 August, the Moor Grifone and Mata, the legendary founder of the city, are borne aloft in procession through the streets of Messina.

Processione della Vara – The image of the Assumption of the Virgin is carried through the town on 15 August.

Special Features

PIAZZA DUOMO AND SURROUNDING AREA

Duomo

After the 1908 earthquake, the **cathedral** was almost completely rebuilt in the style of the Norman original. The façade rises in tiers and is relieved with single-light windows and a small central rose window. The **central doorway★**, one of three, was re-erected using elements of the original fabric (15C). It is flanked by small columns supported by lions, and surmounted by a lunette filled with a *Madonna and Child* from the 16C.

Projecting from the right flank is a small building lit with elegant two-light Catalan Gothic windows.

The beamed and painted **ceiling** contained within replaces the older one, destroyed by bombing raids during the Second World War. The ornamental carved rosettes along the central beams betray the influence of Eastern design.

Treasury – *Access from inside the Duomo. Open 9am-1pm and 3pm-1hr before dusk. €3. ☎ 090 67 51 75.*

On display are a number of religious objects and vestments. The oldest exhibit (from the Middle Ages) is the Pigna, a lamp made of rock crystal. Much of the silver plate was made in Messina, including the arm-shaped reliquaries (the one of San Marziano is inscribed with Moorish and Byzantine patterns), candlesticks, chalices and a fine 17C **monstrance** (containing a host) with two angels and a pelican on top presiding over the rays of divine light.

Orologio astronomico★

The **astronomical clock** is the most interesting component of the 60m/200ft high bell tower to the left of the cathedral. The mechanism dates from 1933 and was built in Strasbourg. It comprises several tiers, each bearing a different display with a separate movement. At the bottom, a two-horse chariot driven by a deity indicates the day of the week; above, the central figure of Death waves his scythe threateningly at the child, youth, soldier or old man – the four ages of man – that pass before him. At the third stage, the Sanctuary of Montalto *(turn left to compare it with the real one)* sets the scene for a group of figures which, according to the time of year, represent the Nativity, Epiphany, Resurrection and Pentecost. At the top, the tableau enacts a scene relating to a local legend whereby the Madonna delivers a letter to the ambassadors of Messina in which she thanks and agrees to protect the inhabitants of the town who were converted to Christianity by St Paul the Apostle: the same **Madonna della Lettera** (Madonna of the Letter), is patron saint of the city. The two young female bell-strikers are the local heroines Dina and Clarenza, who were alive during the period of resistance against the Angevins (1282). The summit is capped with a lion.

The south side of the bell tower *(starting from the bottom)* shows a perpetual calendar, the astronomical cycle marked by the signs of the zodiac, and the various phases of the moon.

A. Picone/Lara Pessina/MESSINA

Astronomical clock

When the clock strikes midday, all the mechanical figures come to life accompanied by a musical air: the lion, the symbol of the vitality of the town, roars three times while the cockerel crows from between the two girls.

Fontana di Orione

In the centre of Piazza del Duomo, is an attractively elegant **fountain**, designed by the Tuscan sculptor Montorsoli to commemorate the inauguration of an aqueduct. Sculpted in a pre-Baroque style (16C), it incorporates allegories of four rivers: the Tiber, Nile, Ebro and Camaro – the River Messina was diverted into the new aqueduct.

Santissima Annunziata dei Catalani

A short way from the cathedral, nestling among fine *palazzi* in Via Garibaldi, sits the Catalan Church. This was built in the 12C when the Normans were in power, and named after the Catalan merchants who patronised it later. The **apse**★ is a fine example of the Norman composite style, incorporating Romanesque elements (small blind arches on slender columns), Moorish influences (geometrical motifs in polychrome stone) and Byzantine features (dome on a drum).

Walking About

The walk described below can either start in Via Garibaldi, Messina's main street, linking Piazza Cairoli in the south (close to the railway station and port) with Piazza Castronuovo, or directly from Piazza del Duomo.

Santa Maria Alemanna

In Via S. Maria dell'Alemagna, which runs across Via Garibaldi. The sad ruin (no roof or façade) still manages to convey something of the original Gothic style, so rare in Sicily, with its pointed arches supported on pilasters and clusters of columns topped by splendid capitals that once articulated the aisles.

From Piazza Duomo take Via Oratorio S. Francesco and turn right into Via XXIV Maggio.

Monte di Pietà

Corner of Via XXlV Maggio and Piazza Crisafulli. The front elevation of this late Mannerist building is ornamented with a massive rusticated doorway framed between rather solid columns and a broken pediment; above, the balcony rests on brackets carved with volutes. The upper storey, destroyed by the earthquake, has not been rebuilt, making the building look unfinished. Today it is used for concerts and recitals. The left side of the building is interrupted by a gate which leads through to what used to be the consecrated ground leading up to majestic symmetrical flights of steps and the Church of Santa Maria della Pietà. Of the church, only the façade survives.

Continue as far as Viale Boccetta.

Chiesa di San Francesco d'Assisi o dell'Immacolata

This monumental church was almost entirely rebuilt following the earthquake of 1908, retaining a few original features such as the three rather austere 13C stone **apses**, relieved in part by tall narrow arches that contain the windows; the two doorways are set into pointed archways that post-date the main building of the church; and the fine rose window on the façade.

Continue as far as Via S. Giovanni di Malta, which runs parallel to Viale Boccetta to the north, then turn right.

Chiesa di San Giovanni di Malta

The west front of this square late-16C building, overlooking Via Placida, is articulated with white stone pilasters, niches and windows (some blind) and, in the upper tier, a gallery.

Worth a Visit

Museo Regionale★

Via della Libertà 465. (♿) Open Tue, Thu and Sat, 9am-1.30pm and 4-6.30pm (3-5.30pm in winter); Wed and Fri, 9am-1.30pm; Sun and public hols, 9am-12.30pm. €4. ☎ 090 36 12 92.

The chronological arrangement of the displays begins with the history of the area and the artistic climate that prevailed through the Byzantine and Norman eras. The first rooms are dedicated to paintings and sculpture: shallow reliefs and capitals. Among the most notable examples, there is a fine early-15C polychrome wooden Crucifix *(third room on the right)* and a glazed terracotta medallion from the Della Robbia workshops of a sweet-faced Madonna gazing down at her Child.

The works in the next room betray the strong influence exerted by the Flemish style: a strong sense of realism and an astute attention to detail characterise the edge of the mantle and cuffs of the garments in the ***Madonna and Child*** attributed to a follower of Petrus Christus (15C). The same exquisite technique is evident in Antonello da Messina's beautiful, though badly damaged ***Polyptych of St Gregory*** (1473). His style assimilates various Northern qualities, namely the International Gothic predilection for linearity (stance of the figures, the crisp folds of falling drapery), and the Flemish fascination for conveying the quality of texture and detail – as the Madonna's clothes demonstrate. The overall balance of composition is achieved with the use of perspective tapering to a single vanishing point and extending out from the central panel through to the side panels.

Antonello da Messina

Antonello "of Messina"was born around 1430 at a time when Sicily was under Spanish rule, and while the town was particularly prosperous. He transferred to the Spanish domain on the mainland, settling in Naples so as to study, possibly in the renowned studio of Colantonio. This proved to be a highly dynamic and stimulating environment. Spain also ruled Flanders at that time and so the artistic currents of Flemish, Spanish and Provençal schools merged here in Naples; Antonello assimilated them all to formulate his own highly personal style of painting. From the Flemish masters, he learnt to paint with oils (becoming the first in the southern part of Italy to practise the new technique; Piero being among the first in northern Italy), aped their realism and copied the way they portrayed textures in exquisite detail. These stylistic elements, however, did not affect the formal – and distinctly Italian – way in which he constructed his compositions and unified his picture space with light. The unified harmony of his paintings is achieved by his use of a rich and warm palette, clear and rational perspective and soft lighting effects. In a different domain, Antonello painted several portraits showing a three-quarter view of his sitter as was common among Flemish artists of the time, rather than the more common Tuscan and Umbrian side profile. His ability to reproduce the different effects of light, in contrast with a plain dark background, concentrates the impact of the picture on the noble yet serene facial features of his sitters. Certainly, his style is further enriched by the influences exchanged with other contemporary artists. During his sojourn in Venice, Antonello met Giovanni Bellini; the encounter made a lasting impression on both artists. Antonello began to use colour tonally and more gently as in the *Annunciation* in Palermo, perhaps the most famous of his Annunciations.

Note how the dais on which the Madonna is seated broadens out into the platform on which the two saints are standing, so making the three figures united in a single space. The predella (central lower panel) defines the limit of the picture plane, as does the necklace hanging down from the step. This early example of a *Sacra Conversazione* may have been pioneered in collaboration with his contemporaries Piero della Francesca and Giovanni Bellini, while Antonello was in Venice between 1475 and 1476 (The *Sacra Conversazione* is a picture composition, usually with the Madonna at its centre, that includes figures of Apostles, saints and martyrs – sometimes donors – as if they existed within a single space and within a single time span).

Other pictures hanging in the same room include the striking *Deposition* by Colijn de Coter: in this the drama of the scene is heightened by the anguished expressions of the mourners bent in supporting the weight of the dead Christ, and in the predominant use of burnt, dull colours.

The adjacent room is devoted to the Messina painter Girolamo Alibrandi. The most striking paintings include the huge *Presentation at the Temple* of 1519 (note the noble expression and gentle features of the woman in the foreground) and *St Paul*. The elegant statue of the *Madonna and Child* in the same room is by Antonello **Gagini**.

The Roman painter Polidoro da Caravaggio and the Florentine sculptor and architect Montorsoli introduced Mannerism to Messina. Their work, together with that of their followers, is displayed in the next galleries. Michelangelo Merisi, better known as **Caravaggio**, spent a year in Messina between 1608 and 1609; during this time he painted the *Adoration of the Shepherds* and the *Resurrection of Lazarus (Room 10)*. The short time he spent here was sufficient to influence contemporary artists living in the city.

The splendid **Senator's Coach★** *(Room 12)*, dated 1742, incorporates a number of exquisitely made furnishings, including small gilded wooden carvings and painted panels.

The top floor of the museum is devoted to displaying decorative and applied arts.

Tours

CAPO PELORO

70km/44mi – allow half a day.

This excursion starts from Messina and follows a panoramic road around the edge of the headland, past the glorious beaches that skirt the tip, before continuing along the Tyrrhenian shore.

The houses that make up the lively little fishing village of **Ganzirri** *(5km/3mi N of Messina along the coast road)* are clustered around two wide saltwater lagoons used for farming shellfish. The road along the "lakeside" bristles with restaurants and pizzerias, and continues to hum with activity late into the summer evenings.

Continuing north for 3.5 km/2mi beyond the Straits of Messina lies **Torre Faro**, a small fishing village overlooked by a lighthouse and great electricity pylons bearing cables across the strait.

Drive through **Lidi di Mortelle** and on to Divieto, before turning inland towards Gesso. On past this little town, after some 6km/4mi, the road that forks right leads up to the top of Antennammare.

Monte Antennammare

The road winds up to the San Rizzo pass. There a second road forks right for the **Santuario di Maria Santissima di Dinnammare** which is situated right on the top of Mount Antennammare (1 130m/3 706ft). From here, a spectacular view spans the **panorama★★** of Messina with its port, Capo Peloro and Calabria to the east, the Ionian coastline with the sickle-s haped promontory of Milazzo, and Rometta perched on a hill to the west.

On the way back, continue down to the crossroads and then turn right. This road coasts its way down the wooded slopes of Colle San Rizzo.

Santa Maria della Valle o Badiazza

The **Benedictine abbey of Santa Maria della Valle**, known also as Santa Maria della Scala, was probably built in the 12C and restored in the 14C. The actual church is not open to the public and the precincts are enclosed behind a tall concrete wall that protects it when the river is in full spate. The exterior, however,has windows set into pointed arches finished in volcanic stone. Through these, the interior can be glimpsed with its two-coloured ribbed vault and sculpted truncated pyramid capitals.

Return to Messina.

IONIAN COAST: MESSINA TO TAORMINA

Approximately 70km/44mi from Messina – allow one day.

This trip follows the coast with brief excursions inland and can be undertaken just as easily in reverse, starting out from Taormina.

Monastero di San Placido Calonerò

On the road to Pezzolo, a short distance before Galati Marina. Open summer, 8am-2pm; otherwise, 8am-8pm. Closed Easter and Christmas holidays. Visitors are advised to contact the Istituto Agrario a few days in advance. ☎ 090 82 11 07; Fax 090 82 12 34.
The **Benedictine monastery**, now the headquarters of a technical institute for agriculture, preserves two attractive 17C cloisters with columns with high dosserets and Ionic capitals. A fine little Durazzo Gothic portal to the right of the atrium leading into the first cloisters, provides access to a vaulted chapel articulated with clustered columns.

Scaletta Zanclea

Scaletta Superiore *(2km/1.2mi inland)* boasts a **castle** that was built originally to serve as a Swabian military outpost (13C); it was eventually acquired by the Ruffo family who used it as a hunting lodge until the 17C. The massive fortress, gentrified by elegant two-light windows on the first floor and single-light windows above, houses the **Museo Civico** and its collections of weaponry and historic documents. *Open summer, daily except Sun and public hols, 9am-1pm and 4-8pm; otherwise, by appointment only. ☎ 090 95 10 10. No charge.*

At Itàla Marina turn right, heading inland. Itàla is situated 2.5km/1.5mi from Itàla Marina.

Itàla

The little hamlet of Croce jostles around the Basilian Church of **San Pietro e San Paolo** which was rebuilt in 1093 by Count Roger, apparently in celebration of a victory over the Arabs. It comprises a tall nave and two lower aisles. The crossing is marked with a dome rising from a square drum. The brick exterior is relieved on the façade with occasional insertions of volcanic stone and by low, in places interlacing, blind arcading inspired by Eastern influences. *Open by appointment only. Call Padre Giovanni on ☎ 090 95 21 54.*

Continuing back along the coast, the road passes **Capo Alì** which is topped by a small round watchtower probably from the Norman period. It then proceeds through the seaside resorts of **Alì Terme**, **Nizza di Sicilia** and **Roccalumera**.

Sàvoca

Approx 3km/1.8mi inland. This picturesque typically medieval town occupies a splendid position on the top of a hill. What is somewhat remarkable is the way this divides into two ridges and yet interconnects with three spurs on which the districts of San Rocco, San Giovanni and Pentefur are built; together they form the star-shaped town.
Beyond the town hall, but still outside the old town sits the **Convento dei Cappuccini**, a Capuchin monastery with a **crypt** that contains the mummified bodies of 32 former town dignitaries and friars from the 17C and 18C. Several of these (some having been daubed with green paint by vandals) are displayed in niches, others in wooden sarcophagi. *Closed for restoration at the time of going to press.* From the sacred area before the church there is a wonderful view of the town, the ruined castle and il Calvario or hill of "Calvary" in the distance.

Go back the same way and turn up Via Borgo and then immediately left on to Via San Michele.

This leads to the gateway to the old town centre. Just beyond the pointed archway on the right stands the 15C Church of **San Michele** with its fine transitional Gothic-Renaissance porches. Alongside sit the ruins of the Archimandrite community precincts (accommodating the highest officers of an Eastern monastic order). As the same street continues, a number of wonderful **views**★ extend over the rooftops and the valley below or up to the ruins of the Norman **castle** and the Church of San Nicolò (or Santa Lucia) differentiated by its peculiar crenellations perched on a rocky spur above. At last, the **Chiesa Madre** comes into view with its fine 16C portal surmounted by a beautifully carved oculus and the coat of arms of Sàvoca, bearing the elderberry *(sambuco)* branch from which the name of the town is supposed to derive. A visit to the town might then conclude with a climb up Calvary hill to the ruins of the Church of Santa Maria delle Sette Piaghe (St Mary of the Seven Sorrows).

The road continues to meander its way (2km/1.2mi) inland to the town of Casalvecchio.

Casalvecchio

This little town, called Palakorìon (old hamlet) in Byzantine times, enjoys a fabulous position with a panoramic view: from the terrace before the **Chiesa Madre di Sant'Onofrio** this **view**★ takes in the Ionian Sea lying off Capo Sant'Alessio and Forza d'Agrò and, to the south, Mount Etna. **Inside**, the church has a fine coffered wooden ceiling ornamented with anthropomorphic figures, and a stone floor inlaid with the local black and red Taormina marble; both date from the 17C.

In a neighbouring former church house is the rather eclectic **Museo Parrocchiale** which displays local farming tools, a silver life-size statue of Sant'Onofrio (1745), a painting of San Nicolò by a follower of Antonelli (1497), liturgical furnishings and sacred vestments. *Contact Signore Carmelo Crisafulli at the town hall for information. ☎ 0942 76 10 30 or 339 62 68 248 (mobile).*

Follow directions for Antillo and, after about 500m/550yd, fork left along a minor road which twists and turns to its destination.

Chiesa di Santi Pietro e Paolo d'Agrò

The **church**, founded by Basilian monks, was largely rebuilt in 1117 and then restored in 1172 by a master builder called Gherardo il Franco; or so the inscription above the architrave of the main doorway claims. It is striking not only on account of its unusual appearance achieved by the use of brick, volcanic stone, limestone and sandstone, but also as a synthesising expression of Byzantine, Arab and Norman influences. The **exterior** is ornamented with decorative banding, interlaced arcading and herringbone patterns. The main façade is graced with a portico flanked by twin towers. The **interior** space is divided into nave and aisles by Corinthian columns with high dosserets that rise to pointed arches. A large ribbed dome contains the central area, hovering on its tall drum suspended by pendentives.

The choir is enclosed by a smaller dome springing from an octagonal drum.

Turn back down towards the coast to Capo Sant'Alessio.

Capo Sant'Alessio★

This lovely rocky headland, distinctively shaped, is crowned with a round fortress on the western side and a polygonal castle on the eastern tip *(neither is open to the public).*

On the south side is the wonderful **beach** of **Sant'Alessio Siculo**.

A road extends from the fortresses to Forza d'Agrò.

Forza d'Agrò

This attractive medieval hamlet caps the furthermost spurs of the Monti Peloritani, enjoying a splendid **prospect★** of the coast broken into inlets and bays. The best viewpoint is probably the terrace of Piazza del Municipio. Behind this climbs a flight of steps through a fine Durazzo Gothic archway up to the sacred area before the **Chiesa della Triade**. The **combination★** of the steps, archway and church façade is especially effective. Tortuous lanes wind their way up the hill towards the castle past the 16C **Chiesa Madre**, which has been remodelled in the Baroque style. The Norman **castle** is now a ruin. Sheltering among the walls is the cemetery: silence and serenity endow this **secluded corner★**, scattered with tombstones, with a particular atmosphere.

Taormina★★★ *See TAORMINA.*

Milazzo

Mylai, the ancient city of the sea, is the natural departure point for the Aeolian Islands, which lie only a few kilometres offshore. This part of Sicily often features in Classical mythology: the promontory, regarded as prime pasture, provided grazing for the flocks of the sun god while the islands were considered to be home to Aeolus, the keeper of the winds, as well as to pretty nymphs, dancing satyrs and sileni (spirits of wild nature later associated with Dionysus) drunk on wine; it was possibly here that Odysseus and his companions were shipwrecked and encountered Polyphemus.

Location

Population: 32 586. Michelin map 565 27M – Milazzo. Milazzo sits at the base of a promontory jutting into the Tyrrhenian Sea. Despite its modern, industrial appearance, the town has a number of important historical and artistic monuments. The oldest part is the medieval centre, perched on a hill leading to the castle, to the north of the city. The lower town, built to a regular grid plan in the 18C, is situated to the south, along the eastern coast. Milazzo is the main port for the Aeolian Islands. *Piazza Caio Duilio 20; ☎ 090 92 22 865; Fax 090 92 22 790; www.comune.milazzo.me.it/turismo/testoturismo.htm*

Neighbouring sights are described in the following chapters: CAPO D'ORLANDO; Isole EOLIE; MESSINA; Golfo di PATTI.

Directory

Transport
Milazzo is linked to Messina by train (40min) and by bus, operated by the Giuntabus company (Via Terranova 6, Messina, ☎ 090 67 37 82). Palermo, approximately 200km/125mi away, can be reached by train (approximately 2hr 30min). Milazzo's railway station is situated in Piazza Marconi, approximately 3km/1.8mi from the historical centre of the town.

Boats to the Aeolian islands
Ferries and hydrofoils operated by SNAV and NGI depart daily from Milazzo to the Aeolian Islands. Taranto Navigazione runs mini-cruises, both during the day and in the evening. *For further information, see Isole EOLIE.*

Where to Eat
• *For all budgets*

Il Covo del Pirata – *Via Marina Garibaldi 2, Milazzo – Closed Wed (except in Aug).* Situated on the seafront, this rustic, ground-floor pizzeria serves excellent pizzas, baked in a wood-fired oven. Very popular with locals.

L'Ugghiularu – *Via Acquaviole 101, Milazzo – ☎ 090 92 84 384 – Closed Wed – €20/38 + €1.50 service.* The cuisine at this trattoria housed in an attractive old olive oil store is simple and based on seasonal ingredients. Well worth a visit.

Al Castello – *Via Federico di Svevia 20, Milazzo – ☎ 090 92 82 175 – Closed Tue (in winter), Mon and Tue at lunchtime (15 Jun-15 Sep) and 10-30 Jan – €22/34.* This pleasant, attractive restaurant enjoys an atmospheric location at the foot of the castle. Outdoor dining by candlelight during the summer months.

Where to Stay
• *Budget*

Jack's Hotel – *Via Colonnello Magistri 47, Milazzo – ☎ 090 92 83 300 – Fax 090 92 87 219 – ▤ – 14 rooms. €44/67 ☕ €3.* This small hotel, conveniently located for both the port and the town centre, is simple and well maintained, with well-furnished rooms. Good value for money.

Taking a Break
Bar Washington – *Lungomare Garibaldi 95, Milazzo – ☎ 090 92 23 813.* A perfect place for a lunchtime snack, this bar also serves *pignolate* (a local speciality made with twists of fried puff pastry with lemon or chocolate icing), a selection of pastries and ice cream.

Special Features

Citadel and castle★
Open daily except Mon. €2. For information on admission times, call ☎ 090 92 21 291; www.comune.milazzo.me.it.

The main fortification of the town was initiated by the Arabs (10C) on what had been an Ancient Greek acropolis, which had been modified and extended over the centuries. Through the **Spanish walls**, there is a large open space with, on the left, the **Duomo Vecchio** (1608), an example of Sicilian Mannerism. At one time this area might have accommodated the houses of those Milazzo citizens charged with public functions; however, after the political and administrative offices were transferred to the lower part of the town, the importance of the cathedral gradually dwindled, until it became used first as a warehouse, then as a prison and finally as a stable or cowshed. The **Aragonese city walls** (15C) are punctuated by

The port and the citadel

five truncated-cone towers: two, set closer together, flank a fine gateway set into a pointed arch bearing the coat of arms of the Spanish monarchs, Ferdinand and Isabella – a shield divided into four sections (representing the monarchs under which Spain was unified), supported by the eagle of St John. Within, stands Frederick II's **castle** with later additions. The fine Gothic doorway is surmounted, however, by the Aragon coat of arms, added in the 1400s. It was here in the great hall that representatives from the five *campate* (regions of Sicily) met to constitute the Sicilian Parliament of 1295. The top of the castle provides a breathtaking view of the Aeolian Islands (from the left: Vulcano, Lipari, Panarea and, on particularly clear days, Stromboli) and the Bay of Tono.

Walking About

The Borgo

The *borgo* is the oldest part of the town: this consists of a medieval quarter stretched along the slope of the hill, loftily presided over by the fortified citadel, where an antiques fair is held on the first weekend of each month.

The entrance to this district coincides with the beginning of Via Impallomeni *(from Piazza Roma)* which is lined on both sides by the Spanish Military Barracks (1585-95). There are many religious buildings within the *borgo*: on the right, in the steep street with the same name, is the **Santuario di San Francesco di Paola**, a church founded by the saint during his stay in the town (1464), remodelled in the 18C. The attractive **façade★** presents an effective interplay of curvilinear stairway, windows and gallery, crowned with an elegant pediment. **Inside**, in the Gesù e Maria chapel, there is an unusual carved wooden altar decorated with gilt and mirrors, set with a charming *Madonna and Child* central panel by Domenico Gagini (1465).

A little further on, up Salita San Francesco, is the Viceroy's residence **(Palazzo dei Vicerè)**, built in the 16C and altered in the 18C when the balconies with Baroque brackets were added. Beyond, on the other side of the road, is the **Chiesa del Santissimo Salvatore**, whose 18C façade was designed by Giovan Battista Vaccarini.

Continuing along Via San Domenico, on the right, is the **Chiesa della Madonna del Rosario** which, until 1782, served as the main seat of the Inquisition Tribunal. Erected in the 16C, it was radically altered during the 18C when the interior was given its stucco decoration and frescoed by the Messina painter Domenico Giordano. Salita Castello, on the left, leads up to the city walls built by the Spanish, the outermost and the most impressive of the walls surrounding the castle.

Città bassa

The lower part of town is the more modern section of Milazzo, built in the 18C when the decision to abandon the old town centre was taken in favour of a flatter site, nearer the sea. At the heart of this part of town is the Piazza Caio Duilio, beside which a fish market takes place every morning. Facing onto the west side of the piazza is Palazzo Marchese Proto (once Garibaldi's headquarters); on the eastern side is the **Chiesa del Carmine**'s elegant **façade★**, composed of a lovely doorway (1620), an architrave sculpted with garlands and volutes, and a niche containing the statue of the Madonna della Consolazione (1632). This is flanked by the graceful frontage of the Convento del Carmine, where municipal offices are now located.

Continue along the old Strada Reale, now Via Umberto I, past the occasional noble *palazzo*, in a poor state of repair. On the parallel street, Via Cumbo Borgia, is the **Duomo Nuovo**, built in the 1930s. Its interior is hung with a few prized paintings: on the high altar, figures of St Peter and St Paul (1531) frame the wooden effigy of St Stephen; these panels are from a dismantled polyptych by Antonello de Saliba, who also painted the *Adoration of the Shepherds*. The luminous *Annunciation* painted with vibrant colours typical of the Venetian School and the *St Nicholas Enthroned with Scenes from his Life* are both attributed to Antonio Guffrè, a painter of the Antonelli School (end of the 15C).

Posted at the crossroads with Via Cristoforo Colombo is the Liberty-style **Villino Greco**, with its fine friezes of stylised flowers and organic decoration.

Tours

CAPO DI MILAZZO

Approximately 8km/5mi by car

Take the **Lungomare Garibaldi** along the seafront, overlooked by the elegant proportions of the 18C façade of Palazzo dei Marchesi D'Amico, and cross the waterfront district of Vaccarella which begins with the piazza before the Church of Santa Maria Maggiore; follow the **panoramic road★** which runs along the eastern side of the Milazzo promontory to the end. Arriving at **Capo dì Milazzo★**, pause to take in the wonderful **view★★** of the surrounding landscape: intense greens merging with the burnt browns of the Mediterranean *maquis* extend over the rocky spur to blend with the dazzling blue of the sea beyond.

From the left side of Piazza Sant'Antonio, a short flight of steps drops down to the **Santuario di Sant'Antonio di Padova** and the bay it overlooks, to which it has lent its name. The place is called after St Antony of Padua, who, it is said, sought refuge in a cave here during a storm in 1221. Since then, it has been a place of pilgrimage; it was transformed into a sanctuary in 1575 under the patronage of a nobleman, Andrea Guerrera; in the 18C it was further endowed with altars and decoration of polychrome marble, and some new panels in shallow relief depicting scenes from the life of the saint.

To return a different route, take the road along the ridge of the little peninsula, passing several of the many elegant villas, and fork right along the road to **Monte Trino**, the highest point on this tongue of land, unfortunately spoilt by the erection of telecommunications transmitters. The name is all that remains of a temple, dedicated, it would seem in Greek and Roman times, to the pagan triad of Apollo, Diana and Isis (or Osiris). From the little piazza before the small **Chiesetta della Santissima Trinità**, there are wonderful **views★** over Milazzo, its citadel and the sickle-shaped promontory.

To the west, the coast opens out into a beautiful long strip of sand. This is followed by the coastal road to the **Grotta di Polifemo**, where Odysseus' mythical meeting with the Cyclops is supposed to have taken place.

In front of the cave stretches the broad beach that lines the glorious **Baia del Tono** (known locally as *Ngonia*, from the Greek word for bay). A little further on may be seen the remains of the former **tuna fishery**, although these are now incorporated into a tourist complex.

A DAY TRIP INLAND

180km/112mi round trip from Milazzo – allow one day.

This excursion follows S 113, occasionally heading inland up the slopes of the ***Monti Peloritani****, the Sicilian extension of the Calabrian Apennines.*

Follow S 113 to Patti as far as San Biagio (for information on the Villa Romana di Terme Vigliatore, see Golfo di PATTI), then take S 185 to Novara di Sicilia. After 5km/3mi, turn right to Montalbano Elicona (44km/27mi from Milazzo).

Montalbano Elicona

Perched at an altitude of 900m/3 000ft on the eastern spur of the Nebrodi mountains, this town offers excellent opportunities for walking through woodland (Bosco di Malabotta) and rambling among the rocky crags of Argimosco. On arrival, the most impressive feature is the great **castle** which dominates the rest of the town. This was erected by Frederick II of Swabia on the site of an earlier small Arab fortress, and destroyed by him following the Guelph uprising in 1232. It was then rebuilt by Frederick II of Aragon in the early 14C, as an elegant fortified residence so typical of that time. Situated on the highest outcrop on the western edge of the town, it is surrounded by a network of narrow, sloping medieval streets, atmospheric in the extreme. Inside the castle complex is a large courtyard in the middle of which stands a chapel complete with traces of frescoes.

It is well worth walking around the ramparts, although this may be awkward in parts *(special care required climbing up)*, so as to take full advantage of the views in every direction. *(♿) Open Apr-Sep, 9am-1pm and 3-7pm; Oct-Nov, 9am-1pm and 3-6pm; Dec-Mar, by appointment only. No charge. ☎ 0941 67 99 38; www.comunedimontalbano.com*

Return to S 185 and turn right to Novara di Sicilia (36km/22mi from Montalbano). This wonderful **scenic road** winds its way through a landscape of pine forests and lush Mediterranean vegetation.

Novara di Sicilia

This small mountain town, between the Peloritani and Nebrodi mountain ranges, is laid out on medieval lines, complete with a towering Saracen castle, now in ruins. In the centre stands the **Duomo**, which shelters a remarkable carved wooden altar, candlesticks and lecterns, sculpted with unusual figures with primitive features.

The road continues inland on S 185 to a mountain pass, **Portella Mandrazzi** (1 125m/3 690ft), from where wonderful views stretch over the Alcantara valley and beyond, to Mount Etna.

From here, it is possible to carry on to Francavilla di Sicilia and to explore the fascinating Valle dell'Alcantara (see TAORMINA).

To continue with the excursion inland, make your way back to S 113, head towards Milazzo and after 5km/3mi, turn right to Castroreale (33km/21mi from Novara di Sicilia).

Castroreale

The ancient town of Cristina, perched upon a series of spurs among the Monti Peloritani, became a dominion of considerable importance with jurisdiction over an extensive area following Frederick II of Aragon's concession of sovereignty in exchange for loyalty during the war against the Angevins. Rechristened Castroreale, it retains many medieval features, interconnecting little streets and alleys that open onto delightful little piazzas, and many churches, several containing a wealth of artworks that testify to the town's glorious past.

The visit starts in Piazza del Duomo.

Chiesa Madre – An elegant Baroque portal graces the façade of the main church in stark contrast with the massive 16C campanile, which was probably used as a watchtower. **Inside** are hung a charming ***St Catherine of Alexandria*** (1534) and *Mother and Child* (1501) by Antonello Gagini and, in the north aisle, Andrea Calamech's *St James the Great (St James the Apostle).* From the terrace, on the east side of the church, there is a magnificent **view★** over the plain of Milazzo; an inscription records further privileges granted to the "royal town" by King Philip IV of Spain in 1639.

Continue along Corso Umberto I, and then turn left towards the 15C **Chiesa della Candelora** – a church dedicated to Candlemas, the feast commemorating the purification of the Blessed Virgin Mary and the presentation of Christ in the Temple – with its simple brick façade and Durazzo portal.

Proceed along Salita Federico II to a round **tower**, all that survives of the castle built by Frederick II of Aragon in 1324. From the top there is a fine **view★** over Castroreale, the little Moorish dome of the Church of the Candelora, and the surrounding countryside beyond.

Head back down to Piazza Peculio; this owes its name to the former Peculio Frumentario (Wheat Store) which has since been replaced by the town hall. This was very probably the Jewish quarter: the arch on the viewing terrace behind Monte di Pietà is supposed to have been that of a synagogue transferred from hereabouts. The piazza is flanked by the 15C Church of the Holy Saviour **(San Salvatore)**, severely damaged in the earthquake of 1978, and its semi-collapsed bell tower (1560) which once formed part of a chain of watchtowers with those of the cathedral and the castle.

Further along Via Guglielmo Siracusa (formerly Via della Moschita), there is a small art gallery on the right.

Pinacoteca di Santa Maria degli Angeli – *Open by appointment only. For further information, contact Signore Bilardo at least two days in advance. ☎ 090 97 46 036. €1.*

This art gallery houses various rare paintings and sculptures, including a panel of St Agatha (c 1420) in the Byzantine style, an unusually delicate Flemish triptych depicting *The Adoration of the Magi* with St Marina and St Barbara, a fine polyptych of *The Nativity* from the Neapolitan studio of GF Criscuolo, a marble statue of St John the Baptist by Calamech (1568) and a silver altar-frontal by Filippo Juvarra (18C).

Museo Civico – *Via G. Siracusa. Open Jul-Aug, 9am-1pm and 4-8pm; Sep-Jun, 9am-1pm and 3-7pm. Closed Wed afternoon and public hols. No charge. ☎ 090 97 46 444; www.castroreale.it*

The municipal museum, in a former oratory dedicated to St Philip Neri, contains sculptures in wood and marble, including the splendid **funeral monument★** of Geronimo Rosso (1506-08), an extremely fine work by **Antonello Gagini**, as well as a number of notable paintings. Among the best are: a 14C Crucifix with scenes from the life of Christ, a lovely *Madonna and Child* by Antonello de Saliba (1503-05) – with the infant portrayed with the face of an adult – a Salvator Mundi (Saviour of the World) panel by Polidoro da Caravaggio betraying the clear influence of Raphael, and an altarpiece depicting St Lawrence by Fra' Simpliciano da Palermo.

Further along the same street is **Sant'Agata**, which was remodelled in the 19C and which contains an *Annunciation* by Antonello Gagini (1519), a statue of St Agatha (1554) by the Florentine sculptor Montorsoli, and an expressive 17C plaster and *papier-mâché* image known as the **"Cristo Lungo"**, which is carried in procession on a 12-metre pole so as to be visible from every corner of the town. *Open Apr-Sep, 6-8.30pm; Oct-Mar, 5-7.30pm. Visitors are advised to book at least two days in advance. ☎ 090 97 46 444 or 090 97 46 514.*

Nearby is the 16C **Santa Marina**, a church incorporating masonry from the Norman period and vestiges of fortifications typical of Spanish defences.

Return once again to S 113 and continue along the road as far as Olivarella, then turn right to Santa Lucia del Mela (20km/12.5mi from Castroreale).

Santa Lucia del Mela

The little town is overshadowed by the silhouette of the **castle** which was built in the 9C by the Arabs, and altered during the Swabian and Aragonese occupations. Little survives other than a massive round tower fortifying the main gateway, part of a triangular bastion, and sections of the defensive walls which shelter the **Santuario della Madonna della Neve** (1673). Inside hangs a lovely *Madonna of the Snow* by **Antonello Gagini** (1529). The terrace to the left of the church affords good views of the surrounding countryside, and of the stone-dressed church corner and window surrounds.

On the way down into the town, there is an elegant Renaissance **doorway**★ in the façade of the **Chiesa Madre di Santa Lucia** (17C): note the lunette containing a relief of the Madonna attended by St Agatha and St Lucy, with the royal eagle, symbol of regal patronage. To the left of the church is Piazza del Duomo and the Bishop's Palace, marked by its heavily rusticated entrance.

Left of the **Chiesa dell'Annunziata** *(in Via Garibaldi)* stands a wonderful 15C campanile with three tiers of single openings surrounded with volcanic stone. The doorway, which dates from 1587, is ornamented with panels of delicate relief illustrating the *Annunciation*, surrounded with a garland of organic decoration.

From Santa Lucia, return to Olivarella and then turn right onto S 113. Follow the road as far as Scala, then turn right to Roccavaldina (20km/12.5mi from Santa Lucia).

Roccavaldina

The main attraction of this little town is the extraordinary apothecary's **pharmacy**★ which in itself is quite unique. The shopfront consists of a fine 16C Tuscan-style doorway flanked by a stone counter from which members of the public used to be served. Inside, arranged on the fabulous old wooden shelves are a rare **collection of maiolica drug jars**★★ (*albarelli*) datable from about 1580. Indeed, what is truly exceptional about this collection is that all the pieces come from the famous Patanazzi family workshop in Urbino, having been commissioned by the Messina herbalist Cesare Candia (whose coat of arms, a dove and three stars on a turquoise background, can be seen on each and every one of the 238 jars assembled). The collection, acquired by a priest from Rocca, has been in the town since 1628; it includes long-necked vases, small jugs with handle and spout, and *albarelli* (typical, tall, pharmacy jars) bearing scenes from the Bible, Classical mythology or the history of Ancient Rome. There are two magnificent display amphorae (note their wonderful handles) decorated, in relief, with characteristic grotesques and a narrative panel: Julius Caesar receiving Senior Captivi *(right)* and the contest of Apollo versus Marsyas who, on losing, was tied to a tree and flayed alive. *For information on admission times and reservations, call ☎ 090 99 48 302.*

Overlooking the same piazza is the 16C **castle**, a transitional building somewhere between a fortress and an aristocratic residence; the massive walls along the right side are tempered by the elegant balconies and their voluted brackets.

On the edge of the town, set in the gardens of the former Capuchin monastery, stands a gracious **municipal villa**, enjoying a privileged situation with a panoramic **view**★ over the promontory of Milazzo and the fortress of Venetico Superiore with its four round towers.

Follow the scenic road for a further 6km/4mi.

Rometta

Strategically positioned at a height of 600m/2 000ft, Rometta has earned its place in history by courageously resisting the Arab invaders: it was the last town to fall into their hands in 965. Little remains of the city walls other than the two pointed gateways, Porta Milazzo and Porta Messina.

The **Chiesa Madre** dedicated to the Madonna of the Assumption, has a fine doorway *(left side)* decorated with a frieze of organic and animal motifs. From the ruins of Frederick II's **castle**, there is a wonderful **view**★ of Capo Milazzo and the Aeolian Islands.

From Rometta, you can either return to Milazzo (22km/14mi) or head towards Villafranca and follow the tour around Capo Peloro (see MESSINA).

Modica★

Twice Modica has been devastated, turned upside down, destroyed or badly damaged, and twice it has pulled itself together ready to face the future. Once was after the earthquake of 1693; the second disaster was a flood in 1902. Today the town is an attractive collection of Baroque churches and picturesque stairways linking the upper and lower sections of town. One of Modica's highlights is the Antica Dolceria Bonajuto, a confectionery shop founded 120 years ago which is renowned for its traditional specialities.

Location

Population: 52 775. Michelin map 565 Q 26 – Ragusa. Modica is divided into two parts: the upper town, dominated by the castle, lies to the north; the lower town, hemmed in by high ground, extends along the two main streets **Via Marchesa Tedeschi** and **Corso Umberto I** that converge to form a Y. The Scalinata di San Giorgio links the two sections of town. ℹ *Corso Umberto I 246; ☎ 0932 75 27 47; Fax 0932 75 28 97.*

Neighbouring sights are described in the following chapters: COMISO; Cava d'ISPICA; NOTO; RAGUSA.

Background

Before the earthquake of 1693, a large proportion of the population lived in troglodyte dwellings cut into the steep limestone cliffs surrounding the modern town. In the centre, stood the castle enclosed on the north side by walls, isolated on its rocky spur. Through the valley flowed two rivers which converged midway to form the River Scicli (or Motucano). Then, as the threat of attack slowly dwindled, the people moved down into the valley; it was not until the terrible earthquake of 1693, however, that the cave dwellings were finally abandoned. The town clustered naturally into a Y-shape around the confluence of the two rivers. Unity was ensured by a succession of 20 bridges between the different banks, transforming the place into a veritable city on water and earning it the epithet "Venice of the South". Then the second disaster struck: a series of freak storms in 1902 raised the water level to a terrifying height of 9m/29ft at the confluence. The town took it all in its stride: the waterways were sealed off and transformed into wide streets that became the main thoroughfares of present-day Modica.

Walking About

Since the 19C, the upper and lower sections of the town have been dramatically linked by a fabulous stairway leading up from Corso Umberto I to San Giorgio, Modica's most beautiful church. This most magnificent among Baroque buildings must surely be the obvious point with which to begin a description of the city.

San Giorgio★★

The flight of almost 300 steps complements the elegant façade, merging with it to produce a most dramatic **composition★★**. Traditionally, its conception has been attributed to Rosario Gagliardi, although some claim the design to result from a collaboration of architects from Noto, notably Paolo Labisi; either way, it was completed in the 19C. The stairway was finished in 1818. The lofty front elevation rises through three levels to a single bell tower; a sense of sweeping movement is imparted by the projecting convex central bay, flanked on each side by twin bays that accommodate the double aisles. A balustrade and a pair of compact volutes act to soften the strong horizontal transition between the ground and first levels. Inside, St George's contains a highly prized chased silver altar front upon which sits a fine **polyptych** (1513) by Bernardino Niger. The three tiers show the Holy Family between St George and St Martin with, above, the Joyful Mysteries and the Glorious Mysteries. The transept floor is inlaid with a 19C meridian line by A Perini. The third

G. Bludzin/MICHELIN

G. Bludzin/MICHELIN

Directory

Transport

The most convenient way of reaching the town is by car, although train (20min from Ragusa and approximately 2hr from Siracusa) and bus services are also available (for information contact the tourist office).

Where to Eat

• *For all budgets*

L'Arco – *Piazza Corrado Rizzone 11, Modica – ☎ 0932 94 27 27 – Closed Mon – €18.* A typical rustic trattoria serving generous portions of home-made, regional cuisine. Good value for money.

Fattoria delle Torri – *Vico Napolitano 14, Modica – ☎ 0932 75 12 86 – Closed Mon – Booking recommended – €29/45.* This traditional restaurant, located in an elegant old *palazzo* in the town centre, serves a range of interesting and creative dishes based on local specialities. Meals can also be taken under the shade of the lemon trees in the attractive outdoor courtyard.

Where to Stay

• *Moderate*

Hotel Bristol – *Via Risorgimento 8/B, Modica – ☎ 0932 76 28 90 – Fax 0932 76 33 30 –* P ♿ *– 27 rooms. €47/88.* Situated in a quiet, residential area in the modern part of the town, this simple, well-kept hotel is ideal for both business visitors and tourists. The rooms here are comfortable and well-appointed, and the staff friendly and welcoming.

Taking a Break

Antica Dolceria Bonajuto – *Corso Umberto I 159, Modica – ☎ 0932 94 12 25 – www.ragusaonline.com/bonajuto/ – Closed Mon.* This confectioner's, founded in 1880, offers delicacies such as *mpanatigghi* (sweet pastries with an unusual filling of minced meat and chocolate); *liccumie* (aubergine and vanilla- and cinnamon-flavoured chocolate made according to the original Aztec recipe); and *riposti* (delicately decorated almond sweets, originally produced for weddings). Also worth sampling are the *aranciate* and *cedrate* (small sweets made with orange and lemon peel) and the *nucatoli* (made with dried figs, almonds, quince and honey).

Caffè dell'Arte – *Corso Umberto I 114, Modica – ☎ 0932 94 58 95 – Closed Wed.* This café is renowned for its *granite* (crushed ice drinks), its excellent *cannoli* and its *cassate*.

chapel on the right contains an Assumption altarpiece by Francesco Paladini. Beside the church stands **Palazzo Polara** which houses the **Pinacoteca Comunale**, and its collection of contemporary paintings. *Open daily except Sun, 9am-1pm. No charge.*

On Via Posteria is the **Casa Natale di Salvatore Quasimodo**, the house where the 20C poet was born, containing furniture and possessions from the writer's study in Milan. *Open Jun-Sep, 10am-1pm and 4.30-7.30pm; Oct-May, 10am-1pm and 3.30-6.30pm. For further information, contact the Cooperativa Etnos. ☎ 0932 75 27 47.*

Continue on down to Corso Umberto I, the main thoroughfare of the Città Bassa (lower town), lined with elegant 18C *palazzi* and religious institutions. At the north end sits **Palazzo Manenti**, ornamented with carved stone portraits of various famous figures living in the 18C. As the street approaches the centre, it passes the lovely undulating façade of **Santa Maria del Soccorso** and, a little further on, the Church of San Pietro.

San Pietro

St Peter's was rebuilt after the earthquake: a flight of steps leads up to the front **façade★**, ornamented with statues representing the twelve Apostles.

Chiesa Rupestre di San Nicola Inferiore

Open Jun-Sep, 10am-1pm and 4.30-7.30pm; Oct-May, 10am-1pm and 3.30-6.30pm. €1.50. For further information, contact the Cooperativa Etnos. ☎ 0932 75 27 47.

In the apse of the rock-hewn church are a series of Byzantine-style frescoes dating from the Norman era. Pride of place is given to Christ Pantocrator (in the centre) surrounded by His almond-shaped aura; at His sides, stand the Madonna and Child and the Archangel Michael, together with a host of saints in attendance. The building, probably consecrated to serve the Greek Orthodox community, consists of a simple hall church: its nave, which terminates with an apse, would originally have been divided by a wall in accordance with Basilian prototypes.

G. Bludzin/MICHELIN

B. Kaufmann/MICHELIN

At the intersection with the other branch of the Y (Via Marchesa Tedeschi) stands **San Domenico** with, beyond, the town hall. This provides a good view of the round tower of the castle above, clinging to its rock, surmounted since the 18C with a clock tower. Almost opposite, the little Via De Leva leads through to the *palazzo* which shares its name, and which has a fine **Chiaramonte Gothic** entranceway. Before the end of the street stands the Baroque **Chiesa del Carmine** which only preserves a doorway with, above, a magnificent rose-window from the original Chiaramonte church. Continue as far as the junction with Via Mercé and turn right: up ahead are the Church of the Madonna delle Grazie and the **Convento dei Padre Mercedari** which now houses the **Museo Civico** and Museo delle Arti e Tradizioni Popolari *(see Worth a Visit)*.

Behind the castle in Via Crispi, sits **Palazzo Tomasi Rosso** with its decorative limestone doorway and balconies; note the stone-carved grimacing masks and acanthus leaves and delicate wrought iron railings.

Via Marchesa Tedeschi, the other arm of the Y, climbs up to *Modica Alta* (upper Modica). At one time, these two towns were legally and administratively autonomous.

Santa Maria di Betlem

This church preserves *(at the far end on the right)*, through an elegant 15C doorway, the attractive **Capella Cabrera**.

An elaborate 19C Nativity scene in the north aisle comprises 60 or so terracotta figures modelled by G Papale.

The street continues uphill past the 19C Baroque-fronted Church of **San Giovanni Evangelista**, elevated up a broad set of steps. At the top (Belvedere del Pizzo), a splendid **view★** extends over the town encompassing, in particular, the Jewish quarter known as *il Cartellone (on the right, beyond Corso Umberto I)*, and the Francavilla district *(the near side of Corso Umberto I)*, the oldest part of town dominated by San Giorgio.

Worth a Visit

Museo delle Arti e Tradizioni Popolari★

In the Convento dei Padri Mercedari. (♿) Open Jun-Oct, 10am-1pm and 4.30-7.30pm; Nov-May, 10am-1pm and 3.30-6.30pm. Closed 1 Jan. €2.50. ☎ 0932 75 27 47.

This museum, dedicated to the rural arts, crafts and practices, displays a vast collection of farming tools, furnishings and handmade bits and pieces. What makes this museum especially unusual and effective is the way objects are presented in their "natural context" as part of an integral arrangement. The reconstituted workshop interiors are self-explanatory: alongside the farmstead, the mainstay of any agricultural peasant community, are the bee-keeper, blacksmith, cobbler, tailor, cartwright, pastry cook, not forgetting the barber's shop.

The monastery also houses the small **Museo Civico**, which displays a collection of artefacts from the local area. *(♿) Open daily except Sun, 9am-1pm. No charge. ☎ 0932 94 50 81.*

Excursions

Scicli

10km/6mi SE. Scicli is tucked away high up in the hinterland, slightly off the beaten track. Its other name, the town of the Siculi, suggests that it is ancient in origin. Affected like the rest of the Val di Noto by the 1693 earthquake, the Scicli of today presents its new and reformed face, risen like a phoenix from the ashes.

The tour starts in Piazza Italia. For information on opening times of the churches, contact the local tourist office (Pro Loco) at Via Castellana 2; ☎ 0932 93 27 82.

The **Chiesa Madre**, dedicated to St Ignatius, shelters the **wooden statue of the Madonna on horseback**: her other name, Madonna delle Milizie, is explained by popular legend. This tells of how she is supposed to have fought at Roger I's side, thus ensuring his victory over the Saracens. Originally, the carved figure was kept in its own sanctuary about 6km/4mi west of the town.

G. Bludzin/MICHELIN

G. Bludzin/MICHELIN

Directory

Festivals

Three festivals are honoured and celebrated by Scicli. The first, the Cavalcata di San Giuseppe, takes place on 18 (evening preparations) and 19 March. This essentially commemorates the flight of Joseph and Mary into Egypt, although it also celebrates the rite of spring after the passage of winter with all the affiliated pagan rituals required. Colour is the festival's dominant element as flowers are used to bedeck the horses' harnesses and great wood bonfires are lit along the route followed by the fugitives, lighting up the garish costumes of the onlookers who throng the streets. Meanwhile the air rings with jingling horse bells and people's voices animated with merriment after the procession, gathering for great feasts partaken in each other's houses.

At Easter, the **Festa dell'Uomo Vivo** celebrates life itself with a lively procession of a statue representing the Resurrected Christ, raced along by young men, through the town's streets.

At the end of May, the **Battaglia delle Milizie** takes place: this consists of a statue of the Madonna on horseback being carried in procession, defeating and trampling over Saracen soldiers (long ago, this festival took place on the Saturday before Easter).

Opposite the church stands **Palazzo Fava**; its corbels are carved with emblems of chivalry. The balcony overlooking San Bartolomeo is especially fine.

On the corner of the piazza, a narrow staircase to the right of the church leads up to Via Duca d'Aosta and **Palazzo Beneventano**. This building, an elegant example of secular late Baroque architecture (18C), is flamboyantly ornamented with corbels sculpted with fantastical figures, decorative pilasters and, over the windows, masks of Moors and Muslims, and aggressive, wild tiger-like animals baring their teeth. The first corner of the house to come into view is ornamented with shields.

Head back down to Piazza Italia and follow Via San Bartolomeo to the end of the street.

The elegantly restrained façade of **Chiesa di San Bartolomeo**, verging on the neo-Classical, rises through three tiers of columns to a bell tower capped with a ribbed dome. Inside, it contains an 18C **Nativity scene**★ fashioned by the Neapolitan craftsman Pietro Padula. All 29 carved wooden figures (originally there were 65) are most beautifully crafted, each endowed with a lovely face and exquisitely rendered costumes.

To the rear of the church is the **Colle di San Matteo**. The caves that punctuate the side of the hill form part of the **Chiafura troglodyte settlement**, which continued to serve as dwellings until the 1960s (the majority of cave-dwellers moved down into the valley below after the earthquake of 1693).

Bird's-eye Views

Two spots provide a good overview of the town's rooftops: one is **Colle della Croce** in front of the 16C-17C Church of Santa Maria della Croce; the other, offering the marginally better prospect, is **Colle di San Matteo** set before a church of the same name, now sadly abandoned. Behind it rise the ruins of a castle that was possibly constructed during the Arab occupation.

Via Mormino Penna – This elegant street passes between the fine Baroque exteriors of several *palazzi* and three churches. The first in line is **San Giovanni Evangelista**, a church with a fine **façade**★ fronting a convex central section reminiscent of the peculiar style of Rosario Gagliardi, to whom it is attributed. The elliptically planned building is decorated inside with neo-Classical stuccowork. A few paces up the street stands a second church, **San Michele** laid out according to the same oval plan as San Giovanni. The 19C building opposite, **Palazzo Spadaro**, preserves its original decoration inside and out (the interior may be viewed during office hours when the local council's cultural affairs department is at work). The street comes to an end before **Santa Teresa**, a church with a late Baroque interior including columns encrusted with stucco.

Walk back along Via Mormino Penna and turn down Via Nazionale to Piazza Busaccasu. The buildings facing onto the square include a Rococo church, **Chiesa del Carmine** and its adjacent convent, and **Palazzo Busacca** complete with clock. From the front of the church may be seen two more churches: Santa Maria della Consolazione and, in the distance, **Santa Maria la Nova**.

G. Bludzin/MICHELIN

B. Kaufmann/MICHELIN

Monreale★★★

Perched high above the Conca d'Oro, the old town of Monreale grew up around the cathedral and the royal palace built by William II. Even today, the life and soul of the town still radiates from around these same buildings, which are surrounded by a warren of narrow streets lined with souvenir shops, bars and small restaurants.

Location

Population: 29 885. Michelin map 565 21M – Palermo The historical centre of the town stretches across the slopes of Monte Reale, with the famous cathedral visible to the east of the town. Visitors are advised to park in one of the car parks in the lower town and head up to the centre by flights of steps. *Piazza Duomo; ☎ 091 63 98 011; Fax 091 63 75 400.*

Neighbouring sights are described in the following chapters: BAGHERIA; CARINI; PALERMO; SOLUNTO.

Background

In Norman times, Monte Reale was a royal hunting ground and the site of a royal hunting lodge.

In addition to the cathedral, this splendid complex of buildings comprising a Benedictine abbey and a royal palace (converted in the late 16C into the Archbishop's Seminary), was initiated by the grandson of Roger II, **William II**, around 1172. Legend relates how the Madonna appeared to him in a dream to suggest that he build a church with money concealed by his father in a hiding place that she would reveal. The building should be so grandiose as to rival the splendour of the greatest cathedrals of other European cities and should outshine the beauty of the Palatine Chapel in Palermo built by his grandfather, Roger. And so the most highly skilled craftsmen came to be employed to work on the project, with no expense spared. To the north, the church was flanked by the royal palace and, to the south, by the Benedictine monastery, of which the magnificent cloisters can still be admired today.

Special Features

DUOMO (Santa Maria La Nuova)★★★

Open 8am-6.30pm (Duomo); 9.30-11.45am and 3.30-5pm (treasury in the Cappella del Crocifisso), €2; ascent to the terraces, 9.30am-5.45pm, €1.50. ☎ 091 64 04 413.

The left side of the Duomo overlooks Piazza Vittorio Emanuele with its Fontana del Tritone. The main front, however, overlooks a smaller piazza which provides access to both the cloisters and a small **public garden** *(last doorway on the right facing the cloisters entrance and across a large courtyard)*, offering a magnificent **view**★★ over the Conca d'Oro.

Mosaics in the main aisle

G. Bludzin/MICHELIN

Directory

Transport

If arriving in Monreale by car from Palermo on Viale Regione Siciliana, take the Calatafimi-Monreale exit and then follow N 186. For visitors without their own transport, bus n°s 309 and 389 connect Piazza dell'Indipendenza with Monreale. For information contact AMAT, ☎ 091 35 01 11.

Where to Eat

Taverna del Pavone – *Vicolo Pensato 18, Monreale – ☎ 091 64 06 209 – bcec@libero.it Closed Mon and 15-30 Jun – €18/21.* This informal restaurant has a friendly, easygoing atmosphere and serves typical Sicilian cuisine at reasonable prices.

Festival

Settimana di musica sacra – This Festival of Sacred Music takes place between September and December, with concerts of sacred, spiritual and liturgical music held in the town's churches. For further information, contact the tourist office.

Exterior

The church is the product of a blend of artistic styles implemented by a combination of craftsmen. The two great towers on either side of the main front are quintessentially Norman in concept, as are the apses (one tall one flanked by two smaller ones), the basilica plan and, therefore, the fundamental arrangement of the cathedral. The superficial decoration applied to the **apses**, on the other hand, is clearly Arab in origin: this can best be **viewed**** from Via dell'Arcivescovado. From the same street, it is possible to make out the vestiges of the original royal palace now incorporated within the Archbishop's Palace.
The apses are articulated with three tiers of intersecting blind arcading: the pointed arches, of varying heights, rise from tall bases through slender columns. The decorative effect is heightened by the use of two different kinds of stone (warm gold-coloured limestone and black lava) as the ribs enclose rectangles filled with miniature circular rose windows traceried with kaleidoscopic star patterns. The same elements are repeated on the façade, although the full impact is marred somewhat by the portico, which was rebuilt in the 18C. This shelters the magnificent great bronze **doors**** **(D)**, designed in 1185 by **Bonanno Pisano** – the architect and sculptor responsible for the famous Leaning Tower of Pisa. It comprises 46 panels illustrating scenes from the Old and New Testaments. The surprisingly modern feel to this work is accomplished by an economical use of figures and a refined degree of stylisation. The two doors are hung within an elaborately moulded stone door frame in which panels of geometric motifs alternate with animals and human figures concealed among branching plant fronds in shallow relief and narrow strips of mosaic.
The entrance from Piazza Vittorio Emanuele, beneath a 16C portico, also consists of bronze **doors*** **(E)** with several narrative panels, this time by Barisano da Trani. The three biblical stories and scenes from the lives of various saints are incoporated among a range of decorative elements, only this time the style is more wooden, more firmly rooted in the Byzantine tradition, even though they were executed four years later.

Interior

Entrance from the west end. Visitors are advised to take coins for the coin-operated lighting of the mosaics.
For a brief moment the elaborate, predominantly golden mantle of mosaics is spellbinding. Gradually the eye grows accustomed to the crowded mass of forms and gleaming designs, focusing on the internal space enclosed by the individual parts of the church. The wide nave is separated from the two much smaller side aisles by columns with splendid capitals, some Corinthian, others of a composite order with acanthus leaves below and representations of Demeter and Persephone (Ceres and Proserpine) above. The capitals and the intrados (curved inner surface of the springer arches) sandwich dosserets decorated with Arab mosaics. Just beyond the halfway mark, the nave is interrupted by a monumental triumphal arch preceding the spacious area contained by the transept and apses, that rise up and above the level of the nave and aisles. This section of the floor is of inlaid marble, as are the skirting and lower part of the walls, echoing Byzantine influences. The wooden ceiling above the choir is 19C.
The church contains the tombs of William I **(F)** and William II **(G)**; the altar in the north transept **(H)** encloses the heart of Louis IX (St Louis), King of France, who died in Tunis in 1270 while his brother Charles I ruled Sicily.
The **Cappella del Crocifisso*** **(K)**, situated in the north apse, is elaborately decked with marble Baroque decoration, with a profusion of inlay work, shallow- and high-relief carving, figurative statues and volutes. The wooden Crucifix dates from the 1400s. The **treasury (L)**, set to one side, houses various reliquaries and other cult objects.

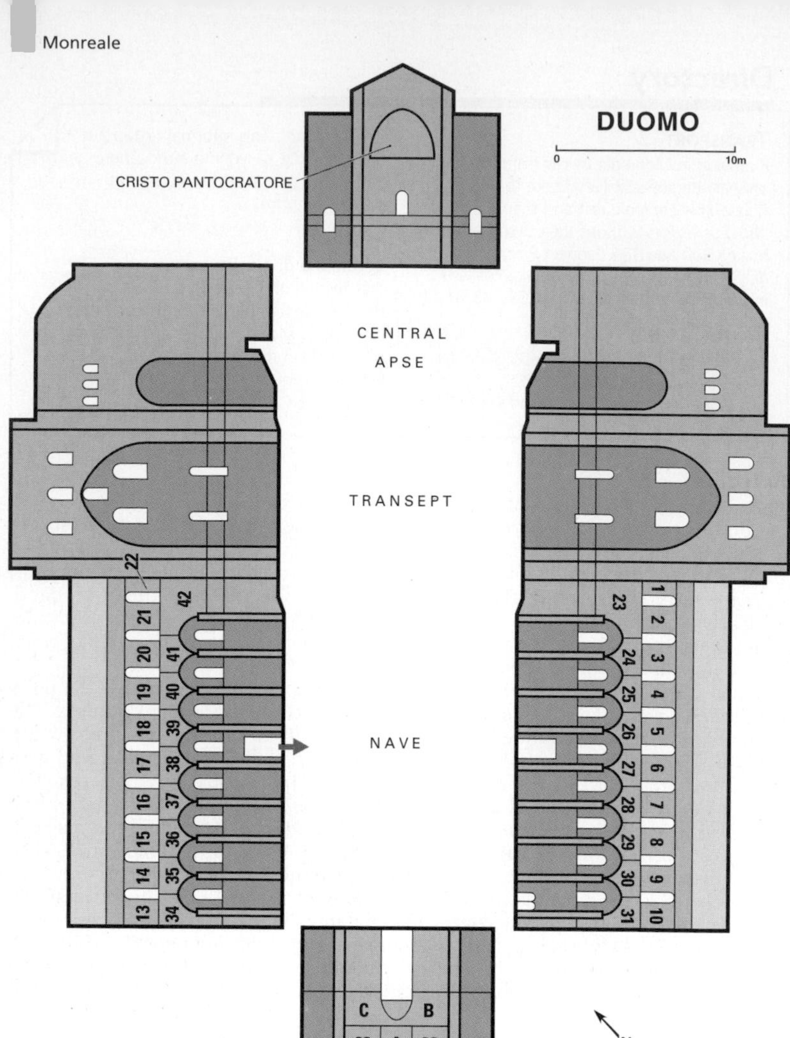

Mosaics★★★

Against a gold background, the characters of the Bible re-enact their stories. The colours are not as bright as those of the contemporary mosaics in the Palatine Chapel, but the figures are represented with greater realism and are endowed with more expressive personality. These mosaics were completed during the late 12C and early 13C by craftsmen from Venice and Sicily. The compositions and their component elements, together with the symbols used, are often the same as those in the Palatine Chapel. The sequential order of the scenes represented follows a precise programme in accordance with recommendations laid down under the papacy of Adrian I by the Seventh General Council at the Second Council of Nicaea, which was convened so as to end the Iconoclastic Controversy (787). This specified that art should be an instrument of religion and the liturgy, and serve to educate the faithful in the teachings of the Christian Church. The mosaics tell the story of Divine Redemption, beginning with the Creation of the Earth and Man, who by committing the act of Original Sin was forced thenceforth to toil in expiation, until God should intervene by choosing the people that He will prepare for salvation *(nave)*. The sending of Christ His own Son represents the realisation of redemption through the sacrifice of His life *(transept)* and works *(aisles)*. Christ's mission is then continued with the foundation of the Church and the example given by those men that followed His example *(smaller apses)*.
The individual scenes are full of realistically portrayed incidental detail: the ropes that bind the scaffolding erected around the Tower of Babel **(29)**; the knives on the table at the Wedding at Cana *(high up on the left-hand side of the crossing)*; the coins

falling from the table upset by Christ when He chased the moneylenders from the temple *(about halfway along the north aisle)*; the astonishing variety of fish depicted in the Creation **(6)** and caught in the fishermen's nets illustrating the Miraculous Draft of Fishes *(north transept)*. Many iconographic symbols are used, such as the cloud *(to denote transportation to another world)* that wraps itself around the figures that have fallen asleep as in the scene of the angel appearing to Joseph *(crossing, on the right)*, or the little dark figure that appears in several scenes, representing the devil – being cast out of those possessed or simply haunting evil people. Note also how the soul of Abel is depicted as a small red figure of spilt blood **(20)**.

Christ Pantocrator majestically fills the **central apse**, with the Virgin and Child below, pictured among angels and Apostles. The lowest tier is populated with saints. Below the arch, in the middle, is the Throne of Judgement.

The vaults of the **lateral apses** accommodate the figures of St Peter *(right)* and St Paul *(left)* with scenes from their lives below.

The life of Christ is depicted in the **chancel**, starting at the crossing where stories from His childhood are related. Christ's adult life is represented in the transept *(starting with south side)*, up until the descent of the Holy Spirit. The aisles illustrate a selection of Christ's miracles.

Below the **triumphal arch**, across the far side of the transept, sit two thrones with mosaic scenes above: the one on the right, above the archbishop's throne, shows William II's symbolic tribute to the church (the king offers up a model of the cathedral to the Madonna); on the left, the royal throne stands as confirmation of the Divine Protection conferred upon the king (Christ Himself crowns William). This latter panel depicts two lions facing each other (Eastern in derivation) in the tympanum: these symbols of Norman power also feature on the armrests of the royal throne.

The **nave** is devoted entirely to the Old Testament: **(1)** The spirit of God moving upon the face of the waters. **(2)** God dividing the light from the darkness in the presence of seven angels (for each day of the Creation). **(3)** The making of the firmament (Heaven) to divide the waters above the heavens from those below. **(4)** Separation of the waters into the seas from the land that was Earth. **(5)** Creation of the sun, the moon and the stars. **(6)** Creation of the birds of the air and the fish of the oceans. **(7)** Creation of Man. **(8)** God resting. **(9)** God leads Adam into the Garden of Eden. **(10)** Adam in the Garden of Eden. **(11)** Creation of Eve. **(12)** Eve is presented to Adam. **(13)** Eve is tempted by the Serpent. **(14)** Original Sin. **(15)** God discovers that Adam and Eve are ashamed of their nudity. **(16)** Adam and Eve are expelled from Earthly Paradise. **(17)** Adam working. Eve is seated with a spindle in her hand. **(18)** Sacrifice of Cain and Abel. *Only the sacrifice of Abel pleases God, symbolised by the ray of light shining straight from the Lord's hand.* **(19)** Cain slays Abel. **(20)** God discovers Cain's crime and curses him. **(21)** Cain is slain by Lamech *(a story from the Jewish tradition and not mentioned in Genesis)*. **(22)** God commands Noah to build an Ark. **(23)** Noah builds the Ark. **(24)** The animals board the Ark. **(25)** Noah welcomes the dove carrying the olive sprig, the sign that the waters have abated. **(26)** The animals come out of the Ark.

(27) Noah's sacrifice as a sign of thanks to God. Behind him is the rainbow, the symbol of God's covenant with Man. **(28)** The grape harvest *(on the left)*. On the right, Noah, drunk andhalf-naked, is discovered by his son, Ham, who calls his brothers to deride him. They are more respectful of their father's dignity and cover his nudity. *Hence the reason for Noah to curse Ham and his descendants, the Canaanites. This is why, henceforth, fathers often express the hope that their sons should not take a Canaanite wife.* **(29)** Noah's descendants unite and build the Tower of Babel in an attempt to reach heaven; this results in chaos. *God, fearing that the force of Man might overthrow Him, caused the people to quarrel with each other, to confound their language and scatter them abroad: this story is often taken to be a parable for upholding Church authority in the face of Man's litigiousness.* **(30)** Abraham, *having settled in the land of Sodom and Gomorrah,* encounters three angels sent by God and invites them to his house. *The angels represent the Trinity.* **(31)** The hospitality of Abraham. **(32)** *God sends two angels to destroy Sodom. Lot, Abraham's nephew, shows them hospitality.* Lot tries to prevent the inhabitants of Sodom from entering the house where the two angels are.

The three following scenes do not come from the Old Testament but relate to the story of St Cassius, St Castus and St Castrense (patron saint of Monreale). **(A)** Cassius and Castus, condemned to being thrown to the lions because they refused to renounce their faith in Christ, are saved when the lions are suddenly tamed and lick their feet. **(B)** Cassius and Castus are taken to a pagan temple causing it to collapse onto the infidels. **(C)** St Castrense cures a man possessed of the Devil who throws himself into the sea and causes a storm.

(33) Sodom in flames while Lot flees with his daughters; his wife, turning round to look back, is transformed into a pillar of salt. **(34)** God appears to Abraham and bids him to sacrifice his only son, Isaac. **(35)** The angel of the Lord stops Abraham from sacrificing his son. **(36)** *Abraham sends a servant to seek a wife for Isaac.* At the well, Rebecca offers up water to Abraham's servant and his camels to drink. **(37)** Rebecca

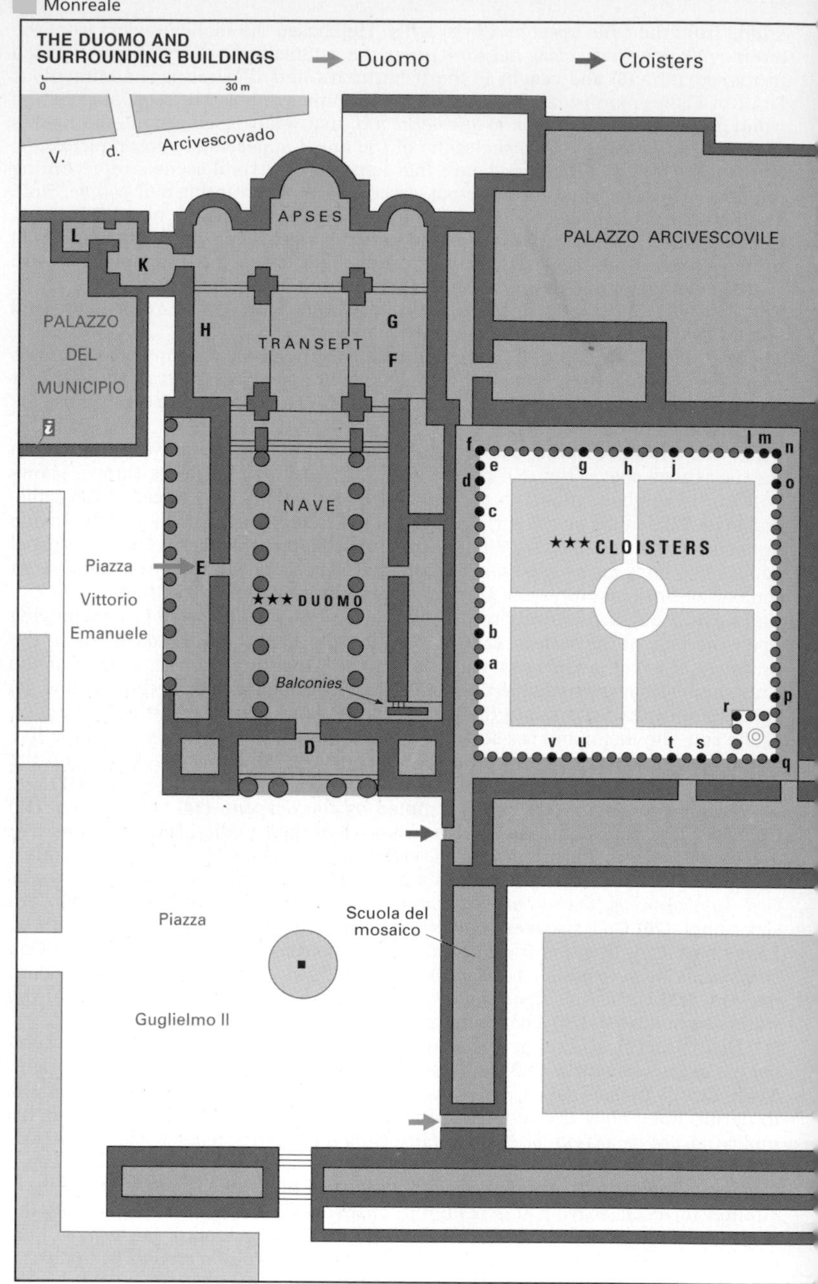

sets out on the journey to her chosen bridegroom, Isaac. **(38)** Isaac with his favourite son Esau, and his second son Jacob. **(39)** Isaac blesses Jacob, believing mistakenly that he is Esau *(depicted on the right, as he returns from hunting). Isaac, who is almost blind in his old age, is deceived by the goatskins covering the arms of Jacob who, unlike his brother, is smooth-skinned.* **(40)** Jacob flees from the vengeful anger of his brother, from whom he has stolen his father Isaac's blessing. **(41)** On his journey, Jacob dreams of a ladder leading from earth up to heaven being ascended by angels. God, at the top, grants him the land on which he has fallen asleep; on awaking, Jacob takes the stones he had been using as pillows and lays them down as a foundation for his city. **(42)** Jacob wrestles with the angel. *On his journey back to his brother Esau's, fearing lest he should be angry, Jacob sent forth his sheep and goats as offerings to him. That night, having made his family ford the stream, an angel approached and wrestled with him until dawn, when the angel blessed Jacob and bestowed upon him a new name: Israel (meaning the one who has fought with God and with Man, and has prevailed).*

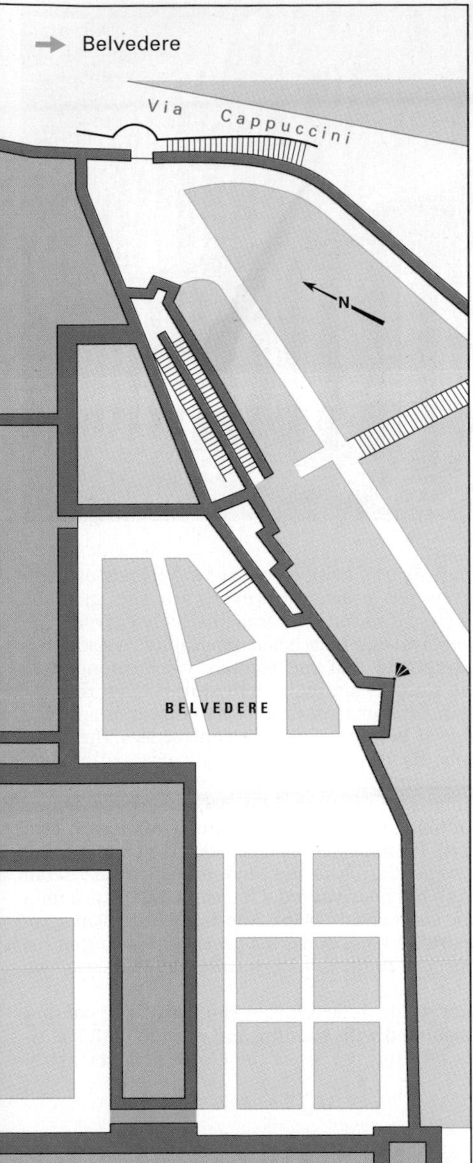

CLOISTERS

- **a** The parable of Dives and Lazarus
- **b** Corinthian capital with windswept leaves
- **c** The story of Samson
- **d** The Massacre of the Innocents
- **e** The Four Evangelists dominated by a mermaid
- **f** The Annunciation
- **g** Owls, symbols of vigilance formerly placed above the monk's cells
- **h** Birds pecking the volutes of the capital
- **j** Joseph sold into slavery in Egypt
- **l** The Resurrection
- **m** Telamons
- **n** Constantine and Helen present the cross of Christ rediscovered on Calvary, symbol of the Church's victory over the Synagogue
- **o** Acrobat
- **p** The cult of Mithras
- **q** The Apostles' mission to evangelise the world: they are depicted in groups of three, in tabernacles protected by a flying angel
- **r** The 12 months of the year
- **s** William II offering Monreale cathedral to the Virgin
- **t** Men of oriental appearance
- **u** Cherubs feeding animals
- **v** The story of Noah

Ascent to the terraces★★★

Access from the far end of the south aisle: but beware, it involves a long and arduous climb. The first outlook provides a marvellous view down over the cloisters. Further round, there is a wonderful view of the **apses**★★. The last, highest section provides magnificent **views**★★ of the Conca d'Oro.

CLOISTERS★★★

(♿) Open Mon-Sat, 9am-7pm; Sun and public hols, 9am-1.30pm. €4. ☎ 091 69 61 319; www.regione.sicilia.it/beniculturali/sopripa
The huge cloisters, one of the finest examples of a building inspired by Islamic architecture, present a series of pointed arches supported by sets of splendid small paired columns, many decorated with polychrome mosaic that is Eastern in inspiration. Those columns marking each corner of the cloisters, together with those at the corner of the tiny square cloisters surrounding the fountain *(southwest corner)*

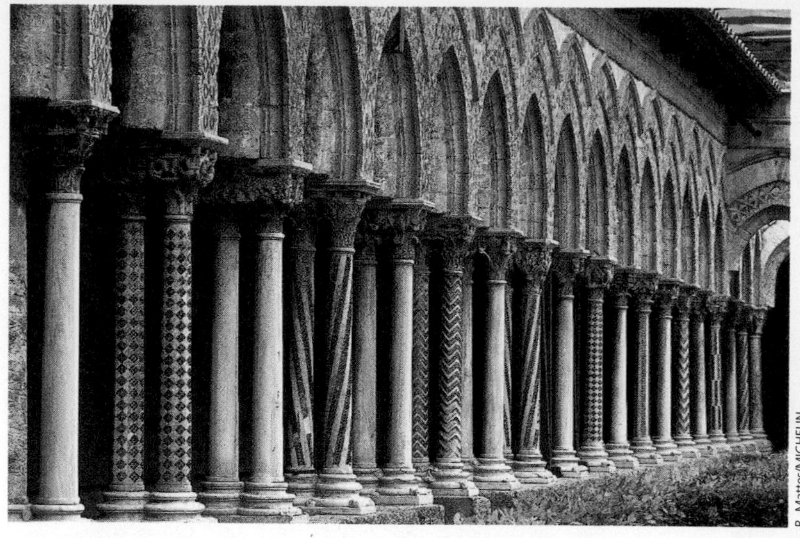
R. Mattes/MICHELIN

are sculpted with animals and human figures interwoven among fronds of luxuriant vegetation. The true jewels in the crown, however, are the fabulous **Romanesque capitals**, each distinctively different and imaginatively carved. The subject matter is drawn from both medieval and Classical iconography. Without following any particular sequence – implying that the capitals were intended as merely decorative – scenes from the Gospels alternate with stories from the Old Testament, symbolic and purely ornamental images, each possessing an originality all of its own. Even the Classical subjects betray a certain inventiveness: the acanthus leaves of the Corinthian capitals, for example, surprisingly natural looking, appear ruffled by the wind **(b)**. To these are added a variety of other subjects: birds stretching down to peck the plant volutes of the capital **(h)**, Atlas figures reaching up to support the weight of the arch **(m)**, cherubs feeding animals **(u)**, exotic characters wearing turbans with snakes **(t)**. Perhaps the most remarkable capital is the one **(s)** in which William II offers up the church to the Madonna: note the detail with which the south side of the church has been carved. One capital depicts a man killing a bull, the sacred symbol of the cult of Mithras **(p)**. Another features an acrobat **(o)**: his position, his weight supported by his arms, his back arched so that his feet rest on the back of his head *(his head in the centre)*, recalls the Trinacria, the ancient symbol of Sicily.

The tiny cloisters in the southwest corner, include a lovely **fountain**. The column in the centre of the circular bowl is sculpted with banding and crested with a cluster of animals. The serenity and grace of this corner of the cloisters is peculiarly evocative of Persian splendour.

Excursions

Castellaccio

3km/1.8mi W. The ruins of the late Norman castle perch on **Monte Caputo**, making for a popular excursion among the locals in the spring and summer as it offers an excellent place for a picnic *(some facilities available)*.

San Martino delle Scale

10km/6mi W of Monreale. Pleasantly situated at a height of 548m/1 797ft, this retreat has long been prized for its cool climate during the burning summer months endured by the coast. The town has assumed the name of the Benedictine monastery that was founded in the 6C by St Gregory the Great, and which was rebuilt and enlarged in the 16C. The **church** preserves a wonderful **wooden intarsia choir stall★** dating from the 16C.

The road leading up to the town affords spectacular **views★★** over the roofs of Monreale, the cathedral, the Conca d'Oro and Palermo.

Mozia★

This tiny island in the middle of the Laguna dello Stagnone (one of four islands in the lagoon) is so small that it is easy to forget the important role that it played in the history of its larger neighbour, Sicily. Yet this site was chosen by the Phoenicians as a suitable location for a vital and later prosperous colony. Its strategic position, surrounded by the shallow waters of the lagoon and naturally protected by Isola Grande on the seaward side, meant that it was coveted as a strategic trading post as much by the Carthaginian as by its Syracusan enemies. In the end, this was to be its undoing: besieged by the Syracusan forces, the old town of Motya was completely destroyed and left abandoned until it was rediscovered at the end of the 19C. Today, visitors to the island are greeted by a profusion of scents and colours: in spring the typical Mediterranean vegetation is especially lush, a perfect excuse in itself for a visit.

Location

Michelin map 565 1N 9 - Trapani. Ferries from the Ettore Infersa saltpans *(saline)* link Mozia with mainland Sicily. For visitors without their own transport, the easiest way to reach the ferry dock is by bus from Marsala. There are no restaurants on the island, so visitors are advised to bring their own provisions.

Neighbouring sights are described in the following chapter: VIA DEL SALE.

Background

THE ISLAND

The ancient Phoenician colony was founded in the 8C BC on one of the four islands of the Stagnone Lagoon now known as the **island of San Pantaleo** (the name it assumed in the high Middle Ages when a group of Basilian monks settled there). Motya, the Phoenician name by which it was known before, is alleged to translate loosely as "spinning centre", after wool carding and spinning cottage industries were instituted on the island. Like most other Phoenician colonies, the island became a commercial trade centre-cum-staging post for Phoenician ships plying the Mediterranean. The 8C BC also saw the beginning of the Greek colonisation of Sicily which, in the main, was concentrated on the east side of the island. It therefore seemed appropriate for the Phoenicians to consolidate their activities in the west, enabling Motya to grow in importance and to evolve into a small town. In the 6C BC, the struggle for Greek or Carthaginian supremacy over Sicily gained momentum, and Motya was forced into taking sides. Hefty defensive walls were erected around the settlement to provide better protection. In 397 BC, the tyrant of Syracuse, Dionysius the Elder, laid siege to the town until at last it capitulated, as every last will to continue was snuffed out. Its surviving inhabitants sought refuge on the mainland, and soon integrated themselves among the people of Lilybaeum, present day Marsala.

The rediscovery of *Motya* is associated with the name of **Joseph Whitaker**, an English nobleman living in the 1880s related to the family that owned a well-established and flourishing business producing and exporting Marsala wines. The house on the island built for Whitaker now accommodates a small museum.

THE LAGOON

Since 1984, the **Laguna dello Stagnone**, Sicily's largest lagoon (2 000ha/5 000 acres), has been designated a nature reserve of special interest – **Riserva Naturale Orientata**. This area extends into the sea, and includes the section of coastline between Punta Alga and Capo San Teodoro. The water here is shallow and very salty, the ideal conditions for salt works to be set up all along the coast and on Isola Grande, where it soon became the main industry; many of these have since dwindled into disuse.

The lagoon harbours four islands: Isola Grande is the largest, Santa Maria is covered in vegetation, San Pantaleo is the most important and Schola is a tiny islet with a few roofless houses that give it an eerie air of decadence.

The most common plant species to thrive here include the Aleppo pine, dwarf palm, bamboo (Isola Grande), **sea marigold** *(Calendula maritima)* which, in Europe, grows only here and in Spain, glasswort or sea samphire (with fleshy branches), sea scilla with its star-like white flowers, the sea lily and the sea rush. The islands are also populated with a multitude of bird species, namely the lark, goldfinch, magpie, Kentish plover, tawny pipit and Sardinian warbler – to mention but a few.

The waters of the Stagnone (which literally means large pool) provide fertile habitats for a broad variety of underwater flora and fauna: sea anemones, murex – collected by the Phoenicians so as to extract a valuable purple dye used for colouring textiles – and over 40 different kinds of fish including sea bass, gilthead, white bream and sole. The seabed also supports colonies of the **Poseidonia oceanica**, a ribbon-leafed seaweed which grows in clusters and produces a flower not unlike an ear of wheat from its centre. This plant is fast becoming a menace to others, spreading itself through the Mediterranean like wildfire: its contribution, however, is to thrive in polluted and slightly stagnant conditions; it stabilises the seabed, oxygenates the water and provides a source of nutrients for other species, thereby playing a role similar to that of the forests on land.

Worth a Visit

♿ *Access to the island and museum, 9am-1pm and 3pm-1hr before dusk. €3 (ferry); €6 (museum).* ☎ *0923 71 25 98.*

As recently as 1971, it was still possible to ride in a horse-drawn cart across the old Phoenician causeway linking the island to the mainland. Given that the causeway lay just below the surface of the water, passengers had the strange impression that they were "walking on water" *(see Porta Nord below)*. This was also the usual means by which the Grillo grapes grown on the island since the 19C were transported for use in making Marsala. In the centre stands the lovely 19C house built by the Whitakers, now a museum.

Excavations

Footpaths run along the perimeter of the island and lead in and among the remains of the Phoenician town (allow 90min; visitors are advised to follow the path in an anti-clockwise direction).

Fortifications – The island lies in the lee of what was once a peninsula – modern day Isola Grande – and was thus naturally protected from attack by the mainland and the shallow waters of the lagoon. In order to increase its natural defences, Motya was enveloped by an enclosure wall with watchtowers in the 6C BC. These fortifications were later modified and reinforced. The footpath skirts the remains of several towers, notably the **east tower** (with a rectangular base) with its staircase up to the ramparts.

Porta Nord – The North Gate is the more important and better preserved of the town's two entrances. The remains of the towers flanking the gateway are still clearly in evidence. Inside, a section of the original main street shows signs of wear, its surface rutted by ancient cart wheels.

On the seaward side, just below the surface of the water, extends a paved causeway linking Motya to Birgi on the mainland. It covered a distance of some 7km/4.5mi and was just wide enough to accommodate two carts abreast. Today, the way is "waymarked" above the surface allowing the keenest visitors to walk the causeway (although the wearing of rubber flip-flops or plastic sandals is highly recommended).

Enter through the gate and proceed along the main street.

Cappiddazzu – This alludes to the areas that lie just inside the North Gate: among the various buildings, the one divided into three aisles may have served a religious function.

Make your way back towards the shore.

Necropolis – A series of stelae and urns indicate the area used for Archaic cremations and burials. A second necropolis was located on the mainland at Birgi, at the far end of the submerged causeway directly opposite.

Tophet – The sacred area consists of an open-air sanctuary where urns containing the remains from human sacrifices to the goddess Tanit and the god Baal Hammon were deposited. At that time, the immolation of firstborn male children was widespread.

A little further along the track, the little island of Schola comes into view: this is the smallest of the Stagnone Lagoon islands, and is distinctively recognisable by its three pink roofless houses.

Cothon – The small rectangular man-made harbour is linked to the sea by a narrow channel. Its exact purpose is not known. Some experts believe it to have been built as a harbour for the smaller, lighter craft that might have plied between the island and the ships moored in the lagoon, ferrying passengers as well as merchandise.

The **Porta Sud** (South Gate) is situated immediately beyond the harbour: like the North Gate, it too is framed by towers. A little further on, the **Casermetta** was reserved for the military: the vertical stone shafts are a typical feature of Phoenician constructions.

G. Bludzin/MICHELIN

The small man-made harbour

The last monument is the **Casa dei Mosaici**, so called because it preserves two fine black and white pebble panels with a winged griffin chasing a deer, and a lion attacking a bull.

Museum – The museum is devoted to displaying artefacts recovered from the island itself, from Lilybaeum (Marsala) and from the necropolis at Birgi, on the shore opposite Motya. In the front courtyard, are arranged a series of stelae from the Tophet. The Phoenician and Punic pottery is simple in shape and devoid of any decoration; the imported Corinthian, Attic and Italiot vases, meanwhile, are decorated with black or red figures. The sculpture collection includes allegorical statuettes of motherhood, like the figurine of the *Great Mother*; terracotta heads betraying a Greek influence; not forgetting the superb **Ephebus of Motya**★★, a noble, proud-looking figure wearing a long, pleated garment, most evidently influenced by Archaic Greek prototypes.

Casa delle Anfore – The House with the Amphorae is located behind the museum, beyond the houses. It owes its name to the simple fact that a considerable number of amphorae were found there.

Nicosia

Clustered around the ruins of its castle, in the highest part of town, the historical centre of Nicosia is a maze of steep, narrow, cobbled streets fronted by churches and *palazzi*, many of which are in need of restoration. Dwellings that have been carved from the rock (now often converted into storerooms or garages) provide a reminder of the troglodyte cave habitations that were commonplace in former times, particularly in southeast Sicily.

Location

Population: 15 051. Michelin map 565 2N 5 – Enna. Situated at an altitude of 700m/2 300ft, the mountain town of Nicosia is perched on four rocky spurs across the southern slopes of the Nebrodi mountains. Signs to the town centre lead visitors to the elegant Piazza Garibaldi, the starting-point for visits to the town. ℹ *Piazza Garibaldi 1; ☎ 0935 67 21 11; Fax 0935 63 84 10.*

Neighbouring sights are described in the following chapter: MADONIE E NEBRODI.

Background

Founded during the Byzantine era when it acquired its eastern-sounding name (possibly a corruption of "Città di San Nicolò"), Nicosia shared the same fate as the rest of Sicily, having passed from Norman hands into Swabian, Aragonese, Castilian and then Bourbon control, but with a difference, as with each successive occupier it managed to resist subordination. This came about because of a strong rivalry between the upper and lower parts of the town, with each faction clinging fiercely to its respective church (San Nicolò and Santa Maria), so as to exclude all

B. Kaufmann/MICHELIN

Nicosia

other preoccupations. This predicament also faced other towns in Sicily (Ragusa and Modica being two examples), but here it assumed an unusual level of determination and aggression. Scuffles would break out in the street during religious processions until, finally, a gate was set up to mark the official division of the town into two. Even as recently as 1957, two crucifixes were borne through the town in separate processions celebrating Good Friday.

Walking About

Piazza Garibaldi

The piazza at the heart of the little town becomes especially atmospheric in the evening when it is suffused with artificial light. It is lined with distinguished-looking buildings, including San Nicolò and the 19C **Palazzo di Città**, which encloses an elegant internal courtyard ornamented with a fine wrought-iron lamp.

Cattedrale di San Nicolò

The cathedral was originally built in the Gothic style (conceived in 1340 as an extension to a chapel), but has undergone several remodellings through the ages. Evidence of its original splendour, however, is to be found in the elegant main **doorway★** decorated with flowers, acanthus leaves and palmettes; the bell tower which, although much altered, retains enough on the second level to suggest the impact of two- and three-arched openings enclosed within elaborate ogive arches. The left flank of the cathedral facing onto Piazza Garibaldi has an entrance ornamented with pointed arches, also from the Gothic period. Further up towards the apsed east end, carved into the external walls, are a set of sample weights and measures. The **interior** results from the many alterations undertaken, not least the ceiling completed in the 19C and crowned, in the dome, by an unusual statue of St Nicholas "suspended" from on high. This 17C figure is by Giovan Battista Li Volsi who, with his son Stefano, also built the **choir stalls★** out of walnut (1622), finely decorated with flowers and *putti*.

The first stalls harbour four scenes depicting *Christ entering Jerusalem (first on the left)* and, opposite, the *Coronation of the Virgin* (note, in the lower section, a representation of Nicosia before the landslide of 1757 which seriously affected the higher part of the town), while the *Martyrdom of St Bartholomew (second on the left)* has as its pennant the *Miracle of St Nicholas.*

The roof of the church, however, holds a secret: above the vault spans another earlier trussed and painted wooden ceiling from the 14C-15C *(closed to the*

Legend of Santa Claus

St Nicholas, or Santa Claus to Anglo-Saxons, was a bishop at Myra in Lycia (southwest Turkey) in the 4C. According to legend, he is reputed to be the mysterious benefactor of three eligible young girls whose father, unable to provide dowries for them, proposed to send them out as prostitutes until the necessary funds were raised. One night, the saint slipped unseen into their house to leave three full bags of coins, thus preserving their moral integrity. And so was born the figure of Santa Claus (or Father Christmas) who bestows gifts on well-behaved children.

public at the time of going to press). Attached to the inside wall of the main façade is an organ by Raffaele della Valle installed in a wooden loft by Stefano Li Volsi. The church preserves examples of Gagini workmanship in the baptismal font and pulpit, and a sculptural arrangement of *Christ in Glory between the Virgin and John the Baptist* attributed to Antonello Gagini *(second chapel on the left)*. The **chapter house** is hung with three fine 17C paintings: *Madonna and Child between John the Baptist and Santa Rosalia* by **Pietro Novelli**, a **St Bartholomew★** by *Lo Spagnoletto* (José de Ribera), in which the flogger and other onlookers are animated by intense realism, and a *Martyrdom of St Sebastian* by **Salvator Rosa**.

Turn up Salita Salomone between buildings from a more splendid age; continue along Via Ansaldi to **Chiesa di San Vincenzo Ferreri** which is frescoed by Guglielmo Borremans, and then on to Santa Maria Maggiore, strategically situated with glorious views of the hills and the lower part of the town.

Santa Maria Maggiore

For information on admission times, call ☎ 0935 63 90 15.

In 1757, a landslide swept away the upper part of the town including Santa Maria Maggiore. Very soon after, work was initiated on a replacement church, slightly taller than its predecessor, while all the local residents set to business in order to meet the cost. The noble La Via family gave a lovely 17C doorway from their *palazzo*; this now adorns the main front. Inside, the eye is immediately caught by the **Cona**, a large marble composition in six tiers illustrating scenes from the life of the Virgin, crowned with a figure of St Michael: a work by **Antonello Gagini** and his pupils. At the end of the south aisle is the throne of Charles V, so called after use by the Emperor when he passed through the town in 1535.

Atop the steep rocks behind the church stood the **castle**, now reduced to a mere ruin *(this is accessible by car along Via San Simone, a road leading uphill from just outside the town centre, thus saving a long walk)*. Little remains of the building other than a pointed entrance archway, in a bastion, and a few vestiges of a tower. From here, a wonderful **view★** extends over the town and the mountains all around.

Returning towards Piazza Garibaldi, take Via Fratelli Testa. On a rise off to the right sits the Chiesa del Santissimo Salvatore.

The church of **Santissimo Salvatore**, graced by a portico, stands on a rise enjoying a fine **view** over the town.

Continue along Via Fratelli Testa, then Via G.B. Li Volsi; at the intersection with Via Umberto I, turn left uphill.

Chiesa dei Cappuccini

Inside is a fine 18C wooden tabernacle attributed to **Bencivinni** and a prized series of paintings by the "Zoppo di Gangi" (The Lame Man of Gangi), **Gaspare Vazzano**, depicting the *Madonna of the Angels, St Barbara and St Lucy*.

Noto★★

In a region populated by olive and almond trees, Noto sits on a plateau dominating the valley of the Asinaro and its citrus plantations. This tiny Baroque jewel endowed with an opulent beauty that verges on the theatrical, is the result of a single tragic event: the earthquake of 1693. During the reconstruction period that followed the earthquake, majestic *palazzi* were built in the soft, local compacted limestone; over time, the stone loses its glaring whiteness and develops a magnificent golden or rosy hue, which is especially attractive when caught in the last rays of the setting sun. Disaster struck once again on 13 May 1996, when, as a result of neglect, the dome of the cathedral collapsed, destroying part of the nave; for the past few years, the cathedral has undergone extensive and occasionally controversial restoration.

Location

Population: 21 608. Michelin map 565 Q 27 – Siracusa. The main monuments in the historical centre are grouped between the central Corso Vittorio Emanuele, which runs through the town from east to west, and Via Cavour, its counterpart to the north. **ℹ** *Piazza XVI Maggio; ☎ 0931 83 67 44.*

Neighbouring sights are described in the following chapters: COMISO; Cava d'ISPICA; MODICA; RAGUSA; SIRACUSA.

Directory

Transport

Noto is 55km/34mi from Ragusa and 30km/19mi from Siracusa, from where there are train (90min and 40min respectively) and bus (1hr to Ragusa and 40min to Siracusa) services. The bus station is situated in Piazzale Marconi, behind the park *(giardino pubblico)*, while the railway station is in Viale Principe di Piemonte, a 10min walk from the historical centre of the town.

Bus services run between Noto and Fontanarossa airport in Catania (approx 80km/50mi).

Sightseeing

Through the streets – Throughout the 18C rectilinear town centre layout, popular districts have sprung up (Agliastrello, Mannarazze, Macchina Ghiaccio, Carmine) among the tightly knit, tortuous and often maze-like streets more usually associated with medieval towns. The Allakatalla association not only provides guided tours of the historic quarters, but also organises "alternative" routes coloured with local stories and popular legend. These veritable leaps into the past are even more captivating in the evening, when the subdued light creates an almost magical atmosphere. For further information, contact **Allakatalla**, Corso Vittorio Emanuele 47; ☎ 0931 83 50 05; Fax 0931 83 60 21; www.allakatalla.it

Where to Eat

• *For all budgets*

Trattoria del Carmine – *Via Ducezio 1/A, Noto – ☎ 0931 83 87 05 – Closed Mon – €12.* A good option after a hard day's sightseeing, this *trattoria* serves good, home-made cooking in a small dining room with tables covered with paper tablecloths.

Trattoria del Crocifisso Da Baglieri – *Via Principe Umberto 46/48, Noto – ☎ 0931 57 11 51 – Closed Wed, one week after Easter and two weeks at the end of Sep – ⊭ – €18.* This simple trattoria takes visitors on an enjoyable trip back in time with its traditional Sicilian atmosphere, regional dishes and reasonable prices.

Where to Stay

• *Budget*

Hotel Al Canisello – *Via Pavese 1, Noto – ☎ 0931 83 57 93 – Fax 0931 83 77 00 – canisello@tin.it – ⊭ – 6 rooms. €60/70 ☕ €3.* This typical 19C farmhouse has thick, whitewashed walls and simple, rustic decor. The old-world atmosphere here is enhanced by floral displays and plain, elegant furnishings.

• *Moderate*

Villa Mediterranea – *Viale Lido, Noto Marina, 7.5km/4.5mi SE of Noto – ☎ 0931 81 23 30 – Fax 0931 81 23 30 – info@villamediterranea.com – Closed Nov-Easter – P ⊭ – 15 rooms. €84/104 ☕.* This attractive Mediterranean-style villa, located on the seafront at Noto Marina, has recently extended its number of guest rooms, while still managing to retain its friendly, family-run atmosphere. Direct access to the beach.

Festival

Primavera barocca – This spring festival, held during the third weekend in May, culminates in the famous **Infiorata**, a flower festival which takes place in Via Nicolaci. Towards the middle of May, the local inhabitants recreate brilliantly coloured tableaux of flowers composed entirely of petals inside the doorways of the *palazzi*. The cobbles of the street are transformed into a gigantic canvas of petals to form designs which vary from year to year.

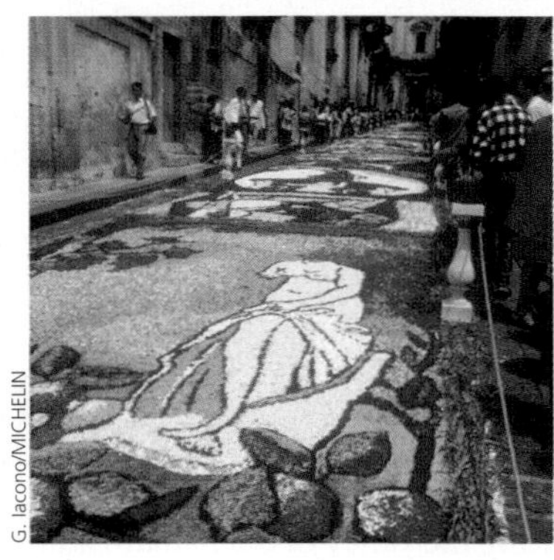

G. Iacono/MICHELIN

Background

Prior to 1693, Noto stood some 10km/6mi away from its present site *(see below, Noto Antica)*. The earthquake completely destroyed the old town, and a broader and less vulnerable site was chosen for the new town, one that might accommodate a straightforward, linear town plan – with intersections at right angles and wide, parallel streets – in accordance with the new Baroque taste. Three of the main streets run on an east to west axis, so that they might always be bathed in sunshine. Three different social categories were catered for: the highest part was reserved for the nobility, the centre for the clergy, while the ordinary people were left to fill the rest of the town. Many Sicilian artists cooperated in the reconstruction of Noto conducted under the supervision of the Duke of Camastra, the acting representative of the Spanish viceroy; these included **Paolo Labisi**, **Vincenzo Sinatra** and **Rosario Gagliardi** who, being a close follower of Borromini, was perhaps one of the most inventive. The town was built like a stage set might be: its perspectives were configured and implemented in an entirely original way, flattered and enhanced with curvaceous forms and curvilinear accents in façades, decorated brackets and keystones, curlicues and volutes, masks, cherubs, and balconies with gracefully bulging wrought-iron railings. Although Noto was rebuilt entirely by local craftsmen, it fits into a much larger picture, as Italian hands modelled, fashioned and realised expressions of the Baroque movement all over Europe.

Walking About

BAROQUE CITY CENTRE**

The main axis is provided by **Corso Vittorio Emanuele** which runs through three piazzas, each with its own church. The street extends from **Porta Reale**, a monumental gateway modelled on a triumphal arch, erected in the 19C. Above the entrance is a pelican, the symbol of self-denial – a reference to King Ferdinand II, who visited the town in 1838 – flanked on one side by a tower (short hand for a fortress and thereby a symbol for strength) and on the other by a *cirneco* (an old Sicilian breed of dog, a symbol of loyalty). Beyond stretches an avenue of trees and to one side the public gardens (Giardino Pubblico) dotted with patches of purple-flowering bougainvillea and palm trees, and the occasional marble bust of a famous local figure.
This is a common meeting-point for the townspeople to congregate and a good spot from where to watch the daily *passeggiata*.

Piazza Immacolata

The square is overlooked by the fairly austere Baroque façade of **San Francesco all'Immacolata** (designed by Sinatra). An impressive stairway leads up to a terrace, with a statue of the Virgin in the centre. The church contains several notable works of art removed from the Franciscan church abandoned in the old town of Noto. These include on the main altar a painted wooden *Virgin and Child* attributed to Antonio Monachello (1564) and, set into the floor of the nave on the right, the tombstone of a Franciscan priest (1575).
To the left of the church, by the entrance to Via San Francesco d'Assisi, sits the lovely **Monastero del Santissimo Salvatore** marked by an elegant tower, once a watchtower, rising tall above the curved frontage. The windows have the most wonderful pot-bellied wrought-iron balconies, echoed across the street at the **Convento di Santa Chiara**, by Gagliardi.

Piazza Municipio*

This is the most majestic and the busiest of the three squares, overlooked on the left by the eye-catching elevation of the Palazzo Ducezio, and on the right by the broad flight of steps to the cathedral entrance, flanked by two beautiful horseshoe-shaped hedges.

Cathedral** – The broad façade with its two tall bell towers do not completely obscure the remains of the dome which tragically collapsed in 1996 destroying a large section of the nave *(restoration work is expected to be completed some time in 2004).*
The wide stairway appears to sweep up from the piazza with a great movement, accentuated no doubt by the two tall exedra side hedges, each with a paved area above, echoing and thereby emphasising their serpentine line. Alongside the cathedral, on the same level, stand the 19C **Palazzo Vescovile** (Bishop's Palace) and

Piazza Municipio

B. Morandi/MICHELIN

Palazzo Landolina di Sant'Alfano, both sober in appearance in contrast with the exuberant style of the other buildings in the square.

On the opposite side of the square sits the **Palazzo Ducezio**, a well-proportioned building with curvilinear elements, enclosed by a classical type of portico designed by Sinatra. The upper section was added in the 1950s.

The main feature on the east side of the square is the façade of the **Basilica del Santissimo Salvatore**.

Via Nicolaci*

Right off Corso Vittorio Emanuele. The eye is naturally drawn along the street as it gently rises up to the **Chiesa di Montevergine** with its fine concave frontage framed between bell towers, designed by Sinatra. Both sides of the street are lined with fine Baroque buildings: on the left, note **Palazzo Nicolaci di Villadorata** with its fabulous **balconies*****. See how the richly carved brackets are ornamented with arrays of fantastical cherubs, horses, mermaids and lions, grotesque figures among which, in the centre, is a figure with distinctively Middle-Eastern features. *Although the palazzo is closed for restoration, it is possible to join a guided tour of the restoration site (by appointment only). €3. ☎ 0931 57 40 80.*

Returning to Corso Vittorio Emanuele, on the left stands the imposing complex of the **Jesuit Church and College** attributed to Gagliardi. The fine central doorway is enclosed between four columns and, at the top, grotesque masks.

Piazza XVI Maggio

The most striking feature on the square is Gagliardi's elegant convex façade for the **Chiesa di San Domenico***, designed with an emphatic use of line and boldly contained by two tiers of columns separated by a high cornice. The interior, predominantly white and encrusted with stucco, is graced with polychrome marble altars. *Closed for restoration at the time of going to press.*

In front of the church lies the delightful **Villetta d'Ercole**, a public garden with an 18C fountain in the centre named after Heracles. Opposite, stands the 19C Teatro Comunale.

The second street on the left off Corso Vittorio Emanuele, Via Ruggero Settimo, leads to the **Chiesa del Carmine**; a church with an elegant concave frontage and a Baroque doorway.

Return to Piazza XVI Maggio so as to turn up Via Bovio, which passes, on the right, the former Carmine convent known as Casa dei Padri Crociferi.

Palazzo Astuto

B. Juge/MICHELIN

Via Cavour

This noble street runs parallel to, but on a level above, Corso Vittorio Emanuele, between a series of interesting buildings: **Palazzo Astuto** (n° 54), whichhas wonderful balconies with bulging wrought-iron railings; and **Palazzo Trigona Cannicarao** (n° 93).

*Beyond the palazzo turn left onto Via Coffa, then left again at the end so as to pass before the late Baroque **Palazzo Impellizzeri**; and turn right onto Via Sallicano.*

Via Sallicano leads right up to the **Chiesa del Santissimo Crocefisso**, designed by Gagliardi, which contains **Francesco Laurana**'s sensitive painting entitled the *Madonna della Neve. Closed for restoration at the time of going to press.*

Excursion

Noto Antica

10km/6mi NW. Along the road to the site of the original Noto there is a sign for **Eremo di San Corrado fuori le Mura**: this 18C sanctuary set amid the green countryside was built beside the cave where St Corrado lived in the 14C. The main road then continues past the **Santuario di Santa Maria della Scala** which preserves a lovely Arabo-Norman arch behind the font. The road leads on to the site where the town of Noto stood before the terrible earthquake of 1693: it was stretched along the ridge of Monte Alveria, squeezed in between two deep gorges, making it easily defensible. Beyond Porta Aurea, the gateway to the now deserted, picturesquely overgrown city, the street system remains intact: how strange, therefore, to think of it as bustling with people in the 17C. A few eerie ruins protrude from the rubble and weeds.

RUINS AND BEAUTIFUL NATURAL LANDSCAPES

85km/53mi – allow at least one day, including the excursion to Cava Grande and the tour of the Riserva di Vendicari.

Cava Grande del Cassìbile★★

Head to Avola and follow signs to Avola Antica (10km/6mi along a winding road). After the town, turn right to a viewpoint where you can park the car.

An excursion to Cava Grande provides the opportunity of exploring a small and forgotten corner of the Iblei mountain landscape, that karst range dominating the southeast part of Sicily. This itinerary off the beaten track will be of particular interest to nature lovers. From the viewpoint, there is a magnificent **view★** over the **Cava Grande Gorge★** plunging down between impressively tall and sheer limestone cliffs. Along the valley bottom winds the river which opens out intermittently to make a succession of tiny lakes, accessible by a path leading down into the gorge. Slightly to the left, a cave may be seen excavated from the rock: this is the **Grotta dei Briganti** (Bandits' Cave), just one of the many rock-hewn dwellings in this settlement, and another example of the type so commonly found throughout the rocky landscape of southeast Sicily. It is thought that this particular cave was used as a tannery.

Descent – It takes half an hour to walk down to the river, or *cava* as it is known locally – allow twice that time to climb back to the top. The track, which at times becomes quite difficult to follow, cuts its way along the river through luxuriant vegetation. After a few hundred metres, the bush gives way to an open clearing around a series of **natural rock pools★★** created by the river, complete with flat, rounded slabs of rock ideal for whiling away a moment or two in the sunshine. In summer, the cool water is very tempting. Furthermore the rock pools are surrounded on all sides by the most idyllic scenery, far removed from anything found elsewhere in Sicily, and so providing an unusual and highly recommended alternative to a swim in the sea off the Syracuse coast.

Return to Avola. Take S 115 to Noto and then S 19 to Capo Passero. A road to the left leads to Eloro.

A Diversion for gourmets

The Baroque town of **Avola** is renowned for its delicious ***mandorla pizzuta***, an almond delicacy which is one of the most famous of all Sicilian pastries. The town is also home to the red **Nero d'Avola** grape variety, the best in Sicily, which is used to add hints of plums and cherries to the best Sicilian red wines. When the grape undergoes a stringent vinification process, resulting in the lowering of the alcohol content, it produces a high-quality red wine with intense, yet harmonious tones.

Eloro

Ancient Helorus was probably founded by the Syracusans some time in the 7C BC. It enjoys a splendid **situation★** on a hill overlooking the sea, not far from the mouth of the River Tellaro.

Excavations – On entering the site, to the east, you see the ruin of a great *stoà* (portico) which once would have marked the entrance to the sacred precinct where the **sanctuary** dedicated to Demeter and Kore was located, now buried below remains of various Byzantine buildings erected later.

Down towards the river lie the remains of a **theatre** *cavea*, badly scarred, unfortunately, when a drainage channel was dug under Fascist rule. Westwards, sits the base of a **temple** thought to have been dedicated to Asclepius (Aesculapius), the son of Apollo and god of medicine and healing. Beyond, northern and western sections of the **enclosure walls** are still much in evidence, as is the **north gate** (complete with the foundations of flanking towers) which marks the beginning of the main street, running on a north to south axis, rutted by cartwheels. In an area east of the principal thoroughfare, set among rectangular buildings, lies an open space that must surely have been the agora (market place).

Return to S 19. After 3km/2mi, turn right towards the Villa Romana del Tellaro.

Villa Romana del Tellaro

(♿) Open 9am-2pm. No charge. ☎ 0931 48 11 11.

Beside the River Tellaro, west of the main Noto-Pachino road, the remains of a Roman villa dating from the second half of the 4C AD have been recovered. These fragments, found in the 1970s while excavations were conducted on a nearby rural complex, seem to suggest that its internal decoration must have been at least as sumptuous as the famous Roman Villa del Casale, near Piazza Armerina.

Tour – The residence is planned around a square peristyle: excavations of the north wing have revealed mosaic floors with geometric designs, notably diamonds and spirals. Three rooms in the northern range preserve mosaics with an intensity of colour far in excess of anything found at the Villa del Casale: these, composed of smaller tesserae, feature hunting scenes, erotic scenes and Achilles' deliverance of the body of Hector to Priam, after avenging the death of his friend Patroclus, a story taken from Homer's *Iliad (unfortunately these mosaics are preserved elsewhere for the time being).*

Before leaving, note on the right, the traces of additional buildings annexed to the main complex – possibly intended as the servants' quarters, and the remains of a wall from the Greek period.

Return to S 19, continue south for a further 4.5km/3mi and then turn left to the Riserva Naturale di Vendicari.

Riserva Naturale di Vendicari★

Open Apr-Oct, 7am-8pm; Nov-Mar, 7am-5.30pm. No charge. Authorisation from the Ispettorato Foreste is required. ☎ *0931 46 24 52.*

The reserve is open throughout the year; the best time of day for birdwatching is the early morning or late afternoon. Needless to say, binoculars are vital.

The Vendicari Nature Reserve was created in 1984, but did not become operational until 1989. It consists of a narrow strip of marshy coastline covering 574ha/1 418 acres and provides a rare, and now completely protected, habitat for migratory species and a highly peculiar kind of sand-loving Mediterranean vegetation. The large stretch of swamp, a hostile environment in many ways because of high salinity levels, has evolved a very unusual ecosystem which continues to attract vast numbers of birds passing through the area on migration.

During the autumn months, it is common to see a variety of waders: grey heron, little egret, white and black stork, greater flamingo. Later lesser black-backed, slender-billed and Audouin's gulls regularly winter in the area. Between November and March, when the level of the water rises, the swamp attracts many species of wintering duck, including teal, shoveler, pintail, mallard, tufted duck, pochard and red-crested pochard. Among the few species to breed here are black-winged stilt (white body, black wings, long red legs) – adopted as the emblem of Vendicari – as well as Kentish plover, little tern, reed warbler and little bittern.

Tour – The track briefly skirts the edge of the **Pantano Grande** before leading off towards the **Torre Sveva** (Swabian Tower), actually erected in the 15C by Peter of Aragon, and the chimney that rises from among the ruins of the **tonnara** (tuna fishery) which functioned until the Second World War. Nearby, set back against the rocks where the waves break over the shore, sit the remains of a Hellenistic **fish-processing plant**: the tanks were used to steep the excess fish before salting them *(tarichos)* or using the by-products to make *garum* or fish paste by breaking down the fish gut and offcuts in sea-water – a highly lucrative commodity that was traded right across the Mediterranean from Phoenician to Roman times.

As regards the flora of the area, Vendicari consists essentially of rock and sand: the rocky subsoil mainly found in the north of the reserve, near **Pantano Piccolo**, supports *garrigue*-type vegetation with cushions of thyme and thorny burnet *(Sarcopoterium spinosum)*. Near **Pantano Roveto**, on the other hand, where sand predominates, sand-loving perennials such as prickly juniper *(Juniperus oxycedrus)* and rosemary grow among the maquis plants.

Follow S 19 for 18km/11mi.

Capo Passero

The extreme southeastern tip of Sicily consists of a headland with a lighthouse: to sea, it marks the point at which the Ionian Sea meets the Canale di Sicilia.

The local **tuna fishery** flourished during the course of this century, and continues to be owned by the Baron of Belmonte who, only in 1994, took part in a *calata*, when the fishermen go out to lay the nets for catching tuna. The complex comprises a canning works, albeit now unused, where the tuna was put into tins, a house for the *Rais* – the quartermaster responsible for overseeing the *mattanza* (the killing of the tuna, *see p 172*) – and a family residence for the owner himself.

A splendid **view**★★ stretches across the water to the open horizon, a seascape which changes tirelessly at the whim of the elements. *Open by appointment only.* ☎ *0931 84 20 18.*

A natural channel separates the **islet of Capo Passero** from the mainland, this can prove to be an especially strategic place to lay nets when the tuna are running. The islet, meanwhile, has been subject to a compulsory purchase so that the colony of dwarf palms growing there might be protected; in consequence the fish-rearing tanks that were there have had to be jettisoned at sea, and tuna fishing in the area has been decimated. As a result, the place is no longer the centre of activity it used to be.

Portapalo di Capo Passero

This comprises the small, picturesque, archetypal fishing village. Naturally, the hub of activity is the harbour where, between noon and 2pm, the fishing boats return and the quays suddenly throng with inquisitive old men and busy housewives come to purchase the fresh catch straight from the sea.

A curious fact about the Mattanza

During the catch, the fishermen used to signal the number of tuna netted in the various chambers: a white and red flag was flown when there were 10; a red flag meant there were 20; a white one meant 30; a red and white one was flown with a white one to signal 40, and so on. If they were unable to estimate the number of fish, they used to wave a sailor's jacket on top of an oar, a gesture known as **u' cappottu**, which meant "we can't count them any more, there are too many".

Palermo★★★

Palermo was once an important staging post on the Grand Tour and a favoured haunt of writers, poets and artists, who were seduced by the city's inherent atmosphere of Eastern exoticism and by its esoteric beauty. Despite the effects of war, rampant modern construction and an undesirable reputation, Palermo has managed to retain its essential fascination, drawing its personality from the many nationalities that have populated its streets over the ages. The Byzantines, Arabs, Normans, Swabians, Angevins and Spanishhave all left their mark on the art and culture of the city. Although parts of the historical centre are still run-down and in need of regeneration, after decades of neglect Palermo is beginning to experience a renaissance, with the restoration of old, forgotten monuments and the proliferation of new cultural projects.

Location

Population: 679 290. Michelin map 565 22M, including a city map. Palermo nestles in a **delightful setting★★** in the middle of a wide bay, enclosed to the north by Monte Pellegrino, and to the south by Capo Zafferano. It is built on the edge of a fertile plain known as the **Conca d'Oro** (meaning the golden shell or the horn of plenty) on account of its lush citrus plantations, palm trees and olive groves. The Viale Regione Siciliana, an extension of the A19 motorway, runs through the outskirts of the city. The historical centre is clustered around the crossroads of the two main streets, Corso Vittorio Emanuele and Via Maqueda; from the Viale Regione Siciliana, take the Corso Calatafimi exit (this street runs into Corso Vittorio Emanuele). Visitors are advised to park their car in one of the large car parks on the outskirts of the city (marked by a P on the map). To get to Via Lincoln from Viale Regione Siciliana, take the Via Basile exit, which is also the junction with S 624 from Sciacca. Ferries and hydrofoils depart from Palermo for Ustica. **B** *Piazza Castelnuovo 34; ☎ 091 58 38 47; Fax 091 58 27 88; www.aapit.pa.it*

Neighbouring sights are described in the following chapters: BAGHERIA; CARINI; CEFALÙ; SOLUNTO; USTICA.

Background

Historical notes – It was the Phoenicians who laid the foundations of the city in the 7C BC, calling it *Ziz,* meaning flower. This, in time, was conquered by the Romans who gave it the name Panormus (from the Greek words meaning "large port or rock") from which "Palermo" (corrupted by the introduction of the Arabic name *Balharm*) has been derived for us today. The city's golden age began under Arab domination (9C), when it was established as one of the main Islamic centres in the west. The town expanded as new quarters were developed beyond the confines of the old centre known as the Cassaro (from the Arabic *Qasr* meaning castle; also the old name of the main street of Palermo, now Corso Vittorio Emanuele); the Kalsa (from *al Halisah* – the chosen one), in particular, flourished down by the seafront and, once fortified, provided a residence for the Emir. In 1072, the city fell into the hands of the Norman **Count Roger**, but the transfer was not a violent one as merchants, artisans and Muslims in general (but also people of other races and religions) were permitted to continue to live and practise their chosen professions as though nothing had changed. Indeed, it was precisely this magnanimity that made it possible for the Arabo-Norman style, that glorious mix of structural and decorative elements, to develop in architecture. The city prospered while benefiting from the wealthy investment of different cultures.

Sicilian Vespers

Charles of Anjou arrived in Palermo in 1266, supported by the Pope. The French were held in scorn by the people, to such an extent that, given their inability to pronounce Italian properly, they were nicknamed *tartaglioni* (stutterers). In 1282, on Easter Monday, in front of the Church of Santo Spirito *(see p 309)*, just as the bell was calling the faithful to Vespers, a French soldier directed an insult at a Sicilian woman, thereby sparking off a reaction of indignation in the crowd. The situation deteriorated and, with the help of the local aristocracy, the quarrel was transformed into a revolt which then spread throughout Sicily. Any Frenchmen unable to pronounce the word *cicero* correctly were massacred, while the others were driven out. Eventually, Peter of Aragon, husband of Costanza d'Altavilla, the daughter of Manfred (the Swabian king ousted by the Angevins), was called upon to rule the island.

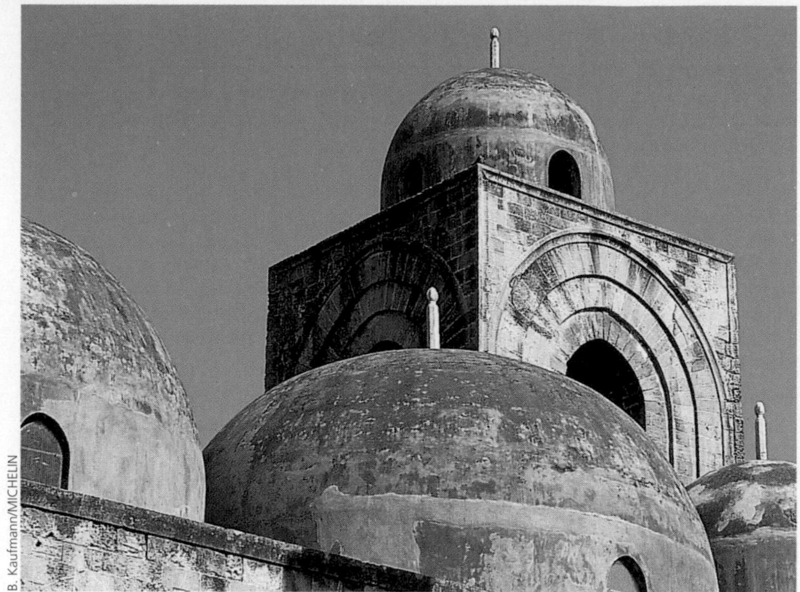
B. Kaufmann/MICHELIN

The red domes of San Giovanni degli Eremiti

Roger II, son of the Count Roger, harbouring a predilection for luxury, built gardens in the Oriental style to complement his sumptuous palaces (La Zisa and La Cuba); he surrounded himself with men of letters, mathematicians, astronomers and intellectuals from far and wide. After a short period of disorder and decadence, Palermo and Sicily passed into the hands of Frederick II of Swabia (1212), under whom the city regained its importance and vigour. The Swabians were succeeded by the Angevins; they in turn were driven out at the end of the War of the Sicilian Vespers, by the Spaniards and, they were succeeded, in the 18C, by the Bourbons of Naples, who embellished the city with Baroque palaces.

The 19C heralded the opening of the city to trade and relations with Europe. The entrepreneurial bourgeoisie became the new economic driving force. The city outgrew its boundaries. The Viale della Libertà, an extension of Via Maqueda, was inaugurated; the surrounding district mushroomed, populated with elegant Liberty-style buildings. Sadly, this was to be the final flurry before a period of stagnation. The city succumbed to the bombing raids of 1943, which badly damaged the historical centre, and there followed an earthquake in 1968. Meanwhile the slow but sure decline of its medieval quarters continued and the construction of large, modern, now crumbling buildings in the suburbs did nothing to improve the city's image. Today, this trend is being reversed as a new sense of determination prompts a systematic re-evaluation, restoration and improved use of the city's magnificent monuments in an attempt to stir this wonderful giant of the East from its protracted slumber.

The *Mandamenti* – Palermo's urban plan is centred around the intersection of two main streets: Corso Vittorio Emanuele and Via Maqueda. Corso Vittorio Emanuele corresponds roughly to the historical **Cassaro** (from the Arabic *al-Qasr*), the city's main artery which once linked the Emirate's palace to the sea and was enclosed at either end by Porta Nuova and Porta Felice. In time the district around the street gradually assumed the same name. Via Maqueda was created at the end of the 16C, when the medieval quarters were demolished and the city was divided into four areas, known as *mandamenti*.

Mandamento Palazzo Reale or Albergheria, to the southwest, coincides with the oldest part of the city: it was here that the Phoenicians settled, followed by the Romans, Arabs and Normans, who built their most important civic buildings in the western section of the district. The eastern part of the *mandamento*, towards Via Maqueda, was originally an irregular and densely populated urban centre, which grew up around Via Albergheria, and included firstly a Muslim quarter (hence *meschita* – mosque – in Via Meschita and Piazza Meschita) and later a Jewish quarter.

Mandamento Monte di Pietà or Capo, to the northwest, was the area mostly inhabited by the Islamic population, where much of the city's artisanal and commercial activity took place. This is still the case today, as shown by the lively Capo market which takes place in this district.

Mandamento Castellammare or Loggia, to the northeast, changed by the creation of Via Roma at the end of the 19C and badly damaged by bombing raids in 1943, included the port area, which brought bustling mercantile activity to the district, and merchants from Amalfi, Pisa, Lucca, Genoa and Catalonia. The historical Vucciria market bears witness to this commercial past.

Mandamento Tribunali or Kalsa, to the southeast, which takes its name from the Court of the Inquisition, which had its headquarters in the Palazzo Chiaramonte, grew up around the Kalsa, the old fortified citadel, and Via Alloro, along which a number of noble mansions were built in the 15C. From the 18C onwards, large aristocratic *palazzi* were built along the seafront, with terraces overlooking the Passeggiata della Marina (the present Foro Italico).

An entrancing place

Many writers have dipped their pen into an inkwell with the intention of encapsulating the elusive spirit of Palermo or of using the city as the backdrop to their stories. Here is an excerpt from a Sicilian text by a writer who transforms Sicily into a dream, evoking images, smells and sounds through words that are sometimes lyrical, sometimes nostalgic and sometimes crude. "To Palermo the red, Palermo the child ... Red, Palermo, which we might imagine the likes of Tyre or Sidon, perhaps Carthage, like the purple of the Phoenicians; of rich red earth, with springs of water where the palm grove rises tall and slender, creating sweet shade, bending with the wind, vibrant with the echo and nostalgia of an oasis, a green mosque, a carpet of comfort and prayer, image of the eternal garden of the Koran. A child because she is sleeping and still, content with her own beauty, having always had to be subservient to foreigners, obedient in particular to her mother, her own natural mother who locks her children in an eternal adolescence.
She settles down, relaxed and happy, in the gentle hollow of a shell ..."
From *La Sicilia Passeggiata* (Strolling through Sicily) by Vincenzo Consolo.

Special Features

PALAZZO DEI NORMANNI AND CAPPELLA PALATINA***

The **Norman Palace** is located at the heart of the original town, probably on a site occupied in Punic times by a fortress. The earliest documents, however, date from the Arab occupation; these confirm this to be where the Emir's palace was once situated, linked to the port by the Cassaro. The castle was abandoned in 938 for reasons of security and the Emir's residence transferred to the Kalsa. The area returned to favour when the Normans re-established a royal seat there, having extended and embellished the palace. Life in the palace revolved around the green hall, an ample space in which regal ceremonies, assemblies and banquets were held. The building comprised various wings, each assigned to different people and functions, interconnected by a terrace or a lush garden ornamented with pools of water and fountains. Four towers punctuated the corners: the Greek, the Pisan, the Joaria (from the Arabic for airy) and the Kirimbi. Sadly, only the

One of the "Quattro Canti" in Piazza Vigliena

G. Bludzin/MICHELIN

Directory

Transport

GETTING TO PALERMO

By air – This is certainly the easiest and quickest way to get to Palermo. **Falcone-Borsellino** airport (once known as Punta-Raisi airport, ☎ 091 70 20 111) is situated 30km/19mi north of Palermo, on the A29 motorway. It is served by a number of airlines operating both domestic and international flights.

There are a number of **car hire** firms at the airport: Avis ☎ 091 59 16 84; Europcar ☎ 091 59 16 88; Hertz ☎ 091 21 31 12; Holiday Car ☎ 091 59 16 87; Maggiore ☎ 091 59 16 81; Sicily by Car ☎ 091 59 12 50.

Connections with the city centre – A bus links the airport with the city centre every 30min from 5am until the arrival of the last flight of the day, stopping in Viale Lazio, Piazza Ruggero Settimo (in front of Politeama Hotel), and at the main railway station. The journey takes approx 1hr and costs €4.65. For information, contact Prestia and Commandè, Stazione Centrale; ☎ 091 58 04 57.

The cost of a **taxi** from the airport to the city is approximately €40. Beware of individuals who offer transport at considerably lower prices.

By car – Close to Palermo the motorway joins the ring road around the city (the Viale Regione Siciliana), from where various exits lead to the major sites of interest. The Corso Calatafimi exit is the most convenient for the historical centre, as this road eventually continues into Corso Vittorio Emanuele, one of the main streets through the old town.

Car parks – The difficulty of finding somewhere to park in Palermo discourages many visitors from driving in the city. Large car parks are found on the outskirts of the city (marked by a P on the map); it is also sometimes possible to park in Via Lincoln, next to the Botanical Gardens, which is a short walk from Piazza della Kalsa

The following guarded car parks are situated in the old town: Piazza Giulio Cesare 43 (railway station); Via Guardione 81 (running parallel with Via Cavour to the north, in the port area); Via Archimede 88 (north of Politeama); Via Sammartino 24 (northwest of Teatro Massimo).

These car parks cost around €20 for 24hr, but often have special arrangements with hotels nearby. Visitors are advised not to leave luggage or valuables in their car.

By boat – Ferries leave for Palermo from Genova (Grandi Navi Veloci, 20hr); Livorno (Grandi Navi Veloci, three times a week, 17hr); Naples (Tirrenia, 10hr and SNAV, 11hr, also a fast service, Apr-Oct, 5hr 30min); Cagliari (Tirrenia, once a week, 13hr 30min). For information and reservations, contact:

Grandi Navi Veloci, Via Fieschi 17, Genova; ☎ 010 55 091; www1.gnv.it/, infopax@grimaldi.it

SNAV, Stazione Marittima, Napoli; ☎ 081 42 85 111; mergelli@tin.it, www.snav.it/

Tirrenia, Molo Angioino, Napoli; ☎ 199 123 199 (from Italy) or 081 31 72 999 (from mobile phones and from abroad); www.gruppotirrenia.it/

By bus – There is a direct daily service between Rome (Stazione Tiburtina and Castro Pretorio), Palermo (Via P. Balsamo 26 and Via Turati 3) and Trapani (Via Ammiraglio Stairi 13), operated by Segesta Internazionale. The service departs Rome at 9pm and Palermo at 6.30pm; journey time 12hr. €35.50 (one-way), €60.50 (round trip). ☎ 091 30 05 56 (weekdays) and 091 32 07 57 (Sat-Sun and public hols).

Palermo can also be reached from all other major towns in Sicily. The main bus companies are SAIS, Via Balsamo 16, ☎ 091 61 66 028; Cuffaro, Via Balsamo 13, ☎ 091 61 61 510; and Segesta, Via Balsamo 26, ☎ 091 61 67 919.

By train – Travelling to Sicily by train from mainland Italy involves crossing the Straits of Messina; the train drives directly onto the ferry; the crossing is included in the price of the train ticket. For information, contact the Italian State Railways *(Ferrovie dello Stato)*, www.fs-on-line.com. For visitors travelling from within Sicily, Palermo has train connections with Messina (approximately 3hr), Caltanissetta (approximately 2hr) and Catania (just over 3hr, but the service is infrequent). Palermo's main railway station is situated in Piazza Giulio Cesare.

GETTING AROUND

It is best to avoid driving in Palermo because of traffic congestion and the difficulty of finding somewhere to park. By far the best way to see the city is by public transport and taxi for longer distances and on foot once in the old town.

A slower, yet nonetheless enjoyable way of soaking up the atmosphere is to take one of the horse-drawn carriages available for hire outside the central station or elsewhere in the city. It is advisable, however, to agree a price before setting off.

Buses – Palermo's city bus services are operated by AMAT, Via Stabile, on the corner of Via Ruggero Settimo; ☎ 091 72 91 111; www.amat.pa.it/index.html. There are two types of bus ticket: one valid for up to two hours (€1) or one for a full day (€3.35);

M. Magni/MICHELIN

the latter is worth purchasing if public transport is likely to be used several times in the course of the day.

Radio Taxis – Autoradio Taxi ☎ 091 51 27 27; Radio Taxi Trinacria ☎ 091 22 54 55.

SIGHTSEEING

The tourist office publishes a monthly magazine with information on events taking place in the city, plus opening times for museums, churches and *palazzi*.

Combined tickets – There are combined tickets for the Galleria Regionale di Palazzo Abatellis, Museo Archeologico Regionale and Palazzo Mirto (€7.75; valid for two days); the Chiostro di Monreale, Cuba, Zisa and Chiostro di San Giovanni degli Eremiti (€7.75; valid for two days); the Galleria di Palazzo Abatellis and Palazzo Mirto (€5.15; valid for one day); and the Museo Archeologico Regionale and Palazzo Mirto (€5.15; valid for one day).

Guided tours – The **CST** (Compania Siciliana Turismo) organises visits to several of the main sights in combination with a visit to the Duomo at Monreale every Saturday morning. On other days of the week, it also arranges accompanied day trips to Segesta, Erice and Trapani; Mount Etna and Taormina; Agrigento and Piazza Armerina; Il Capo market; Mondello and the Capuchin Catacombs in Palermo (half-day visits only). The CST office is located at Via Emerico Amari 124; ☎ 091 74 39 654; Fax 091 58 22 18; www.compagniasicilianaturismo.it

The **AMAT** (Azienda Municipale dei Trasporti) organises various bus tours around the sights of the city and Monreale. Tours leave at 9am and last approximately 4hr. €11.50 (transport only). Via Stabile, on the corner of Via Ruggero Settimo; ☎ 091 72 91 111.

The **Cooperativa Solidarietà** offers tours to the historical *mandamenti* and a themed tour entitled *"I Beati Paoli"*. 3hr, €7.75. For further information, call ☎ 091 58 04 33. It was in the Capo district that a large number of the *Beati Paoli* stories were set. This massively popular novel by Luigi Natoli was published in instalments between 1909 and 1910, capturing the imagination of large numbers of Palermitani who read it avidly and who spent hours speculating on the suspense maintained with each new edition. Its vivid style succeeds in painting a uncompromising yet faithful picture of Palermo in times past.

"Palermo sottosopra" – The **qanat** are artificial underground canals, built on an almost imperceptible slope, which absorb moisture from the water table and transport it for miles underground. First built in Persia around the 7C-6C BC, these canals were adopted in Europe after the fall of the Roman Empire. The *qanat* were built by the *muqanni* or water masters, who passed on their skills from father to son and spent their short lives building these miraculous masterpieces. The *qanat* open to the public in Palermo date from the Norman period. The tour *(approximately 2hr; €8.50)* is an experience not to be missed, in which visitors are taken underground dressed in overalls and equipped with a speleologist's helmet, and are then led along the narrow canals by a CAI guide. It is advisable to wear a bathing costume underneath the waterproof overalls (you are unlikely to keep dry!) and to bring a towel and a change of underwear. *For further information, contact the Cooperativa Solidarietà a few days in advance; ☎ 091 58 04 33.*

100 open churches – The aim of this excellent initiative is to provide access to a number of buildings hitherto closed to the public. The idea is to appoint groups of volunteers to administrate and oversee opening times (ideally 9am-5pm) and provide guided tours. Those buildings to have benefited from the scheme so far include a number of churches (Sant'Eulalia dei Catalani, Santa Maria dei Miracoli, Madonna della Mercè, Madonna dei Rimedi, San Carlo, Santa Caterina, dell'Itria or dei Cocchieri, Santa Ninfa dei Crociferi, Sant'Orsola, Santa Teresa alla Kalsa), the Convento di Santa Maria del Gesù and Stand Florio. For information and reservations, ☎ 091 740 60 35.

Where to Eat

• ***Budget***

SICILIAN FAST FOOD

Local specialities include snacks such as *u sfinciuni* or *sfincione* (pizza topped with tomato, anchovies, onion and breadcrumbs), *pani ca' meusa* or *panino con la milza* (roll filled with charcoal-grilled pork offal), *panelle* (fried chickpea flour pancakes) and *babbaluci* (tiny marinated snails sold in paper cornets), which are often sold in the local markets.

Antica Focacceria San Francesco – *Via A. Paternostro 58, Palermo – ☎ 091 32 02 64 – info@afsf.it* Situated in the heart of the old town opposite San Francesco church, this old-style café has marble tables and an original counter made from a cast-iron stove. An excellent selection of *focaccia farcita* (flat pizza dough baked with various fillings), *arancini di riso* (deliciously moist, deep-fried rice balls sometimes with tomatoes and peas stuffed with meat sauce, otherwise filled with melted mozzarella), *torte salate* (Sicilian savoury "cakes"), fried ricotta cheese, and *sfincione*.

Di Martino – *Via Mazzini 54, Palermo –* ⊄. This café is a perfect retreat after visiting 19C Palermo or the Museo d'Arte Moderna. A good selection of delicious *panini* (rolls) which can be eaten at the tables outside.

Focacceria Basile – *Via Bara all'Olivella 76, Quartiere Massimo, Palermo – ☎ 091 33 56 28 – Closed Sun and evenings (except Sat).* This attractive trattoria-cum-*rosticceria* has a long counter displaying takeaway pizza and *focacce*, an open-view kitchen which prepares fast cooked meals and two somewhat plain dining rooms.

Focacceria Basile 2 – *Piazza Nasce 5, Quartiere Politeama, Palermo – ☎ 091 61 10 203 – Closed Sun.* Run by the same family as the Focacceria Basile in Via Bara all'Olivella, this pleasant *rosticceria* prepares a range of snacks and Sicilian-style fast food, such as *arancini*, *caponate* (a tomato and aubergine mixture) and *panini con la milza*.

Giannettino – *Piazza R. Settimo 8/11, Palermo – ☎ 091 61 14 560.* One of the best addresses in the city for pizzas, *calzoni*, rolls and other typical Sicilian snacks. The café has a pleasant sitting area for those who want to eat in, as well as offering a takeaway service.

I Cuochini – *Via R. Settimo 68, Palermo – ☎ 091 58 11 58 – Open 8.30am-2.30pm and 4.30-7.30pm. Closed Sun.* This tiny shop, located for the past 170 years in the inner courtyard of the Palazzo del Barone di Stefano, sells an irresistible range of Sicilian specialities, such as pizza, *panzerotti* (fried pastries) and *arancini*. Not to be missed!

RESTAURANTS

Villa Cicara – *Via G. Filangeri 10 (Piazza Magione), Palermo – ☎ 091 61 77 777 – Closed Tue (Jan-Mar) – €15/22.* The dining room of this restaurant is decorated in rustic style, with old tools on the wall and a large wrought-iron chandelier. Guests can also dine in the garden, surrounded by orange and pomegranate trees, a large palm tree and a host of other plants.

Hostaria da Ciccio – *Via Firenze 6 (at the intersection with Via Roma 178), Palermo – ☎ 091 32 91 43 – €18/25.* This trattoria, founded towards the end of the 1930s, has two small dining rooms and a pleasant outdoor summer dining area. The restaurant still specialises in traditional Sicilian dishes and fresh fish and neither the authentic atmosphere nor the excellent quality of the cuisine has changed since it first opened.

Casa del Brodo – *Corso Vittorio Emanuele 175, Palermo – ☎ 091 32 16 55 – casadelbrodo@gestelnet.it – ▤ – €18/30.* Founded over 100 years ago, this restaurant once had a rustic feel which has been replaced by a more elegant ambience. With its attractive blue tablecloths, copious *antipasti* buffet laid out in the corridor between the two dining rooms, and excellent Sicilian cuisine focusing on fish specialities, this restaurant offers good value for money.

Ai vecchietti di Minchiapititto – *Via P. Paternostro 28, Palermo – ☎ 091 58 56 06 – ▤ – €20/34.* This restaurant, housed in a 19C building, has two small rustic-style dining rooms with vaulted ceilings and brick arches. In summer, meals are served outside in a small garden.

La Cambusa – *Piazza Marina 16, Palermo – ☎ 091 58 45 74 – leopoldo@lacambusa.it – Closed Mon and in Dec – €21/27 + 10% service.* Overlooking Piazza Marina, this elegant, quiet restaurant specialises in fish dishes. Excellent *antipasti* buffet.

• Moderate

Capricci di Sicilia – *Via Istituto Pignatelli 6 (on the corner of Piazza Sturzo), Palermo – ☎ 091 32 77 77 – Closed Mon (except Jul and Aug) – ▤ – €25/40.* Mime artists and street vendors occasionally make an appearance at this lively restaurant with simple decor and informal service. The food here is excellent, with an emphasis on regional specialities.

Trattoria Biondo – *Via Carducci 15 (N of Piazza Castelnuovo), Palermo – ☎ 091 58 36 62 – Closed Wed and 30 Jul-15 Sep – ▤ – €24/33 + 10% service.* Situated near Teatro Politeama in the historical centre of Palermo, this restaurant specialises in Mediterranean cuisine. The ambience is rustic and friendly, with bottles, old wine and tomato crates, gourds and other small objects brightening the decor. Note that a 10% service charge is added to your bill.

Al Genio – *Piazza S. Carlo 9 (near Piazza Rivoluzione), Palermo – ☎ 091 61 66 642 – Closed Mon and at lunchtime (Jun-Sep) – €25/30.* This restaurant in Palermo's old quarter has two dining rooms with vaulted ceilings, one with exposed stonework. Run by the same family for generations, the Al Genio specialises in genuine Sicilian cuisine.

Santandrea – *Piazza Sant'Andrea 4 (Vucciria), Palermo – ☎ 091 33 49 99 – Closed Tue and Wed lunchtimes; Mon and Sun (Jul-Aug) and Jan – ▤ – Booking recommended – €28/45.* This pleasant restaurant in the heart of the Vucciria district serves traditional Sicilian cuisine.

Where to Stay

• Budget

Hotel Cavour – *Via A. Manzoni 11 (5th floor with a lift), Palermo – ☎ 091 61 62 759 – Fax 091 61 62 759 – giopintos@tiscalinet.it – ▭ – 10 rooms. €24/52.* This recently renovated hotel on the fifth floor of an old *palazzo* is conveniently located near the railway station. It has light, airy rooms with high ceilings and simple, functional furnishings.

Hotel Moderno – *Via Roma 276 (3rd and 4th floor with a lift), Palermo – ☎ 091 58 86 83 – Fax 091 58 82 60 – ▤ – 38 rooms. €46.50/62 ☕ €2.60.* A friendly, family-run hotel, where the staff go out of their way to make guests feel welcome. The fair-sized rooms are complemented by simple, functional furnishings.

Hotel Azzurro di Lampedusa – *Via Roma 111 (5th floor with a lift), Palermo – ☎ 091 61 66 881 – Fax 091 61 00 105 – azzurrolampedusa@tiscalinet.it – ▤ ⚹ – 12 rooms. €62/72 ☕.* Well located in a *palazzo* right in the historical centre, this hotel offers rooms with all necessary creature comforts. Excellent value for money.

• Moderate

Hotel Gardenia – *Via M. Stabile 136 (7th floor with a lift), Palermo – ☎ 091 32 27 61 – Fax 091 33 37 32 – gardeniahotel@gardeniahotel.com – ▤ – 16 rooms. €62/84 ☕ €5.* A small family-run hotel on the seventh floor of a building in the old town. Some of the simply furnished rooms have private balconies overlooking the heart of the city. Good value for money.

Hotel Posta – *Via A. Gagini 77, Palermo – ☎ 091 58 73 38 – Fax 091 58 73 47 – info@hotelposta.it – – 27 rooms. €67/88* . Situated behind the busy Via Roma, this family-run hotel with 27 simple, but comfortable rooms is popular with actors performing in the nearby Teatro Massimo.

• ***Expensive***

Massimo Plaza Hotel – *Via Maqueda 437, Palermo – ☎ 091 32 56 57 – Fax 091 32 57 11 – booking@massimoplazahotel.com – – 15 rooms. €100/145* . This elegant hotel, situated right opposite the neo-Classical Teatro Massimo, offers excellent service and comfortable rooms decorated in warm colours, with parquet floors and tasteful furnishings.

Hotel Principe di Villafranca – *Via G. Turrisi Colonna 4, Palermo – ☎ 091 61 18 523 – Fax 091 58 87 05 – info@principedivillafranca.it – – 34 rooms. €126/180* . The hotel's small, bright and tastefully decorated reception area comes as a pleasant surprise. Comfortable lounges, antique furniture, attractive paintings, a small library and high quality bedrooms.

Centrale Palace Hotel – *Corso Vittorio Emanuele 327, Palermo – ☎ 091 33 66 66 – Fax 091 33 48 81 – cphotel@tin.it – – 63 rooms. €150/214* . The elegant and tasteful Centrale Palace is located in a 17C mansion and offers excellent hospitality. This hotel has pleasant lounges, including a superb panoramic restaurant on the top floor.

AN ART NOUVEAU MASTERPIECE

Villa Igiea Gd H. – *Salita Belmonte 43 – ☎ 091 63 12 111 – Fax 091 54 76 54 – villa-igiea@thi.it – 108 rooms. €206/340* . Housed in a 15C building, this hotel was restored in the early 20C and decorated in magnificent Art Nouveau style. Excellent service and charming rooms with private balconies.

Taking a Break

POLITEAMA DISTRICT

Antico Caffè – *Via Principe di Belmonte 107-115, Palermo.* One of the oldest cafés in Palermo, the traditional Antico Caffè enjoys a splendid setting on Via Principe Belmonte. First opened in 1860, it continues to serve excellent cakes and pastries on its attractive terrace.

Bar-Pasticceria Mazzara – *Via Magliocco 15, Palermo – ☎ 091 32 14 43.* This famous bar was where Giuseppe Tomasi di Lampedusa, author of *The Leopard*, used to stop for breakfast. The bar started out as a *pasticceria* (the *cassata*, *cannoli*, typical Sicilian cakes and pastries, and ice cream are excellent), then extended its activities to include a *rosticceria*, self-service restaurant and pizzeria.

Enoteca Picone – *Via G. Marconi 36, Palermo – ☎ 091 33 13 00 – Closed Sun.* This traditional, family-run wine bar, founded in 1946, has one of the best cellars in Palermo, with a choice of over 4 000 different wines. Wine tasting has developed into an art form in these rustic, elegant surroundings, where the wine is accompanied by cold meats, cheeses and other local specialities.

I Quaderni di Mamma Andrea – *Via Principe di Scordia 67, Palermo – ☎ 091 33 48 35 – Open Mon-Fri, 8.30am-1pm and 4-7.30pm; Sat, 8.30am-1pm.* Since 1990, Mamma Andrea has specialised in jams, cakes, liqueurs, honey and other delicacies, with the emphasis on high quality and sophistication.

NEAR THE GIARDINO INGLESE

Bar Costa – *Via Gabriele d'Annunzio 15 (N of the Giardino), Palermo – Closed Tue.* This bar specialises in all kinds of cakes and pastries, including delicious orange and lemon mousses.

Pasticceria-Caffetteria Castiglione – *Via Catania 96, Palermo – ☎ 091 30 49 19 – Closed Mon.* A perfect setting for a cup of coffee accompanied by a delicious cake or pastry, this café is situated away from the more famous tourist areas, not far from the English Garden.

Stancampiano – *Via E. Notarbartolo 51, Palermo – ☎ 091 62 54 099.* This *gelateria* has the largest selection of ice creams in Palermo. Take your pick from a choice of cones or tubs or do as the Sicilians do and enjoy your ice cream accompanied by a brioche.

OTHER DISTRICTS

Gelateria di Ciccio – *Corso dei Mille 73, Palermo – ☎ 091 61 61 537.* Only a few hundred metres from the railway station, this ice cream parlour, dating from 1940, offers a range of over 50 different flavours of ice cream. A welcome oasis in the summer months.

Oscar – *Via Mariano Migliaccio 39, Palermo – ☎ 091 68 22 381 – Open 8am-9pm – Closed Tue.* Sicilian *cassata*, *torta Devil* (Devil's Cake, the house speciality), almond pastries and a whole range of other delicacies can be sampled at this *pasticceria*, considered by many to be the best in Palermo. Slightly off the beaten track, but well worth the effort.

Shows

Cantieri culturali alla Zisa – *Via Gili 4, Palermo – ☎ 091 65 24 942.* The old Ducrot warehouses, near Castello della Zisa, were once home to a well-known furniture factory. Nowadays, theyhave been transformed into public rooms which host a range of exhibitions, concerts and plays.

Lo Spasimo – *Via Spasimo (Piazza Magione), Palermo – ☎ 091 61 61 486.* The Santa Maria dello Spasimo complex, home to the Scuola Europea di Musica Jazz, provides an atmospheric setting for a range of cultural events *(see p 296)*.

IL TEATRO DEI PUPI

The name synonymous with the ancient tradition of the puppet theatre in Palermo, is that of the Cuticchio family. For generations not only have these highly skilled puppeteers put on performances, they have themselves made the actual puppets. Sadly, puppet shows no longer attract the same large crowds they used to. At one time they were the talk of the day, followed by everyone and, as such, provided work not only for puppeteers (of which there were many companies in business), but also for many a skilled craftsman who specialised in giving form to their fabulous creations. A simple suit of armour, for example, might comprise some 35 to 36 individual parts before being assembled by hand.

Teatro di Mimmo Cuticchio – *Via Bara all'Olivella 95, Palermo – ☎ 091 32 34 00.* This theatre is the setting for performances by the Mimmo Cuticchio puppet company. The workshop opposite *(open to the public)* is used to store the company's puppets, as well as its stage machinery.

Teatro Ippogrifo – *Vicolo Ragusi 6 (near the Quattro Canti), Palermo – ☎ 091 32 91 94; 347 06 76 368 (mobile) – Performances at 6pm (for a minimum audience of 20 people).* This theatre company belongs to Nino Cuticchio, a member of one of Sicily's most famous puppet-making families. The puppet workshop is located at Via Bara all'Olivella 38.

Teatroarte-Cuticchio – *Via dei Benedettini 9, Palermo – ☎ 347 45 47 613.* Founded by Girolamo Cuticchio in 1946, this renowned company is now run by his sons. The puppet workshop is situated on the same premises.

Shopping

LOCAL MARKETS

The most colourful and picturesque markets are, without doubt, those selling food, with their array of multicoloured awnings, their brightly painted stalls decked with assortments of fruit, vegetables or fish, lit with bare light bulbs.

La Vucciria – This historic market is certainly Palermo's most famous, always bustling with colour and noise, and is the most important food market in the city. It takes place set back from the waterfront in Via Cassari-Argenteria and the surrounding area (stretching as far as Piazza San Domenico).

D. Boggini/MICHELIN

The origin of the name is controversial: some maintain that it comes from the French term *boucherie* (butcher), others are of the opinion that it refers to the deafening clamour of the traders' voices drawing attention to their wares.

Ballarò – Ballarò market is held in the area stretching from Piazza Casa Professa to Corso Tukory. The food stalls cluster around Piazza del Carmine, while clothing and second-hand items can be found near **Casa Professa.** A lively atmosphere, especially in the morning.

Il Capo – The first, more picturesque, food section is along Via Carini and Via Beati Paoli; the clothing and shoe stalls congregate in Via Sant'Agostino and Via Bandiera. In addition to the brightly coloured stalls, it is worth noting the interestingly named streets in this area, such as Sedie Volanti (flying chairs) and Gioia Mia (my love).

Mercato delle Pulci – A range of antique and modern bric-a-brac can be found in the flea market (located between Piazza Peranni and Corso Amedeo), where haggling over prices is mandatory!

I Lattarini – The name of this market derives from the Arabic *suk-el-attarin* (grocery market). Once a food market, its stalls now sell clothing, work tools and ironmongery.

SHOPS

The city's most elegant shops are concentrated in the new development along Via della Libertà, Via Roma and Via Maqueda. The pedestrianised **Via Principe di Belmonte** is also lined with elegant shops; the central section of the street has been planted with trees to provide shade for tables spilling onto the pavement from its many bars. In the bustling **Via Calderai** *(which crosses Via Maqueda south of Piazza Bellini)* there are a number of arts and crafts shops selling firedogs for fireplaces, chairs, china and crockery. The small Via **Bara all'Olivella** *(opposite Teatro Massimo)* is lined with handicraft shops specialising in ceramics, woodwork and puppets.

Enoteca Picone – *Via G. Marconi 36, Palermo – ☎ 091 33 13 00 – Closed Sun. See Taking a Break.*

Enoteca Sicilia – *Via Maqueda 92, Palermo – ☎ 091 61 62 288 – Open 9am-12.30pm. Closed public hols.* €8. This permanent exhibition of Sicilian wine labels is housed in the beautiful Palazzo Ramacca. A wine tasting is included in the price of the guided tour (two wines, which change daily).

Franco Bertolino – *Salita Ramires 8, Palermo – ☎ 0347 05 76 923 – Open Mon-Sat, 9am-8pm.* Bertolino is one of the last remaining artists to specialise in the production of the traditional, colourful Sicilian carts. His workshop, boutique and small museum are housed in an old building near the cathedral.

Il Laboratorio Italiano – *Via Principe di Villafranca 2, Palermo – ☎ 091 32 02 82 – Open Mon-Sat, 9am-7.30pm.* A range of fine, hand-crafted ceramics are exhibited and sold in the three rooms of this small workshop. A reputable address, renowned for its unusual and original items.

La Bottega d'Arte di Angela Tripi – *Corso Vittorio Emanuele 450-452, Palermo – ☎ 091 65 12 787 – tripi@tripi.it – Open Mon-Sat, 9.30am-7.30pm.* Situated near the cathedral in Palazzo Santa Ninfa, this workshop specialising in small terracotta statues for cribs is famous throughout the world. A superb showcase of high-quality craftwork.

Vincenzo Argento e Figli – *Corso Vittorio Emanuele 445, Palermo – ☎ 091 61 13 680 – Open Mon-Sat from 10am (shop); performance at 6pm.* The old artistic tradition of making puppets has been handed down through the generations in this long-established family business, founded in 1893. Today, the shop continues to sell an incredible variety of puppets.

Opening hours – Most shops are closed on Monday morning (food shops close on Wednesday afternoon). Shops generally open between 9am and 1pm and from 3.30 to 7.30pm (4-8pm on Saturday afternoon).

Festivals

U' Fistino – This festival, held in honour of the city's patron saint, Santa Rosalia, takes place on 14 and 15 July, with processions, costumed parades and firework displays.

Festa dei Morti – On 2 November, in celebration of All Souls' Day, children receive gifts and sweets from their departed loved ones.

Festival di Morgana – This gathering of puppeteers and performers from around the world is held at the Museo Internazionale delle Marionette from the end of November to mid-December.

central part of the original complex survives today, together with the massive Pisan Tower; the dome is a later addition dating from when an observatory was installed there in 1791. The palace then endured a period of abandonment and decline that lasted well into the 17C when, under the Spanish viceroys, it was restored. It was then that the impressive south front and the beautiful internal courtyard with its three storeys of loggias were inserted.

Today, the *palazzo* serves as the seat of the Sicilian Parliament (or ARS: Assemblea Regionale Siciliana). The entrance hall, with a monumental staircase (where a senator's beautiful carriage is displayed), dates from 1735.

Cappella Palatina

Open Mon-Fri, 9am-noon and 3-5pm; Sat, 9am-noon; Sun, 9-10am and noon-1pm. Closed public hols. No charge. ☎ 091 70 54 879.

On the first floor (take the staircase on the left). Before entering the Palatine Chapel, it is worth pausing a moment to admire the superb **courtyard** enclosed by three superimposed loggias. Set into the wall on the left is an inscription in Latin, Greek and Arabic that sings the praises of a water-clock made during the reign of Roger II. The chapel was built by the king between 1130 – the year of his coronation – and 1140. In the beginning it would have stood alone, with the apse at the east end. Then, through the course of time, it became incorporated into a complex of other buildings which now conceal it completely. Currently, the entrance is via the narthex that precedes the chapel proper. What can still be seen is the exterior of the side wall (corresponding to the north aisle) with its two-tier decoration. The lower section echoes the decorative arrangement at the same level inside: slabs of white marble surrounded by *pietra dura* decoration (inlay of semi-precious stones). The upper tier comprises composite panels dating from the 19C, depicting scenes from the life of David. At the rear, next to the entrance, Roger II is represented handing a decree instituting the royal ecclesiastical body to the *ciantro* (literally a singer, but, in this case, the person in charge of the chapel).

Once inside, attention is immediately drawn to the fabulous Arabo-Norman interior decoration of blazing gold set off by the marble.

Structure – The internal space, with a rectangular ground plan, is divided into two parts: the first section is divided into three aisles by 10 granite columns; the second, up five steps, comprises the chancel, which is contained within a marble balustrade. On the right, near the division of the two halves, is the double **ambo**, supported by four beautiful columns and two small pilasters, with integrated lecterns borne by the eagle of St John and the lion of St Mark. To one side is the fine Paschal **candlestick** (12C), a wonderful piece of sculpture, tall, slender and richly decorated: its square pedestal is formed by four lions intent on mauling two men and two animals; a braid of plant-like branches intertwines the figures of wild beasts and an armed man preparing to defend himself. Above, Christ sits in a mandorla supported by angels, holding the Gospels in his hand while, below, a figure in bishop's clothing kneels before him (possibly Roger II himself). Two tiers of birds (vultures pecking the tails of slender storks) support three figures representing the three ages of man. The acute sense of realism of these figures might suggest they are of a later date; perhaps the figures were added when the candlestick was moved, and required further refinement.

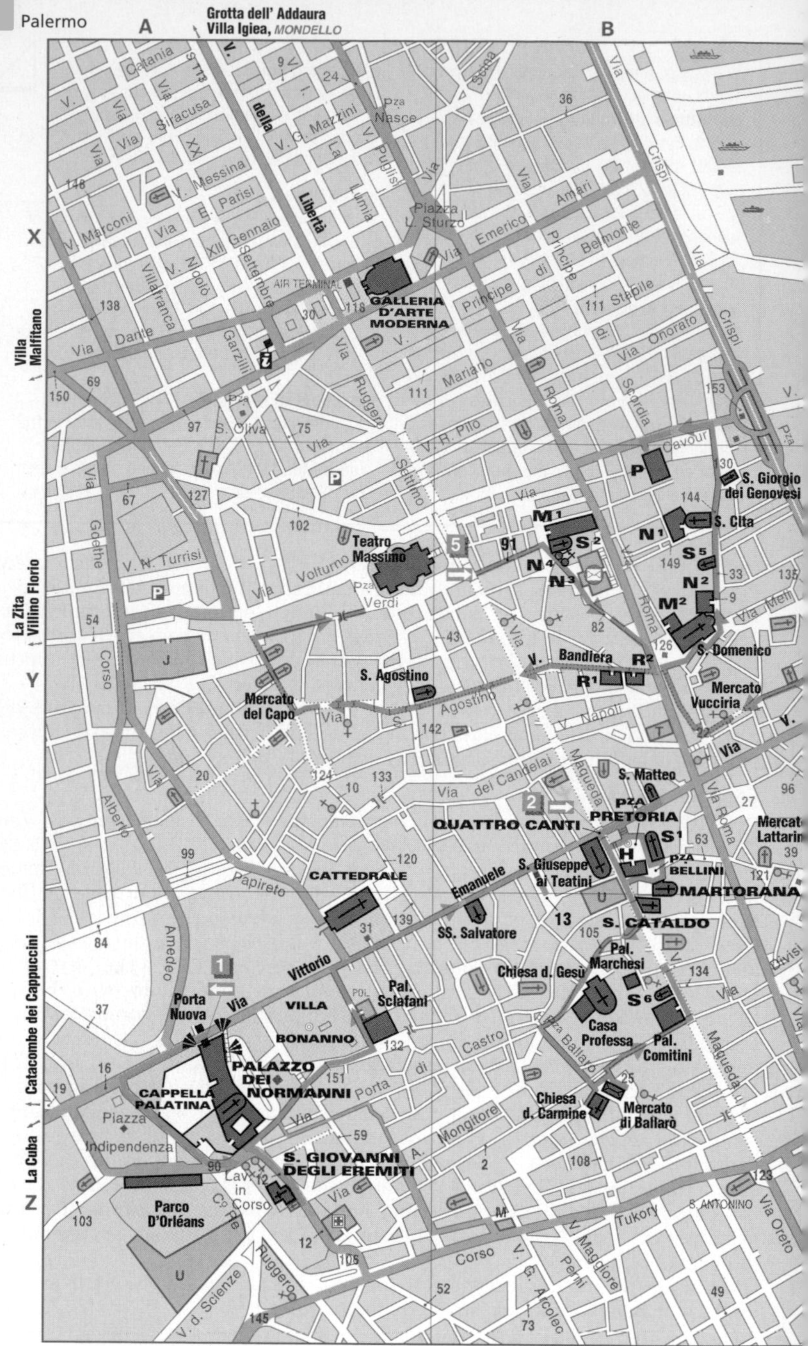

Set against the back wall of the chapel is the majestic **royal throne**, which also forms an integral part of the mosaic above depicting Christ seated, attended by the Archangels St Michael and St Gabriel (representing death and birth respectively) and by the Apostles St Peter and St Paul (founders of the Christian Church). The actual throne is inlaid with mosaic and porphyry; the coat of arms in the centre is that of the House of Aragon. The porphyry octagon probably bore the image of the reigning monarch.

The pavement comprises a geometric arrangement of marble tiles and mosaic, that form large Oriental-style rectangles.

The remarkable **wooden muqarnas ceiling★★** in the central nave, a masterpiece by North African artists, depicts a number of scenes from daily life (unfortunately not visible to the naked eye): courtly and hunting scenes, drinking, dancing, games of chess, animals etc. This exceptional work of art comprises the most extensive cycle of Fatimid painting to have survived to the present day.

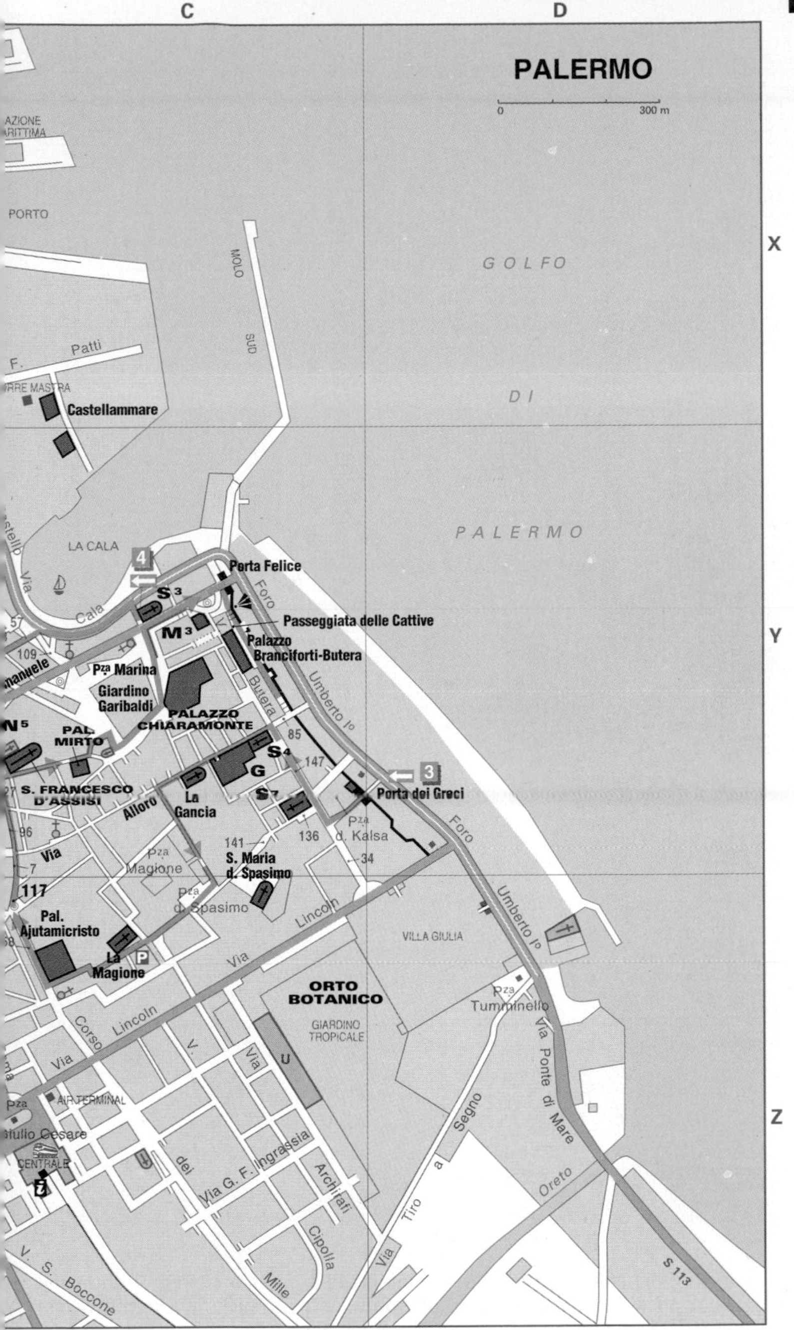

Mosaics – The exquisite mosaics comprise tesserae of coloured paste (cement and pigment) and glass onto which gold leaf has been applied, imparting an overall brilliance. They recount the story of the Old Testament *(nave)*, a selection of the most important episodes in the life of Christ *(chancel)*, and of St Peter and St Paul *(aisles)*. The silent witnesses include a host of Prophets, angels and saints, either shown full-length or enclosed in medallions.

The mosaics were executed in two different phases: the oldest ones date from the 1140s, the ones in the nave, echoing the style of those at Monreale, date from the 1160s and 1170s.

The sequence of scenes in the nave serves a single function, and that is didactic: this is a prime example of teaching through pictures. Of particular note is the illustration of the earth being separated from the sea: the terrestrial globe is shown as a sphere of water in which there are three areas of land (America and Oceania had not yet been discovered). These are divided by sea which takes the form of a Y

PALERMO

Albergheria (Via) **BZ** 3
Alloro (Via) **CY**
Amari (Via E.) **BX**
Amedeo (Corso A.) **AYZ**
Aragona (Piazza) **CY** 6
Aragona (Via) **CY** 7
Archimede (Via) **AX** 9
Archirafi (Via) **CZ**
Arcoleo (Via G.) **BZ**
Ballarò (Piazza) **BZ**
Bandiera (Via) **BY**
Beati Paoli (Via) **AY** 10
Bellini (Piazza) **BY**
Benedettini (Via d.) **AZ** 12
Boccone (Via S.) **CZ**
Bologni (Piazza) **BYZ** 13
Butera (Via) **CY**
Cala (Via) **CY**
Calatafimi (Corso) **AZ** 16
Candelai (Via d.) **BY**
Cappuccinelle (Via d.) **AY** 20
Cappuccini (Via d.) **AZ** 19
Caracciolo (Piazza) **BY** 22
Carini (Via I.) **AX** 24
Carmine (Piazza d.) **BZ** 25
Cassa di Risparmio (Piazza) **BY** 27
Cassari (Via) **BCY** 28
Castello (Piazza) **BCY**
Castelnuovo (Piazza) **AX** 30
Catania (Via) **AX**
Cattedrale (Piazza d.) **AZ** 31
Cavalieri di Malta (Largo) **BY** 33
Cavour (Via) **BXY**
Cervello (Via) **CY** 34
Cipolla (Via) **CZ**
Collegio di Maria (Via) **BX** 36
Colonna Rotta (Via) **AZ** 37
Crispi (Via) **BX**
Croce dei Vespri (Piazza d.) **BY** 39
Dante (Via) **AX**
Divisi (Via) **BZ**
Don Sturzo (Piazza) **ABX**
Donizetti (Via G.) **ABY** 43
Errante (Via V.) **BZ** 49
Filiciuzza (Via) **ABZ** 52
Finocchiaro Aprile (Corso) **AY** 54
Fonderia (Piazza) **CY** 57
Garibaldi (Via) **CZ** 58
Garzilli (Via N.) **AX**
Generale Cadorna (Via) **AZ** 59
Giudici (Discesa d.) **BY** 63
Giulio Cesare (Piazza) **CZ**
Goethe (Via) **AY**
Indipendenza (Piazza) **AZ**
Ingrassia (Via G. F.) **CZ**
Juvara Cluviero (Via) **AY** 67
Kalsa (Piazza d.) **CY**
La Lumia (Via I.) **AX**
Latini (Via B.) **AX** 69
Libertà (Via d.) **AX**
Lincoln (Via) **CZDY**
Maggiore Perni (Via) **BZ**
Magione (Piazza d.) **CYZ**
Maqueda (Via) **BYZ**
Marconi (Via) **AX**
Marina (Piazza) **CY**
Marino (Via S.) **BZ** 73
Mazzini (Via G.) **AX**
Meccio (Via S.) **AX** 75
Meli (Via) **BY**
Messina (Via) **AX**
Mille (Corso d.) **CZ**
Mongitore (Via A.) **ABZ**
Monteleone (Via) **BY** 82
Mosca (Via G.) **AZ** 84
Mura delle Cattive (Salita) **CY** 85
Napoli (Via) **BY**
Nasce (Piazza) **AX**
Onorato (Via) **BX**
Oreto (Via) **BZ**
Orleans (Piazza) **AZ** 90
Orologio (Via) **BY** 91
Papireto (Via) **AYZ**
Parisi (Via E.) **AX**
Paternostro (Via A.) **BCY** 96
Paternostro (Via P.) **AX** 97
Patti (Via F.) **BCX**
Peranni (Piazza D.) **AY** 99
Pignatelli d'Aragona (Via) **AY** 102
Pilo (Via R.) **BXY**
Pisani (Corso P.) **AZ** 103
Ponte di Mare (Via) **DZ**
Ponticello (Via) **BZ** 105
Porta di Castro (Via) **ABZ**
Porta Montalto (Piazza) **AZ** 106
Porta S. Agata (Via) **BZ** 108
Porto Salvo (Via) **CY** 109
Pretoria (Piazza) **BY**
Principe di Belmonte (Via) **BX**
Principe di Scordia (Via) **BX**
Principe Granatelli (Via) **ABX** 111
Puglisi (Via) **AX**
Quattro Canti (Piazza Vigliena) **BY**
Rao (Via C.) **CZ**
Rivoluzione (Piazza) **CZ** 117
Roma (Via) **BXCZ**
Ruggero Settimo (Piazza) **AX** 118
Ruggero Settimo (Via) **AXY**
S. Agata (Via) **AY** 120
S. Agostino (Via) **AYZ**
S. Anna (Piazza) **BY** 121
S. Antonino (Piazza) **BZ** 123
S. Cosmo (Piazza) **AY** 124
S. Domenico (Piazza) **BY** 126
S. Francesco da Paola (Piazza) **AY** 127
S. Francesco d'Assisi (Piazza) **CY** 129
S. Giorgio dei Genovesi (Piazza) **BY** 130
S. Giovanni Decollato (Piazzetta) **AZ** 132
S. Isidoro alla Guilla (Piazza) **AY** 133
S. Oliva (Piazza) **AX**
S. Orsola (Vicolo) **BZ** 134
S. Sebastiano (Via) **BY** 135
S. Teresa (Via) **CY** 136
Sammartino (Via) **AX** 138
Scienze (Via d.) **AZ**
Scina (Via) **BX**
Scuole (Via d.) **AZ** 139
Siracusa (Via) **AX**
Spasimo (Piazza d.) **CYZ**
Spasimo (Via d.) **CY** 141
Spirito Santo (Via d.) **ABY** 142
Squarcialupo (Via) **BY** 144
Stabile (Via M.) **AYBX**
Stazzone (Piazza) **AZ** 145
Tiro a Segno (Via) **DZ**
Torremuzza (Via) **CY** 147
Tukory (Corso) **ABZ**
Tumminello (Piazza) **DZ**
Turrisi (Via N.) **AY**
Turrisi Colonna (Via) **AX** 148
Umberto I° (Foro) **CDYZ**
Valverde (Via) **BY** 149
Verdi (Piazza) **ABY**
Villafranca (Via) **AX**
Virgilio (Piazza) **AX** 150
Vittoria (Piazza d.) **AZ** 151
Vittorio Emanuele (Via) **AZCY**
Volturno (Via) **AY**
XII Gennaio (Via) **AX**
XIII Vittime (Piazza) **BX** 153
XX Settembre (Via) **AX**

Cappella Palatina **AZ**
Casa Professa **BZ**
Castellammare **CXY**
Catacombe dei Cappuccini **AZ**
Cattedrale **AZ**
Chiesa del Carmine **BZ**
Chiesa del Gesù **BZ**
Chiesa di S. Spirito **ABZ**
Galleria d'Arte Moderna (Teatro Politeama) **AX**
Galleria Regionale di Sicilia (Pal. Abatellis) **CY G**
Giardino Garibaldi **CY**
Grotta dell'Addaura **AX**
La Gancia **CY**
La Magione **CZ**
La Cuba **AZ**
La Ziza **AY**
Martorana **BY**
Mercata Vucciria **BY**
Mercato di Ballarò **BZ**
Mercato di Capo **AY**
Mercato Lattarini **BY**
Museo Archeologico Regionale **BY M1**
Museo Internazionale delle Marionette **CY M3**
Museo del Risorgimento **BY M2**
Oratorio del Rosario di S. Cita **BY N1**
Oratorio del Rosario di S. Domenico **BY N2**
Oratorio di S. Caterina d'Alessandria **BY N3**
Oratorio di S. Filippo Neri **BY N4**
Oratorio di S. Lorenzo **CY N5**
Orto Botanico **CDZ**
Palazzo Ajutamicristo **CZ**
Palazzo Branciforti-Butera **CY**
Palazzo Chiaramonte **CY**
Palazzo Comitini **BZ**
Palazzo dei Normanni **AZ**
Palazzo Marchesi **BZ**
Palazzo Mirto **CY**
Palazzo Oneto di Sperlinga **BY R1**
Palazzo Pretorio (Municipio) **BY H**
Palazzo Sclafani **AZ**
Palazzo Termine **BY R2**
Parco d'Orléans **AZ**
Passeggiata delle Cattive **CY**
Ponte dell'Ammiraglio **CDZ**
Porta dei Greci **CY**
Porta Felice **CY**
Porta Nuova **AZ**
Prefettura **BY P**
Quattro Canti **BYZ**
S. Agostino **AY**
S. Cataldo **BZ**
S. Caterina **BY S1**
S. Cita **BY**
S. Domenico **BY**
S. Francesco d'Assisi **CY**
S. Giorgio dei Genovesi **BY**
S. Giovanni degli Eremiti **AZ**
S. Giuseppe ai Teatini **BY**
S. Ignazio all'Olivella **BY S2**
S. Maria della Catena **CY S3**
S. Maria della Pietà **CY S4**
S. Maria dello Spasimo **CYZ**
S. Maria di Valverde **BY S5**
S. Matteo **BY**
S. Orsola **BZ S6**
S. Teresa alla Kalsa **CY S7**
SS. Salvatore **BZ**
Teatro Massimo **AY**
Villa Bonanno **AZ**
Villa Igiea **AX**
Villa Malfitano **AX**
Vucciria **BY**

– the symbol of the Holy Trinity; the firmament, all around, is not yet illuminated by stars. Look out also for the **Creation of Adam**: note the striking resemblance in the face of Adam with that of God, thereby underlining the inscription in Latin: *"creavit ds ominem at imaginem sua"* (And God created Man in His own image). The scene recounting the story of **Original Sin** sounds an unusual note as both Adam and Eve are shown with the forbidden fruit in their mouths as they reach for a second one. The section that follows on from the second half of the panel illustrating the **Sacrifice of Cain and Abel**, when the latter lies to the Lord, up to the scene showing the family of Noah (including Noah himself) was substantially remodelled in the 19C: this is evident from the radical change in style. *To read the Old Testament scenes in the nave, begin from the top of the right-hand side of the nave and follow the length of the top register along the left hand side of the nave; continue with the second register, starting again on the right-hand side of the nave. For an explanation of the lesser known biblical stories, see the description of the mosaics in MONREALE.*

In contrast, the iconography of the scenes in the **chancel** is modified for contemplation by the clergy and is therefore conducive to reflection rather than teaching by example. This explains why the scenes from the life of Christ are not arranged sequentially but in order of importance *(note especially above the right-hand apse).*

The **cupola** above the choir contains the figure of Christ Pantocrator, flanked by the three Archangels (St Gabriel, St Michael and St Raphael) and Tobit, and four angels. Biblical figures line the inside of the drum, and the Evangelists fill the pendentives (triangular corner sections).

The Annunciation is represented above the arch of the apse, placed there as a reminder of the Word of God that foretold Christ in Benediction (in the vault) and the enthroned Madonna, the Queen of Heaven. On the underside of the arch, at its apex, is a medallion containing the Throne of Justice, the Cross hung with the crown of thorns, and the dove.

In the **south transept**, pride of place is given to the figure of St Paul (apse vault) surrounded by scenes from the life of Christ; the barrel vault has a medallion filled with the symbol of Pentecost, a dove flying down among the Apostles (figures below). The story of the *Nativity* is particularly well related: the three kings are represented on their journey towards Bethlehem and the Christ Child. (Note that the Magi on the left wear Phrygian caps, a pointed hat with the top folded forward, to denote the fact that they come from the East. Historically, the Magi were astrologers of the Persian court, priests of the cult of Mithras, which was widespread throughout the Roman Empire.) St Joseph, on the left of the Virgin Mary, is seated on a typical type of Sicilian chair. The blue lunette below the scene symbolises the washing of the Christ Child.

Dominating the **north transept** is St Andrew (apse vault), but only since the 14C when he replaced the original mosaics of St Peter; beside him is the Hodegetria Madonna and Child (Guide or Instructress pointing to the Way of Redemption based on an icon said tohave been painted by St Luke). To one side, St John the Baptist preaches in the desert.

Some of the mosaics in the apse were substantially reworked in the 18C.

The **aisles** are covered with scenes from the life of St Paul *(starting from the beginning of the south aisle)* and St Peter *(last section of the south aisle, along the length of the north aisle).*

Royal Apartments**

(♿) Guided tours only (30min), Mon, Fri and Sat, 9am-noon. Groups by appointment only. No charge. Fax 091 70 54 737; www.ars.sicilia.it

The visit begins in the Salone d'Ercole (1560), now the chamber of the Sicilian Parliament, so called after the large frescoes by Giuseppe Velasquez (19C) depicting the *Twelve Labours of Heracles* *(see p 388)*. Today, only six panels are visible (the others being hidden behind the gallery), namely *(starting from the far end of the hall)* Heracles and the giants (not, in fact, related to the Labours), the slaying of the many-headed Hydra of Lerna, the capture of the Ceryneian hind, the taming of the three-headed dog Cerberus, the capture of the Erymanthean boar, and the Cretan Bull. The frescoed ceiling illustrates the birth, triumph and death of the hero.

Across the hall of the viceroys is a small entrance room which once constituted the heart of the **Joaria**, one of the Norman palace's original towers, now incorporated into other buildings. The wall apertures were designed to provide ventilation, allowing cool and warm air to circulate through the cavities between one wall and another. On the left is the most interesting room in the palace, **Sala di Ruggero II**, which is decorated in a way that is reminiscent of the Palatine Chapel. From the high marble panelling, framed within friezes of mosaic, springs the golden mantle that covers the upper sections of the wall and ceiling. Hunting scenes alternate with symbolic animals such as the peacock (for eternity, as it was alleged that its flesh would never decompose) and the lion (for royalty and strength); all are portrayed in accordance with an Eastern iconography, which demanded that they be shown in pairs, one facing the other. Representations are exquisitely detailed, as the figures wander through a typically Sicilian landscape with palms and citrus trees. At the centre of the ceiling is a medallion with the Imperial emblem: an eagle holding a hare between its talons. There follows a number of other 18C and 19C rooms, including the Yellow Hall (or Hall of Mirrors), named after the beautiful gold candlesticks it contains.

Osservatorio Astronomico

Top floor of the Pisan Tower. Open 9.30am-12.30pm. Closed Sat-Sun, public hols and in Aug. ☎ 091 23 34 43; www.astropa.unipa.it

The **astronomical observatory** houses a museum of old instruments used in astronomy, meteorology, seismology and topography; visitors are able to relive a fundamental event in astronomy: the discovery of the first asteroid, on this very spot, on 1 January 1801, by Father Piazzi. From the top, there is a fabulous bird's-eye **view***** over Palermo.

CAPPELLA PALATINA

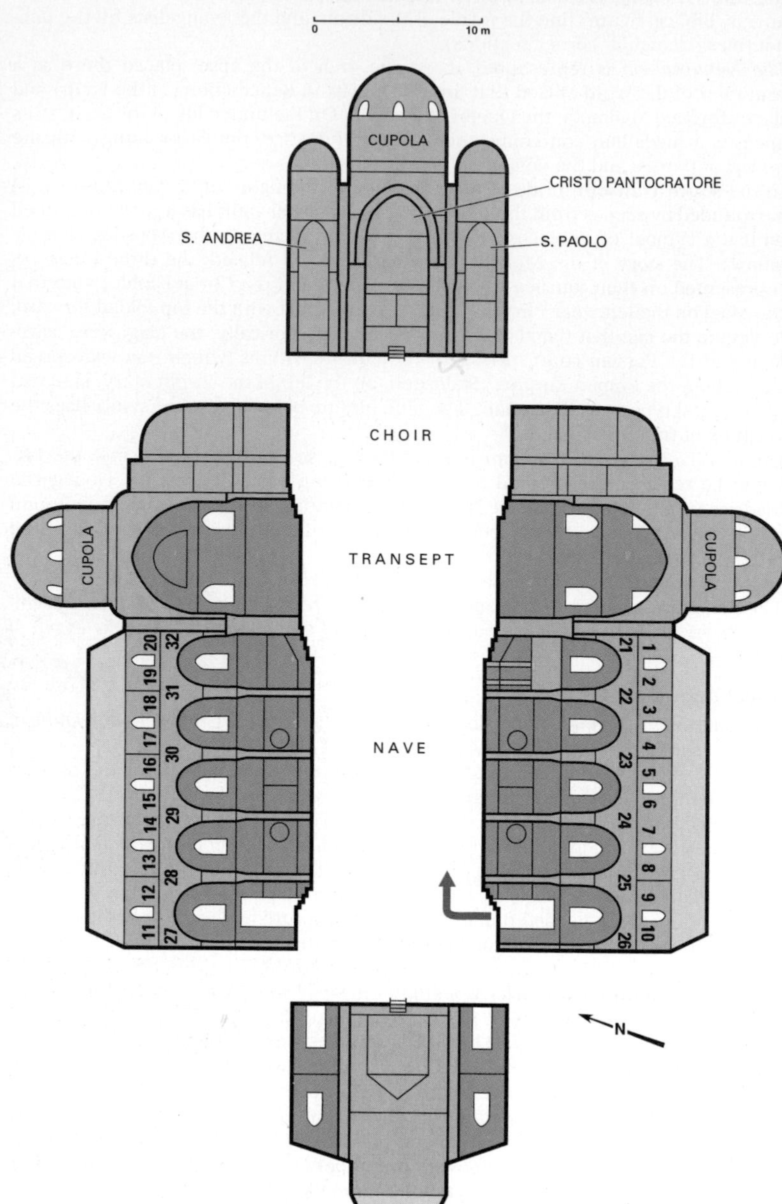

1 The creation of light and of the seas
2 The dry land separated from the waters
3 The creation of plants and trees
4 The creation of the sun, moon and stars
5 The creation of fish and birds
6 The creation of land animals
7 The creation of Adam
8 God resting from his labours
9 God pointing out the tree to Adam
10 The creation of Eve
11 Original sin
12 The shame of Adam and Eve
13 Paradise lost
14 Adam and Eve at work
15 The sacrifice of Cain and Abel
16 Cain kills Abel and lies to God
17 Lamech confesses to his two wives that he has killed two men
18 Enoch taken up to heaven on account of his deep faith
19 Noah with his wife and three sons
20 Building the Ark
21 Return of the dove
22 God tells Noah to leave the Ark
23 Noah planting a vineyard and getting drunk
24 Noah's descendants build the city of Babel
25 Abraham meets three angels and offers them hospitality
26 Lot on the threshold of his house tries to restrain the Sodomites
27 Destruction of Sodom, and Lot leaving the city
28 God tells Abraham to sacrifice Isaac, but an angel intervenes
29 Rebecca at the well and departure for Canaan
30 Isaac blessing Jacob
31 Jacob's dream
32 Jacob wrestling with the angel

Walking About

Unless otherwise stated, churches are generally open in the morning and late afternoon.

THE HISTORIC QUARTER 1

For the Palazzo dei Normanni, see above.

Porta Nuova

Built under the Emperor Charles V, the gateway is topped by a Renaissance-style loggia; note at the end of the pitched roof, the Imperial eagle. Beyond the gate stretches **Corso Vittorio Emanuele**, a long, straight road which runs across town to **Porta Felice**.

Palazzo e Parco d'Orléans

This is the house and garden in which Louis Philippe d'Orléans, the future King of France, lived in exile from 1810 to 1814. Today, it is used by the Sicilian regional authorities. The garden has magnificent banyan trees *(Ficus magnolioides)* with their spectacular array of roots, and various exotic animals.

San Giovanni degli Eremiti★★

Open Mon-Sat, 9am-7pm; Sun and public hols, 9am-1.30pm (last admission 30min before closing). €4. ☎ 091 69 61 319; www.regione.sicilia.it/beniculturali/sopripa

The Church of **St John of the Hermits** and its garden are situated not far from Palazzo dei Normanni, providing a tiny haven of peace where even the noise of the Palermo traffic seems muffled.

In a luxuriant garden of palm trees, agaves, bougainvillea, orange trees, Chinese mandarin trees and shrubs of various kinds, stands the church that was built around the middle of the 12C at the request of King **Roger II**. This is one of the most famous Arabo-Norman monuments in Palermo. Its simple, square forms which enclose spaces consisting of perfect cubes rise to a red roof with five squat domes (echoing the profile of San Cataldo not far away), all clearly the work of Moorish craftsmen. The interior, simple and bare, is shaped into a Latin-cross plan: the central space is divided into two halves above which hover two domes. The transept is subdivided into three, each part contained by a dome; the south bay rises first to become a bell tower that is then capped by a dome.

At one time, the church was flanked by its monastery, the abbot of which was employed as the king's private confessor. Today, only the delightful little 13C **cloisters**★ with their paired columns remain.

Villa Bonanno★

These lovely public gardens lie behind the Palazzo Reale (Norman Palace). Excavations conducted in one part of the garden have revealed the **remains of Roman patrician houses** containing mosaics featuring the seasons and Orpheus, now housed in the Museo Archeologico Regionale *(see Worth a Visit)*. In the upper part of the garden, near the Norman Palace, stands an elaborate 17C monument to Philip V of Bourbon.

Palazzo Sclafani

The front of the building (1330) overlooking Piazzetta San Giovanni Decollato is ornamented with fine Gothic two-light windows within interlacing arches so typical of the Arabo-Norman style, and an elegant cusped doorway surmounted by the royal eagle. It is from this *palazzo* that the famous fresco *The Triumph of Death* was transferred to the Galleria Regionale di Sicilia.

Cattedrale★

Palermo's cathedral is an imposing edifice. It was built in the late 12C in the Sicilian-Norman style, but has undergone considerable alteration over the centuries. A notable addition from the 15C is the Catalan Gothic south porch with, on the outermost wall, the symbols of the four Evan-

Cathedral apses

B. Kaufmann/MICHELIN

gelists (St Mark's lion and St Matthew's angel on the right, St Luke's ox and St John's eagle on the left), its fine inner doorway and its beautiful, carved wooden doors. The neo-Classical dome was added in the 18C, when the interior was also completely refurbished. The original fabric of the building, however, can still be seen in the **apses★** which retain their typical yet effective geometric decoration.

Inside, the first chapel on the right contains the tombs of members of the Swabian and Norman royal families: Frederick II, his wife Costanza of Aragon, Henry VI and, at the rear, Roger II and his daughter Costanza d'Altavilla.

Treasury and crypt – *Access from the south transept. Open Mon-Sat, 10am-12.30pm and 2-4pm. €1 (treasury); €1.50 (treasury and crypt).*

The **treasury** contains a fine carved ivory staff made in Sicily in the 17C, and jewels belonging to Queen Costanza of Aragon. Among these are various rings and the magnificent **Imperial gold crown★** set with precious stones, pearls and enamels.

A number of tombs from different periods are preserved in the crypt, a large proportion belonging to former bishops. Note the Classical Roman sarcophagus decorated with the figures of the nine Muses, Apollo, and a seated man wearing a toga.

Chiesa del Santissimo Salvatore

Open 9am-12.30pm and 3.30-5pm. Closed Tue. ☎ 091 32 33 92.

The present oval Church of the Holy Saviour, built on the foundations of a Norman predecessor, was designed in the late 17C by **Paolo Amato**. The interior is richly decorated in the Baroque style complete with polychrome marble and stucco. Within the dome may be discerned fragments of a large fresco of the *Triumph of St Basil* (1763). Today, the church is principally used as an auditorium.

Further along Corso Vittorio Emanuele is **Piazza Bologni**: among the alignment of fine 18C buildings sits **Palazzo Alliata di Villafranca** which displays proudly the elaborate coats of arms of two aristocratic families including that of the Bologna family. In the centre of the piazza is a statue of Charles V, the Spanish monarch.

FROM THE QUATTRO CANTI TO THE ALBERGHERIA 2

I "Quattro Canti"★★ (Piazza Vigliena)

The intersection of Palermo's two main thoroughfares, Via Vittorio Emanuele and Via Maqueda, is marked by a spacious octagon: the infilled corners of the square are furnished by four elegant 18C Baroque *palazzo* façades, their elevations subdivided into sections with Classical columns (Doric, Ionic and Corinthian), with, at the centre of each, an elaborate fountain dedicated to one of the four seasons. The niches of the middle storey contain statues of the four Spanish kings of Sicily, those in the upper level contain effigies representing the patron saints of Palermo, who protected the districts lying behind them: St Christina, St Ninfa, St Oliva and St Agatha (who was subsequently replaced by St Rosalia) *(see p 311)*.

San Matteo

For information on admission times, call ☎ 091 33 48 33.

The Church of St Matthew was built in the mid-17C. Its façade consists of three orders, the niches and projecting surfaces of which contrast to produce striking *chiaroscuro* effects. The richly decorated interior reflects the church's ties with the Unione dei Miseremini, founded with the aim of hearing masses for souls suffering in Purgatory. The valuable works of art here include two beautiful canvases by P Novelli (*The Presentation at the Temple* and *The Marriage of the Virgin*, fourth chapel in the side aisle), the 18C frescoes in the vault and dome by Vito d'Anna, and the statue of *Faith and Justice* to the side of the presbytery and the lunette portraying *Christ Freeing Souls from the Flames of Purgatory* opposite, by Giacomo Serpotta. Serpotta himself is buried in the crypt of the church (access from the left aisle).

Piazza Pretoria★★

At the centre of this lovely piazza is a spectacular **fountain★★** by the 16C Florentine sculptor Francesco Camilliani, originally intended as a garden ornament for some Tuscan villa. Comprising concentric circles of gods and goddesses, nymphs, monsters, animals' heads, allegories, ornamental staircases and balustrades, this fountain is a veritable Mount Olympus. Spouting water brings the whole to life, animating it with sparkling light, yet never upsetting the balance of the composition: a rare quality often found in Tuscan Renaissance works of art.

The top basin is divided into four sections; below each is a smaller bowl which, in turn, is overlooked by one of the four allegories of the rivers of Palermo: Gabriele, Maredolce, Papireto and Oreto. Among the statuettes guarding the ramps is Ceres, the Classical patroness of Sicily, who holds a sheaf of wheat and a horn of plenty. The wrought-iron railing surrounding the fountain is by Giovan Battista Basile.

The piazza is bounded by fine buildings: to one side rises the dome of **Santa Caterina**; on the south axis stands the **Palazzo Pretorio** (also known as Palazzo Senatorio or Palazzo delle Aquile), the city hall. Across the road is the church of San Giuseppe ai Teatini.

B. Kaufmann/MICHELIN

The fountain in Piazza Pretoria

Palazzo Pretorio

Open Sat, 8am-1pm. No charge. For further information, call ☎ 091 74 01 111.
Concealed by the present rather austere exterior, the result of 19C renovations, lie the vestiges of a succession of earlier façades in various styles, the oldest of which dates from the 1300s. Since then, it has been the seat of the City Council. The main entrance, especially on the inside, is ornamented with a profusion of Baroque elements (1691), including spiral columns; beyond, lies an attractive courtyard with a monumental staircase up to the *piano nobile*. Here, on the first floor, there is a shallow relief *(on the left)* of a crowned Ceres, a homage to the patroness of Sicily. The rooms open to the public include the **Sala dei Lapidi** lined with marble tablets bearing inscriptions and now used for Council meetings (note, in passing the magnificent central 17C chandelier carved from a single piece of wood), and **Sala Garibaldi**, named after the Italian hero who addressed the assembled crowds from the balcony in 1860. A glass case on the right contains some fine weapons and scabbards inlaid with gold and mother-of-pearl belonging to Napoleon Bonaparte.

San Giuseppe ai Teatini

Piazza Pretoria is bordered by the side of this striking Baroque church. The most eye-catching element is the original campanile which rises to an octagonal section with spiral columns at the top. The sides are ornamented with flaming vases. The **interior★**, in the form of a Latin cross, is theatrical, endowed as it is with a majestic ceiling, stunning white and gold stucco decoration and frescoes on a grand scale. Each aisle bay is capped with a small round dome, itself encrusted with stucco. Set diagonally from the rear wall are two fine organ cases. To either side of the entrance is one of a pair of unusually impressive 18C **stoups★**, each consisting of an angel in flight with a basin in its arms.

Frutta Martorana

Frutta martorana, also known as *pasta reale* and one of the most typical kinds of Sicilian *pasticcerie*, is named after the church of the same name. According to tradition, the origins of this delicacy can be traced back to medieval times when every convent specialised in making a different kind of confectionery. The ones made by the Benedictine convent of la Martorana in early November for the feast day of All Saints, were of marzipan, shaped and coloured to resemble various fruits. The tradition continues today: during the Fiera dei Morti at the beginning of November the district between Via Spicuzza and Piazza Olivella is invaded by brightly coloured stalls selling *frutta martorana*, dolls made from sugar and children's toys.

Marzipan is also of medieval origin: the term is derived from the Arabic *mauthaban* which originally denoted a coin, then a unit of measurement and, finally, the container used to store the paste, made of almonds, sugar and white of egg.

S. Sauvignier/MICHELIN

Piazza Bellini★

This small square is contained by three churches: **Santa Caterina** (dating from the end of the 16C, with an 18C dome), la Martorana and San Cataldo which, with its three red domes, endows the square with an Eastern flavour.

La Martorana★★

Open Mon-Sat, 8am-1pm and 3.30-7pm (5.30pm in winter); Sun and public hols, 8.30am-1pm. ☎ 091 61 61 692.

This church is named after Eloisa Martorana who, in 1194, founded the nearby Benedictine convent, to which the church served as a chapel. The church, in fact dedicated to **Santa Maria dell'Ammiraglio** (St Mary of the Admiral), had been founded in 1143 at the request of George of Antioch, an admiral in the fleet of Roger II.

The linearity of the Norman original is unfortunately concealed behind the Baroque façade (on the south side of the church) that faces onto the piazza. The main entrance is through a fine portico-cum-bell tower, articulated by three orders of columns and double arch openings. At one time, this was free-standing; it was attached to the church in the 16C when the latter was extended by two bays, at the same time as the apse was replaced by a square choir.

Mass is celebrated according to the Greek Orthodox liturgy.

Interior – The building is divided into two parts. The first two bays, added in the 16C, were frescoed in the 17C; the older church shelters a wonderful array of glorious **mosaics★★** that strictly conform to Byzantine iconography, possibly executed by the same craftsmen who were employed at the Capella Palatina. The wall which once constituted the main façade has two mosaic panels representing George of Antioch prostrate at the feet of the Virgin *(on the left)* and Roger II receiving the crown from Christ *(on the right)*. Filling the nave dome is Christ Pantocrator surrounded by four Archangels (St Michael, St Gabriel, St Raphael and St Uriel). In the register below are eight Prophets and, in the pendentives, the four Evangelists. In the nave vault may be seen the Nativity *(on the left)* and the Death (Dormition) of the Virgin.

The gratings of the nuns' gallery are a fine example of wrought-iron work.

San Cataldo★★

Open 8.30am-1pm. Closed public hols. ☎ 091 87 28 047.

The church, the main seat of the Knights of the Holy Sepulchre, was built during the Norman period (12C). A distinctive Moorish quality is imparted by the combination of its rather severe square forms, crenellated walls, perforated window screens and characteristic bulbous red domes (likened by the Italians to a eunuch's hat).

The austere interior is articulated into three aisles by antique columns stolen from more ancient buildings. The nave is crowned with three domes, each supported on squinches. The polychrome marble paving is original.

Chiesa del Gesù di Casa Professa

When the Jesuits arrived in Sicily in the mid-16C, the Spanish government gave them its generous support. It was here that they founded their first church, although this was considerably altered before arriving at its present form at the end of the same century. Sadly, the church suffered serious damage during the bombing of 1943 and has been partially rebuilt.

Its sober façade is in marked contrast to the Baroque exuberance of the interior which is encrusted with stucco and *pietra dura* decoration. The **chancel decor★** executed by the Serpotta brothers is especially fine, populated with a euphoric display of cherubs engaged in all manner of activities: gathering grapes, holding garlands of flowers, torches, musical instruments, rulers, set squares, and lances with which they pierce devils.

The second chapel on the right has two fine paintings by **Pietro Novelli**: *St Philip of Agira* and ***St Paul the Hermit★***, in which the last figure on the left is a self-portrait of the artist.

The **sacristy** is furnished with a splendidly carved cupboard (16C).

Count of Cagliostro

Giuseppe Balsamo was born in Palermo in 1743. He became fascinated by occult science and founded a Masonic lodge; assuming the name Count of Cagliostro, he embarked upon his travels around Europe practising the "arts" of healing and magic with his miraculous "water of eternal youth". In France, he became involved in court intrigues which led to him being imprisoned in the Bastille. Following his return to Italy, fortune still refused to smile upon him and he was again arrested. This time, accused of belonging to the sect of the *Illuminati*, he was incarcerated in the fortress of San Leo, in the Montefeltro near Urbino. Here, he died in poverty, and his body was taken to the cemetery in Palermo. His house is located off Piazza Ballarò, in Via Cagliostro.

Next to the church stands **Casa Professa**; this houses the **municipal library** which contains a large number of incunabula and manuscripts. The first and second room (reading rooms) are hung with the portraits of 300 illustrious men.

Chiesa del Carmine

Open 8.30am-noon. ☎ 091 65 12 018.

Piazza del Carmine, in front of the Church of Our Lady of Mount Carmel, is brought to life each day by the picturesque **Ballarò food market**. Before entering the church, it is worth taking the time to admire from afar the splendid tile-covered **dome** supported by four giant Atlas figures.

Inside the church, the two most interesting features are the sumptuous **altars★** in the transepts, decorated with pairs of golden twisting columns on which spirals of stucco tell the story of the life of the Virgin Mary *(on the left)* and of Christ *(on the right)*. They are the work of Giacomo and Giuseppe Serpotta. Above the left-hand altar is a fine canvas of *La Madonna del Carmine* (Our Lady of Mount Carmel), dating from the 15C.

Return to Via Maqueda. Palazzo Comitini stands on the left at the corner of the street (see Worth a Visit).

Sant'Orsola

For information on admission times, call ☎ 091 32 19 88.

This 17C church was once the headquarters of the Compagnia dell'Orazione della Morte, an organisation responsible for burying the deceased of the district. The façade is late Renaissance in style and the interior 18C with unusual communicating chapels. In the last chapel to the right, decorated by Serpotta, the usual rejoicing *putti* are replaced by skeletons and dangling bones.

Camera dello Scirocco di Palazzo Marchesi

From Piazzetta SS Quaranta Martiri, go into passageway n° 14 (to the left of the tower), and from the courtyard take the staircase on the left. Ring the bell if the door is closed. For information, call ☎ 091 58 45 65 (Assessorato al Centro Storico). No charge.

One of the oldest of the Palermo *scirocco rooms* is under the cloisters of the 15C **Palazzo Marchesi**, at a depth of 8m/26ft. An enormous Arabic cistern, once used for the city's water supply, has been found next to this room.

Le Camere dello Scirocco

The custom of excavating artificial caves under the seigniorial mansions of Palermo can be traced as far back as the 15C. These caves provided refuge on days when the scorching southeast wind swept through the city, drying out both mind and body. Palermo's limestone soil was ideal for this purpose and the presence of numerous springs allowed for the construction of small pools in which to escape the heat.

LA KALSA AND VIA ALLORO 3

The Kalsa district, which lies behind the port, was razed by Allied bombing raids in 1943, during which a large number of lives were lost and countless buildings destroyed. The ruins were thrown into the sea and, as a result, the Foro Italico now stands a little way from the seafront. This fascinating district, full of contradictions, is at present subject to major reconstruction, with the creation of new squares (such as **Piazza Magione**, laid out like an English meadow), *palazzi* and monuments, and the opening of cultural centres of international renown, such as the Chiesa dello Spasimo and Teatro Garibaldi. Although much remains to be done, new life is being breathed into the historic heart of Arabo-Norman Palermo.

The heart of the quarter is Piazza della Kalsa, although the district itself stretches as far as Corso Vittorio Emanuele, and contains many of the city's most interesting monuments.

The main entrance to the quarter is the **Porta dei Greci** beyond which lies the piazza and the church of **Santa Teresa alla Kalsa**, a monumental Baroque church built between 1686 and 1706 by **Paolo Amato**, including an imposing façade with two orders of Corinthian columns.

Turning onto Via Torremuzza, note the beautiful stone-framed Noviziato dei Crociferi at n° 20 and, further along on the opposite side of the street, **Santa Maria della Pietà** designed by Giacomo Amata: inside, in the section reserved for the closed order of Dominican nuns which founded the church, is a choir screen emblazoned with a rising sun.

Via Alloro

Throughout the Middle Ages, this served as the quarter's main street. Today, most of the elegant *palazzi* that once lined the thoroughfare have, sadly, either been destroyed or have fallen into disrepair. The few surviving buildings include Palazzo Abatellis and, next to it, the lovely Chiesa della Gancia.

Palazzo Abatellis★

This magnificent *palazzo*, built in Catalan-Gothic style with some Renaissance features, was designed by Matteo Carnelivari, who worked in Palermo towards the end of the 15C. Its elegant front has a great square central doorway ornamented with fasces (bundles of rods, an Ancient symbol of authority), and a series of two- and three-light windows. The *palazzo* is arranged around an attractive square courtyard and now houses the Galleria Regionale di Sicilia *(see Worth a Visit)*.

La Gancia

The church dedicated to **Santa Maria degli Angeli** was originally built by the Franciscans in the late 15C; numerous alterations have since modified its appearance, particularly the interior. The exterior retains from the original its square profile and rustication. On the side of the church flanking Via Alloro, note the *Buca della Salvezza*: this "Hole of Salvation" was made by two patriots who had hidden in the crypt of the church during the anti-Bourbon rebellion of 1860 so that they could be pulled to safety by a handful of local people.

The **interior**★ gives the impression of being Baroque although elements date from several different periods. The fine wooden ceiling painted with stars on a blue background, the magnificent **organ**★★ by Raffaele della Valle, the elegant marble **pulpit** and Antonello Gagini's relief tondi of the *Annunciation (on either side of the altar)* all date from the 16C. Most of the superficial decoration, notably the stuccowork in the nave and in some of the chapels by the Serpotta brothers, unfortunately in poor condition, dates from the 17C. Among the parts of the original fabric that survive are some very fine details including an original ***novice monk***★ peeping out over the top of a cornice in the chapel to the left of the altar.

Cross Piazza della Magione.

Santa Maria dello Spasimo★

The church and convent were built just inside the walls of the Kalsa in 1506. The patron of the project was Giacomo Basilicò who, to mark the occasion, commissioned **Raphael** to paint a picture of the anguish of the Madonna before the Cross (now in the Prado in Madrid). Building work on the church was slow and not yet completed when the Turkish threat made it necessary to build a new bastion just behind the church. In turn the complex was transformed into a fortress, a theatre, a hospice for plague victims (1624) then, later, for the poor (1835) and finally a hospital; it was eventually abandoned in 1986. The church and old hospital have been restored and transformed into unusual venues for cultural events (the church currently houses the Scuola Europea di Music Jazz). The section that is currently accessible to the public is the part arranged around the 16C cloisters: this is endowed with simple lines. Beyond sits the **church**★, the only example of Northern Gothic in Sicily. The tall, slender nave reaches up towards the open sky without a roof and ends with a lovely polygonal **apse**. The original entrance is given prominence by a *pronaos* in which were installed two side chapels. The one on the left is still visible, complete with its distinctive little bulbous dome. This, in turn, provides access to the old Spanish bastion, now laid out as a garden. The whole complex is most evocative, particularly when caught by the rays of the setting sun.

La Magione

An attractive little avenue of palm trees leads up to the Romanesque church, which was founded in the 12C by Matteo d'Ajello, a prominent official in the service of the Norman sovereigns. In 1193, it was given by Emperor Henry VI to the Order of Teutonic Knights, in whose hands it remained for more than 300 years. The **front elevation**★ rises through three tiers of pointed arches which at the lowest level are ornamented with decorative features and enclose the doorways. The interior, divided into three aisles, is simple and austere. The church also has fine **cloisters** from the original Cistercian monastery, unfortunately severely damaged during the Second World War. Vestiges of pre-existing constructions, including a 10C Arab tower, are visible from the cloisters.

Via della Magione runs along the side of **Palazzo Ajutamicristo**, a large 15C building designed by **Matteo Carnelivari**.

Piazza della Rivoluzione

This delightful little square is so called because it was here that the anti-Bourbon rebellion of 1848 was sparked off. In the centre is a fountain embellished by the 17C **Genio di Palermo**; this statue, which symbolises the city, depicts a king feeding a serpent.

Head back to Via Alloro. The walk continues with the monuments located to the north of Via Alloro.

San Francesco d'Assisi★

Very little of the original 13C church survives. It succumbed to damage, repair and alteration on successive occasions, but owes its current appearance to the fact that, last time it was restored, great efforts were made to respect its original design. The simple front elevation includes a fine rose window and magnificent Gothic **portal★** from the original 13C structure. Inside, a strong sense of airiness and space, so typical of Franciscan churches, has been preserved despite subsequent structural remodelling. Of note are eight statues by Giovanni Serpotta, and the fine entrance **doorway★** to the Mastrantonio Chapel, by **Francesco Laurana** and **Pietro di Bonitate** *(fourth chapel on the left).*

Oratorio di San Lorenzo★★★

Closed for restoration at the time of going to press. For further information, contact the Chiesa di San Francesco, ☎ 091 61 62 819.

This masterpiece created by a mature **Giacomo Serpotta** has been described as a "cave of white coral". On the walls, paintings alternating with statues of the Virtues illustrate scenes from the life of St Francis (to the right) and St Lawrence (to the left); the martyrdom of the latter is depicted opposite these works. Nude thinkers on the upper sections of the walls recall figures by Michelangelo. The lofty detachment of the Virtues and the veiled sadness of the nudes contrast sharply with the triumph of the delightful rejoicing *putti*, depicted in the most imaginative poses (note the figure making a soap bubble and the two characters kissing each other tenderly). However, the innocent vitality of these figures is in stark contrast to events that have taken place in the church, the most notorious of which was the theft in 1969 of Caravaggio's *Nativity*, painted to hang above the altar of the church.

Keeping the Chiesa di San Francesco to your left, continue to Palazzo Mirto (see Worth a Visit).

Piazza Marina

In the centre of the piazza, which in itself lies at the very heart of medieval Palermo, is an attractive garden, the **Giardino Garibaldi**, which is planted with magnificent **banyan trees★★** with their large, exposed, trunk-like roots.

The piazza is enclosed on all sides by fine buildings: Palazzo Galletti (n° 46), Palazzo Notarbartolo (n° 51) and Palazzo Chiaramonte. Diametrically opposite this, on the far side, sits the lovely **Fontana del Garraffo**, (from the Arabic *gharraf*, meaning abundant water) which was constructed at the close of the 17C by G Vitaliano, to designs by Paolo Amato.

Palazzo Chiaramonte★

This splendid *palazzo* was built in 1307 for the Chiaramonte family, one of the wealthiest and most powerful dynasties of the Aragonese period. The building also came to be called **Lo Steri** from *Hosterium*, a fortified residence, an obvious function given its clean, square form. It passed into the hands of the Spanish viceroys, and served as the headquarters of the Court of the Inquisition from the 17C until 1782, when the institution was abolished in Sicily.

The main front is ornamented by two tiers of elegant two- and three-light **windows★★** (note the fabulous stone inlays on the underside of the arches on the first floor). The style, which in essence was distilled from the Gothic, is so distinctive as to be described simply as Chiaramonte; this may be discerned in many other Sicilian civic buildings of the same period.

The Museo Internazionale delle Marionette is situated close to the *palazzo (see Worth a Visit).*

Close by stands the monumental **Porta Felice** (1582), which marks the eastern end of Via Vittorio Emanuele. This is designed in the late Renaissance style, its two massive upright elements softened by an interplay of volutes and openings surmounted by pediments. The 17C **Loggiato di San Bartolomeo** can be seen close to the gate. This recently restored building, part of an old hospital destroyed by the 1943 bombing raids, is now a venue for exhibitions and cultural events.

The Foro Italica, the old **Passeggiata alla Marina**, starts at Porta Felice. From the 16C onwards this promenade, with its esplanade overlooking the sea, was a popular meeting-place and area for strolling for Palermo's elegant aristocracy, as well as the site of festivals and parades. A number of fine *palazzi* were built here, including the 18C **Palazzo Branciforti-Butera**, with terraces that enjoyed splendid and exclusive sea views. In 1847 the German writer Fanny Lewald was to write in *Diogena*: "Night never completely falls in Palermo, especially along the seafront, which is perhaps one of the most beautiful promenades in Europe ...Under the row of terraces along the *corso*, starting at seven, the evening *passeggiata* takes place. At ten o'clock the orchestra strikes up and the music continues until midnight; it is only around ten that the marina really comes to life." The atmosphere of days gone by is evoked by the natural beauty of the setting and the neo-Classical bandstand *(immediately after the crossroads with Via Alloro).*

Passeggiata delle Cattive

Built in 1823 along the wall which marked the end of the Passeggiata alla Marina, this promenade owes its unusual name to the popular expression *"mura di li cattivi"*, which translates as the "wall of the wayward women". The walkway provided widows with a higher degree of privacy (as well as a better view) than the promenade below. The splendid seafront façade of the Palazzo Branciforti-Butera can be admired from here.

FROM THE OLD HARBOUR TO THE VUCCIRIA 4

The *cala*, the city's ancient harbour, was once protected by the **Castellammare**, which was built by the Arabs, and later transformed for use as a fortress, prison and private residence. The massive construction was, however, badly damaged in 1922 when the new jetty was extended. A description of the Cala quarter which extends behind the old harbour must begin with the church, as this was where the chains that were used to close off the area were kept through the centuries, hence its dedication to Santa Maria della Catena.

La Vucciria *by Renato Guttuso*

Santa Maria della Catena★

Open 9am-1pm. Closed Sat and in Aug. ☎ 091 60 67 111.

The design of the church is attributed to Matteo Carnelivari. Its elevation is dominated by the broad square portico with three arches; behind these are doorways set with low reliefs by Vincenzo Gagini. A decorative fretwork stone cornice runs along the top and sides of the portico (the flight of steps in front of the church was added at a later date). The overall style is transitional Gothic-Renaissance (1490). The lovely interior is articulated by blind arcading into square bays with pointed cross-arches, the stone ribs being offset by the white vault. The chancel is lit by traceried two-light windows. The second chapel on the right contains fragments of a frescoed Madonna and, on the altar, symbolic chains.

The church is especially evocative at sunset, when the façade is dramatically set alight by the colours of the setting sun.

Further along the broad curve of the harbour lies Piazza Fonderia, beyond which (between Via Cassari and Piazza San Domenico) extends the picturesque and historic **Vucciria** market.

San Domenico

Open Jul-Sep, Mon-Sat, 9.30-10.30am, Sun and public hols, 9.30-11.30am; Oct-Jun, call ahead for admission times. ☎ 091 32 95 88; www.domenicani-palermo.it

Before the church stretches an attractive **piazza** with, at its centre, a statue of the Madonna raised on a column.

The church was initiated in the 17C and completed a century later. The Baroque front elevation rises in three ordered tiers of Doric and Corinthian columns and square pilasters framing a statue of St Dominic. The spacious interior is divided

into nave and aisles, with a side chapel off each bay. A fine scheme of inlaid *pietra dura* decoration ornaments the fourth chapel on the right and the Chapel of the Rosary in the north transept. Adjacent to the church are lovely 14C **cloisters** with paired columns.
The neighbouring buildings accommodate the **Sicilian Historical Society** (Società Siciliana per la Storia Patria) which, in turn, has its own small **Museo del Risorgimento** containing mementoes of Garibaldi. From the windows of the museum, there is a splendid view of the cloisters of San Domenico.

Oratorio del Rosario di San Domenico***

For information on admission times, call ☎ 329 61 95 122.
The oratory is a veritable treasury of stucco decoration by **Giacomo Serpotta**, who succeeded, as always, in conferring a profound sense of movement to the antics of his cherubs. These are characterised by a spontaneous playfulness so often found in children; their unusually expressive faces, exuding happiness or thoughtfulness, highlight Serpotta's skill at working with stucco, a medium devoid of any inherent life of its own when compared to stone or marble.
The stucco or plasterwork provides frames for a series of paintings relating to the Joyful Mysteries of the Rosary *(left and rear walls)*, some of which are by **Pietro Novelli**, and the Sorrowful Mysteries of the Rosary *(right wall)*, which include a *Flagellation* by Matthias Stomer. In the niches which alternate with the paintings, are allegories of the Virtues, a series of extraordinary female figures remarkable for their poise and for the delicate way in which their drapery is rendered. In some instances they are attended by *putti*; the statue of Meekness, for example, holding a dove, is flanked by a *putto* dressed in a monk's attire stretching a podgy little hand towards her.
In the large ovals above the paintings, Serpotta has depicted scenes from the Apocalypse of St John: note how the figure of the Devil writhes as he falls, having been driven from heaven.
Above the dome of the altar, more winged cherubs hold up a great sheet. On the high altar itself, sits the splendid painting by Anthony Van Dyck of the *Madonna of the Rosary* (1628) with St Dominic and the patron saints of Palermo; this, in turn, is framed by two allegorical female figures who look onto the scene as if witnessing a theatrical performance. The ceiling, frescoed by Pietro Novelli, illustrates the *Coronation of the Virgin*.

Santa Maria di Valverde

Open 9am-1pm. ☎ 091 33 27 79 (Parrocchia di San Mamiliano).
An elegant marble portal by Pietro Amato (1691) leads into this small church. The **interior** is extravagantly decorated in the Baroque style using different types of marble, sculpted into soft drapery on the side altars. In the first chapel on the right, dedicated to Saint Lucy, note the delicate perspectives created by the different marbles.

Santa Cita

Open 9am-1pm. For afternoon admission times, call ☎ 091 33 27 79. If the chapel crypt is closed, contact the nuns in the nearby Istituto del Sacro Cuore.
This church was badly damaged by the bombing raids in 1943, which destroyed its side aisles. Note the beautiful **marble chancel arch*** by Antonello Gagini in the presbytery: the Nativity and Dormition of the Virgin are represented inside the arch; Dominican saints can be seen in the pilaster panels on the arch, and portraits of St Thomas Aquinas and St Peter the Martyr grace the two medallion tondi, on the corners. In the eight coffers of the arch intrados are episodes of the life of St Zita. Also worthy of note is the beautiful **Cappella del Rosario** to the right of the presbytery, with its delicate stuccowork and polychrome marquetry. Access to the **crypt** *(cripta della Cappella Lanza)*, decorated with different types of marble, is from the chapel to the left of the presbytery.

Oratorio del Rosario di Santa Cita***

Access from Via Valverde or Via da S. Cita. Open 9am-1pm and 3-5pm; Sun, contact the nuns in the nearby Istituto del Sacro Cuore. Donations welcome. ☎ 091 33 27 79.
The oratory is a remarkable work by the leading Baroque decorator **Giacomo Serpotta**, who worked here between 1686 and 1718. A host of angels and cherubs are endowed with carefree expressions and realistic attitudes, completely intent on playing among themselves, climbing up onto the window frames, larking about with garlands of flowers, turning their backs irreverently, crying, sleeping, and hugging their knees deep in thought.
The eye is immediately drawn towards the wall at the back of the nave where a great drape hangs across the entire wall, supported by a struggling crowd of cherubs. A central panel depicts in relief the Battle of Lepanto; this is flanked by two

SCALA

Stucco decoration in Santa Cita: cherubs and the Battle of Lepanto

emaciated youths, symbolising the horrors of war. All around the oratory, even below the side windows, are panels depicting the Mysteries of the Rosary. On the left wall begin the series relating to the Joyful Mysteries: the Annunciation, Visitation, Nativity and Presentation at the Temple. On the right are the Sorrowful Mysteries: Jesus in the Garden at Gethsemane, the Flagellation, Crowning of Thorns, and Calvary. At the far end are a second series of Joyful Mysteries *(starting bottom left)*: the Resurrection, Ascension, Descent of the Holy Spirit, and the Assumption of Mary. At the top, in the centre, the Crowning of Mary.

The high altar has a fine painting by Carlo Maratta of the Madonna of the Rosary (1690).

The eight windows along the side walls are "guarded" by allegorical figures.

A little further on, sits **San Giorgio dei Genovesi** overlooking its own piazza: this is one of the rare expressions of the late Renaisssance. It was built by a community of Genoan merchants to shelter those among them who died in Palermo ; having been deconsecrated, the former church is now used to house temporary exhibitions. *Open during exhibitions only.*

In Via Cavour, is the **Prefettura**: a Venetian neo-Gothic building that was once known as the Villa Whitaker, having been erected by one of the 12 grandchildren of Ingham, the British Marsala magnate *(see p 239)*.

FROM VIA ROMA TO THE CAPO QUARTER 5

Via dell'Orologio, on the right just before Teatro Massimo on Via Maqueda, provides an unexpected view of one of Sant'Ignazio's two bell towers, whose clock has lent its name to the street.

Sant'Ignazio all'Olivella

This fine Baroque church was initiated in the late 16C on the site where, according to tradition, the villa of the family of Santa Rosalia once stood. An interpretation of Olivella would confirm this: *Olim villa*, once a villa (was here). The front incorporates two bell towers which add a certain freedom to the overall composition.

Inside, an eye-catching inscription in bright red proclaims *jahvé* in the centre of the Gloria behind the altar. The first chapel on the right contains a great wealth of decorative inlay in the form of polychrome *pietra dura*.

Access to the Oratorio di San Filippo Neri (or Sant'Ignazio) is from the south transept.

The Museo Archeologico Regionale stands next to the church *(see Worth a Visit)*.

Oratorio di San Filippo Neri

Access from the piazza or from Sant'Ignazio. Open Mon-Fri, 5.30-6pm; weekday mornings and Sat, by appointment only. ☎ 091 58 68 67.

This was designed by the architect **Venanzio Marvuglia**. Inside, the stuccowork illustrates the Gloria: the attractive composition with the angel surrounded by groups of cherubs in twos and threes, is the work of **Ignazio Marabitti**.

Oratorio di Santa Caterina d'Alessandria★

Via Monteleone 50; ring the bell. Open Thu, 1-2.45pm. ☎ 091 87 28 047.

Although more static and less vigorous than work by his father Giacomo, this stuccowork by **Procopio Serpotta** elegantly portrays various scenes from the life of St Catherine, the protector of scholars, alongside allegories of the sciences: Rhetoric, Ethics, Geography and Astrology to the right; Dialectics, Physics, Geometry and Theology to the left and, under the beautiful triple-arched tribune of the entrance wall, Knowledge and Science. The ceiling is decorated with delicate foliage patterns.

Continue along Via Monteleone as far as the crossroads with Via Roma.

On the far side of Piazza San Domenico, directly opposite the church, is the narrow **Via Bandiera** which marks the outer fringe of the **Capo market**, and has a number of fine buildings, notably **Palazzo Termine** (n° 14) built in 1573 with hints of the Spanish style. Its most striking features are the lovely two-light stone traceried windows divided by slender columns; the window on the corner was added during restoration at the beginning of this century. Next door is **Palazzo Oneto di Sperlinga**, an elegant 18C residence.

Chiesa di Sant'Agostino

The splendid 13C St Augustine's was built at the request of the Chiaramonte and Sclafani families. The **front★** is graced with a beautiful entrance decorated with duotone geometric and flower motifs, and a lovely rose window. The Gaginiesque side entrance in Via Sant'Agostino is also worthy of note. The interior is largely dominated by Baroque alterations, which include stuccoes by followers of the Serpotta School, signed on the shelf under the second statue on the right with Serpotta's mark, a lizard (*serpe* in Sicilian).

The heart of the quarter which lies further along Via Sant'Agostino, is brought to life every morning by a busy market, the **mercato di Capo**. Notice in Via Cappuccinelle (n° 6) the shop sign above the **Panifico Morello**: this consists of an elegant Liberty-style mosaic panel with a female figure enclosed within a "niche" of wheat sheaves, with a lotus-flower motif below and further wheat sheaves above.

To continue with the walk described below, take Via Porta Carini and then turn right into Via Mura di San Vito to Piazza Verdi.

CITTÀ NUOVA

At the beginning of the 19C, the city underwent a period of considerable expansion. The wealthy merchant bourgeoisie chose the northwest side of the city to build fine residences in keeping with the new aesthetic taste, lavishly decorated with wrought-iron work, glass and floral panels. The hub of high society shifted from Via Maqueda to its extension, which took the name of Via Ruggero Settimo and, a little further on, **Via della Libertà**. Here they built the great temples of opera, two theatres – the Massimo and the Politeama – and a large number of modern *palazzi* scattered through the neighbouring streets. Even today, a walk along Via XX Settembre, Via Dante and Via Siracusa, to name but three, will reveal a flavour of the splendour promoted by the wealthy upper-middle classes in the late 19C.

A TOUR OF THE MAIN LIBERTY-STYLE BUILDINGS

Besides the ones described below, Palermo's best Liberty-style residences include **Palazzo Dato** with its pink external detailing on the corner of Via XX Settembre and Via XII Gennaio; Ernesto Basile's **Villa Favaloro Di Stefano** in Piazza Virgilio and the **Villino Ida** at 15 Via Siracusa, with its fine wrought-iron balcony and tiled frieze.

Another must, albeit in a completely different part of the city, is the **Villa Igiea** *(Salita Belmonte 43, ☎ 091 63 12 111)*. This very large building is scenically positioned on the slopes of Monte Pellegrino. It began life as a nursing home for Igiea Florio (who suffered from tuberculosis), adapted from a pre-existing neo-Gothic building to designs by Ernesto Basile for an exotically luxurious home. The dining room in particular, now the **Sala Basile★** *(accessible by request and subsequent permission from the hotel staff, who are always very helpful)*, was completely renovated: lovely wooden panelling was installed, and the interior decoration with beautiful female figures surrounded by delicate, long-stalked flowers was commissioned from Ettore de Maria Bergler, a well-known Liberty-style painter. On the walls of the corridor are photographs depicting illustrious guests who stayed here in the past, including many European kings and queens.

Teatro Massimo★

Guided tours, 10am-3.30pm. Closed Mon. €3. ☎ 800 65 58 58; www.teatromassimo.it
This opera house is one of the largest in Europe. The front of this imposing neo-Classical structure is composed of six columns and a broad triangular pediment, modelled on the *pronaos* of an ancient temple. Set back, a great dome rises from its high drum. The initial design was completed by Giovan Battista Basile in 1875; building work was concluded by his son Ernesto, who took it upon himself to add the two small, distinctive Liberty-style kiosks in front of the theatre (the one on the right, built of wood and wrought iron, is known as the Vicari al Massimo Kiosk, while the one on the left, made of iron, is the Ribaudo Kiosk). The **interior** is highly elegant. The ceiling of the auditorium is adorned with a magnificent gilded wheel, decorated with a representation of the Triumph of Opera. On the upper floor, the Royal Lounge leads into the Royal Box.

Grand hotel et des Palmes

This building came to prominence in the mid-1800s when used as a residence by Ben Ingham, the Englishman who played a key role in the history of Marsala *(see p 239)*. Soon converted into a hotel *(Via Roma 398, ☎ 091 58 39 33)*, it has provided hospitality to all the persons of note passing through the city: musicians (Wagner finished *Parsifal* here – his stool remains), painters (sketches by Guttuso and Fiume furnish one of the salons), writers, politicians past and present (President Andreotti for one), great names from the theatre world and countless numbers of aristocrats have silently passed through its corridors over the years. It has provided an objective context for important political occasions, newsworthy events, mysterious incidents linked to the world of *omertà* (tacit complicity demanded by the Mafia) and intrigues. It was here, in 1957, that a secret dinner was held for the top henchmen of the Italian and American Mafia; that a secret agent disappeared in mysterious circumstances, having fallen from the seventh floor straight through the skylight of the great hall of mirrors (before being immediately rushed "to hospital" by two equally mysterious figures on standby); it was here that, in 1933, the French writer Raymond Roussel ended his dissolute and tragic life by committing suicide (or overdosing on hallucinogenic drugs). Another strange story involves the Baron of Castelvetrano who lived hidden away in his suite on the first floor for more than half a century. This enforced exile was allegedly levied upon him for having killed a boy guilty of petty theft; the sentence was pronounced by the father of the unfortunate victim.

Teatro Politeama

The Politeama Theatre, as imposing and built in the same neo-Classical style as the Teatro Massimo, faces onto the vast Piazza Castelnuovo. Its façade is dominated by a quadriga of bronze horses.

Inside, it accommodates the Galleria d'Arte Moderna Empedocle Restivo *(see Worth a Visit)*.

The delightful Villa Malfitano *(see Worth a Visit)* stands at the end of Via Dante, which heads west from Piazza Castelnuovo.

Teatro Politeama

G. Bludzin/MICHELIN

At n° 36 Viale Regina Margherita *(the street which runs across Via Dante near Villa Malfitano)* stands **Villino Florio★**, a magnificent house built for one of the most powerful families in Sicily in the 19C: the Florio. It is, without doubt, one of the finest examples of the Palermo Liberty style. Designed by Ernesto Basile, it was originally surrounded by a large garden.

Worth a Visit

IN THE HISTORIC CENTRE

Galleria Regionale di Sicilia★★

Via Alloro 4. Open Mon-Sat, 9am-2pm (also 3-8pm Tue and Thu); Sun and public hols, 9am-1.30pm (last admission 30min before closing). €4. ☎ 091 62 30 011.

The gallery's internal layout is most interesting having been completed in the 1950s by Carlo Scarpa, one of Italy's foremost contemporary interior designers. For each important work of art, the designer has contrived a tailor-made solution in terms of support and background, using different materials and colours so as to display it in the best possible manner while exploiting natural daylight to the full.

The gallery collects together sculptures and paintings from the medieval period. The first exhibit to draw attention on the ground floor is the magnificent fresco of the ***Triumph of Death★★★*** *(Room II)*, from the Palazzo Sclafani. The title probably refers to the 13th Tarot card as the cards, which were highly popular in the Middle Ages, were also known as *Trionfi* (Triumphs). The painting shows the cruel and realistic figure of Death, astride a skeletal horse and armed with a bow and arrows, in the act of striking down men and women in the full flush of youth. Note, in particular, how colder shades of colour have been used to portray Death, the horse, and the faces of those who have been struck by his arrows. On the left, among the group of beggars and the afflicted who have been "spared" by the terrible rider, is painted a figure *(top)* who gazes out from the picture at the observer; the brush in his right hand denotes this to be a self-portrait of the unknown author of the picture. The modernity with which some of the details – such as the stylised nose of the horse – have been rendered is quite extraordinary.

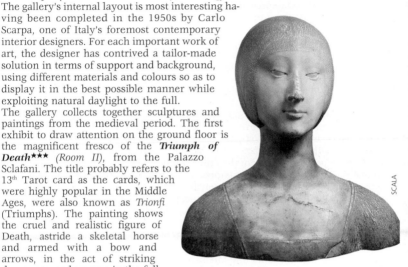

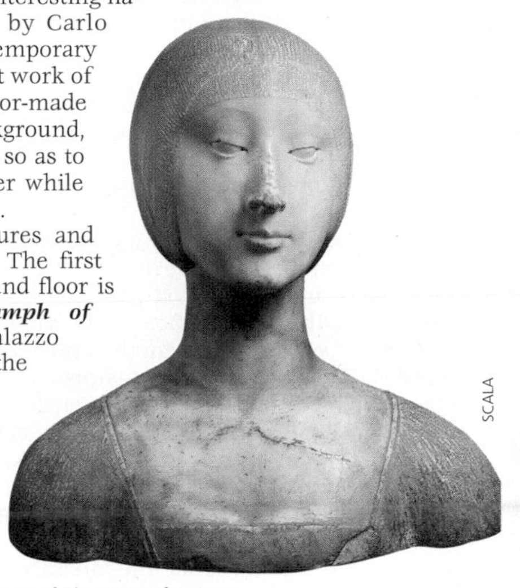
SCALA

Bust of Eleonora of Aragon

The admirable ***bust of Eleonora of Aragon★★*** *(Room IV)*, with its gentle expression and delicate features, together with the bust of a young woman, are by the sculptor **Francesco Laurana** who worked in Sicily in the 15C. This was also when the Gagini family were active and works by them are to be found all over the island. Included in the gallery is a fine ***Madonna and Child★*** by **Antonello da Messina**.

The first floor is entirely devoted to painting (with many works from the Sicilian School). Note the lovely portable Byzantine icon *(first room opposite the entrance)* with scenes from the life of Christ, and, in Antonello da Messina's glorious ***Annunciation★★***, the peaceful expression of acceptance in the face of the Virgin. In the room devoted to Flemish painting is the famous ***Malvagna Triptych★★*** (1510) by **Mabuse** which shows the Virgin and Child surrounded by angels singing and playing musical instruments in a lavishly decorated frame, set against an equally fabulous landscape background.

Museo Archeologico Regionale★★

Piazza Olivella. (♿) Open 8.30am-7pm (last admission at 6.30pm). €4; €7.75 (combined ticket with Palazzo Abatellis and Palazzo Mirto). ☎ 091 61 16 805.

The Regional Archaeological Museum is installed in the 16C confines of the Olivella monastery which, with the adjoining Baroque church of **Sant'Ignazio all'Olivella** *(see above)* was founded in the 17C by the fathers of St Philip Neri. The museum contains a magnificent collection of artefacts recovered from Sicilian sites, in particular those from Selinunte.

Ground floor – The visit begins in **small cloisters★** with a hexagonal fountain in the centre. At the back, high up in the wall, is a beautiful single-light window with a decorative surround. The portico shelters an assortment of Punic and Roman anchors (also on display in the large cloisters). One small room devoted to Phoenician art displays two sarcophagi from 6C BC with organic decoration. Another is dedicated to Egyptian and Punic finds, including the hieroglyphic inscription known as the **Palermo Stone** (the other three parts are in Cairo and London) which narrates 700 years of Egyptian history, and a Punic one recovered near the harbour at Marsala bearing the figure of a priest before a perfume burner, worshipping the god Tanit.

Beyond are the large cloisters, off which are arranged a series of rooms devoted to artefacts from **Selinunte**. The first displays the twin stelae formed by pairs of busts representing the gods of the Underworld, both in shallow relief and in the round. This leads into the Sala Gabrici *(interactive information terminals)* which contains a reconstruction of the front elevation of Temple C and a selection of the original triglyphs. Sala Marconi has various lion masks with waterspouts from the Temple of Victory at Himera. The exhibits in the following larger room are principally from Selinunte, including the range of marvellous **metopes★★**. The six metopes date from 575 BC and were discovered in the fortifications of Selinunte's acropolis. As these are the only sculptures of their kind to have been discovered in the region, experts believe that there may have been a sculpture school in the city. Some of the metopes represent the gods worshipped in Selinunte, such as the Apollonian triad (Apollo, Artemis and their mother Latona), Demeter and Persephone. The oldest (smaller) artefacts, notably from a 6C BC Archaic temple, are displayed below the window on the right: one fragment depicts the Rape of Europa by Zeus in the guise of a bull. On the left are three more marvellous metopes from Temple C (6C BC), brightened by traces of colour on the bodies and clothes. The high relief, which in places verges on being in the round, shows Perseus severing the head of Medusa while from her breast springs Pegasus, the winged horse born from her spilt blood *(central scene)*; above is the figure of Athena with, to the left, the four-horse chariot of the sun god Apollo and, to the right, Heracles capturing the Cercopi (two thieving brothers) and hanging them from a stick. These works demonstrate perfect mastery of the art of composition.

Against the back wall are four metopes from Temple E: these are considered to be the finest in terms of their expressiveness, their sense of movement and their realism which has been described as "modern" in concept. Starting from the left, these show Heracles fighting with an Amazon, Hera before Zeus (who, seated, lifts the veil from her face), Actaeon being transformed into a stag (the muzzle of the animal can just be seen behind the head of Actaeon as he is attacked by the dogs), and Athena fighting the giant Enceladus. The four rooms filled with Etruscan finds contain some fine cinerary urns and *bucchero* ware.

First floor – Among the various **bronzes** from the Greek, Roman and Punic periods, are a couple of truly superb ones: **Heracles catching the stag★**, perhaps the central decoration for a fountain and, more particularly, the fabulously lifelike bronze **Ram★★**, a Hellenistic work of extraordinary quality, from Syracuse. This masterpiece, which dates from the 3C BC, was originally part of a pair that adorned the tyrants' palace on the island of Ortygia. It is exceptional for its detailed features and skilful execution and is one of the most important works of art in the museum.

The following room displays small marble statues include a fine **Satyr★**, a Roman copy of an original by Praxiteles.

Second floor – On this floor are arranged the museum's prehistoric collections and a selection of its finest Greek vases, Roman mosaics and frescoes. The room with the mosaics includes panels illustrating **Orpheus with the animals★** (3C AD), the seasons, and representations of allegories and myths closely associated with the cult of Dionysus found in Palermo.

Museo Internazionale delle Marionette★★

Via Butera 1. ▤ *Open 9am-1pm and 4-7pm. Closed Sat-Sun and public hols. €3.* ☎ *091 32 80 60; www.museomarionettepalermo.it*

The International Puppet Museum contains a fabulously rich collection of *pupi* (Sicilian puppets based on characters from the French *chansons de geste*), marionettes (articulated puppets operated with strings), shadow puppets, scenery and panels from all over the world. The first rooms are devoted to Sicilian puppets, many being presented "on stage". Notice, in particular, the delicate facial features of Gaspare Canino's theatre puppets (19C). The second section presents the European tradition, including such renowned figures as the English *Punch and Judy*, and the non-European, which comprises a vast Oriental collection: Chinese glove-puppets; string-puppets from India, Burma, Vietnam, Thailand and Africa; shadow puppets from Turkey, India and Malaysia (made of leather). All the caricatures are evocatively displayed in semi-darkness (for preservation purposes) as if to suggest the remoteness of their origins in the distant past and from far afield. In Room IV a *hsaing waing* has been arranged: this consists of a Burmese orchestra pit where, an hour before the performance, musicians used to sit and play pieces of music that constituted a symbolic rite. The final section is dedicated to special puppets destined for a violent, spectacular death. The museum also has an active theatre *(details of performances are available from the museum)*. The walls are hung with decorative puppeteers' posters, which were used by storytellers to illustrate their stories.

Palazzo Mirto★

Via Merlo 2. Open 9am-6.30pm (1pm Sun and public hols). €2.50; €5 or €7.75 (combined tickets for two or three museums). ☎ 091 61 64 751; www.regionesiciliana.it

The *palazzo* that provides the princes of Lanzi Filangeri with a residence has been altered several times to meet the family's needs. Its current form dates from the late 18C. Just inside, on the left, are the magnificent **stables★** (19C) complete with stalls and ornamental bronze horse-heads. A red marble staircase leads up to the first floor which is still furnished in the main with original pieces. Among the rooms open to the public there is the **Chinese sitting room★** with its leather-covered floor, painted silk walls depicting scenes from everyday life, and fine *trompe l'oeil* ceiling: this was used as an intimate smoking room or for playing cards. The next room, a small vestibule, contains a good set of 19C Neapolitan plates decorated with people in costume; it is said that the service was used for masked balls and that each guest was supposed to sit in front of the plate featuring their particular costume. Leading from the vestibule is another unusual **smoking room★** this time panelled with painted and embossed leather, a material suited to such rooms because it does not become impregnated with smoke.

The most striking element of the **Pompadour sitting room★** is the beautiful wall silks embroidered with flowers. The mosaic floor is the only original one.

The dining room contains a Meissen service (18C) exquisitely painted with flowers and birds.

Palazzo Comitini

Via Maqueda 100. ♿ Open 9.30am-1.30pm (also 3-5pm Thu). Closed Sat-Sun and public hols. No charge. ☎ 091 66 28 260; Fax 091 66 28 254.

The *palazzo* (1768-71), built for the Prince of Gravina, incorporates two older ones belonging to the Roccafiorita-Bonanno and Gravina di Palagonia families. The fronthas two large entrances and nine openings (now windows) on the ground floor, and a series of bulbous balconies (evocatively described in Italian as *a petto d'oca* which translates as "goose breasted") on the first floor. The building was radically altered in 1931 with the addition of another floor for use as the administrative offices for the Province of Palermo. A wide staircase leads up from the internal courtyard to the loggia on the first floor and the Sala delle Armi (Armoury), now the Salone dei Commessi: the two masks flanking the doorway served as torch extinguishers. Off to the left is the Green Room, furnished with a fine 18C Murano glass lamp. **Sala Martorana★**, now the seat of the Provincial Council, is lined throughout with 18C wood panelling inlayed with mirrors; these add luminosity to the room and enhance the impact of the ceiling which is frescoed with *The Triumph of True Love*: the chariot of Wisdom has overcome Avarice, Falsehood and Perfidy; as it crushes Eros and Envy, it is celebrated by cherubs bearing garlands of flowers. The theme is picked up in the four corner medallions which depict the four Virtues: Fortitude, Temperance, Prudence and Justice. Sadly, the tiled floor is in poor condition.

Adjacent to the Sala del Presidente, at one time the prince's bedroom, are two small boudoirs; these are panelled in wood and furnished with shelves bearing early-20C maiolica plates.

THE MODERN CITY

Villa Malfitano★★

Via Dante. Guided tours only (30min), 9am-1pm. Closed Sun, public hols and 15 Jul. €2. ☎ 091 68 20 522.

The famous Liberty-style Villa Malfitano, contained within its glorious **garden★★**, was begun in 1886 by **Joseph Whitaker**, a grandson of the mighty **Ingham**, that English gentleman-cum-wine-merchant who came to live in Sicily in 1806. Ingham was an entrepreneur who managed to build himself a commercial empire out of a Marsala wine business he founded and developed until it became one of the three leading producers, and a large steamship company. In stark contrast to his grandfather, Joseph was fascinated by ornithology and archaeology: to satisfy his interests he travelled to Tunisia, where he studied the birds (later writing a treatise on the subject), and initiated a programme of excavation on the island of Mozia which he had purchased *(see MOZIA)*. Another of his passions was botany: he arranged to have trees sent from all over the world so that he could plant them around his villa; these gardens soon comprised a whole range of rare and exotic species: palm trees, Dragon's Blood trees, the only example in Europe of *Araucaria Rouler* and an enormous banyan tree. The villa soon became one of the main points of reference for high society at that time. Lavish parties were held there and important guests, such as the reigning monarchs of Great Britain and Italy, were received and entertained. The point came when the villa would epitomise the pre-eminence of the family. It was remodelled upon the Villa Favard in Florence, and endowed with elegant wrought-iron verandas which reflect a taste for the new Liberty style (the one at the back is especially beautiful).

The gardens at Villa Malfitano

The internal furnishings are exquisitely chosen: a profusion of Oriental items (often purchased at the most famous English auction rooms) include, for example, a pair of *cloisonné* elephants from the Royal Palace in Beijing, and a pair of large wading-birds riding on the back of a turtle, a group symbolising the four elements (the birds represent the air, the turtles water, the snake wound around the neck and held in the beak of the bird represents the earth and the lantern which acts as a lamp symbolises fire). The best craftsmen from the area and the most famous local artists were employed to work on the villa (the dining-room furniture was all made in Palermo, except for the table, which is English). Worthy of particular note is the *Safari in Tunisia* by Lo Jacono (in the corridor) and the pastel portrait of Joseph's daughters by Ettore de Maria Bergler, which hangs above the lovely spiral staircase leading up to the first floor, decorated in the then fashionable Pompeian style, as is the ceiling of the corridor.

The real highlight of the Whitaker house, however, is the **decoration** conceived by the same artist for the **Sala d'Estate** (Summer Room): this consists of a *trompe l'oeil* composition covering the entire room (walls and ceiling), transforming the enclosed space into a cool veranda surrounded by vegetation.

Galleria d'Arte Moderna Empedocle Restivo★

Via Turati 10. Open daily except Mon, 9am-8pm (1pm Sun and public hols). €3. ☎ 091 74 07 625; www.comunepalermo.it

The Empedocle Restivo Gallery of Modern Art is contained within an elegant Liberty-style interior (note the large, wrought-iron lights). The collection comprises a highly prized selection of 19C and 20C paintings and sculptures by a number of Sicilian artists and a few foreign artists.

The sculptures include a delightful *Faun* by **Trentacoste**, a marble figurine of Classical proportions, but gracefully coiled upon itself like a spiral ready to burst free.

Sicilian 19C art developed in different directions while simultaneously giving rise to a new generation of concepts. Artists specialised in using the medium they found most congenial. The great themes tackled often revolved around psychological introspection, interspersed with neo-Classical composure, history and landscape. From this period stem the portraits by Patania, such as his *Study of a Sick Priest* in which the man's suffering is rendered with piercing realism, and those by Salvatore Lo Forte, who managed to impart to his subjects so much strength of character. This is also the age of patriotism, which Erulo Eruli encapsulated in his great composition *The Sicilian Vespers*: the incident, in fact, is set in the 19C, with the subject transposed into an example of heroic rebellion against all kinds of foreign domination.

Different trends may also be detected in the style and expression of the various landscape painters represented: Lo Jacono's realism *(Wind in the Mountains)* becomes loaded with feeling in the works of A Leto who painted "impressions" by dabbing strong, warm colours onto his canvas (three studies for *The Rope-makers*); Michele Catti absorbed all the tenets of Impressionism before painting his hazy landscapes with horizons lost in infinity, as in *Last Leaves*. Onofrio Tomaselli *(The Carusi)* adds a note of compassion (in the sense of the Latin word, implying a sharing of pain) with his bold use of warm colours. A few works both from the Italian and other foreign schools exemplify the new trends that emerged at the close of the 19C and the beginning of the 20C: Expressionism in the *Nativity* by Lienz, Symbolism in the works of Von Stuck *(The Sin)*, and Pointillism in Terzi's *Summer Morning*.

The last few rooms collect together paintings from the 1930s and the years following the Second World War: *The Tram* by Sironi, with its cold colours; *The Schoolchildren* by F Casorati, with its geometric lines that seem to accentuate the sadness and immobility of the children (what is haunting is the blank, staring eyes of one child in the foreground); an expressive *Self-portrait* by Guttuso. These rooms also accommodate a number of sculptures, including the fine *Acrobat* by T Bertolino, with its curving, sinuous lines.

Albero di Falcone

At the beginning of Via Notarbartolo (which intersects with Viale della Libertà just beyond the English Garden), on the right heading towards the ring road. "Falcone's Tree" stands outside the house of Giovanni Falcone, the judge who was killed by a Mafia bomb in 1992. Since his death, the tree, situated in front of the military sentrybox, seems to have become a token shrine in its own right: messages, photographs, and small offerings bear witness to the people's esteem and affection for Falcone and for Borsellino, another Mafia victim.

Museo della Fondazione Mormino

Viale della Libertà 52. Open 9am-1pm and 3-5pm. Closed Sat afternoon, Sun and public hols. No charge. ☎ 091 60 85 972; www.aesnet.it/fondasicilia

The Mormino Foundation Museum is housed on the first floor of the Banco di Sicilia (Villa Zito). It was formed to display an accumulation of art work, original creations and recovered artefacts acquired over the years by the Banco di Sicilia. The first rooms are devoted to artefacts recovered during the excavations of Selinunte, Himera, Solunto and Terravecchia di Cuti, a small town further inland where a village from the 6C-5C BC was unearthed. A second section displays maiolica from Sicily and from the rest of Italy (with a few examples from Turkey and China). The third section is devoted to a large collection of 13C-19C coins and medals; this is complemented by a fine series of Sicilian engravings on the walls. N° 936 in particular, dating from the 16C, provides a view of Palermo as it was, completely surrounded by defensive walls: Palazzo Reale can be pinpointed at the top and, to its left, San Giovanni degli Eremiti; at right angles to the *palazzo* runs the axis of present-day Via Vittorio Emanuele, which continues down to the harbour; this is guarded on the left by the Castellammare falling into ruin; in the centre is La Martorana.

On the ground floor is displayed the bank's philatelic collection with stamps dating from the era of the Kingdom of the Two Sicilies.

Villa Trabia

Via Salinas. Take Via Latini, which then becomes Via Cusmano, as far as Piazza D. Siculo; Via Salinas is one of the streets leading off this square. A wonderful garden surrounds the villa, built in the 18C and bought the following year by Giuseppe Lanza Branciforte, prince of Trabia and Butera. The current appearance of the villa is the result of the many alterations undertaken at the end of the last century. The building, now used as municipal offices, has a splendid entrance with a monumental staircase.

Onofrio Tomaselli, I Carusi

Civica Galleria d'Arte Moderna E. Restivo, Palermo

BEYOND THE CITY GATES

Catacombe dei Cappuccini★★

Via Cappuccini. Open 9am-noon and 3-5pm. €1.30. ☏ 091 21 21 17.

The Capuchin Catacombs hold a certain macabre fascination: in simple terms they consist of a maze of corridors containing thousands of mummified bodies, contorted in expression and posture, perfectly dressed, appended (as if they had been hanged, with a rope around the neck) to the walls, in niches or propped up against the wall. The overwhelming sense of tragedy, which never fails to touch visitors, is heightened by the fact that these figures are shut away behind railings. The catacombs contain the remains of almost 8 000 Capuchin friars (the oldest corpses date from the late 16C), as well as those of illustrious or wealthy Palermitani, children and virgins, each category having been allotted its own special area. What is particularly extraordinary is the condition of the corpses, preserved intact by the special environmental conditions causing gradual desiccation. In especially good condition is the body of a little two-year old girl who died in 1920; she is so well preserved that she seems merely asleep; her body was injected with a concoction of chemicals (the doctor who administered them died without revealing his secret potion).

In the cemetery adjacent to the Capuchin monastery is the tomb of Giuseppe Tomasi di Lampedusa, author of *The Leopard,* who died in 1957 *(third avenue on the left).*

La Cuba★

Corso Calatafimi 100. (♿) Open summer, 9am-7pm; otherwise, 9am-6.30pm; Sun and public hols, 9am-1pm. €2. ☏ 091 52 02 99.

The Cuba Sottana, now incorporated into military barracks, was probably surrounded by a vast artificial lake that was known as the Pescheria (fishpond). In the old stables, just inside the entrance on the right, is a model reconstruction of how the palace must have looked originally. On the wall, the engraved Kufic inscription celebrates the completion of the building, thereby confirming that it was erected in 1180 at the request of William II.

The decoration of the building is exquisitely simple: above a series of tall pointed arches of differing widths are inserted various other smaller openings. La Cuba was built according to a rectangular plan, with four small projections at the centre of each side. The internal space was divided into three parts (the first, or last in the order of our visit, also accommodated two service rooms). In the central section there is an eight-sided star-shaped pool: from here the water would trickle gently into the Pescheria without breaking the surface so as not to disturb the reflections of the building and garden.

THE GREEN PARKS OF PALERMO

The parks around Palermo in the time of the Arabs and the Normans covered great areas of land. The one lying west of the city, known as the **Genoard** or the Paradise on Earth, was chosen by the sovereigns as an apt place for a summer residence or a pleasure palace in the Oriental sense of the word: a peaceful-haven set among gardens of exotic plants, with pools containing fish, watercourses and even wild animals from distant lands. Such were the dreams that inspired the building of the city's many parks, which included **la Zisa** and the much-restored **Scibene Castle**, which is still visible from Viale Tasca Lanza *(from Via Pitrè, the continuation of Via Cappuccini, turn right after passing Viale Regione Siciliana)*. Also of importance were the **Cuba Sottana** and **Cuba Soprana**, now part of the crumbling Villa Napoli complex (a few arches are just visible; *entrance at Corso Calatafimi 575*). In the latter stands **la Cubola**, a small, square pavilion surmounted by the characteristic bulbous red dome, which is accessible from Via Zancla *(heading towards the centre, cross Corso Calatafimi to your left, and Viale Regione Siciliana shortly after)*.

This passion for gardens has continued over the centuries, so that the city now has many havens of peace, planted with a host of exotic plants and trees. These veritable corners of paradise are ideal for relaxing or strolling amid the greenery: the exotic garden of San Giovanni degli Eremiti, Villa Bonanno, Villa Giulia, the Botanical Gardens, Villa Malfitano, Villa Trabia, Giardino Garibaldi in Piazza Marina, or the beautiful **English Garden**, extremely well kept, with an enormous number of palms, cactuses, parasol (maritime) pines and banyans, where walking is a sheer delight.

La Zisa★

Piazza Guglielmo il Buono. (♿) Open Mar-Oct, 9am-7.30pm (2pm Sun and public hols); Nov-Feb, 9am-7pm (1.30pm Sun and public hols); last admission 30min before closing. €4. ☏ 091 69 61 319; www.regione.sicilia.it/beniculturali/sopripa

The name is derived from *El Aziz,* meaning the splendid or noble one. Today, sadly, only the shell of the palace remains, yet this retains an undeniable aura. It was initiated by William I and completed by his son William II between 1166 and 1175; work on the building was entrusted entirely to Moorish craftsmen. In the 14C, after a period of neglect, it was transformed into a fortress, then into a depository for objects contaminated by the plague (16C), before being converted (and then extensively altered) into a *palazzo* for some noble family; recent restoration-has endeavoured to return it to its original state.

Tour – The main attraction on the ground floor is the room with the fountain: built on a cruciform plan, open at the front, the room has two square pools that collect water from the main channel in the centre of the room, fed from a waterspout. The upper section of the walls carries a mosaic frieze of peacocks and arches. From here are arranged a succession of rooms, each equipped with a special ventilation system whereby draughts of cool air could circulate through gaps in the walls. The niches and windows have *muqarnas*, a highly decorative honeycomb of miniature vaults and stalactite pendants, a characteristic feature in Islamic architecture. The *palazzo* houses a collection of objects, mainly from Egypt (from the Mameluke and Ottoman periods), that typify the art and style of furnishings that might once have adorned the original palace. The 15C *mushrabiyya*, a sort of perforated wooden screen placed in front of doors and windows as protection against excessive heat and light, are particularly fine.

Albergo delle Povere

Corso Calatafimi 217. Open to the public during exhibitions and conferences. This complex was originally intended at the end of the 18C as a hospice for the poor of the city; in the 19C, it was reserved for spinsters who set up a weaving workshop there; it is now used for temporary exhibitions and conferences.

The **fountain** in front is 17C. The complex, which includes the buildings on the other side of the road, consists of two parts arranged round two large, beautiful cloisters; these, in turn, are connected by a central courtyard onto which faces the Church of Holy Trinity. The left wing still shelters Opera Pia, a charity providing assistance to the poor; the right wing serves as operational headquarters for the exclusive carabinieri hit-squad unit charged with protecting Sicily's artistic heritage. Facilities include exhibition rooms and a lecture hall with a capacity for 350 people.

AND, IF YOU GET THE CHANCE ...

... take up position at one end of the semicircular wall enclosing the fountain and get someone else to stand at the other end; a mere whisper will carry from one side to the other. Who needs a mobile phone?

Orto Botanico★

Via Lincoln 38. Open Mon-Fri, 9am-5pm; Sat-Sun and public hols, 9am-1pm. Closed on national hols. €3. ☎ 091 62 38 241.

The Botanical Gardens have occupied their present site since 1789. The French architect Dufourny designed not only the gardens but also a series of buildings for use as research laboratories and experimentation. The gardens contain a huge range of different species, including fine examples of Oriental and exotic plants, such as the majestic Dendrocalamus giganteus – a giant kind of bamboo – or the incredible **banyan tree★★** *(Ficus magnoloides)*, the tallest and most wide-spreading tree in the garden. There are various South American plants such as *Chorisias* and *Bombacaceae* characterised by their strange, swollen, prickly trunks, brought to Palermo in the late 19C. From the large, deep pink flowers develop the fruits which, when mature, split open, dropping their seeds and their enveloping thick-hairy padding, once used like horse hair. One greenhouse contains a fine variety of cactus; note, at the entrance, the enormous *barili d'oro* (literally "barrels of gold" – also ironically called "mother-in-law's chairs").

Ponte dell'Ammiraglio

Corso dei Mille. The picturesque medieval bridge once straddled the waters of the River Oreto, which was then diverted. It was built in 1113 by George of Antioch, an admiral serving under **Roger II**.

San Giovanni dei Lebbrosi★

Via Cappello (a road to the left off Corso dei Mille, beyond the Ponte dell'Ammiraglio). St John of the Lepers may be the oldest Norman church in Sicily. Its most charming feature is the red dome which caps the bell tower-cum-entrance. The church is supposed to have been founded in 1070 (although some say it may have been a century later).

Chiesa di Santo Spirito or dei Vespri

Inside the cemetery of Santa Orsola, in Piazza di Santa Orsola (from Piazzetta Montalto take Via Colomba and then turn right into Via dei Vespri). Open 8.30am-1.30pm. ☎ 091 42 26 91.

The Church of the Holy Spirit or of the Vespers was built in 1178 during the reign of Roger II. It came to fame on 31 March 1282 when, during Evensong (Vespers), a French soldier insulted a Sicilian woman, provoking the bystanders to jump to her defence and so providing a pretext for an outburst of growing resentment towards the invaders from beyond the Alps. The incident sparked off the War of the Sicilian Vespers which, in turn, led to the eviction of the French from the island.

The front of the church, although incomplete, points proudly upwards, while a decorative system of duotone interlacing arches, typical of Norman art, extends down the sides to the apses.
The interior is austere and simple (largely thanks to the restoration work carried out in the late 19C, when it was restored to its original state by removing the elaborate decoration added during the Baroque era); the internal space is divided into a nave and flanking aisles by pointed arches that spring from round piers. The east end comprises three apses, in accordance with the Norman tradition. The painted *Christ on the Cross* above the altar is 16C.

Santuario di Santa Maria di Gesù

Follow Viale della Regione Siciliana to the intersection with Via Oreto (the southern extension of Via Maqueda). Turn right along Via Santa Maria di Gesù (look out for the green sign above the shoe shop on the corner). Open Mon-Sat, 9am-12.30pm; Sun and public hols, 11.30am-12.30pm. ☎ 091 44 51 95.
The 15C Sanctuary of St Mary of Jesus occupies a peacefully serene and cool spot on the slopes of Monte Grifone. The way to it leads through a cemetery where, traditionally, aristocratic families have kept their mausoleums. The area in front of the church is surrounded by fine patrician tombs mainly from the 19C or the beginning of the 20C, including the Liberty-style chapel belonging to the princes of Lanza di Scalea. The main entrance has a marble surround decorated with delicate shallow reliefs depicting Christ among angels and Apostles. The doorway on the left side is Gothic in style; it has attractive capitals carved with organic decoration. **Inside**, the chancel has two bays articulated by pointed arches; Antonio Alliata's marble sarcophagus is attributed to Antonello Gagini (in the chancel, high up on the right); there is a rare **wooden statue of the Virgin★** (1470); and a fine coffered wooden **ceiling**, painted with flowers and angels (early 16C), spans the entrance to the church and the organ above it. It is also worth taking note of the brightly coloured wooden organ loft, painted with scenes from the life of St Francis (1932).

Parco della Favorita

3km/1.8mi N. Follow Viale della Libertà as far as Piazza Vittorio Veneto. Turn right into Piazza dei Leoni; from here Viale del Fante runs alongside the park as far as the Chinese palace. The large park situated at the foot of Monte Pellegrino was created in 1799 by Ferdinand III of Bourbon, when the Napoleonic troops drove him out of Naples (where he had reigned as Ferdinand IV). The parkland, donated to the king by a number of noble families from Palermo, became his private hunting estate; he had a house built there, the delightful **Chinese palace**, a curiously shaped building with an exotic decor, designed by Marvuglia. The servants quarters were accommodated in the building next door which was similar in style to the first, but arranged around a lovely courtyard onto which faced the kitchens (connected to the palace by an underground passageway); this now houses the Museo Etnografico G Pitré.
Museo Etnografico Pitré – *Viale Duca degli Abruzzi 1, Parco della Favorita. (♿) Open daily except Fri, 8.30am-8pm (last admission 7.30pm). Closed public hols (except Sat-Sun) and Easter. €3. ☎ 091 74 04 893.*
The Pitré Ethnographic Museum houses a large quantity of artefacts associated with local folklore, the aim being to explain their significance and customary use, especially in rural areas. Reconstructions of houses, tools, needlework and embroidery, fabrics, a wonderful 17C wrought-iron bedhead, everyday pottery, "Sunday-best" clothes for high days and holidays, splendid engraved horn goblets and gourd containers for water or wine provide an introduction to life in Sicily in days past. In the rooms around the courtyard are displayed various examples of Sicilian carts, all decorated with incredibly elaborate carving, painting and wrought-iron work *(pause to admire the intricate detail of these exhibits)*, two 17C council carriages, and children's toys. Amulets and trinkets linked with magic and popular superstitions, together with the fine collection of handmade votive objects, bear witness to the strong faith of the country people. The museum also has a library *(open mornings only)* of books about popular traditions in Sicily and beyond.

> **Where to Eat**
> **Pizzeria Tonnara Florio** – *Discesa Tonnara 4, Arenella district – ☎ 091 63 75 611 – www.tonnaraflorio.it – Closed Mon evening –* ▤. This attractive Liberty-style building, unfortunately in need of restoration, has a beautiful garden and a number of rooms once used for processing tuna and repairing fishing boats.
> The building now houses a nightclub and a pizzeria.

Villa Niscemi★

Piazza Niscemi, at the end of Viale del Fante. Open 9am-dusk (gardens); Sun only, 9am-1pm (villa). No charge. ☎ 091 74 04 801.
Next to the Parco della Favorita stand the gardens and beautiful country villa that once belonged to the princes Valguarnera di Niscemi. Bought by the local

authorities in 1987 and now used as their headquarters, the villa has several frescoed rooms decorated with 18C furnishings. One of the most attractive rooms is the Salone delle Quattro Stagioni, adorned with a fresco of Charlemagne that is depicted on the Valguarnera coat of arms.

Excursions

Monte Pellegrino

14km/9mi N. From Viale della Libertà, turn right into Via Imperatore Federico and then head along Via Bonanno. The road up Monte Pellegrino offers magnificent **views★★★** over Palermo and the Conca d'Oro; in places it is crossed by a wide, much steeper, paved path dating from the 17C (used by those going up on foot). As the road climbs, it passes on the left, the **Castello Utveggio**, a massive pink construction that can also be seen from the city; it then continues on to the **Santuario di Santa Rosalia** (17C), a sanctuary built around the cave where, according to legend, St Rosalia lived. It is also said that this was where her bones were found in 1624 and that these, when carried in procession down through the city, liberated it from the plague. Following this event, St Rosalia became the patron saint of Palermo. The cave is covered with zinc guttering which helps collect the dripping water from the walls, as this is considered to have miraculous properties.

Further on up, the road comes to a lookout point which, though dominated by a statue of the saint, provides breathtaking **views★** out to sea.

Grotte dell'Addaura★

Between Mondello and Arenella. Take Via Crispi and follow the Lungomare Cristoforo Colombo as far as Punta di Priola. If approaching from Monte Pellegrino, continue along Via Bonanno, turn right into Viale Regina Margherita, then right again along the seafront. Closed at the time of going to press. For further information, contact the Soprintendenza di Palermo ☎ 091 69 61 319; Fax 091 67 02 070

A series of caves among the lower slopes of Monte Pellegrino have revealed that they were inhabited during Palaeolithic times (5th millennium BC). In one of these caves have been found various extraordinary **rock engravings**, possibly associated with some initiation ceremony or a ritual. The engravings consist of animals and a group of **nine human figures★** wearing strange headdresses, standing in a circle around another two figures arching their bodies and holding their arms stretched out in front of them, almost as if they are dancing.

Mondello

11km/7mi N of Palermo. Continue along the seafront. The road passes below the tall rugged slopes of Monte Pellegrino. This area, now an elegant holiday resort, was "discovered" at the beginning of the century by well-to-do Palermitani who decided that it provided the ideal conditions for a weekend away or for a short seaside holiday. As a result, large numbers of elegant villas (many of which still stand) sprang up along the seafront, the length of Viale Principe Scalea (Villa Margherita at n° 36), Via Margherita di Savoia (especially at the beginning) or in the streets behind, like n° 7 Via Cà da Mosto (Villino Lentini).

> **WHERE TO EAT**
>
> **Bye bye blues** – *Via del Garofalo 23, Mondello – ☎ 091 68 41 415 – info@byebyeblues.it – Closed Tue, at lunchtime on weekdays and Nov – – Booking recommended – €23/39.* This restaurant is well worth a visit for its original atmosphere and inventive cuisine, with a good balance of meat and fish dishes. It also has an excellent wine list.

Tour

INLAND FROM PALERMO

120km/75mi – allow one day. This day trip combining archaeology, art and natural landscapes passes through attractive verdant scenery which is almost Alpine in places. The first section of the tour offers splendid views of the bay.

From Viale Regione Siciliana, take the Calatafimi-Monreale exit and follow S 186 to Monreale (8km/5mi).

Monreale★★★ *See MONREALE*

Return to S 186.

After Pioppo and the turn off to San Giuseppe Jato, there is a magnificent **view★** of Palermo and the sea.

After Giacalone, turn left onto S 624 (the Palermo-Sciacca road). Turn off this road at San Cipirello (25km/16mi) and take the road signposted Corleone and Tagliavia. A turning on the left a short distance further on is marked with yellow signs for Scavi del Monte Jato. The road winds uphill for 5km/3mi (the asphalt gradually peters out into a dirt track that is fairly badly rutted in parts). A short, final section must be undertaken on foot.

Scavi del Monte Jato

Open daily except Mon, 8am-dusk. No charge. ☏ 091 85 72 976.

Founded by the Elimi (or the Sicani) as early as the 1st millennium BC, Jetae enjoyed its period of greatest splendour in the 3C BC. The houses erected during Swabian times occupy large sections of the Greco-Roman settlement (note in particular those in the area around the *cavea* of the theatre), contributing, in many cases, to their ultimate destruction, especially as building materials were systematically pillaged from those surviving constructions that, until then, had borne the test of time.

On the west side of the **agora** or market place (300 BC) stand a portico and a *bouleuterion*, a council chamber with a capacity of 200 people; between the two doorways, the orator would stand to address the assembly. West of the agora is the **theatre** (late 4C-early 3C BC), which, with its 35 tiers of seats, was able to accommodate an audience of approximately 4 400. The **house with the peristyle** was built over two storeys, around a porticoed courtyard; the north side is distinctively arranged with three reception rooms. The position of the doorways, offset from the central axis (so as to accommodate the couches they used when eating), implies they were dining or banqueting rooms. One preserves its original *opus signinum* floor, complete with the inlaid inscription of thanks and farewell that a departing guest might give after a banquet. In the northwestern corner of the peristyle is the bathroom, equipped with bath (note the drainage channel) and, in the servant's quarters behind it, traces of the fireplace that would have been used to heat the water.

The **Temple of Aphrodite** *(opposite the south side of the house, on the far side of the paved street)*, erected in about 550 BC in typically Greek style, bears witness to the earliest cultural exchanges between the indigenous population and the Greek world.

Museo Civico di San Cipirello

San Cipirello, Via Roma 320. ♿ Open summer, daily, 9am-noon and 4-7pm; otherwise, Mon-Sat, 9am-1pm and 3-7pm, Sun and public hols, 9am-noon and 2-6pm. No charge. ☏ 091 85 73 083.

This municipal museum displays the artefacts recovered from the archaeological excavations at Monte Jato. The most significant pieces are undoubtedly the sculptures that adorned the theatre: two maenads and two satyrs, followers of Dionysus, god of the theatre (and wine), and a crouching lion. Furthermore, the history of the town may be traced through the pottery found there: indigenous pottery with incised decoration, Greek black-figure ware, Roman red-gloss terra sigillata or Samian ware, and glazed ceramics from the Middle Ages. At one end of the room, the roof from the building erected on the stage of the theatre *(skene)* has been in part reconstructed with tiles bearing the inscription (meaning "of the theatre").

Follow S 624 towards Palermo and take the turn-off to Piana degli Albanesi.

The road affords magnificent views of the valley as it climbs up to **Portella della Ginestra**, where a monument commemorates a massacre perpetrated by the bandit Salvatore Giuliano in 1947, before descending to **Piana degli Albanesi** *(12km/7.5mi)*.

The Albanian community in Sicily

Towards the middle of the 15C, the area occupied by the Balkans was invaded by the Turks. Many inhabitants emigrated, some settled in Molise and Apulia. A century later, an Albanian *condottiere* (mercenary) was summoned by Alfonso of Aragon to contain a spate of revolts thereabouts: the soldiers then stayed in southern Italy, particularly in Calabria, before trickling through into Sicily over the ensuing years, and arriving at Piana degli Albanesi. Here they were welcomed with open arms and obtained permission to continue practising their faith in accordance with the Greek Orthodox Church. The Church granted them ever-greater administrative and religious autonomy, enabling them to maintain their traditions, language and literature. One of their most important communities is centred around Piano degli Albanesi and, although completely integrated within the local population, the Albanians retain their own ancient traditions, especially during religious festivals. Two of the most important festivals are Epiphany (12 days after Christmas) and Easter, when the locals don their most splendid costumes, typically embroidered with gold and silver, before pouring out onto the main street, Corso Giorgio Kastriota, and rallying before the churches of Santa Maria Odigitria, nearby San Giorgio (actually in Via Barbato) and San Demetrio, the town's main church. Outward signs of their heritage are evident at all times in the local dialect they speak and in the Greek Orthodox masses they celebrate; even the road signs and street names are inscribed in two languages. The town itself has another name, *Hora*, meaning the town.

Although there are no actual Albanian specialities as such to have gained popularity in Sicily, at least one typical Palermo sweetmeat is said to be of Albanian origin. It is the *gelu i muluni* which consists of watermelon sweetened with sugar and thickened, pieces of chocolate, candied pumpkin, pistachio nuts, cinnamon and vanilla, and served with ice cream.

P

To the southeast of the town lies the **Lago di Piana degli Albanesi**, a lovely man-made lake nestling silently amid the lushly green countryside: a view of this pastoral idyll may be espied from the Basilian monastery just above the town.

From Piana degli Albanesi follow signs to Ficuzza (20km/12.5mi S). The winding road leads upwards and offers splendid views of the town and man-made lake.

Palazzo Reale and Bosco della Ficuzza

Open summer, 9.30am-1.30pm and 3.30-7.30pm; otherwise, 10am-1pm and 2-5pm. For information on trips in the forest, contact the Centro di Recupero della Fauna Selvatica (same opening times as the palace), ☎ 091 84 60 107.

The small village of Ficuzza is arranged around the piazza in front of this **hunting lodge** built for Ferdinando III of Bourbon at the beginning of the 19C. The limestone walls of Rocca Busambra (1 613m/5 290ft) act as an impressive backdrop to the elegant neo-Classical lines of the building. The rather bare interior has a beautiful **dining room** decorated with stuccowork depicting hunting scenes. Attractive gardens *(parco reale)* lie behind the palace.

G. Iacono/MICHELIN

Palazzo Reale with Rocca Busambra in the background

To the right of the palace, the **Centro di Recupero della Fauna selvatica di Ficuzza** (Ficuzza Wildlife Protection Centre) provides visitors with a wealth of information on local fauna.

A road to the left of the palace leads into the woods and is the starting-point for a number of excursions.

The **Bosco della Ficuzza**, once a royal hunting ground, is a plateau covering approximately 7 000ha/17 300 acres of land dominated by Rocca Busambra. The forest comprises mainly holm oak, maple, oak and cork oak, while its rich fauna includes porcupines, martens, hedgehogs, tortoises, golden eagles and peregrine falcons.

From Ficuzza, return to the main road and head towards Godrano and Cefalà Diana (17km/10.5mi E).

Cefalà Diana

The town deserves a visit even if it is solely on account of its 10C **Turkish baths**, the only example of its kind in Sicily. In the town, it is worth making a detour to see the ruins of a 13C **castle** of which a single square tower and fragments of the defensive outer walls remain. The place once served as a defensive outpost between Palermo and Agrigento, on what is now a major road. During the ensuing centuries it was used as a grain depot until, in the 18C, it became a noble residence. Other attractions include, in the main piazza, a series of expressive bronze sculptures by a contemporary artist from Corleone, Biagio Governali; the panels of the Door of Miracles of San Francesco di Paola; and the highly dramatic War Memorial and Monument to the Emigrants.

The baths – *Open May-Oct, daily except Mon, 9am-1pm (also 3-7pm Sun and public hols); Nov-Apr, daily except Mon, 9am-1pm (also 3-5pm Sun and public hols). No charge. ☎ 091 82 01 184.*

These are located just over 1km/0.6mi outside the town, beside the River Cefalà, within their tastefully restored complex. The original date for the baths is difficult to ascertain accurately although it is certainly pre-1570. It is thought that the outer buildings were probably used to accommodate those afflicted by aches and pains who came to bathe in the hot sulphurous springs to relieve their rheumatism.

The rectangular brick building consists of a large room enclosed by a fine barrel vault, in the floor of which there are three pools – although at one time there was only one much larger one. This first section is separated from the elevated rear portion of the room by an elegant screen consisting of an arcade of three raised or Moorish-style arches supported on slender marble columns, terracotta capitals and dosserets (high blocks, inserted above the *abacus*). Beyond the screen is another, smaller pool, where the hot water bubbling out from the ground was collected before being channelled into the large pool. The vault is punctuated with ventilation holes, while the walls have niches which might have been used by bathers for their discarded clothes.

Return to the main road and continue as far as the junction with S 121. Follow signs back to Palermo (87km/54mi).

Pantalica★

This area of wild, rugged scenery combines the archaeological interest of the necropoli at Pantalica with the attractive natural landscapes of the Anapo Valley.

Location

Michelin map 565 P 27 – Siracusa. The archaeological site is accessible from both Ferla and Sortino; the former provides better views of the necropolis and avoid-shaving to climb down to the river bed, cross the river and climb up the other side. The protected natural area can be reached either from the Floridia-Sortino road or from Cassaro, to the south of Ferla (*see below for details*). The first option is of greater environmental and archaeological interest.

Neighbouring sights are described in the following chapters: CALTAGIRONE; SIRACUSA.

Background

Pantalica, identified as the ancient Hybla (founded, it is alleged, like Megara Hyblaea, in 728 BC by a group of colonists from Megara with the blessing of their last king Hyblon), has been inhabited since the Bronze Age. Towards the middle of the 13C BC, the Sicani moved inland from their original settlements in the coastal regions to a chosen site at Pantalica, as the coast at this time was subjected to attack and regular waves of settlers, and was therefore no longer secure. The narrow valley through which the River Anapo ran, together with the Cavagrande (which becomes the Calcinara in its final section) were naturally defensible in that they comprised two deep gorges with one means of access (the saddle of Filiporto, to the west); furthermore, the area had two rivers that were considered of inestimable value. Today, little survives of the original town, which was probably destroyed by the Syracusans before the foundation of Akrai in 664 BC, save for an incredible number of tombs in the steep limestone cliffs (which must have been excavated with huge effort probably using bronze or stone axes, given that iron had not yet been discovered). New life was breathed into Pantalica by the Byzantines, who installed small communities in rock-hewn dwellings there. It is probable that the site continued to be occupied during the Arab and Norman periods before being completely abandoned until the beginning of the 20C, when the archaeologist Paolo Orsi began excavating.

Worth a Visit

Archaeological site★

Always open. No charge. ☎ *0931 48 11 11.*

More than 5 000 burial chambers honeycomb the walls of this quarry to make five necropoli through successive periods. The earliest in the north and northwest necropoli (13C-11C BC) are elliptical in shape, whereas the most recent (850-730 BC) are rectangular. What is distinctive about these tombs is the way in which they are organised into compact family units, rather than into the more usual extended groups.

Follow the signs for Pantalica from Ferla; after 9km, stop and park at Sella di Filiporto *(yellow sign)*, the ancient gateway to the town, where the remains of the fortification trench can still be seen. From here, a path runs along the southern edge of the upland plateau from which, looking back, the **Filiporto necropolis** can be seen within a broad amphitheatre of rock. Further along the way there are splendid **views★★** over the Anapo gorge below; the path then continues down to a

Byzantine settlement with rectangular rock-hewn dwellings, and to the Oratory of San Micidiario. Follow the path and, after about 1km/0.6mi, turn left for the **anaktoron** or Prince's Palace; this is also accessible by car, by continuing along the main road some 1.5km/0.9mi (note in passing the **northwest necropolis** on the left) and then taking a short path *(yellow sign)*. The site accommodates the remains of a megalithic construction which, demonstrating clear Mycenean influences, was thought by Orsi to have been built by Mycenean workmen in the service of the prince.

Return to the car. 11km/7mi before Ferla the tarred road peters out (note the Byzantine village of Cavetta just before this). Leave the car and take the steep path down, enjoying, along the way, the marvellous **views**★★ of the gorge of Calcinara and of the vast **northern necropolis** enclosed by the wall on the opposite side *(20min on foot to the river)*.

Protected Natural Area★

Access – *There are two entrances to the Anapo Valley, via the Fusco gate (off the Floridia-Sortino road, turn left after about 12km/7mi at the fork marked with a yellow sign for Valle dell'Anapo; 700m/770yd further along, continue left – red road with wooden barrier), or via the Cassaro gate (from Ferla, follow the signs for Cassaro; at the first fork, turn left and continue to the bridge over the river; the Ponte Diga gate is located thereabouts – 4km/2.5mi from Ferla). Open May-Oct, 8am-7.30pm; Nov-Apr, 8am-5pm. No charge. ☎ 0931 46 24 52.*

An expedition through the protected area (soon to become a nature reserve) around the Anapo Valley reveals an extraordinary **landscape** comprising a succession of gorges defined by vertical cliffs, along which ran the old Syracuse-Ragusa-Vizzini railway. For those who do not wish to walk the whole route (13km/8mi), there is an alternative, clearly marked track which both natural and archaeological points of interest, leading to the **Cavetta necropolis** *(on the right immediately after the first tunnel)*, the **southern necropolis** *(on both sides after the second tunnel)* and the **Filiporto necropolis** *(after 4km/2.5mi in the wall on the right)*. Furthermore, at the start of the alternative route, immediately on the right (level with a pier of the fallen bridge), can be seen a series of vents associated with the Galermi aqueduct, built by the tyrant Gelon to convey water from the river to Syracuse, which continues to be used for irrigation purposes.

Horse-drawn transport

The section from Pantalica to the Case Specchi refuge can be taken by horse-drawn carriage (maximum 14 people). This service must be booked in writing, two weeks in advance, by contacting the Ispettorato Dipartimentale delle Foreste, Via S. Giovanni alle Catacombe 7, Siracusa. For further information, call ☎ 0931 46 24 52. If taking the walking tour (highly recommended), visitors are advised to bring a torch for the tunnel sections.

Flora and fauna

The geological formation known as the **cave iblee** (or Hyblaean quarries), a series of deep canyons cutting through the landscape, harbours a broad range of plants in a concentrated area. The tree varieties that make up the thickly wooded section up the rocky slopes include white and black poplars, and willows; there is also a profusion of tamarisks, oleanders, wild orchids and the nettle *Urtica rupestris*, a relic from the Ice Age. Clinging to the slopes elsewhere are patches of Mediterranean maquis: forest of holm and cork oaks interspersed with, in the more arid parts exposed to the sun, an aromatic scrub of sage, thyme, giant fennel, euphorbia and thorny broom. The Oriental plane tree deserves a special mention as it only grows wild in a very few places in Italy; the threat of a spreading fungus, a pathogenic canker, seems to have been checked here for the time being, thanks to appropriate measures.

As regards fauna, the Anapo Valley also accommodates a large number of different species: foxes, pine martens, porcupines, hares and hedgehogs; painted frogs and other amphibians; dippers, stonechats, kingfishers, partridges and a pair of peregrine falcons.

Excursions

Ferla

Isolated on the limestone upland plateau crossed by the River Anapo, the town boasts several 18C religious buildings. **San Antonio**, built on a Greek-cross plan overlooking an attractive square-cum-forecourt cobbled with geometric designs, has an elegant frontage comprising five convex panels, articulated with columns, and surmounted by two towers, one incomplete. Inside, the stucco and painted wall and ceiling decoration, panels and statues combine to make a charming Baroque whole. *Open Mon-Sat, 4-6pm; Sun and public hols, 10-11.30am and 4-6.30pm. For information and reservations (at least three days in advance), call ☎ 0931 87 00 81.*

The church belonging to the Montevergine monastery, enclosed within a secluded square, has a harmonious front and a bell tower, designed with concave and convex lines (18C).

The **Museo dell'Opra dei Pupi** is in the former monastery of St Francis. This museum contains the puppet theatre and puppets which once belonged to the puppeteer Ignazio Puglisi (1904-86), a collection which is organised by theme, with rooms dedicated to monsters (devils, skeletons and giants), to Paladins and Saracens, and to the *cartoni*, large sections of cardboard portraying the puppets, used as a background. One of the last rooms is dedicated to the characters of farce which spoke in Sicilian dialect and brought the show to an end. *Open Mon-Fri, 10am-noon; Sat-Sun and public hols, by appointment only. Closed 10 Sep. No charge. ☎ 0931 95 207.*

Pantelleria★★

The island of Pantelleria is endowed with a jagged coastline bathed by clear blue sea, that hides a wealth of varied marine life; its rocky slopes, fashioned by drystone walling into terraces fit for cultivation, together with the typical local houses known as *dammusi*, combine to confer upon the island an exceptional and unique beauty. The distinctive colours of the soil and bedrock, which for the most part are basaltic, have earned Pantelleria the nickname, "black pearl of the Mediterranean". This "rich land of offerings" (the translation of its current name, whose origins are late Greek or Byzantine) is famous for its Solimano and Passito di Pantelleria wines. The island's wild beauty makes it popular with the jet set and personalities from the world of film and television, many of whom have holiday homes here.

Location

Population 7 375. Michelin map 565 Q 17-18 – Trapani. Pantelleria is the largest of Sicily's satellite islands with a surface area of 83km²/32sq mi; it is also the most westerly, lying a mere 84km/52mi from the African continent, at the same latitude as Tunisia. Its warm climate, however, is constantly being tempered by ever-present strong winds blowing in from the sea, hence the justification for the island's Arabic name *Qawsarah or Bent el Rion*, meaning Daughter of the Wind. 🅘 *Piazza Cavour 1; ☎ 0923 91 18 38.*

Background

Volcanic land – The highest point on the island is Montagna Grande (836m/2 742ft), an ancient crater. The rocky black lava coastline is riddled with caves and small headlands projecting into the sea. The land mass, being volcanic, is extremely fertile and well drained, and therefore suited to the cultivation of the vine. Solimano, a sparkling wine with a delicate bouquet, together with the Passito di Pantelleria, made with *zibibbo* grapes, are the principal specialities of the island. Second to these are salted capers, which are harvested from plants that produce abundant numbers of exquisitely delicate flowers.

Traditional dammusi

G. Iacono/MICHELIN

Directory

Transport

The quickest and easiest way of getting to the island from mainland Italy is by **air**. There are direct flights from Trapani and Palermo; during the summer, services also operate from Rome and Milan. A shuttle bus links the airport, situated 5km/3mi south of Pantelleria town, to Piazza Cavour in Pantelleria.

Those already in Sicily, ideally in the area of Trapani, might like to consider the **ferry** travelling overnight on the outward journey (6hr) and returning by day (5hr). For information and reservations, contact **Siremar** (Gruppo Tirrenia), ☎ 199 123 199 (from Italy) or 081 31 72 999 (from abroad and mobile phones); www.gruppotirrenia.it/siremar/html/home/mainframeset.htm **Ustica Lines** (Via Amm. Staiti 23, Trapani; ☎ 0923 22 200, info@usticalines.it, www.usticalines.it) operates a **hydrofoil** service (2hr 30min) from June to September.

Sightseeing and Tourist Information

The best way of exploring the island is by car, enabling visitors to discover the island's many surprises at a leisurely pace. The road running around the island is asphalted but very narrow. Bus services from Piazza Cavour link Pantelleria with other parts of the island.

Several tour operators, some private, are able to provide information on the types of accommodation and facilities available. Most can also arrange holiday packages, car and boat rentals. **Pro Loco** ☎ 0923 91 18 38; **Associazione Turistica Pantelleria** ☎ 0923 91 29 48; **Promozione Turistica di Pantelleria** ☎ 0923 91 22 57.

To explore the coast from the sea, rubber dinghies may be hired; organised boat trips are also provided.

Where to Eat

• For all budgets

La Favarotta – *Località Khamma Fuori, Khamma – ☎ 0923 91 53 47 – ⊄ – €20.* This restaurant offers welcome respite during the heat of summer. Located inland at an altitude of 400m/1 300ft, the menu here nevertheless includes a number of excellent fish dishes.

La Nicchia – *Scauri Basso, Scauri – ☎ 0923 91 63 42 – Open Sat-Sun only. Closed at lunchtime and Jan-Feb – €27/35.* At La Nicchia, guests can choose between dining on an outdoor terrace with tables and wooden chairs, in the indoor dining room where the pizza kitchen is open to view, or beneath a delightful pergola at the end of the garden, surrounded by colourful flowers and plants.

I Mulini – *Kania 12, Tracino – ☎ 0923 91 53 98 – imulini@galactica.it – Closed Nov-Easter – €30/49.* This picturesque restaurant housed in an old mill has been tastefully restored in traditional style. The restaurant specialises in simple, local cuisine.

Where to Stay

If you are planning to stay one or more nights on the island, it is well worth renting a *dammuso*, one of the typical local Arab-style houses *(see above)*. Tourist information providers will be happy to give information on terms and conditions.

• Budget

Port Hotel – *Via Borgo Italia 71, Pantelleria – ☎ 0923 91 12 99 – Fax 0923 91 22 03 – porthotel@pantelleria.com – 43 rooms. €39/63* ☕. This simple white building on the seafront near the port is both comfortable and well maintained. Although the rooms are quite small, their attractive blue and white decor is both pleasant and refreshing.

• Moderate

Albergo Papuscia – *Contrada Sopra Portella 28, Tracino – ☎ 0923 91 54 63 – Fax 0923 91 54 63 – albergopapuscia@tiscalinet.it – Closed Dec-Easter – ⊄ – 11 double rooms. €77* ☕. This small, friendly hotel in the upper part of the town has rooms in traditional *dammusi* with typical walls of lava rock. Guest areas include a bar and simple restaurant, with a veranda for the summer months.

Shopping

Visitors should not leave the island without buying some capers and a bottle of the excellent dessert wine, the Passito di Pantelleria, for which the island is renowned. These can be bought from shops in the built-up areas or from the farms where they are produced.

S. Sauvignier/MICHELIN

Various phenomena provoked by volcanic activity are still much in evidence on Pantelleria: hot springs emerge from the sea floor just off the coast, sulphuric vapour emanates from natural caves, and jets of steam (known locally as *favare*) are intermittently emitted from the volcanic rock, especially in the vicinity of the craters *(see below)*.

Evolution of a house style – The first residents of Pantelleria may have come from Africa in Neolithic times to extract its black gold, namely obsidian which, at that time, was highly sought after. Near to a village dating from this period, with fortifications of a type found elsewhere only at Los Millares in Spain (near Almería), are a number of megalithic funerary structures of a kind that is distinctive to the island, known locally as **sesi** *(see below)*, yet reminiscent in shape of the *nuraghi* of Sardinia.

Next came the Phoenicians: they called the island Kossura and provided it with a large harbour on the exact spot occupied by the island's main port today. There followed waves of Carthaginians, Romans, Vandals, Byzantines and Arabs, who boosted the local agriculture by introducing cotton, olives and figs, and improving the cultivation of the vine. Many of the island's farming communities preserve their Arab names: Khamma, Gadir, Rakhali, Bukkuram, Bugeber and Mursia.

During the Second World War, Pantelleria's key strategic position right in the middle of the Canale di Sicilia separating North Africa from Italy, earned it the attentions of the Fascist government, which began to fortify the place. As a result, it was subjected to systematic bombing raids in 1943 by the Allies based on the Tunisian coast.

The traditional type of house found on Pantelleria is the **dammuso**; this is Arab in origin. The square constructions are built with square stones (now only used to face the exterior). The roof doubles as a terrace, but rather than being completely flat, the surface is gently undulating so as to permit rainwater to be channelled away, and subsequently collected for domestic use. At one time, each individual house constituted a single residential unit, more often than not divided into two rooms: one for human habitation, the other for sheltering animals. Nowadays, however, many have been bought up and converted into summer homes, often grouped into a residential complex comprising several units.

The inhabitants of Pantelleria, who by trade tend traditionally to be farmers rather than sailors, have tried to resolve the problem posed by the strong winds that blow during the greater part of the year and prevent trees from growing tall (even the olive trees have been adapted and helped by man to grow at ground level by pruning them into a circular fan of low-lying espaliers). The solution they have devised is the **Pantelleria garden**, a circular or square enclosure with high stone walls, in which one or more citrus trees might grow, protected from the wind. Sometimes these gardens are physically attached to a house, others might be situated in the centre of a field – an oasis of green, especially when seen from the air.

Worth a Visit

TOUR OF THE ISLAND BY CAR★★

Approx 40km/25mi round trip.

A scenic coast road provides glorious views of the landscape.

Pantelleria

The houses of the island's main built-up area are clustered around the harbour, having been reconstructed without any formal planning after the Second World War. The main landmark is the **Castello Barbacane**; this was probably founded in Roman times, since when it has been demolished and rebuilt on a number of occasions. It owes its present appearance to Frederick II of Swabia.

Follow the west coast, heading south.

Neolithic Village

The archaeological site is situated some 3km/1.8mi beyond Mursia and the **Kuddie Rosse**, ancient craters of a reddish colour. The only discernible feature among the low stone field boundary walls and scattered piles of rubble is the **Sese Grande★** (just beyond the quarry, at the end of a long wall, continue left some 50m/55yd. The *sese* lies behind a villa, on the left.) This structure rises from an elliptical base of large blocks of lava into a kind of tower. It is surrounded by an ornamental ledge which spirals its way up to the top. The base has 12 entrances serving as many low passages that interconnect the same number of domed funerary chambers. Here, the dead were entombed in the foetal position, with the head pointing towards the west, surrounded by their personal grave goods.

A little further on, the rocky black **Punta Fram** points out to sea. Past the tip of the headland, a flight of steps leads down from the right side of the road, to the **Grotta di Sataria** which contains pools of water fed by hot springs.

Scauri★

High up on the cliff edge, enjoying a spectacular **position★**, Scauri overlooks its picturesque little harbour, fed by hot springs. Marvellous **views★** are to be had from the cemetery.

After continuing some way along the coast, park the car and walk into Nikà.

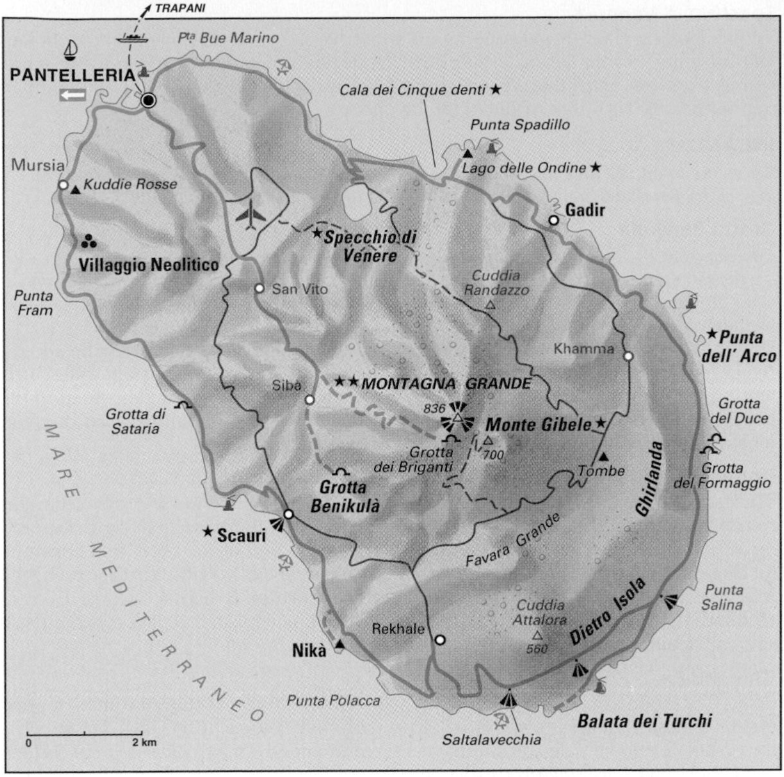

Nikà

30min on foot there and back. The minuscule fishing village is stituated in a lava gorge. Among the nearby rocks emerge a number of hot springs.

Back on the coastal road, turn left at the junction for **Rekhale**, one of the few villages that preserve *dammusi* and Pantelleria gardens in their original state.

Return to the coast, which at this point drops steeply down to the sea. After a bend in the road appears **Saltalavecchia** (which literally translates as the "old lady's leap"), a village perched on the cliff at one of the highest points; enjoy the very dramatic **view**★★ down a sheer face to the sea, over 150m/500ft below *(be very careful here as the ground can give way).*

Balata dei Turchi

This was where the Saracens used to land on the island unseen. It is one of the few sheltered coves with access to the sea (a broad, flat rock), protected from the wind and therefore overgrown with tall vegetation, notably bushes of wild juniper and sweet-smelling pines.

Dietro Isola

The road provides splendid **views**★★ out over the coastline which here is dominated by this great headland.

Punto dell'Arco★

At the far end of the promontory sits the **Arco dell'Elefante**★, a spectacular naturally formed archway of grey lava which, in colour and shape, resembles the head and trunk of an elephant.

Gadir

The little harbour full of fishing smacks bubbles with water from thermal springs (in the harbour hollow).

A short way beyond, a path leads off to the right of the road to the lighthouse on **Punta Spadillo**. When the lighthouse comes into view, branch left along a second track towards a collection of abandoned houses, then climb up to the batteries. Behind the white one, follow the path downhill between low lava walls; it eventually opens out by the tiny **Lago delle Ondine**★ (lake of waves). Almost completely surrounded by glorious tall cliffs and wonderful boulders of volcanic rock, this lava hollow collects water from the breaking waves to form a small emerald-green pool of stillness.

After the fine **Cala dei Cinque Denti**★ (the bay with five teeth), turn left at the fork.

Specchio di Venere★

Venus' looking glass (besides being an attractive purple wild flower) is a delicious lake of green water fed by a sulphur-rich spring on its western flank. Its name comes from the myth that Venus studied her reflection in this lake when comparing her beauty with that of her rival Psyche.

INLAND★★

Leave the town of Pantelleria by the airport road and continue to Sibà. Beyond the village is the Benikulà Cave or Bagno Asciutto (natural sauna).

Grotta Benikulà

Coming from the direction of Sibà, there are no signs: access to the cave is down a road on the left (signposted from the other direction). Leave the car and proceed on foot. It takes 10min to walk there and back. Those intending to indulge in a sauna should take a swimming costume and a towel.

Looking down over the valley from above, two Pantelleria gardens may be seen. Inside the cave, the temperature of the steam rises the deeper in one goes. It is worth pausing at the cave entrance, entering only once you are accustomed to the heat. It is advisable not to spend too long inside as the temperature can be overwhelming.

La Montagna Grande★★

The road up to the Montagna Grande offers magnificent **views★★** over the surrounding landscape. The mountain is covered with pine forest *(with prescribed picnic sites)*. Leave the car by the building marking the end of the road, and continue on foot past two other buildings (a *dammuso* and a chapel); a little further on to the left, a series of stone steps leads up to the **Grotta dei Briganti**, a large cave in which the temperature is constantly warm, which is why in the past it served as a refuge for outlaws (hence its name).

Ghirlanda

Costa Ghirlanda, on the east side of the island, conceals a number of tombs of indeterminable age. Access to them is by an extremely bumpy dirt track for which a four-wheel drive vehicle (or a horse) is recommended. In an oak wood *(on the left)* is a collection of rock-hewn **tombs**, which local tradition claims to be Byzantine. The exceptional beauty of this mysterious place alone makes the excursion worthwhile.

Monte Gibele★

This old volcano, now extinct, provides the perfect context for an agreeable walk. From Rakhali, head inland and, at the junction, fork right until a path appears on the left. Continue on foot. The path leads to the crater, now covered in vegetation. On the way, the track skirts past the **Favara Grande**, a powerful geyser which issues jets of boiling hot steam.

TOUR OF THE ISLAND BY BOAT★★

The perfect complement to an exploration of the island's land mass, is to go off and discover her other splendid attributes by sea. The opaque blackness of the lava rocks contrasts sharply with the deep blue sea which, in places, appears an emerald green. The coastline is interrupted by little, delightfully secluded creeks, ravines and intriguing caves. Starting out from Pantelleria, a clockwise tour of the island will first reveal the jagged and low-lying north coast; in the area of Cuddia Randazzo, the rocks assume strange black profiles which can be construed as figures of animals or other weird creatures. There follows a series of inlets and caves, perfect for swimming. Then comes the **Arco dell'Elefante★** *(see above)* and a further succession of caves and hollows divided by pillars of lava. The most dramatic grottoes are situated between Punta Duca and Punta Polacca, however **Grotta del Duce**, **Grotta del Formaggio** and Grotta della Pila dell'Acqua can only be fully explored by the smallest craft. This is the most spectacular stretch of the island's coast, with its towering great cliffs reaching far into the sky and large monolithic rocks pointing sharply out of the sea until, at last, the drama culminates in a view of **Saltalavecchia**. Ever taller rocky outcrops follow (sections of coastline around Scauri), before the coast becomes characterised by flatter and low-lying boulders as in the vicinity of Cala dell'Alga.

Golfo di Patti

This stretch of coastline offers magnificent views of impressive rocky cliffs, beautiful beaches and extensive lagoons, backed by the northern slopes of the Peloritani and Nebrodi mountains. In addition to its stunning natural landscapes, the region is also home to archaeological sites of major interest, such as the Roman villas at Patti and Terme Vigliatore, and the ruins of the Greek city of Tyndaris.

Location

Michelin map 565 27M - Messina. The bay stretches for 30km/19mi from Capo Calavà to Capo Milazzo, which juts out into the sea like a sickle. The broad sweep of beach which stretches along the ample width of the bay is dotted with seaside resorts, such as Gioiosa Marea, Marina di Patti, Oliveri and Falcone, and is briefly interrupted halfway by Capo Tindari, crowned by its sanctuary. *Piazza Marconi 11, Patti; ☎ 0941 24 11 36; Fax 0941 24 11 36.*

Neighbouring sights are described in the following chapters: CAPO D'ORLANDO; MILAZZO.

TOUR

40km/25mi – allow half a day.

Patti

This small town in the hinterland extends down to the sea at Marina di Patti, where the remains of a Roman villa were recently discovered *(see below).* The old town centre still retains its medieval network of narrow streets, spanned by arches, clustered around the cathedral.

Elevated to a bishopric by Roger II in 1131, then nominated a royal town by Frederick III of Aragon in 1312, Patti received the title of *magnanima* (generous) from Charles V for having made a generous tribute to the crown. Very little remains of this glorious period of the town's history, Patti having succumbed to repeated earthquakes (particularly the one in 1693).

The present **cathedral** building dates from the 18C, its beautiful 15C **portal** having been restored to the main façade. The small clusters of columns which flank the main entrance have magnificent capitals, typical of the late Romanesque, carved with grotesques: two-headed, winged animals and fantastical semi-human monsters. **Inside** stands the **sarcophagus of Queen Adelasia** *(in the right transept)* – wife of Roger I – a 16C restoration of the 1118 original. *For information on admission times, call ☎ 0941 84 08 13.*

On the northern side of the town, beside the River Montagnareale, is Porta San Michele, the only fragment of the Aragonese defensive town walls to survive. Beyond the gate sits the little church of **San Michele**, which contains a fine marble ciborium by Antonello Gagini (1538) and a triptych featuring a group of angels flanked by St Agatha and Mary Magdalene.

Where to eat

Il Casaro – *Via Luca della Robbia 3, Marina di Patti – ☎ 0941 36 74 75 – Closed Mon, Dec and Jan – Booking recommended – €18/30.* This popular eatery, a former pub converted to a restaurant by the new, dynamic owner, enjoys a good reputation in the area. Facilities here include a dining room with an attractive bar-counter, a delightful wooden veranda, and a small garden for summer dining. Good-quality cuisine at reasonable prices.

Villa Romana di Patti

In Patti Marina, near the underpass of the motorway on the right. Open 9am-2hr before dusk. €2. ☎ 0941 36 15 93.

The large Imperial Roman villa was discovered during construction work on the motorway. The complex is arranged around a peristyle with a columned portico from which lead various rooms, including one with three apses, paved with mosaic featuring geometric motifs and depictions of domestic and wild animals. There would also have been baths on the east side of the house.

Follow S 113 for 9km/6mi, then turn left to Tyndaris.

Tindari★

From the east, Tyndaris appears backed up against a succession of hills that emerge from the sea and rise to form a land mass resembling a great dragon slumbering peacefully; perched high upon its head stands the sanctuary, a discernible landmark from afar. As the road winds down the dragon's back, wonderful **views★** open out over the bay of Patti and the beaches that sweep right round to Capo Milazzo.

The **sanctuary**, a relatively recent addition to the landscape, shelters a Byzantine Black Virgin which attracts large bands of pilgrims, notably around the Marian feasts of the Visitation (31 May) and the Birth of the Virgin (8 September).

THE CITY OF CASTOR AND POLLUX

The Greek colony of **Tyndaris** was founded by the tyrant of Syracuse, Dionysius the Elder, in 396 BC to accommodate refugees from Sparta at the end of the Peloponnese War (404 BC). The name refers to the Dioscuri, Castor and Polydeuces/Pollux, sons of Leda and Zeus and brothers of Helen (whose abduction was the catalyst for the Trojan War) and Clytaemnestra. Leda was the wife of the mythical hero Tyndareus of Sparta, who was said to have fathered Castor, while Pollux was believed to have been fathered by Zeus. Consequently, the Dioscuri are also known as the Tyndaridi. The link between the town and the heavenly twins is taken up on coins and mosaics.

The new town, occupying a raised, yet naturally defensible position, developed its strategic importance in policing the sea between Messina and the Aeolian Islands. Despite its impressively solid defensive fortifications on the landward side, the town fell into the hands of the Carthaginians. Later, under Roman dominion, it flourished through a period of great prosperity, prompting a range of public buildings such as schools, markets and public baths to be constructed or redeveloped. The theatre, which was built by the Greeks, was modified so as to accommodate the demands of its new audience.

Thereafter, Tyndaris progressively declined: a landslide destroyed part of the city including its most important features, and further damage was then incurred by the Arab conquest in the 9C.

At the foot of the rock face are the **Laghetti di Marinello**, visible from the terrace before the church *(see below)*.

Archaeological Site★ – *Open 9am-2hr before dusk. €2. ☎ 0941 36 90 23; www.regione.sicilia.it*

The path up to the top of Capo Tindari passes alongside sections of the defensive **walls** built during the reign of Dionysius; these were later reinforced and replaced by a double barrier of square stone blocks. The walls were only built around the vulnerable parts of the town, which was laid out on a regular grid system with three wide *decumani* (main thoroughfares) interconnected by *cardini* at right angles. The natural inclination of the site facilitated an efficient drainage system along the secondary streets.

A small **antiquarium**, just beyond the entrance to the site on the left, displays artefacts recovered from the excavations.

The **Insula romana** comprises an entire block to the south of the main axis or *decumanus superiore*, complete with baths, taverns and houses including a large patrician house which preserves fragments of mosaic.

The arcaded remains of the **basilica** give some suggestion of the scale and elegance of the original building. Even though the ruin has been classified as a basilica or public meeting house, its true function is still uncertain: it may possibly be a part of some monumental *propylaeum* (gateway) for the agora or main square of the city. It is built of large square blocks of sandstone, and must have comprised five great arches. The central archway, also the widest, provided access to a barrel-vaulted passage spanning the main road.

Turn left on to the decumanus superiore.

The **theatre** was built by the Greeks (late 4C BC) in such a way as to take full advantage of the natural lie of the land, with the *cavea* (auditorium) facing the sea and the Aeolian Islands. It was adapted in Imperial times for staging gladiator fights.

FESTIVAL

The Tindari Estate festival is held in the theatre at Tindari from the last week in July to the third week in August. The festival's programme includes prose readings, dance performances and classical and contemporary music concerts.

Follow S 113 for 3.5km/2mi, then turn left to Oliveri.

Laghetti di Marinello

This is the name given to the pools of water left by the tide on the wide sandy strip below Capo Tindari, some of which contain a rich variety of aquatic plants. The area also attracts an interesting selection of birds: gulls and migratory species, including grebes, coots and little egrets. According to legend, these rock pools came into being to save a little girl who otherwise would have fallen to her death from the top of the headland because of her mother, who refused to have faith in the Black Virgin; she was saved when the sea miraculously withdrew to leave a soft landing pad of sand that cushioned her fall. In 1982, one of the rock pools assumed the profile of a veiled woman, identified by the local people as the Madonna of the sanctuary.

These pools can be reached on foot (about 30min) from Oliveri. The beach tails off into a glorious **bay★★** of clear blue water. In summer this is a veritable paradise for bathers although the beach is rarely crowded *(swimmers are strongly recommended not to bathe in the actual pools, since the water is stagnant: it is preferable to swim in the bay).*

Return to the main road, continuing along it for 6.5km/4mi to the district of San Biagio.

B. Kaufmann/MICHELIN

The Laghetti di Marinello

Villa Romana di Terme Vigliatore★

Open 9am-2hr before dusk. ☎ *090 97 40 488.*

The luxury suburban residence, dating from the 1C AD, has not been excavated fully. The villa comprises the actual residential quarters *(on the left)* and a small baths complex for the owners of the villa and their guests *(on the right).*

To the left extends a square **peristyle** with eight columns down each side (of which only part has been excavated). Straight ahead is a large **tablinum** (archive room) with an *opus sectile* floor made up of black and white stone pieces laid in geometric patterns, surrounded with a marble tile border. The rooms on the left served as a kitchen (adjacent to the *tablinum*) or bedrooms.

The most interesting part of the complex, however, is the private baths *(to the right of the entrance to the site)*, which were extended in two different phases. First there is the semicircular bath, to the left of which is the **frigidarium** paved with a fine black and white mosaic depicting a boat with two oarsmen and a fisherman (with a line). Around the central panel are dolphins (at the four corners), with a swordfish above. The heating system of the various sections of the baths is clearly visible. Hot air from a furnace located behind the complex circulated by convection through the cavities in the walls formed by rectangular pipes and between the ground and the floor, which was raised by little columns of bricks known as *suspensurae*.

From Terme Vigliatore visitors can either continue to Milazzo (see MILAZZO) or follow the tour described on p 253.

Piazza Armerina

Piazza Armerina is best known for the fabulous nearby Imperial Villa of Casale, yet its attractive historic centre clustered around a Baroque cathedral is worthy of interest in its own right. The town comes to life each 13 and 14 August, when the townsfolk don medieval garb in order to re-enact the arrival of the Gran Conte Ruggero d'Altavilla (Roger De Hauteville) and his troops.

Location

Population: 22 530. Michelin map 565 O 25 – Enna. The town sits in pleasant rolling countryside at an altitude of 700m/2 300ft. Behind a mass of modern constructions, the narrow streets of the historic centre wind their way uphill to the cathedral, which stands at the highest point of the town. Piazza Armerina is the closest settlement to the famous Villa del Casale and visitors travelling from Enna or Caltagirone must first drive through Piazza Armerina to reach the villa. **ℹ** *Viale Generale Muscarà,* ☎ *0935 68 02 01.*

Neighbouring sights are described in the following chapters: CALTAGIRONE; CALTANISSETTA; ENNA; VILLA IMPERIALE DEL CASALE.

Walking About

MEDIEVAL QUARTER★

The little town is visible from a good distance away with, at its centre, the Duomo dominating the highest point (721m/2 364ft). Around the great church grew up the old town, threaded by a jumble of narrow medieval streets, lined by fine Renaissance and Baroque town houses.

Duomo – The monumental Baroque building, crowned with a great dome, towers over its own **piazza**, an open space enclosed by the likes of the Baroque **Palazzo Trigona**.

The current church stands upon the 15C foundations of another, from which a bell tower survives on the right side, with Catalan Gothic windows on the two lower levels and Renaissance equivalents above. The front elevation comprises a broad façade ornamented with pilasters and engaged columns; a sandstone string course articulates the horizontal planes, balancing the important emphasis given to the elegant central doorway framed by spiral columns, surmounted by a single, wide, square window, above which is the eagle, the heraldic emblem of the Trigona family who originally commissioned the church.

Inside, it preserves a number of notable works of art. Immediately on the right, through a Gagini-style Renaissance archway, stnads the baptismal font. Above the main altar, at the far end of the nave, is the **Madonna delle Vittorie★**. This Byzantine image is popularly linked to the banner given at the Council of Melfi, the capital of the Norman kingdom of Puglia, where several councils were held, by Pope Nicholas II to his legate Roger I "to go before him and inspire his army in its future campaigns". In the little chapel to the left of the chancel is a fine **painted wooden cross★** from 1455, with the Resurrection depicted on the back. Overlooking the nave there are two gilded wooden organ cases; one ornamented with a medallion enclosing the Trinacria, the ancient symbol of Sicily *(on the left)*, the other showing Count Roger on horseback *(on the right)*.

A walk through the streets

In Via Cavour, behind the Duomo, stands a 17C **Franciscan complex** (now a hospital); its sandstone and brick church is marked by a bell tower with a conical spire covered in maiolica tiles. The south face of the convent buildings includes an elegant **balcony** supported by Baroque brackets, designed by GV Gagini.

Continue on down the street to Slargo Santa Rosalia and **Palazzo Canicarao**, which now comprise commercial offices (Azienda di Promozione Turistica). The main buildings enclosing **Piazza Garibaldi** include the **Chiesa di Fundrò**, dedicated to St Roch, and the 18C Palazzo di Città.

Turn down Via Vittorio Emanuele which opens out before two church façades face to face: **Chiesa di Sant'Ignazio di Loyola** is preceded by a staircase that divides into two above the

The majestic dome of the cathedral

R. Mattes/MICHELIN

Directory

Where to Eat

Al Fogher – *S 117 bis, 3km/1.8mi N of Piazza Armerina – ☎ 0935 68 41 23 – Closed Sun evening and Mon – Booking recommended – €29/42.* Efficiently run by an enthusiastic, entrepreneurial couple (he runs the kitchen, while she takes care of the dining room), the Al Fogher is one of the best-known restaurants in Sicily. Traditional, authentic Sicilian fare with a contemporary twist.

Where to Stay

• ***Budget***

Mosaici–da Battiato Hotel – *Contrada Paratore Casale 11, 3.5km/2mi W of Piazza Armerina – ☎ 0935 68 54 53 – Fax 0935 68 54 53 – Closed 20 Nov-25 Dec –* *– 23 rooms. €35/45* *€4 –* A simple, well-maintained hotel in an ideal location for visitors wishing to explore the delights of Piazza Armerina and admire the mosaics at the Villa Casale.

Ostello del Borgo – *Piazza San Giovanni 6, Piazza Armerina – ☎ 0935 68 70 19 – Fax 0935 68 69 43 – info@ostellodelborgo.it –* *€39/52* . Don't be deceived by the name – this is not a hostel in the normal sense of the word, but accommodation provided in a wing of the former monastery of St John. Some of the monks' cells have been converted into spacious, comfortable guest rooms.

Festivals

Palio dei Normanni – From 12 to 14 August, the town of Piazza Armerina sees the re-enactment of the legendary arrival of Roger de Hauteville (Ruggero d'Altavilla) in the town. This is followed by jousting and a procession in which the statue of the Madonna and Child with two angels, kept in the cathedral, is carried through the streets to be presented to the town by the Count *(see below)*.

first flight; **Chiesa di Sant'Anna** has a noticeably convex façade. Above, towers the solid, square profile of the **Aragonese castle** (1392-96). From here, return to Piazza Duomo so as to take Via Monte down to the **Chiesa di San Martino di Tours**, which was founded in 1163.

ON THE OUTSKIRTS

On the western side of town, at the far end of Via Sant'Andrea, stands a 12C hermitage, **l'Eremo di Sant'Andrea** and, a little further on, the precincts of **Santa Maria del Gesù** (17C), now sadly abandoned but which preserves nonetheless its fine portico with a loggia above.

The Palio and its legend

It all stems from the people's huge admiration for the great Count Roger: in those days, the town was held by the Saracens, the infidels, so the Norman advance in Sicily was considered a kind of holy war. Very soon, the inhabitants of Piazza rose in revolt, acclaiming Roger Guiscard de Hauteville (known in Italy as Ruggero d'Altavilla) as their leader. On arrival, the paid mercenary/*condottiere* gave the town a banner which earned great admiration from the faithful. The banner was then furled and put away until the mid-1300s, when it was recovered and borne with great ceremony to the town church. As if by a miracle, the plague which was then decimating the town, suddenly died out and the banner became a cult object. According to tradition, the standard in question is the one bearing the Madonna delle Vittorie, now in the cathedral.

Excursions

Villa Imperiale del Casale★★★ *5km/3mi SW. See VILLA IMPERIALE DEL CASALE.*

Aidone

From Piazza Armerina take S 228 (7km/4mi NE). The small town, a few kilometres from the ruins of Morgantina, accommodates the **Museo Archeologico Regionale**: this small regional museum in a former Capuchin monastery displays prehistoric and protohistoric artefacts found in the immediate area. Access to the museum is through the Church of San Francesco, which contains a lovely 17C wooden tabernacle. The exhibits include some fine antefixes from the mid-6C BC, bearing masks of gorgons, lions and maenads. *Open 9am-7pm. €3. ☎ 0935 87 307.*

Scavi di Morgantina

From Aidone follow signs for Scavi di Morgantina (approx 7km/4mi NE of Aidone). Open Apr-Sep, 8am-6.30pm; Oct-Mar, 8am-4pm. €2.60. ☎ 0935 87 307.

The area of **Serra Orlando** has been inhabited since the Bronze Age. During the Iron Age, one particular settlement on the hill became the focal point of the area, and it was this that grew to become Morgantina, probably named after the king of the Morgeti, an Italic tribe from central-southern Italy. In the 5C BC, the town was refounded a short distance beyond the original, at Serra Orlando. The archaeological site has been excavated since 1955: the excavations have brought to light the remains of the Siculi centre that was colonised by the Greeks, grew to prominence in the 1C AD, and was then abandoned.

The **site** extends from one hill, into a small valley and up the next rise. The **agora**, a small **theatre** and, on the northern hill, fragments of mosaics under protective roofing are all in evidence.

Ragusa★★

Ragusa is one of the towns where life was thrown into disarray by the earthquake of January 1693. As in so many other towns, after the earthquake the inhabitants turned their efforts to re-erecting their town. However, there were conflicting opinions about the best way to do this. Rebuilding began in the newly cleared open spaces according to the Baroque ideal vision for a city, planned with wide avenues bisected by perpendicular streets, piazzas and avenues providing calculated vistas of the great monuments, most notably the Cathedral of San Giovanni. Attention was then turned to rebuilding Ibla, the oldest part of the town. Ibla is a delightful medieval site which is fascinating for the contrast between its exuberant Baroque architecture and complex network of narrow, medieval streets.

Location

Population: 69 735. Michelin map 565 Q 26. Ragusa is actually two cities in one: the less interesting upper, more modern town, built to a regular street plan, and the charming lower town situated to the east, which, because of its narrow medieval layout, is best explored on foot. *In Palazzo La Rocca, Via Capitano Bocchieri 33, Ibla; ☎ 0932 62 14 21.*

Neighbouring sights are described in the following chapters: CALTAGIRONE; COMISO; Cava d'ISPICA; MODICA; NOTO.

Walking About

RAGUSA IBLA★★

A visit to the old town will logically begin from the long stairway of Santa Maria delle Scale, which leads down from the new (higher) part of town to the heart of Ragusa Ibla. At certain points, it provides the most splendid **views★★** of the town's rooftops, notably the dome of Santa Maria dell'Itria *(left)* and the neo-Classical dome of the cathedral.

Santa Maria delle Scale was largely rebuilt in the 18C; from the original fabric of the earlier church it preserves the Gothic south aisle, with its elegant **pointed arches★**. Below the second archway is a large Gagini School terracotta panel depicting the Dormition of the Virgin.

In Ibla itself, as if guarding the entrance to the Salita Commendatore *(on the right)*, stands the statue of San Francesco di Paola set against a corner of **Palazzo Cosentini**, which has beautiful **balconies★★** and brackets carved with caricatured figures and masks. This comprises one of the most secluded corners of town, with a warren of intersecting stepped alleyways among which are hidden a number of interesting buildings.

The Church of **Santa Maria dell'Itria** is notable outside for its campanile ornamented at the top with lovely floral panels of maiolica from Caltagirone. Inside, the church contains various chapels articulated with lovely columns, all different (note the spiral columns of the chapels flanking the main altar). Just beyond the church is **Palazzo Nicastro★★** or Vecchia Cancelleria (1760) – the old prison: note its marvellous doorway surmounted by an attractive balcony. The steep slope downhill on the left emerges in front of the flight of steps leading up to the elegantly convex front of the **Chiesa del Purgatorio**.

To get to Via Bocchieri, follow Via del Mercato, turn right into Via Solarino and then left into Via S. Agnese, which leads into Via Tenente di Stefano.

Santa Maria dell'Itria

Palazzo La Rocca

Azienda Autonoma Provinciale del Turismo headquarters. This Baroque *palazzo* still bears traces of the original medieval building that preceded it. An elegant double staircase shows the way up to the main entrance on the first floor where the tourist office is located. The six **balconies★★** along the main façade are ornamented with portrait heads of real people of the day: note the flute, lute and trumpet players, and a mother nursing a baby.

M. Guillot/MICHELIN

San Giorgio

Duomo di San Giorgio★★

When seen from a distance, the most striking feature is the neo-Classical dome with its blue lantern articulated with Corinthian columns, added in the 19C. From the piazza, on the other hand, the eye is drawn up the steep and imposing flight of steps to the wonderful pink façade. The elegant and harmoniously proportioned front elevation comprises a central, slightly convex bay contained by three tiers of columns, flanked by a side bay surmounted by a volute. Delicately carved decoration ornaments the doorway and cornice. The figure of St George on horseback driving a spear into the dragon, is incorporated both into the façade (above the left volute), and as the centrepiece of the beautiful railings at the bottom of the steps. The building was erected in the 18C by **Rosario Gagliardi**.

The **interior**, divided into nave and aisles, has the same frieze along the nave as the one on the exterior, thereby linking the two into an ideal whole.

Piazza

The space before the Duomo is rectangular in shape and set at a slight angle to the church, on a slope. The other buildings enclosing it include **Palazzo Arezzi** which has a wonderful balcony projecting over an archway through to the street beyond; further on, on the opposite side of the square, stands **Palazzo Donnafugata** with its delightful little wooden balcony.

San Giuseppe★

Silence should be observed in the church which is part of the Benedictine monastery.

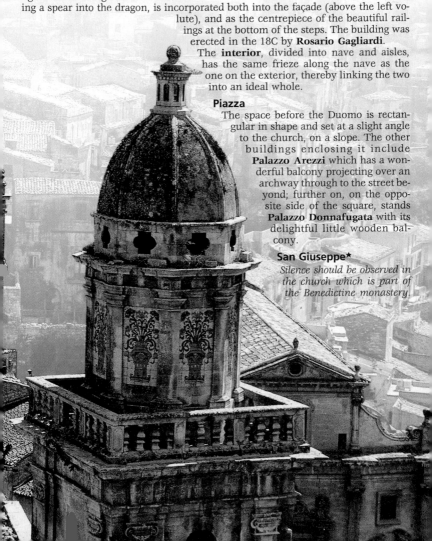

Directory

TRANSPORT

There are daily bus services from Agrigento (2hr 30min), Catania airport (2hr), Palermo (4hr) and Siracusa (approximately 2hr), as well as a train service from Siracusa. Both trains and buses arrive in the modern town. For further information and timetables, contact the tourist office.

WHERE TO EAT

• ***For all budgets***

Il Barocco – *Via Orfanotrofio 29, Ibla – ☎ 0932 65 23 97 – ilbarocco@hot.mail.com – Closed Wed –* ▤ *– €22/26.* This restaurant/pizzeria in the town centre has bright, colourful decor and an informal and homely atmosphere.

Baglio la Pergola – *Contrada Selvaggio (in the stadium district), Ragusa – ☎ 0932 68 64 30 – info@lapergolarg.it – Closed Tue –* ▤ *– €23/33.* A varied selection of main courses and pizzas are on the menu in this restaurant in a typical country *baglio* or stronghold. The traditional Sicilian specialities are particularly recommended.

Locanda Don Serafino – *Via Orfanotrofio 39, Ibla – ☎ 0932 24 87 78 – info@locandadonserafino.it – Closed Tue – €25/41.* The main features of this pleasant restaurant are a piano bar, perfect for an after-dinner drink, and a dining room housed in the converted stables of an aristocratic mansion. The culinary emphasis here is distinctly Sicilian.

WHERE TO STAY

• ***Moderate***

Hotel Montreal – *Via S. Giuseppe 6 (on the corner of Corso Italia), Ragusa – ☎ 0932 62 11 33 – Fax 0932 62 10 26 – montreal@sicily-hotels.it –* ▤ ♿ *– 50 rooms. €58/83* ☕. Despite its lack of frills, this old-fashioned hotel is friendly, impeccably clean and in a good central location.

• ***Expensive***

Eremo della Giubiliana – *Contrada Giubiliana, 7.5km/4.5mi SW of Ragusa – ☎ 0932 66 91 19 – Fax 0932 66 91 29 – info@eremodellagiubiliana.it – Closed 7 Jan-1 Apr –* ⛱ P ▤ *– 9 rooms. €156/240* ☕. This attractive and unusual hotel is housed in a beautifully restored old monastery in the heart of Ibla's upper town. High levels of comfort and the facilities expected of a hotel of this category.

SEASIDE RESORTS

Ragusa is situated close to some of the most popular seaside resorts in southern Sicily, characterised by fine sandy beaches, sand dunes and rocky cliffs. Sampieri, Donnalucata and Scoglitti are perfect for a relaxing holiday, while Marina di Ragusa and Marina di Modica, both of which are exposed to the wind and therefore very popular with surfers and windsurfers, are more suited to outdoor enthusiasts and night owls.

FESTIVALS

I Misteri – This parade and torchlit procession takes place on Good Friday.

Festa di San Giorgio – A re-enactment of the martyrdom of St George is held in Ragusa on the last Sunday in May, ending with a grand firework display.

The elegant front elevation bears a remarkable resemblance to that of San Giorgio, and for this reason has been attributed to Gagliardi. It rises through three tiers of Corinthian columns and figurative statues. The **interior**, an oval space, is enclosed below an oval dome; the splendid floor is a striking combination of maiolica tiles and black pitchstone. Note the gratings which enabled the enclosed nuns to follow mass out of sight of the congregation.

Follow Via XXV Aprile.

Giardino Ibleo

These public gardens containing several religious buildings are laid out at the far end of Ragusa Ibla. Just outside the entrance, on the right, stands the elaborate Catalan Gothic portal of **San Giorgio Vecchio** (15C).

The church just inside the gardens, on the left, is **San Giacomo**, better known as Chiesa del Crocefisso because of the wooden effigy contained within, left of the main altar. It dates in the main from the 14C (the 1693 earthquake caused the lateral aisles to collapse; these were never rebuilt), and encloses a ceiling painted with historical panels from 1754 – unfortunately several are missing. The *trompe l'oeil* dome is especially effective. *For information on admission times, call ☎ 0932 62 14 21.*

To the side of the garden stands the **Chiesa dei Cappuccini**. This contains a lovely **triptych★** by **Pietro Novelli** showing the Virgin Mary flanked by St Agatha and St Lucy. The figure in the left-hand section of the central panel looking out of the picture is a self-portrait.

A wonderful **view** from the gardens extends over the Irminio Valley.

Archaeological excavation conducted on a site just beyond the garden has unearthed a street and residential quarter dating from the Classical period underlying various medieval constructions.

Further along Via Pescheria, on the right-hand side, note the **Chiesa di San Francesco all'Immacolata.** The church, largely rebuilt in the 17C, preserves a 13C Chiaramonte doorway *(west flank)*.

NEW TOWN

The "modern" town has been developed on a framework of straight, parallel streets intersecting at right angles to each other, to form a regular grid-like pattern up the side of the Patro hill. The elegant **Via Roma** bisects the town on a parallel axis to the side of the hill; the perpendicular **Corso Italia** runs down towards Ibla between wonderful buildings.

On the right is Piazza San Giovanni, overlooked by the church with which it shares its name.

Cattedrale di San Giovanni – The cathedral dates from the early 18C. Its imposing Baroque front elevation, flanked by its campanile, has a broad, raised terrace.

Further along Corso Italia, on the left, is the 19C Chiesa del Collegio di Maria Addolorata, with **Palazzo Lupis** – note the fine brackets – beyond. There follows Via San Vito *(right)*: n° 156 is **Palazzo Zacco**, marked by a great coat of arms supported on decorative brackets on the corner. Note the balcony **brackets** projecting from the lateral façade carved with figures and grotesques. Back in Corso Italia, but a short distance further along on the left, rises **Palazzo Bertini** which was built towards the end of the 18C. Three large **masks★** peer down from the carved window keystones, as if watching the pedestrian traffic. According to tradition, these personify a pauper, who is ugly, hungry and toothless *(left)*; a nobleman, serene in the assurance of his social status; and a merchant, wearing a turban and a self-satisfied expression, assured by the weight of money in his pocket.

Museo Archeologico Ibleo – *Via Natalelli; under the Ponte Nuovo, on the first floor of a building, above a garage.*

The local archaeological museum displays artefacts recovered from the surrounding area. Among the most interesting exhibits is a reconstruction of the Classical necropoli at Camarina and Rito, and one of the kiln at Scornavacche. *Open 9am-1.30pm and 4-7.30pm. €2. ☎ 0932 62 29 63.*

Tour

SEASIDE

110km/69mi from Ragusa, finishing in Comiso – allow one day. From Ragusa take S 194 to Modica (12km/7.5mi SE).

Modica *See MODICA*

Take S 115 to Pozzallo (20km/12.5mi SE).

Pozzallo

This sleepy hamlet lies on the edge of a long beach. Its most characteristic landmark is the **Torre dei Conti Cabrera**, which was originally built by the local count as a watchtower at a time when pirates frequently assaulted the community. Although destroyed by the 1693 earthquake, it has been rebuilt as it was.

Continue along the coast road.

This coast road passes the resorts of **Marina di Modica** and **Sampieri**.

Turn right at the junction to Scicli and continue 10km/6mi to the town (see p 258).

After 6km/4mi the coast road passes through the **Riserva Naturale della Foce dell'Irpinio**, before arriving at **Marina di Ragusa**⛱, a popular seaside resort in summer.

The **Parco Archeologico di Kaucana** is located nearby, between Punta Secca and Casuzze. There are two entrances to the archaeological site: one along the coastal road, the other on the road from Punta Secca to Marina di Ragusa. It encloses the ruins of a residential area and a small palaeo-Christian church. *Closed for restoration at the time of going to press. ☎ 0932 91 61 42.*

Continue along the coast road.

C CAPPELLO SCULPTURE COLLECTION

Carmelo Cappello, a native of Ragusa (b 1912), began to work in the 1930s. His style, which evolved from being highly figurative in the early years to becoming pure abstraction in his latest creations, is well represented in this small, but interesting collection. *Il freddoloso* (*Shivering with Cold* – 1938), one of his most famous works, is a realistic figure charged with great expression. In the later works, facial features become abstracted by being reduced to a minimum: compare the expressive faces of the two women with well-defined noses and eyes (though no hair or mouth) in *Le prime stelle (The First Stars)* to the faces of the two athletes in Acrobati (1953-54). In this latter work, individual personality and detail has been distilled, abstracted and replaced by a concentration on rhythm and movement of line. Cappello's latest works are austere studies of pure line, clinically cold (an impression imparted by the polished steel) yet which twist and merge, attempting to encapsulate in form the fluid dynamics of the universe.

The collection is housed in the industrial estate (ASI) south of Ragusa, in Contrada Mugno *(the junction at Km 321.700 on S 115). Open Mon-Thu, 9am-12.30pm and 3.30-5pm; Fri, 9am-12.30pm. Closed Sat-Sun.*

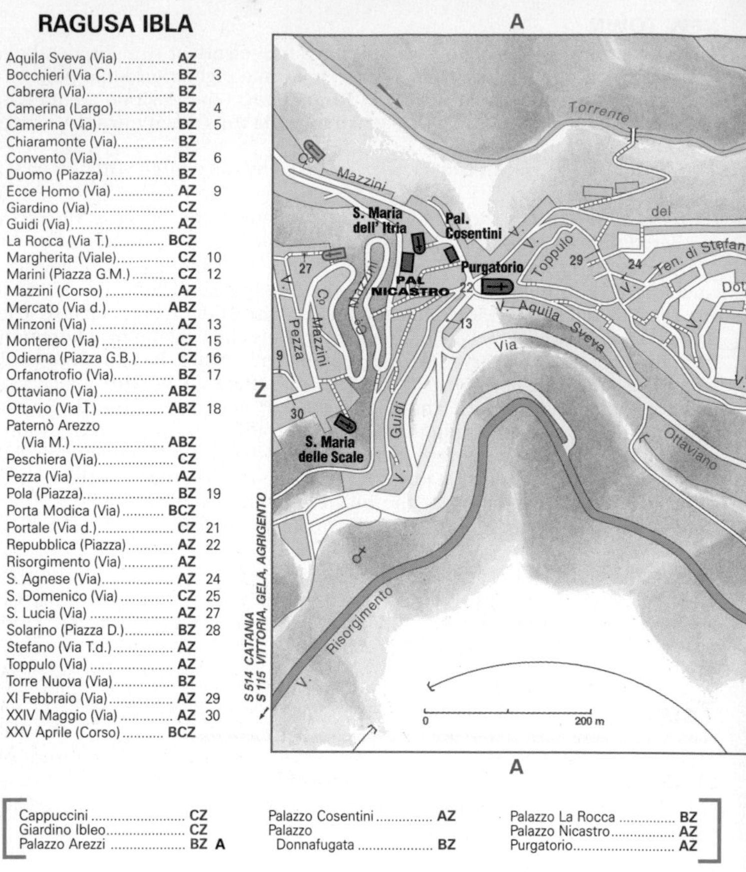

Rovine di Camarina

Open 9am-2pm and 3-6pm. €2.50. ☎ 0932 82 60 04.

Camarina was founded in 598 BC as a Greek town at the behest of Syracuse; it suffered assaults on many occasions, only to be rebuilt and then finally destroyed by the Romansin 258 BC. **Excavation** has revealed the remains of a temple dedicated to Athena (incorporated in the masonry of the 19C building which now houses the museum), sections of plateia B, the market-place and stoa – the portico over the covered market – and a residential quarter dating from Hellenistic times *(marked by the fence on the other side of the road).*

Museo Archeologico Regionale di Camarina – *(♿) Open 9am-2pm and 3-6pm (last admission 30min before closing). €2.50. ☎ 0932 82 60 04.*

In the first room the most recent finds recovered as a result of ongoing work are displayed; these are gradually replaced and transferred to the permanent collection. The layout is therefore subject to reorganisation. The sea off Camarina has proved to conceal a wealth of treasures lost in numerous wrecks: a wonderful **Corinthian bronze helmet★** (6C-5C BC), an Attic-Etruscan helmet (4C BC), an elegant bronze and enamel perfume container (2C AD), and a hoard of more than 1 000 bronze coins (AD 275). There is also an unusual set of **lead weights** recovered from the seabed from the area below the market-place. The museum possesses a vast collection of Corinthian (older and therefore more crudely made) and Attic **amphorae★**. The Etruscan and Punic amphorae are different, being more elongated. The section devoted to the Archaic period contains a fine aryballos (a small bucket-like vessel used for drawing water from a well) decorated with two lions facing each other (228T1), from the necropolis at Rifriscolaro.

From Camarina head inland to Donnafugata (12km/7.5mi).

Castello di Donnafugata★

♿ Guided tours only, Tue-Fri, 9am-1pm (also afternoon visits in summer); Sat-Sun, 9am-4pm. Closed Mon. €5. ☎ 0932 61 93 33.

The oldest part of the castle (which includes the square tower) dates back to the mid-17C when the Donnafugata fiefdom was acquired by Vincenzo Arezzo La Rocca. The building was continuously altered until the early 20C, when Corrado Arezzo transformed the façade into what can be seen today.

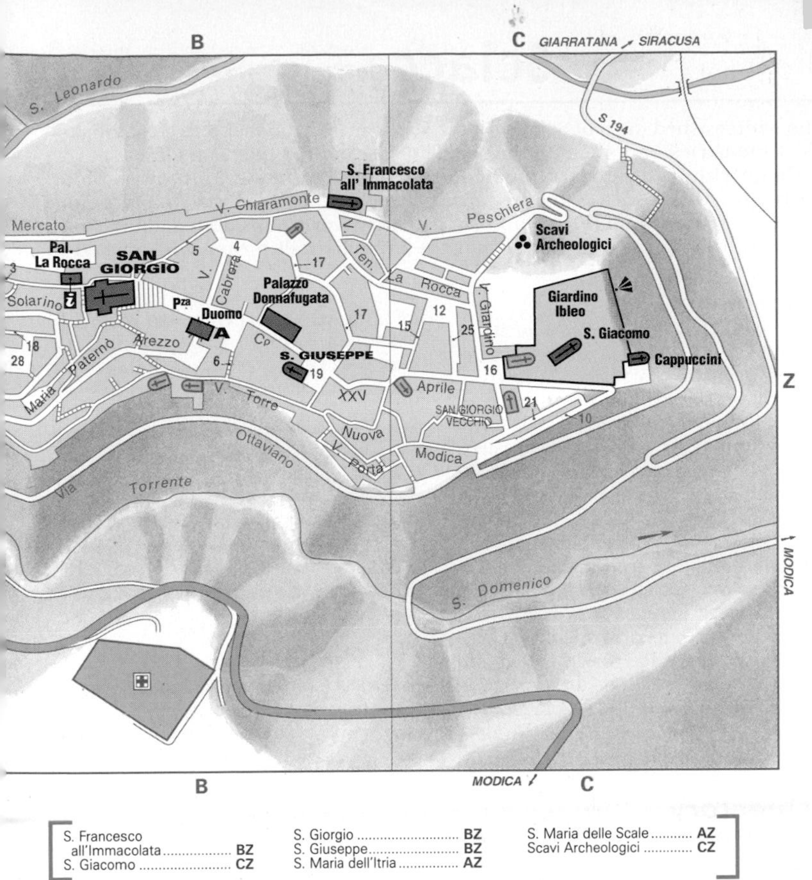

What is striking about the exterior of the castle is the elegant Venetian Gothic loggia which dominates the central section of the main façade. The trefoil arches become a recurrent motif repeated in the two-light windows throughout the building.

Origins of the name Donnafugata

The name, which is Arabic in origin, is misleading. It does not, in fact, refer, as first appearances might suggest, to a woman fleeing some tyrannical husband or father (*fuga* in Italian means "escape" or "flight"), nor to one of the legends that linger in some popular memory, but is a free interpretation and transcription of *Ayn as Jafât* (meaning Fountain of Health), which in Sicilian dialect became Ronnafuata and so was corrupted to its modern form.

Gardens – The large garden, shaded first by large banyan trees *(Ficus magnolioides)*, then by other Mediterranean and exotic species (succulents and cluster pines), conceals various follies intended to charm and bemuse its visitors, like the round temple and a coffee house (where refreshments could be taken), the stone maze and several artificial caves encrusted with fake stalactites (below the temple).

Villa – The first floor is open to the public. At the top of the black stone (*pietra pece* in Italian) staircase, ornamented with neo-Classical statues, is the **Salone degli Stemmi**, named after the armorial crests of great Sicilian noble families painted on the walls. Among the suites of rooms are some with delicately painted *trompe l'oeil* ceilings. These include the stucco-decorated **Salone degli Specchi** (the Hall of Mirrors), the **Billiard Room** and **Music Room**, each with painted landscapes projecting out beyond the walls, and the bedroom of the Princess of Navarre, paved in black *pietra pece* (a bitumous limestone mined locally, from which pitch is made) and white limestone where, it is said, Princess Bianca was kept segregated from Count Cabrera (an anachronistic legend, given that the princess lived in the 14C). The **Stanza del Signore** and the **Fumoir** are beautifully furnished; the decoration of the latter, a smoking room, is perfectly appropriate to its function. It is papered with pipe motifs and the ceiling is painted with medallions filled with playing cards and beautiful peacocks at the corners.

The castle has been featured in the making of many well-known films including the *La Giara* scene in the film *Chaos* by the Taviani brothers.

From here, continue to Comiso (16km/10mi N, see COMISO).

Sciacca

The whitewashed town of Sciacca is striking for its Arab feel. Long-established local industries here include the thermal spa and fishing, as a glance at the harbour with its fleet of fishing boats and backdrop of attractive and colourful houses will testify. Sciacca's main attraction, however, is its prodigious output of maiolica on sale in a host of pottery workshops dotted about town. It was in the waters off Sciacca that the French airship *Dixmude* crashed in 1923.

Location

Population: 41 1626. Michelin map 565 O 21 – Agrigento. Physical stamina is required for a visit to Sciacca, a town of steep streets perched on a flank of Monte Kronio by the sea's edge. Natural terracing divides the town into three sections: the narrow, winding streets of the medieval district of Terravecchia lie to the north of Via Licata; the town's major monuments can be seen between Via Licata and Piazza Scandaliato; while the port area extends beyond Piazza Scandaliato. Sciacca has countless flights of steps and narrow alleyways, so visitors are advised to park their car and explore the town on foot. *Corso Vittorio Emanuele 94, ☎ 0925 86 247 and Corso Vittorio Emanuele 84; ☎ 0925 21 182; www.aziendaturismosciacca.it/home.htm*

Neighbouring sights are described in the following chapters: AGRIGENTO; CASTELVETRANO; Antica città di SELINUNTE.

The Island that Came and Went

July 1831: at the time, anyone looking out to sea from Sciacca was unlikely to imagine what was about to happen. For, in a very short space of time, a great land mass emerged from the water. Rather than being some monster rising from the underworld, this apparition was a volcanic outcrop that gently settled back into a truncated cone. This precipitated a huge stir and prompted a host of heatedly contested theories. The island was christened **Ferdinandea**, in honour of the reigning Spanish monarch. But it was short lived: after a mere five months, the island disappeared into oblivion.

Directory

Where to Eat

• *For all budgets*

Porto San Paolo – *Largo San Paolo 1, Sciacca – ☎ 0925 27 982 – Closed Wed, two weeks in Nov and two weeks in Apr – – €18/30 + 10% service.* The Porto San Paolo specialises in fish dishes. Choose between the rustic ambience and wood decor of the dining room and the summer veranda overlooking the port.

Villa Palocla – *Contrada Raganella, 4km/2.5mi W of Sciacca – ☎ 0925 90 28 12 – info@villapalocla.it – – €20/30 + 10% service.* This villa has a truly Sicilian flavour, with its garden planted with fragrant citrus trees surrounding a mid-18C, late Baroque style building. Offering both accommodation and a restaurant, the Villa Palocla's menu is dominated by an excellent range of fish dishes.

Hostaria del Vicolo – *Vicolo Sammaritano 10, Sciacca – ☎ 0925 23 071 – Closed Mon and 14 Oct-1 Nov – – €23/36.* This small, elegant restaurant in the heart of Sciacca serves typical, traditional Sicilian cuisine enlivened with contemporary touches. Good wine list.

Where to Stay

Also see p 154.

SCIACCA

• *Budget*

Verdetecnica – *Via Monte Kronio 22, Sciacca – ☎ 0925 81 133 – Fax 0925 81 133 – verdetecnica@tin.it – – 6 apartments €70.* A small gem of a hotel situated on a hill overlooking Sciacca and comprising six apartments, all equipped with bathroom and kitchen of varying sizes. Simple decor, in tune with the surrounding countryside. Minimum stay of five days in August.

SAMBUCA DI SICILIA

• *Budget*

Lago Arancio Vacanze – *Contrada Arancio, Sambuca di Sicilia – ☎ 0923 94 60 03 – Fax 0923 94 13 71 – €25/50.* This small rural hotel with just a handful of rooms enjoys a panoramic and peaceful location. Activities on offer at the lake include canoeing, water-skiing and fishing.

Taking a Break

Bar Roma – *Piazza Dogana 12, Sciacca, ☎ 0925 21 239.* Aurelio Licata, the owner of this bar, is famous for his lemon *granita* (crushed ice drink), which, served with a delicious brioche, is considered a typical Sicilian breakfast.

Festivals

Carnevale – Sciacca's carnival is one of the most famous in Sicily, with a magnificent procession of allegorical carts.

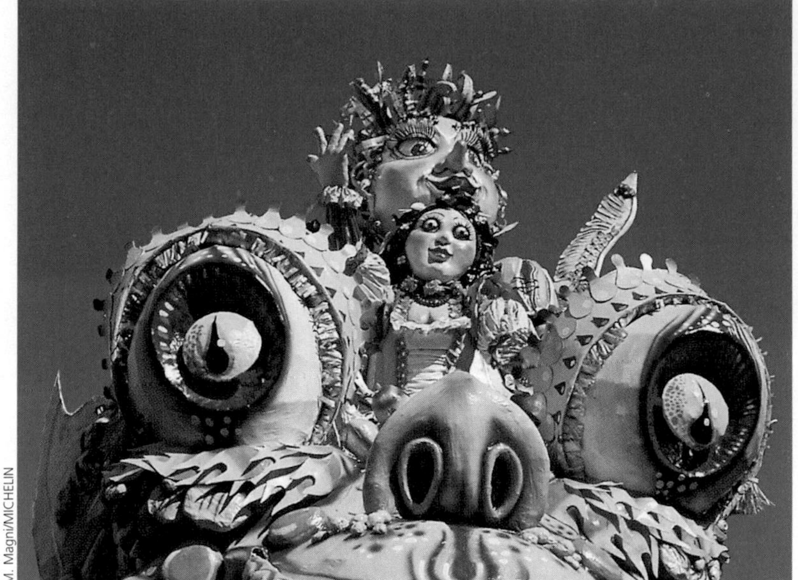
M. Magni/MICHELIN

Carnival colours

Walking About

HISTORIC CENTRE

The perfect kernel at the heart of Sciacca is **Piazza Scandaliato** with its broad terrace overlooking the multicoloured harbour packed with boats, and the open sea beyond. Dominating the west side of the square is the 18C Church of **San Domenico**; the longer flank accommodates the former **Jesuit College** (complete with fine 17C cloisters), now used as the town hall. Behind lies Piazza del Duomo.

Duomo

The cathedral was founded by the Normans (from which time only the exterior wall of the three apses survives), and rebuilt in the 1600s. The Baroque façade remains unfinished. The **interior** nave and side aisles preserve various works of interest. The barrel-vaulted nave is frescoed (1829) by the local artist Tommaso Rossi with the Apocalypse and several episodes from the life of Mary Magdelene. The chapel to the right of the chancel contains a lovely Renaissance marble altarpiece (1581) by Antonio Gagini; its walls are hung with paintings of scenes from Christ's Passion.

The central thoroughfare, **Corso Vittorio Emanuele**, runs to the right of the Duomo, past the 15C-17C **Palazzo Arone Tagliavia** *(on the right)*, its fine castellated frontage accommodating three pointed entrances and, above the central arch, a lovely three-light Gothic window. A little further on the left sits the 19C Imperial-style **Palazzo San Giacomo** (or Tagliavia), with its south-facing façade graced with four sphinx-like herms. The Venetian neo-Gothic front of the building overlooks Piazza Friscia.

In **Viale della Vittoria** which leads off the piazza, on the right, stands the **Convento di San Francesco**. This, after being completely restored, has been transformed into a conference-cum-exhibition centre. The fine monastery cloisters display sculptures by contemporary artists, including three large *Bathers* by Bergomi (1989). *Open Mon-Sat, 8am-1pm. Closed on national hols. No charge. For information on afternoon admission times, call ☎ 0925 96 11 11; www.termesciacca.it*

At the far end of Viale della Vittoria, **Santa Maria delle Giummare** (entrance in Via Valverde) rises tall above the surrounding buildings. This was founded by the Normans and rebuilt in the 16C. The actual church is contained within the main body of the building (which has a Baroque doorway); the two square "towers" provide residential quarters for the dependent monastery. The austerity of the battlemented façade is in part relieved by two decorative two-light windows.

A little further on the right lie the ruins of **Castello della Luna**. This was built in the late 14C, rebuilt in the 16C and almost completely destroyed in the 19C. Today, only the perimeter walls and an imposing cylindrical tower remain. The street passes in front of the castle before leading down to the lovely Norman church, San Nicolò la Latina.

San Nicolò la Latina

Open summer, 6.30-7pm; otherwise 5.30-6pm. Donations welcome. ☎ 0925 21 315.
This church was founded in the early part of the 12C by Giulietta, the daughter of Roger I. Its simple façade has a doorway with a heavily moulded surround, and three similarly accented single openings above (the two side ones are blind). The interior comprises a Latin-cross plan, complete with nave, short transepts and three semicircular apses typical of transitional Arabo-Norman prototypes. The light filters through small, single openings set deep into the wall, reminiscent of arrow-slits.

Climb back up to the castle ruins and follow Via Giglio to the town gate, **Porta di San Calogero**, where remains of the medieval walls may be seen. On Piazza Noceto is situated **Santa Maria dell'Itria**, an annexe to the larger Chiesa Madre with a fine Baroque façade, **San Michele Arcangelo** (17C-18C). Inside it shelters a lovely 18C gallery and a carved, painted wooden organ case set against the back wall; on the right look for the fine Catalan Gothic cross and, in the south aisle, an altarpiece of St Jerome dating from 1454.

Continue down towards Corso Vittorio Emanuele to the junction with Via Licata which accommodates two fine 18C buildings: Palazzo Inveges, and further up on the right, Palazzo Ragusa. At the next intersection with Via Gerardi, turn left: on the corner with Corso Vittorio Emanuele is the **Palazzo Steripinto**, a Catalan-style *palazzo* dating from the 15C. Its splendid façade is articulated with diamond-cut rustication and two-light openings; it is battlemented with Ghibelline merlons.

Via Gerardi opens out into Piazza del Carmine, named after the Carmine church which stands there, laid out before the 16C town gateway, **Porta San Salvatore**, ornamented by two lions facing each other. The Norman-built **Chiesa del Carmine**, although remodelled several times, retains its original rose window.

Santa Margherita

Open Mon-Fri, 8am-2pm and 4.30-7pm; Sat, 8am-2pm only; Sun and public hols by appointment only. ☎ 0925 20 478; www.comune.sciacca.Ag.it
The original church fabric dates from the 13C; the alterations were implemented in the late 16C. The main front has a lovely Catalan Gothic doorway, although the Renaissance-Gothic side door on the left side with *St Margaret and the Dragon* by Pietro da Bonitate and Francesco Laurana (apparently only the figure of Mary Magdalene on the left jamb is his) is more famous. Inside, the coffered ceiling is painted to suggest a star-spangled sky. A monumental 19C organ takes up most of the back wall, and a splendid marble altarpiece in the right chapel relates scenes from the life of St Margaret.

The other church nearby with a fine stone doorway is **Chiesa di San Gerlando.** A little further on the left stands the 15C **Palazzo Perollo**: its main façade has three late Gothic three-light windows and its inner courtyard is furnished with a lovely, although dilapidated, Catalan staircase.

Worth a Visit

Palazzo Scaglione★

Piazza Don Minzoni (near the Duomo). Open 9am-1pm and 3-7pm. Closed Mon afternoon, Sun and public hols. No charge. ☎ 0925 28 025.
This 18C residence, now a museum, displays the *objets d'art* and other works of art collected in the 19C by Francesco Scaglione. All the rooms are crowded with pictures – the majority by Sicilian painters – engravings, coins, archaeological artefacts, bronze sculptures and ceramics in a clear demonstration of the eclecticism and encyclopaedic collecting mania so typical of the period. The last room contains a fine 18C ivory and mother-of-pearl crucifix. The *palazzo* has maiolica floors and frescoed ceilings throughout.

Thermal baths

Viale delle Terme, SE of the town. Open 8am-1pm. Closed Sun and national hols. No charge. For information on afternoon admission times, call ☎ 0925 96 11 11; www.termesciacca.it
The thermal treatments in the region surrounding Sciacca have been famous since Antiquity, yet it was only sometime in the mid-19C that a spa was opened outside the town centre in the Valle dei Bagni *(this has still to be restored and reopened)*. The most modern thermal facilities at the **Nuovo Stabilimento Termale** date from 1938: this extensive, Liberty-style complex lies southeast of the town, right by the edge of the sea, in its own private landscaped gardens. Here, the naturally occurring sulphurous waters are used in mud therapy (for relieving arthritis), balneotherapy (recommended for osteo-arthritis and skin conditions) and inhalation

treatments. Other such degenerative conditions are treated with various therapies also available from the Stufe di San Calogero on Monte Kronio, and at the thermal pools at Molinelli. These baths are supplemented by mineral-rich waters that issue from the ground at a constant temperature of 34° C. Such treatments have proved effective for skin conditions as well.

Excursions

Monte Kronio

Leave Sciacca along Via Porta S. Calogero. 7km/4mi. The haul to the summit provides ample opportunity to survey the wonderfully spacious **panorama★★** panning in an arc of 240° over the coast, the plain of Sciacca and the bare mountains inland. At the top sits the **Santuario di San Calogero**, built by the Franciscans. The natural occurrence of caves in which hot vapours are caught has been exploited to provide steam baths since Antiquity. The largest and most well known is the Stufe di San Calogero. The rational explanation for the phenomenon is that a vein of hot water runs deep within the mountain; when it comes into contact with direct heat the water evaporates and escapes upwards, mingling with the air as it rises through the fissures and cracks in the rock, to break through into the open at a temperature of 40°C.

The vapours are considered by the Italians as having great therapeutic powers, especially in cases of rheumatism, skin disease, gynaecological problems and allergic reactions.

The son of the Earth and the Sky

The name of this isolated peak (386m/1 266ft), set in a deserted landscape, suggests an immediate association with Cronus (Greek Kronos), the god of time and one of the oldest figures of the pantheon, born out of a union between Mother Earth (Gaea) and her son, the god of heaven (Uranus). Banished to Tartarus along with his other siblings (the Titans) by his father, Cronus was assisted by his mother in rising up against Uranus and castrating him; there followed a Golden Age on earth that lasted until his youngest (oldest in Homer) son Zeus, assisted by the Cyclops and the Hundred-handed Giants, declared war on Mount Olympus and the other Titans: at this point the myths vary in detail. According to some, the gods were defeated by thunderbolts and falling stones before being imprisoned in Tartarus; other accounts prevalent in Sicily relate how Zeus inveigled the gods by inebriating them with ambrosia and honeyed mead, chaining them up as they slept, and relegating them to a group of islands called the Isole dei Beati (Islands of the Blessed).

The other legendary hero associated with this place is Daedalus who, being an expert on labyrinths, as is well known, decided to redirect the boiling vapours that emanated from cracks in the rock in order to harness their power: and so the origins of the *stufe vaporose* – the steamy caves – are explained.

Stufe di San Calogero – *Open daily except Sun, 8am-1pm. Closed on national hols. €1. For information on afternoon admission times, call ☎ 0925 96 11 11; www.termesciacca.it*

The caves were either inhabited or regularly used for religious practices until the Bronze Age; they were finally abandoned some time around 2 000 BC when steam began to pour into them, possibly as a result of a landslide, making permanent occupation impossible. After a period of complete neglect, the caves began to be used again some time during the Greek occupation, possibly as a result of the steam being seen to emanate from the mountainside and interpreted as a mysterious (and hence divine) phenomenon. Indeed, numerous artefacts have been recovered from the caves, especially vases and votive figurines *(some of which are displayed in the archaeological museum at Agrigento).* The various names by which the caves are now known are those bestowed upon them by a monk who came here in the 4C; having quickly realised the therapeutic potential of the vapours, he set about dividing the caves into rooms with stone benches on which to seat his patients. The largest caves include l'Antro di Dedalo and the Grotta degli Animali. The Grotta del Santo nearby, probably provided living quarters for St Calogero, who is depicted in the maiolica icon above the altar (15C).

Today, the caves are incorporated in the modern spa complex Grande Albergo delle Stufe.

Next to the Stufe, a small **antiquarium** displays artefacts found in the immediate vicinity. *Open Tue-Sat, 9am-1pm and 3-7pm; Mon, Sun and public hols, 9am-1pm. No charge. ☎ 0925 28 989.*

Castello Incantato

2km/1.2mi W: take Via Figuli out of Sciacca and follow signs for Agrigento (S 115). (♿) Open Apr-Sep, daily except Mon, 10am-noon and 4-8pm; Oct-Mar, daily except Mon, 9am-1pm and 3-5pm. Donations welcome. ☎ 0925 99 30 44; www.comune.sciacca.ag.it

This incredible garden, peopled with sculpted stone heads, was conceived in 1913 by Filippo Bentivegna (1888-1967). Over a period of half a century, *Filippu delli Testi* – as he is called here – sculpted these faces out of the rock in every corner of his extensive estate, with expressions that range from the worried to the serene.

Tour

VALLE DEL BELICE AND VALLE DEL SOSIO

160km/100mi – allow one day.

Take S 115 towards Castelvetrano and then S 188 as far as Portella Misilbesi. From here turn right to Sambuca di Sicilia, still following S 188.

The road skirts around **Lago Arancio**, a man-made lake of major environmental importance because of the storks that inhabit the area. The lake is now a LIPU (Lega Italiana Protezione Uccelli – Italian Association for the Protection of Birds) reserve.

Sambuca di Sicilia

The town reclines lazily on a gentle slope. Noble *palazzi* run the length of the central street Corso Umberto I: at the far end, a stairway provides access to a viewing terrace; behind stands the hamlet's main church.

From Sambuca, follow signs for Scavi di Monte Adranone (7km/4mi).

Scavi di Monte Adranone

Open Tue-Sat, 9am-1pm and 3-7pm; Sun and public hols, 9am-1pm. No charge. ☎ 0925 28 989.

The Ancient Greek settlement (6C BC) overlies another earlier, indigenous, one. The site, perched high on a mountain top, overlooking the surrounding countryside, is naturally defended on one side and reinforced by strong defensive walls on the other two, making it into a vaguely triangular area. The town, loosely identified with Adranon, a place documented by the Classical historian Diodorus Siculus, was probably destroyed in 250 BC during the First Punic War.

Tour – Outside the walls, on the southeastern side, lay the **necropolis** containing subterranean funeral chambers, including the **Tomba della Regina** lined with square-cut blocks of tufa.

A short distance further on stands the **Porta Sud** (south gate) framed between turrets. The building nestling within has been identified as a farmstead. The way up to the **acropolis** passes on the right a large rectangular construction, probably intended for public use; ahead extends a complex of stores, shops and houses. At the top, the **acropolis** overlooks the entire valley: the **view★★** up here pans round in a complete circle, taking in the rooftops of the livinghamlet of Sambuca and **Lago Arancio** below.

The most significant building would have been the large **Punic Temple** with, on the right, its large cistern. The rectangular temple wouldhave comprised an inner sanctum open to the sky, with a *cella* adjacent on the eastern side.

Continue along the road for a few kilometres and then turn right to Bisacquino.

The road runs through an attractive **landscape★** of rolling hills and steep mountains, passing the panoramic abbey of **Santa Maria del Bosco** (16C-17C) on the right. The abbey was badly damaged by the terrible earthquake which struck the Belice region in 1968.

Bisacquino

The birthplace of Frank Capra (1897-1991), the director of the film *It's A Wonderful Life*, Bisacquino is a small town attractively perched on the slopes of Monte Triona. Dominated by the impressive dome of the 18C Chiesa Madre, the town has an intricate Arab-influenced layout. The majolica bell tower of Santa Maria delle Grazie stands on the same square as the church. The town's other monument of note is the unusual triangular-shaped bell tower of San Francesco, also decorated with majolica. A number of typical scenes relating to rural life and traditional tradeshave been recreated in the interesting **Museo Etnologico** in Via Orsini. *Open Mon-Fri, 8am-2pm (also 3-6pm Tue and Thu); Sat-Sun, by appointment only. No charge. ☎ 091 83 08 047.*

From Bisacquino follow S 188c towards Palermo and take the exit to the 17C sanctuary of the **Madonna del Balzo**. A stunning **view★★** of the surrounding area can be enjoyed 900m/2 950ft above the clearing opposite the sanctuary.

Return to S 188. From Bisacquino, head towards Palazzo Adriano.

The road passes the small **Lago Gammauta**, which can be explored by making a short diversion.

Palazzo Adriano

The focal point of this village, in which Tornatore filmed part of *Nuovo Cinema Paradiso*, is the attractive **Piazza Umberto I★**. This elegant square is paved with white stone and lined with buildings that show a certain harmony of architectural style, including the Greek-Byzantine church of Santa Maria A Catholic church of Santa Maria del Lume. Houses to the n clustered around the castle ruins.

From Palazzo the road continues to Prizzi, passing through tain scenery.

Prizzi

Standing at an altitude of over 1 000m/3 300ft, Prizzi enj framed by the Sicani mountains. An unusual measurem erected immediately after the unification of Italy, can be a Corso Umberto I. A little further on, the attractive **Piazza Sparacio** – not much more than a widening of the street between the houses – is decorated with murals, which, in combination with other façades in the town, form a kind of open-air museum. The oldest part of town, with its network of narrow streets winding around the Chiesa Madre and the castle, is situated to the north of Corso Umberto. The town comes to life on Easter Sunday, when the Ballo dei Diavoli festival is held here.

Return to S 188 and retrace your route for 30km/19mi. Turn left at the junction to **Chiusa Sclàfani**, an attractive town which has retained its historic medieval centre. The town is built around a Benedictine monastery, which has an attractive garden next door.

10km/6mi after Chiusa Sclàfani, follow signs to Caltabellotta.

Caltabellotta

The two roads up to the town offer wonderful **views★★** over the surrounding valley; the route via **Sant'Anna** is especially scenic. Caltabellotta enjoys a fabulous **position★★**, 900m/2 950ft above sea level. Its name (deriving from the Arabic *Kal'at al-ballut* meaning Fortress of the Oaks) seems to conjure up a picture of the town precariously clinging to a bare spur of rock. Given its high position, which made it difficult to storm, Caltabellotta came to be considered over the centuries as a place of safety, and as a consequence became transformed into a military outpost. It was here that the Angevins signed a peace treaty that sealed an end to the War of the Sicilian Vespers (1302).

The tallest point is claimed by the chapel and hermitage of San Pellegrino, and the ruins of the Norman castle that blend into the landscape. At the foot of the castle stand the extant Arabo-Norman **Chiesa Matrice** and **Chiesa del Salvatore** with its fine late Gothic doorway.

The road heading down to Sciacca offers splendid **views★★** of the valley below.

Segesta★★★

Only the pure, harmonious lines of the Doric temple and the evocative Ancient theatre, which is still used today for plays and concerts, remain of this city.

Location

Michelin map 565 2N 0 – Trapani. Segesta occupies a splendid **position★★**, among gently sloping hills of yellow ochre and ruddy brown that, at times, are thrown into marked contrast by patches of variegated greens around the excavated areas. This timeless landscape is presided over by the majestic silhouette of the Doric temple, one of the most perfectly preserved monuments to survive from Antiquity, standing on a hill surrounded by a deep valley, framed by Monte Bernardo and Monte Barbaro where the theatre is situated.

Neighbouring sights are described in the following chapters: ERICE; GIBELLINA.

Background

Ancient Segesta was probably founded by the Elimi; under Greek sponsorship, it soon ranked, like Erice (Eryx), among the leading towns of the Mediterranean basin. In the 5C BC, it was pitched against its great rival Selinunte (Selinus). In an attempt to rally its defences against this threat, Segesta appealed for help from Athens in 415 BC, but these reinforcements were defeated by Syracuse whose forces were allied to Selinunte. In 409 BC, Segesta turned to Carthage for support; on landing in Sicily, these troops destroyed both Selinus and Himera. In turn, Segesta was destroyed by the Syracusan tyrant Agathocles in 307 BC but rose again under the Romans. Subsequent developments are not documented, although it is thought that the city probably succumbed to further damage by the Vandals in the

B. Kaufmann/MICHELIN

5C AD. What is certain is that the area was inhabited in medieval times, as ruins of a Norman castle and a small three-apsed basilica (later abandoned and rebuilt as a hermitage in the 15C), situated in the northern part of the ancient acropolis, testify. This part of the site extended over two areas separated by a hollow. The south-eastern section was predominantly residential, whereas the north was populated by public buildings, including the theatre.

Worth a Visit

Temple open in summer, 9am-7pm; otherwise, 9am-5pm. Last admission 1hr before closing. €4. A shuttle bus service operates to the theatre (€1). Bar and restaurant. ☎ 0924 95 23 56.

Tempio★★★

Built in 430 BC (although scholars are divided about its exact date), the temple is a Doric building of extraordinarily harmonious proportions.

The 36 columns of the peristyle are almost completely intact, their gloriously mellow golden-tinged limestone flattered by their smooth finish. The fact that the shafts are unfluted, coupled with the absence of a *cella*, has prompted the suggestion that the temple was abandoned before completion. This theory is dismissed by some scholars who claim that the lack of a *cella* (which usually comprised the first part of the sanctuary to be undertaken) might indicate that the building was intended to consist merely of a peristyle, making it a pseudo-temple. Furthermore, the mystery surrounding the purpose such a construction would serve is exacerbated by the lack of any indication as to which deity might have been the dedicatee.

The road up to the theatre *(approx 2km/1.2mi: regular minibus service)* provides fabulous **views**★★ back over the temple. Before the theatre, on the right, are the remains of the Hermitage of San Leone, with a single apse, built over the foundation of an earlier three-apsed church and, behind it, the ruins of the Norman castle.

Teatro★

The theatre was built in the 3C BC during the Hellenistic period, while the area was under Roman domination. It consists of a perfect semicircle with a diameter of 63m/207ft, apparently slotted into a rocky slope. The tiers of seats face west towards the hills, beyond which, to the right, may be glimpsed the broad Bay of Castellammare.

FESTIVALS

In July and August, the theatre hosts an impressive programme of concerts and contemporary and classical plays. The atmosphere at the theatre is particularly moving during the performances of music, poetry and literature, known as *albe* (dawn), which take place at 5am. For further information, contact the Calatafimi Segesta tourist office on ☎ 0924 95 46 19.

Antica città di Selinunte★★

Selinunte is derived from the name for the sweet-smelling he... called *Selinon*: wild celery *(Heleioselinon – Apium graveolens)*. This he... widely used to crown victors at the Isthmian games and to make wreaths for adorning the tombs of the dead. It grew in profusion in this part of Sicily and appears on the first coins minted by the town.

Location

Michelin map 565 O 20 – Trapani. The archaeological site is divided into four areas: the first, spread across the hill on the eastern side, contains three large temples, one-having been re-erected in 1957; the second, on the hill to the west and surrounded by walls, comprises the acropolis, south of the third area, where the ruins of the ancient town can be seen; the fourth, lying west of the acropolis, beyond the River Modione, also consisted of a sacred precinct complete with temples and sanctuaries. From the motorway, take the Castelvetrano exit and follow S 115d to Marinella. Bus services run to the site from Agrigento, Castelvetrano, Marsala, Mazara del Vallo and Trapani. It is possible to drive from the eastern temples to the acropolis.

Neighbouring sights are described in the following chapters: CASTELVETRANO; MAZARA DEL VALLO; SCIACCA.

For accommodation in the area, see CASTELVETRANO.

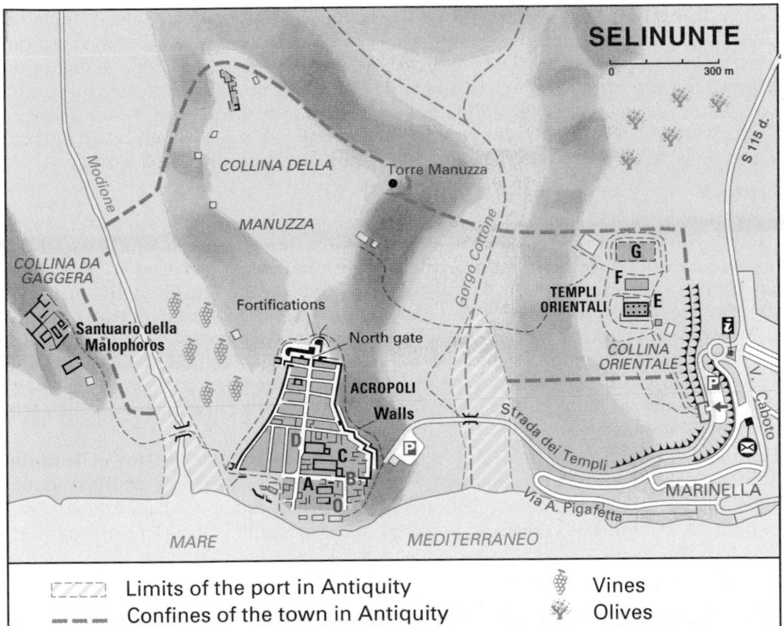

Background

The colony was founded by settlers from Megara Hyblaea during the 7C BC. Thereafter, Selinunte enjoyed a short but intensive period of prosperity (almost two centuries of splendour), perhaps thanks to prudent government practised by the continuous line of successive tyrants. Evidence of the town's flowering is to be found in the extensive area allocated to sacred ritual and public use, concentrated in distinctive districts.

For a long time, Selinunte allied itself to Carthage, in the hope of securing support in the conflict with its rival, Segesta, although, in the end, it was destroyed in 409 BC by the Carthaginian Hannibal, who used ferociously cruel methods in winning supremacy: this resulted in the death of 16 000 Selinuntini and the capture of a further 5 000 as prisoners (according to the account given by Diodorus Siculus). When the survivors begged him for their freedom and for the temples of the city to be spared in return for a substantial payment, Hannibal consented; once he had the cash in hand, he sacked the temples and pulled down the walls.

Selinunte invested every last effort in repairing the damage and, against the odds, struggled to survive until the Second Punic War, when it was razed to the ground.

…rth a Visit

…Open 9am-3hr before dusk. €4. ☎ 0924 46 277.

The ruins are scattered over an almost deserted area, having been completely abandoned since Silenunte's downfall: the ruined temples continue to point their impressive great columns to the sky; other buildings, reduced to heaps of rubble, probably by an earthquake, inspire a tragic air of utter desolation. The fine metopes which once adorned several of the temple friezes are displayed in the archaeological museum in Palermo.

In the absence of any sure knowledge as to which gods the temples were dedicated to, scholars have identified them with letters of the alphabet.

To complete the picture, it is well worth visiting the quarries from where the stone was brought *(see below)*.

Templi orientali

The first of the eastern temples to come into view is **Temple E**, which, re-erected in 1957, was dedicated to Hera. It dates from the 5C BC and has a complex ground plan. The entrance to the *pronaos* was from the east-facing side, up several steps and through the colonnade. Only the capitals remain, lying on the ground, from the two free-standing columns that marked the doorway. Beyond lay the *cella* off which opened a small secret chamber (the *adytum*) where the statue of the deity was kept. Behind this opened the *opisthodomus*, which was identical to the *pronaos*. On the right, lie the ruins of **Temple F**, on a smaller scale than Temple E and probably dedicated to Athena.

Lastly, **Temple G** – the second largest Greek temple in Sicily, after the Temple of Olympian Zeus at Agrigento – would have been the most impressive. Conceived on simply gigantic proportions – 17 columns long and 8 wide, each with a diameter of almost 3.5m and a height of more than 16m/53ft – it was probably dedicated to Apollo. Today, it is reduced to a mass of fragments scattered over the ground. The cylindrical blocks with which the columns were built, each weighing several tons, retain distinctive grooves that suggest to scholars that the temple was never completed.

Acropoli

Drive from the eastern temples car park to the next one. The acropolis stretched across a hill on the far side of the dip called Gorgo di Cottone, through which the River Cottone flowed down to the sea where the town's **harbour** *(now overgrown)* was situated. The site was enclosed within defensive walls built in the 6C-5C BC. The streets were laid out according to the Classical town plan proposed by Hippodamus of Miletus, with three main arteries bisected at right angles by a grid of smaller streets. This area contained the town's public and religious buildings, together with a few houses for the highest ranking members of society.

The path skirts a section of the powerful graduated **walls** surrounding the eastern side of the acropolis.

Temples – The first to be made out as the track climbs uphill is the ruin of **Temple A**. Within the wall with the doorway into the *naos* are two spiral staircases, the most ancient examples known to date. This precinct, however, is dominated by 14 of the 17 columns of **Temple C**, which were re-erected in 1925. This, the earliest

Temple C towers over the other ruins

surviving temple at Selinus (initiated early 6C BC), was probably dedicated to Apollo or Heracles. It is hard to imagine the full impact of the pediment (ornamented with a clay Gorgon's head in shallow relief) as it lies broken on the ground. It is from this temple that the finest metopes, now in the archaeological museum in Palermo, come; there is also a reconstruction of the pediment there. It is interesting to follow the evolution in building techniques implemented during the temple's construction: the columns on the south side are monolithic, whereas the others are composed of cylindrical segments, being far easier to transport. Traces of three further temples have been identified in the acropolis.

Fortifications – At the far end of the *decumanus maximus* rises the curtain wall which once surrounded the acropolis. What may now be seen consists, in fact, of the fortifications built using recycled building stone (the columns split lengthways come from an unidentified temple from an unknown site) after the site was destroyed in 409 BC. Beyond the north gate, the **Porta Nord**, stands an impressive three-storey structure comprising two superimposed galleries surmounted by a series of arches which allowed for soldiers and equipment to move quickly through them.

Ancient town

The residential part of the town was situated on the hill of Manuzza: from the 4C BC, this area was gradually abandoned and used as a necropolis for burials.

Santuario della Malophoros

The sanctuary may be reached by following the track that extends from the first cardo to the left of the decumanus maximus (from the acropolis); allow 20min there and back.
The sanctuary is in honour of Demeter Malophoros (she who bears the pomegranate), the goddess of plants and thereby the protector of farmers and growers. It was built inside a sacred precinct *(temenos)* on the opposite side of the River Modione, where a harbour and the town's trading emporium were located. Beyond the propylaeum (identifiable by the remains of columns) stands a large sacrificial altar. A channel bearing water from the Gaggera mountain spring separates it from the temple. The latter, without columns or foundations, comprised a *pronaos*, a *cella* and an *adytum* containing a statue of the deity.

Excursion

Cave di Cusa*

20km/12mi NW of Selinunte. Head towards Campobello di Mazara, then follow signs to Cave di Cusa. Open 9am-dusk.
The Cusa quarries were the main source of building stone for the temples of Selinunte. The stone, a fine-grained and resistant kind of tufa particularly suitable for building, was quarried for more than 150 years, from the first half of the 6C BC. Work at the quarry ground to a brief halt following the outbreak of war when Selinunte was forced to confront the Carthaginian onslaught (resulting in the destruction of the town). The quarries and the houses of the 150 people who worked here were abandoned suddenly, as shown by the enormous blocks of rock destined for the temples that remain half-quarried here.

The great cylindrical blocks which lie scattered on the ground or await to be quarried (some 60 in number) are a characteristic feature of the quarry, which is 1.8km/1mi long and extends along a ridge from east to west.

In the first section of the quarry, some blocks sit cut and ready for transporting; others barely sketched out, are ready for the stonecutter. At the far end of the quarry is a capital in the making. Its cylindrical mass tapers from a square base into the 12 wedges intended as the *echinus* or ovolo moulding below the abacus. The cracks still show the marks made by picks.

A LONG AND COMPLEX TECHNIQUE

Once the dimensions and profile of the piece to be extracted had been marked out, a double groove about half a metre deep was dug around it to enable the stonemasons to work and cut the block *in situ*. The tools used included picks, bronze saws and wedges. To split the harder layers, wooden wedges were inserted into cracks and then dampened with water so that, as they swelled, the stone would crack open. The block was then severed at the base and removed by means of winches or slid down ramps. The deep U-shaped grooves visible in some of the square blocks were made so that a rope could be fed through them for lifting. Many blocks have a square hole at either end. Into these sockets were fitted special shafts that enabled the blocks to be moved and set in place. The blocks were transported on wooden frames with wheels, and pulled by oxen and slaves. A wide rocky track led from the quarries to Selinunte.

Siracusa★★★

Siracusa (Syracuse) has for ever depended upon the sea, rallying herself around the Island of Ortygia, overlooking a wonderful bay on the east coast. Its name is synonymous with an Ancient Greek past, taking in a series of valiant tyrants and the rivalry between Athens and Carthage. This past has left a number of vestiges for the modern-day visitor to see and enjoy. Alongside this dramatic historical background, there exists another less obvious past that can be explored among the streets of Ortygia, where time seems to stand still somewhere between the medieval and Baroque eras. This pleasant working-class district is dotted with crumbling *palazzi*, which are at long last being restored to their original splendour.

Location

Population: 126 271. Michelin map 565 P 27. The historical centre of Siracusa is situated on the island of Ortygia, linked to the mainland and the modern city by the Ponte Nuovo, the only road access to the island (visitors are advised to leave their car in this area). Just behind Ortygia lies the district of Akradina, the modern and commercial part of town crossed by Corso Gelone. The Neapolis quarter, literally meaning "new town", contains the archaeological area and can be seen to the northwest of Akradina, while to the east of Neapolis lies Tyche, a residential area in Ancient times and so called because a temple here was dedicated to the goddess of fortune (from the Greek *Tyche* – fortune or luck). Dominating the remainder of the city is the area known as Epipolae (meaning "upper town"); this section of the city was guarded and defended by the castle of Euryalus, built in the most strategic position in Siracusa. ℹ *Via Maestranza 33; ☎ 0931 46 42 55; Fax 0931 60 204, www.flashcom.it/aatsr/*

Neighbouring sights are described in the following chapters: CATANIA; NOTO; PANTALICA.

Background

Syracuse was colonised some time in the 8C BC by Greeks from Corinth, who settled on the island of **Ortygia**. Soon this power base was seized by a succession of mighty tyrants. Under their rule the city enjoyed success and great splendour (5C-4C BC); its population stabilised at the 300 000 mark, and it established its supremacy over the rest of Sicily. Between 416 BC and 413 BC, there developed a furious conflict between Syracuse and Athens, the Athenian warriors being led by the great general Alcibiades. So the people of Syracuse endured one of the most famous and cruel periods of ancient history. At last the city fell to the Romans, and so to subsequent invaders – barbarians, Byzantines, Arabs and Normans.

Tyrants of Syracuse – The tyrant in Antiquity corresponds with the modern dictator, and several such figures populate the history of Sicily during the Hellenistic period, particularly in Syracuse.

Gelon, already tyrant of Gela, extended his dominion to Syracuse in 485 BC. His expansionist ambitions baited the hostile Carthaginians to such an extent as to provoke open conflict. Gelon, in alliance with **Theron**, the tyrant of Akragas

Ortygia

D. Boggini/MICHELIN

Directory

Transport

The nearest airport is Fontanarossa airport in Catania, which is linked to Siracusa by buses which run daily (1hr).

Buses leave from Piazzale San Antonio to Catania (approximately 1hr), Palermo (4hr), Ragusa (2hr) and a number of other destinations. For further information, contact the following two bus companies: AST, ☎ 0931 46 27 11, and SAIS, ☎ 0931 66 710.

A train service also operates from Siracusa to Catania (1hr 30min), Messina (3hr), Ragusa (approximately 2hr) and Taormina (2hr 15min).

Sightseeing

Antico mercato d'Ortigia – Siracusa's old covered market (Via Trento 2), built at the beginning of the 20C but abandoned in the mid-1980s, is now home to a number of tourist agencies selling excursions, guided tours, tickets for local transport and cultural events, and audioguides. For information, call ☎ 0931 44 92 01; www.anticomercato.it

Combined tickets – All tickets are valid for two days. €8: Museo Archeologico Regionale Paolo Orsi, Galleria Regionale di Palazzo Bellomo and Zona archeologica della Neapolis; €5: Museo Archeologico Regionale Paolo Orsi and Galleria Regionale di Palazzo Bellomo; €6: Museo Archeologico Regionale Paolo Orsi and Zona archeologica della Neapolis.

Siracusa by sea – Boat trips around the **Porto Grande and Ortygia★** by motor launch are operated by **Motonave Selene**. Excursions along the coast provide a different perspective on the town. Outings last on average 35min, but can be extended on request; they can also include lunch or dinner by prior arrangement. Those timed around sunset and nightfall, when monuments are floodlit, are especially enjoyable. This is also the only means of seeing Castello Maniace. Trips run Mar-Nov (and at other times of year, depending on sea and weather conditions) by appointment only. ☎ 0931 62 776, 0931 79 10 33; Fax 0931 46 12 01, or 368 66 67 21 /347 12 75 680 (mobile phone on board).

Where to Eat

• ***For all budgets***

Giardino di Epicuro – *Largo della Gancia 5 (at the end of Via Nizza), Siracusa – ☎ 0931 46 89 96 – Closed Wed – Booking recommended – €20/50.* This pleasant, relaxed restaurant in the heart of the historical centre serves a selection of fish dishes and a good choice of pizzas.

Darsena da Jannuzzo – *Riva Garibaldi 6 (turn right as soon as you arrive in the Ortygia district), Siracusa – ☎ 0931 61 522 – Closed Wed – ▤ – €25/35.* The main reason for visiting the Darsena da Jannuzzo can be seen at the restaurant entrance where a splendid display of fish is on display. The simple but delicious cuisine here is served either in the unassuming dining room or on the veranda, with its view of the canal.

Where to Stay

• ***Moderate***

Bed & Breakfast Dolce Casa – *Via Lido Sacramento 4, Loc. Isola (take S 115 towards Noto, then turn left to Loc. Isola) – ☎ 0931 72 11 35 – Fax 0931 72 11 35 – contact@bbdolcecasa.it – ▤ – 10 rooms. €52/83* ☕. Situated halfway between Siracusa and the sea, this private villa has been converted into a friendly B&B. The light, spacious rooms, furnished in rustic style with the occasional romantic touch, and the beautiful garden adorned with palm and pine trees, ensure a relaxed and pleasant stay.

Agriturismo La Perciata – *Via Spinagallo 77, 14km/9mi SW of Siracusa on P 14 (from Maremonti, head to Canicattini, then take the turn-off to Floridia) – ☎ 0931 71 73 66 – Fax 0931 62 301 – perciata@perciata.it – Restaurant closed lunchtime Jun-Sep – ▤ – 11 rooms. €65/82* ☕ *– Restaurant. €20/25.* This Mediterranean-style villa amid an oasis of greenery is ideal for a relaxing holiday. Activities on offer here include tennis, horse-riding and hydro-massage. Comfortable rooms and apartments with elegant, rustic decor.

Hotel Gutkowski – *Lungomare Vittorini 26, Siracusa – ☎ 0931 46 58 61 – Fax 0931 48 05 05 – info@guthotel.it – ▤ – 13 rooms. €73/88* ☕. Careful attention to detail is evident throughout this hotel, with its elegant entrance on the ground floor, delightful panoramic sun-terrace and tastefully decorated rooms.

• ***Expensive***

Albergo Domus Mariae – *Via Vittorio Veneto 76, Siracusa – ☎ 0931 24 854 – Fax 0931 24 858 – domusmariae@sistemia.it – ▤ – 13 rooms. €93/130* ☕. The spacious guest rooms in this traditional hotel run by Ursuline nuns are furnished with both elegance and taste. The pleasant sun-terrace offers attractive views of the Mediterranean.

Taking a Break

Enoteca "Capriccio" – *Via dell'Amalfitania 11, Siracusa – ☎ 0931 46 49 18 – Open 10am-10pm.* This wine bar serves an excellent selection of Sicilian wines, including the more unusual *Rosolio al mandarino* and *Rosolio alla cannella*.

Gelateria Bianca Salvatore – *Corso Umberto I, Siracusa.* Customers are spoilt for choice at this reasonably priced *gelateria*, which has a selection of 30 different flavours of ice cream served either in a cup or cone. Pleasant shady terrace from which you can watch the world go by.

Pasticceria-Gelateria Dolcidea – *Viale Regina Margherita 23, Siracusa –*

☎ *0931 22 920.* Enjoy a range of typical Sicilian ice cream and *granite* on the small, shady terrace outside this *gelateria* close to the Porto Piccolo.

Shows

Teatro dei Pupi del Fratelli Mauceri – *Via della Giudecca 17, Siracusa – ☎ 0931 46 55 40 – Shop open Mon-Sat, 9am-noon and 4-7pm.* This small theatre in the heart of the Ortygia district is run by the Mauceri brothers, whose puppet performances offer an entertaining insight into traditional Sicilian culture. Make sure you also visit the nearby Alfredo Mauceri workshop, where the puppets are made.

Shopping

Galleria Bellomo – *Via Capodieci 15, Siracusa – ☎ 0931 61 340 – Open Mon-Sat, 10am-1pm and 4.30-7pm; Sun 10.30am-1pm.* This workshop-cum-gallery, opened in 1980, displays a fascinating collection of papyrus items made by the owner, Signora Massara, who inherited her love for papyrus from her father-in-law.

Galleria del Papiro – *Via Ruggero Settimo 35, Siracusa – ☎ 339 15 02 337 (mobile) – Open Mon-Sat, 9.30am-1pm and 3.30-7pm.* The artist Alessandro Romano uses papyrus as the raw material for his works of art, many of which are exhibited and on sale in this gallery.

Seaside Resorts

The coast to the south of Siracusa has a number of attractive sandy beaches, such as **Arenella**, with its stretches of rocky coastline and picturesque creeks, including Ognina, a paradise for diving enthusiasts. The most beautiful beach in the area is Fontane Bianche, 20km/12mi south of the city.

Istituto Nazionale del Dramma Antico, Siracusa

Festivals

Classical theatre – In May and June, the Greek theatre is the setting for performances of Classical Greek and Latin plays. For information, contact the Istituto Nazionale del Dramma Antico, Corso Matteotti 29, Siracusa; ☎ 0931 67 415; Fax 0931 21 424; www.indafondazione.org/

Festa di Santa Lucia – The festival of Siracusa's patron saint, St Lucy, is celebrated on 13 December.

(Agrigento), succeeded in defeating them at the famous battle of Himera in 480 BC. He was succeeded by his brother **Hieron I** (478-467 BC), and it was during his reign that Cumae was assisted in averting the Etruscan threat (474 BC): from this battle there exists a bronze helmet, found at Olympia and now displayed in the British Museum in London.

After a brief period of democracy, punctuated by battles against Athens, the famous **Dionysius the Elder** acceded to the throne (405-367 BC). He refused the discredited title of tyrant and adopted instead that of ***strategòs autokrátor***, meaning absolute general. This shrewd strategist underpinned his government with popular consensus, which he secured with gifts and favours, and by his reputation as the defender against the Punic threat, which he did not, however, succeed in eliminating. During his tyrannical rule, Syracuse became an independent and mighty force in its own right. On a more personal level, Dionysius I appears to have been haunted with suspicions, ever fearful that someone might be plotting against him. His fears developed into manias of persecution and culminated in his decision to retreat with his court to the castle of Ortygia, which he made into an impregnable private fortress. The story of his life is dotted with strange happenings from which werehatched numerous malicious rumours, half fiction and half fact. Such writers as Valerius Maximus, Cicero and Plutarch describe how the tyrant was so distrustful of the barbarians that he entrusted the task of shaving to his own daughters but, fearing that even they might be tempted to murder him, he insisted that sharpened walnut shells be used rather than razors or scissors; he had a small ditch dug around his marital bed with a small bridge that he could remove when he retired for the night and, to show that the life of a ruler was fraught with danger, he had a sharp sword suspended from a single horse hair above the head of an envious member of his court called Damocles (hence the expression "the sword of Damocles" to allude to a looming threat). His greed, it is said, led him to take possession of the golden mantle from the statue of Zeus, replacing it with a woollen one.

Upon his death, he was succeeded on the throne by his young son **Dionysius (II) the Younger**, who lacked the political astuteness of his father; he was briefly toppled by his uncle **Dion** in 357 BC who, in turn, was assassinated four years later (Dion's life is celebrated in a poem by William Wordsworth). Dionysius II was expelled a second time following a desperate plea from the Syracusans to the mother-city Corinth; in 344 BC **Timoleon**, an effective general, was sent to the rescue; as a wise and moderate statesman he restored peace to Sicily. There followed **Agathocles**, who in order to secure power harboured no qualms in murdering members of the aristocracy; his attempts to rout the Carthaginians from Sicily were unsuccessful (culminating in his defeat at Himera in 310 BC).

The last tyrant to govern Syracuse was **Hieron II** (269-216 BC), a mild and just ruler celebrated by Theocritus *(Idyll xvi)*, who oversaw the last golden age of Syracuse and signed up to an alliance with Rome against the Carthaginians in the First Punic War. In 212 BC, despite the clever devices designed by Archimedes, the town fell to Roman rule and became the capital of the Roman Province of Sicily.

Archimedes – There exists no reliable source of information for details on the life of Archimedes, the famous mathematician, born in Syracuse in 287 BC. It is said that he was so absent-minded and absorbed by his research that he even forgot to eat and drink; his servants were forced to drag him by force to the public baths and, even there, he continued to draw geometric shapes in the ash. It was while he was soaking in his bath that he came upon the principle which was to ensure his fame endured thereafter: a body immersed in a liquid is subject to a force equal to the weight of the volume of the liquid that has been displaced. Thrilled with his discovery, he is supposed to have stood up suddenly and rushed out of the house shouting "Eureka!" (I've got it!).

Besides his contributions to the study of arithmetic, geometry, physics, astronomy and engineering, Archimedes is credited with several significant mechanical inventions, notably the Archimedes Screw – a cylinder containing a spiral screw for moving liquid uphill, like a pump *(see p 382)*; the cogwheel; celestial spheres; and burning glasses – a combination of lenses and mirrors with which he succeeded in setting fire to the Roman fleet. According to tradition, Archimedes was so deeply involved in his calculations when the Romans succeeded in penetrating the city, that he died from a sword wound inflicted by a Roman soldier, more or less oblivious of what was happening.

Poetic muses – Syracuse played its own part in developing its artistic prominence in Antiquity. Several of its rulers became so taken with the power of patronage and the benefits of promoting the arts that, before long, established foreign poets and writers were being welcomed to their court. Some, like Dionysius the Elder, tried to establish themselves as writers but without any great success. The first to take a truly effective interest was Hieron I, who proclaimed himself protector of poets and invited to his court such illustrious figures as Bacchylides, Xenophon and Simonides, and highly competitive rival poets **Pindar** and **Aeschylus**, the latter one of the most eminent early Greek dramatists and author of *The Persians* (c 470 BC) and *The Women of Etna* (now lost); both plays are known to have been performed in the Greek theatre in Neapolis.

By contrast, **Plato** was to endure difficult relations with Syracuse, most particularly with its rulers. Dionysius the Elder welcomed him reluctantly, only to expel him shortly afterwards; after his demise, the philosopher returned (under the protection of the regent Dion), only to be expelled a second time – by Dionysius II – after failing to persuade the tyrant to accept the principles of his Utopian state (outlined later in his *Republic*).

Theocritus, the protagonist of a kind of bucolic poetry at which Virgil was later to excel, was probably a native of Syracuse.

In more recent times, **Salvatore Quasimodo** (1901-68) was born in Siracusa. A poet obsessed with the malaise of life, which he expressed in verses that became ever more terse and concise, he won the Nobel Prize for literature in 1959.

Special Features

PARCO ARCHEOLOGICO DELLA NEAPOLIS★★★

♿ *Open Apr-Oct, 9am-6pm; Nov-Mar, 9am-3pm. €4.50.* ☎ *0931 48 11 11.*

There are two different entrances: one is in Via Rizzo and the other in Viale Paradiso. To follow the itinerary prescribed below, begin from the entrance in Via Rizzo.

Teatro Greco★★★

This is one of the most impressive theatres to survive from Antiquity. The *cavea* was completely cut out from the bedrock, taking advantage of the natural slope of Colle Temenite. The date of construction has been established as the 5C BC, largely on the basis of factual reports documenting the first performance of Aeschylus' play *The Persians*. It is also known who the builder was, namely a certain Damocopus, known as Myrilla, because he used unguents *(miroi)* at the official opening of the theatre.

The theatre was modified by Hieron II in the 3C BC, when it was divided into nine wedge-shaped sections, and a passageway was inserted around the *cavea* about halfway up. The wall in front of each section is inscribed with the name of a

H. Champollion/MICHELIN

famous person or deity. Today, certain letters may still be distinguished, including those spelling out Olympian Zeus (ΔΙΟΣ ΟΛΥΜΠΙΩΥ) in the central section; to the right, facing the stage, appear the letters naming Hieron II himself (ΒΑΣΙΛΙΕΟΣ ΙΗΡΩΝΩΣ – *of King Hieron*), his wife ΒΑΣΙΛΙΣΣΑΣ ΦΙΛΙΣΤΙΔΩΣ – *of Queen Philistis*) and his daughter-in-law (ΒΑΣΙΛΙΣΣΑΣ ΝΗΡΗΙΔΟΣ – *of Queen Nereis*). It was altered in Roman times so as to host water sports (it is thought) and gladiatorial combats before the amphitheatre *(see below)* was completed. Later it was put to other uses. In fact, the Spaniards installed various water-driven millstones in it: the furrows left by two mill-wheels in the central part of the *cavea* may still be seen, as can the drainage channel bearing the water away.

Behind the *cavea* is a large open area with, in the centre, the **Grotta del Ninfeo** (Nymph's Cave). The rectangular tank set before it was filled with water drawn from the aqueduct that was built by the Greeks to carry water over a distance of some 35km/22mi from the rio Bottigliera, a tributary of the River Anapo, near Pantalica *(see PANTALICA)*. Having fallen into disuse during the Middle Ages, the aqueduct was restored in the 16C by the Marchese di Sortinoto in order to power the watermills erected in the theatre.

To the left extends the **Via dei Sepolcri** (Street of Tombs). Pockmarking the rock face on each side are a series of Byzantine tombs and votive niches in which offerings used to be placed.

The limestone quarries

The *latomie*, from the Greek *litos* – a stone – and *temnos* – a cut – are the ancient quarries that supplied blocks of limestone for the construction of public buildings and grand houses. Quarrying was initiated after a suitable site was selected on the grounds that it might yield regular, good-quality blocks of stone. Crevices were made in the bedrock into which wooden wedges were inserted; these were then dampened to make them expand, causing the rock to split.

In the search for layers of compacted rock, the quarrymen would excavate funnel-like tunnels that gradually broadened out the deeper they were dug. Pillars of rock would be left to prop up the ceilings of these hollows. It has been calculated that in such a way, enormous quantities of material could be efficiently quarried. Once the quarry was exhausted, the cavities would be used as prisons, as described by Cicero in his *Speeches against Verres* (or *Verrine Orations*): it is highly probable that the 7 000 Athenian prisoners captured in 413 BC were held in the *latomie*; all of these perished after eight months of incarceration there, save for the few who were lucky enough to be sold as slaves or those who, according to legend, were able to recite verses by Euripides from memory. The caves, it should be noted, would have been very different in those days: they would have been wider, darker and more suited to accommodating large numbers of prisoners; what we see today has been severely affected by falls of rock dislodged, for the most part, by earth tremors. In later times, the quarries have hosted lengthy funeral rites, have served as refuges, and been used as garden allotments. Only recently was it thought appropriate to reassess their historical importance and restore them.

A map locating all the *latomie* (12 have been identified but some are buried below buildings) reveals how they lie in a kind of arc that corresponds to the limestone terrace formation skirting what is more or less the edge of the two ancient quarters of Neapolis and Tyche. An overview *(from beside the Greek theatre)* provides a better understanding of the layout, for where the ceiling has collapsed as a result of earth tremors, it is possible to see a number of the stone supports or pit props still *in situ*.

After the **Latomia del Paradiso**, continuing along the arc, from west to east, they appear in the following order: **Latomia Intagliatella**, **Latomia di Santa Venera**, **Latomia del Casale** and **Latomia dei Cappuccini**. This last one is perhaps the most majestic and spectacular of them all, on account of its steep limestone walls.

Orecchio di Dionisio★★★
The haunting cave known as the Ear of Dionysius is situated in one of the most striking former limestone quarries *(latomie)* in Siracusa: the one that is aptly named **Latomia del Paradiso★★**, now a delightful garden shaded with orange trees, palm trees and magnolias. As its name suggests, the cave resembles an auricle (cavity inside the ear), both in the shape of the entrance and the winding internal space beyond. It was the artist Caravaggio who gave the cave its name during his visit to Sicily in the early 1600s on hearing the intriguing explanation of how Dionysius the Elder was able to hear his enemies without seeing them, thanks to the cave's extraordinary echo.

The smoothness of the walls, so tall and even, together with the maze-like interior permanently swathed in shadow, make it difficult to imagine that the Ear of Dionysius was once a quarry. In fact, its peculiar shape is explained by the way the limestone was quarried. A small crack was made in the surface at the top; this was then broadened into a narrow channel that was gradually excavated downwards (possibly with the aid of water) until the good stone was reached. The cave has amazing acoustics which the occasional guide or visitor will put to the test by suddenly bursting into song.

Many stories concerning the cave once quarrying ceased are circulated by guides and guidebooks: the most likely hypothesis is that it was used as a prison (like all the other *latomie*); the most imaginative tells of how it came to be used as a hearing trumpet by Dionysius; others say it was used by choirs performing at the nearby theatre.

The neighbouring **Grotta dei Cordari** earned its name from its use until fairly recently by rope-makers for twisting long stretches of sisal and twine, as it provided them with a pleasantly cool area in which to work. Although only visible from the outside (for safety reasons), it clearly shows how it was quarried.

Ara di Ierone II
This enormous altar, some 200m/650ft long and partly carved out of the rock, was commissioned by the tyrant Hieron II in the 3C BC for public sacrifices. Originally, a large rectangular area may have stretched out in front, probably with a portico and a central pool.

Anfiteatro Romano★
The Roman amphitheatre was built during the Imperial era. Its situation makes best use of the natural lie of the land and required only half of the *cavea* to be cut out of the bedrock. This is the best preserved section. The other half of the circle was built using large blocks of stone which have been pillaged through the successive centuries. Two entrances may be discerned: one on the north and one on the south side. The rectangular pit in the centre of the arena is connected to the southern entrance by a ditch. This "technical" area was reserved for the stage machinery apparatus that provided performances with special effects.

Opposite the entrance to the amphitheatre stands the pre-Romanesque Church of **San Nicolò dei Cordari** (11C). To its right, sits a water tank built by the Romans for collecting water that was used to flood the amphitheatre for performances of *naumachiae* (re-enactments of sea battles) and for cleaning the arena after the gory fights between gladiators and wild animals.

Tomba di Archimede
Visible from the outside only from the corner of Via Romagnoli and Via Teracati. At the eastern end of Latomia Intagliatella are the **Grotticelli Necropolis**. Among the many cavities hollowed out of the rock, one is ornamented with Doric columns (badly damaged), pediment and tympanum. This "Tomb of Archimedes" actually conceals a Roman *columbarium* (a chamber lined with niches for funerary urns).

Walking About

ORTYGIA★★★
"Sicanio praetenta sinu iacet insula contra
Plemyrium undosum; nomen dixere priores
Ortygiam. Alpheum fama est huc Elidis amnem
occultas egisse vias subter mare, qui nunc
ore, Arethusa, tuo Siculis confunditur undis."

"Stretched in front of a Sicanian bay lies an island, over against wave-beaten Plemyrium; men of old called it Ortygia. Hither, so runs the tale, Alpheus, river of Elis, forced a secret course beneath the sea, and now at thy fountain, Arethusa, mingles with the Sicilian waves."

Virgil, *The Aeneid*, Book III (lines 692-695).

SIRACUSA

Agatocle (Via) .... BCY
Agrigento (Via) .... BCY 2
Archimede (Piazza) .... CZ 3
Arsenale (Via d.) .... BCY
Bainsizza (Via) .... BY
Bengasi (Via) .... BZ
Cadorna (Viale L.) .... BY
Capodieci (Via) .... CZ 4
Cappuccini (Piazza) .... CY
Castello Maniace (Via) .... CZ 6
Catania (Via) .... BY 7
Columba (Via) .... AYZ
Crispi (Via F.) .... BY 9

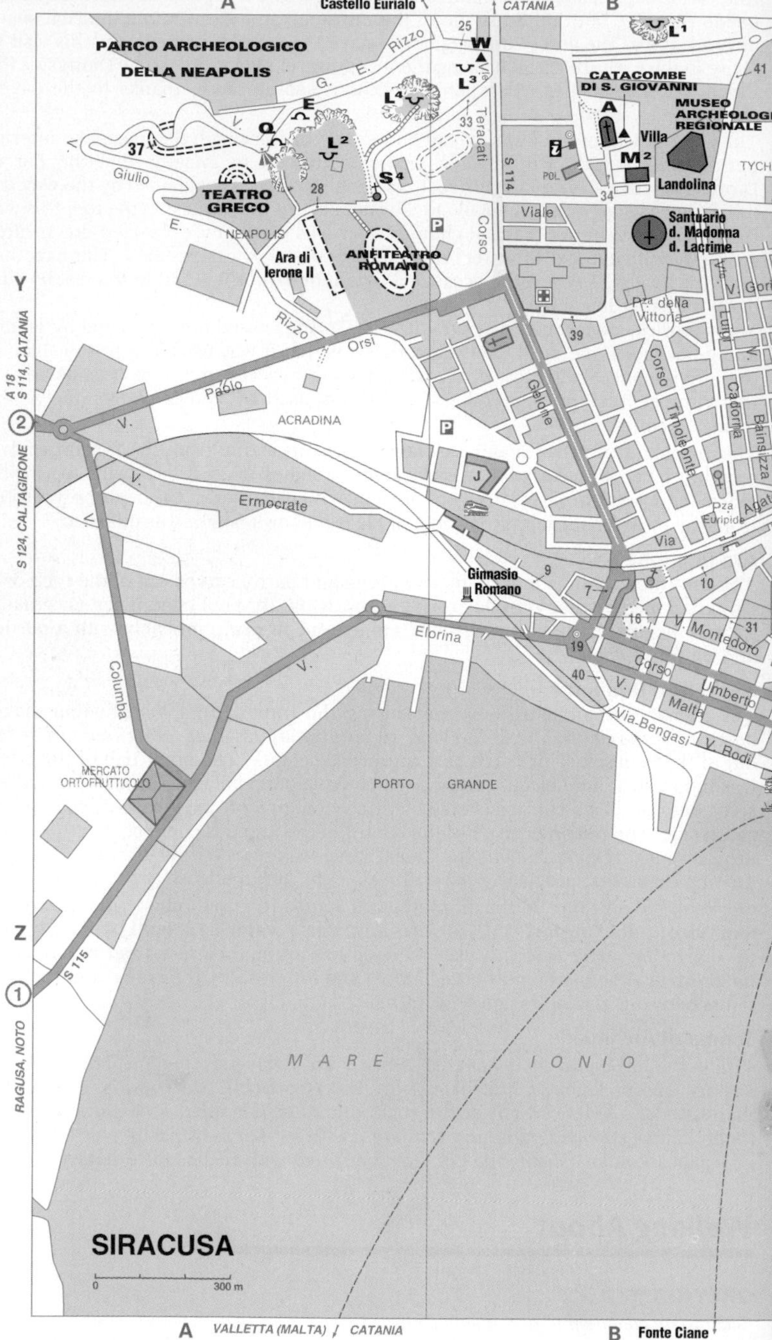

There are so many wonderful buildings and interesting outlooks as to make it impossible to set an itinerary including all that might be worth seeing. The descriptions given below therefore mention only the most interesting streets, leaving a large section of the historical city without commentary for visitors to explore at will according to inclination. A word of advice: remember to raise your gaze as often as possible so as not to miss any understated secret lurking in the narrow streets among their splendid buildings.

Diaz (Viale A.) .... BY 10
Dionisio il Grande (Riviera) ..... CY 12
Duomo (Piazza) .... CZ 13
Elorina (Via) .... ABZ
Ermocrate (Via) .... AY
Euripide (Piazza) .... BY
Foro Siracusano .... BYZ 16
Gelone (Corso) .... BY
Gorizia (Via) .... BY
Maestranza (Via d.) .... CZ 18

Malta (Via) .... BZ
Marconi (Piazzale) .... BZ 19
Matteotti (Corso G.) .... CZ 21
Mergulensi (Via) .... CZ 22
Mirabella (Via) .... CZ 24
Montedoro (Via) .... BZ
Montegrappa (Via) .... CY
Necropoli Grotticelle (Via d.) ..... BY 25
Nizza (Via) .... CZ
Orsi (Viale P.) .... ABY
Pancali (Piazza) .... CZ 27
Paradiso (Via) .... AY 28
Passeggio Adorno .... CZ
Piave (Via) .... BCY
Puglia (Via) .... CY 30
Regina Margherita (Viale) .... BYZ 31
Rizzo (Viale G. E.) .... AY
Rodi (Via) .... BZ
Roma (Via) .... CZ
Romagnoli (Via) .... ABY 33
S. Giovanni (Viale) .... BY 34
S. Lucia (Piazza) .... CY
S. Martino (Via) .... CZ 36
Sepolcri (Via d.) .... AY 37
Svevia (Piazza F. d.) .... CZ 38
Teocrito (Viale) .... BCY
Teracati (Viale) .... BY
Testaferrata (Via G.) .... BY 39
Timoleonte (Corso) .... BY
Torino (Via) .... CY
Tripoli (Via) .... BZ 40
Umberto I (Corso) .... BZ
Vittoria (Piazza d.) .... BY
Vittorio Veneto (Via) .... CZ
Von Platen (Via A.) .... BY 41
XX Settembre (Via) .... CZ 42

Anfiteatro Romano .... AY
Ara di Ierone II .... AY
Basilica di S. Giovanni Evangelista .... BY **A**
Basilica di S. Lucia extra Mœnia .... CY
Belvedere di S. Giacomo ..... CZ
Castello Maniace .... CZ
Catacombe di S. Giovanni ... BY
Chiesa dei Gesuiti .... CZ **C1**
Chiesa dello Spirito Santo ... CZ
Duomo .... CZ **D**
Fonte Aretusa .... CZ
Forte Vigliena .... CZ
Galleria Civica d'Arte Moderna .... CZ **M1**
Ginnasio Romano .... BY
Grotta dei Cordari .... AY **E**
Latomia dei Cappuccini .... CY
Latomia del Casale .... BY **L1**
Latomia del Paradiso .... AY **L2**
Latomia di S. Venera .... BY **L3**
Latomia Intagliatella .... AY **L4**
Museo Archeologico Regionale Paolo Orsi .... BY
Museo del Papiro .... BY **M2**
Orecchio di Dionisio .... AY **Q**
Palazzo Bellomo .... CZ
Palazzo Beneventano del Bosco .... CZ **R1**
Palazzo del Senato .... CZ **R2**
Palazzo Mergulese-Montalto CZ **R4**
Parco Archeologico della Neapolis .... AY
Porta Marina .... CZ
S. Benedetto .... CZ **C2**
S. Filippo Neri .... CZ **S1**
S. Francesco all'Immacolata CZ **S2**
S. Lucia .... CZ **S3**
S. Martino .... CZ
S. Nicolò dei Cordari .... AY **S4**
S. Pietro .... CZ
Santuario della Madonna delle Lacrime .... BY
Teatro Greco .... AY
Tempio di Apollo .... CZ **V**
Tomba di Archimede .... BY **W**
Villa Landolina .... BY

The island, the most ancient area of settlement, is linked to the mainland by the Ponte Nuovo, a natural extension of one of the main thoroughfares of Siracusa, Corso Umberto I. A powerful awareness of the sea and all things associated with it pervades this area: the harbour, filled with colourful boats, moored or going about their business, stretches both to the right and to the left.
As the eye roams the seafront, its attention is caught by the lovely neo-Gothic *palazzo* on the corner: this red-plastered house with two-light windows was once

the home of the poet and writer **Antonio Cardile** (b Messina 1883, d Siracusa 1951). Its distinctive appearance may perhaps arouse the curiosity of visitors to these parts, inspiring them to take a walk around the perimeter of the island, and explore the intriguing quality of the place, absorbing its atmosphere, quieter and more peaceful than elsewhere, and contemplating the attenuated sounds that signal life within its walls. To the right lies the sea; to the left, the old Spanish walls stand as a reminder of times when (until 1800) the old town was fortified.
The bold linearity of the **Porta Marina** is interrupted by a decorative Catalan aedicule framing the entrance to Passeggio Adorno, a walkway created along the top of the walls in the 19C.
Finally, a glance will also take in the great Porto Grande, the scene of several major naval battles.

Fonte Aretusa★

The Fountain of Arethusa played a significant part in persuading the first group of colonists to settle here in Antiquity. Legend relates how Arethusa, one of Artemis' nymphs, tormented by the demonstrations of love from a hunter named Alpheus, turned to the goddess for help. Artemis intervened by turning Arethusa into a stream so that she might escape underground and re-emerge on the island of Ortygia as a beautifully clear freshwater spring or fountain. Alpheus, meanwhile, was not to be defeated: he, too, changed himself into an underground river, crossed the Ionian Sea and came up in Ortygia having mingled his waters with those of Arethusa.
Today, the fountain sustains palm trees and clumps of papyrus, ducks and drakes. The façades of the houses painted in pastel shades make for an attractive picture, a harmonious three-dimensional visual entity that extends along the streets of the island.
Looming on the horizon on the far side, sits the solid profile of the **Castello Maniace**, a sandstone fortress built by Frederick II of Swabia in the first half of the 13C. Its name honours the Byzantine general, George Maniakes who, in 1038, tried to rescue Ortygia from the Arabs, and then fortified the island, especially the area where Frederick II would later rebuild the castle. The massive square structure is a typical example of Swabian building: the architectural features are both functional and cosmetic, suggesting that the castle was conceived to function as a defensive stronghold and also as a bold visual reminder of Swabian authority. *The castle is closed for restoration at the time of going to press, but will reopen to the public once work has finished. For further information, contact the tourist office on ☎ 0931 46 42 55.*
Cross the tip of the island to reach the eastern shore, from where a series of wonderful views extend over the castle (the best view, however, is from the sea); pass before the Church of **Santo Spirito**, with its fine three-tiered white façade unified by volutes and decorative pilasters. A little further long, in Via **S. Martino**, the Church of **San Martino**, whose origins date back to the 6C, is fronted by a fine Catalan-Gothic style doorway.
Continue along Via S. Martino to the Church of **San Benedetto**, with its fine coffered ceiling, and the adjacent Galleria Regionale di Palazzo Bellomo *(see Worth a Visit)*.

Take Via Capodieci, then turn right into Via Vergini.

Piazza Duomo★★

The attractively presented irregular square precedes the cathedral, curving gently at one end to accommodate its majestic front elevation. The open space becomes especially effective when the cathedral façade is dramatically caught by the setting sun or floodlit after nightfall. The other fine Baroque buildings enclosing the square include the striking **Palazzo Beneventano del Bosco**, which conceals a lovely internal courtyard, and opposite, **Palazzo del Senato**, whose inner courtyard displays an 18C senator's carriage; at the far end stands the Church of **Santa Lucia**. Next to Santa Lucia, the former convent and Church of Montevergini houses the Galleria Civica di Arte Contemporanea *(see Worth a Visit)*.

Duomo★

The area now occupied by the cathedral has been a place of worship since early Antiquity. A temple erected in the 6C BC was replaced by a temple dedicated to Athena, honouring the goddess with some of the profits from the fateful and decisive defeat of the Carthaginians at Himera (480 BC). In the 7C AD, the temple was incorporated into a Christian church: walls were raised between the columns of the peristyle and a double arcade of eight arches was inserted in the *cella* to provide two lateral aisles. Still today, the majestic Doric columns may be seen along the left side of the church, both inside and outside the building. Possibly converted into a mosque during the Arab domination, it was restored for Christian use by the Normans. The 1693 earthquake caused the front façade to collapse; it was rebuilt in the Baroque style (18C) by the Palermo architect Andrea Palma. He used the

column as the basic unit module for his design. The entrance is preceded by an atrium screening a fine doorway flanked by a pair of twisted columns, the spirals of which are decorated with vines and grapes (a symbol of the Passion).
Inside, the right side of the south aisle incorporates the columns of the temple; today these frame the entrance into the lateral chapels. The first bay on the right contains a lovely font made from a Greek marble krater, supported by seven small 13C wrought-iron lions.
The next **chapel**, dedicated to **St Lucy**, is furnished with an 18C silver altar-front. The silver figure of the saint in the niche is by Pietro Rizzo (1599). Elsewhere, the cathedral is furnished with several statues by the various **Gagini**: the *Virgin* is by **Domenico**; *St Lucy* is by **Antonello Gagini** *(north aisle)*; the *Madonna della Neve* in the north apse is also by Antonello.

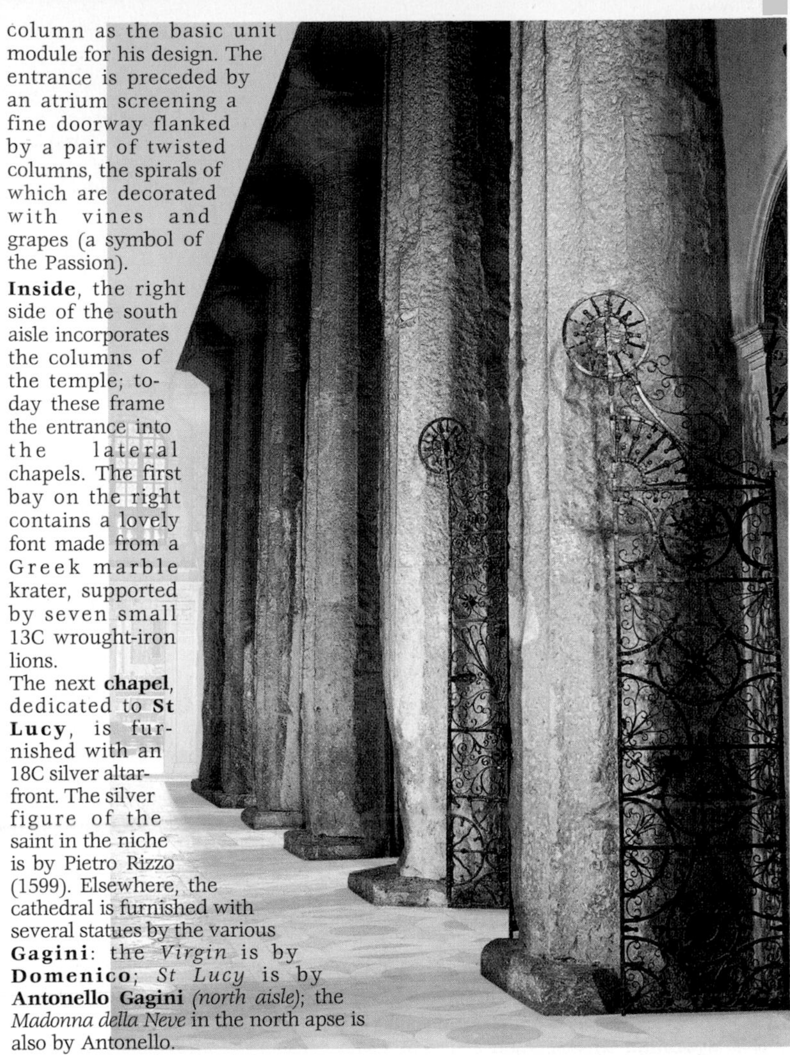

H. Champollion/MICHELIN

The Greek columns of the cathedral

Via Landolina, north of the piazza, accommodates the powerfully fronted **Chiesa dei Gesuiti**.
From the church, make your way to the nearby **Piazza Archimede**. This square was constructed more recently. Presiding over the central space, overlooked by fine buildings, is the 19C fountain of Artemis.

Palazzo Mergulese-Montalto★

Via Montalto. This superb, although rather dilapidated, *palazzo* dates from the 14C. The main elevation rises through two storeys separated by an indented string course. The upper section is ornamented with wonderful highly elaborate **windows★★**, set into richly carved arched settings subdivided by delicately slender twisted columns. The ground floor is graced with a pointed arched entrance surmounted by a decorative aedicule.
Return to Piazza Archimede.

Via della Maestranza★

Not only is Via della Maestranza one of Ortygia's main thoroughfares, it is also one of the oldest. It threads its way between a succession of aristocratic residences, predominantly Baroque in style. Among the most interesting, look out for: **Palazzo Interlandi Pizzuti** (n° 10) and, a little further on, **Palazzo Impellizzeri** (n° 17) with its sinuously linear arrangement of curved windows and balconies. **Palazzo Bonanno** (n° 33), which now accommodates the headquarters of the tourist office, is an austere medieval building sheltering a lovely inner courtyard and a loggia on the first floor. At n° 72 stands the imposing **Palazzo Romeo Bufardeci**, with its exuberant frontage and Rococo balconies.
The street opens out into a small square before the Church of **San Francesco all'Immacolata** flanked by a 19C bell tower. The light-coloured, curved and elegant front elevation is gracefully articulated with columns and pilasters. At one time the

church used to host a ritual rooted in Antiquity: during the night of the 28 November the *Svelata* (literally, the unveiling) took place, during which an image of the Madonna was unveiled. This event was timed to occur in the early hours of the morning before dawn (so that people could go off to work, in an era when the working day started very early) after a long vigil accompanied by local bands.

Almost at the end of the street may be discerned the curved façade of **Palazzo Rizza** (n° 110). **Palazzo Impellizzeri** (n° 99) dominates the street, rising to its full height through a sumptuous and highly original frieze ornamented with human faces and grotesque masks, surmounted with organic decorations.

Behind this last section of the street extends the **Quartiere della Giudecca**, a quarter that retains its medieval street plan, threaded by narrow streets. During the 16C a considerable community of Jews settled and thrived there until expelled.

At the end of the street the **Belvedere S. Giacomo**, once a defensive bastion, offers a splendid **view**★ of Siracusa. The nearby **Forte Vigliena** can be seen on the right.

Mastrarua

Renamed Via Vittorio Veneto, this street was once the main thoroughfare of Ortygia. This was the route followed by kings as they entered the town, by official parades and royal processions. It is logical, therefore, that it should be lined with fine *palazzi*. **Palazzo Blanco** (n° 41) is graced outside with a niche in which stands a statue of St Anthony; it has a lovely internal courtyard and staircase within. **Casa Mezia** (n° 47) has a doorway surmounted by a projecting griffin. Beyond the Church of **San Filippo Neri** there follows **Palazzo Interlandi** and **Palazzo Monforte**, badly damaged alas. This last *palazzo* marks the corner with Via Mirabella, which also contains yet more fine buildings. Note, right opposite Palazzo Monforte, the elegant **Palazzo Bongiovanni**: the doorway is surmounted by a mask and, above, a lion holding a scroll bearing the date 1772 which, in turn, acts as a central support for a balcony; its central window is ornamented with volutes.

Continue along Via Mirabella.

A small diversion to the right allows for a detour past the neo-Gothic **Palazzo Gargallo** (Archivio Distrettuale Notarile – Records Office). Another **Palazzo Gargallo** graces Piazzetta del Carmine (n° 34), built in the same style. Via Mirabella also heralds the beginning of the Arab quarter, characterised by extremely narrow streets known as *ronchi*. One of these streets conceals the palaeo-Christian Church of **San Pietro** distinguished by its fine doorway, which is now used for concerts and presentations. A little further along Via Mirabella stands the Church of **San Tommaso** which was founded in Norman times (12C). Turn back along the Mastrarua; n° 111 has a lovely doorway decorated with monstrous creatures. N° 136, is the birthplace of the writer, **Elio Vittorini** (1908-66).

Tempio di Apollo

This temple of Apollo, built in the 6C BC, is the oldest peripteral Doric temple (that is, enclosed by columns) in Sicily. According to one inscription it was dedicated to Apollo; according to Cicero it was dedicated to Artemis – before being transformed into a Byzantine church, then a mosque, and back again into a church by the Normans. The remains of the peristyle columns and part of the wall of the sacred precinct are still in evidence.

Corso Matteotti, described as the drawing room of Ortygia, leads off the piazza, flanked on either side by elegant shops.

Worth a Visit

Museo Archeologico Regionale Paolo Orsi★★

(♿) Open Tue-Sat, 9am-2pm (also 3.30-7.30pm Mon, Wed and Sat); Sun and public hols, call for information; last admission 1hr before closing. €4. ☎ 0931 46 40 22; www.regione.sicilia.it

The Paolo Orsi Museum nestles in the garden of **Villa Landolina**, virtually hidden from view. Its importance lies in the fact that it provides a fundamental benchmark in the understanding of Sicily's prehistory right up to the period of the sub-colonies of Syracuse.

The museum presents the inception and development of the various cultural phases in chronological order. The three main sections, all extremely well laid out, are provided with a centrally located introductory area, below which, in the basement, is an auditorium where audio-visual presentations are given *(see programme schedule at the entrance).*

Section A: Prehistory and protohistory – Displays open with a collection of fossils and minerals, skeletons and prehistoric animal remains along with an exhaustive supply of information about the fauna of the island. The models of two dwarf elephants found in the Grotta di Spinagallo in Siracusa (the originals are in the Museo di Paleontologia in Rome) are of particular interest; these were thought to have been at the root of the Cyclops myth, through a mistaken interpretation of the hole created by the elephant's trunk. There follow various human artefacts representing the Palaeolithic and Neolithic eras, followed by specimens dating from successive phases. The majority of artefacts comprise fragments of pottery, including a large red-burnished **vase★** from Pantalica – a simple yet highly sophisticated tall-footed shape.

Finally, a number of hoards are shown alongside groups of bronze objects (spearheads, belts and buckles) recovered from containers that had been concealed or hidden (underground or in a cavity).

Section B: Greek colonisation – These objects mark and illustrate the foundation and development of Greek colonies in eastern Sicily. The three Ionic colonies were Naxos, Katane and Leontinoi, from where the beautiful headless marble ***kouros*** (Archaic male figure) came. The two Doric colonies were Megara Hyblaea and Syracuse, both of which are extremely well represented. The singular limestone figure of the ***Mother-goddess*★** nursing twins (6C BC) was recovered from the necropolis at Megara Hyblaea. Seated and headless, the figure powerfully embodies maternity, extending her arms to embrace and contain the two babies which seem to melt into her, as if the three bodies were one.

Museo Archeologico, Siracusa/SCALA

Mother-goddess from Megara Hyblaea (6C BC)

The Syracuse collection is vast and includes two famous exhibits which are often reproduced: a polychrome shallow-relief clay panel with a **gorgon**, and the bronze statuette of a horse, the symbol of the museum, found in the necropolis at Fusco. At the entrance to this section devoted to Syracuse, is temporarily displayed the splendid headless statue of ***Venus Anadyomene*★** or Landolina Venus (after the man who discovered her). This Roman copy of an original by Praxiteles is one of many made in Antiquity (others include the Medici Venus, the Capitoline Venus) characterised by soft sinuous lines. The poise with which she holds the drapery is somehow underlined by the very delicate way in which the light fabric falls into folds that echo the perfect shape of a shell.

Section C: Sub-colonies and Hellenised centres – The first part, devoted to the sub-colonies of Syracuse, contains various fine anthropomorphous figures, including a clay *acroterion* representing a **rider on horseback**.

The second part deals with the history of minor centres. Note the tall clay sculpted enthroned figure of **Demeter** or **Kore** dating from the latter half of the 6C BC.

The third and last part of this section is devoted to Agrigento and Gela. The striking painted **Gorgon's mask**, part of a decorative temple frieze, comes from Gela as does the fine Attic red-figure *pelike* (two-handled vase) by the painter Polygnotos. Three wooden **Archaic statuettes** are rare examples of votive art: although these were probably extremely widespread, in most cases the wood will have perished and disintegrated with time.

Catacombe di San Giovanni★★

Open daily except Mon, 9am-1pm and 2.30-5.30pm: €3.50. ☎ 0931 36 456; www.kalosnet.it

The catacombs are situated in the Akradina area which, until Roman times, was reserved for the cult of the dead. Unlike the Roman catacombs elsewhere in mainland Italy that are excavated from fragile tufa which restricted their size (lest they collapse), these in Siracusa are cut out from a layer of hard limestone and therefore could be extended into considerably larger underground chambers.

This complex system of catacombs was developed around the tomb of St Marcian, one of the early Christian martyrs (4C-5C). The extensive network of rectilinear tunnels depends upon a central axis that probably followed the lines of an abandoned Greek aqueduct. At right angles to this principal artery lead a series of minor vein-like passageways. The chambers vary in size according to whether they accommodated a single person or several (maximum 20 people). Interspersed among these large cavities are a number of smaller and shallower hollows for children (at a time when the infant mortality rate was high). At intervals, there appear round or square areas used by the Christians for interring martyrs and saints. The most significant of these is the *Rotonda di Adelfia,* in which a wonderful sarcophagus was found intact, carved with biblical scenes *(awaiting to be displayed, possibly on the second floor of the archaeological museum).* Note also, beside the main gallery, the Greco-Roman conical cisterns that have later been used as burial chambers.

Cripta di San Marciano – The Crypt of St Marcian, situated near the necropolis, marks the place where the martyr is alleged to have met his death. The Greek-cross chamber lies some 5m/16ft below ground level. The far wall accommodates three semicircular apses: the right one is the altar where St Paul is supposed to have preached on his return from Malta in AD 60 (*Acts of the Apostles*, Ch 28 v12); against the right wall of the central apse sits the tomb that is popularly believed to be that of the martyr. The peep-hole inserted on one side was to enable the pilgrims to see the body of the saint and to allow a cloth to be passed over it that might then be considered a special relic-cum-keepsake. The four corners below the central vault are marked with pilasters and Byzantine capitals bearing representations of the Evangelists.

B. Kaufmann/MICHELIN

The basilica of San Giovanni Evangelista

Basilica di San Giovanni Evangelista – The church stands over the crypt of St Marcian. This picturesque ruin, open to the sky, is one of the most atmospheric spots in all Siracusa, especially at sunset, and even more intensely on saints' days and holidays when Mass is celebrated. The basilica was founded in association with the martyr's crypt, for it was usual to mark a sacred burial place with a shrine of some kind. The basilica was destroyed by the Arabs, and restored by the Normans. The main frontage of the Norman church, ornamented with a lovely rose-window, is still visible on the left flank. The main damage was incurred during an earthquake when the roof collapsed, never to be rebuilt. The front portico has been reconstructed using 15C building materials.

The interior, now partly taken over by clumps of tree spurge *(Euphorbia dendroides)*, preserves its original Byzantine main altar.

Museo del Papiro

Open daily except Mon, 9am-2pm. No charge. ☎ 0931 61 616; www.sistemia.it/museopapiro

The rediscovery of papyrus in Syracuse can be attributed to Saverio Landolina who, in the 18C, reassessed the value of the plant, which was being used by the local population at that time for decorative purposes. He also succeeded in reinventing the means of making paper (with several examples displayed in the museum).

Santuario della Madonna delle Lacrime

Open 7am-1pm and 3-8pm. ☎ 0931 21 446; www.madonnadellelacrime.it

The rather cumbersome mass of this singular modern conical structure in reinforced concrete (80m/262ft in diameter and 74m/243ft high) dominates the skyline from a long way off. The construction of such an imposing building was prompted by a miraculous event that occurred in 1953 (when an unassuming

Papyrus

Cyperus papyrus is a plant which grows vigorously in Egypt; it has also been known to man in Siracusa, along the banks of the River Ciane *(see Excursions)*, since Antiquity. It consists of a perennial marsh plant which grows in various forms and sizes, and produces a profusion of tall stems ending with ruffs of bracts (inflorescence). In Ancient Egypt, it was used in all kinds of different ways that exploited its amazing versatility: stems were bundled together to build lightweight boats; it was used for making ropes, baskets and trays, for weaving fabric for clothes and wigs, even for making shoes (such as sandals). The ruff at the top was used to make fans and parasols for civil or religious ceremonies and funeral rites. It has even been suggested that the most tender spongy part of the stalk might have been eaten.
The most famous product made from papyrus is paper, although this involves a fairly complex process. The variable factors include the age of the plant and the stabilising treatment following the bleaching process. Strips are laid in two perpendicular layers one on top of the other, pressed and dried. The resulting sheet has a flat surface (with horizontal fibres) suitable for writing, backed and supported by the vertical fibres. It is interesting to note that in many languages the word for paper actually comes from the word "papyrus" (French *papier*, German *Papier*, Spanish *papel*, Welsh *papur* and so on).
The material displayed in the museum covers all the possible applications of papyrus. This includes documents from the time of the pharaohs (fragments of the *Book of the Dead*); objects made of rope; fans all made from the same variety of plant; featherweight boats with slightly raised prows and sterns adept for navigating through shallow waters and marshy areas, and still very much in use by hunters and fishermen in Africa. The last section is dedicated to paper, its actual production (reconstruction of a workbench) as well as the pigments and instruments used by scribes.

painting of the Madonna began to shed tears), since when the shrine has attracted large numbers of pilgrims. The architects of this project were the Frenchmen M Andrault and P Parat, and the Italian structural engineer R Morandi. **Inside★**, a dizzy sensation of lofty height is provided and accentuated by the use of vertical windows extending upwards to the apex of the roof.

Basilica di Santa Lucia extra Mœnia

This basilica faces onto its own piazza: a wide, rectangular area imbued with peace. According to tradition, it was erected to mark the spot where the saint was martyred in 303, as Caravaggio suggests in his painting of the subject *(now in Palazzo Bellomo)*. The original Byzantine church underwent a considerable number of changes over the years to arrive at its present form in the 15C-16C. The oldest extant parts are the front entrance, the three semicircular apses and the two lower tiers of the bell tower (12C). The painted wooden ceiling is 17C. Below the church lie the **Catacombs of Santa Lucia** *(closed to the public)*, which by their very existence might substantiate the truth as to whether the saint was indeed martyred here.
Still in the same square, the small octagonal building by Giovanni Vermexio, a 17C architect, contains the tomb of the saint. Her actual relics, however, were transported to Constantinople in the 11C by the Byzantine general George Maniakes, and thence to Venice following the fall of Constantinople during the Fourth Crusade. They are now preserved in the Duomo here.

Ginnasio Romano

The Roman Gymnsasium, situated on Via Elorina just beyond the **Foro Siracusano**, formed with the Forum a part of the market place of ancient Akradina. The name, however, is erroneous. In fact, it was part of a complex building that comprised a *quadroporticus*, with a small theatre – rows of seating are still visible in the *cavea* part – and a small marble temple which served as a stage set.

Santa Lucia

St Lucy, the patron saint of Siracusa, lived here in the 4C, hence the reason why so many local churches are dedicated to her, including the Duomo. The date of 13 December (her *dies natalis*, when the saint's earthly life came to end and her spiritual life began) is celebrated with a procession headed by the silver statue of the saint from the Duomo to the place where she was entombed.

IN ORTYGIA

Galleria Regionale di Palazzo Bellomo★

Open daily except Mon, 9am-2pm (also 3-7pm Wed); last admission 30min before closing. €2.50. ☎ 0931 69 511.
Palazzo Bellomo, first built under Swabian rule (13C), was extended and raised in the 15C. Such is the reason for the two markedly different styles: at ground level, the combination of the pointed archway and narrow arrow-slit openings give it the appearance of a fortress; the first floor has elegant three-light windows separated with slender columns. The *palazzo* was built as a private residence before being acquired by the nuns from the adjoining convent of St Benedict in the 18C. Today it is all part of the same museum. The Church of **San Benedetto** standing alongside contains a fine coffered ceiling.

Inside, the *palazzo* shelters a lovely internal porticoed courtyard with a staircase leading to the first floor. The top part of the parapet is ornamented with rosettes and trilobate tracery. At the top of the first flight of stairs, note the fine Flamboyant aedicule above the doorway.

Museum – The museum is dedicated in the main to Sicilian art. However, Byzantine influences clearly pervade a series of paintings *(Room IV)* by Venetian artists working in Crete (at a time when it formed part of the Venetian Empire). These show *The Creation* (six panels), *Original Sin* and *Earthly Paradise*. The upper floor is largely devoted to painting: perhaps the most striking, despite being damaged, is the ***Annunciation**** by **Antonello da Messina**. As with other paintings by the same artist, there is an inherent Flemish quality to this picture especially in its minute attention to detail (the saint's mantle, crowded landscape through the window); the overall formality, spacious composition and precise definition of perspective is more typically Italian. The ***Entombment of St Lucy**** by **Caravaggio** might even be modelled on the saint's actual tomb in the catacombs nearby in Siracusa which bear her name. The characteristically dramatic and provocative style of this artist's work is here evident in the arrangement of the crowd: the main figures jostling around the saint, who lies dead upon the ground, are the gravediggers, including one in the foreground turning his back to the onlooker. Atmosphere is imparted by the strong light which, in turn, casts disturbing shadows.

The museum also displays an eclectic collection of objects: furnishings, holy vestments, Nativity figures, furniture and ceramics.

Galleria Civica d'Arte Contemporanea

(♿) Open mid-May to mid-Sep, Tue-Sun, 9am-1pm and 5-9pm, Mon, 5-9pm only; mid-Sep to mid-May, Tue-Fri, 9am-1pm and 4-8pm, Sat-Sun and public hols, 9am-1pm and 5-9pm, Mon, 4-8pm only. No charge. ☎ 0931 24 902.

The former convent and Church of Montevergini *(entrance in Via delle Vergini)* presently houses the municipal collection of contemporary art. This consists mainly of paintings by Italian artists (Sergio Fermariello, Marco Cingolani, Aldo Damioli, Enrico de Paris).

Excursions

Castello Eurialo*

9km/5.5mi NW along Via Epipoli, in the Belvedere district. Open 9am-1hr before dusk. No charge. ☎ 0931 71 17 73.

The road up to the fortress gives some idea of the scale of the defensive reinforcements imposed on the city by Dionysius the Elder. In addition to fortifying Ortygia, the able strategist decided to build a wall around the entire settlement, encompassing the districts of Tyche and Neapolis which, until then, had stood outside the city limits and had therefore been easy prey for attack. With this in mind, he ordered the construction of the imposing **Walls of Dionysius** (*mura dionigiane* – 27km/17mi) across the Epipolae high plateau enclosing the north side of the town. The fortification comprised two parallel walls built of rectangular limestone blocks, infilled with rubble. The enclosure reached 10m/33ft in height and 3m/10ft in width; posterns were placed at regular intervals around the perimeter so as to allow traffic to flow freely, and to provide constant surveillance in case of any thought of attack by the enemy. The gates of the castle, being vulnerable, were flanked by defensive towers. One section of the wall is visible along the road up to Belvedere *(on the left)*.

The top of the ridge provided a strategic position for the castle. Its name, Euryalus, is derived from the headland on which it stood, which vaguely resembles the head of a nail (Greek: *euryelos*). The fortress is one of the most impressive Greek defences to have survived from Antiquity. Its heart is ringed with a series of three consecutive ditches linked by a warren of underground passages that enabled garrisons to operate independently, while at the same time enabling any material fired by the enemy into the ditches to be removed before it incurred any damage. Should the enemy ever succeed in entering the castle precinct, it would have been completely disorientated. The entrance to the archaeological area coincides with the first of these ditches. A little further on, the second deep trench lined with vertical walls may be discerned before, finally, arriving at the third, making this a veritable Chinese-puzzle masterpiece of defensive design. Three tall square piers in the third ditch lead to the assumption that there must have been a drawbridge apparatus providing access to the inner stronghold (or keep). The east side is riddled with a series of communicating passageways; one measuring some 200m/650ft in length led to a pincer-type gateway *(trypilon)* and a way out of the fortress. The west side of the ditch accommodated various underground rooms for storing supplies.

Behind stood the square keep, preceded by an impressive series of defensive towers. Within the confines of the keep itself there is an open area with three square cisterns, visible on the right. The far corner provides a fine **view*** down to Siracusa *(opposite)* and the plain stretching away to the left.

Tempio di Giove Olimpico

3km/1.8mi out of town along Via Elorina, signposted right. The Temple of Olympian Zeus, built some time in the 6C BC, occupies a splendid position, slightly raised above the surrounding landscape. Its majestic appearance must have been worthy of the supreme power it represented.

Fonte Ciane★★

8km/5mi SE. In high season, visitors should turn up and wait until enough people arrive to form a group. Booking is recommended out of season. Visitors are advised to contact Signore Vella for further information, ☎ 0931 39 889 or 368 72 96 040 (mobile).

The River Ciane, which almost merges with the nearby River Anapo, is the main link with the internal area of Pantalica *(see PANTALICA)*. Its mouth is a favourite starting-point for **boat trips★★**. Shortly after setting off, a splendid view of the Grand Harbour of Siracusa opens out before you. The boat then continues through lush vegetation: predominantly reeds, ancient ash trees, and eucalyptus, before entering a narrow gorge and emerging in a luxuriant grove of swaying papyrus rising from the water. It was here, according to the myth transcribed by Ovid (*Metamorphoses: The Rape of Proserpine*, Book 5, l 409-437), that Cyane the water nymph, wooed by Anapus, tried to obstruct Pluto from abducting Persephone and, as a result, was transformed into a spring.

Lara Pessina/MICHELIN

Luxuriant clumps of papyrus

Tour

ARCHAEOLOGICAL SITES

Approximately 80km/50mi – allow one day

From Siracusa, take S 114 towards Catania.

Thapsos

Open daily except Sun and public hols, 9am-2pm. No charge. For information and reservations, contact the Soprintendenza a few days in advance. ☎ 0931 48 11 11.

The Magnisi peninsula which separates the Bay of Augusta from the Bay of Siracusa is tenuously connected to the mainland by a narrow isthmus of sand. Archaeological discoveries have now ascertained that, in the Middle Bronze Age (15C-13C BC), there grew up one of the most important prehistoric cultures here; this is further underlined by the recovery of Mycenean and Maltese ceramics that suggest Thapsos continued thereafter to be a trading emporium of considerable importance.

Archaeological site – Excavation has revealed a number of substantial remains from a settlement, including various round huts from the 15C-14C BC: several of these preserve the holes in which the roof poles were held, and the central hearth. From a subsequent phase (13C-12C BC), there survive traces of a more sophisticated residential complex comprising a series of rectangular chambers arranged around a cobbled courtyard; these concur with Mycenean prototypes. Note also, on a slope to the west of the site, the cisterns for collecting rainwater and the small ditch by which it was channelled to the settlement.

Further south along the dirt track edging the area of excavation, on the left, may be seen fragments of the Early Bronze Age fortifications, complete with extant foundations for lookout towers.

A few hundred metres beyond this extends a vast **necropolis** containing some 450 burial chambers. These consist of small man-made hollows preceded by a vestibule, which in most cases consists of a small shaft, *dromos* passageway or tunnel (these are more evident along the seashore where the sea has eroded the external wall). The burial chambers are round with conical ceilings; in some, the walls accommodate shallow niches (visible in one tomb where the ceiling has collapsed) in which the grave goods were deposited. These chambers were used for extended groups of people (complete families and dependants), and were designed to serve several generations. Entombment was by inhumation.

Return to the coast road and continue in the direction of Augusta.

Megara Hyblaea

(♿) Open Apr-Oct, 9am-6pm; Nov-Mar, 9am-3pm. No charge. ☎ 0931 48 11 11.

The Greek colony of Megara Hyblaea, founded by the Megarians of Greece in 728 BC, was twice razed to the ground: once in 483 BC by Gelon, the tyrant of Gela, and again by the Romans in 213 BC. The archaeological site is situated in a strange landscape, stranded between the sea and the chimneys of the Augusta oil refinery.

Excavations – The **necropolis** lies outside the town walls, alongside the older enclosure walls *(before crossing the railway bridge, by the bend, take the dirt track off to the right).*

Beyond the entrance extends one of the *decumani* that once led to the **agora** (market-place). One of the particular characteristics of the site is the clear evidence of successive building phases as Archaic constructions give way to Hellenistic ones above. On the left of the piazza sits a sanctuary, recognisable by the semicircular north end wall. Follow D 1, a street on the left, which passes alongside a large **Hellenistic house** from the 4C-2C BC (entrance marked by iron steps): this comprises some 20 rooms arranged around two courtyards, a rectangular one with a well in the middle, and a second diamond-shaped one. Some rooms preserve remains of *opus signinum* floors (an amalgam of clay particles mixed with minute pieces of rubble, bound together with lime). In each case, the thresholds of the various internal doorways are clearly visible, together with the grooves into which fit the door jambs. To the left of the *agora*, lie the **Hellenistic baths**. The boiler is discernible (below the metal walkway) as is a round room used for ablutions which once would have been ringed with basins. Further along C 1 (right of the baths) is a *Pritaneo* (where magistrates would meet) from the Archaic period (6C BC) built of characteristic square, regular-cut stones. The *decumanus* continues beyond the square, as far as the **West Gate** and fortifications from the Hellenistic period, built with regular blocks and reinforced with defence towers.

Continue N for 15km/9mi.

Augusta

Augusta today is an important Italian commercial port, and an industrial conglomeration, concerned primarily with oil refineries and the production of "green" (lead-free) petrol. The town has incurred considerable damage over the years as a result of the 1693 earthquake, the Allied bombing of 1943, and following major seismic tremors as recently as 1990.

The town was founded by Frederick II on account of its strategic position with regard to defending the Bay of Augusta: hence the overpowering defensive quality of the Swabian castle, despite its neglected state of repair. The entrance to the citadel is by the **Spanish Gate**, flanked by two imposing bastions.

The main axis of the old town is Corso Principe Umberto, the commercial thoroughfare which runs north to south.

Brucoli

This charming fishing village clusters around its picturesque little **harbour** which lies in the mouth of the River Porcaria. The 15C **castle** *(closed to the public)* occupying the very tip of the headland where the village has grown up, enjoys a marvellous **view**★ of the harbour on one side and the ample Golfo di Brucoli on the other.

Head towards Lentini (25km/15mi W of Brucoli).

Lentini

This small agricultural town, which was badly affected by the earthquake of 1693, is dependent on growing citrus fruits. The centre of town is marked by the **Chiesa Madre** dedicated to Sant'Alfio (a hugely popular saint here and in the hamlets around Etna); preserved in its palaeo-Christian underground vault are the relics, it is alleged, of St Alfio, St Filadelfio and St Cirino, as well as a 9C Byzantine image of the Hodegetria Madonna (Guide or Instructress pointing to the Way of Redemption based on an icon said to have been painted by St Luke). A small **archaeological museum** displays artefacts recovered from the excavations at Leontinoi. *Closed for restoration at the time of going to press.*

Leontinoi

Access is easiest via Carlentini. For information on admission times, call ☎ 095 78 32 962.

This area has been inhabited since protohistoric times (as the bases of huts on Collina di Metapiccola testify: these may be reached by a track that leads off to the right from the entrance to the archaeological zone). In 729 BC it was targeted by the Chalcidians of Naxos as a good place to found a colony. It was here that the philosopher **Gorgias** was born.

Excavation has brought to light the remains of various monumental pyramidal tombs and walling beyond. The Syracusan gate serves as the main entrance to the town. The way leads on towards what is assumed to be the site of an acropolis (on Colle San Mauro) where vestiges of a temple have been found. The track climbs up past the circular base of what was perhaps a defence tower. From the top, a wonderful view extends over Lentini and, in the distance, a man-made lake known as the **Biviere**. The mound to the left is Colle di Sant'Egidio where the town's necropolis was located, complete with tombs excavated from the base rock.

Case del Biviere★

In the Contrada Biviere: from Lentini railway station, turn right and follow the sign for SP 67 to Valsavoia. By the fork in the road, on the right, stands a villa with a large green entrance. The garden is open by appointment only; to make a reservation, phone or send a fax at least two weeks in advance. Brunch, drinks, lunch or tea can be booked for groups. €5. ☎ 095 78 31 449; Fax 095 78 35 575.

According to legend, when Heracles came to these parts intending to present the skin of the Nemean lion to Ceres, he fell in love with the area and created a lake which would bear his name; this was subsequently changed to Biviere (to mean drinking trough or fish-farm) during the Arab occupation. The house was built on the eastern edge of the lake which was infilled during the 1930s; when it came to be restored to its original state, it was made smaller and removed to some distance from the villa. The lovely gardens that now surround the house were initiated in 1967 at the behest of the Borghese princes. They comprise a broad variety of Mediterranean species including yuccas, palms, flowering trees (jacaranda, originally from Brazil, and Judas trees), together with more exotic plants such as *Xanthorrea arborea* and *Encefaloartus horridus* – the silvery blue prickly cycad which was thought to exist only in fossil form before it was discovered growing in Tanzania.

The stone jetties of the old port are home to a fine collection of succulent plants.

Where to Stay

Agriturismo Casa dello Scirocco – *Contrada Piscitello, Carlentini, 3km/1.8mi SE of Lentini – ☎ 095 44 77 09 – Fax 095 78 36 120 – www.casadelloscirocco.it – 🏊 – 50 beds €40/80.* ☕. This interesting establishment with an evocative name is located in a complex of caves which date back to the pre-Greek era. It comprises a villa founded in ancient times, equipped with a ventilation system which keeps the house cool during hot weather.

Rovine di Solunto★

Solus or Soluntum, one of Sicily's three Punic towns (with Motya and Palermo), enjoys a splendid position on the slopes of the Monte Catalfano headland, with views over the sea beyond Capo Zafferano.

Location

Michelin map 565 22M-Palermo. Because of Solunto's hilly **location★★** much of the walking around the magnificent ruins is uphill. For this reason, the site is best avoided during the hottest part of the day.

Neighbouring sights are described in the following chapters: BAGHERIA; CEFALÙ; MONREALE; PALERMO; TERMINI.

Worth a Visit

Access – *Starting from Bagheria, cross the level crossing near the station and turn down S 113 towards Porticello. A minor road forks left towards the hill. Open Mar-Oct, Mon-Sat, 9am-6.30pm, Sun and public hols, 9am-1pm; Nov-Feb, Mon-Sat, 9am-4.30pm, Sun and public hols, 9am-1pm. €2. ☎ 091 90 45 57.*

Solunto was founded by the Carthaginians in the 4C BC, possibly beside or among the ruins of an old Phoenician town; a century later it succumbed to Roman rule. The name has two origins: one legendary and associated with the evil creature **Soluntus**, who was defeated by Hercules in this very area; the other more plausible explanation links it to the Carthaginian word *Selaim*, meaning crag.

The urban layout conforms with the Classical principles upheld by Hippodamus of Miletus, arranged orthogonally with a *decumanus maximus* and perpendicular side streets enclosing *insulae* (blocks); a network of intersecting narrow passages was inserted to drain away water. The precipitous site required terraces to be built, and for additional living space to be accommodated in tall houses. Although the upper storeys no longer survive, the flights of steps providing access are still visible.

The way up to the ruins passes the **Antiquarium** just inside the gate, which displays artefacts recovered from the site, including a fragment of fresco with a tragic mask.

Baths

The thermal baths complex preserves the under-floor brick supports which enabled hot air to circulate and heat the rooms from below, and a small room with a mosaic floor which served as a bath.

Via dell'Agorà

The *decumanus maximus* is partly paved in stone and, rather unusually, in terracotta. It bisects the town on a south-west to north-east axis, extending to the forum, here designated with the Greek name agora.

Gymnasium

This is the name commonly given to the patrician house with an atrium and a peristyle, from which there remain three Doric columns and part of the entablature, complete with architrave, frieze of metopes and triglyphs and cornice. At the rear, a staircase would have provided access to the floor above.

Via Ippodamo da Mileto

This is a *cardo*: from the bottom, a magnificent **view**★★ extends over the bay of Palermo and Monte Pellegrino.

Casa di Leda

This large patrician house is so called because it contains a wall frescoed with Leda and the Swan. The house is arranged around a peristyle (as indicated by the stump of a corner column and cavities for the other columns) with an *impluvium* in which rainwater was collected (surrounded by a mosaic cornice with black and white volutes) before being piped to an oval cistern set before and below it. One of the rooms facing out onto the peristyle is frescoed in Pompeiian style. At the sides of this room, probably a *triclinium* (dining room), steps would have led to the first floor.

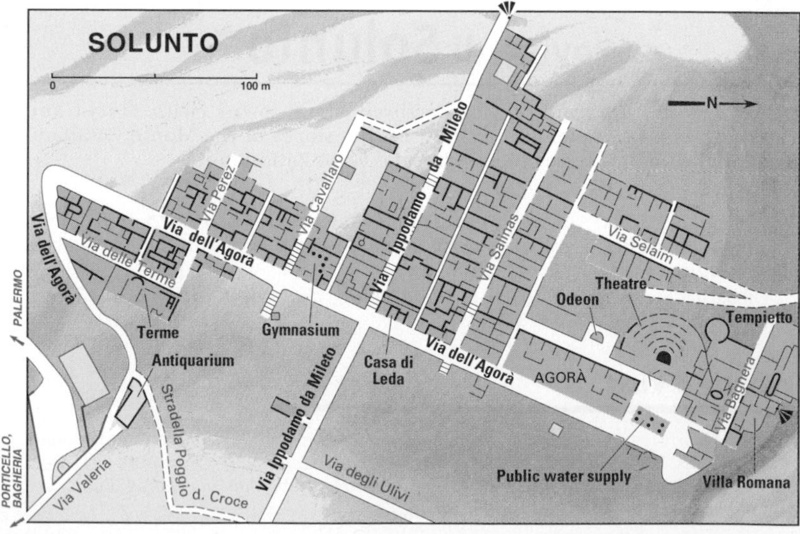

Agora

The square, enclosed on all sides by public buildings, was lined with shops *(at the far end)*. On the east side, there was a large **public cistern**: note the bases of the 26 columns that supported the roof.

Theatre

Little survives of the theatre: its shape, however, is still discernible from the air. It was built with rows of seating cut in part from the bedrock – as with the theatre at Segesta. The original building dates from Hellenistic times, although this was substantially altered in Roman times: note how the orchestra is now semicircular; the Greek orchestra would have been larger and have formed almost two-thirds of a circle.

The small round construction on the eastern side probably constituted a **small temple** used for initiation rites associated with the cult of the gods.

Odeon

The small theatre was intended for musical performances or council meetings: the parts still in evidence include the orchestra and a few rows of *cavea* seating.

Villa Romana

This spacious two-storey house was graced with a peristyle. The stairs indicate the way up to the first floor.

From the villa, there is a beautiful view of Capo Zafferano and the little town of **Sant'Elia**. On the right, at the far end of the bay, crowning the tip of the headland, stand the ruins of the **medieval castle of Solanto**.

Taormina★★★

Taormina stands high up on a rocky plateau 200m/650ft above sea level, in a fabulous position★★★ overlooking the sea, right opposite Mount Etna. Its beautiful landscapes and memorable sights – in particular its magnificent theatre – have made the town famous worldwide. Since the 18C it has been a popular destination for travellers, although it has only developed into a substantial tourist resort in the last 30 years. Many foreigners, especially British and German, have decided to build villas in the town and many illustrious personalities have sojourned there, including the German Emperor Wilhelm II and King Edward VII, such famous families as the Rothschilds and the Krupps, writers such as DH Lawrence, and, more recently, stars and members of the international jet set. From April to September, Taormina's appeal is lessened somewhat by the crowds of tourists who invade the town, although it remains a highlight of a trip to Sicily at any time of year.

Location

Population: 10 697. Michelin map 565 2N 7 – Messina. As it is extremely difficult to find somewhere to park in the historical centre, visitors are advised to leave their car in one of the well-signposted car parks along the road leading into the town and to walk into the centre. The historical centre is best explored on foot, and the reward for tackling the many flights of steps and steep slopes (avoid the hottest part of the day) is the magnificent view from the top of the town. ℹ *Piazza S. Caterina (Palazzo Corvaja); ☎ 0942 23 243; Fax 0942 24 941; www.taormina-network.it*

Neighbouring sights are described in the following chapters: ACIREALE; ETNA; GIARDINI NAXOS; MESSINA.

Background

Legend and history – Legend relates how the crew aboard a Greek vessel that was sailing along the eastern coast of Sicily had the impudence to be distracted while making a sacrifice to Neptune, the god of the sea. The god, outraged, sent forth such a strong wind that the boat was shipwrecked. Just one of the sailors escaped death and the anger of the god, and succeeded in reaching the beach at Capo Schisò. Fascinated by the area, the lonely survivor, Theocles, decided to return to Greece to persuade a band of his compatriots to come to Sicily and found a colony. This was **Nasso**, modern-day Naxos *(see GIARDINI NAXOS).*

There is a seed of truth in the legend: for a Greek colony was indeed founded here in the 8C BC, and its people prospered quietly until 403 BC when Dionysius, the tyrant of Syracuse, decided to extend his territory by including this part of the island; following their defeat, the colonists were allowed to settle on the plateau of Monte Tauro (200m/650ft above sea level) which hitherto had been occupied by the Siculi. From that time, records begin to refer to the settlement of *Tauromenion*, modern Taormina. At first the town was allied with Rome, and was then conquered by Octavian; when the Roman Empire fell, it became the capital of Byzantine

The Greek theatre with Mount Etna in the background

B. Morandi/MICHELIN

Directory

Transport

Trains and buses run to and from Catania (approximately 1hr), Messina (1hr) and Siracusa (2hr 30min). There is also a daily bus service from the town to Fontanarossa airport at Catania. Taormina-Giardini train station is situated in Villagonia, 3km/1.8mi from the centre. The bus station is on Via Pirandello.

Excursions from Taormina

The CST (Compagnia Siciliana Turismo) bus company offers a number of excursions to places of interest, including Siracusa, Agrigento, Piazza Armerina, Palermo, the Aeolian Islands, the Alcantara gorge and Etna. For further information, contact CST, Corso Umberto 101; ☎ 0942 62 60 88; Fax 0942 23 304; www.tin.it./cst

Where to Eat

For further restaurant options, see GIARDINI NAXOS.

In addition to the restaurants listed below, the district to the west of Corso Umberto I is teeming with typical outdoor Sicilian restaurants set out on discreet terraces or in secluded gardens.

• ***Budget***

Porta Messina – *Largo Giove Serapide 4, Taormina – ☎ 0942 23 205.*
The list of pizzas in this friendly restaurant is endless, with more unusual options for those who are ready to experiment.

La Piazzetta – *Vicolo F. Paladini 5/7, Taormina – ☎ 0942 62 63 17 – www.paginegialle.it/ristorantelapiazzetta – Closed Mon (except Jul and Aug), Nov and Jan – €20/34 +10% service.* The cuisine at this friendly, family-run establishment with a typical village-restaurant atmosphere is distinctly Mediterranean, with an emphasis on fish. Pleasant terrace.

Il Baccanale – *Porta Filea 1, Taormina – ☎ 0942 62 53 90 – Closed Thu (except Apr-Sep) – – €23/35.* This restaurant serving fine Sicilian cuisine is popular with foreign tourists and enjoys a rustic atmosphere with outdoor tables on a small piazza.

Al Saraceno – *Via Madonna della Rocca 18, Taormina – ☎ 0942 63 20 15 – info@alsaraceno.it – Closed Mon (except Jul and Aug) and Nov – – €24/33.* This recently restored restaurant is situated along the street running from the Castello Saraceno. On fine days the splendid view from the spacious terrace on the first floor extends as far as the Straits of Messina. Fresh fish and pizza are the house specialities.

• ***Moderate***

Al Duomo – *Vico Ebrei 11, Taormina – ☎ 0942 62 56 56 – info@ristorantealduomo.it – Closed Mon, Jan and Nov – – Booking recommended – €33/41.* The highlights of Al Duomo are its delightful terrace with a view of the cathedral and its excellent local cuisine.

Il Delfino–da Angelo – *Via Nazionale, Mazzarò, 5.5km/3.5mi S of Taormina on S 114 – ☎ 0942 23 004 – Closed Nov-15 Mar – €27/37.* Combine lunch with a dip in the sea at this attractive restaurant situated right on the beach.

Where to Stay

For further accommodation options, see GIARDINI NAXOS.

• ***Budget***

Bed & Breakfast Villa Regina – *Punta San Giorgio, Castelmola, 5km/3mi NE of Taormina – ☎ 0942 28 228 – Fax 0942 28 083 – intelisano@tao.it – Closed Nov-Feb – 10 rooms. €30/50 ☕ €8.* This simple guesthouse has a cool, shady garden and a delightful view of Taormina and the coast. Ideal for those in need of a peaceful and relaxing break.

• ***Moderate***

Hotel Villa Schuler – *Piazzetta Bastione, Via Roma, Taormina – ☎ 0942 23 481 – Fax 0942 23 522 – www.villaschuler.com – Closed Dec-Feb – ♿ – 26 rooms. €70/124 ☕.* Converted into a hotel in 1905, this old house in the historical centre is surrounded by a Mediterranean garden full of tropical flowers and plants. The hotel retains some of its late-19C atmosphere and has old-fashioned, comfortable rooms.

Andromaco Palace Hotel – *Via Fontana Vecchia, Taormina – ☎ 0942 23 436 – Fax 0942 24 985 – info@andromaco.it – – 20 rooms. €85/120 ☕.* Despite its rather grand name, this elegant family-run hotel close to the town centre is both cosy and romantic, with simple, yet comfortable furnishings and panoramic views.

Hotel Del Corso – *Corso Umberto 238, Taormina – ☎ 0942 62 86 98 – Fax 0942 62 98 56 – hoteldelcorso@tiscalinet.it – Closed Jan and Feb – 15 rooms. €83/124 ☕.* This well-known, recently restored Taormina hotel has been under new management since 2000. Although the reception area is small, the dining room is elegant and the rooms tastefully decorated.

• ***Expensive***

Hotel Isabella – *Corso Umberto 58, Taormina – ☎ 0942 23 153 – Fax 0942 23 155 – – 32 rooms. €105/160 ☕.* The perfect destination for those who prefer the town to the beach. This top-quality hotel is elegant, efficiently run and enjoys an excellent location in the town centre. Breakfast is taken on a delightful terrace with views of the Greek theatre.

Hotel Villa Sonia – *Via Porta Mola 9, Castelmola, 5km/3mi NW of Taormina – ☎ 0942 28 082 – Fax 0942 28 083 – intelisano@tao.it – Closed Nov-20 Dec and 6 Jan-28 Feb – ♿ – 35 rooms. €119/191 ☕.* Situated at the entrance to the charming village of Castelmola, this attractive villa is tastefully decorated with period items and Sicilian handicrafts.

IN THE FOOTSTEPS OF KINGS AND ARTISTS

Grand Hotel Timeo – *Via Teatro Greco 59, Taormina* – ☎ *0942 23 801 – Fax 0942 62 85 01 – ricevimento.timeo@framon–hotels.it* – – *87 rooms. €262/277* . This superbly located hotel helped to establish Taormina's reputation. Recently restored to its former period splendour, the hotel offers all the modern creature comforts expected of a high-quality establishment.

Taking a Break

Caffè Wunderbar – *Piazza IX Aprile 7, Taormina* – ☎ *0942 62 53 02.* Greta Garbo and Tennessee Williams enjoyed meeting for cocktails in this famous café at the foot of the Torre dell'Orologio, in one of the most attractive corners of Taormina. The interior is elegant in style, while the terrace enjoys magnificent views of the Bay of Naxos. Not to be missed!

Mocambo Bar – *Piazza IX Aprile 8, Taormina* – ☎ *0942 23 350.* "Take a seat at the Mocambo and watch the world go by ..." is the advice given by the owners of this bar-*pasticceria*, which enjoys a superb location overlooking the beautiful Piazza IX Aprile. Open from breakfast to after dinner, this bar has a pleasant atmosphere throughout the day.

Pasticceria Saint Honoré – *Corso Umberto I 208, Taormina* – ☎ *094 22 48 77 – Open 7am-midnight.* You're spoilt for choice in this *pasticceria* with its wide selection of cakes, ice creams, pastries and *torroni* (a type of nougat). Alternatively, enjoy a cooling glass of *granita* on the Saint Honoré's terrace.

Shopping

La Bottega del Buongustaio – *Via G. di Giovanni 17, Taormina* – ☎ *094 26 25 769 – Open 9am-8.30pm.* Set back from the hustle and bustle of Corso Umberto, this shop specialises in DOC-label Sicilian produce, including wines, liqueurs, sauces, preserves, honey, pasta and olive oil. An excellent address for those wishing to take home some of the island's gastronomic specialities.

Festivals

Festa del costume e del carretto siciliani – Held in April and May, this festival celebrates the Sicilian cart and local costume, hosting a number of traditional folk shows.

Taormina arte – This international music, theatre and film festival takes place from July to September. For information, call ☎ 0942 21 142; www.taormina-arte.com

Sicily. Shortly after the arrival of the Arabs it was destroyed, only to be immediately rebuilt and, in 1079, to be conquered by the Norman Count Roger d'Altavilla, under whom it enjoyed a long period of prosperity.
In the centuries that followed, it became a Spanish dominion before succumbing to French and then Bourbon rule, until the Unification of Italy.

Special Feature

Theatre***

(♿) Open 9am-2hr before dusk. €4. ☎ *0942 23 220; www.regione.sicilia.it*
The theatre was built by the Ancient Greeks (Hellenistic period), and then transformed and enlarged by the Romans. What survives today dates from the 2C AD. The amphitheatre is built in such a way as to exploit the natural lie of the land: several of the *cavea* steps are cut directly from the bedrock. The Greek theatre conformed with the correct application of the Classical orders; it included a semicircular *orchestra* section reserved for musicians, chorus and dancers. The Romans removed the lower tier of steps when converting the orchestra into an arena (circular, therefore), a shape better suited to hosting circus games; they also added a corridor to provide access for gladiators and wild animals.
The red of the bricks, the white of the marble columns which still adorn the stage, and the intense blue of the sky above are the predominant colours in this idyllic landscape. From the top of the *cavea* (auditorium), visitors and spectators can absorb the full impact of the glorious **panoramic view***** spread before the majestic presence of Mount Etna, its summit often capped with snow, sloping gently down and into the sea which, in turn, silently laps at the undulating coastline below. The magical prospect is extended all along the top of the *cavea* as far as the opposite left-hand corner where the outlook encompasses Taormina itself.
The theatre, which continues to be used, has hosted in the past the *David di Donatello* prize, one of the most prestigious events in the Italian film industry. It now hosts *Taormina Arte*, an international festival of cinema, theatre, ballet and music, which takes place during the summer months.

Walking About

The centre of Taormina, now reserved for pedestrians, radiates from the main thoroughfare Corso Umberto I, from which it is possible to reach all, or almost all, the main sights.

Corso Umberto I*

What a pleasure it is to stroll along this peaceful thoroughfare beginning at **Porta Messina** as it gently climbs up to **Porta Catania**, past its elegant shops, restaurants and cafés. Behind this front, most especially off to the left near the bottom, extends an intricate network of side streets full of unexpected sights and smells (like the sweet scent of marzipan fruits and almond paste wafting up from back-street sweet-shop kitchens). Just beyond Porta Messina, at the entrance to the street, stands the 17C **Chiesa di San Pancrazio**. This is dedicated to St Pancras who, according to legend, was the first Bishop of Taormina. The church, meanwhile, sits among the foundations of a temple dedicated to Zeus Serapis (notice the remains of the Ancient wall incorporated into the building's left flank). The façade includes an attractive portal of Taormina stone, framed on each side by niches containing statues of saints.

Along the course of the street there are three lovely piazzas.

Piazza Vittorio Emanuele

This square occupies the site of the ancient Roman Forum. Behind the **Chiesa di Santa Caterina** with its fine Baroque pink marble and Taormina stone doorway, vestiges of ancient buildings can be seen. These red-brick ruins belong to an **Odeon**, a small covered theatre from the Roman period (1C AD).

Palazzo Corvaja

The main heart of the building, which includes the square tower and the central section overlooking the internal courtyard, dates from the period of Arab domination. The left wing and the staircase up to the first floor were added in the 13C; the right wing dates from the 15C. Having been abandoned and left to become completely dilapidated over the years, it was completely restored after the Second World War. A succession of styles is clearly discernible: the top of the tower is Arab, the two-light windows of the state room (13C) and the elegant front entrance are Catalan Gothic (the stairway in front of it is ornamented with shallow relief panels depicting scenes from Genesis, unfortunately badly damaged), the Sala del Parlamento *(in the right wing)* is Norman – it is so called because the Sicilian parliament used to meet here in the 15C.

The offices located off the courtyard, on the right, are in part occupied by APT, the Sicilian Tourist Authorities; they also display various typical Sicilian puppets and splendidly ornate Sicilian carts.

On the first floor of the *palazzo* is the **Museo Siciliano di Arte e Tradizioni Popolari**, housing a collection of carts, puppets, costumes, embroidery, cribs and a series of ex-votos. *Open daily except Mon, 9am-1pm and 4-8pm. €2.50. ☎ 0942 23 243.*

Naumachie

In a side-street off to the left. The name technically refers to the simulated naval battles that the Romans so enjoyed watching. In this case, it relates to a red-brick wall dating from the Roman period that has been reinforced by a system of blind arcading. In fact, it probably served as a supporting wall for a large reservoir of water and formed part of a rectangular building, possibly a gymnasium.

Piazza IX Aprile*

This delightful little square overlooks the sea offering wonderful **views**** over the bay and across to Mount Etna. It is enclosed on the other three sides by the bare façade of San Giuseppe (17C), San Agostino (now a library) and the Torre dell'Orologio, which sits on an open loggia that provides a through way to the 15C part of the town. The extant building dates from the late 17C, when the clock was added, although it would appear that the foundations date as far back as the 6C AD, when the tower formed an integral part of the town's defences. The piazza serves as a standard meeting-place which means it is often crowded with people happy to while away the time at one of the bars with tables outside.

Piazza Duomo

A splendid Baroque **fountain** in Taormina stone rises from a circular base at the centre of the square. The largest basin facing eastwards at one time served as a drinking trough. Elevated in the centre, it bears the symbol of the town, a centaur, which here takes on a female form with, instead of the usual four legs, two legs and two arms holding an orb and a sceptre, the attributes of power.

Duomo

The 13C cathedral is dedicated in honour of St Nicholas of Bari. The front elevation has a starkly simple façade, relieved only by a Renaissance doorway flanked by single-light windows, surmounted by a rose window. The crenellations along the roof line have earned it the name of "cathedral-fortress". The left lateral wall has a fine entrance set into a pointed arch ornamented along the edge with vines; the rose window is aligned with the transept.

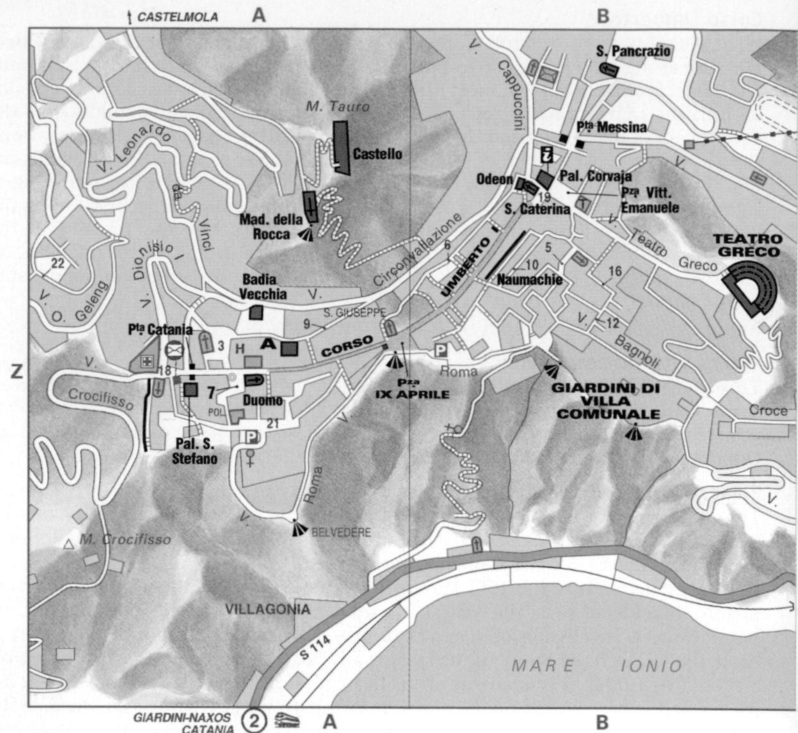

Interior – The fabric of the building is Gothic; the ground plan is a Latin cross. The nave is separated from the side aisles by an arcade of pointed arches, which spring from column shafts of pink marble. The clerestory above comprises simple single-light windows that illuminate the nave. Over the second altar in the south aisle sits a fine 16C polyptych by Antonello de Saliba.

TAORMINA'S PALAZZI*

The old town centre is dotted with fine *palazzi* which share various features: most are Gothic in style with Arabo-Norman touches, most are built of black lava stone and white Syracuse stone in a combination to provide geometric patterning and other decorative effects such as articulating arches, arcades and doorways. The application of such simple ideas animates the elevations of Taormina's most interesting town houses.

Palazzo di Santo Stefano

Turn left up Via del Ghetto just before Porta Catania. This fine building dates from the 15C. It was built for the Dukes of Santo Stefano, who formed part of the De Spuches family whose origins were Spanish. The bold rustication gives it the appearance of a fortified residence. The most effective decorative element is the two-tone (black lava and white Syracuse stone) geometric frieze which runs the length of the upper storey. The two levels which articulate the elevation have two-light windows: those on the second floor are set into elaborate arches.

The *palazzo* presently accommodates the **Fondazione Mazzullo**, which hosts permanent exhibitions of sculpture and drawings by the artist Graniti (and the occasional temporary show, notably during Advent when a display of terracotta Nativity scenes is arranged). A recurrent theme among the works in lava, granite and bronze, is the expression of pain: this is especially notable in a series of *Executions by Firing Squad* in which crumpled bodies are depicted as mutilated and incomplete, yet powerfully expressive; and in the *Wounded Cat* that is roughly hewn in stone. In contrast, what is striking about the female busts is their impenetrable facial expressions portrayed through features that in some are barely delineated, and in others are perfectly modelled – as in the *Amazon* and *Sappho*. *Open 9am-1pm and 4-8pm. No charge.*

Badia Vecchia

Via Dionisio 1. The name may derive from the false impression that the building had been an abbey. Its solid proportions are reminiscent of the Palazzo di Santo Stefano, as is the two-tone lace-like frieze between the first and second floors. Attractive two-light windows open above the frieze. The building is home to the **Museo Archeologico**. *Open 9am-1pm and 4-6pm. No charge. ☎ 0942 62 01 12.*

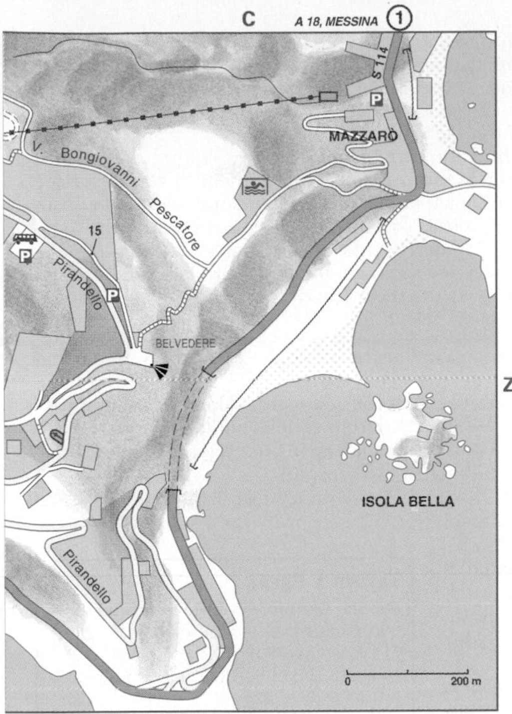

TAORMINA

Carmine (Piazza d.)	AZ	3
Don Bosco (Via)	BZ	6
Duomo (Piazza d.)	AZ	7
Fazzello (Via)	AZ	9
Giardinazzo (Via)	BZ	10
Ginnasio (Via d.)	BZ	12
Giovanni (Via d.)	BZ	13
Guardiola Vecchia (Via)	BCZ	15
Jallia Bassia (Via)	BZ	16
S. Antonio (Piazza)	AZ	18
S. Caterina (Largo)	BZ	19
S. Domenico (Piazzale)	AZ	21
Umberto I (Corso)	ABZ	
Von Gloeden (Via W.)	AZ	22

Palazzo Ciampoli	AZ	A

Palazzo Ciampoli

Providing a backdrop to the steps of Salita Palazzo Ciampoli, to the right of Corso Umberto I, just before Piazza Duomo. Despite its poor condition and an unsightly old discotheque sign (it having closed a few years ago and made way for a hotel), the façade of this *palazzo* is composed of two levels separated by a decoratively engraved stone panel. The entrance is set into an elegantly pointed arch, and is surmounted by a shield bearing the date when the palace was built: 1412.

Palazzo Corvaja *See p 365*.

I giardini di Villa Comunale★★

Via Roma. The gardens are planted with a huge variety of flowering plants and shrubs ranging from the most common to the exotic. During the times when it was still under private ownership, a series of follies were erected in various eclectic styles with a touch of the exotic. The most unusual consists of a conglomeration of arches and arcades which, at a glance, might be construed as a beehive, hence the name *(the Beehives)* appropriated to it by its owner, Lady Florence Trevelyan. An enthusiastic ornithologist, she used these follies for bird-watching purposes.

The little road that runs along the seaward edge provides a fine view of Mount Etna and the south coast.

Excursions

Beaches

A cable car links Taormina with Mazzarò on the coast. From Mazzarò a bus service operates to the other beaches (€3.50 there and back for the cable car + bus; ask for a Funibus ticket). The cable car runs every 15min and the bus every 30min.

While Taormina perches high up on its headland, the sea laps gently at the wonderful beaches below. The little bay of **Mazzarò** is enclosed on the south side by **Capo Sant'Andrea**, which is riddled with caves and grottoes, including one known as the Blue Grotto (Grotta Azzurra). The sound of fishermen calling for people to join a boat trip echoes the lengths of all the beaches. Beyond the headland is the delightful **bay★★** that sweeps round to **Isola Bella**, which is tenuously linked to the main shore by an extremely narrow strip of land. The island is part of the WWF Isola Bella Regional Reserve *(entrance at Km 47.2 on S 114; for further information, contact Viale S. Pancrazio 25, Taormina; ☎/Fax 0942 62 83 88)*. The longest beaches, **Spisone** and **Mazzeo**, extend north of Mazzarò.

Castello

4km/2.5mi along the road to Castelmola; a track turns up to the right. The castle can also be reached on foot by following the signs for "Salita Castello", up a series of broad steps, from Via Circonvallazione (about 1km/0.6mi there and back) in Taormina, or by taking Salita Branco, which starts in Via Dietro i Cappuccini. Avoid undertaking this walk in the midday sun or at the height of summer!

The **castle** stands isolated on the summit of Monte Tauro (398m/1 305ft). Just below it stands the **Santuario della Madonna della Rocca**: the little terrace before the church offers a fine **view**★★ of Taormina's ancient theatre and town. A footpath continues up to the castle, which consists of a medieval fortress built on the foundations of a former acropolis from Antiquity. Little of the trapezoidal-shaped building survives other than the old walls and the fragments of a tower. From here, yet another splendid **view**★★ extends over the theatre and Taormina.

Castelmola★

5km/3mi NW. This little village, occupying a strategic **position**★ up behind Taormina, centres around the picturesque little Piazzetta del Duomo; from here, an intricate network of tiny paved streets extends outwards. Magnificent glimpses of the surrounding landscape may be snatched from various points, most especially from Piazzetta di Sant'Antonino, where the **view**★ opens out towards Mount Etna, the north coast and the beaches nestling below Taormina.

The staircase on the right side of this piazza used to lead up from one of the old town gates to the castle; it was moved here when the road was built. The ruined **castle**, of which little remains other than sections of the 16C walls, maintains a good view of Monte Venere (beyond the cemetery) and the lesser Monte Ziretto.

The **Chiesa dell'Annunziata** next to the cemetery, although of Norman foundation, has been completely rebuilt; it preserves an attractive doorway sculpted in white stone.

A regional speciality typical of these parts is almond liqueur, a potent concoction which, it is claimed, was invented by the local inhabitants of Castelmola.

Taking a Break

Bar San Giorgio – *Piazza S. Antonio 1 – 98030 Castelmola – 5km/3mi NW of Taormina* – ☎ 0942 28 228. Established at the beginning of the 20C, this traditional café enjoys a wonderful location in the quiet Piazza S. Antonio, with superb views of Taormina and the sea. Past customers have included Charles Rolls and Henry Royce as well as John D Rockefeller, and the café continues to be popular with celebrities. Specialities include *vino alla mandorla* (almond liqueur).

Tour

THE ALCANTARA VALLEY

60km/37mi – allow approximately one day (including the visit to the gorges and the walk along the river bed).

Etna looms over the Alcantara Valley, alternately featuring among the hills then disappearing behind them as the road winds its way, providing an ever-changing kaleidoscope of marvellous **views**★.

Giardini Naxos ⌂⌂ – *See GIARDINI NAXOS*.

Continuing along the road, on the left, appear some disconcerting olive-wood sculptures by Francesco Lo Giudice, known as *Il Mago* (the magician).

Gole dell'Alcantara★

For information, contact the Ente Parco Fluviale dell'Alcantara, ☎ 0942 98 10 38; www.parcoalcantara.it/ The gorge is accessible when the water level is low, for a stretch of 50m/55yd to 200m/220yd. At the entrance to the gorge, waders can be hired to keep out the perennially freezing cold waters of the river. Under normal conditions, it is possible to walk upriver from May until September. During the rest of the year, only the entrance to the gorge is accessible. There is a lift to take visitors back up to the top of the gorge. Special camping facilities are available nearby. Open May-Oct, 7am-8pm; Nov-Apr, 7am-5pm. €2. Rental of boots and waders €6.70. Prices are subject to change. ☎ 0942 98 50 10.

The gorge – The descent on foot affords a spectacular **view**★ of the entrance to the gorge.

Once level with the river bed, the salt cliffs tower some 50m/165ft above the narrow tongue of water: geometric black forms seem to confront each other ominously as they surge skywards. Their axes intersect, forming pentagonal and hexagonal prisms, irregular shapes which, in interplay with the light, create forms both graceful and monstrous. Their massive bulk, exaggerated by shadow, seems accentuated

The Origins of the Alcantara Gorge

Lost in the mists of time, a small volcano north of Mount Etna woke and poured forth enormous quantities of lava which flowed down to the sea and beyond, to form Capo Schisò. The tortuous route taken by the river of lava was followed by a torrent of water which ploughed a channel through it, smoothing the lava and clearing away the aggregate. Towards the end of its journey, the water encountered more friable ground and, sweeping onwards, exposed two sheer cliffs of very hard basalt that had cooled and hardened into fascinating prism-like shapes. This is the gorge, only part of which is now accessible.
The name of the river, and of its valley, *Al Qantarah*, dates back to the period of Arab occupation and refers to the arched bridge built by the Romans that was capable of withstanding the force of the river in full spate, still an impressive sight even today.

further up the gorge, where the world suddenly seems to be composed of three elements: rock, water and sky. All the while, the sun defines contour and profile by casting its bright light deep into the darkness; occasionally this is refracted into a thousand tiny mirrors by minuscule droplets of water that have been ejected by the waterfalls, which then collect together into rivulets that stream down the sheer rock face.

Motta Camastra

A road off to the right leads to the small town which stands at an altitude of 453m/1 486ft.

Francavilla di Sicilia

It was here on 21 June 1719 that a violent battle took place between some Spaniards and Austrians, an event that is recorded for posterity by a series of prints preserved in the Capuchin monastery which stands on top of the hill nearby. Founded in the 16C, the monastery still has a few original cells and houses a small museum about life in this offshoot of the Franciscan Order. In the church there are several works of art, including an 18C wooden aumbry (small cupboard) for the vessels of the Eucharist bearing a pelican plucking the flesh from its breast to feed its young, a symbol of the sacrifice of Christ.

M. Magni/MICHELIN

Walking in the Alcantara Gorge

Castiglione di Sicilia

Castel Leone (now reduced to a ruin) dominates the town from on high, set as it is on its amazing rocky spur of tufa as if fused to the earth. The **site★** of the castle has been a lookout point since ancient times. From here stretch magnificent **views★★** over the town and Etna. To the east lie the ruins of a fortress dating from 750 BC.
The main monuments are clustered around the highest part of the town.

Legend

At one time the Alcantara River flowed calmly along its course without crags, rapids or sheer drops, making the valley fertile. The people who lived there, however, were evil: they hurt each other and had no respect for nature.
Two brothers lived in the valley and cultivated a field of wheat. One was blind. When the time came to divide up the harvest, the sighted farmer took the grain measure and began to share out the wheat. One measure for himself and one for his brother. Then, overtaken by greed, he decided to keep most of the harvest for himself. An eagle, happening to fly overhead, witnessed what was happening and reported the incident to God, who hurled a thunderbolt at the cheat, killing him outright. The thunderbolt also struck the heap of grain that had unjustly been set aside, turning it into a mountain of red earth from which poured a river of lava which flowed down to the sea.
Legend from the book entitled *Al Qantarah* by L Danzuso and E Zinna.

The 18C church, **San Antonio**, has a concave façade and a campanile built of lava with an onion-shaped dome. The interior, decked with polychrome marble, has a magnificent triumphal arch (1796). There is a fine wooden organ in the chancel.

San Pietro preserves in its campanile some of the primitive Norman original tower, relieved by blind arcading. **Santa Maria della Catena**, preceded by a flight of steps, has a fine doorway with spiral columns.

Off the road to Mojo Alcantara, a right fork leads to the remains of a **Byzantine chapel** (or *cuba*) dating from the 7C-9C.

Mojo Alcantara

The name of this little town comes from a small volcano which, when it erupted, gave rise to the creation of the gorge. Today, it is a green, innocuous-looking cone.

Randazzo★ *See p 209*.

From Randazzo it is possible to join the Circumtenea *(see ETNA)* or continue on towards the Nebrodi Mountains *(see NEBRODI E MADONIE)*.

Termini Imerese

Famous since Antiquity for its hot springs, from which emanates water rich in chloro-iodide salts at a temperature of 43 °C, Termini also has an important commercial harbour and an extensive industrial area. It is especially busy at carnival time when allegorical floats process through the streets with groups of revellers in fancy dress – a long-running tradition of which the town is especially proud.

Location

Population: 27 923. Michelin map 565 2N 3 – Palermo. Termini comprises an old upper town and a modern, industrial lower town, linked by a series of narrow streets and flights of steps. Most of the major monuments are to be found in the upper town, which is best explored on foot. ℹ *Palazzo Civico, Piazza Duomo; ☎ 091 81 41 700.*

Neighbouring sights are described in the following chapters: BAGHERIA; CEFALÙ; SOLUNTO.

Walking About

A good place to start exploring the town is Piazza Duomo, overlooked by the Palazzo del Comune containing a former Council Chamber decorated with frescoes by Vincenzo La Barbera (1610) depicting the history of the town.

Duomo

Open daily except Fri, 9am-noon and 3.30-8.30pm. ☎ 091 81 41 291.

The cathedral was largely rebuilt in the 17C. Inside, it has a fine marble relief Madonna del Ponte *(fourth chapel on the right)* by Ignazio Marabitti (1842). A lovely wooden statue of the Immacolata by Quattrocchi (1799) adorns the chapel dedicated to the Immaculate Conception, and the chapel of San Bartolomeo is furnished with an interesting Venetian-style Rococo sedan chair once used for taking communion to the sick.

The Museo Civico can be seen in Via Museo Civico on the opposite side of the piazza to the Duomo *(see Worth a Visit)*.

From behind the Duomo, Via Belvedere leads up to a terrace that provides extensive **views** of the coast. A little further on, on the left, is an attractive little church dedicated to **Santa Caterina d'Alessandria** (14C); above the fine pointed arch doorway is set a shallow relief of the saint. Just beyond lies the shaded gardens of **Villa Palmeri**, where the remains of the **Roman Curia** can still be seen. From the park, follow Via Anfiteatro down to the ruined **Roman amphitheatre** (1C AD), its ambulatory piers still much in evidence.

Return to Piazza Duomo and follow Via Mazzini; on the right stands the 17C **Chiesa del Monte**, which was long used as the town's Pantheon (mausoleum for dignitaries).

TAKING A BREAK

For instant refreshment on a hot summer's day, try the exquisite home-made ice creams and water-ices *(granita)* on sale at the Gelateria Cicciuzzu, situated on the Belvedere terrace just behind the Duomo.

FESTIVAL

Carnevale – The towns's traditional carnival includes a procession of allegorical floats and other events around the town.

Città bassa
Return to the car and drive down to the lower part of town along the Serpentina Balsamo. A lane leading off a left bend provides a perfect opportunity to stop and take in the lovely view of the pale blue tiled dome of the **Chiesa dell'Annunziata**.

Piazza delle Terme, at the bottom, is dominated by the Grande Albergo delle Terme, built in the 19C to designs by the architect Damiani Almeyda.

Worth a Visit

Museo Civico
In Via Museo Civico, on the opposite side of the piazza to the Duomo. (♿) Open daily except Mon and public hols, 9am-1.30pm and 4-7pm. No charge. ☎ 091 81 28 279.
The museum is well laid out with helpful information boards; it comprises an archaeological collection and a section dedicated to art. The first rooms display material from Palaeolithic and Neolithic times recovered from local caves; excavated artefacts from Himera, including two fine red-figure Attic craters (5C BC); coinage from the Ancient Greek, Roman and Punic periods. Finally, a large room is dedicated to Hellenistic and Roman pottery: grave goods such as oil lamps, small receptacles and ointment jars; figurines dressed in togas found in the forum and the House of Stenius (1C AD); portraits including one of Agrippina, the mother of Caligula, which still bears traces of paint; terracotta pipe from the aqueduct of Cornelius; and Roman inscriptions.
The chapel of San Michele Arcangelo frescoed by Nicolò da Pettineo leads off the archaeology department. It also contains a *Madonna and Saints* triptych by **Gaspare da Pesaro** (1453), a two-faced marble cross (15C) by followers of the Gagini, and an interesting 15C wooden composition unusual in that it depicts the Trinity as a *Pietà* (with the Holy Spirit personified).
Reached through the chapel and up to the floor above, the **art gallery** is hung with paintings from the 17C-19C. Notable works include a Flemish *Annunciation* (16C), several pieces by the local painter Vittorio La Barbera (*Crucifixion*, 17C), a *St Sebastian* by Solimena and, in a small room at the far end, a tiny portable Byzantine-style 18C panel triptych.

Excursions

Acquedotto Cornelio
Take the road to Caccamo, and turn left *(yellow sign)*; after some 300m/330yd, on a bend, the Roman aqueduct comes into view on the left, its two tiers of arcades spanning the valley formed by the River Barratina.

Caccamo *9km/5.5mi S.*
Clinging to a rocky precipice among the lower spurs of Monte San Calogero, this pretty little town, overlooked by its impressive castle, was probably founded by the Phoenicians.

Castle★ – *Entrance from Via Termitana. Open in Aug, 9am-12.15pm and 4-7.15pm; otherwise, 9am-12.15pm and 3-6.15pm. Closed 1 Jan and 25 Dec. No charge. For information, call ☎ 091 81 03 111 (office hours).*
This is one of the best preserved castles in Sicily. It stands on a rocky spur and is arranged on several different levels, the result of spiralling extensions being added through the 14C, 15C and 17C. The main unit, complete with all the features of a small fortress, probably dates from the 11C. The defensive elements were reinforced by the Chiaramonte, while in the 17C, under Amato ownership, these were relaxed as the castle was transformed into a noble residence with terraces, and single- and two-arched windows were inserted.

Tour – Beyond the first gate, a 17C ramp leads up to a second gate. The broad, paved courtyard provides access to the Torre Mastra, from the top of which magnificent **views★** open out in a full circle to include Termini Imerese, Mongerbina, Capo Zafferano, Rocca Busambra and the Vicari Castle. A fine 18C doorway leads through to the Sala delle Armi or Salone della Congiura where the rebellious barons gathered before confronting William the Bad. The interior of the castle has recently undergone radical renovation. The apartments to the left of the Weapons Hall give access to the Torre Gibellina; the rooms to the right include the Salotto dei Nobili with its lovely five-bay window, before leading out onto a terrace with a panoramic view.

Return to Corso Umberto I and turn right to Piazza Duomo.

Piazza Duomo★ – The square provides an attractive open space split between two levels. The elevated northern side is fronted by a harmonious group of buildings, namely the **Palazzo del Monte di Pietà** (17C) flanked on the left by the **Oratorio del Santissimo Sacramento** and the **Chiesa delle Anime Sante del Purgatorio**

on the right. This very special arrangement constitutes a sort of theatrical stage from which to survey the lower part of the square: the balustrade, which serves both to separate and to link the two levels, is surmounted by four statues representing the Blessed Giovanni Liccio, Santa Rosalia, San Nicasio and San Teotista.

Chiesa Madre – The main church, dedicated to St George, stands on the western side of the piazza. On one side it clings to the rocky spur which rises to the castle, while on the other, it is supported by sturdy arcades and bastions. **Inside** hangs the dramatic, strongly highlighted painting of *The Miracle of Sant'Isidoro Agricola* (1641) by Mattia Stomer, while in the chapel of the Holy Sacrament, above the inlaid marble altar sits an unusual ciborium ornamented with marble reliefs by the Gagini School (15C). Also worth noting in passing, are the white marble font beside the high altar (1466) and the entablature over the sacristy entrance *(right transept)* with its delicate low reliefs by **Francesco Laurana**.

Down Corso Umberto I, and off to the right, is Piazza San Marco which is lined with the buildings of a former Franciscan monastery, the Church of the Annunciation with its twin bell towers, the Chiesa della Badia, and what was the 14C church of **San Marco** (the doorway with its pointed arch is still visible).

San Benedetto alla Badia – The single-nave church has a superb majolica **floor** attributed to Nicolò Sarzana from Palermo (18C), although this is badly damaged in places and mostly covered by carpets. When possible, it is worth climbing up to the women's gallery, once the preserve of nuns of a closed order from the convent which stood adjacent to the church. From the gallery there is an excellent view of the whole church, and, in particular, of the very fine wrought-iron railings (18C) at the far end. It is worth admiring the **stuccoes** in the apse by Bartolomeo Sanseverino (18C): the lunette, above, depicts *The Supper at Emmaus*; the statues on either side of the altar are allegories of *Chastity* and *Obedience*.

Return to Corso Umberto I. Just before Piazza Torina turn left uphill.

Santa Maria degli Angeli (or San Domenico) – The two-aisled church has a fine trussed **wooden ceiling** ornamented with paintings of Dominican saints (severely damaged by humidity). In the chapel dedicated to Santa Maria degli Angeli *(on the right)* is a lovely *Madonna and Child* by Antonello Gagini (1516), and, on the underside of the main arch, a series of small paintings by Vincenzo La Barbera depicting *The Mysteries of the Rosary* (17C).

Before leaving Caccamo, it is well worth walking to the far side of town and turning right (signposted "Centro Storico"): at a certain point somewhere along this almost circular route, there is a wonderful **view★** over the whole town with, down below the **Torre Pizzarone** – at one time part of the town's external defences – the Torre delle Campane (now the cathedral bell tower), and the purpose-built bell tower standing on the left of the Chiesa dell'Annunziata.

Scavi di Himera

18km/11mi E. Open Mon-Sat, 9am-6.30pm; Sun and public hols, 9am-1pm. €2. ☎ 091 81 40 128.

Himera was founded in 648 BC by colonists from Zancle (modern Messina). In 480 BC, it was here that the Carthaginians suffered a crushing defeat at the hands of the allied forces of Agrigento and Syracuse. Its demise came in 408 BC, however, when a second wave of invading Carthaginians first conquered, then razed the town to the ground for good.

The ancient town is sited at the top of a hill south of the main Messina-Palermo road. Here, sections of wall and part of the sacred area with three temples have been brought to light. Further along the road up to the site is the **antiquarium**, used to display artefacts found on site.

The most significant and best-preserved structure, however, is the **Temple of Victory** (5C BC), which stands at the bottom of the hill, on the northern side of the main road. It seems probable that the Greeks forced the Carthaginians to build this temple to celebrate their victory in 480 BC. Possibly dedicated to Athena, it would-have been a Doric temple with six columns at the front and 14 down each side; stumpy vestiges of columns, the *cella*, the *pronaos* and the *opisthodomus* are clearly visible. The eaves were marvellously decorated with sculpted lions' heads, now in the archaeological museum in Palermo.

San Nicola l'Arena

13km/8mi W. A **castle** with three round towers overlooks the picturesque little harbour of this seaside resort. An old shed on theharbour front still preserves various boats used for tuna fishing.

In the distance (westwards) stands a lookout tower, situated on Capo Grosso.

Trapani

Trapani, the ancient Drepanum, extends along a curving tongue of land that ends in two horns – one occupied by the Torre di Ligny, the other by a *lazaretto* (a house for the reception of the diseased poor, especially lepers). According to legend, this was formed by the sickle that was dropped by the goddess of agriculture Demeter (Ceres) while she desperately sought her daughter Persephone, who had been carried off to Hades. The inner edge of the sickle *(north)*, sheltered by the Tramontana reef, provides protected anchorages and moorings for fishing boats. Each morning, on the shore opposite, is held a picturesque fish market *(pescheria)*.

Location

Population: 69 221. Michelin map 565 19M Most visitors arriving in Trapani will drive along the central Via Fardella, which crosses the modern section of town and leads to the medieval district at the end of the headland. Most of the town's monuments of interest are located in the old town, which is best explored on foot. Trapani is the main port for the Egadi Islands and Pantelleria. ℹ *Piazza Saturno;* ☎ *0923 29 00; Fax 0923 24 004.*

Neighbouring sights are described in the following chapters: Isole EGADI; ERICE; MARSALA; MOZIA; PANTELLERIA; VIA DEL SALE.

Walking About

CENTRO STORICO★

The medieval districts of the old part of town are situated on the headland pointing out to sea. The tip was developed by the Spanish in the 14C *(quartiere Palazzo)* and remodelled in the Baroque style later. The oldest section, built in true Moorish fashion around a tight network of interconnecting narrow streets, stretches back along the peninsula; this would originally have been enclosed by walls.

Rua Nova

Now named Via Garibaldi, the "New Road" was laid in the 13C by the Aragonese. Today, it is lined with fine 18C *palazzi* and churches, including the statue-crested **Palazzo Riccio di Morana**, **Palazzo Milo** and **Badia Nuova** (Santa Maria del Soccorso), the interior of which is decorated with Baroque polychrome marble and two elaborate **galleries★** supported by angels. *Open 8.15am-1pm.* ☎ *0923 43 21 11.* Palazzo Burgio opposite is graced with a fine 16C doorway.

Via Torrearsa is lined with elegant shops to the left and leads down to the Pescheria (fish market) on the right. Beyond the intersection, Via Garibaldi continues as Via Libertà, past the splendid **Palazzo Fardello di Mokarta** (the inner courtyard is enclosed within a portico and a round-arched loggia) and Palazzo Melilli with its 16C doorway.

The harbour

B. Kaufmann/MICHELIN

TRAPANI

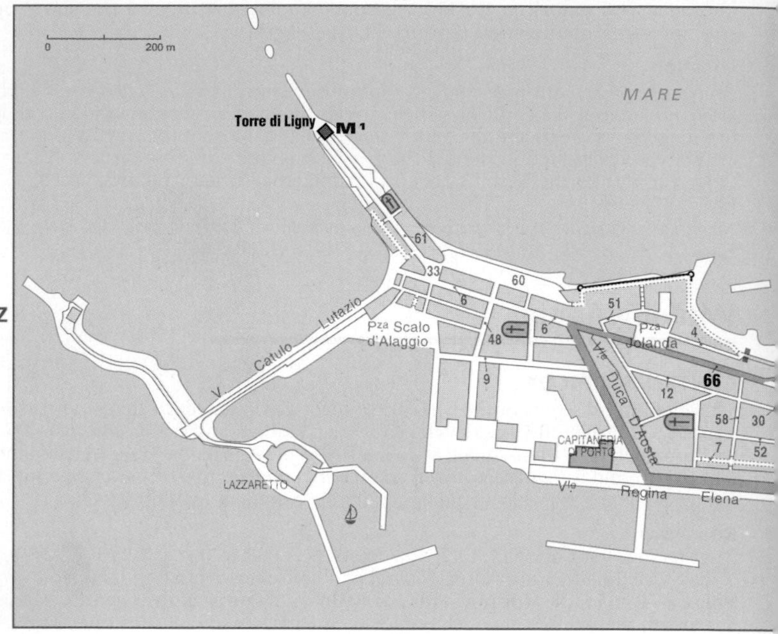

Directory

Transport

Trapani is approximately 150km/95mi from Agrigento and 100km/60mi from Palermo, to which it is connected by both bus and train (3hr 30min and 2hr respectively). The bus and train stations are both situated in Piazza Umberto I. For further information and timetables contact the tourist office. Birgi airport, 15km/9mi south of the town (☎ 0923 84 25 02), operates services from Trapani to Pantelleria.

Ferry services to the Egadi Islands and Pantelleria leave from Trapani, with sailings operated by **Siremar** (Gruppo Tirrenia), ☎ 199 123 199 (from Italy) or 081 31 72 999 (from mobiles and abroad); www.gruppotirrenia.it/siremar/html/home/mainframeset.htm

Where to Eat

One of Trapani's most typical dishes is *cuscus di pesce*, which originates from North Africa and has been adapted by the addition of locally caught fish.

• *For all budgets*

Ai Lumi Tavernetta – *Corso Vittorio Emanuele 75, Trapani – ☎ 0923 87 24 18 – info@ailumi.it – Closed Sun and Jul – ☒ – Booking recommended – €24/36.* The reasonably priced menu at this attractive, fashionable restaurant in the centre of town includes fish and meat dishes with a strong emphasis on traditional, local cuisine.

Taverna Paradiso – *Lungomare Dante Alighieri 22, Trapani – ☎ 0923 22 303 – ☒ – Booking recommended – €30/38.* Situated right on the seafront, this friendly, attractive restaurant specialises in fish dishes, especially tuna, the most popular fish in this part of Sicily.

Where to Stay

See ERICE: Directory.

Festival

Settimana Santa – Holy Week celebrations culminate in the **Processione dei Misteri** on Good Friday as 20 groups of sculpted figures are carried through the streets all day and the following night. At other times, the statues are kept in the **Church of the Purgatorio** (in the town centre, in Via San Francesco); made of wood, cloth and glue by local craftsmen, they date from between 1650 and 1720.

Roma (Via) .... BZ 49
S. Anna (Via) .... AZ 51
S. Francesco d'Assisi (Via) .... AZ 52
S. Francesco di Paola (Largo) .... BZ 54
Scalo d'Alaggio (Piazza) ... AZ
Scarlatti (Piazza) .... BZ 55
Scontrino (Via) .... BZ 57
Serisso (Via) .... AZ 58
Sirene (Viale d.) .... AZ 60
Spalti (Via) .... BZ
Staiti (Via A.) .... BZ

Torre di Ligny (Via) .... AZ 61
Torrearsa (Via) .... BZ
Umberto I (Piazza) .... BZ 63
Vallona (Via) .... BZ 64
Vespri (Via) .... BZ
Virgilio (Via) .... BZ
Vittorio Emanuele (Corso) .... AZ 66
Vittorio Emanuele (Piazza) .... BZ 67
Vittorio Veneto (Piazza) .... BZ
XX Settembre (Via) .... BZ 69
XXX Gennaio (Via) .... BZ

Annunziata .... BZ
Badia Nuova .... BZ
Biblioteca Fardelliana .... BZ B
Cattedrale .... BZ
Collegio .... BZ
Museo della Preistoria e di Archeologia Marina .... AZ M1
Palazzo Ciambra .... BZ
Palazzo Fardella di Mokarta .... BZ
Palazzo Milo .... BZ R
Palazzo Riccio di Morana .... BZ
Palazzo Senatorio (o Cavarretta). BZ S
S. Agostino .... BZ
S. Maria del Gesù .... BZ
Torre di Ligny .... AZ

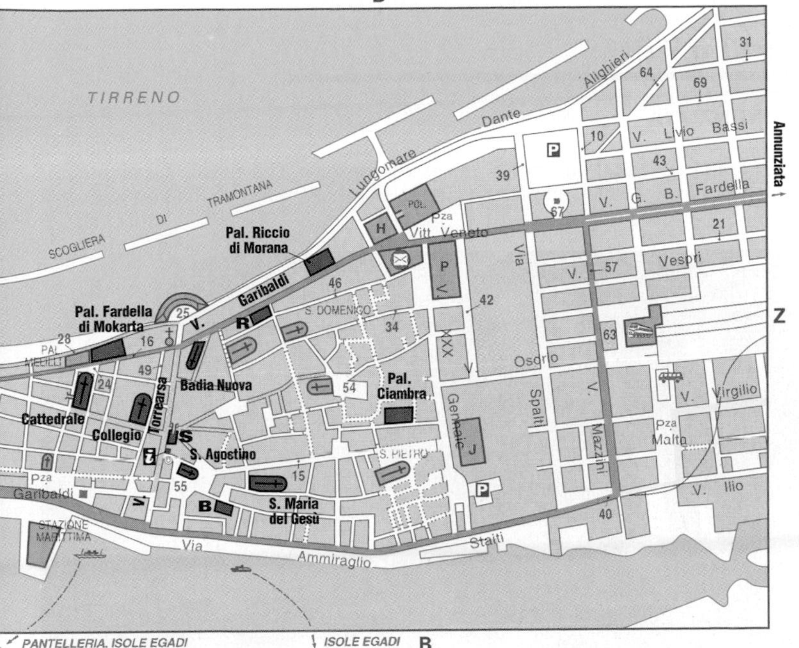

Turn left into Corso Vittorio Emanuele.

Rua Grande

The second principal thoroughfare constructed in the 13C (the modern Corso Vittorio Emanuele) stretches between elegant Baroque buildings such as the Palazzo Berardo Ferro (n(86) and the Sede del Vescovado (Bishop's Palace).

Cattedrale – *Open Mon-Fri, 9am-noon and 5-6pm; Sat, 9am-noon; Sun and public hols, 10.30-11.30am and 5.30-6.30pm. Donations welcome.* ☎ *0923 23 362; www.parrocchie.org.trapani/cattedrale*

The cathedral dedicated to St Lawrence was erected in the 17C on the site of an earlier 14C building. The front elevation, put up a century later (1740), is a marvellous expression of the Baroque. Inside, it contains a number of paintings by Flemish artists: a *Nativity (third chapel on the right)*, a crucifixion and a **Deposition** *(fourth chapel on the left)*.

Chiesa del Collegio dei Gesuiti – *Closed for restoration at the time of going to press.* The 17C church has an imposing Mannerist façade ornamented with pilasters and female caryatid figures.

Palazzo Senatorio (Cavaretta) – This lovely *palazzo* stands dramatically across the end of the street. Its elaborate façade rises through two orders of columns and statues up to a pair of large clocks. Alongside stands a 13C bell tower.

Sant'Agostino

This church, built by the Knights Templar in the 14C, was badly damaged during the Second World War. The lovely **rose window★** and the Gothic doorway are original.

The Fountain of Saturn in front of the church was built in 1342 to commemorate the building of an aqueduct.

Not far away, the **Biblioteca Fardelliana** displays a series of interesting topographical engravings from the Gatto collection, including views of the Trapani area from the 17C to the 20C. *Open Jul and Sep, 9am-1.30pm; Aug, 10am-1pm; Oct-Jun, Mon-Fri, 9am-1.30pm and 3-7.30pm, Sat, 9am-1.30pm only. Closed Sun, public hols and 7 Aug. No charge.* ☎ *0923 21 506.*

Santa Maria del Gesù

Open Mon-Fri, 7.30-10am (also 5-6pm Thu). Closed public hols. ☎ 0923 87 20 21.
This church with its fine Catalan doorway dates from the beginning of the 16C. Inside the church, the Cappella Staiti (in the right aisle at the back of the church) houses the **Madonna degli Angeli★** by Andrea della Robbia, underneath a magnificent marble tribune by Antonello Gagini (1521).
Head along Corso Italia. Turn left by the church of San Pietro, then immediately right.

Palazzo Ciambra (della Giudecca)

This fine example of the Plateresque (Spanish renaissance) style (16C) has heavy rustication to emphasise the doors and windows, as well as the front of the tower.

Worth a Visit

L'ANNUNZIATA

In Via Pepoli at the far eastern end of town (in the direction of Palermo) stands the large Carmelite institution known as the Annunziata. The actual church adjoins the former convent which now houses the town's main museum, the Museo Pepoli.

R. Mattes/MICHELIN

The Easter procession

Santuario dell'Annunziata★

For information on admission times, contact the parish priest several days in advance on ☎ 0923 53 91 84. Donations welcome.
The church, although built in the early 14C, was transformed and enlarged in the course of the 18C. The original front elevation is ornamented with a Chiaramonte Gothic portal, surmounted by an elaborate **rose window** above.
The **Cappella dei Marinai** (16C) along the left flank, comprises a lovely Renaissance tufa building surmounted by a dome. Inside, it is decorated with a fusion of styles drawn from Eastern and Renaissance sources: recurring elements include the shell which appears in the side niches, pendentives and apse.
The **Cappella della Madonna** extends like a Lady Chapel from behind the main altar of the church. Access is through a fine Renaissance arch designed by the Gagini (16C) with bronze gates dating from 1591. On the altar sits the delicate figure of the **Madonna of Trapani** (14C), attributed to Nino Pisano. Off the right side of the nave, near the door, lies the **Cappella dei Pescatori** (16C) enclosed with a frescoed octagonal dome.

Museo Pepoli★

Open Mon-Sat, 9am-1.30pm; Sun and public hols, 9am-12.30pm. €2.50. ☎ 0923 55 32 69.
The ex-Carmelite convent beside the Santuario dell'Annunziata provides a magnificent setting for the museum and its fine collections of historic artefacts from prehistoric times to the 19C.
The ground floor is devoted to sculpture. The Gagini family is well represented, with four graceful statues of saints; the most striking is probably the figure of *St James the Greater* by **Antonello Gagini**.

A sumptuous polychrome marble staircase leads up to the first-floor **art gallery**: the most notable paintings are the **Trapani polyptych★** (15C), a **Pietà★** by the Neapolitan Roberto di Oderisio (14C) and a lovely *Madonna and Child with Angels* by Pastura (1478-1509). Works from the Neapolitan School include a fine *St Bartholomew* by Ribera.
The medium most favoured by the local artists and craftsmen is the Mediterranean red coral (pink coral comes from China). Examples displayed here include liturgical objects and various pieces of jewellery (look out for those made by Matteo Bavera, 17C). There is also a wonderful series of 16 small figurative groups carved out of wood and dressed in cloth depicting the *Slaughter of the Innocents* (17C).
The local **pottery "industry"** is represented by a pair of fine maiolica panels depicting the **mattanza** (the ritual killing of the tuna fish) and a view of Trapani (17C).

THE TIP OF THE HEADLAND

Museo della Preistoria e di Archeologia Marina

Closed for restoration at the time of going to press. ☎ 0923 29 000.
The **Torre di Ligny**, built in 1671 as a defensive bastion on the tip of the "sickle", houses a collection of archaeological artefacts; informative panels complete with illustrations outline the prehistoric era in Sicily. Most of the medieval objects were recovered from the many shipwrecks found nearby. Among the most interesting things on display are the Spanish amphorae.
From the terrace at the top of the tower extends a fine view over the town and across to the Egadi Islands.

Ustica★★

This tiny volcanic island (8.6km²/3.2sq mi), the summit of a large submerged volcano, is the oldest of the Sicilian outer archipelago, having emerged long before the Aeolian Islands. Both the way the volcano was formed and the blackness of its lava have determined the choice of a name derived from the Latin *Ustum*, meaning burnt. Its jagged coastline shelters a series of wonderful caves, bays and creeks. Local residents eke out a living from fishing and tourism; additional income is presently being generated by developing the range of crops grown (vines, vegetables, cereals and especially lentils).

Location

Population: 1 360. Michelin map 565 K 21 – Palermo. Situated 60km/37mi from Palermo, this tiny island is dotted with rocky inlets and is best discovered by boat. A road and several footpaths allow visitors to explore the island's interior. The western coast is now part of a marine national park. ℹ *Piazza Umberto I; ☎ 091 84 49 456.*

Background

Ustica was inhabited continuously from the late Neolithic until the end of the Classical period, when it was left to serve as a refuge for pirates. A handful of settlers moved there from Lipari in the Bourbon era. Until the 1950s, it was used as a penal colony. Tourism developed when underwater diving enthusiasts came to explore the surrounding beautifully limpid waters and wonderfully rugged coastline. In 1987 it was designated a marine national park. In Italy, the name of this island is indelibly linked to the tragic plane crash here in 1980, when 81 people on board a flight from Palermo to Bologna lost their lives.

Riserva Naturale Marina di Ustica

Directory

Transport

Direct services operate out of Palermo. Crossings by ferry (2hr 30min) and hydrofoil (1hr 10min) are provided by **Siremar**, (Gruppo Tirrenia), ☎ 199 123 199 (from Italy) or 081 31 72 999 (from mobiles and abroad); www.gruppotirrenia.it/siremar/html/home/mainframeset.htm.

During the summer season, a hydrofoil service calling at Trapani-Favignana-Levanzo-Ustica-Naples is operated by Ustica Lines. The Ustica-Naples leg takes approximately 4hr. Contact **Ustica Lines**, Via. Amm. Staiti 23, Trapani; ☎ 0923 22 200; info@usticalines.it; www.usticalines.it

Sightseeing

The standard means of transport available include hired mopeds and a regular minibus service around the island in both directions. Extremely good value bus passes, valid for a week, two weeks or a month, are available from the town hall.

Where to Eat

• For all budgets

La Luna sul Porto – *Corso Vittorio Emanuele II 11, Ustica – ☎ 091 84 49 799 – Closed Sun (in winter) – ⊠ – Booking recommended – €15/30.* This pleasant restaurant is run by an Italian woman from Piedmont who fell in love with Ustica over 10 years ago. Simple service, reasonable prices and a lovely view of the port from the outdoor terrace.

Mario – *Piazza Umberto I 21, Ustica – ☎ 091 84 49 505 – Closed Mon (in winter) and Jan – €26.* Dine outdoors in summer and in the restaurant's cosy dining room in winter. A firm favourite for genuine, simple Sicilian cuisine in this delightful corner of the Mediterranean.

Where to Stay

• Budget

Hotel Diana – *Contrada San Paolo – ☎ 091 84 49 109 – Fax 091 84 49 109 – www.hoteldiana.to.it – Closed Nov-Feb – ⊠ – 30 rooms. €31/62* ☕. This circular hotel enjoys a quiet location outside Ustica town, with impressive panoramic views. The only disadvantage to the irregularly shaped rooms is the space taken up by the beds. Good restaurant.

• Moderate

Hotel Clelia – *Via Sindaco I° 29, Ustica – ☎ 091 84 49 039 – Fax 091 84 49 459 – hotelclelia@tin.it – 26 rooms. €35/105* ☕. Once a small *pensione*, this hotel has recently been renovated and now offers higher levels of comfort and better facilities. Pleasant rooms with all necessary creature comforts.

Sport and Leisure

Those who love the sea and enjoy swimming should not forget to bring a mask, snorkel and fins: snorkelling will introduce the visitor to a spectacular underwater world and add a new perspective to their appreciation of the natural beauty of Ustica.

Every year, a special week-long sub-aqua course is organised, including theoretical and practical diving lessons (marine archaeology, marine biology, modern recovery techniques for lifting artefacts from the seabed) and guided tours. For further information, apply to the Riserva Marina or to Archeologia Viva, ☎ 055 50 62 303.

Festival

Rassegna Internazionale delle Attività subacquee – An International Review of Underwater Activities is organised annually during the summer (usually in May, June or September). This gathering includes a range of different events, such as exhibitions and other activities. For detailed information, contact the Azienda di Promozione Turistica in Palermo, ☎ 091 58 38 47.

Special Features

MARINE NATIONAL PARK

The nature reserve was brought into being in 1987 to preserve and protect the huge natural diversity of flora and fauna present in their submarine habitats off Ustica's coastline. The National Park comprises three zones. **Zone A**, classified as **riserva**

Riserva Naturale Marina di Ustica

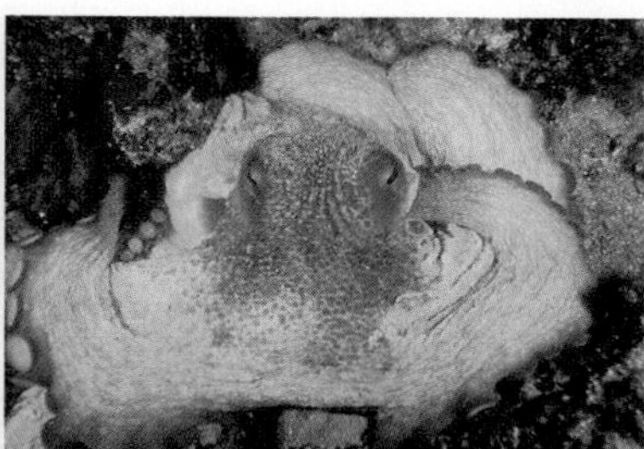

integrale, extends along the west flank of the island from Cala Sidotti to Caletta and as far as 350m/1148ft offshore (marked with special yellow buoys): swimming is permitted, fishing and boating are prohibited.

Zone B, classified as **riserva generale**, extends beyond Zone A from Punta Cavazzi to Punta Omo Morto (thereby including the entire length of the southwest to the northeast coastline, to a distance of 3 nautical miles (5.5km) offshore): here swimming is permitted as is underwater photography (but not fishing with a speargun), hook-and-line fishing and commercial fishing (on acquisition of a permit from the Commune).

Zone C, classified as a **riserva parziale**, applies to the rest of the coast: here national fishing regulations apply and speargun fishing is permitted.

The submerged world

The sea around Ustica is especially clean and pollution free (lying in the middle of an inward current from the Atlantic Ocean). It therefore provides ideal conditions for multitudes of different species of aquatic flora and fauna to live and proliferate. One striking sight is the vast meadow of *Poseidonia oceanica*, a truly beneficial seaweed, nicknamed the "lungs of the Mediterranean" (because it oxygenates the water), to be found up to a depth of 40m/131ft. Just below the surface, the water often shimmers with passing shoals of white bream, two-banded bream, the dark Ray's bream which emerge from their eggs as piercingly blue fry, voracious-looking grey mullet (at the worst they only tickle), saddled bream, salpas, and the brilliantly coloured rainbow wrasse. The patches s haded by some over hanging rock attract groups of cardinal fish; the rock face itself shelters colonies of beautiful orange "flowered" madrepore, which sometimes cover vast sections at a time with colourful sponges (for those unfamiliar with these, sponges come in s hades of black, white, yellow and orange, in s hapes compact, long, thin and string-like). Little groupers also cower in the s hadow of the rocks, but emerge, peeking with curiosity, as anything or anyone approaches. At greater depths lurk the larger fish – notably grey mullet. Here the underwater landscape harbours shy moray eels, lobsters, mantis prawns and shrimps (in the caves), sea urchins, sea bream, enormous white bream, splendid red gorgonians, and black coral (a pale yellow "living" skin covers the ossified darker interior). With a bit of luck, tuna, ocean sunfish, turtles and barracuda might also make a brief appearance on the scene.

What's on offer – There are various possibilities both for scuba-divers and snorkellers. Those who do not like to get wet can still participate in the underwater world by taking a trip (by day or by night) on the motorised glass-bottomed boat called the *Aquario*, which carries up to 20 passengers.

There are two other reserve centres located at Torre dello Spalmatore (the twin of Torre Santa Maria) – where conferences and other special delegations are hosted – and at Caletta – from where guided tours to the Grotta Segreta start; the **aquarium** there reconstitutes 13 different environments corresponding to the various habitats found at different depths. *Open 10am-1pm and 3-6pm.* €2.50. ☎ *091 84 49 456.*

Guided tours – The west coast, the area designated *riserva integrale* (most highly restricted), harbours two secret and pink-hued grottoes: **Grotta Segreta** and **Grotta Rosata**. The entrance to the latter is hidden by rocks whether approaching by land or by sea; its descriptive name effectively sums up the pink marbling of the palest tone to shades of "antique pink" imparted by a distinctive kind of algae.

For those who prefer to enjoy the sea from above or from just below the surface, the reserve authorities lay on **sea-watching** trips (with a commentary) in the *riserva integrale:* these involve a guide pointing out the specific organisms and fish as they appear (accustomed as they have become to the presence of man, they appear almost tame).

Scuba-diving – Highlights for any scuba-diving enthusiast include the **Grotta dei Gamberi**, near Punta Gavazzi, where incredibly delicate fan-like red gorgonians thrive (at a depth of approx 42m/138ft), and the **sub-aqua archaeological trail** off

Riserva Naturale Marina di Ustica

the lighthouse-topped headland Punta Gavazzi (depths of 9m/30ft-17m/56ft, marked by an orange buoy), where many artefacts – anchors and Roman amphorae – can be admired *in situ*.

Another popular haunt is the **Scoglio del Medico**: this consists of an outcrop of basalt riddled with caves and gorges that plunge to great depths, and so provides a spectacular underwater **seascape★★**. **Secca di Colombara** (40m/131ft below) is spectacular in a different way, populated as it is by rainbow-coloured arrays of sponges and gorgonians.

Worth a Visit

Ustica★

A small hamlet centres on the largest bay, populating the bowl around the harbour. A single road and various flights of steps, flanked with magnificent hibiscus bushes, lead up to the main town above. A characteristic feature of the houses peculiar to Ustica is the relatively recent practice of painting their exteriors with artistic murals: landscape scenes, *trompe l'œils*, portraits, still-life paintings, and any other fanciful composition that might spring to mind. The most eye-catching building is the **Torre di Santa Maria** which houses the **Museo Archeologico** and its collections of artefacts recovered from the prehistoric village at I Faraglioni and from Hellenistic and Roman tombs found on Capo Falconiera. Note, in particular, the unusual circular fire basket in four sections (and thus transportable) and the lovely tall two-handled cups. *Closed Mon. €2.50. For further information, contact the Riserva Naturale Marina, ☎ 091 84 49 456.*

Capo Falconiera – At the far end of the central piazza where the Chiesa Madre is situated, turn right past the Stations of the Cross. From here, a stepped path on the left climbs to the top. The ruins of a Bourbon fortress and a 3C BC settlement were positioned up here doubtless because the site could be well defended and because it surveyed traffic into the only harbour on the island at Cala Santa Maria (still the port today). Naturally restricted by space and inaccessibility, the area was extended by cutting terraces into the rock: as a result, three tiers of housing are stacked one above the other. Many of the cisterns for collecting rainwater are clearly in evidence as is a staircase cut into the rock (right at the top). At the foot of the fortress, remnants of a contemporary hypogeum necropolis (with underground chambers) have been discovered together with a second necropolis with burial sites (and hypogea) dating from palaeo-Christian times (5C-6C AD). From here, a **view★** stretches from the harbour to the centre of the island, marked with the distinctive profiles of Monte Costa del Fallo and Monte Guardia dei Turchi.

Villaggio preistorico★

The village can still be seen through a fence.

An extensive Bronze Age settlement has been discovered at Colombaia, in the vicinity of **I Faraglioni**. This comprises a collection of foundations for circular huts that were re-used later for square-based constructions of a type similar to a kind of prehistoric house found on the Island of Panarea. The residential area is bisected by a single "high street"; this would indicate that the settlement was developed according to a town plan (albeit fairly basic) with a consideration for public areas, something unusual for the time (usually, the huts were randomly arranged). The village was protected by a strong set of **enclosure walls** (the surviving section suggests it was elliptical in shape) formed by two curtain walls 6m/19ft thick at the base, fortified by semicircular towers. The missing sections of curtain walling and the presence of huts founded on bedrock, have been read as evidence that the rock was joined at that time to the mainland, and that the collapse (probably caused by an earthquake) caused the village to be abandoned suddenly.

Coast

The jagged coastline is interrupted by a number of caves which can be explored either by boat (fishermen in the harbour volunteer their services to visitors, using

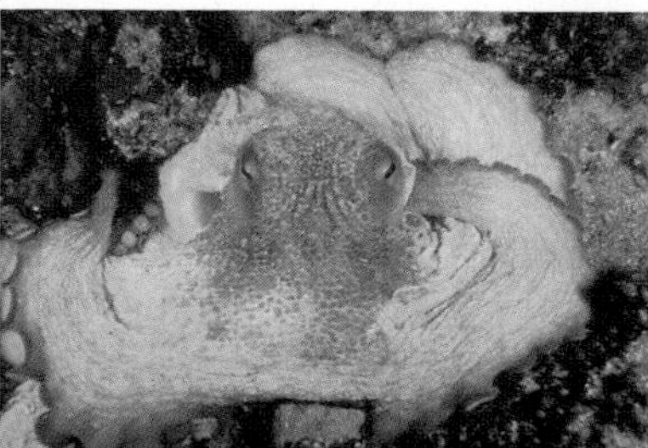

Riserva Naturale Marina di Ustica

boats that are small enough to enter the narrowest caves) or by land. Small beaches (Cala Sidoti, Punta dello Spalmatore, al Faro) succeed lovely rocky bays – including one enclosing the **piscina naturale★** (a natural pool popular with bathers) along the west coast of the island. Conversely, the east coast shelters magnificent caves like Grotta Azzurra, Grotta Verde and Grotta delle Barche, which are best explored with mask and snorkel; the Grotta delle Barche can also be reached on foot by a lovely **path★** that threads its way through pines and past tall hedges of prickly pears from Torre di Santa Maria, along the side of the hill, providing marvellous **views★** of the sea and the coast.

La Via del Sale★

The road from Trapani to Marsala skirts round the edge of the lagoon and the island of Mozia providing fine views★★ of the local salt works: panels of mirror-like water, framed by thin strips of earth, synchronise to form an irregular and multicoloured scene. In places, the profile of a windmill may be discerned, a reminder of times past when they provided the main means of pumping the water and grinding the salt.

Location

Michelin map 565 1N 9 – Trapani. The white saltpans lie to the south of Trapani and extend along the coast almost as far as Marsala. They offer a particularly striking sight in summer when the salt is ready to be collected: then, the pinkish hues of the concentrated saline contained in the outer pans contrast with those towards the centre of a deeper colour, while the innermost, now dry, sparkle in the sunshine.

Neighbouring sights are described in the following chapters: ERICE; MARSALA; MOZIA; TRAPANI.

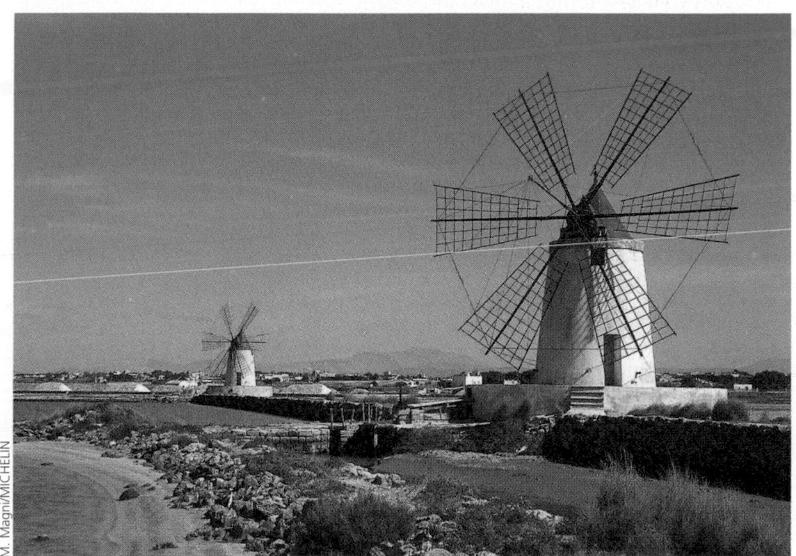

M. Magni/MICHELIN

Background

Ancient origins – The coastal area between Trapani and Marsala came to be exploited back in the time of the Phoenicians who, realising the extremely favourable conditions available, set about building basins in which to collect salt; this valuable commodity they then exported all over the Mediterranean. So this otherwise barren stretch of land came to be systematically worked: from the shallow water, the searing temperatures and arid winds (which also facilitate evaporation, of course) was born a tough but beneficial industry to produce the precious element, so vital to the survival of man. One of the foremost and fundamental properties of salt is its ability to preserve food, a quality with which the earliest peoples were familiar, using it to treat perishables for the lean winter months or simply during transportation. After the Phoenicians, however, there are no reliable references to the saltpans around Trapani until the Norman era when Frederick II himself alludes to them in the Constitutions of Melfi, making them a Crown monopoly. From this date on, the rise in status of the port of Trapani may be tracked fairly easily. The economic success of the saltpans, meanwhile, shows that major fluctuations in output shadowed the rise and fall in fortunes of the territory as it succumbed to various external events beyond its control. War, epidemic, transitions of government from one rule to another influenced the production and trading of salt just as it would any other field. On the whole, the area was profitable, as was the commercial activity itself, and that is why it has continued, albeit with fits and starts, until the present day. The salt is still being extracted, although the methods used (and the effort expended) have changed as processes have become mechanised. The picturesque windmills that characterise the landscape are no longer employed and the back-breaking demands on the manual workers have been minimised.

Automating the salt works

Mechanisation – The most important individual pieces of machinery used in the cultivation and processing of salt, in the past at least, were the classic Dutch windmill, the American windmill, which was introduced in the early 1950s, and the Archimedes screw.

The **Dutch windmill** comprises a conical building, capped with a conical roof, and six trapezoidal vanes consisting of cloth sails attached to wooden frames that catch the wind and propel a system of mechanical gears. Inside the building, a complex system of interconnected cogs and wheels, shafts and stays allow the circular roof (and, hence, the sails) to be orientated according to the direction of the wind and so exploit the natural resource to grind the salt (in this case) or to pump water (if the windmill is situated between two pans). Should the mill be required to pump water, the gearing is harnessed to an Archimedes screw.

The main difference between the **American windmill** and its smaller Dutch counterpart is its sophistication: it has a massive wheel of 24 iron vanes (instead of six meagre wooden ones) and a greater degree of automation (including a gearing system allowing the roof to regulate itself automatically to catch the wind). The mechanical technology has in most cases been installed inside the pre-existing base of a disused Dutch windmill; the other alteration required involves the mounting of three cogged wheels to the upper wall that must carry the extended sails.

The **Archimedes screw**, the most efficient tool for pumping water from any depth (as it can be activated in a few centimetres of liquid), is powered by hand or by means of a windmill. In simple terms, the screw consists of a rotating shaft with small wooden blades attached to form a continuous spiral. The screw is surrounded by closely fitted staves and bound with metallic strips to make it watertight.

Manpower – Few people were ever fully employed to work the saltpans all year round other than the *curatolo*, the trustworthy overseer, and the miller, who was responsible for maintaining the windmill in proper working order. Additional workers were employed on a seasonal basis. The harvest involved the hiring of various labourers. In July, a team would begin by breaking up the crust of salt; other tasks involving creating small channels for the remaining water to be drained away into the *vasu cultivu* (where it was stored until the following year). Next, the salt was shovelled into small piles in neat rows, thereby allowing any damp residue to dry out. For the actual harvest to begin in earnest, a band of 20 men or *venna* would be hired; they were charged with filling baskets with salt and emptying them on the dike in much larger piles. In the autumn, the heaps were covered with tiles by the *curatolo*.

G. Bludzin/MICHELIN

TOUR

30km/19mi excursion between Trapani and Marsala along SP 21 – allow one day, including a visit to the Island of Mozia.

Trapani *See TRAPANI.*

From Trapani, follow the coast road *(SP 21)* to Marsala, which provides a succession of fine **views★★** over the saltpans of Trapani and Paceco and those at Stagnone. The first stop is **Nubia**, the headquarters of the WWF, formerly the World Wide Fund for Nature *(Via Garibaldi 138)*, which manages the **Riserva Naturale Salina di Trapani e Paceco**, a saltwater nature reserve habitat where 170 species of bird – resident and migratory – have been recorded. Indeed, it is not unusual to see migrating flamingos, storks, cranes and herons. *(♿) Open 9am-6pm (5pm Oct-Mar). Closed 25 Nov and public hols. ☎ 0923 86 77 00.*

Museo del Sale di Nubia

Open Mon-Sat, 9.30am-1pm and 3.30-6.30pm (5pm in winter); Sun, 9.30am-1pm only. Guided tours available (30min). Audio-visual presentation. €1. ☎ 0923 86 71 42.
A small, yet highly interesting salt museum has been set up in a 300-year-old salt worker's house: it recounts the different stages involved in collecting salt from the saltpans and displays various specialist tools adapted for its extraction and harvest, including mill gearing, windmill vanes, cogwheels, spikes and sprockets. Additional information about the methods and practices are further clarified by means of explanatory boards and photographs of salt workers in action.

Le saline

The salt works in front of the museum successfully demonstrate how and why the different saltpans interact, as well as describing the successive phases in the "cultivation" and extraction of the crystallised salt.

A canal supplements the two large basins on the outer edge of the complex known as the *fridde* (a corruption of *freddo* meaning cold) because of the temperature of the incoming water. The *Mulino Americano* (literally the American mill – *see Automating the salt works above*) located between these two basins uses an Archimedes screw contraption (of a type displayed in the museum) to transfer water into the *vasu cultivu*, where it blends with the yeast-like residue of the previous crop. The greater the saline concentration (measured in Baum), interestingly enough, the warmer the water. From here, the water is drained to the *ruffiana*, an intermediary stage between the *vasu* and the *caure*, where the water temperature is considerably warmer and the salinity attains 23 Baum. Next in line comes the *sintine*, where the high concentration of salt and the high temperature combine to lend a pinkish tinge to the solution, and so begin the last stages in the process. The water now passes into the salting pans or *caseddri*, where layers of pure salt crystals are allowed to form (27-28 Baum) in preparation for harvest twice a year, usually around mid-July and mid-August. The conical piles of sand, aligned the length of the *arione*, are left open to the elements to be rinsed through by the rain, before being covered with "Roman" tiles for protection from heavy downpours and dirt.

From Nubia, return to the main road and continue towards the Stagnone lagoon, where the most spectacular saltpans are located. A sign indicates the way to the Ettore e Infersa salt works.

Working windmill

Wind permitting, the mill operates in summer, Wed and Sat, 4-6pm; rest of the year, Sat-Sun and public hols, by appointment only. €2.50. For further information, contact Saline Ettore e Infersa, ☎ 0923 96 69 36.
This 16C windmill, once indispensable for grinding salt, survives today solely because of the love and attention lavished upon it by its owners (Saline Ettore e Infersa); presently restored to working order, it demonstrates what is involved and inspires a romantic fascination in the practices of times past in the young minds of modern generations.

The sails can rotate at a speed of 20kph/12.5mph and generate a power equivalent to 120 horsepower (30/40hp are required to activate the grinder in the ground-floor rooms alone).

Mozia★ *See MOZIA.*

The coast road picks its way to Marsala along a most pleasant route, which can be particularly spectacular at sunset.

Marsala *See MARSALA.*

Villa Imperiale del Casale★★★

This splendid, imposing Roman villa owes its fame to its magnificent mosaic floors – thought to be the work of North African artists – which are striking for the variety of colours used and subjects depicted. The Villa Imperiale del Casale was declared a UNESCO World Heritage Site in 1997.

Location

Michelin map 565 O 25 – Enna. To get to the villa from Caltagirone or Enna, cross Piazza Armerina and then take the Caltanissetta road (there are no direct links to this road from S 117b).

Neighbouring sights are described in the following chapters: CALTAGIRONE; CALTANISSETTA; ENNA; PIAZZA ARMERINA.

For information on hotels and restaurants, see PIAZZA ARMERINA.

Background

This country villa was built between the end of the 3C and the beginning of the 4C AD, undoubtedly by someone of importance, possibly a member of the Imperial family: one of the most likely candidates seems to be Maximian, one of the tetrarchs who jointly ruled the Empire from AD 286 to 305. Surrounded by large estates, the villa was only occupied occasionally until the 12C. It was destroyed by a fire, then buried in mud following floods and a subsequent landslide in about 1161; it was only partially rediscovered at the end of the 19C.

The large complex (c 3 500m^2/37 600sq ft) was built on different levels. The main entrance **(A)** led into a polygonal courtyard, which provided access to the large peristyle overlooked by guest rooms (to the north – note: the map given has north pointing downwards) and the owner's private apartments (to the east). Beyond the guest rooms were the servants' quarters **(B)**, complete with kitchen. The private apartments used by the members of the household were divided into two by a large basilica for meetings and official receptions. At the rear of these buildings stands a

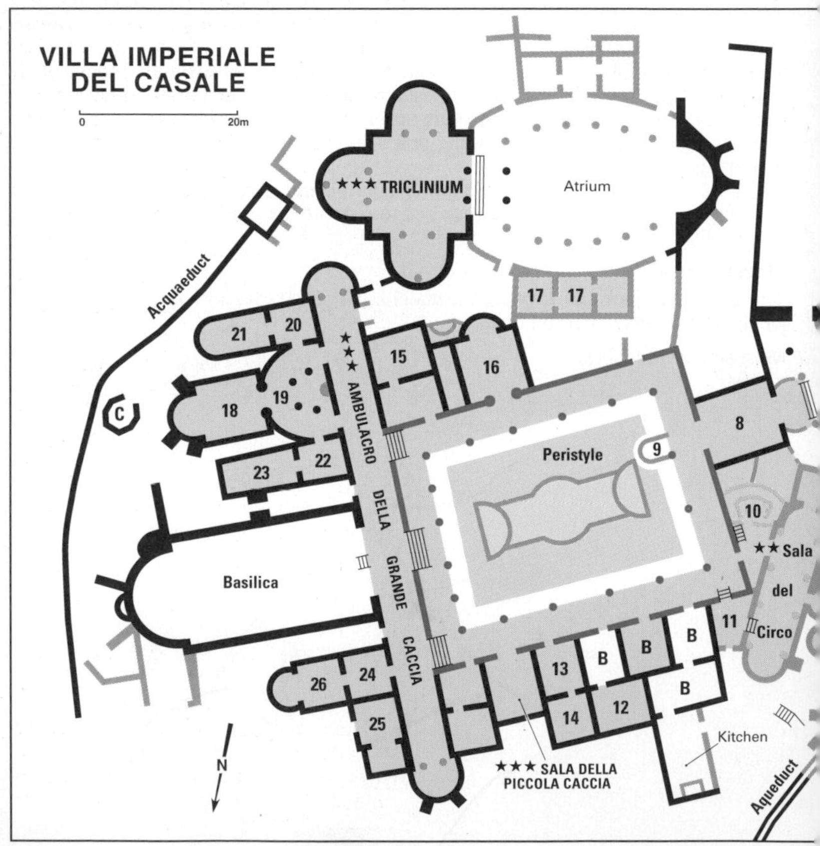

small separate octagonal latrine reserved for members of the family **(C)**. The living area was situated to the south of the complex and consisted of a large elliptical atrium which gave onto a large apsed triclinium (dining room) **(24)**, six small rooms and service amenities **(D)**.
The western part of the complex housed the baths. The water was supplied by two aqueducts connected to a third which, in turn, was fed by the River Gela which flows only a few metres away.
Mosaics – What makes the villa unique is its floors, which consist almost entirely of mosaics that fortunately survive in excellent condition. The majority of panels are polychrome and feature a wide range of subjects: mythological scenes, incidents from daily life, special occasions – a great hunt, circus games, feast days honouring the gods and a grape harvest – alternate with geometric decoration incorporating medallions, stars and key patterns in a wonderful array of colours. What is particularly remarkable is the evocative way in which movement and action is portrayed thereby animating the various scenes with realism. The rare skill with which the wild and exotic animals have been portrayed has been interpreted as the work of North African craftsmen.
In order that the various scenes might be seen from the best angle, the panels are laid facing the entrance to each room: the full impact, therefore, is delivered to the visitor as he or she enters the room.

Worth a Visit

It is advisable to visit the villa early in the morning, especially in summer when conditions can become unpleasant due to the large number of tour groups and the heat generated by the plexiglass roofs. Open 8.30am-7.30pm (last admission 6.30pm). €4.50. ☎ 0935 68 73 02.

Terme

Information on the villa's baths can also be found under Insights and Images: Art.
Just inside the entrance to the steam baths, on the left, is a section of the **aqueduct** that supplied the villa with water. Immediately beyond is the suite of rooms which makes up the thermal complex. In the first are installed the great furnaces *(praefurnia)* **(1)** which heated the water in order to generate steam that was then circulated through cavities below the floors and in the walls, thereby heating the rooms. Sections of pipes which once ran along the length of the room can still be seen in the walls. The underfloor heating is visible in the **Tepidarium (3)**: small brick columns support the actual floor, leaving a large cavity between the floor and the ground through which hot air could circulate freely. This room was maintained at a moderate temperature for use immediately after the **Caldaria (2)** where saunas and the hot baths were taken.

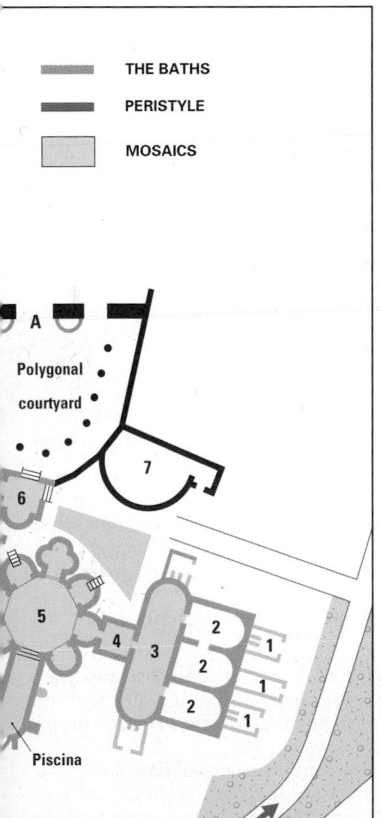

Sala delle Unzioni (4) – The function of the small square anointing room is reflected in the mosaic decoration. Slaves are shown preparing oil and unguents for application and massaging the bodies of the bathers *(the figures at the top left)*, with some of the tools of their trade: the *strigile*, a sort of curved spatula with a handle used for scraping and cleaning the skin, and a jar of oil *(the figure at the top right)*. Below, Tite and Cassi (from the names of the two slaves on the cloth draped around their hips) hold a bucket and a brush. The latter wears a pointed hat, of a kind typical in Syria.
Frigidarium (5) – The octagonal room set aside for cold baths has a fine central mosaic with a marine theme: cherub fishermen surrounded by tritons, nereids (sea nymphs) and dolphins.

One recess is filled with a man sitting on a leopard skin, attended by two servants.

From the *frigidarium*, the **piscina** and the end of the aqueduct can just be seen.

Beyond the **shrine of Venus (6)**, thus called because fragments of a statue of the goddess were found there, is the **polygonal courtyard** articulated by a colonnade. In the centre are the remains of the *impluvium* – a basin or cistern in which rainwater is collected from the surrounding roofs. From here the water was channelled towards the great **latrina (7)**.

The main entrance to the villa was from the courtyard: on the south side can be seen the remains of the entrance **(A)** comprising a central door flanked by two side doors.

Peristilium

Pass through the **vestibule (8)**. The mosaic features figures bearing a candlestick, a branch of laurel and, below, a figure with a diptych (a small book consisting of two panels) from which he might read a welcome addressed to the master of the house and any guests. Directly opposite is the **lararium (9)**, where statues of the household gods, the *lares*, were kept.

The imposing rectangular portico (eight columns on the short sides, 10 on the longer sides) is dominated by a great fountain with a small statue as its centrepiece.

Peristilium mosaic★★ – Running along all four sides of the portico is a beautiful mosaic ornamented with round medallions set among squares with, at the corners, birds and leaves. The medallions feature the heads of both wild and domestic animals (bears, tigers, wild boars and panthers; horses and cows).

Piccola latrina (10)

The floor mosaic depicts animals, including a wild ass, a cheetah, a hare and a partridge.

Sala del Circo★★

The long room, apsed at both ends, represents a circus, identified as the Circus Maximus in Rome. The decoration illustrates a chariot race, the final event in the festival honouring Ceres, the goddess of plenty and the harvest, whose cult was particularly popular in nearby Enna *(see ENNA: Mythology)*. The scene is shown in great detail. Above the *spina*, the central line around which the horses are racing, the winner receives his prize, the victory palm, handed to him by a magistrate dressed in a toga, while another character blows a horn to signal the end of the race. On the left, around the bend in the track, are the spectators, among whom a boy picks his way distributing bread. The right-hand bend is dominated by a view of three temples dedicated to Jupiter, Rome and Heracles, before which a charioteer is being dressed: one child holds out his helmet, while a second gives him the whip.

The charioteers are dressed in green, white, blue or red tunics to indicate to which of the four competing factions they belong.

Along the south side of the peristyle are a series of rooms reserved for guests. Access to these was via a second **vestibule (11)**, which is decorated with mosaics showing the lady of the house with her children and her servants holding lengths of cloth and a box containing oils. Other rooms **(B)** comprised the servants' quarters, complete with kitchen in which the oven can still be seen.

Sala della Danza (12)

The mosaic, which is unfortunately incomplete, nevertheless gives an impression of women and men dancing. One girl in particular, at the top left, moves sinuously with a veil over her head.

Sala delle Quattro Stagioni (13)

The four seasons, after which this room is named, are represented in medallions, personified by two women (spring and autumn), differentiated by their clothing, and two men (summer and winter), each with a bare shoulder.

Sala degli Amorini Pescatori★★ (14)

A few cupid-like cherubs concentrate on fishing with lines, tridents and nets while others play in the water with dolphins. In the upper section may be seen the shore, where a large building stands, fronted by a columned portico, among palm trees and umbrella pines.

The walls bear traces of frescoes depicting a further number of cherubs.

Sala della Piccola Caccia★★★

Here, in the **Room of the Small Hunt**, five panels depict the most important moments in the heat of the hunt. In the top left corner, a hunter walks with his dogs on a lead, before releasing them and encouraging them to chase after a fox *(on the right)*.

In order to give thanks for favourable conditions and a successful day, a sacrifice is offered to Diana, the goddess of hunting, a statue of whom is shown set on a column, in the middle ground. Two high-ranking officials burn incense on the altar while, behind them, a wild boar is brought forth in a net *(on the left)* and another hunter *(on the right)* holds up a hare that he has caught. The whole of the central part of the mosaic is dominated by a banqueting scene. Shaded by a red awning slung between the trees, game is being cooked over a fire. There is a pause in the day's activity: the horses are tethered, the nets are hung on branches, the huntsmen, arranged in a semicircle, relax around the fire taking refreshment. All around are hunting scenes: at the top left, two falconers seek out birds hidden among the branches of a tree; on the right, in the bushes, a man encourages his dogs to follow a hare and, below, a huntsman on horseback tries to coax out another hare from under a bush. The last panel depicts the netting of deer and the hunt for a boar which, having injured the leg of a man (shown resting on the ground, on the left), is being hemmed in by fellow hunters as they plunge a spear into its chest.

Ambulacro della Grande Caccia★★★

The fabulous Corridor of the Great Hunt, 60m/200ft long with a recess at each end, is the most engaging and monumental part of the whole villa. The floor mosaic depicts an incredibly elaborate hunting scene. Panthers, lions, antelopes, wild boar, ostrich, dromedaries, elephants, hippopotamuses and rhinoceroses are captured and put into cages or bound prior to being loaded onto ships destined for Rome, where they will be shown to acclaim in the great amphitheatres. What makes this composition so extraordinary is the variety of its scenes, the realism with which men are shown vying with wild beasts, the strong sense of action and movement, the wealth of and articulate attention to detail. Note, for example, how the limbs of animals shown underwater are portrayed in a different colour to the parts above the surface.

Just beyond the midway point is a group of three figures: the central one is presumed to be the Emperor Maximian, protected by the shields of two soldiers. Further on, another scene shows the same tremendous sophistication of detail: a tiger pounces on a crystal ball in which an image of the animal is reflected. Nearby, a curious scene provoking considerable controversy illustrates a winged griffin holding a wooden box in its talons from which the head of a boy peeps out. Some maintain that the boy acts as human bait to attract the animal, while others interpret the scene as a warning against the cruelty of hunting, and that the protagonists have swapped roles.

In the right recess, Africa is depicted as a female figure with an ivory tusk, flanked by an elephant, a tiger and, above left, an Arab-style phoenix – that mythical bird symbolising immortality which took its own life by throwing itself into the flames, only to be reborn from its ashes.

Along the eastern side of this long corridor opened rooms used by the owners of the villa, including, in the middle, the basilica destined for audiences and receptions *(for a description of these rooms, see below)*.

A scene from the mosaic of the Great Hunt

Sala delle Dieci Ragazze in Bikini** (15)

In the Room of the Ten Girls, the mosaic shows two rows of girls dressed in outfits that bear an uncanny resemblance to the modern two-piece bikini. In fact, they are pictured in their underwear, which was also commonly used when doing gymnastic exercises. The upper part was called the *fascia pectoralis* and the lower part *subligatur*. The young women concentrate on performing their various exercises: weightlifting, discus throwing, running and playing ballgames. In the bottom row, the girl wearing a toga is about to crown and award the palm of victory to another girl who has been performing exercises with a hoop, trundling it with the aid of a stick.

Diaeta di Orfeo* (16)

The Chamber of Orpheus is so called because it was reserved for playing music. At the centre is Orpheus (scarcely visible), seated on a rock, playing the lyre and enchanting all the animals which surround him. In the apse behind is a statue of the god Apollo.

The south wing of the villa accommodated the principal reception rooms: a spacious central atrium is flanked by six small units (three on each side) and a large apsed *triclinium* where meals were served. Two of the three rooms on the north side (17) contain mosaics of cherubs harvesting grapes from the vines.

R. Mattes/MICHELIN

Girls in "bikinis"

Triclinium***

The large central square space extends into three broad apses.

Central area – The main mosaic is dedicated to the **Twelve Labours of Heracles** (Hercules to the Romans). Only some of them are recognisable. On the left is the Cretan Bull (or Bull of Minos), the famous and powerful animal sent from the waters by Poseidon to Minos, which having been captured by Heracles was eventually sacrificed to Athene by Theseus at Marathon *(see p 127)*. Beside it is the Hydra of Lerna, whose many heads, one of which was immortal, were chopped off by the hero. In this case, the monster is represented with the body of a water snake and a single, immortal head. The Hydra, the younger sister of Cerberus, acted, with her brother, as guardian of the Underworld, her realm being the deep waters near Lerna, on the border with Argos. In this Labour, Heracles is assisted by his nephew and friend Iolaus, the figure, it is assumed, depicted next to the hero in the left apse. At the top, in the centre, is the great Nemean Lion, which terrorised a mountainous area. Having killed the monster, Heracles wore its pelt as a cloak and its head as a helmet. In honour of this great deed, Zeus, the divine father of Heracles, brought the lion to the heavens, making it into one of the constellations of the zodiac.

On the right is the Hind of Artemis, which Heracles captured among the hills of Ceryneia in Arcadia. To the left of the animal is Cerberus, the many-headed huge and savage dog which was brought by Heracles from the gates of the Underworld.

Left apse – This mosaic represents the **glorification of Heracles**, who is depicted in the centre, holding the hand of his friend Iolaus *(on the left)*, while Zeus bestows a laurel wreath on his head.

The panel below illustrates the metamorphoses of **Daphne** into a laurel *(on the left)* and of **Cyparissus** into a cypress *(on the right)*. This serves as a reminder of why laurel is twisted into crowns honouring the heads of brave warriors, emperors and poets: Daphne was the nymph loved and pursued by Apollo; to escape his clutches she prayed to her father, a river god, and her mother, Earth, to be turned into a laurel tree. In consolation Apollo made himself a laurel wreath which, from then on, was awarded as a prize at the Pythian Games held in Apollo's honour.

Central apse – The scene represents a **battle of the giants**: five huge creatureshave been struck by Heracles' poisoned arrows. Except for the central figure, the others have snakes' tails for legs. One of the Labours consisted of Heracles stealing the Oxen of Geryon and carrying them back to Greece. The return journey is particularly animated with exploits *(see Insights and Images: The Ancient Greeks in Sicily)*; it was as he crossed Italy that he encountered the giants, one of whom was called Alcyoneus, and fought them by the Flegraean Fields (near Naples).

In the mosaic below, **Hesione**, the daughter of Laomedon, king of Troy, is threatened by a sea monster sent by Poseidon, an incident resulting from Laomedon's failure to honour his agreement to pay Poseidon and Apollo for their assistance in building the walls of Troy. The only way to safeguard the city from the sea monster was to sacrifice Hesione. Heracles undertook to slay the monster on condition Laomedon should give him his famous horses; when the king again reneged on his promise, Heracles raised an army against Troy and gave Hesione to Telamon. On the right is Endymion, who was thrown into perpetual sleep, awaiting Selene, the moon, his lover.

Right apse – This mosaic depicts the story of **Ambrosia and Lycurgus**. On the left, three maenads (literally *mad women*) attack Lycurgus, a legendary king of Thrace who, having surprised Dionysus (engaged in a bacchanal) on his land, chased him off, killing many maenads and satyrs. Among them, he even tried to kill Ambrosia who, in the scene depicted, is changing into a vine. Behind the maenads are the figures of Pan, Dionysus and Silenus.

Continue along the wall of the aqueduct. Just before a small hexagonal latrine **(C)**, some steps on the left lead into room 18.

Diaeta di Arione (18)

The chamber of Arion was probably dedicated to making music and reading poetry, judging by the mosaic decoration which depicts the poet and musician Arion sitting on the back of a dolphin in the middle of the sea, holding a lyre and surrounded by sea nymphs, tritons and cherubs astride wild beasts and sea monsters. Here is another example of the precise and minute detail demonstrated elsewhere by the mosaicists: one nymph on the right holds a mirror in which her face is reflected.

Atrio degli Amorini Pescatori★★ (19)

The mosaic illustrates a delightful variety of fishing scenes which run right around the semicircular portico.

Vestibolo del Piccolo Circo★★ (20)

The Vestibule of the Small Circus takes its name from another circus scene, this time with children as the protagonists. Racing around the turning-posts are the chariots drawn *(starting from the top right and working anti-clockwise)* by flamingos, white geese, waders and wood pigeons. Each pair of birds also seems to symbolise a season, as the motifs on their collars would suggest: roses (spring), ears of wheat (summer), bunches of grapes (autumn) and leaves (winter).

Cubicolo dei Musici e degli Attori (21)

This particular *cubiculum* probably served as a bedroom for the owner's daughter. In the apse, two girls sit at the foot of a tree making crowns of flowers. The decoration of the rectangular room is divided into three areas populated by musicians and actors. The letters inscribed in the medallions in the second and third sections allude to musical notes.

Vestibolo di Eros e Pan (22)

Dominating the antechamber is the central horned and cloven-hoofed figure of Pan, the god of the woodlands, flocks and shepherds, fighting Eros, the god of love. Next to Pan is the judge, wearing a laurel wreath. Behind the two contestants is the audience made up of satyrs and maenads (carrying a thyrsus – the rod entwined with vine and ivy more often attributed to Dionysus) supporting the god of the woodlands, and the family of the owners of the house supporting Eros. The fight symbolises the difficulty for anyone who is ugly (Pan) to vanquish love. In the background, on a table, are aligned four hats set with diadems and palm leaves and, below, two bags full of money, as the writing indicates.

Cubicolo dei Fanciulli Cacciatori★ (23)

This *cubiculum* was probably the bedroom of the son of the house-owner. The mosaic divides into two parts, which in turn are subdivided into three sections. At the top, girls collect flowers and make garlands; a boy carries two rose-filled baskets on his shoulders. Lower down, hunting scenes show children killing a hare, capturing a duck and killing a small antelope.

Walk around the large **basilica**, noting the fragments of the floor tiled with marble.

Vestibolo di Ulisse e Polifemo★ (24)

These mosaics illustrate the famous story of Odysseus (Ulysses to the Romans) outwitting the Cyclops Polyphemus (shown here with three eyes) with a cup of wine intended to intoxicate him and send him to sleep. Behind him, the hero's companions are filling another cup.

Cubicolo della Scena Erotica★ (25)

Surrounded by images of the four seasons (in the hexagonal medallions), a polygonal medallion enclosed within a laurel wreath shows a young man embracing a loosely clad girl. This is one of the few rooms that still bears traces of wall paintings depicting dancing figures.

In the room behind the vestibule **(26)** is a **mosaic★** with **fruit**, realistically represented with exquisite delicacy, set within medallions and among complex geometrical shapes, while the apse is ornamented with a delicate flower composition against a pale background.

Notes

Notes

Index

Index

PALERMO .... Place, sight, tourist attraction covered as a chapter in the guide
Petralia Soprana .... Place of interest
Accommodation .... Pratical information
Serpotta, Giacomo .... People, events and artistic styles